923

XM 105

ISSUE | No. _4241_ | **LABEL**

Return to .... Library
on or before latest date below.

30 OCT

DE GAULLE

The apotheosis of de Gaulle. Having asked his followers to stay "a few paces behind" he begins his triumphal march down the Champs Elysées on August 26 1944. (*See page 245*)

DE GAULLE

A Biography by Aidan Crawley

THE LITERARY GUILD
LONDON

This edition published *1969* by
The Literary Guild, *9* Grape Street, London *WC2*
By arrangement with Messrs Wm. Collins Sons & Co. Ltd.

© Crawley Features Ltd. *1969*

Printed in Great Britain
Collins Clear-Type Press
London and Glasgow

To Andrew, Harriet and Randall

CONTENTS

8 CONTENTS

LIST OF PLATES

ACKNOWLEDGMENTS

I would like to thank especially Dr. David Thomson, Master of Sidney Sussex, Cambridge, who read the book in manuscript and made invaluable suggestions; the Hon. Mrs. Vanessa Thomas who, as Sir Gladwyn Jebb's daughter, lived in Paris through some of the crucial years of the story, and has read the proofs; Mrs. Kay Sykes who typed the first draft of the book and Mrs. Philippa Windsor-Jones who typed and corrected the final draft. The Rev. S. B-R. Poole, of Littlebourne near Canterbury, took infinite pains in preparing the index.

I owe a great debt to the staff of the Library at the House of Commons who were unfailingly helpful, even through all-night sittings.

It will be obvious from the References and Bibliographical Notes to how many authors and publishers I owe a debt of gratitude. In particular I would like to extend my thanks to:

Messrs. George Weidenfeld and Nicolson for permission to quote from *The Memoirs of General de Gaulle*; Robert Hale Ltd. (*The De Gaulle Revolution* and *France 1940–1955* by Alexander Werth); Cassell and Co. Ltd. (*History of the Second World War* by Winston S. Churchill); Hutchinson (*France and Her Army* by Charles de Gaulle); Routledge and Kegan Paul (*Basic Verités* by Charles Peguy); William Heinemann (*Pétain and de Gaulle* by J. R. Tournoux); Berger-Levrault (*Charles de Gaulle* by Lucien Nachin and *Le Fils de l'Épee* by Charles de Gaulle); Librairie Ernest Flammarion (*Venu de ma Montagne* and *Au Coeur de la Melée* by Paul Reynaud); Fayard (*De Gaulle entre deux Mondes* by Paul-Marie de la Gorce) and the Librairie Plon (*La Tragédie du General* by J. R. Tournoux).

I express my gratitude to *Paris Match* for leave to reproduce some of the photographs, and to the *Daily Express* for all the help given in obtaining them.

Above all I must thank my wife, Virginia Cowles, for her constant encouragement and expert criticism.

PREFACE

There have been many biographies of de Gaulle, mostly by Frenchmen. My justification for adding to their number is that an Englishman writes with a different bias, and after a decade of Gaullist power in France it is time an English point of view was presented. Also there have been published in the last few years so many studies, criticisms, volumes of anecdotes, memoirs and documents relating to particular incidents in de Gaulle's life, that they need blending into the story. I have told it from the beginning because de Gaulle's early life has a fascination of its own and his later life is unintelligible without knowledge of what went before.

During eleven years as a British Member of Parliament—from 1945–51 and 1962–67—and two as a junior Service Minister, I met many of the military commanders, leading politicians and civil servants on both sides of the channel who have helped shape the events in which de Gaulle has played his part. All whom I approached were generous in their help, although for the sake of brevity and because many still wish to remain anonymous, I mention only a few.

In France Professor Bertrand de Jouvenal and his wife Hélène gave me constant help and encouragement. M. Gaston Palewski, Gaullist since 1940, and now President of the Constitutional Council, opened many doors. M. Geoffroy de Courcel, de Gaulle's aide-de-camp in 1940 and Ambassador in London in the 1960s, was good enough to see me and, through his Embassy, to provide the text of several of de Gaulle's speeches. I talked with M. René Massigli, once de Gaulle's Foreign Minister and later Ambassador in London; M. Charles Morazé, political adviser to de Gaulle from 1956–58; M. Emanuel d'Astier de la Vigerie, resistance leader and Minister of the Interior during the Liberation; General Béthouart, de Gaulle's contemporary at St. Cyr; the late M. Paul Reynaud who supported de Gaulle in the 1930s, gave him office when Prime Minister in June, 1940, and attacked him bitterly after his return to power; M. Georges Bidault, Chairman of the National Council of Resistance, 1943–4, Foreign Secretary and Prime Minister and then head of the O.A.S. during many of the attempts on de Gaulle's life; M. Jacques Soustelle, head of Fighting France's intelligence, Minister of Information after De Gaulle's return to power in 1958, then an exile in Switzerland; M. Alfred Fabre-Luce, Vichyite and satirist; Professor Rougier, who acted as Pétain's emissary to London in 1940.

In London I have had discussions with members of de Gaulle's personal staff in the 1940s, members of the British intelligence services and secretaries of the Cabinet Offices at different periods. Journalists, including Mr. Harold King, Reuter's correspondent in Paris for most of de Gaulle's life and a passionate supporter, have been helpful as always. I am particularly grateful to Mr. Harold Macmillan and Mr. Edward Heath for allowing me to question them over the negotiations for Britain's entry into the Common Market.

I should add that every opinion not directly attributed is mine and that no one with whom I have talked bears any responsibility for my interpretation of events.

CHAPTER I

DESTINED FOR A SOLDIER

Charles de Gaulle's father, Henri, had always wanted to be a soldier.

He served as a lieutenant in the Franco-Prussian war and, at the siege of Paris in 1870, was wounded during one of the skirmishes around Le Bourget. But he had no money and after the capitulation was forced to leave the army, which he loved, and to take up teaching. Being a devout Catholic and a royalist he refused to take a post in the state lycée and taught only in church schools.

Henri followed his own father's example by marrying into the Maillot family of Lille. His wife was his cousin, Jeanne Maillot-Delannoy, a deeply religious woman, two of whose sisters were nuns. Her mother was a Delannoy from whose family Franklin Delano Roosevelt may have descended.

Henri was teaching in Lille when he married and his first two sons were born in the Maillot house in the ancient Flemish quarter of the city; the eldest, Xavier, in 1887 and the second, christened Charles André Marie Joseph, on November 22, 1890. The three other children, Jacques, Pierre and Marie-Agnès, were born soon afterwards when the family had moved to Paris where Henri became the lay headmaster of the Jesuit College of the Immaculate Conception. In Paris the de Gaulles lived first in the huge buildings of the Jesuit College, 389 Rue Vaugirard, near the Gate of Versailles; then in the Avenue Dusquesne, near the *École Militaire*; finally in the Place St. François Xavier close to the Invalides, which came to symbolise for the young Charles "all the glories of France" and all his dreams for the future.

Charles de Gaulle described his father as a "thoughtful, cultivated, traditional man" imbued with a feeling for the dignity of France, who made him aware of her past. Henri's love of history had led him to make some researches into the origins of his own family. In the evenings or on Sundays, sitting round the fire, he would tell his children about their ancestors. The family's true origin was never determined. It might have been Celtic or Flemish. But Henri thought the name itself might have come from the word *gaule*, a long pole used to beat olives from the trees in the Middle Ages.* True history began with a Richard de Gaulle, who in the thirteenth century received the fief of Elbeuf in Normandy. From then onwards the records were fairly continuous.

The hero of the family was a Sieur Jehan de Gaulle who took part in the last great charge of feudal knights against the English archers at the Battle of Agincourt. Charles's face would glow with pride when his father recounted how Jehan, having survived the slaughter of French chivalry, refused to acknowledge England's Henry V as King of France and followed the defeated Charles VI to Bourges. According to a family tradition this same Jehan, a few years later, was one of the six men-at-arms who accompanied Joan of Arc on her first journey to visit "the Dauphin" at Chinon.

During the sixteenth and seventeenth centuries the de Gaulles lapsed into obscurity. In the eighteenth century they emerged again as Crown lawyers and, not surprisingly, one of them found himself in prison during the Revolution. He survived, however, and later became Director of Transport and Posts in Napoleon's *Grande Armée*. His son, Julian Philippe, the grandfather of Charles de Gaulle, was born in Paris in 1801 and with him began both the scholastic tradition which has been carried down to the present day, and the connection with the Maillot family of Lille. For not only did Julian Philippe and his wife Josephine Maillot become recognised historians but two of their sons, Charles de Gaulle's uncles, followed in their footsteps. Their work was esoteric. Julian Philippe edited a life of St. Louis for the Society for the History of France and wrote a long history of Paris. His wife wrote biographies of Chateaubriand and O'Connell, the liberator of Ireland, and edited a magazine which published the works of Proudhon and other social reformers. Of their sons Charles, who was a cripple, wrote a history of the Celts which was also an impassioned plea for the unity of all Celtic races, and Jules, the third son, compiled one of the first systematic catalogues of Hymenoptera—four-winged insects—and became a member of the *Institut de France*.

From his earliest days, therefore, Charles was steeped in history. The de Gaulles rarely entertained but, when his uncles visited his father, the grown-ups would sit in a circle discussing the past while Charles sat quietly in a corner listening. England was the arch-enemy. He was soon familiar with the campaigns of the Hundred Years' War, of Louis XIV and Napoleon. Even when the conversation moved to

* Henri's theory may have been known in scholastic circles, for in November, 1940, a group of Paris students marched round the Arc de Triomphe each carrying two poles (deux gaules) as a gesture of defiance to the uncomprehending Germans.

the present it was still the British who were frustrating the French, in Siam or Egypt. When Charles was eight the two countries were on the brink of war over Fashoda. It was in character that none of Henri's children were ever allowed to learn English.

But Charles's upbringing implanted in him an instinct which was even stronger than rivalry with England. His parents not only loved history, they idolised France. Charles himself was later to say that his mother had "an uncompromising passion for her country equal to her religious piety";[1] his father's feelings were more gentle but no less profound. Yet it was a sombre idolatry, peculiar to families like the de Gaulles who lived largely in the past. For neither of Charles's parents had ever fully recovered from the catastrophe of the 1870s. The shock was the greater because it was so unexpected. When Napoleon III declared war in 1870 most of the rulers of Europe expected the French to reach the Rhine in a few days and Berlin within a few weeks. Prussia, even after its defeat of Austria in 1866, was still a small state; France had been the dominant military power on the Continent for more than two centuries.

"The odds are fearfully against us in the awful struggle which is about to commence," wrote the Crown Princess of Prussia to her mother, Queen Victoria.[2] When she spoke of the possible annihilation of Prussia she was only echoing the predictions of many well-informed people. "My thoughts are constantly with you, wishing my two daughters safe here," replied the Queen on June 20 in a distraught letter in which she urged her second daughter, Princess Alice, wife of the Grand Duke of Hesse and the Rhine, to leave Darmstadt for fear of falling into French hands.

Of course, there were those who saw things more clearly. Some diplomats, sickened by the flattery and mutual admiration which characterised the court of Napoleon III, correctly assessed both the quality of the French army and the mood of the people. "There is no real patriotism in France, there is only chauvinism and that is not quite the same thing,"[3] was the verdict of the Italian ambassador; he went on to say that he did not believe the French army capable of resisting a well-disciplined foe. A Russian colleague remarked how indifferent the French people were to everything that did not personally concern them and felt that no people who talked so much and were so obsessed with money could win a war. The French people themselves were far less confident than they sounded in 1870. The crowds in the street might shout "*à Berlin*," but before the battle started there was a general premonition of disaster and the most common topic of conversation was the probability of the Emperor's fall.

The de Gaulles and the Maillots were not Buonapartists. The first Emperor had exhausted France, his nephew was an adventurer; but in the absence of a monarchy, the army enshrined all the greatness of France in their eyes, and when it was so ignominiously defeated the light went out of their lives. As Charles was one day to say of himself after an even greater disaster, his parents carried the dishonour of France on their backs. One of his earliest and most painful memories was of his mother describing her feelings when she saw her own mother in tears at the news that Bazaine had capitulated. Henri would often tell the story of the siege of Paris, in which he had taken part, and each year, when the children were young, he used to take them to the cemetery at Le Bourget and read to them the inscription to the dead of 1870; "The sword of France, broken in their valiant hands, will once more be re-forged by their descendants."

Charles not only shared the sense of humiliation, but burned to avenge it. "Nothing saddened me more profoundly," he wrote, looking back on his childhood, "than our weaknesses and our mistakes . . . the surrender at Fashoda, the Dreyfus case, social conflicts, religious strife."[4] There seemed no end to France's degradation. While Charles was a boy, England, Germany and Russia wielded political and military power in the world and France was either ignored or forced to pick up the crumbs which fell from their tables. Successive crises in the Balkans were settled without effective French intervention. Although France had a major interest in the construction and management of the Suez Canal, de Lesseps was unable to raise the money to buy the bankrupt Khedive's shares in the Canal Company because the British objected to wholly French ownership. In 1876 Disraeli rubbed salt into the wound by doing it instead. Six years later, when Gladstone had once again succeeded Disraeli, the French were forced to refuse the British offer of a joint occupation of Egypt because the payment of the German indemnity had crippled her finances and she was reluctant to divert troops from her own frontier.

Fashoda, which so mortified the young Charles, nearly brought the two countries to war. In 1896 the British were in the process of reconquering the Egyptian Sudan and securing control of the Nile waters near its source. The French, intent on completing a continuous belt of territory under the French flag from the Atlantic to the Indian Ocean, sent a force under General Marchand to occupy Fashoda which lay across the British path. On September 25, 1898, Kitchener, the British commander, reached Fashoda and, finding General Marchand's troops in occupation, summoned him to withdraw. The rivalry of centuries once more brought feelings in both countries to boiling-point.

But the new Foreign Minister, M. Delcassé, recognised that France was in no position to wage a colonial war without command of the sea and the French troops were ordered to retire.* The boy Charles drank in these bitter dregs and yearned to render "some signal service" to restore his country's fortunes.

Although his elder brother Xavier was intellectually more brilliant, it was Charles who was the leader of the five de Gaulle children. He was precocious and domineering and loved to play practical jokes on his family, their friends and the servants. *"Parfaitement diable, horriblement diable,"*[5] said one of his victims, and no doubt he was right. Like other families the children developed their own language, but it was not of the usual kind which entailed a simple juggling of syllables. Charles made his brothers and sister learn to speak French backwards —*"ne suov zella."* It was not easy but he overrode all objections and the children became quite fluent. Charles shared the passion of his generation for playing soldiers and his father bought him a splendid collection of those now almost forgotten toys. But whether the armies were spread out on the nursery floor or consisted of gangs of boys drawn from the neighbourhood, he played with unusual seriousness and intensity. According to his father he could understand a military campaign at the age of five. Whatever the war in which they were engaged, Xavier, Jacques and Pierre were made to represent enemies or allies while Charles insisted always on representing France. Once his younger brother Pierre, of whom he was particularly fond, was found crying. When asked why by his mother, he said that Charles had slapped his face. Pierre, who was supposed to be a crusader, had been carrying a dispatch scribbled on a piece of paper, but when captured by the "Saracens" had failed to eat the message as ordered by his elder brother. This was not an isolated incident. Charles was so often cold and forbidding that his family used to say that he must have been born in an ice house.

Charles had a passion for reading and devoured French history books even on his holidays. Until 1907 when the Third Republic expelled the Jesuits from France, he was taught at the Jesuit College at which his father was the lay head. He was a good classical scholar and developed an interest in philosophy at an early age. According to his sister, his favourite authors were Pascal, St. Augustine and

* A formal reconciliation was achieved in the First World War. In his little book *Souvenirs of France*, Rudyard Kipling recalls a review of French troops by Joffre and Kitchener during which Kitchener shook hands and talked with General Marchand in front of the whole line. Kipling felt the *"frisson"* which went through the ranks as the troops watched the reunion.

Froissart whose chronicles he was said to have read by the time he was six. He liked music but dreaded his piano lessons. At one time he had ambitions to become a monk and work overseas as a missionary in the French Empire. But when on his tenth birthday his father took him to see Rostand's new masterpiece *L'Aiglon*, he was so profoundly moved by Cyrano de Bergerac that he decided to become a soldier and never thereafter wavered in his determination.

Charles's decision delighted his parents and his father, in particular, encouraged him and upheld his resolve. He had some anxious moments. Charles was never idle, but the curriculum at the Jesuit College bored him and he began to neglect it. He liked reading philosophy and started to write poetry. In his last year at the College, which was also the last year of its existence, his father took him to task and warned him that unless he tried harder he would not be able to pass into the Military College of St. Cyr. From then on Charles got down to work. At the age of seventeen, after the Jesuit College had closed, he went to the *Collège d'Antoing* on the Belgian frontier, coming back to Paris for the final year before the examinations. His father's words bore fruit. In 1909 Charles passed first in his class into St. Cyr.

Charles was now nineteen and already a strong and rather strange character. He was a head taller than most young men of his age, and with his large nose, weak chin, wide ears and rather gangling movements, had a commanding but unprepossessing appearance. As yet girls were of no interest to him. He was not unfriendly, but was unusually serious and liked going for long walks with a chosen friend. He had his day-dreams, but he was already capable of contemplation. He was not as religious as his parents but saw the Church as part of the fabric of French life and went to mass fairly regularly. He was still unsure of what he believed but was evolving his own ethical code and tended to be uncompromising in asserting what he thought right and wrong.

Hitherto this solitary self-assertive young man had led a sheltered, almost cloistered life. His chief companions were his brothers and sister and his holidays, when he was not at home, were spent with relations. But those relations belonged to a small, conservative caste which, intellectually and politically, had cut itself off from the main stream of French life. By the beginning of the twentieth century the majority of French people no longer nurtured a sense of humiliation. Momentarily they might flare up at British high-handedness on the Nile, but within a few years they had shrugged it off and entered the *entente cordiale*. They longed for revenge against Germany but they were far too practical, too deeply engrossed in making money or harassed with the difficulty of earning it, to brood over past mistakes. As a whole the French had come to terms with their defeat. Property was intact and those who owned it dominated French life and were intensely mercenary. A foreigner who had lived in France through the Prussian occupation noticed that peasants and merchants seemed to relish making money out of the invader. To his shocked inquiry a tradesman replied, "it does not matter to whom we sell our potatoes; what is important is to sell them."[6] During the next thirty years, as Charles de Gaulle was growing up, this hard-headedness increased. The French aristocracy, formerly so inbred, shrewdly married into wealthy Jewish, American or bourgeois families. The peasants contracted marriages for their children to prevent the fragmentation of their land. Foreigners might still see traces of the Revolution in the familiarity with which waiters shook hands with distinguished clients or in the boldness with which peasant families, up for the day from the country, invaded the smartest cafés; but although there were frequent strikes and occasionally riots, the Revolutionary spirit had been crushed by the savage repression of the Commune and, even at the turn of the century, socialism had not yet got a grip on the masses.

And while the bourgeoisie reigned Paris had become the intellectual centre of the world. The poets, painters, philosophers and writers who inhabited the Left Bank of the Seine found the atmosphere of a struggling Republic more congenial than cities dominated by the courts and conventions of monarchical Europe. They might have little chance of marrying a rich bourgeoise but they could mix with all and sundry in the cafés, get cheap meals at restaurants "full of culinary magic"[7] and buy a bunch of violets for a sou. The streets belonged to everyone. "One walked and talked and slept with whomever one pleased and cared not a hoot for others." It was the Paris in which Stefan Zweig, a young Austrian poet, paid court to the German master Rainer Maria Rilke. It was the Paris of Rodin, Sarah Bernhardt and that other beautiful actress, Cécile Sorel; of the wealthy Jaurés, the prophet of socialism. It was the Paris of Flaubert, Guy de Maupassant and Anatole France. In Paris the Curies were discovering radium and Clemenceau was a rising barrister. It was the Paris in which Captain Dreyfus was falsely convicted of being a spy and where Zola had risked all in writing J'Accuse.

But this was not the Paris of the young Charles de Gaulle. It was not that he did not enjoy himself in his own way. He loved the Great Exhibition, he went to the theatre, he read poetry and he was as thrilled as the rest of his countrymen when Blériot flew the Channel. But he did not engage in the great social and political controversies which were rending France and making her a leader in the battle of ideas. For him the dispute between Church and State, the liberal revolt against racialism, the socialist onslaught against property, the destination of the Republic felt by traditionalists like his parents, were and were always to remain regrettable examples of "strife" and "conflict." Even at the age of nineteen argument was distasteful to him. He liked to ponder and pronounce, but when challenged he would end the conversation with a quip or relapse into silence, provoking one of his contemporaries into the remark that when Charles had found a slogan he had said all there was to say.

The Dreyfus case must have been of particular concern to him. Charles de Gaulle was a child when it began, but before it ended he had already made up his mind to become a soldier and its repercussions were still causing havoc in the army long after he entered St. Cyr. Yet neither then nor later does he seem to have taken a firm stand. This is remarkable, for in every family in the country the case became the chief topic of conversation. The great debate sucked into its vortex all the issues which divided French society, the Republic against the Church, anti-Semitism, the role of the army in the State, the basic principles of justice. Fathers quarrelled with children, lovers parted, life-long friendships were broken. Until the disaster of 1940 nothing was again to cause such violent feeling.

Briefly the facts were that, at the end of October, 1894, Captain Alfred Dreyfus, a Jewish officer who held an important position in the Intelligence Service of the General Staff, was arrested on a charge of selling secret information to the Germans. He was tried *in camera* by a military court, convicted, degraded and sent to prison on Devil's Island. But the following summer a new chief of French Military Intelligence, a Colonel Picquart, discovered that evidence produced at the trial had been faked and, although information had been sold to the Germans, it had been sold by someone else. Yet it took eleven years, which included a second trial at which Dreyfus was again convicted, before the Captain was finally reinstated. And during those eleven years Frenchmen learned to hate each other more bitterly than they had during the religious wars. The France which the de Gaulles idolised, the France in which the army, the church and the law had stood for integrity and decency, was dragged through the mud.

It was the army which suffered most. In the early years after the trial successive Ministers of War, the military hierarchy and most officers with a Catholic background not only upheld the verdict of the Court Martial but persecuted their opponents. Officers who were suspected of being republicans or even seen reading Clemenceau's newspaper *L'Aurore*, which took Dreyfus's side, were demoted or dismissed. Jews within the army and without were attacked in the street and beaten up. After Dreyfus had been "pardoned" in 1899, mainly because of the savage treatment he had received on Devil's Island, the tide began to turn. From then on it was the Catholics who were persecuted. A purge, the forerunner of so many others in the twentieth century, decimated the officer Corps for the second time. "Good" republicans were set to spy upon their brother officers and to report conversations. The attendance of Roman Catholics at Mass was recorded and regular worship became a ground for suspicion and even a bar to promotion. Officers in the same regiment refused to shake hands, duels multiplied. In 1906 the French Federation of Trade Unions passed a resolution extolling anti-militaristic propaganda and called on its members to make it even bolder and more effective. In the year before Charles de Gaulle entered St. Cyr the number of candidates dropped by half.

In later life Charles de Gaulle was to say that in the Dreyfus affair he was on the side of the Republic. No doubt this was broadly true. It was one of the few differences he had with his father. One of his uncles once told Charles that, when he visited his brother at the Jesuit College and asked after the two eldest boys who were pupils there, Henri replied, "Oh, they seem to be doing quite well. The only trouble with them is that they are both Republicans." But it was a lukewarm republicanism which the young Charles professed. He broke no heads in the cause of Dreyfus. In one of his later books he alludes briefly to the Dreyfus case. His attitude is equivocal. He refers to the "probability" of a miscarriage of justice but goes on to record the horror with which such a probability was rebutted by a military hierarchy dedicated to the service of the country.[8] He deplored the intrigues to which the case gave rise and ended by blaming the press for magnifying the whole affair.

The truth was that, intellectually, Charles was rather timid. He was clear-headed enough to see that the monarchy was dead, but was fascinated by Maurras, who was the monarchists' philosopher. He was aware that religious beliefs were everywhere being challenged, but the thinkers he most admired were those, like Bergson, who set out to prove that the new knowledge only confirmed the spiritual nature of the universe. He had sympathy with socialist aspirations but, even as a young man, never joined the socialist party. One thing alone excited him—patriotism. A love of France, he felt, ought to unite men and obliterate all their differences.

Charles deliberately cultivated the romanticism in his nature. Of a

flourishing school of romantic poets, the one he most enjoyed was
Charles Péguy. Péguy was little known in his lifetime, but has since
had an enormous influence in France. His writing became the inspiration of the Resistance in the Second World War. Péguy was proud of
having been born a peasant and of having earned his own education
through state scholarships; yet he hated what he called "the modern
world," the world of the bourgeoisie, and dreamed of a harmonious
city in which all men would be poor and honest and love each other.
He spent sixteen years writing about Joan of Arc. Yet Péguy had a
message and it was a message which Charles de Gaulle drank in so
deeply that he made it his own. Péguy's thought, Péguy's words and
phrases were to appear and reappear, sometimes almost verbatim, in
the speeches and lectures he was to deliver and the books he was to
write. Péguy held that a brave man, for the sake of truth, must break
with his friends not once but as often as truth demanded it. He must
accept solitude. Péguy hated weakness, particularly the insidious weakness which induces men to compromise with their enemies or to surrender their principles: "Nothing is as murderous as weakness and
cowardice. Nothing is as humane as firmness."[9] Above all Péguy worshipped France and the French, and glorified the profession of arms.
The French, he wrote were:

> Intelligent people
> Before you are through talking they have understood
> Hard working people
> Before you are through talking the work is done
> Military people
> Before you are through talking the battle is begun—[10]

To Péguy the French were the Elect of God, the successors to the
Hebrews, a people without whom God would be at a loss because, if
there were no Frenchmen, no one would understand what he was
doing. As for war, it was the ultimate test of honesty and courage:

> Blessed are those who die in great battles
> Stretched out on the ground in the face of God.[11]

It was with Péguy's verses ringing in his ears, that Charles went off to
join the army. Nothing that had happened had dampened his enthusiasm. "When I joined the army," he wrote, "it was the greatest thing
in the world. Beneath all the criticisms and insults that were lavished on
it, it was looking forward with certainty and even a muffled hopefulness to the approaching days when everything would depend upon
it."[12] A new law obliged all young men accepted at St. Cyr to do a
year's military service before entering the Academy. Charles did his
service from October, 1909, to October, 1910, in the ninth company of

the 33rd Infantry Regiment stationed at Arras. He used to say later that the most valuable lesson he learned from this year in the ranks was that, if you did the opposite of what the N.C.O.s told you to do, you might get on fairly well—exactly the contrary of what he would have said had he been an Englishman. He neither disgraced nor distinguished himself and became a corporal. Yet he must have been a little out of the ordinary, for the only anecdote which emerges from his preliminary service shows that he struck the imagination of the first officer who commanded him in exactly the same light as he struck Sir Winston Churchill thirty years later. When Captain Tuguy, in charge of the ninth company, was asked why he had not promoted such a dedicated young man to be sergeant he replied: "Would you have me nominate as sergeant a boy who would only be at his ease as the Grand Constable?"*

In the autumn of 1910 Charles de Gaulle entered the Military Academy of St. Cyr. On his contemporaries he made the impression that might have been expected. His appearance earned him the nicknames of "*Le Grand Charles*" or "*La Grande Asperge*," and because of his aloof and rather arrogant manner, he was also known as "The Cock" and "The Peacock." One at least of the names has stuck. He was not, however, one of the leading lights of the Academy. General Béthouart, who was in the same class and, in 1940, commanded the French troops in the battle for Norway, remembers him only dimly as a clever student who had few friends. Nevertheless, Charles passed out thirteenth in a class of two hundred and eleven which was headed by the future Marshal Juin. Now came a crucial decision. Charles's placing allowed him to choose the regiment he was to join. The cavalry regiments were not only the most fashionable but, for generations, had thrown up most of those who reached the highest positions in the French army. At a time when *l'attaque à l'outrance* was considered the essence of military gospel, this was perfectly logical. Charles was more than ordinarily ambitious and his friends expected him to opt for the *Cuirassiers*. But Charles had other ideas. Not only was he not built for a horseman, he had secretly come to the conclusion that the day of the cavalry was over and that in the war that he and so many others already believed inevitable, the infantry would offer far wider scope. He chose, therefore, to return to the regiment in which he had already served. At the end of 1912 Charles, now Sub-Lieutenant de Gaulle, went back to the 33rd Infantry at Arras.

* Sir Winston Churchill, reflecting on his meeting with de Gaulle in the garden of 10 Downing Street in June, 1940, wrote: "I felt, there goes the Constable of France."

For the next two years Charles de Gaulle was busy learning his profession. Arras, which then had a population of some 26,000, had been a garrison town since 1815 and was a link in the chain which guarded France's northern frontier. It was neither a gay nor a beautiful city. The slate roofs and grey buildings as often as not matched the grey sky, and the barracks, sited near the ruins of one of Vauban's fortresses, were devoid of luxuries. All this, however, suited Charles who was a northerner and felt at home in these rather dour surroundings. A group of St. Cyrards had joined the regiment with him and one, Lucien Nachin, later wrote a little book, based on letters which passed between a few friends and notes on conversations taken at the time. Nachin is important because he was Charles de Gaulle's first disciple. He admits that, to many people, de Gaulle appeared cold and aloof but he puts this down to his being a great reader. Nachin himself found him warm and gentle. According to Nachin, within a month of their arrival in Arras, everyone was talking about de Gaulle. Heads turned in the street as he passed and those who came in close contact with him were convinced that one day the young lieutenant would become President of France. This eulogy was born of hindsight, for by the time Nachin put his recollections on paper de Gaulle had celebrated his triumph as the saviour of his country. But there is no doubt that even as a young man de Gaulle could cast a spell. He repelled more people than he captivated but he was never mediocre and could not be ignored.

Captain Salicetti, who commanded the 6th Company, put de Gaulle in charge of recruits and Nachin describes the enthusiasm and solemnity which the young sub-lieutenant set about instructing "the hardy miners and patient peasants" who formed the bulk of the area's intake. Every week Charles held a special meeting of the N.C.O.s under his command and discussed the technical problems thrown up by the general course of instruction; he would draw them out and give each a sense of his own responsibility, "communicating the ardent flame which animated him."[13] "His reputation quickly spread beyond the little corner of the Parade Ground reserved for the instruction of his company. People talked about him, but always with an inflection of admiration or respect . . ."

At the end of his first year Charles gave a dinner to his contemporary "Cyrards" in the regiment and let himself go on the subject of an officer's duty and career. One can picture the scene, the young officers all in uniform—for even off-duty they never wore mufti—their wine glasses full, sitting round the table when the meal was over, listening to the first of many monologues which it was somehow impossible to interrupt. No doubt Charles was compelling, for he had read and thought more than most. He carried in his head the words of Barrès, Psychari, Péguy and a whole school of French poets and writers who for the past decade had been extolling the profession of arms. And although at the end of 1913 the war clouds had temporarily lifted, he still believed that war must come and openly looked forward to it. His guests, says Nachin, were profoundly moved.

But Charles's two years at Arras had a special importance for a more personal reason. While he had been at St. Cyr the 33rd Regiment had received a new commanding officer. His name was Philippe Pétain. It is unlikely that this change had influenced Charles's decision to return to Arras, for no special renown attached to Colonel Pétain's name. On the contrary, he had had a difficult and unsatisfactory career. As he said himself, had been old in all his ranks, an old lieutenant, an old captain and now, at fifty-six, an old colonel. It was generally understood that the command of a line regiment was to be his last appointment, the prelude to an early retirement. To prepare for that Pétain had already bought himself a small property near St. Omer.

However, Pétain's failure had not been due to any shortcomings as a regimental officer. The son of a peasant, he had enlisted in the years following the Prussian occupation and had risen entirely through his own ability. He was a strict disciplinarian dedicated to his profession and imbued with a burning desire to avenge France's defeat. His difficulties arose because he had views on strategy and tactics which ran counter to those held by the General Staff and which he expressed in uncompromising terms.

Pétain—and in this as in other things de Gaulle was to follow him—had no time for the French Empire. In his view the acquisition of territory spread across the globe involved a burden which France was unable to support. He saw neither glamour nor military value in campaigns against ill-armed, undisciplined tribes in Asia or Africa. The employment of French troops overseas merely weakened the army where it should be strongest, on the northern and eastern frontiers of France. Since the expansion of the Empire had been the policy of successive governments for thirty years and colonial wars the arena in which most of the military hierarchy had won distinction, these views were ill-received. Pétain made them the more unpalatable by his gift for terse expression.

But Pétain had been at loggerheads with his military superiors over an even more important matter. He had attended the *École Supérieure de Guerre* in 1900 and had sufficiently impressed his instructors to be appointed lecturer at the National School of Fire-power in the following year. Here he began a campaign which he was to maintain for the rest of his life. The prevailing view among the French General Staff was that the secret of victory in war lay always in attack. Attack dislocated the enemies' plans and gave the attacker the initiative. Pétain took a different line. He was impressed above all with the accuracy and effectiveness of modern weapons and believed that these would dominate any future battle. While the military hierarchy was proclaiming that heavy artillery was of little use, that bayonets were more effective than bullets, while even Foch was scoffing at military aircraft as mere sport, Pétain began preaching the overwhelming importance of fire-power. "The offensive, it is fire-power which advances. Defence, it is fire-power which stops the enemy. Guns conquer, the infantry occupies."[14] Pétain's lectures caused consternation. To a man like Colonel de Grandmaison, a lecturer on the General Staff, he seemed to be destroying the offensive spirit and undermining the morale of the army. For a time Pétain was without employment. But he had supporters, among them Foch, commandant of the *École Supérieure*, who considered him "a remarkable student and even thinker."[15] In 1909, the year in which de Gaulle did his military service, Pétain was appointed assistant professor for infantry tactics at the school and the following year occupied the professorial chair. He was an impressive lecturer, speaking without notes and with great economy of words. His tall figure and piercing blue eyes dominated the audience which included several members of the General Staff. For the younger officers there was standing room only.

Pétain maintained and developed his thesis. The artillery must no longer be considered a separate arm but must be at once the shield and spearhead of the infantry. He projected the idea of the creeping barrage behind which infantry could advance from carefully selected strongpoints. He emphasised the new dimension which fire-power had given to defence. But although Foch sang his praises and said that "his teaching at the school had been of the highest order from every point of view," Pétain had made powerful enemies. Foch recommended him for the rank of full colonel but when General Franchet d'Esperey wished to nominate him for promotion to Brigadier so as later to be able to give him a Division, he received a curt reply from the Ministry of War. Pétain was never to be a divisional commander. It was with this sentence hanging over him that Pétain had accepted the colonelcy of the 33rd Regiment at Arras.

Everything about Pétain appealed to the young Lieutenant de Gaulle. The gulf between a sub-lieutenant and a colonel thirty-four years his senior was too wide for any intimacy and Pétain increased the gulf by cultivating unapproachability. He believed that a commander should keep his distance from his subordinates. But Pétain really commanded. He knew everything that went on in his regiment, was quick to censure, sparing in praise. He looked his part to perfection. Tall, fair haired, with eyes of so clear a blue that everyone who met him remarked upon them, he held himself erect whether sitting or standing; he looked magnificent on a horse. To Sub-Lieutenant de Gaulle, Pétain seemed the embodiment of authority. "My first colonel—Pétain—taught the art and meaning of command," he wrote later.[16]

What particularly impressed de Gaulle was Pétain's capacity to think for himself and the fearless manner in which he expressed criticism. At the end of his first year of service he was to witness a typical example. The culminating point of the manoeuvres in the autumn of 1913, in which the 33rd Regiment took part, was a splendid charge of three regiments against a village on top of a hill. After a perfunctory bombardment by artillery, the troops, dressed in red trousers and blue tunics, advanced with fixed bayonets, flags flying, the bands in front, to take the village by storm. General Gallet, who was in command, seemed delighted. When Pétain's turn came to offer comment during the discussion which followed the exercise he began: "I am sure that General Gallet decided, in order the more forcibly to impress you, to present in this exercise the synthesis of all the faults a modern army must no longer commit."[17]

Such irony goes far to explain why Pétain had so often been passed over in promotion, but it delighted the young Charles de Gaulle. Irony was a cult he was to develop himself and, like Pétain, to use to make senior officers appear ridiculous in front of their subordinates. However he never dared try it on Pétain. Far apart in age though they were the two men had much in common. General Sérigny, Pétain's friend for thirty years, described him as "cold, almost glacial"; Charles's relations were still making jokes about his being reared in an ice house. In everything to do with his profession Pétain was meticulous; so was the young lieutenant. Both were careful of their appearance and scrupulous over the meaning of words. Both had a firm belief in their own powers and despised mediocrity; but whereas Pétain could conceal his disdain de Gaulle could seldom help showing it. Both men regarded the French Army as the one stable and unifying force in France.

Of course they also differed. Pétain could relax whereas de Gaulle could only mark time. There is a charming story told of Pétain as a young officer paying a visit to a Casino in the south of France. He had put ten francs—a large sum for him—on a number at the roulette table and to his delight heard the number called by the croupier. Three hundred and sixty francs were pushed towards him. But just as he was about to pick the money up he glanced across the table and saw his commanding officer standing opposite, looking at him. Young officers were not allowed to gamble. Without a word Pétain turned away leaving the money where it was. De Gaulle has never gambled in his life.

Pétain could not resist women. He was a bachelor until he was sixty-two and during those years "his uniform flitted from skirt to skirt." Even during the first world war Pétain's Chief of Staff had the utmost difficulty in keeping women away from his headquarters. General Sérigny recounts that one day he received in great secrecy a telegram decoded by the French Secret Service which the German ambassador in Madrid had sent to his own government.[18] In it the ambassador announced that he had at last been able to engage a mistress for the French General at a salary of 12,000 pesetas a month. General Sérigny showed Pétain the telegram and asked him if he had any suspicion who the woman might be who had been chosen by the enemy. Pétain, after a pause, replied "yes." Sérigny thereupon took advantage of the occasion to warn the General once more about his relations with women, after which "their visits became a little less frequent." However Pétain was not fundamentally flippant. As a captain he had fallen in love with a Mlle. Hardin but when he asked for her hand her father had refused. He did not believe that the prospects of a young officer were good enough. His daughter married someone else. Pétain swore that he would never marry any other girl and when the war was over and Mme. Vardon, as she had become, was left a widow, Pétain made her Madame la Maréchale. They remained devoted for the rest of Pétain's life. Charles de Gaulle, on the other hand, was reticent about women even when young. He hated the coarse jokes that Pétain used to tell. A woman who knew him over many years said that she always felt that Charles regarded her sex either as a source of physical pleasure or a waste of time. But other than his wife, no woman's name has ever been linked with de Gaulle's, and he has been an exemplary husband and father.

But these differences in character did not bother the young lieutenant de Gaulle. At Arras, Pétain became his hero. "He was a great man," he wrote after the war, and although in de Gaulle's eyes the greatness was to fall away, he never retracted his opinion of Pétain in his prime. On his side Pétain had taken favourable notice of his tall, ungainly but dedicated second lieutenant. Two comments from de Gaulle's personal military dossier, both written in 1913 and signed by Pétain read as follows:

"Passed out of St. Cyr thirteenth out of 211, has proved from the beginning to be an officer of real worth who raises high hopes for the future. Throws his whole heart into his job as instructor. Gave a brilliant lecture on the causes of the conflict in the Balkan Peninsular."[19]

The second entry is dated Arras, October, 1913, the day de Gaulle was promoted to lieutenant:

"Very intelligent, passionately devoted to his profession. Handled his section perfectly on manoeuvres. Worthy of all praise."

This high opinion in the man who was soon to become Commander in Chief of the French armies was to stand Charles de Gaulle in good stead in the years to come. For Pétain did not forget, and was to become de Gaulle's friend and protector. Although at the time their relationship was distant and formal, at Arras a bond was formed between Charles de Gaulle and his colonel which, with one exception, was to prove the most important of his life.

* * *

While Charles was learning the rudiments of his profession the European powers had moved to the brink of war and then retreated. In July, 1911, while de Gaulle was at St. Cyr, the Kaiser suddenly sent a gun-boat into the little West African harbour of Agadir and threatened to denounce the agreement which had been reached giving France virtual control over Morocco. For three weeks the world held its breath expecting war to break out at any moment. Ironically the decision rested with Britain, who was not directly involved and whose Liberal cabinet had struggled for five years to maintain the peace. Lloyd George, the Chancellor of the Exchequer, and the young Home Secretary, Winston Churchill, had both opposed increases in the British fleet demanded by the Admiralty in the hope that Germany might curtail her naval building programme. It was upon this overwhelming desire for peace in London that the Kaiser was relying when he attempted to overawe the French. But Grey, the British Foreign Secretary, was alarmed at the Kaiser's sudden move and on July 21 Lloyd George made a speech at the Mansion House in which he indicated that if Britain were to be treated "as if she were of no account in the Cabinet of Nations" then "peace at that price" would be too great a humiliation. Lloyd George's audience of city magnates scarcely

applauded such a platitudinous statement, but in the Chancelleries of
Europe it echoed like a thunderclap. If Lloyd George counselled resistance it meant that England would fight alongside France. The Kaiser
drew back. In 1912, when the Balkan League, encouraged by Russia,
attacked Turkey and provided Lieutenant de Gaulle with the subject
of a "brilliant lecture," Germany supported Britain and successfully
limited the conflict and in the following year brought it to a close. By
the end of 1913 hopes of peace were brighter than for a decade. The
people of Europe dreaded war. The socialists, gaining ground everywhere, held conference after conference to try and organise passive
resistance among workers which would make war impossible. In
France the law extending military service to three years had been
fought almost as bitterly as the Dreyfus case. When in June, 1914, the
Liberal and Socialist parties led by Caillaux and Jaurés swept into
power at the General Election and a new left-wing government was
formed under M. Viviani, it seemed as if the forces of moderation
were firmly in the ascendant.

But in 1914 parliaments were even less a guarantee of peace than
they are to-day. Great issues were decided by monarchs, goaded or
restrained by a handful of advisers or by small inner cabinets which
often presented their colleagues and supporters with a *fait accompli*. In
the end the desire of the Russians to promote pan-Slavism in the
Balkans at the expense of the Austro-Hungarian and Turkish empires,
and the determination of the Kaiser to build a navy which would free
him from the irksome limitations imposed by the British command of
the sea, bedevilled every attempt to halt the armaments race. Poincaré,
elected President of France at the beginning of 1913, had done all in
his power to further Russian preparations for war and in defiance of
French public opinion, had stimulated the vociferous minority of his
own countrymen who clamoured for revenge upon Germany. When
the Archduke Franz Ferdinand of Austria was murdered by Serbian
terrorists in July, 1914, those who had desired war were to have their
way.

Yet France was not really ready for such a trial of strength. Although General Joffre, "a silent solid man" trained as an army engineer
who had reluctantly accepted the post of Commander in Chief after
the dismissal of General Michel in 1911, had put an end to the purges
and counter-purges within the officer corps and done much to restore
morale, there were fatal weaknesses in the High Command. Michel's
correct assessment of the German plan of campaign through Belgium
had been discarded in favour of an offensive plan by which the French
hoped to recapture the lost provinces of Alsace and Lorraine. Yet,

according to a French senator, the manoeuvres of 1914 had shown that the army was "badly equipped, badly trained and badly led." Joffre held an inquiry and removed three corps commanders. But no last minute changes could make good the shortage of heavy machine guns or the absence of any heavy artillery—the lack of that essential fire-power for which Colonel Pétain had pleaded so obdurately.

None of these fatal deficiencies were then apparent to the young Lieutenant de Gaulle. The "muffled hopefulness" with which he had looked forward to the great ordeal need be no longer suppressed. "I admit," he wrote later, "that in the prime of youth I envisaged without horror and magnified in advance this adventure into the unknown."[20] It was all quite natural, particularly in a young man of his class and up-bringing. Thousands of others in Britain, Germany, Russia and Austria were feeling the same. In London Raymond Asquith was telling Cosmo Lang, the future Archbishop of Canterbury, what a relief it was only to have to do what one was told to do in a cause in which one believed. In France the enthusiasm of youth was the more striking because of the turmoil through which the country had just passed. To de Gaulle it seemed as if a miracle was taking place, the miracle of the "Union Sacré" in which differences of class, religion, political belief were suddenly extinguished in a wave of patriotism. The unity for which he had longed was suddenly there, standing before him in the long line of recruits who had flocked to the colours and were waiting eagerly to be trained.

The ecstasy Charles felt when war was declared burst through the pages of one of his later books. "It is only necessary for France to draw the sword for every fervour to merge in unison . . . Everything which can contribute to such an upsurge—patriotism, religious faith, hope, hatred of the enemy—is at once strengthened by mass approbation. On the other hand theories which one might have thought would be obstacles to such a movement of opinion suddenly disappear. Not a group stands out against mobilisation. Not a trade union seeks to hinder it by a strike. In parliament there is not a vote missing to pass the necessary credits for war. The number of defaulters among those called up, officially estimated at 13%, turns out to be no more than 1.5%. Three hundred and fifty thousand volunteers besieged the recruiting offices. Frenchmen living abroad forced their way on to trains and ships so as to return to their country. Suspects listed under Carnet B begged to be allowed to go to the Front. One sees 3,000 peace-time deserters rush to the frontiers demanding the right to fight."[21]

Lieutenant de Gaulle marched to the attack with the first battalion of the 33rd Regiment which formed part of the second division of General Lanrezac's 5th Army on the Meuse. This division was one of the first to be engaged and on August 15, 1914—a day about which Charles had had strange premonitions that it would be his last—he was slightly wounded while defending the bridge at Dinant. De Gaulle was sent back to Arras for a minor operation, but fearing he might fall into the hands of the advancing Germans, left hospital and took a taxi at his own expense to Paris where he was operated upon a second time. Next day he left hospital again, hiring a car to get away from the Capital which was being encircled. Rejoining his regiment three months later he found it under new command, for Pétain had already been given a brigade. The new Colonel, Claudel, made him his adjutant, a role which de Gaulle so interpreted as to allow him to make frequent reconnaissances beyond the front line for which, in January, 1915, he was mentioned in despatches. In February Colonel Claudel was succeeded by Lieutenant Colonel Boudhors and it was still as adjutant that de Gaulle took part in the battle of Champagne, which was launched partly to give relief to the Russians who were being hard pressed in Poland.

By now de Gaulle was an acting captain and a veteran. He had shown both stamina and courage and seemed to bear a charmed life. He disdained trenches and would never bend down even in the front line, yet no sniper ever hit him. At times he seems to have been guilty of senseless bravado. Once, when inspecting his company with two lieutenants, de Gaulle saw a mortar shell coming straight towards them. His companions saw it too and threw themselves on the ground. De Gaulle remained standing waiting for the explosion; the shell burst quite close but nobody was injured. As the smoke cleared away and the lieutenants picked themselves up de Gaulle turned to them and asked, "Were you afraid, Gentlemen?" Yet de Gaulle was also becoming disillusioned. An officer in his regiment, describing the conditions under which they were fighting, wrote "on our side heavy artillery was non-existent, munitions scarce; the enemy was protected by thick networks of barbed-wire which we were quite powerless to breach. The assaults were costly and fruitless, the gains insignificant, the losses enormous."[22] It was the same story along the whole battle-front, and de Gaulle began to rail against commanders who could sacrifice the flower of French manhood so futilely. Lacking all diffidence he delivered his protests in person, first at division headquarters and finally at the 5th Army's General Staff. It made no difference.

De Gaulle was wounded again near Mesnil-les-Hurlus in March, 1915, and this time took five months to recover. He rejoined his regi-

1. Charles de Gaulle at the age of 7 with his sister Marie Agnès and his brother Xavier

2. De Gaulle the footballer

ment at the end of July near Berry-au-Bac, to find himself engaged in intensive trench warfare. Then fate gave a twist to his career. Six months later the battle of Verdun was at its height and Pétain, who had broken all records by rising from the command of a brigade to that of an army corps in two months, was put in command of all the armies defending the fortress. The first corps of the 5th Army was assigned to him to stem the German attack. Thus de Gaulle once more came under the command of his old colonel.

The 33rd Regiment went into the front-line at Douaumont straight from the lorries which had transported them. They fought a terrific battle for six days holding, losing and regaining the line under a bombardment which reduced the village to rubble. In the end de Gaulle's Company was practically wiped out and he himself wounded in the thigh and taken prisoner while unconscious. For this action de Gaulle was awarded the *Croix de Chevalier de la Légion d'Honneur*. The citation was unusual. "Captain de Gaulle, a company commander, renowned for his high intellectual and moral qualities, when his battalion had been decimated after suffering a terrible bombardment, finding that his company was being attacked from all sides by the enemy, led his men in a furious hand to hand fight, the only solution which he felt compatible with his view of military honour. Fell in the battle. An officer without equal in every respect."[23] Such a tribute could only have been paid by a man who knew de Gaulle personally. It was signed by Pétain. When de Gaulle regained consciousness he found that the German soldier who was tending him was the same man whom a little while before he had been doing his utmost to kill. It was February, 1916. For the rest of the war he was to remain a prisoner.

* * *

For a young man who had dreamed such dreams of glory and who, in each successive battle, had shown that he preferred death to captivity, the monotony and frustration of prison life must have been especially galling. However de Gaulle made the most of his time. He learned German, read the German newspapers to keep abreast of the war (the Allied communiqués were printed without censorship), studied and pondered the military situation and lectured his fellow prisoners remorselessly on everything from the ideal form of State to the future "war of movement." Many of the ideas which he was afterwards to develop germinated behind the walls of Fort Nine as he struggled to combine the principle Pétain had taught him—the overriding importance of fire-power—with some means of breaking down the static warfare to which the development of heavy artillery and the machine gun had led. Once again he earned the nickname of "Constable of France."

De Gaulle also tried to escape. He got outside the walls or wire five times but each time was quickly recaptured. His height was a disadvantage but he does not seem to have taken much trouble to conceal it. Once, having got out through a tunnel, he was caught walking across country in broad daylight. Like most prisoners de Gaulle was posted from camp to camp. He began at Szuczyn in Poland and ended at Fort Nine, Ingolstadt, Bavaria, the Colditz of the First World War where intrepid escapers were finally lodged. It was an international community, amusingly described by the English cricketer, Lieutenant A. J. Evans in his book *The Escape Club*. Tardieu, Berger-Levrault, Catroux, Tukatchevsky, Garros the air ace, were all inmates who at some time were to cross de Gaulle's path again. He remained at Ingolstadt until the Armistice.

De Gaulle was spared one experience by being made a prisoner. He did not live through the mutiny of the French army in 1917. Yet it has a place in his life because of the role which Marshal Pétain played.

The mutiny is an extraordinary story. The awful losses against which de Gaulle had protested in 1916 continued throughout the year and reached a peak in Nivelle's disastrous offensive the following spring. The French army was exhausted. Billeting conditions were appalling, food scarce and bad, first-aid primitive and leave often countermanded. For some time the troops had been the prey of an insidious peace propaganda, financed by the Germans but encouraged by Louis Malvy, the Minister of the Interior. Morale had suffered. The Russian revolution in February had given a new zest to subversion and strengthened the hands of the defeatists. Many Frenchmen, both inside and outside the army, began to feel that the war could not be won.

Then suddenly, at the end of April, 1917, the mutinies began. The first refusal to obey orders occurred in the 4th Army in Champagne on April 29. It spread like wildfire. Men who had survived the massacre brought about by Nivelle's obstinacy refused to go back into the line. Two Russian brigades deposed their officers, introduced Soviets and refused to fight. Their example was infectious. Whole units in the rear threw down their arms and made off for home shouting "death to officers" and singing revolutionary songs. Officers were spat upon and man-handled. Two regiments commandeered lorries and, fully armed, began to drive to Paris. By June the mutiny had spread to five army corps and affected fifty-four divisions. The French army was paralysed.

Troops still manned the front-line but they would neither move out of it nor into it except on their own terms.

And yet the news never leaked out. Although thousands of French citizens had witnessed the disorders, and pitched battles between loyal troops and mutineers had been fought, only the barest hint of the true state of affairs reached France's allies and little more the majority of Frenchmen. Pétain gave Sir Douglas Haig, the British Commander in Chief, an inkling of what was happening when he explained that the French could no longer give their promised support to the British attack on the Messine Ridge. Trenchard, a commander of the Royal Flying Corps, actually witnessed mutiny when his car was held up for six hours in a village by "a rabble of soldiers and refugees." But no British Commander informed his government and Lloyd George and the British Cabinet remained in ignorance until after it was all over. Until the beginning of June not even the French President, M. Poincaré, knew the truth. When Painlevé, the Minister of War, explained the situation to the War Cabinet in the presence of Pétain, who had succeeded Nivelle as Commander in Chief, Poincaré was dumbfounded. He asked what would happen if the Germans attacked. Pétain replied that there were only two dependable divisions between Soissons and Paris. The Germans, had they known, could have reached the capital in a few days.

It was Pétain's greatest achievement to have restored the morale of the French army and to have made it capable within a year of taking the major part in the final battles under Foch which ended the war. He did it by a mixture of ruthlessness and sympathy, by meeting grievances as well as by punishing ringleaders. And he did it in time. At a critical moment in the great German offensive in the spring of 1918, when it looked as if the British line might break, he was able to send Haig reinforcements and to take over a sector of the front. He repaid the debt he owed to Haig for the part the British had played the year before. No subsequent failure, neither his defeatism in 1918 or 1940, can detract from the laurels Pétain earned in that shattering year.

De Gaulle in Fort Nine knew none of these things. When he returned and learned about them he became an even more devoted admirer of the Marshal and soon one of his inner circle of friends.

CHAPTER II

CLIMBING THE LADDER

Charles de Gaulle always regarded the two and a half years he had spent as a prisoner as a tremendous handicap in his military career. And he was right. While he had been alternately tunnelling and lecturing in prison camps, those of his contemporaries who survived the holocaust had risen in rank and gained invaluable experience both on the battlefield and on the Staff. The probability that he would have been killed had he remained free was of no comfort to him. He had been left behind in the race and somehow had to make up lost ground.

Yet the continuity of his life had never been wholly broken. De Gaulle was essentially the scholar-soldier, and in prison he had greatly extended his knowledge. Having learned German he had soaked himself in the daily happenings of an enemy country at war, through the newspapers and through conversations with his guards. He had continued to read history and studied the German philosophers. He had written as well as lectured. And he had done all this not merely to pass the time but deliberately, to develop his own thought and powers of expression. Before he left Ingolstadt he carefully collected all his notes and put them in a suitcase to which he clung through all the vicissitudes of the journey home. This was his stock-in-trade.

The Armistice came just before de Gaulle's twenty-eighth birthday and he arrived in France just after it. He had been granted the substantive rank of captain. From Paris he went straight to his parents' country home in the Dordogne, but devoted son though he was, peace and quiet were the last things he wanted. He longed for action and after a few weeks with his parents went in search of it.

In Europe in 1919 there was no shortage of causes for which a man could still fight. The Armistice had halted Armageddon but under its umbrella a host of minor quarrels had broken out. The break-up of four empires had let loose the forces of suppressed nationalism from the Rhine to the Don. Separatist movements blossomed in Bavaria, Bessarabia, the Ukraine. Greece was on the point of attacking Turkey. The Rumanians invaded Hungary. Poles, Czechs and Yugoslavs were at each other's throats over the frontiers of their newly constituted countries. But the greatest threat to the peace which allied statesmen were planning at Versailles came as a result of the Russian revolution. The Bolsheviks were winning the civil war inside Russia and as a result revolutionary cells in every country emerged from the shadows and entered the struggle for power. In Hungary Bela Kun succeeded in maintaining a communist dictatorship for several months. Poland, however, was the key. If the communists could capture this new buffer state which had risen from the ashes of war, they would dominate eastern Europe and carry the threat of revolution to every country between the Oder and the Atlantic. In 1919 the issue hung in the balance.

The Ukraine, which had been fighting the Red and White armies alternately for its independence since the revolution, suddenly found itself at war with Poland in Eastern Galicia. The Poles won and almost immediately became the allies of the Ukrainians fighting the Red Army. Under an agreement concluded between Petlura, the Ukrainian leader, and Pilsudski, the socialist revolutionary who had become nationalist leader in Warsaw, Polish troops entered the Ukraine at the beginning of 1919. However they were hard pressed and needed reinforcements. It was then that Pilsudski turned to France. A large number of Poles had escaped to France during the war and Pilsudski asked if a mission could visit France and recruit a Polish division. Nothing could have suited the French government better. The collapse of the Russian Empire had left France without her traditional ally in eastern Europe. Clemenceau, spurred on by Foch, had already decided that, if the Bolsheviks could not be overthrown within their own borders, they must be sealed off. This meant strengthening both Poland and Rumania. Accordingly in April, 1919, the Polish General, Joseph Haller, arrived in France and began recruiting.

To Charles de Gaulle, fretting over lost seniority and chafing at inactivity, General Haller seemed heaven-sent. The Polish struggle appealed to him. The fierce patriotism of the Poles matched his own, whereas the internationalism preached by the communists seemed to be undermining the most natural and noble feelings of mankind. It was with something of the spirit in which his ancestors had gone off to the Crusades that in May, 1919, Charles joined the 4th Division of Polish *chasseurs*. A few months later he was on his way to Warsaw.

By the time de Gaulle's division arrived, the war was beginning to go against the Ukrainians. Exhausted by three years of civil war following immediately upon the struggle against Germany, their enthusiasm for Petlura was waning. The Polish troops received less and less Ukrainian support. The 4th Division was sent up to Volhynie where, for several months of hard fighting, it held up the advance of the Red Army. But by June, 1920, the Polish army under General Rydz-Smigly was forced to evacuate Kiev. The following month the Red Army, led by the former Czarist officer and de Gaulle's fellow prisoner of war, Tukatchevsky, crossed the Polish frontier and within three weeks was only fifteen miles from Warsaw. On July 23 the Poles sued for an armistice. It looked not only as if de Gaulle's adventure but the whole fabric of allied and above all of French policy in eastern Europe was going to collapse.

The Allied governments made feverish efforts to forestall this by getting the Russians to accept a conference. This the Russians did. But the Bolshevik leaders were both clever and confident. Before negotiations began they circulated the terms upon which they agreed to recognise Poland's independence. Like the Lublin Committee twenty-five years later, the Bolsheviks laid down conditions that would immediately have brought the country under communist dictatorship. Since none of the Allies was in a position to send troops, pressure was brought to bear on the Poles to accept. And then, suddenly, what Sir Winston Churchill described as "the miracle of the Vistula" happened. Although negotiations for an armistice were still in progress and the International Conference was due to open at Minsk, the battle for Warsaw suddenly exploded. While de Gaulle's division stood firm in front of Modlin, Pilsudski attacked the Red Army's southern flank and within four days the battle was over. The Russian army was virtually destroyed and 70,000 prisoners taken. Poland was saved.

Weygand, who headed a small French mission to Warsaw and has often been given more credit for the Polish victory than he would himself accept, had watched the fighting in front of the capital and had noticed de Gaulle. He gave him his fourth mention in dispatches. He described him as a remarkably intrepid officer with exceptional intellectual and moral qualities. Charles de Gaulle's gamble had come off. He had once again proved to himself and his superiors that he was a good fighting soldier. He could return to France with improved chances of promotion. But then a curious thing happened. Another Frenchman, Colonel Mercier, who was in charge of the Polish officers' school at Rembertow, just outside Warsaw, offered de Gaulle the post of lecturer in infantry training. De Gaulle accepted. No doubt he was inspired by the prospect of helping to build the country he had just defended and perhaps garrison duties in France seemed dull in comparison; but it was a surprising step for a young man so in love with his own country to take. It seemed almost as if de Gaulle had made up his mind that the best way to get on was to stay abroad. His lectures, based on those he had prepared at Ingolstadt, at once attracted attention and Chief of Staff of the Polish army, General Stanislas Haller (a cousin of General Joseph Haller) proposed to appoint him professor at the new *École de Guerre*. Again de Gaulle would have accepted, but at this point the French Ministry of War intervened. Whether because of Weygand's recommendation or the long memory of his old commander, Marshal Pétain, now Inspector-General of the French army and Vice-President of the War Council, de Gaulle was recalled to France. In October, 1921, he was appointed lecturer in French military history at St. Cyr. The aftermath of the First World War was over. De Gaulle at last had his foot on the ladder.

*   *   *

Charles de Gaulle returned from Poland not merely to a new job but to a new life. According to some of his contemporaries Charles had always spoken rather cynically of marriage. If this was so he was soon to eat his words. While on leave in Paris in 1919 he had been introduced at the *Salon d'Automne* to the daughter of a wealthy biscuit manufacturer in Calais, Yvonne Vendroux. She was dark, pretty, well educated but shy. A few days later Yvonne accompanied her brother Jacques to Paris. At the Ball of the *École Polytechnique* in Versailles she met de Gaulle again. He was no great dancer, but during a waltz he asked her to marry him and she accepted. Before he went back to Poland they had become unofficially engaged. On his next leave they were married. The wedding took place from the Vendroux's house in Calais on April 21, 1921.

When he took up his position at St. Cyr, therefore, de Gaulle had a home and a wife with a strong personality and some money of her own. This was fortunate, for inflation was doubling the cost of living every few months and, since army pay lagged far behind prices, most young officers were having a hard struggle. The young de Gaulles were by no means a typical army couple. They took a flat on the Left Bank in Paris at No 4 Boulevard des Invalides and were able to spend their holidays with de Gaulle's relations in Lille or his wife's parents at the Château de Septfontaines in the Ardennes near Charleville. Apart from their families neither Charles nor Yvonne was very sociable. Yvonne preferred the country to Paris and Charles, besides being absorbed in his career, had just begun work on his first book. They were happy and self-contained.

The next three years were critical for Charles. As he well knew the

lectureship at St. Cyr was a test. If he did well then the approbation
of both Pétain and Weygand might sweep away the obstacles to quick
promotion and allow him to make good the years he had lost. If he
blotted his copy book then a regimental command and early retirement
were probably the best that he could hope for. The period of history
that Charles was to cover in his lectures started with Napoleon I and
finished at the end of the nineteenth century.* His treatment of it was
not original. The main theme, the grandeur of France which providence
had created for some exalted and exceptional destiny, might have been
written by Maurras, Péguy or Barrès in 1913. Echoing the anti-
Buonapartist views of his parents, he was harsh on Napoleon who had
left France "crushed, invaded, drained of blood and of courage, smaller
than when he took control, condemned to accept bad frontiers, the
evils of which have never been redressed . . ."[1] But he remarked that
even to-day crowds came from all over the world to render homage to
his memory and succumbed before his tomb to the "thrill of his
grandeur." He was critical of French military leadership but held that
the courage of the French troops had redeemed the defeat of 1870 and
turned the disastrous battle of the frontiers in 1914 into a moral victory.

Above all de Gaulle stressed the themes dear to the heart of Pétain,
the importance of fire-power and the irrelevance of colonial expansion.
At heart de Gaulle was always a metropolitan Frenchman. Expenditure
of life and treasure in Africa in the nineteenth century, and particularly
in Algiers, he told his pupils, gave France only the illusions of glory.
Her losses weakened her and the spread of her responsibilities was a
distraction which prevented her statesmen from exercising their true
influence in Europe. Even the Crimean War was a mistake, for however brilliant French feats of arms, the weakening of Russia and Austria
meant that France was strengthening the rising power of Germany
and condemning herself to a rivalry the effects of which she would
have to support alone.

All this made an excellent impression which was enhanced by his
natural ability as a lecturer. He enunciated beautifully, spoke lucidly
and used few gestures. And de Gaulle had presence. He held himself
erect and was always immaculately dressed in long black riding-boots
and a sky-blue uniform with a stiff collar. His unusual height was
emphasised by being tapered at both ends. And, whether strictly correct
or not, he always wore white gloves which his young wife used to wash
herself to make sure they were absolutely clean. Young cadets with a

---

* Although no written version of these lectures exists, much of the substance was
reproduced in the book *France and her army* which de Gaulle began writing a year
later. It was published in 1938 by Berger-Levrault.

sharp eye for any eccentricity are not the easiest audience to hold; but while de Gaulle was speaking there was absolute silence. Yet in spite of this success, during his last two years as a lecturer at St. Cyr, de Gaulle was not only to undo the good impression he had made but to bring his career to the very verge of ruin. If it had not been for Pétain his final lecture at St. Cyr might have been the last that he delivered.

The goal of all ambitious young officers was to serve for a period on the General Staff, the road to which lay through the *École Supérieure de Guerre* which had been re-opened in 1919. Not having served on any General Staff during the war, de Gaulle was not automatically qualified to apply for admission and during his first year as assistant professor at St. Cyr he prepared himself for the competitive examination. He was accepted and entered on his two year course in November, 1922. For a year therefore he was professor and pupil at the same time.

Owing to the war the intake into the *École Supérieure* was unusual. The prestige of French arms was such, after the victory of 1918, that the Forty-fourth course, to which de Gaulle belonged, was international in character. Thirty-one of the 206 officers came from fourteen foreign countries. (Four were American; there were no British.) Even more unusual, most of the professors and students had had actual experience of fighting. All the professors had commanded in the field and inevitably used first-hand knowledge in their teaching. On the other hand students, who had been at the receiving end of these commands, could also draw upon their own experience from many different fronts. Their attitude to their professors was more critical and their criticism better informed than would be the case for another quarter of a century. Inevitably there was friction. The professors tended to emphasise the strategy and tactics which had led to Allied—in their eyes mainly French—victory and to draw conclusions from the immediate past which seemed valid for the foreseeable future. In particular the fighting on the Western Front seemed to have given overwhelming confirmation to the view of Marshal Pétain that, in modern war, fire-power was decisive. It was because this teaching had gone unheeded that the Allies suffered such appalling casualties in the first three years of the war; it was because of his own direction of the battle of Verdun and subsequent allied offensives that the Allies had gained victory in the end.

With these truths in mind the professors at the *École Supérieure* in the 1920s developed a theory of warfare which seemed to them of mathematical certainty. Artillery and the machine gun dominated the battle. *A priori* it was possible to build a line and behind that line to build up certain selected positions from which attacks could be launched as fire-power slowly advanced. Tanks could help, but only in conjunction with the infantry advancing behind a barrage.

This *a priori* school of thought was forcibly represented at the *École Supérieure* by its Commandant, Colonel Moyrand, an old colleague of Marshal Joffre, a man of high character with a brilliant war record. But his teaching was not accepted without demur by all his pupils. Many of them had been at the battle of Verdun and had learned by bitter experience the truth of Pétain's dictum; but some had also seen the fighting in 1918, when de Gaulle was a prisoner of war, and had drawn their own conclusions about the possible use of tanks and armoured vehicles. A few had already attended the "School for New Machines," which had been founded in 1919 under General Estienne, where ideas based on the independent use of tanks and motorised infantry were being developed.

One of de Gaulle's contemporaries at the *École Supérieure*, Captain Chauvin, had already expressed disagreement publicly with the fashionable view that tanks should only be used as infantry protection. Captain Chauvin, who had passed out first in his class from the tank school, was giving lectures in various garrison towns at this time, advocating the use of tanks as an automatous force with a strategic purpose. A young lieutenant, Cailloux, went further and tried to demonstrate during one of the exercises how tanks could be used by themselves for a forward thrust. But these young Turks were not taken seriously by the professors at the *École Supérieure*. Cailloux in particular was told to go away and play with his "toys."

The further the Forty-fourth Course went in its study, the wider the gap between the professors and pupils became. Cailloux, who was later to become a general, spoke of it as a "divorce" which was obscured by discipline and traditional respect for most of the time but which became open and absolute whenever exercises were thrown open to discussion. What the young officers hoped for was an imaginative appraisal of war in the future designed to take advantage of the fact that the Allies had a new form of mobile fire-power in the tank,which was forbidden to the Germans. What they got were detailed lessons in the art of combining infantry, artillery and—to a lesser degree— tanks, but always in the context of trench warfare to which the professors appeared to see no alternative.

De Gaulle had not yet made a special study of tanks, but he sensed a rigidity in the attitude of his professors and was soon known as the one who asked the most awkward questions. His memory was prodigious. On one occasion the Course was touring the battlefields round Metz, where French troops had fought gallantly but in vain in the 1870s. When they reached a certain village which had been the scene of a battle in that campaign, some of the officers asked the Commandant, General Dufieux, if they might recapitulate the action. The General agreed and called upon one of the more senior, a Major, to describe it. Taken by surprise the officer did his best, but was frequently at a loss for the name of a commander or the number of a unit. As he paused a muffled voice could be heard in the rear giving him the information he required. The pauses became longer, the prompting louder and most persistent until de Gaulle, whose voice it was, having been pushed to the front by his colleagues, took over from the Major and delivered a dazzling account of the fighting, naming each regiment in turn and describing in detail the part it had played. The Commandant, both amused and pleased, congratulated de Gaulle and some of his brother officers expressed envy of his memory. "Yes," replied de Gaulle, "that doesn't come in my sleep. I have cultivated my memory a great deal. From childhood I have memorised whole acts of classical plays. I know *Cyrano de Bergerac* by heart. With my brothers and sister I used to speak French backwards, *'el Siaçnarf.'* At first we did not get further than *'Riover ua, ruojnob, ut sav tnemmoc.'* I have continued to oil the machinery."[2]

However, de Gaulle's arrogance could also antagonise his instructors and provoke serious criticism. His personal file, at the end of the first year of the course, contained the following: "A lively intelligence, wide general culture, facility in expressing himself, sees the position correctly in the field, gives clear orders, has decision, very hard working.

"A very developed personality, great confidence in himself. Could achieve excellent results if he admitted mistakes with a little better grace and if he consented more easily to allow his point of view to be disputed. Has succeeded very well in all branches of the army."[3]

At the end of the second year, Colonel Moyrand himself had written some special notes on de Gaulle. "A very intelligent officer, cultivated and serious; has brilliance and facility; greatly gifted; much stuff in him.

"Unfortunately spoils his incontestable qualities by his excessive assurance, his severity towards the opinions of others and his attitude of being a King in Exile. Moreover, he appears to have more aptitude for general studies and for the synthesis of a problem than for its detailed examination and the practicalities of its execution.

"Exercised the command of an army corps during the first part of manoeuvres; showed decision in his task and calmness and the power to command, but also sometimes a failure of judgment; adopted solutions which were irrelevant to the situation, which he, however, honestly admitted.

"In the end fulfilled correctly, although impinging a little on the scope of his colleagues, the functions of Chief of the First Bureau of the Army Corps and Chief of Staff of the division."[4]

The truth was that de Gaulle presented a difficult problem for the professors of the *École Supérieure de Guerre*. They recognised his ability but were concerned that his character might disqualify him from exercising the highest command. Commenting later in life on the notes he had written, General Moyrand, as he had then become, wrote: "De Gaulle was an interesting but also a delicate and difficult case. He had great qualities. He was very egotistic. I thought him out of the ordinary. He mixed little with the other students. When he came to the auditorium he was almost always alone."[5] The other professors had similar reservations.

His fellow students were divided. A young man who keeps much to himself is never likely to be popular and de Gaulle made no attempt to court popularity. He commanded admiration but was also intensely irritating. He had answers for everything and expressed firm opinions on any subject under discussion. As always he disliked argument and when he saw himself being drawn into one would quickly withdraw, extricating himself with some epigram. His favourite was "*Tout est dans tout.*"

One of Charles's closest companions on the course was the future General André Laffargue, at the time a captain and two years Charles's junior.* Laffargue began by disliking him for his undisguised conceit, but gradually changed his opinion and found de Gaulle, on better acquaintance, neither disdainful nor haughty but original, possessed of humour and even gaiety. On the other hand he thought de Gaulle lacked balance and lived too much in a world of abstraction. Captain Chauvin, another member of the course, makes a rather similar comment: "In intelligence his superiority is as clear as in the realm of culture. Although his eyes are wide open to what goes on around him —more in relation to things than to men—he seems to rely on an intense inner life."[6]

Yet de Gaulle could unbend. Returning by bus or train from an exercise he would join with his cavernous voice in bawdy songs and once revealed that, in a period of extreme boredom in Poland, he had "gone on a binge" which had lasted five or six days. What he most enjoyed, however, was an olympian sally at the expense of more

* General Laffargue was later very critical of de Gaulle and gave evidence on behalf of Pétain at the latter's trial.

frivolous companions. One evening in the Mess the officers of the Forty-fourth Course arranged a special bull-fight in honour of some new arrivals from Spain. Laffargue, who took part, describes how he and several others rode on the backs of brother officers impersonating either the bull or the picador. De Gaulle, he says, took no part in the proceedings but moved about the room like a "silent phantom" watching every detail. At the height of the *corrida* Laffargue happened to pass close to de Gaulle, "galloping" with the legs of another officer; he heard de Gaulle remark sonorously, "in every association between men there is always one who will manage to get carried by the other."[7]

De Gaulle's companions enjoyed his wit; they found his ill-concealed sense of superiority more difficult to stomach. At the end of an exercise in which de Gaulle had been paired off with Chauvin they lay down together, their backs to the same oak tree, to smoke and rest. Their thoughts wandered. They discussed the future. Suddenly Chauvin heard himself saying: "*Mon cher*, I must tell you something which will no doubt make you smile. I have a curious feeling that you are pledged to a great destiny." Half-surprised at what he had said, Chauvin expected a dig in the ribs accompanied by some tart rejoinder. Instead there was silence. He turned his head and saw his companion gazing into the far distance. Then slowly and with emphasis de Gaulle replied: "Yes. I think so too."[8]

De Gaulle's disputes with his professors reached a climax during the final exercise, held near Bar-sur-Aube, in the summer of 1924. It was a full-scale "battle" in which Colonel Moyrand, the professor of general tactics, was to lead one side; de Gaulle the other. For the day, therefore, he became commander of an Army Corps with all the other officers on the course filling subordinate positions. Throughout the day Colonel Moyrand directed the manoeuvres facing the young captain with a variety of situations requiring quick decisions. De Gaulle acquitted himself admirably and was deemed to have won the battle.

The discussion of the exercise was held that evening in the classroom of the college at Bar-sur-Aube. Colonel Moyrand presided, de Gaulle sitting with some difficulty at a school desk in the front row. From the colonel's manner it soon became clear that he was not so much concerned with the discussion as with justification. The colonel maintained that de Gaulle had won the day because he had applied the *a priori* principle. De Gaulle disagreed, explaining calmly and politely that his method was empirical. The class, listening, realised that a clash of wills was taking place and that the result might affect de Gaulle's future. At the end the argument became heated. Colonel

Moyrand, visibly annoyed, put a question which was plainly irrelevant to what had gone before: "Where, then, was the baggage train of the left-hand regiment of your right-hand division?"[9]

Scarcely turning his head, de Gaulle said to his Chief of Staff: "Châteauvieux, please be good enough to answer."

"But it is you that I ask, de Gaulle," said Colonel Moyrand, now furious. "Colonel," replied de Gaulle more calmly than ever, "you gave me the responsibilities of an army commander. If I had also assumed those of my subordinates I should not have been able adequately to fulfil my mission. *De minimis non curat Praetor*. Châteauvieux, please reply to the colonel."

Colonel Moyrand, controlling himself with difficulty, retorted: "Very well. We know that you consider many tasks beneath you. I am now clear in my mind about you."

Since this was the final exercise, de Gaulle's clash with Moyrand was bound to have a disproportionate effect on his future career.

As passing-out day for the Forty-fourth Course approached there was a great deal of discussion among students and professors about the grading that de Gaulle would receive. There were three grades corresponding to "very good," "good," and "passable," and degrees within each grade ranging from A to E. Most of the students took it for granted that de Gaulle would be in the first grade, but argued about which degree he would be awarded. The majority of the professors, on the other hand, were in favour of relegating him to the third "passable" grade in view of his extreme self-confidence and resentment of criticism. The discussion was so animated and prolonged that wind of it—as well as of the altercation between Colonel Moyrand and de Gaulle over the final exercise—spread far beyond the confines of the *École Supérieure* and finally reached the ears of the Inspector-General of the Army, Marshal Pétain.

Ever since his days as colonel of the 33rd Regiment, Pétain had taken an interest in de Gaulle and since the latter's return from Poland had included him in the small group of young officers to which he gave his confidence. Mme. Pétain has said that in these years de Gaulle was a frequent visitor to their home. When de Gaulle's first son was born on December 28, 1921, the Pétains came to the christening and although the Marshal was not a Godfather, the boy was called Philippe in his honour. Above the baby's cot hung a framed picture of the Marshal with a signed inscription which read: "To my young friend Philippe de Gaulle, wishing that he might combine in his life all the qualities and all the gifts of his father, affectionately, Philippe Pétain."[10] Pétain's name was always on Charles's lips and although he spoke of the Marshal with some awe he was not above boasting of his association with the great man. On his side Pétain not only thought highly of de Gaulle but was particularly sympathetic over his difficulties with the *École Supérieure*. Having himself fallen foul of his superiors through a too blunt expression of his views when lecturing there, he understood exactly what the younger man was up against and was determined to help him. In Pétain's eyes the school was due for a snub and he took some pleasure in preparing one.

First Pétain made his own inquiries into the conduct of the final exercise held by the Forty-fourth Course. While on a tour of inspection he invited de Gaulle to explain his views in person. The Marshal was impressed and pronounced laconically that de Gaulle had been right. He also let it be known that he would regard the placing of de Gaulle in the third grade as a miscarriage of justice.

But although General Dufieux, the school's commandant, bowed to the Marshal's insistence and overruled his professors, he did no more than place de Gaulle in the second grade of "good." This was a great blow. It meant that de Gaulle had lost the right to apply for a post on the General Staff. Publicly he might protest that this was the last thing he wanted; inwardly he was furious. There is no question that he had expected to pass out with the highest honours and had never understood the resentment his arrogance and sarcasm had caused. Fuming, he remarked that he would never enter the school again except as commandant and that then people would see how things had changed.

The effects of this set-back were immediately apparent. In October, 1924, de Gaulle was posted to the Fourth Bureau of the staff of the "Land Army," which dealt with transport and supplies. After a few months, still in the same Bureau, he was transferred to the General Staff of the Army of the Rhine at Mainz, where he was entrusted in particular with the problems of refrigeration. Such postings were plainly intended to humiliate him and he became so depressed that at one time he even considered leaving the army. But his innate belief in himself came to his rescue and, not for the last time in his life, he emerged from the depths of depression more determined than ever to pursue his military career. "It is nice to be promoted," he wrote to his friend Lucien Nachin, "but the important thing is to make a mark."[11]

For some time Charles de Gaulle had been working on the notes he had brought back with him from Ingolstadt. Although a prisoner he had been fascinated by the spectacle of a great people going down to defeat. He had gleaned much from newspapers and conversations with his guards. In the intervening years he had written five essays in which he had attempted to analyse the main causes of German disintegration. The episodes he selected were the disobedience of General Von Kluck which, in de Gaulle's eyes, lost the Germans the battle of the Marne; the declaration of unrestricted submarine warfare; the relations of the Germans with their allies; the collapse of morale among the German people. Just before he went to Mainz he managed to get the essays published as a book under the title *La Discorde chez l'Ennemi*. The essays were readable and thorough but added nothing original to the many analyses of the war which were appearing at the time. The main interest in the book lies in the introduction, where de Gaulle ascribes the betrayal of a valiant people's sacrifice to the "Cult of the Superman" which had infected its leader and made them insensible and even contemptuous of the sufferings of the masses. De Gaulle had so much of the cult himself that this came as a surprise, particularly to those who knew him. It seemed inconsistent with the philosophy of leadership which he had already begun to preach. However de Gaulle was making a narrow and perhaps a valid point. He had never been and was never to become a militarist in the sense that he believed the army should be a political power. But in Germany this is what had happened. Because of the cult Hindenburg and Ludendorff had been accorded such adulation that they, and not the civil government, had wielded the real power. It was this, de Gaulle felt, that was primarily responsible for the German catastrophe.

But the book did not make the mark de Gaulle had hoped. Simply by publishing it he antagonised those who regarded any appeal by a serving officer to a wider audience as a backstairs method of pursuing an argument. Although his essays were well received by the few who read them, less than 1,000 copies of the book were sold and it was soon forgotten. Yet for Charles himself the publication was a turning point. Seeing normal avenues of promotion blocked, he had made up his mind to force his own way to the front. If his immediate superiors would not listen to him, he would appeal over their heads to the highest echelons of the army, to politicians and the public. It was a dangerous course which many have tried in all walks of life but in which few have succeeded. Yet for the next fifteen years it was to be de Gaulle's chief weapon in his struggle for recognition.

Meanwhile, at Mainz, de Gaulle's concern for refrigeration was almost symbolic. He went to the Rhineland at a time when France's relations not only with the Germans but with her former Anglo-Saxon allies had only just subsided below boiling-point. The French were in the process of evacuating the Ruhr which, under Poincaré, they occupied nearly two years before. Reluctantly and with bad grace they were abandoning the attempt to create independent governments in the Rhineland and the Saar which they had hoped would separate these territories from Germany and bring them under French domination.

French fears of a recrudescence of German nationalism were certainly justified. The myth that the German army had never been defeated on the field of battle but had been stabbed in the back by revolutionaries in Berlin, had been assiduously cultivated and was widely believed. Democracy was despised by both Conservatives and Communists and all parties were united in their determination to evade the terms of the Treaty of Versailles. Hitler had gone almost unpunished after his bloody failure in Munich earlier that year and his movement was growing; political murders were common and the murderer seldom caught. Exploiting this unrest, the Nationalist parties were working for rearmament and revenge.

Nevertheless the French attempt to dismember Germany had only made matters worse. The occupation of the Ruhr was a pretext by which France hoped to gain permanent possession of the Rhineland and subjugate German heavy industry to the *Comité des Forges*. But by arming the "separatists" and setting up puppet governments, the French were themselves breaking the treaty which they had imposed upon Germany and the brutality with which they perpetrated a succession of illegal acts antagonised even moderate German opinion. Pretending to be neutral in a local quarrel, French troops disarmed, arrested and expelled tens of thousands of German police, civil servants and patriotic citizens and stood by while their "separatist" riff-raff stormed government buildings and shot down innocent people in the streets. Certainly Germany was ruined. The savings of the middle classes had been wiped out by an inflation in which, at its peak, one dollar exchanged for four thousand two hundred billion marks. But France had gained nothing but hatred and Poincaré's fall from power in 1924 showed that even in his own country opinion was turning against him.

Although the last French troops left the Ruhr three months after de Gaulle arrived in Mainz, the "New Era" inaugurated by the Dawes Plan for Reparations was never more than a façade. The Germany that was readmitted to the Comity of Nations under the Treaty of Locarno was dedicated to revenge and above all to revenge on France. Even Stresemann was secretly an ally of Von Seeckt. Charles de Gaulle sensed this at once. He was, in any case, more in sympathy with Poincaré than his successor Herriot. In his lectures at St. Cyr he had stressed the vulnerability of France's northern and eastern frontiers;

he was then, and for another thirty years remained, a staunch advocate of the dismemberment of Germany and the restoration of its eighteenth century pattern of independent principalities. As a member of the General Staff of the Army of the Rhine he knew a good deal about the reorganisation of the German army which was taking place under the noses of the Allied Control Commission. The Germans he met confirmed his view that, as a people, they had never accepted defeat. "We are plunged in the darkness which preceded the dawn of a new world, or at any rate the world we have known," he wrote to Nachin. "Still, one must live and it is probable that in order to live one must one day fight . . . For my part I am happy to prepare myself for that day."[12] But his preparation was now to take a surprising turn.

Marshal Pétain had not forgotten Charles de Gaulle and was waiting for an opportunity to make use of his talents. Since the war there had been little discussion of the basic character of the French army. In 1921 a new "Law of Recruitment" had been passed, ordaining three years' military service. The army which emerged was territorially based and locally trained, a citizen army of the type which had failed so tragically in 1870 but which, because of the "miracle of the Marne," had eventually triumphed in 1918. The livelier spirits in the military hierarchy had been demanding a drastic overhaul of the whole system for some years. But the politicians had been hard to move. As Millerand followed Clemenceau; Briand, Millerand; Poincaré, Briand; and Herriot, Poincaré as head of the French government, each in turn had let sleeping dogs lie. The French army was still the strongest in the world and there seemed little to worry about. Then in 1924 the socialist government led by Herriot and Blum, bent on finding money to improve the French social services, began to talk of reducing the period of conscription from three years to two or even one.

The members of the *Conseil Supérieur de Guerre* became alarmed. They had been made uncomfortably aware of the British refusal to support French occupation of the Ruhr and saw clearly that, if France was to maintain her military superiority over the Germans, she would have to do so alone. But she needed a different kind of army. It was in these circumstances, towards the end of 1924, that Marshal Pétain, pressed by his *Chef de Cabinet*, Colonel Bouvard, initiated a review of the role and structure of the French army. So as not to alarm the politicians it was to take the form of a history in which the role of French arms and military institutions was to be traced throughout the ages. The final chapters were to suggest the reorganisation necessary if the army was to meet the threat of the future. As Colonel Bouvard was shortly retiring he needed a younger man to take charge of the work. The choice fell on de Gaulle. Since it was necessary for de Gaulle's career that he should spend some time on an army General Staff, the Marshal waited. It was not until October, 1925, therefore, that de Gaulle was recalled from Germany to Paris and made a member of Pétain's staff.

He went quickly to work. What Pétain was really aiming at was the construction of a fortified zone in the north east of France. De Gaulle was therefore instructed to prepare informed opinion for such a development by a historical survey of the role played by the permanent fortresses of the past. The theme suited him perfectly. He was a student of Vauban, the architect of Louis XIV's line of fortresses, and having fought the battle of the frontiers in 1919, was only too conscious of his country's vulnerability. He finished the essay in two months and published it in the *Revue Militaire Française* on December 1 under the title of *Rôle Historique Des Places Françaises*. Beginning from the time France attained her then boundaries, de Gaulle emphasised the weakness which the creation of Belgium constituted in the north, stressed the power and ambition of the Germans, the attraction which Paris held for them and the easy access afforded to it by the northern French plains; "the fortification of its territory is a permanent national necessity for France," he concluded.

Nothing de Gaulle was to write for another thirty years had such a success; as the theme had been dictated by the *Conseil Supérieur*, he had for once pleased the military hierarchy. The article was acclaimed as a masterly presentation of the case for the fortification of the north-eastern frontier. When in 1925 M. Poincaré once again became Premier, he and his Minister of War, M. Maginot, began the preparation of the famous line of fortresses which was to bear the latter's name. De Gaulle was pleased and proud. This time, however, some of his friends were disturbed; de Gaulle seemed to be advocating a purely defensive role for the French army. Nachin wrote querying the wisdom of a plan which might induce a false sense of security as well as disclose in advance France's main line of defence. De Gaulle replied at once, in January, 1926, and again in 1927. He claimed that Vauban's fortresses, few in number but impregnable, had "barred" the main routes into France and greatly reduced the mobility of Louis XIV's enemies; a modern system of fortifications, stretching from the Rhine to the North Sea, could perform a similar function. He defended himself against Nachin's criticisms by arguing that such a system should be part of a national defence plan, a concern of government rather than the High Command in the same way that the power of the economy was part of the defence plan. The High Command, which could not of course be confined to defence, would include the fortifications as one of its permanent assets. It was not, however, an asset on which an entire strategy could or should be based.

There is no question that Nachin was right and de Gaulle's argument specious. It was naïve to suggest that a government could spend milliards on a vast system of fortifications without at the same time inculcating a defensive attitude in its High Command. The essay reveals how slowly de Gaulle's tactical ideas had evolved. At the *École Supérieure* he had shown an interest in tanks and armoured vehicles but, like Pétain, he still regarded them as subjects for research and experiment. He was never an innovator like General Fuller and Captain Liddell Hart in England, who were already pressing for armoured divisions of the type which the Germans were soon to form and which were to prove so decisive in the Second World War. He never really grasped the implications of their power. It was to be many years before the lessons which contemporaries like Cailloux and Chauvin had so quickly learned became part of his thinking. It remains one of the ironies of history that de Gaulle, who was to become one of the fiercest critics of the "Maginot mentality," was himself one of the originators of the Maginot Line.

All that, however, lay in the future. What mattered in 1925 was that de Gaulle was restored to favour, able to play an important role as a member of Pétain's staff. Pétain himself was delighted and decided to take immediate advantage of de Gaulle's success. He had continued to brood on de Gaulle's grading at the *École Supérieure de Guerre* and when a member of his own staff, General Hering, described by one of his contemporaries as "the sworn enemy of all conformism," became the new commandant at the school in 1926, the Marshal returned to the charge. He told General Hering that de Gaulle's grading had been a scandal amounting to a miscarriage of justice and that reparation was due both to de Gaulle and himself. He wanted "to give a lesson to some of these professors—a lesson they will understand."[13] Pétain was well aware that the honour of lecturing at the school was reserved for those who had passed out in the first grade; he also knew how chagrined de Gaulle had been at missing this opportunity. He now decided, in defiance of all precedent, to make amends.

While de Gaulle was writing further chapters of the history of the French army through the summer and autumn of 1926, the Marshal continued to see General Hering and finally prevailed upon him to organise a series of lectures which de Gaulle would deliver and over which he, the Marshal, would preside in person. It is impossible to imagine a greater snub to the school's hierarchy. De Gaulle, still a captain, was to be brought in from outside to lecture not only to the students but to the professors themselves, under the eye of one of the most renowned Marshals of France.

Although de Gaulle must have been aware of the resentment he might cause, he did not hesitate. On April 27, 1927, he arrived at the *École Supérieure* to deliver his first lecture. The small band of professors was assembled in a room behind the school's auditorium. De Gaulle, immaculate and aloof, joined them. The Marshal arrived with General Hering. All drew back to let the Marshal enter the auditorium. But Pétain stopped and turning to de Gaulle made him go first saying: "It is the professor's privilege to lead the way. Once across the threshold the professor has the right to teach what he will. It is a sacred principle. It is thus that I applied it myself, giving vent to ideas different from my time."[14]

The procession filed into the auditorium with de Gaulle at its head. The professors took their places in the front row among the students. De Gaulle, in full uniform, mounted the stage. With the same slow and deliberate movements he had affected as a lecturer at St. Cyr, he took off his *képi* and laid it on the table, laid his sword beside it, took off his white gloves and waited for the Marshal to open the proceedings. The Marshal spoke one sentence: "Gentlemen, Captain de Gaulle is going to expound to you his ideas; I ask you to listen with attention."[15]

With his opening words de Gaulle resumed the attack on the fashionable *a priori* theory of warfare which he had waged against Colonel Moyrand in the same room two years before.

"The action of war," he began, "assumes essentially the character of contingency . . . The enemy may present himself in an infinite number of ways; he disposes of means of which it is impossible to know the exact force; his intentions are susceptible of taking an infinite number of directions."[16]

De Gaulle spoke fluently, without gestures, without notes, standing still or striding backwards and forwards across the stage. He quoted from memory Greek and French philosophers, writers like Bergson and Anatole France, all the great Continental commanders from Caesar and Hannibal onwards. The more he spoke, the more uncomfortable and angry the professors in the front row became. For de Gaulle's theme was the vital role of leadership, and the picture he painted of the leader was at once a criticism of his superiors, a justification of himself and a veiled but unmistakable tribute to the Marshal. He quoted a passage from Bergson in which the philosopher contends that the human intellect is at peace when contemplating solid matter, ill at ease when facing the changing realities of life. He called upon instinct to redress the balance.

"Great men of war have always been conscious of the role and the value of instinct. What Alexander called his hope, Caesar his fortune, Napoleon his star, is not this simply the certitude that a particular gift has put them in such a special relationship with reality that they can always dominate events?"

He quoted Flaubert's picture of the young Hannibal already clothed "with the indefinable splendour of those who are destined for great enterprises."

"Great leaders," he said, "possess the facility of isolating themselves morally, of keeping a hidden part of themselves free for meditation, a mystery, a secret, whereas the immense majority of men only dissimulate their interests." Leaders "calculated their gestures in such a way as to strike people's minds vividly, while common people took no such trouble."

When de Gaulle reached his peroration he threw caution to the winds. The period in which they lived, he said bluntly, was not propitious for the making or the selection of military leaders. The strain of war had weakened men's wills, undermined their morale and turned opinion against the profession of arms. "Powerful personalities, organised for struggle, for severe tests and great events, do not always present those facile advantages, that superficial seduction which earns approval in ordinary life. Such men are usually sharp, awkward, even ungainly. If the mass of the people admits in its heart their superiority and gives them a certain tacit respect, it is rare that they are loved or that men favour them. The choice that governs careers is more often influenced by that which pleases than that which deserves."

No one in the audience can have missed his meaning. No doubt he had in mind the Marshal's early struggles, his supercession and imminent retirement in 1913; but the reference to his own recent experiences was plain. There was a buzz of comment as the officers dispersed. Some praised de Gaulle's loftiness of thought, his lucidity; others criticised his condescension and arrogance and complained that they had learned nothing. The Marshal departed and it was left to General Hering to bear the brunt of the professors' onslaught. They complained bitterly that he had imposed "this de Gaulle" on them and that they had been humiliated by having to listen to the speaker's panegyric of himself. "He is out of his mind. Plainly he thinks he is Napoleon," said one.

Tactfully General Hering explained that they were wrong, that the picture of the leader de Gaulle had painted was not himself but the Marshal. The whole lecture in fact had been a eulogy of the Marshal. In any case, he added, if great men or men who thought they were great had no pride they would never achieve their destiny. The professors were not propitiated. They granted de Gaulle only one thing, a stupendous memory. He seemed to know everything by heart, they said enviously. All the more humiliating to have to listen to him again.

For the following two weeks the scene was repeated. The Marshal came and sat in the front row with the professors, giving nothing away by his expression but secretly enjoying their discomfiture. De Gaulle, immaculate as ever, took the stage and held forth, captivating some by his eloquence, infuriating many more by his increasing self-confidence. "Here's Hannibal!" murmured someone who remembered de Gaulle's allusion in his first lecture to Flaubert's description: "The indefinable splendour of those who are destined to great enterprises."

His theme in the second lecture was "Character" and "Discipline." He began by regretting, as he had done at St. Cyr, the colonial role which the army had played since 1815. These minor wars had sapped the élan of the army. Thereafter he enlarged upon what he had said about leaders: "Faced with an event, it is upon himself that the man of action relies . . . Instead of sheltering beneath the hierarchy or hiding behind written instructions or covering himself with written reports, he stands upright and alone . . ."

Sometimes de Gaulle, walking backwards and forwards on the stage, looked directly at the Marshal and seemed to be addressing him personally. The man of character, he said, is distant because authority does not come without prestige nor prestige without keeping one's distance. "Beneath him men murmur under their breath about his haughtiness and his exaction. But once in action criticism is silenced. Men's wills, men's hopes turn to him like iron to a magnet . . ." Yet, he added, such a man's conduct of affairs seldom pleases his superiors.

The third lecture, on "Prestige," was an elaboration of the first two and much of it repetitive. The professors were not merely indignant, they were bored. They protested again and again to General Hering who patiently answered them. Yet loyal though Hering was he could not counteract the impression de Gaulle had made. The good graces he had earned with his article on the northern fortifications were entirely dissipated. A small group among his listeners, which included his old friend Captain Chauvin, sang his praises and hoped that his lectures had inspired a new generation of officers with a sense of the nobility of the profession of arms. But the majority had neither understood not appreciated them. Even Nachin admits that the lectures were "above the heads" of most of those who heard them and provoked "a latent hostility" to de Gaulle which made the officers instinctively resist his teaching.

De Gaulle, however, was quite unabashed. Pleased with the stir he had created, he obtained permission to deliver the lectures again, this time to a wider audience. Under the patronage of *Le Cercle Fustel de Coulanges*, a Society which had close links with the neo-Fascist organisation *L'Action Française*, it was arranged that he should repeat them at the Sorbonne in the autumn of 1927. Now at last, he felt he would make his mark, for instead of addressing a captive and partly disgruntled audience he would be addressing politicians, professors, retired officers and undergraduates.

Once again his performance was impeccable. The hall was full and de Gaulle easily mastered some young communist hecklers who staged a demonstration. And yet the lectures fell flat. Instead of being besieged with letters and further invitations to speak, de Gaulle was ignored. He did not wish to join *L'Action Française* and no other political organisation sought him out. No prominent politician took him up. The professorship of the *École Supérieure* was further away than ever.

The truth, which anybody less egotistic might have sensed, was that the lectures were a personal *tour de force*. They achieved their object at the *École Supérieure* because of the circumstances in which they were delivered. But they contained no startling new military or philosophical proposition and there was no reason why a disquisition on personal leadership from a captain who seemed to have been passed over for promotion, should have created a stir in academic or political circles. As a recruit to a fascist organisation de Gaulle might have made his mark; but as an officer publicly expounding his personal philosophy, even though he was known to be the protégé of France's most renowned living Marshal, he could only appear slightly ridiculous.

The lectures are of interest therefore only in the light of de Gaulle's later life. They were his confession of faith and they became important when he did. There is scarcely an event in his subsequent career which is not illuminated by reference to them. But at the time no one outside a tight and jealous little military circle was interested.

This fact was now borne in upon de Gaulle in a particularly painful way. Pétain himself began to lose interest. The capacity to withdraw into oneself, to keep subordinates at a distance, which de Gaulle had praised as a hallmark of leadership, was now applied by the Marshal to the Captain. No doubt Pétain had genuinely wished to further de Gaulle's career but he had also used him and used him effectively. Having obtained his twin objectives of gaining acceptance of his plan of fortifying the frontiers and snubbing the professors at the *École Supérieure*, the Marshal turned to more important affairs—in particular to the construction of the Maginot Line. De Gaulle was mortified to find that the history of the French army which Pétain had commissioned was now forgotten. De Gaulle had finished the first three chapters and prepared the outline of four more. The Marshal was in no hurry to have them completed. When extracts from the second and third chapters appeared in the *Revue Militaire* they attracted little attention. Pétain made no comment.

A little book by de Gaulle which was published at the same time suffered a similar fate. *Le Flambeau* is a historical dialogue between three soldiers covering the period from the Revolution to the Restoration of the Monarchy. It is not without grandeur and faithfully echoes all that de Gaulle felt about the history of France. It is a lament for the failure of political and military leadership and a glorification of the soldier and the profession of arms. "We serve France," says the young St. Cyrard Canrobert, "men pass, one régime follows another but France remains," and he goes on to quote Marshal Saxe, the great eighteenth century commander: "We others, soldiers, are like the overcoats men remember only when it rains. For the moment it is not raining. But when the storm comes the rest will run to us and we shall become the mantle of France."[17]

But in 1927 the storm which de Gaulle had so often prophesied seemed to be receding and with it his own fortunes. *Le Flambeau* sold only a few hundred copies and passed into oblivion. De Gaulle felt neglected and deeply depressed. The bitterness he then felt towards the Marshal was to come to the surface years later in the phrase he often repeated: "The Marshal was a great man who for me died in 1925." Fortunately this was not true. The Marshal was very much alive and was still to render de Gaulle great service. De Gaulle did not, in fact, turn against him until much later. On the contrary he still counted himself one of Pétain's inner circle and looked to him for help. But there was no denying that the immediate future looked bleak. De Gaulle's work on the history of the French army had lapsed. The road to the General Staff was still blocked. He had failed to force himself upon the intellectual world of Paris. Like Pétain before him he seemed condemned to becoming nothing more than a regimental officer. After twelve years as a captain de Gaulle was now, at last, gazetted Major. In December, 1927, he left Marshal Pétain's staff with a warm personal recommendation, and was posted to command the Nineteenth Infantry Battalion, part of the force occupying the Rhineland at Trèves. One crumb of comfort was to reach his ears. When making the appointment General Matter, Director of the Infantry, remarked to Colonel Nachin: "I am posting a future Commander-in-Chief."[18]

* * *

The Germany to which de Gaulle returned at the end of 1927 was very different from the Germany which he had left three years before. The recovery which had been started by the London Agreement was in full swing. By 1928 Germany was receiving more than twice as much in loans as she was paying out in reparations. The currency was stable and industry was booming. The production of foodstuffs and manufactures had risen so fast that Germany was already challenging Britain as the largest exporter in Europe. The internal war-debt of more than one hundred and sixty million marks had been almost wiped out and German credit was as high as that of any country in the world.

Politically Germany had been reinstated as a great power. The Treaty of Locarno had guaranteed existing German frontiers in the west, put an end to the supervision of the Allied Control Commission and paved the way for the admission of Germany to the League of Nations in 1936 with a permanent seat on the Council. In the elections held six months after de Gaulle's arrival in Trèves the moderate parties gained a big majority and the new government was formed with a Social Democrat, Hermann Muller, as Chancellor and Stresemann still as Foreign Secretary. The Weimar Republic seemed at last to be establishing itself.

But the appearance both of prosperity and political stability was deceptive. Wages were low and the numbers of unemployed often rose above two million. Trade Unions, which had been destroyed by inflation, had never recovered their power. The peasants and middle classes, having lost their savings, lived on credit or speculation. Prices and taxes were high. In spite of the increase in exports the balance of payments was unfavourable; foreign loans were not being repaid. The mood of the people was sullen. At the extremes the Communists still hoped for revolution but were incapable of organising it; the militant nationalist groups, including Hitler's National Socialists who had won eight hundred thousand votes in the May elections, still plotted to overthrow the Republic by force. Violence and political murder were common. The presence of Hindenburg as President gave the Republic a respectable façade, but behind it moderate men of all parties lived in fear. A nationalist dictatorship, bent on freeing Germany from the last restraints of the Treaty of Versailles, was already on the horizon.

De Gaulle knew his Germany and at once fastened on what was beneath the surface. Three years earlier he had sensed that the people had never accepted defeat; now he was convinced they were out to avenge it. "The force of events is destroying what remains in Europe of the agreed and precious safeguards," he wrote a few months after his arrival. "The *anschluss* is near at hand and then Germany will take back by force or agreement, all that was wrung from her for the advantage of Poland. After which they will reclaim Alsace. All that seems to me written in the stars."[19] Yet to be right and unable to influence events only made relegation the more unbearable. De Gaulle concentrated on his battalion.

De Gaulle was pleased with the young officers in his regiment and found them far keener and more alive than their elders. The men were mainly Basque, short, dark and used to hard climbing in the Pyrenees. They marched with a short, very quick step from which de Gaulle was mercifully spared because as Major he rode a horse. To relieve the tedium of garrison life the training programme prescribed long periods under canvas interspersed with divisional and army corps manoeuvres. De Gaulle soon had the battalion in splendid shape and equally soon got himself into trouble.

It began, absurdly enough, over the beret. The thought of de Gaulle in the large floppy Alpine beret worn by the *Chasseurs Alpins* is incongruous, and perhaps he felt ridiculous. If so he decided to emphasise the fact. Traditionally the regiment wore the beret on the left side of the head; de Gaulle preferred the right and made his own battalion conform to his wishes. His commanding officer protested but, as there was nothing in the regulations to prevent him, de Gaulle persisted. It was an irritating and unnecessary way of drawing attention to himself. More serious disagreements were to follow.

In the autumn of 1928 de Gaulle had crossed the Moselle with his battalion as part of an exercise. In the middle of the winter, which was particularly severe, he proposed to repeat the exercise across the ice with which the river was now covered. All the preparations were made and the battalion was ready to move when a message came from headquarters forbidding him to make the crossing. De Gaulle obeyed the order but was infuriated by the interference. The exercise had been carried out from the camp at Bitche. When the time came to return to Trèves de Gaulle decided to revive an old tradition of the regiment and complete the homeward journey by a forced march, entering the city by night. He told nobody of his decision, but with two stages of the march still remaining, he handed over the battalion to his deputy and went ahead on horseback with two cyclists. An hour later the column found him mounted at a crossroads. De Gaulle ordered a halt of an hour, summoned his officers and told them that the battalion would complete the march to Trèves that night.

There were many objections. The doctor feared that the effort might be too much for the young recruits, the captains protested that all the arrangements for bivouacking had been made and that, in any case, such an order required the permission of the General. De Gaulle cut them short saying that he accepted full responsibility and would give them written orders. The march began and long after nightfall the battalion clattered through the streets of Trèves, the band playing the regimental tune of "Sidi Brahin."

Not a man had fallen out but the authorities of the occupied town complained to the Divisional Commander who at once instituted an inquiry. De Gaulle's colleagues prophesied dire punishment, for he had broken not only the rule against forced marches but also against untimely entry into the town. De Gaulle replied calmly that they would find they were wrong. He came from Pétain's entourage and all would be well. And de Gaulle proved right. Against all precedent no action was taken.

But de Gaulle was incapable of taking a hint. Other self-willed men, Lyautey, Orde Wingate, T. E. Lawrence, defied authority and yet enhanced their own prestige through transparent disinterestedness or because their immediate goal justified the risks they were taking. In de Gaulle's case there were no such extenuating circumstances. A mystical love of France was no valid excuse for insubordination in a battalion commander. He seemed to his immediate superiors to be suffering from an exaggerated sense of self-importance and to be prepared to assert it even at the expense of those under his command. As might have been expected, his next brush with authority nearly proved fatal.

It began, paradoxically, on a note of commendation. That same winter an epidemic of influenza swept the army of the Rhine so severely that a hundred and forty-three men died. A group of parliamentary deputies, pressed by their constituents who had lost or feared losing their sons or relations, demanded of M. Poincaré that he appoint a parliamentary commission to investigate. The commission was high-powered and comprised such well known politicians as Daladier, Ramadier, Félix Gouin, Vincent Auriol, Herriot, Guy la Chambre, Jacques Doriot. When it visited the Rhineland it included Trèves in its itinerary.

The regiment at Trèves had not been so severely hit by the epidemic as many others, but of the three battalions de Gaulle's had suffered worst. In the report of the Commission the units in which the greatest precautions had been taken were listed, and among them was the Nineteenth Battalion of *Chasseurs Alpins*.

When the report was debated in parliament de Gaulle came in for extravagant praise. Colonel Picot, a member of the Commission who unofficially represented the Ministry of War, having listed all the precautions taken by Major de Gaulle, said that the deaths in the battalion could have nothing to do with the way the men were treated, for it was admirably commanded. He cited in particular the regimental funeral that had been accorded a machine gunner named Gouraud who had died. As Infantryman Gouraud had no family de Gaulle had ordained that he himself and the Captain of the Machine Gun Company should wear mourning in his honour. "There is a leader, a commander!" declaimed Picot to loud applause.[20]

De Gaulle was neither pleased nor taken in by these eulogies. He was certainly scrupulous in looking after his men but he knew that Colonel Picot, on behalf of the Ministry, was out to show that the severity of the epidemic had nothing to do with laxity on the part of the army, and was using de Gaulle to prove his case. "The Nineteenth Battalion," wrote de Gaulle at the time, "had not been nearly so hard hit by the epidemic as Colonel Picot tried to make out in order to prove something quite different. The whole story is lamentable for itself and for its consequences."[21]

But the story was not quite over. With memories of 1917 in their minds, the Government sent Marshal Pétain, who was still Inspector-General of the Forces, to visit the Army of the Rhine and restore morale. He reported that all was well. Hardly had he left, however, than a widespread movement began among the troops to get themselves exchanged into units in France. The winter was bitterly cold and they saw no reason why others should not take their turn of the rigours of the Rhine. Deputies were written to and a sort of shuttle service began which interfered with training and further lowered morale.

De Gaulle, determined to keep his own battalion intact, issued an order, which was read out daily, that any infantryman who took steps to get himself posted would be punished. However, one of his men had already written to his Deputy and shortly afterwards an official telegram arrived sanctioning his exchange. Instead of acting upon it, de Gaulle put the man in gaol. This time there was serious trouble. The Deputy complained, the Ministry of War asked questions, the Commander in Chief of the Rhine Army, General Guillaumat, summoned de Gaulle before him. He was told that he might be placed on the non-active list.

The General's summons allowed de Gaulle a little time, so he immediately took a train to Paris and presented himself at Marshal Pétain's headquarters, saying that he was in grave difficulties and had come to see "Le Patron." Pétain received him at once. Apart from his belief in de Gaulle as a soldier there was a deeper and more personal reason why the Marshal should wish to help him at this time, for at the beginning of the year de Gaulle's third child, Anne, had been born a mongol. Both parents were distraught. In a letter to a friend Mme. de Gaulle had written: "Charles and I would give everything, health, fortune, advancement, career if only Anne could be a little girl like others."[22] Those who saw de Gaulle with his daughter during the fifteen years of her life know that this is true. The infinite patience and love he bestowed on her, the hours he spent playing with her and trying to interest her, revealed a side of his nature that none except his family and a few intimates suspected. But Pétain was an intimate and knew the strain under which de Gaulle was suffering. He got in touch at once with M. Painlévé, the Minister of War, and managed to arrange things.

Fortunately the infantryman had applied for his exchange before de Gaulle had issued his order and could therefore be released without undermining de Gaulle's position. General Guillaumat's summons was cancelled and in spite of increasing resentment within the General Staff of the Army of the Rhine against a man who imposed such discipline on others but ignored it himself when he chose, de Gaulle returned to Trèves to finish his period of command. "I took a nasty thorn from his foot," the Marshal was to say later.[23] It was an understatement. Pétain had literally saved de Gaulle's career.

De Gaulle was not insensible of what the Marshal had done for him. Twice Pétain had seen him slip and twice he had lifted him up and put his feet firmly back on the ladder. Now he had rescued him from disgrace. At Trèves de Gaulle spoke of him not only with admiration but as a great man to whom he owed a special debt. Yet it was not in his nature to harbour gratitude. A quarter of a century later, when the Marshal might have expected the debt to be repaid in some small measure, de Gaulle appeared to have forgotten how much he owed his former chief. Far from recalling the incident at Trèves he referred to Pétain in the late twenties as a man already senile. Had that been true de Gaulle would certainly never have been in a position to assume the leadership of France. The fact was that both were hard men with occasional soft spots. De Gaulle's softness was reserved for other than Pétain.

At the time, however, it seemed as if the old master-pupil relationship might blossom into a new intimacy. De Gaulle wrote to Nachin saying that he was busy with the preparation of the Marshal's speech for his reception at the *Académie Française*, where he was to succeed to the Chair rendered empty by the death of Marshal Foch. Pétain was particularly anxious about the eulogy of Foch he was obliged to pronounce, for he himself had reservations. But by now de Gaulle's reputation was causing difficulties even among his old colleagues on the

Marshal's staff. In the end Pétain's advisers persuaded him not to use de Gaulle on the grounds that his literary ambitions were too great and that he might claim the authorship of the speech. The matter was allowed to drop. As Pétain showed no interest in reviving the history of the French army which de Gaulle was anxious to complete, de Gaulle had to resign himself to seeing out the last few months of his command at Trèves. "Having tasted silence," he commented acidly, "the Emperor ended by being enslaved by it."[24]

In Germany the effect of the collapse of the American Stock Exchange was already being felt and support for the Republic was dwindling. The Nationalists were openly preparing an authoritarian régime and the National Socialists a programme of revenge and world domination. But in France and Britain no one seemed to heed the danger. De Gaulle was near despair. "Oh, the bitterness there is in being in harness in these days. Nevertheless one must be. In a few years they will turn to my Basques to save the country," he wrote to Nachin.[25] Rather than stay and witness the paralysis he felt creeping over the leaders of his country he decided to go abroad and see something of the Empire and that colonial army whose role he had so often criticised. As his time to leave Trèves approached he applied to be posted to the General Staff of the Army of the Levant. He left France for Beirut at the end of 1929 and was to be away for more than two years.

CHAPTER III

AGAINST THE GRAIN

After the storms of the Rhineland, the Levant was an oasis. Attachment to the General Staff in Beirut did not mean that de Gaulle had joined the French colonial army. He had no executive position. He was an observer, able to travel and form judgments at leisure without feeling compelled to transmit them to his superiors.

De Gaulle had never before left the European continent, yet he seems to have been curiously unmoved by his first sight of the cradle of western civilisation. As a historian and churchman every name must have been familiar. From Beirut he climbed the Lebanon mountains, pocketed cones from the remnants of Solomon's cedars, passed over the top and down into the Bekaa valley to the great Roman ruins of Baalbek, skirted Mount Hermon on the way to Damascus and drove out into the desert to visit the Foreign Legion at their post on the edge of Queen Zenobia's fabulous Grecian ruins at Palmyra. He visited the great Crusader castles and gazed in awe at the massive ruins of Belfort across the Litany valley. He listened to the creaking of the huge water wheels performing their age old task of irrigation on the road past Homs and Hama to Aleppo. He searched in vain for traces of the ports of Tyre and Sidon. Yet neither in his letters nor in the little military history he was soon to start writing does he mention these things except as points of geographical reference. De Gaulle was interested only in the reasons why France was in the Levant at all and in the role she was playing there. Neither seemed to him satisfactory.

French influence in the Levant began with the Crusades and was sustained through the Middle Ages by missionaries who settled in the coastal regions and in Syria. In spite of spasmodic Moslem persecutions French fathers managed to convert and educate a considerable minority of the Syrian peoples. With the prospect of the collapse of the Turkish Empire during the first world war, religious influence turned into political interest.

In 1916 two experts in Middle-Eastern affairs, Sir Mark Sykes on behalf of Great Britain and M. Georges Picot on behalf of France, had

3. The four de Gaulle brothers in uniform. *Below*: De Gaulle at Saint Cyr with a group of friends

4. De Gaulle as a prisoner of war in 1916 (*See page* 33)

drawn up a secret agreement by which, when Turkey was defeated, the French should take northern Syria as their sphere of interest and the British southern Syria (including Palestine) and Iraq. It was on the basis of this agreement that the mandates of the League of Nations were eventually conferred, giving both Britain and France the right to maintain troops in the areas.

Unfortunately the British, without the knowledge of the French, had a year earlier concluded another secret agreement, this time with the Arabs, in which they had promised that most of Syria should form part of an independent Arab kingdom to be ruled over by Feisal and Abdullah, sons of the Sherif of Mecca, who had led the Arab revolt which, with Lawrence's help, had played a valuable part in Allenby's campaign. Such contradictory promises could not be resolved peaceably. Soon after the World War ended the French turned on the Arabs, drove Feisal from Damascus by force and brought the whole of Syria under their control. The British created Arab kingdoms in Iraq and Jordan but further compromised the future by creating a home for the Jews in Palestine and ruling that country themselves. The seeds of the conflict which still bedevils the Near East and has more than once threatened to bring on a Third World War had been sown. The Arabs felt betrayed, the French and British were deeply suspicious of each other, the vision of Israel had been born. When de Gaulle arrived in Beirut an uneasy calm had lasted for ten years.

Besides travelling the length and breadth of Syria de Gaulle visited Egypt, Palestine and Iraq. The more he saw, the less he liked the role that France was playing. "The Levant is a crossroads where everything passes: religions, armies, Empires, merchandise, and yet nothing changes. We have been here for ten years. My impression is that we have scarcely penetrated beneath the surface and that the people are as much strangers to us (and we to them) as they were before . . .",[1] he wrote in a letter home after he had been in the country six months. He was irritated by the Arabs who could never be brought to do anything for themselves "without constraint"; he was even more irritated with Frenchmen who were content to adopt the oriental habit of putting everything off until to-morrow. He felt and wrote that France should either make an effort to build roads, to irrigate and teach the rudiments of agriculture or get out. "There is one man and I believe only one, who understands Syria well and knows what to do here; it is Colonel Catroux. For that reason, of course, he has left."[2] Twelve years later it was de Gaulle himself who enabled Catroux to return.

French mandatory rule, therefore, began in strife and continued in discord. The French found the whole spirit of the mandate, with the emphasis on bringing the inhabitants as rapidly as possible to a condition in which they could govern themselves, contrary to the tradition of their Empire in which all men were educated to aspire to French citizenship and where colonial territories elected representatives to the Metropolitan Government in France. They continued to expand French education and support the indigenous catholic churches. They created a large force of local levies in both Lebanon and Syria and set up an enlightened political-military service to maintain peace between the still warring tribes of Bedouin in the desert; but they never entered whole-heartedly into the political education of a volatile people or made the Arabs feel that independence was a genuine goal.

To the end of his appointment de Gaulle remained convinced that, in the Levant, France was wasting her time. He did not, however, say so publicly and finished his attachment without antagonising the Staff on which he served. This in itself was an achievement and did not pass unnoticed. Pétain, watchful as ever, had been waiting for an opportunity to bring de Gaulle back into the fold. One of the Marshal's last acts before retiring from the Vice-presidency of the *Conseil Supérieur de Guerre* was to appoint de Gaulle one of its secretaries. De Gaulle returned to Paris in the spring of 1931.

*   *   *

De Gaulle came home to find Europe reeling from the effects of the collapse of the American stock-exchange. The whole capitalist system seemed to be crumbling. In Germany the number of unemployed had already passed three million and was still rising, reparation payments had ceased, the banks were on the point of failing. Stresemann was dead and the "Grand Coalition" of the centre parties had given way to the government representing the Conservative Nationalists under Dr. Bruening. Hitler was already a force waiting to pounce should Bruening fail. In the elections of the previous autumn his National Socialists had received six and a half million votes.

In Britain nearly ten per cent of the working population was unemployed, the pound was weakening and the minority Labour Government, unable to check unemployment, was shortly to give way to a "National" Government led by Mr. Ramsay MacDonald but relying for its existence on the support of Mr. Baldwin and the Conservative Party. In France the full effects of the financial crisis were just beginning to be felt. Although unemployment was less severe than in countries more dependent upon imports, it had begun to rise; trade and the national revenues were contracting; stringent economies which must inevitably affect the army had to be made in the budget.

De Gaulle was in no hurry to plunge into the maelstrom. He was lucky in that Pétain's successor on the *Conseil Supérieur* was none other than General Weygand who, ten years previously, had commended him so highly. Weygand at once confirmed de Gaulle's appointment to the secretariat. But de Gaulle had many months of leave due to him and decided to use them in picking up the threads of political and military developments and tying up the loose ends of work he had left unfinished before he went to Syria.

First he turned again to the three lectures he had given at the *École Supérieure* and the Sorbonne in 1927. He revised them and added two additional chapters, one on doctrine, much of which had already appeared in an article in 1925 and which continued his attack on the *a priori* school of military thinking, the other on politics and the soldier. The whole was then published as a long essay in 1932 under the title *Le Fil de l'Épée*, dedicated to Marshal Pétain "with the homage of a respectful and profound devotion." It is by far the most interesting of the books de Gaulle wrote before the Second World War. The lectures had been his confession of faith as a soldier; in the essay he broadens his theme so as to make an impassioned plea to his whole generation to awaken to reality and prepare themselves for the struggle that was to come.

Comparing the book to the lectures one is struck by the degree to which de Gaulle's stay in Syria had calmed and matured him. He was no longer the angry young man sneering at the obtuseness of his elders. The intolerance of views opposed to his own, upon which his instructors had commented so unfavourably, had given way to a sympathy which made him far more persuasive. In France as in England appeasement was in the air. De Gaulle tried to awaken his countrymen to its fatal consequences not by scoffing at their fears but by insisting that war must always be an integral part of life. "War is the worst of plagues, but it has made the world as we know it," he wrote. "Having suffered the cruelties imposed by force the masses react passionately. A sort of mystique spreads everywhere which not only leads men to curse war but inclines them to think it has been banished for ever just because they wish so much it could be."[3]

De Gaulle knew that his appeal would fall mainly on deaf ears but he hoped that a few who mattered would listen while there was still time. He was searching for a new leader who would shake people from their daily absorption in the business of living and give them a new sense of purpose and discipline. It was the same appeal that Oswald Mosley was making in England, but whereas Mosley was aping Hitler and Mussolini, de Gaulle was trying to rouse people to meet the danger the new dictators represented by a searching examination of themselves. He wanted a combined élite of politicians, soldiers and civil servants to study the social, economic and military problems of defence and put France into a state of readiness. He thought it natural that states- men, struggling to create a new understanding between nations, should find military problems anathema, "if only because no one likes paying bills."[4] Yet soldiers and statesmen do have to collaborate whether they like it or not. "It is time," he wrote, "that the military élite again becomes conscious of its pre-eminent role, that it lifts its head and gazes at the peaks. To give edge to the sword it is necessary to restore the philosophy of those who wield it."[5]

Le Fil de l'Épée did not antagonise the military hierarchy in the way that de Gaulle's lectures had done five years earlier. One military critic wrote: "there is an audacity in pitching one's thought on such an elevated plane from the outset, merit in sustaining such an effort with- out weakening; but there is the ever present risk of finding oneself obliged to become the man who symbolises these ideas, of contracting the moral obligation of representing the living reality. Nevertheless Major de Gaulle is of a stature to assume this responsibility."[6] But there were few who shared such a belief. De Gaulle, after all, was an obscure officer, backward in promotion with no reputation as a writer or as a journalist. To the general public he was quite unknown. Other books, propounding the ideas which de Gaulle had criticised so savagely at the École Supérieure, had a far wider circulation and attracted much more attention. It was not until another twenty years had passed and de Gaulle had fulfilled the role assigned to him by his critic that men turned again to this slim little volume. The second edition of Le Fil de l'Épée, published in 1946, sold many more copies than the first and was translated into many languages. For by then men had come to realise that this essay had all along been de Gaulle's Mein Kampf, that the soul of the man lies unfolded in these few pages and that if one is to understand de Gaulle and interpret his character one must go back to the thoughts expressed when he was seeking, not to practise them himself on the world's stage, but to influence others to do what it still lay in their power to do.

But although Le Fil de l'Épée caused little stir, de Gaulle never gave up hope. The essay was only the first shot in a campaign to change the military and economic thinking of those who guided the destinies of France which he carried on for the next eight years. It is certainly the most disinterested and in some ways the most attractive period of his life. While others who rebelled against the supine ineffectiveness of French policy attempted to seize power through *coups d'état*, de Gaulle remained the servant, critical but loyal, of the statesmen and soldiers who formed the *Conseil Supérieur*, the prospective disciple of any leader who would assume the mantle of his thoughts. Whether he was accompanying M. Tardieu to Geneva for the talks on disarmament or attending as an "expert" the endless round of meetings and conferences through which his masters conducted their defence policy, he continued relentlessly to press his views.

Throughout these years de Gaulle lived more gregariously than at any other period of his life. He had a flat in Paris, and in 1933 had bought the Château de la Boisserie at Colombey-les-Deux-Églises on the upper Marne. His wife and three children, Philippe, Élisabeth and Anne, lived mostly in the country so that during the week he was free to devote himself entirely to his self-appointed mission. The isolation into which he had so often withdrawn as a regimental officer was broken down by the nature of his work at the Secretariat and by his burning desire to win support for his ideas for the regeneration of France.

Much of his time was spent with a remarkable man, Lieutenant-Colonel Émile Mayer who, with his son-in-law, M. Grunebaum Ballin, ran the publishing house of Berger-Levrault. Mayer, who had been a friend of Marshals Joffre and Foch and had foreseen both trench warfare and the tank before 1914, had published a steady stream of articles and books on military affairs and conducted a voluminous correspondence with all the leading men of his time. Every Sunday morning in his house on the Boulevard Beauséjour he held a literary salon to which came writers, politicians and soldiers. De Gaulle soon became a regular visitor. Every Monday a rather wider group which included Émile Mayer and also several Deputies, used to meet for lunch at the Brasserie Dusmenil opposite the Montparnasse station, not far from de Gaulle's office. It was here that he met socialists like Philippe Serre and Pierre Bourdet, writers like Baratier, Duval, Giroud, and neo-fascists like Le Cour-Grandmaison. De Gaulle still visited Marshal Pétain and still attended the annual dinner which the Marshal gave at the Café de Paris to all his old collaborators; but as de Gaulle's campaign for the reform of the army developed he was to find the Marshal less and less amenable to his ideas. The two men, whose lives had been hitherto so closely intertwined and who had each in his own way done so much for the other, began to grow apart. De Gaulle was less concerned than most of his group with the political complexion of the government. To him all the political parties seemed blind to what was going on in Europe and he applied himself with equal fervour to any man who would listen. When in May, 1932, as a result of the General Election, Herriot and Léon Blum assumed power on behalf of the socialist majority, he canvassed the members of their parties relentlessly. The internationalism of the socialists, the pacifism which permeated the rank and file of the party throughout Western Europe, were the antithesis of his own political philosophy; but if men were sincere he never despaired of converting them. When late that year M. Herriot and Paul-Boncourt proposed an international *Force de Frappe* to be put at the disposal of the League of Nations it seemed that here was an idea which embodied at least some of de Gaulle's thinking. But the idea came to nothing. Herriot's plan to give the League of Nations an effective peace-keeping force was rejected by the British and, far from undertaking any new military commitments, the French socialist government actually reduced its own military budget.

Then in 1933 Hitler came to power. Within a few months he had suppressed all other parties, broken up the Disarmament Conference on the ground that it denied Germany a position of equality with the other powers, and left the League of Nations. Beginning his notorious exercise in psychological point-counter-point, talking peace and preparing war, he then suggested that France and Germany should both limit their armies to three hundred thousand men. Fortunately the French turned this offer down for, as any reader of *Mein Kampf* could have foretold, Hitler had not the slightest intention of observing the limit himself. He then proclaimed the unrestricted rearmament of Germany which had been taking place secretly for many years.

Hitler's blatant intentions crystallised de Gaulle's thinking. In May of that year he had written an article for the *Revue Politique et Parlementaire* in which he had outlined the reforms he thought necessary for the French army. Now, in October, he sat down to elaborate them. Using the notes he had made for the final chapter of the history of the French army which Pétain had commissioned ten years before, he finished his book in three months. It was published early in 1934 under the title *L'Armée de Métier*.

Several of de Gaulle's biographers have claimed that, with this book, he launched ideas which were adopted by the Germans and, in the shape of Panzer Divisions, eventually caused the downfall of France. M. Paul Reynaud, who warmly supported de Gaulle's thesis in the French Parliament, makes the same claim in his memoirs. These claims are without foundation.

There was nothing original in de Gaulle's military thinking. The mobile armoured striking force manned by long-service men which he advocated had been widely discussed ever since 1918 and was already coming into existence in Britain and Germany. In France itself General Estienne, the founder of the Tank School, had published a study in 1922 calling for the creation of a specialised armoured corps of one hundred thousand men manoeuvring four thousand tanks; in 1928 General Doumenc, who was to hold high command in the Second World War, had made a similar proposal to the General Staff. In both 1924 and 1931 these ideas had been aired in the French parliament by M. Reynaud and M. Louis Dumat. Over the years Colonel Allehaut had also written consistently on the same subject.

Nevertheless the leading protagonists of the armoured striking force were British. The tank was a British invention and in the years after 1918 General Fuller, who had been the first tank commander, and Captain Liddell Hart, the military thinker and historian, had produced a series of books and articles on mobile armoured warfare which became the basis for experiments carried out in the British Army in the 1920s. Results of these experiments were published.

Although he never acknowledged it de Gaulle had carefully studied Liddell Hart's work. Liddell Hart's ideas on the need for reviving the mobility of infantry through a wider use of mechanical transport as well as by new tactics based upon the use of tanks had first found expression in the new manual of infantry training produced in Britain after the war. This manual had been widely studied in France and when Liddell Hart revisited the battlefields in 1921 he was asked by some French officers to write a critique of the French post-war *Règlement d'Infanterie* which was subsequently published in the semi-official *Revue Militaire Générale*. His essay on the development of a new model army so impressed Marshal Pétain that, in the winter of 1926–7, Liddell-Hart received an official invitation to visit the French Army again and express his views. De Gaulle was then on Marshal Pétain's staff. The critique which Liddell Hart wrote ends with the following paragraphs:

"I know well that the suggestion of changing to a professional army has little hope of acceptance in France, where the fear of a military dictatorship is a political obsession, and where the belief that a conscript army is necessarily a cheap military insurance has a deeply rooted hold on the public mind.

"But France has been such a pioneer in mechanical development and mechanisation has such obvious advantages and so few drawbacks for a country whose military problem is primarily European, that she will surely awaken to the fact that here lies the science-sent means to offset her declining population and to buttress her military position by a revival in modern form of that mobility which has been her tradition and her spirit. For in the mobility of her forces she found of old the secret of her greatest successes, and it is essentially suited to the temperament of her people.

"Thus, even if her Government shrink from a complete change, it may be that, realising the precipice to which the present path is trending, they will seek a compromise solution and cut down mere quantity in order to afford the cost of converting part of their present forces into a mechanised striking force of highly trained long-service volunteers, to form a spearhead to the national army which could be expanded and developed after the outbreak of war."[7]

Liddell Hart's critique was officially circulated throughout the French Army on the orders of Marshal Pétain. It is inconceivable that de Gaulle did not read it and read it carefully. The surprising thing is that he made no use of it until almost ten years had passed. The Germans were much quicker. Liddell Hart's essay *The Development of the New Model Army*, published in England in 1924, was translated into German and studied by the German General Staffs. General Guderian and many other German writers have acknowledged that it was to the ideas of Captain Liddell Hart and General Fuller that the development of the Panzer Divisions owed its origin. By the time de Gaulle's book appeared the Germans already had three armoured divisions in the process of formation. Guderian only read de Gaulle's book in 1937 by which time the pattern of the German armoured division had already been decided. The truth is that *L'Armée de Métier* was not a technical book at all, and only a late comer in the many studies of mobile warfare which were being produced in European countries. Out of the one hundred and twenty odd pages only ten were devoted to a description of the force itself and these the German General Von Thoma described as "rather up in the clouds." Liddell Hart himself has commented "so far as can be deduced from his hazy outline, the division he pictured would have been a clumsy monstrosity, impossible to manoeuvre ..."[8] As for the Air Force, de Gaulle saw it only as a useful means of "camouflaging" tanks by spraying smoke screens from above. In the edition published in 1934 the tactical use of aircraft in conjunction with tanks is not foreseen at all.*

* Later de Gaulle rectified this deficiency. In a second edition published in London in 1940, he interpolated a passage bringing his views on the tactical role of aircraft up to date. But he failed to mention that this passage was not included in the original.

But although *L'Armée de Métier* only sold seven hundred and fifty copies in its first edition it was an important book because it revived this neglected discussion in France at a crucial moment. The Maginot Line was not a complete defence. It lacked depth, might be pierced by tanks, neutralised by gas or over-passed in the air. Above all it stopped at Malmédy and left the whole Belgian frontier unguarded. De Gaulle was sceptical of the Belgian alliance and doubted whether the British would be able to help in time. France would have to face the German onslaught alone. He therefore called for a striking force of six mechanised and largely armoured divisions, manned by professional volunteers, which could be moved swiftly to repair any breach in the fortifications or any thrust through Belgium. It should also be ready to make a "preventive" invasion of Germany if the situation called for it. Anticipating the traditional French fears of a professional army he pictured his force as an "armoured spearhead" mounted on the "wooden shaft" of the conscript armies. Both, he argued, were essential to French security.

The book appeared at a moment of crisis in the Fourth Republic. In the spring of 1934 its very existence was in danger. The refusal of successive Ministers of Finance to devalue the franc had resulted in chronic unemployment and high prices. A scandal in the municipality of Bayonne involving a Levantine named Stavisky, who was found dead after being charged with fraud, and also a former Minister of Colonies and two Deputies, had produced an ugly mood particularly among peasants and small traders. The para-military organisations of the parties of the right tried to exploit the general discontent. On February 6, 1934, immense crowds, some of them armed, started marching through the streets of Paris towards the Chamber of Deputies converging on the Place de la Concorde. They were stopped on the bridge over the Seine by a police barricade which they eventually charged. The police opened fire. Twenty people were killed and several hundred wounded. Inside the Chamber, Deputies debated in uproar, expecting any moment to be invaded by the mob. The President, with an overcoat hidden under his desk so that if necessary he could flee in disguise, suspended the sitting for some hours. But the columns turned back and although they remained in the streets throughout the night seemed bereft of real leadership. By the morning they had dispersed.

Three days later an even larger demonstration, organised by the communists in protest against the *Croix du Feu* who were believed to be the organisers of the Fascist demonstration, filled the streets again. This time, however, there were no casualties. Had any leader, either Communist or Fascist, been ready for a revolution he could probably have seized power; for the "Régime of Parties" was generally despised and the Deputies were in a state of panic. But the moment passed. M. Daladier resigned and M. Doumergue was called upon to form a government of reconstruction. He at once appointed a Commission of constitutional reform and summoned Marshal Pétain, whose name had been mentioned as a possible ruler if the revolt of February 6 had succeeded, to become his Minister of Defence.

After such a crisis and with his hero and patron holding the key position de Gaulle's opportunity seemed to have come at last. Over the past decade he had often summoned the Marshal to his aid; he could surely now gain his ear. However the two men had already drifted far apart. Pétain's views had hardened. In spite of the encouragement he had always given de Gaulle he himself had been unable to follow the logic of his own military thinking and transfer the "superiority of fire-power" into the armoured vehicles which science now offered him. As Nachin had predicted, Pétain settled for a defensive strategy. In spite of the staggering fact that the Maginot Line left the whole of France's northern frontier undefended, Pétain put his entire faith in it. In the debate on defence which took place in June he asked only that, in order that the Line should be properly manned, National Service should be extended from one to two years. Pétain was supported by the fallen Prime Minister Daladier, who believed in "concrete" rather than armour, and feared any formation capable of an offensive action. When both Weygand and his successor Gamelin protested, Pétain replied blandly that he did not think that next time the Germans would come through Belgium. Nobody dared contradict him. Once Pétain had won his vote de Gaulle reluctantly decided that it was useless to approach him or to attempt to change his ideas. He had to look elsewhere for support.

The champion he found was the most brilliant and fearless of the many talented men who had held office in France since the war. Paul Reynaud, who had already been Minister of Finance and the Colonies, was in the middle of a long struggle against financial orthodoxy. He believed that France could recover economically only by following the British and American examples and devaluing her currency. It was to be another four years before his view was accepted. Reynaud had already heard of de Gaulle from Jean Auburtin, a member of Émile Mayer's entourage. In December, 1934, Gaston Palewski, Reynaud's *Chef de Cabinet*, took de Gaulle to see him. When de Gaulle entered the room Reynaud was on the point of leaving. To de Gaulle's initial appeal he replied that he was already too deeply involved in the battle for devaluation to undertake a new cause. He offered to find someone else to support de Gaulle's project. "I have already tried," said de Gaulle, "it is either you or no one." Reynaud paused. He was overworked and already the target of much abuse. He did not want to shoulder another crusade. But there was something so compelling in de Gaulle's manner that he sat down again and said, "All right, I will listen to you."[9]

De Gaulle developed his theme in a voice surprisingly gentle for so large a man, leaning towards Reynaud and occasionally spreading wide his hands and forearms in a gesture the world has come to know. In the end Reynaud promised to present a counter-proposal in the Assembly based on de Gaulle's armoured corps of a hundred thousand regular soldiers when the Government's plan to increase National Service from one year to two years came up for debate.*

The debate took place on March 15, 1935. Doumergue's Government had fallen and Pétain had resigned as Minister of Defence. Flandin was Prime Minister and General Maurin had succeeded Pétain. Reynaud presented a formidable case. He pointed out that behind the German shock-divisions, capable of delivering an annihilating attack, was "an army in depth" ready to exploit a breakthrough. "You read the German newspapers, Gentlemen, as I do. You know what the Germans say. Never again a war of four years which exhausts the victor as much as the vanquished. This time we must strike in overwhelming force immediately."[10] Was France ready to strike back? The British had already doubled their Air Force and Mr. Baldwin had declared in the House of Commons that Britain's frontier was no longer the English Channel but the Rhine. To be able to retaliate France, a land power, must have a specialised armoured corps capable of the same devastating assault as the German shock troops.

But although many of the Deputies, Léon Blum in particular, were impressed, Reynaud failed to win a majority. The Socialists were afraid that a highly trained professional army might become the tool of those who wished to set up a dictatorship in France; many of the right-wing Deputies were more afraid of Communism than the Germans and were already prepared to come to terms with Hitler; the French people were too pacifist, perhaps still too exhausted, for its representatives to contemplate a change which seemed to accept the inevitability of war.

When General Maurin rose to reply for the Government he had little difficulty in carrying the Chamber with him. "How can anyone believe that we could think again of taking the offensive when we have

* M. Reynaud, who has described this scene in his book *Venu de ma Montagne*, also gave a vivid account of it to the author in 1965.

spent milliards to establish a fortified barrier?" he asked. "Are we to be so mad as to advance in front of this barrier—on I do not know what kind of adventure? That, Gentlemen, shows you the mind of the Government. For the Government, at least as far as I am concerned, knows perfectly what the plan of the next war will be."[11] M. Daladier once more backed up the Minister, saying that a professional corps of shock troops was more dangerous to the internal security of the state than anyone imagined.

Neither de Gaulle nor Reynaud accepted defeat in the Assembly as final. Immediately after the debate they went to work on a detailed project which Reynaud was to put privately before the Defence Commission of the Chamber. De Gaulle briefed him on the costs— £85,000,000 approximately spread over five years for material alone— and warned him not to fall for the argument that an armoured corps, if decided upon, could be created by simple administrative instructions without special legislation. If Reynaud did that, nothing would come of it. Reynaud appeared before the Commission on March 28 and again argued cogently. But although he was courteously received the Commission unanimously rejected his plan. It was, they said, "contrary to logic and to history."

Reynaud had shot his bolt. He never lost interest and was to return to the question in many future debates. But his frontal attack had failed and he was soon to be immersed in the Abyssinian war and thereafter in a succession of crises. For the moment de Gaulle's hopes of influencing the Government had been dashed. Nevertheless he persevered in the only way open to him. In the same month in which he had approached Reynaud, de Gaulle had applied to have an article *How to Create a Professional Army* published in the *Revue Militaire Française*. His request had been refused by the Vice-Chief of Staff, General Colson, in a letter which de Gaulle later forwarded to Reynaud.[12]

Ministry of War   *Paris, December* 17, 1934

My dear de Gaulle,

You have sent me a projected article *How to Create a Professional Army* which you intend to ask to be inserted in the *Revue Militaire Française*.

I have read this article, as I have read your previous studies, with all the interest which it incontestably deserves.

Nevertheless I believe that its insertion cannot be accepted for, although the *Revue Militaire Française* leaves full responsibility to its authors for the ideas set out in their articles, it is nevertheless true that this *Revue*, published with the agreement of the General Staff of the Army, stems morally at least from the Ministry of War.

Moreover the latter is unalterably opposed to any distinction which, by separating our military forces into two categories, might risk contrasting in men's minds a professional army with the national army.

It is therefore inopportune to publish in the *Revue Militaire Française* ideas which risk running counter or might induce others to run counter to the views of the Ministry.

This is not to say, once again, that there is nothing to learn in your ideas; we are learning from them, you may be sure, and moreover you will see the results.

Cordially,
Colson

Having been denied official sanction de Gaulle now rewrote the article and got it published in the June issue of the *Weekly Review*. In it he tried to answer some of the main arguments made against his project in the Chamber and took particular pains to show that the professional army he advocated was not to take the place of the traditional army but to be its spearhead. The article was little more than a gesture but André Pironneau, the Editor of *L'École de Paris*, supported him, and Lucien Nachin and Jean Auburtin wrote other articles praising his theme. In the Chamber, Philippe Serre on the Left and Le Cour-Grandmaison on the Right kept the question alive.

But de Gaulle was struggling against the main tide of opinion not only in France but in Western Europe as a whole. In England, in the previous year, Lord Cecil's famous peace ballot had shown that a huge majority of the people still clung to the belief that the League of Nations might somehow keep them out of war. Yet whenever the question of the use of force arose, by which alone the will of the League might have been made effective, the British always drew back. When the Emperor Haile Selassie appealed to the League of Nations against Italian aggression, even Winston Churchill advised caution. "Go just as far as the French," he said to Sir Samuel Hoare, "drag them with you but do not forget their weakness or ask the impossible of Laval."[13] Hoare took the advice, but the pact he made with Laval at the expense of the Ethiopians caused such a revulsion of feeling in Britain that he was forced to resign. The French, remembering the Ruhr and the violent criticisms which Lloyd George and other leading statesmen had launched against their every attempt to enforce the Treaty of Versailles, no longer had any faith in their ally. Three months later, when the British at Geneva proposed oil sanctions against Italy, Flandin, on behalf of the French Government, rejected the motion. A week later, on March 7, 1936, Hitler re-occupied the Rhineland with some detachments of the S.S.

*　　*　　*

When General Guderian was interviewed by French officers after the war he remarked: "If you French had intervened in the Rhineland in 1936 we should have been sunk and Hitler would have fallen."[14] Hitler himself knew the risks he was taking. "The forty-eight hours after the march into the Rhineland," he said later, "were the most nerve-racking in my life. If the French had then marched into the Rhineland we would have had to withdraw with our tails between our legs, for the military resources at our disposal would have been wholly inadequate for even a moderate resistance."[15]

But the situation confronting the French Government was not as simple as Hitler or his Generals later implied. Certainly the German action was a flagrant violation of the Treaty of Versailles and infringed the spirit of the Treaty of Locarno which Hitler had freely signed. Yet it did not necessarily infringe the latter. The Treaty of Locarno had allowed for the reoccupation of the Rhineland by the Allies only if they deemed a German action to be a preliminary to an attack on France or Belgium. This intention Hitler emphatically denied. He went further, and now that Germany had regained control of her territory, offered to settle all outstanding disputes with France.

The French were in an appalling difficulty. If action were to be taken it had to be taken immediately, yet they could not be sure that any other signatory to the Treaty of Locarno would support it. The British Ambassador in Paris counselled vigorously against the despatch of French troops. Although Russia was not a signatory, Mr. Litvinov in Moscow did the same. The French Chiefs of Staff were unanimously opposed to the general mobilisation they considered necessary if French troops were to be used. General Maurin, the Minister of Defence, said in Cabinet: "Mobilise the army? You know very well you have no intention of making war. You will simply injure the morale of the troops."[16] M. Sarraut, the Prime Minister, and M. Flandin, now Foreign Secretary, felt that France should move but could not carry enough of their colleagues. The moment passed and the matter was referred to the League of Nations.

It is easy with hindsight to pronounce that this was the best and perhaps the last chance of thwarting Hitler without war, but in the light of world opinion as it then was it is difficult to see how the French Government could have acted differently. French public opinion was overwhelmingly hostile to the use of force. The Socialists and centre parties felt that the Germans had a right to control their own country, the Conservatives and neo-fascists resented the idea of marching against Hitler in alliance with Soviet Russia. In Britain feeling was much the same. When M. Flandin visited London a week after the Germans had moved, to urge that the signatories to the Treaty of Locarno enforce its terms and oblige the Germans to withdraw, he was met with an overwhelming refusal. Duped and mesmerised by Hitler, the British were prepared to twist every letter of the Treaty to avoid action which might conceivably end in war. Most British Ministers took the view that Hitler's occupation of the Rhineland was legitimate and French objections unreasonable. Eden, the Foreign Secretary, wanted action under the League of Nations, but only if France or Belgium were attacked. Mr. Baldwin, the Prime Minister, was even less bellicose: "In Europe we have no more desire than to keep calm, keep our heads and continue to try and bring France and Germany together in a friendship with ourselves," he said in the House of Commons on March 12. Even Churchill, who had steadfastly warned his countrymen of the dangers attendant upon the rise of Hitler, wrote in the London *Evening Standard* on March 13: "Instead of retaliating with arms, as the previous generation would have, France has taken the correct course by appealing to the League of Nations." If France had acted alone there is no doubt that England would have attempted to mediate. Unless the French had been immediately successful it is possible that, by dividing his chief adversaries, Hitler might have become stronger than ever.

De Gaulle did not share his countrymen's qualms. "We should have acted with surprise, brutality, speed," he wrote to Jean Auburtin.[17] To another friend he remarked that, if France had had the professional army he had advocated, there would have been no need for the general mobilisation which had so daunted the High Command. And yet he did not abandon his struggle. The aftermath of Hitler's success seemed for the moment to offer new hope. A general election was held in April and the French people, alarmed not so much by Hitler as by the growth of Fascism in France, turned to the combination of Communists, Socialists and Radicals known as the *Front Populaire* and gave it an overwhelming majority. Léon Blum, the new Prime Minister, at once embarked upon a major programme of internal reform which included not only a shorter working week, higher salaries and wages and nationalisation of the arms industries, but also a large increase in the defence budget.

In the previous year Blum had taken a leading part in the debates on Reynaud's project for a mobile striking force and knew the name of Reynaud's military adviser. In October, 1936, on the very day that King Leopold declared Belgian neutrality, Blum invited de Gaulle to see him. "I saw enter," wrote Blum while in prison in 1941, "a man calmly at ease, almost placid, whose height and breadth of shoulders seemed almost gigantic. If I tried to convey in words the impression which has remained with me across the years, not only of his vivacity but of his quality, his bearing . . . it is that one felt that on first meeting him that he was a man 'all of one piece' . . . The man who then presented himself, who looked at me so calmly, who spoke to me in such measured and gentle tones, could not, on his own showing, be concerned with more than one idea at a time, one plan, one belief."[18]

Blum told de Gaulle that the new Government planned large expenditure on national defence, particularly on tanks and aircraft. De Gaulle replied that almost all the aircraft were defensive "interceptors" and that the tanks, slow with short-ranged guns, were designed solely for the support of infantry instead of for independent operations. "We are going," he said, "to spend as much money as would be needed for the mechanised army and we shall not have that army."[19]

They discussed what would happen if, as now seemed certain, Hitler turned on Vienna, Prague and Warsaw. De Gaulle pointed out that the only way to stop such a move was for the French to march to the Rhine. Blum recoiled. Like his predecessors he seemed incapable of contemplating offensive action even as a deterrent and showed the same blind faith in the Maginot Line. De Gaulle tried to shake him but in vain.

Before they parted Blum intimated that he would like to appoint de Gaulle to the Staff of the Minister of War. But de Gaulle remarked that he had already been entered for the new course at the Centre of Higher Military Studies and the matter was dropped. He had made his last bid to give France the army she needed and he had failed. Although now officially in retirement Marshal Pétain had won.

For the army with which France was eventually to face Hitler was based upon the original instruction "on the tactical employment of large units" inspired by Pétain in 1921 and developed under his guidance and influence in the intervening years. Neither Weygand, who succeeded Pétain as Commander in Chief Designate in 1931, nor Gamelin, who succeeded Weygand and was to lead France into war in

1939, had been able to introduce any fundamental changes. Weygand, while accepting a purely defensive strategy, had at least wanted to fortify the Belgian frontier; Pétain had prevailed against him on the grounds that the Germans were unlikely to launch an attack through the Ardennes. Gamelin went further. In 1936 and 1937, after de Gaulle's meeting with Léon Blum and during the discussions on the defence programme put forward by the *Front Populaire*, he raised the question of armoured divisions. He argued that France needed something stronger than the Panzer divisions with which to counter attack. The Supreme War Council of which de Gaulle's old enemy at the *École Supérieure de Guerre*, General Dufieux, was a member, voted almost unanimously against him. But as Gamelin said under interrogation after the war, it was Pétain's influence behind the scenes which counted: "We couldn't say: 'Don't listen to Marshal Pétain,' nor could we argue with him in official meetings or in the press. What we did do was to prescribe the opposite of what he said in our instructions or in our criticisms of manoeuvres."

In 1938, in an introduction to a book by General Chauvineau entitled *Is an Invasion any longer possible?*, Pétain wrote of tanks: "They are expensive, rare and relatively slow to move into position. The time necessary for them to develop their action can be used by the defence to bring up their reserves. There is also, on the ground, the mortal barrage which can destroy them, a combination of mines and anti-tank weapons."[20] The furthest Pétain would go was to admit that the technical possibility of tanks and of armoured divisions had not been sufficiently studied. As a result the War Council was to order experiments to be carried out in 1938 on the possible employment of one armoured division; but even these experiments were postponed because of the Munich crisis and the actual composition of the division was not decided upon until just before the outbreak of war. Although by 1939 the French possessed more tanks than the Germans, they were designed solely as infantry support and split up into small units dispersed throughout the army. The Germans had six armoured divisions by 1939 and ten by May, 1940. Pétain's prestige had triumphed over de Gaulle's imagination. The old man's inability to adopt the ideas of the younger whom he had once thought the hope of the French Army, condemned France to defeat.

De Gaulle played no part in these latter day discussions. From the time of his interview with Blum he resigned himself to the fate he foresaw for France. For a moment, indeed, it looked as though he might pass into retirement. When his name came forward for promotion to full Colonel at the end of 1936, Gamelin opposed it. Reynaud inter-

vened with Daladier, Blum's Minister of Defence, and de Gaulle was
gazetted at the end of 1937 on Daladier's insistence. He at once enrolled for the course at the new centre for Higher Military Studies in
Paris and was accepted for the year 1938. As usual, he was unpopular
among his colleagues. Colonel Groussard, who was later to come to
London on a mission from Vichy, described him as "courteous but
cold, keeping a distance between himself and others which didn't
encourage the offer of a drink."[21] Another member of the course, who
had just returned from Indo-China, was infuriated when, instead of
being asked his opinion, he was forced to listen to de Gaulle's lengthy
solution of the whole Far Eastern problem although this was a part of
the world to which de Gaulle had never been. Nevertheless, de Gaulle
was made Director of Studies for his course and, besides attending
lectures, delivered many himself on the use of tanks in battle. Since the
War Council was at last considering experiments in the use of tanks his
views on this occasion aroused no controversy and even earned him
a reward. While the course was in progress he had applied for the
command of a regiment of tanks as full Colonel and his request was
granted.

There is no doubt that de Gaulle looked upon the Tank Regiment
as his war station and probably his last command. He made typical
preparations. He did not have the vivid premonitions of death which
he had experienced in 1914 but he expected it and wished to meet it
in an orderly manner. Although he was now one of the leading tank
experts in the French Army and had just been lecturing the highest
ranking commanders in the use of tanks in battle, he at once enrolled
for a course of practical instruction with the 501st Tank Regiment
stationed at Versailles. If he was to command in battle he would at
least know his weapon at first hand. At the same time he tidied up
his literary life and fired the last salvo in the propaganda barrage with
which he had tried to awaken his countrymen over so many years.
But the book he published in 1938 had a surprising and rather tragic
sequel.

Ever since 1925 he had carried with him from the Rhine to Paris,
from Paris to the Levant and back again, the manuscript of the History
of the French Army which he had begun on Pétain's instructions when
he had first joined the Marshal's staff. From time to time he had corrected and added to it. Now, urged on by his old friend Émile Mayer,
he determined to finish and publish it as "the final warning which,
from my modest place, I addressed to my country on the eve of the
cataclysm."[22] It appeared under the title *La France et son Armée*.

It was not quite the cannonade which might have been expected.

The military history, the vulnerability and glory of France were all there, but instead of containing a blue-print for the modernisation of the French Army and a final devastating criticism of what existed, the last chapter gave a vivid but almost irrelevant description of his own experiences in the First World War. It was as if de Gaulle had despaired of reforming the machine and was appealing only to the spirit which animated it. This really was the book's message. On the eve of Hitler's war, as all through her history, the soul of France was mirrored in her army. Even if the mirror was still distorted by a mute longing for peace, the moment was at hand when the French people would turn again to their men of action. The fate of France already lay in their hands.

But with an irony which was symbolic of the feeling in the country, this appeal for unity in action was to sever the last links which bound de Gaulle himself to his oldest and most steadfast benefactor.

Since the study on which the book was based had been initiated by Pétain, de Gaulle naturally informed him of his intention of publishing it. Pétain objected; the study had been official and must therefore remain anonymous. A visit by de Gaulle made the old man relent, but he insisted that he himself write the dedication. De Gaulle accepted this but he failed to warn the Marshal that it was too late to include it in the first edition. When the book was published, therefore, it appeared with the dedication which de Gaulle had written himself which read:

> To
> The Marshal Pétain
> who wanted this book written,
> who directed with his advice
> the writing of the first five chapters
> and thanks to whom
> the last two are the history
> of our victory[23]

Pétain at once wrote to the publisher complaining that the dedication contained two inaccuracies: he had never wanted the book published and had agreed only out of friendship for de Gaulle; the first chapter as well as the last two were entirely de Gaulle's. As de Gaulle had already accepted Pétain's corrected dedication there was nothing to argue about. He wrote at once to the Marshal explaining what had happened and adding that he regarded his wishes as an order which would be obeyed when the second edition was published. However Pétain, urged on by one or two of his then collaborators who were jealous of the favour he had always shown de Gaulle, magnified the incident into a quarrel. He spoke of de Gaulle as a man "without heart" and, when he met him in Metz in October at the wedding of General Giraud's daughter, refused to speak to him. Unfortunately the book sold slowly and the war broke out before a second edition was needed. De Gaulle was unable to keep his word and Pétain's dedication never appeared. The Marshal never forgave him. The two men were to meet again and to have one curt exchange. But the friendship from which both had gained so much over a quarter of a century was at an end.

CHAPTER IV

ONSLAUGHT

While de Gaulle and Pétain were squabbling over the dedication of a book the world was moving inexorably towards war. The Fascist Dictators, emboldened by their successes in 1936, had moved from aggression to aggression. Having occupied the Rhineland without opposition Hitler had immediately started fortifying it, thus denying France the only means of effectively supporting its allies in Eastern Europe by a swift attack across the Rhine. Hitler then turned his attention towards each of these allies in turn. In the Agreement which he had signed with Dr. Kurt von Schuschnigg in 1936, Hitler had guaranteed Austrian independence and accepted the outlawry of the Austrian Nazi Party. In February 1938, after months of increasing Nazi agitation, Schuschnigg was summoned to Berchtesgaden and presented with an ultimatum which gave the Austrian Nazis control of the country. Schuschnigg accepted, but since Nazi agitation increased he submitted the Treaty to a Referendum. On March 11, two days before voting was to take place, German troops marched into Vienna; next day they appeared on the Italian frontier at the Brenner Pass. Mussolini, who had vigorously protested against just such an action three years before, had been debauched into acquiescence.

De Gaulle observed these events "without surprise but not without pain," from the eastern frontier which had dominated so much of his military thinking. In the autumn of 1938 he had taken up his command of the 507th Tank Regiment at Metz, the ancient fortress of which General Giraud was now Governor. Having been at the centre of the great defence controversy for so long he felt strangely isolated; but he had cut himself off deliberately and now drove himself into the task of training men to use tanks with the same fierce energy he had shown with his *Chasseurs Alpins* ten years before. Although his regiment was part of an infantry division, the tanks themselves were modern and it was up to him to develop the principles upon which they should be used. "After some detailed experience," he wrote in a letter towards the end of the year, "I find myself more than ever convinced of the soundness of the ideas which I tried to spread and 'which, alas, have up till now been listened to far more willingly by the Germans than by my own compatriots. The possibility of manoeuvre and attack can no longer be demanded on land except from tanks. The age of infantry is finished except as a defensive arm. Artillery keeps its relative value but from now on it is in support of tanks it must be used before all else. It remains to recognise these facts and to organise the French army accordingly, making it an instrument of manoeuvre and shock-attack based upon tanks; that is to say an armoured corps.

"Moreover this corps, given its relative importance and the cost of the material devoted to it, can only be formed for the moment out of specialists like the marine and aviation. We are entering the era of professional armies. All the prejudice in the world won't stop this development. Happily for us the Germans have also got some good military conformists and although they are doing a great deal for the Panzer Corps, the aviation and the marine, they are not making much effort to organise mass support . . ."[1]

If by "mass support" de Gaulle meant a failure to organise German industry to sustain a long war, he had shrewdly picked on Hitler's greatest weakness. At the time, however, the support seemed adequate. All through 1938 the strength of the Dictators had grown. Even before the seizure of Austria the Rome-Berlin Axis had been extended to Tokyo after Hitler had recognised the Japanese conquest of Manchuria. At one stroke the Far Eastern empires of Britain, France and Holland were threatened. In Europe the destruction of Czechoslovakia followed inevitably upon the seizure of Austria. The acquiescence of the democracies in the fusion of two Germanic peoples enabled Hitler to incite German minorities in whatever country they lived to demand autonomy as a means to domination. Throughout the summer of 1938 the claims of Herr Henlein, Nazi leader of the Germans in Czechoslovakia, became more exorbitant, Hitler's diatribes, published daily in the controlled German press, more strident. By September, tension had reached such a point that the first steps towards mobilisation were taken in France and in Britain certain classes of reservists were called up. Forty million gas masks were distributed to the civilian population. "Events show with terrible clarity how right you have been," wrote de Gaulle on September 24 to Paul Reynaud, once more a Minister. "My regiment is ready. As for me I see without surprise the greatest events in the history of France approaching and I am sure you are destined to play a preponderant role in them."[2] But the great events were once again to be postponed. A few days later, on September 29, the

French Prime Minister, Daladier, joined Chamberlain and Mussolini at Munich and signed the "Agreement" by which the dismemberment of Czechoslovakia was begun.

When Reynaud learned the terms which Beneš, the Czech Prime Minister, was forced to accept, he said to General Gamelin, the French Commander in Chief, "all you have to do now is to find thirty-five divisions."[3] De Gaulle was even more laconic. To a Major in his regiment who asked him what he thought ought now to be done, he replied "make war." But in both France and Britain such men were in a small minority. The House of Commons and the British people were overwhelmingly in favour of Chamberlain's desperate attempts to appease Hitler; in France Daladier received similar support. Hundreds of thousands of Parisians flocked spontaneously into the streets to celebrate a great "victory" for peace. "Our Premier and the Minister of Foreign Affairs have preserved peace for us . . . peace with dignity and honour," wrote Jean Prouvost in *Paris Soir*, and most of the other newspapers echoed his sentiments.

Had the Munich Agreement been a calculated device by which France and Britain had hoped to save time so as to put their defences in order, it might have had some justification. But it was no such thing. Both Chamberlain and Daladier genuinely believed they had gained "peace in our time." Although Hitler had already broken every pledge he had made, used every concession granted as a means of extorting another and was following, almost slavishly, the creed and method he had set out so clearly in *Mein Kampf*, Daladier and even more Chamberlain accepted his word. With what *The Times* described as "realism" they stressed Hitler's "courtesy" and welcomed his peaceful "intentions." Led by such "boobies," as de Gaulle was later to call them, it is not surprising that the people of France and Britain exulted and snatched at the pretence that the latest pause in aggression was permanent peace. Yet within three weeks of signing the Munich Agreement Hitler had given secret orders that it was to be ignored and the German occupation of Czechoslovakia began.

From Metz de Gaulle exploded with frustration at the inactive routine which was forced upon him. "The commander of a unit," he wrote in a letter, "is quite simply a person who uses his time and his means to struggle against his superiors right through the ranks of the hierarchy and including the Ministry, to try and keep his effectives, his material, his cadres and his own goodwill against the tumult of orders, circulars, prescriptions, and general and absurd rules which are always contradictory and which would have soon reduced to nothing the various small units of the army if in fact one had applied them.

Luckily one does not apply them except to safeguard appearances by rendering reports."[4]

But de Gaulle could not confine himself to private remonstrance. He had said that the only answer to Munich was to make war. As the prophet of the mobile armoured striking force he found himself in command of a regiment of modern tanks. It was too much to expect that he would not attempt to put his theories into practice. In the last manoeuvres before war broke out he did just that. Defying his superiors and often throwing the exercise into chaos, he used his tank regiment independently as if it had been an armoured brigade. At once there was an outcry. Infantry commanders protested that tanks used without infantry support would have been destroyed—by machine guns. De Gaulle replied that, once the tanks had passed, nothing of the infantry would have been left. General de la Porte du Theil, who was in charge of the manoeuvres, upheld de Gaulle, but General Giraud, the overall commander, told him that he was riding upon clouds and reiterated the doctrines so soon to be shattered that tanks could only open the way for infantry and must never be far ahead of them.

Provoked by what had become routine opposition from Higher Command, de Gaulle began once more to lobby politicians. After Hitler had completed the occupation of Czechoslovakia by a formal invasion in March, 1939, he believed that even the most myopic of his compatriots must see that new decisions had to be taken. Reynaud was preoccupied with finance, but Frédéric-Dupont, who belonged to the same political party, was sufficiently perturbed by what de Gaulle told him of the state of the French defences to seek a special interview with General Gamelin and ask him his view on de Gaulle's theories. Three years before Gamelin had asked the *Conseil de Guerre* to study the need for armoured divisions "urgently." The study had in fact been carried out and a decision was about to be taken to form two such divisions as an experiment. Yet Gamelin would not be hurried and in any case had no clear idea how the divisions should be used. He replied to Frédéric-Dupont: "I do not believe in the theories of Colonel de Gaulle. These theories are neither wise nor realistic. Certainly tanks are necessary, that is understood, but to believe that with tanks one can pierce the positions of the enemy, this is not serious thinking."[5] Soon Gamelin was to change his mind once more but for the moment there was nothing de Gaulle could do but wait.

As the spring of 1939 wore on the last futile scenes of the inter-war tragedy were played out. With Czechoslovakia occupied Hitler began his clamour against the Poles. The Danzig Corridor took the place of Sudetenland in the centre of the stage. Now that Franco had won the

Spanish Civil War, Marshal Pétain was sent as French Ambassador to Madrid to try to offset, through the prestige of his name, some of the credit the Italians had won through their military aid. A few days later, on March 31, Mr. Chamberlain, who nine months before had refused even to contemplate action on behalf of Czechoslovakia because neither British nor French troops could protect its frontier, gave an unsolicited guarantee to come to the aid of an even more remote and less known country, Poland. But neither in France nor Britain was rearmament pressed with any real urgency. It is true that Mr. Chamberlain countermanded the instruction that nothing should be done to disturb trade or that rearmament should not be on a scale that might alarm the Germans or Italians, but he took none of the controls necessary to enable industry to speed up the 1934 rearmament programme. The French, having again turned their backs on an armoured force, refused to extend the Maginot Line and accepted a forty-hour week throughout industry.

During the summer a final note of farce was added by the negotiations in Moscow. Eighteen months earlier, in March 1938, when the dispute over Czechoslovakia was approaching its crisis, Russia invited France to complete the Franco-Soviet Pact by a military convention which would commit both countries to action in the event of a German attack on the nations of Central Europe. The French Government under Daladier refused, the Communists and the left-wing Socialists being too weak to overcome the hostility to the Soviets of the Moderates in the *Front Populaire*. The Russian offer was taken up in Britain by Winston Churchill who, with a group of Conservative friends, vigorously pressed the Prime Minister to form an effective alliance with Russia. Chamberlain refused in his turn. He mistrusted Russia and doubted whether her army and air force were efficient, particularly since Stalin—on information of a plot supplied by Beneš, the Czechoslovakian President—had "purged" so many senior officers. He did not see how a military action by Britain or Russia could prevent the Germans overrunning Czechoslovakia and above all, as he clearly explained to the House of Commons, he did not wish to form an alliance which might be interpreted as hostile to Germany.

Now, in the summer of 1939, France and Britain approached the Soviet government to try and conclude the agreement they had rejected so disdainfully the year before in order to implement the guarantee they had given to Russia's old enemy Poland. Having been rebutted, the Russians were naturally suspicious and cautious, but in April they stated their requirements quite clearly and after three months' haggling, during which the atmosphere of mutual suspicion increased, the Allies accepted the Russian basis for a pact and in August sent a joint military mission to settle the details. Even now the Allies were half-hearted. The Russian delegation was headed by Marshal Voroshilov with full powers to conclude an agreement. The French and British mission had vague instructions and no full powers. The Russians had prepared a detailed plan which they immediately put forward. The French and British had no plan and strict limitations on the amount of information they could exchange. Voroshilov came straight to the point and asked whether Poland and Rumania were prepared to allow Russian troops to enter their territory; if not there was no point in continuing the discussion. The Allies could give no answer. As Stalin was later to tell Churchill, the Russians concluded that Britain and France would not declare war over Poland and aimed simply at embroiling the Russians with Germany. With a cynicism which the Allies thoroughly deserved Stalin had already sent an envoy to Berlin. While the allied missions were still struggling to keep negotiations alive, Hitler announced that Ribbentrop was leaving for Moscow. He arrived on August 23 and signed the mutual-aid agreement that evening under the very noses of his enemies. The fate of Poland was sealed; war was now only a matter of days.

"When, in September 1939, the French Government followed the British Cabinet's example, and consented to join in the conflict already begun in Poland, I had not the least doubt that it did so with the illusion that, in spite of the state of war, we would not fight all out. It was therefore without astonishment that, as commander of the tanks of the 5th Army in Alsace, I saw our mobilised forces settle down into stagnation, while Poland was struck down in two weeks by the Panzer divisions and the air squadrons. It is true that Soviet intervention hastened the crushing of the Poles. But in Stalin's decision to make common cause with Hitler one could discern his conviction that the French would remain stationary, that the Reich therefore had its hands free and that it was better to share than to be its prey. While the enemy forces were almost all being used on the Vistula, we did nothing really, apart from a few token actions, by way of placing ourselves on the Rhine. We did nothing, either, to check Italy by giving her the choice between a French invasion and pledges of her neutrality. We did nothing, lastly, to realise immediately the junction with Belgium by gaining Liège and the Albert Canal."[6]

De Gaulle's damning indictment of French strategy on the outbreak of war, written some fifteen years later, received powerful support from the Germans when the war was over. At the Nuremberg Trials General Jodl was to say that, in 1939, Germany was only saved from catastrophe because the one hundred and ten French and British divisions remained inactive against the twenty-five German divisions in the west. General Keitel, Chief of the German General Staff, supported him. "We were surprised to see that France did not attack Germany during the Polish campaign. Sudden attack would have encountered only a curtain of twenty-five divisions, including reserves, and would have met with but feeble resistance from us."[7] But both the Generals and de Gaulle were indulging in special pleading. The Germans wished to humiliate the French whose presence at Nuremberg they particularly resented; de Gaulle ten years later was seeking to justify his whole movement, which had recently been rejected by the country, by pretending that France, differently led, might have won the war at the outset. Pétain and Vichy alone were to blame for France's defeat.

The truth was very different. For all the brave slogans of the phoney war France in 1939 was profoundly defeatist. Although thousands were to die bravely, there was scarcely a thinking Frenchman who really believed that, when the Germans attacked, they would be halted. The whole world expected Hitler to advance through Belgium. Yet France's northern frontier was unfortified and the French had tamely acquiesced in Belgian neutrality. Throughout 1939 it had been the British who had put the main pressure on King Leopold, albeit unsuccessfully. A government which faced Hitler's Germany so complacently could not be said to have been serious in wishing to defend itself.

And the government reflected opinion in the country. In 1914 Frenchmen spoke of the *"Union Sacré"*; in 1939 they were so divided that many of their leaders would not speak to each other at all. Communists and Socialists so distrusted the Fascist organisations of the bourgeoisie that they made no attempt to equip France industrially to meet the German menace; during the holiday month of August, 1939, production of military aircraft fell to thirteen machines. The bourgeoisie and the professional classes so feared the spread of the Soviet system that they not only prevented any effective alliance with Russia but came to prefer collaboration with the dictators to resistance with only Britain as an ally. Men like Flandin, whose first instinct had been to move into the Rhineland, Ybarnégeray, who had favoured the occupation of the Ruhr, as well as more pliable politicians such as Chautemps or Baudouin who were all, nonetheless, patriotic Frenchmen brought up in the tradition of French greatness, had become convinced that collaboration with Hitler was France's only hope. Less moderate men like Doriot and Darnand, the former socialists Déat and Marquet, publicists like Le Grix, Bailby, writers like Charles

Maurras who despised the Republic and its democratic institutions but in another age would have been patriotic royalists or Buonapartists, preached active support of the dictators and in some cases accepted large sums of money to further Nazi and Fascist propaganda. Quisling happened to be a Norwegian but there were many Frenchmen who deserved the name. By 1939 the French Fifth Column was every bit as numerous and even more effective than its counterpart in the Netherlands or Scandinavian countries. Even the centre parties, the right-wing Socialists and Radicals led by men like Blum and Herriot who were deeply opposed to fascism in all its forms, abdicated from any serious attempt to check aggression and earned the nickname "Re-signed Nationalists." They opposed dictatorship in France but abroad their policy was to do nothing without Britain.

After all the excuses have been made, it cannot be denied that, from 1919 to 1940, Britain failed to rise to a single international challenge. The British knew in 1919 and 1920 that the Germans were already evading the Treaty of Versailles and planning rearmament and revenge yet, while deploring the French occupation of the Ruhr, they did nothing to prevent this recrudescence of militant German nationalism. They rejected M. Briand's attempt to begin the unification of Western Europe in 1930 and M. Herriot's efforts to create an international army for the League of Nations in 1932. When Hitler began rearming, the British sabotaged any prospect of collective action to restrain him by signing a naval agreement which they hoped would prevent his fleet outstripping their own but left the French Fleet in a position of inferiority. Mr. Eden's efforts to have sanctions imposed upon Italy over Abyssinia were so watered down that Laval was able to make his agreement with Hoare. From that moment all faith in the League of Nations died.

When Hitler entered the Rhineland the British held their breath for fear the French might drive him out. The rape of Austria was welcomed in London as the natural union of two Germanic peoples. When Czechoslovakia's turn came, the British rejected M. Daladier's overtures for joint action to save her and treated Dr. Beneš almost as a delinquent when he refused to complete his country's suicide as quickly as the British desired. The British lent money to Germany without caring how it was spent and were still lending vast sums as late as 1938. They turned a blind eye to the mass persecutions that accompanied Hitler's acts, even though they were informed of them in detail by the refugees who flocked to British shores. Finally the British gave an unsolicited guarantee to Poland, not because they had any hope of taking action which could save her, but because they knew, as a result of the Hitler-Stalin pact, that once Poland was partitioned Hitler would turn west. It was a record of craven diplomacy and mistaken political judgment which had not been equalled in British history since the time of King Edward II. And at every stage, British short-sightedness had a decisive influence upon France.

For although the French were militarily and economically strong enough to stand on their own and to give a lead which in almost every case Britain would have been bound to follow, they were spiritually too exhausted to do so. History had paralysed them. Political aggression had died with the first Napoleon. The idea of the military offensive, blunted at Sedan, had been finally killed by General Nivelle in 1917. When Pétain decided that France's military strategy should be confined to the defence of its own frontiers he was doing no more than give expression to her physical and intellectual prostration. He is doubly guilty for having failed to complete the fortification of those frontiers or supply any mobile striking force to repel the armoured attack he knew must come where the frontier was open, but he represented militarily the escapism of the age.

But France could not afford escapism. The tragedy of her association with Britain lay in the geography of the two countries. Britain could be diplomatically craven because the sea gave her time. If France was to avoid meeting a German onslaught alone for the third time she had to take preventive action, yet each time she wanted to take the initiative and turned to Britain for support, Britain turned her down. She could never bring herself to take action alone.

Whatever claims de Gaulle might make in later years, therefore, there was not the smallest prospect that the French would attack or effectively resist the Germans in September 1939. What is astounding is that the British did not recognise the true state of affairs. Reports from France were conflicting. The British Ambassador in Paris was under no illusions, but as he had described those who, like M. Reynaud, wished to resist the Germans at the time of Munich as a "small noisy corrupt war group," his opinions were suspect. Churchill, on the other hand, had implicit faith in the French army. He visited the Rhine sector at the invitation of the Supreme Commander, General Gamelin, in August, 1939, and was so impressed by what he saw and by the figures which he was shown that he said to General Georges, the Commander in Chief of the French Armies in the field, "But you are the masters." He had accepted completely the French reliance upon a purely defensive strategy which, as he was later to write in his memoirs, "imposed itself irresistibly" upon him. With Churchill mesmerised, any chance that France's ally might have made good the deficiencies in her fighting spirit or strategic thinking disappeared. In their hearts the British were thankful that the French would take the first shock. They would fulfill their commitments and do their best to help but they had neither the will nor the capacity to change the character of the phoney war.

*   *   *

At the time no one was more painfully aware of the true state of French morale than de Gaulle. On the outbreak of war he had gone to Wangenbourg, in Lower Alsace, to take command of all the tanks of the 5th Army under General Bourret. Bourret was an excellent general and a good picker of men. His Chief of Staff was de Lattre de Tassigny. But although both de Gaulle's superiors appreciated him, they could not prevent his own tank regiment from being broken up according to plan. Having framed it to act as a single striking force de Gaulle had the mortification of seeing its three battalions sent as separate units to support the infantry in different parts of the line. Thereafter, while Ministers tried to persuade the French people over the radio that the phoney war had already achieved a victory comparable to the Marne in 1915, de Gaulle waited in agonised frustration for the blows to fall.

Twice he tried to rouse those in authority to an awareness of their danger. In November 1939 he addressed a note to the High Command about the lessons to be learned from the German campaign in Poland. He did not advocate an advance into Germany but harped on his old theme, now vindicated on the eastern front, of the vulnerability of extended and static fronts to the penetration of armoured columns. The note was acknowledged, de Gaulle's old enemy General Dufieux commenting briefly that such views must be rejected.

In January 1940, he wrote a more elaborate memorandum in the same sense and, since it was impossible to get it printed, distributed cyclostyled copies to eighty of the leading personalities in the High Command, the government, and the political world. It was a final statement of all that he had thought and written for twenty years, applied to the immediate situation. The Germans were about to attack France with a powerful mechanised force; unless France somehow rallied equivalent "units of riposte" she would be annihilated. "The internal combustion engine," he wrote, "endows modern means of destruction with such force, speed and range that the present conflict will be marked, sooner or later, by movements, surprises, breakthroughs and pursuit, the scale and rapidity of which will infinitely exceed those of the most lightning events of the past . . . It is high time for France to draw the conclusion."[8]

At the end of the month de Gaulle went to dine with M. Reynaud in Paris and met Léon Blum who later recorded something of what had passed. "The Colonel, who had just been given the command of the tanks of the army of Alsace, speaking quietly, in a voice devoid of bitterness and looking at us calmly said, 'What I have is nothing. Deeply anxious, I play my part in complete mystification. I have got no armoured division under my command for the good reason that none exists. A few dozen light tanks which are attached to my command are merely a speck of dust. I am afraid that the lessons of Poland, clear as they are, are being rejected deliberately. People do not want to see that what succeeded there should be possible here. Believe me, everything remains to be done on our side and if we don't succeed in time we shall lose this war miserably and we shall lose it by our own faults'."[9]

In his own memoirs de Gaulle says that Blum asked him to forecast the course of the war. " 'The problem,' I answered, 'is whether in the spring the Germans will attack westwards to take Paris or eastwards to reach Moscow.' 'Do you think so?' said Léon Blum, astonished. 'The Germans attack to the east? But why should they go and lose themselves in the depths of Russian territory? Attack to the west? But what could they do against the Maginot Line?' "[10] As they left Reynaud's flat de Gaulle mentioned his memorandum to Blum and asked him if he might send him a copy. Blum received it a few days later and, in his memoirs, said that for the first time he understood the true situation of the war. But Blum was out of office; elsewhere the memorandum appeared to have as little effect as its predecessors. Daladier, the Premier, ignored it and Gamelin, having read it, was confirmed in his view that its author was a dangerous man. Yet a change was about to take place. During the early months of the war the only strategy open to Gamelin—in view of public opinion in France and Britain—had been to do everything possible to distract the attention of the Germans and postpone the day when they would attack in the west. Hence his support, which many people found surprising at the time, for the forlorn adventures in Norway and Finland which prompted de Gaulle to remark that it looked as though France was more anxious to attack Stalin than Hitler. But although Gamelin would not take lessons from de Gaulle he had been impressed by the success of the Panzer divisions in Poland and, during the last three months of 1939, had been pressing forward the formation of the armoured divisions which had been agreed to the year before. The first was formed in January 1940, the second in March and a third was scheduled for April. This was repentance from the condemned cell, but it was better than nothing. And then suddenly a gleam of light was injected into the gathering gloom. On March 21, after the collapse of Finland, the Chamber overthrew Daladier and Paul Reynaud was asked to form a government. To de Gaulle it seemed that at the last minute a hope of reprieve was being offered his doomed country.

*   *   *

Reynaud at once summoned de Gaulle to Paris. He wanted help in preparing the speech he was to make to the Assembly. Leaving Metz in a state of considerable excitement, de Gaulle reviewed the situation in the train. The only hope lay in a clean sweep in the Ministry of Defence and, so far as possible, in the High Command as well. If he could persuade Reynaud to introduce men into the government who would revolutionise the army and the economic organisation behind it in the shortest possible time, it might yet be possible to avert disaster. By the time he had reached Paris he had marshalled his arguments and was confident of victory. He did not know that Reynaud had already thrown away the opportunity.

Of course Reynaud was in a difficulty. His tenure of office depended upon a delicate balance of forces within the Assembly. He had to temporise and appease. But there were certain key posts to which, if he was to be able to carry out his intention of prosecuting the war more vigorously, he had to appoint men who shared his views. Yet instead of taking the Ministry of Defence himself and putting Daladier in the Foreign Office as he had intended, he allowed M. Herriot, who carried the majority of the Radical Socialist group, to over-persuade him. Daladier was left in charge of defence. Reynaud added Foreign Affairs to his own burdens and gave Chautemps, a convinced appeaser, the Vice-Presidency of the Council.

De Gaulle arrived in Paris to find that these appointments had already been made. His heart sank. Reynaud wanted to use him and proposed that he should take the secretaryship of the War Committee. But Daladier replied that if the proposal was endorsed he would resign and recommend that de Gaulle take his place. He did not dislike de Gaulle personally but knew that the latter's ideas on defence meant the reversal of all that he had been working for as Minister for the last four years. But Reynaud could not take the plunge. Instead of jumping at the opportunity that Daladier had offered him, Reynaud chose Baudouin, a man who had always advocated closer understanding with Germany, in de Gaulle's stead. Even when it came to including socialists in his government, Reynaud did not dare appoint

5. De Gaulle with President Lebrun early in 1940. *Below*: The last government of the Third Republic. From left to right: Frossard, Chichery, Reynaud, Jean Prouvost, Février, Yvon Delbos, Pernod, de Gaulle

6. Young Frenchmen joining the Free French movement at Olympia. 1940

Marshal Pétain with Marshal Goering in 1941. Darlan is on the right

those, like Blum, whom he knew would support the war. The arch-enemy of appeasement abroad had become an appeaser at home. Even so, Reynaud only received a vote of confidence by a majority of one.

De Gaulle's forebodings deepened as he listened to the debate in which Reynaud presented his Cabinet to the Assembly. It seemed to him that no one spoke except those "who considered themselves injured by the new coalition." The danger in which the country stood, the necessity of the national effort, the co-operation of the Free World, were mentioned only to adorn claims and complaints."[11] But he stayed on for a few days with the new Prime Minister, hoping for a change but becoming more and more depressed with the political atmosphere in which the main topic of conversation seemed to be how to bring the war to an early end. Everything was being discussed: help for Finland, how to bomb Baku, what parts of French Africa would buy over Mussolini, whether Pétain should become Commander in Chief or even Head of State if Reynaud fell—everything except how to fight the Germans.

It was a relief to be asked to lunch with General Gamelin at his headquarters in Vincennes. In spite of their differences de Gaulle admired Gamelin "in whom intelligence, fineness of perception, and self-control attained a very high degree."[12] He must have suspected that some special reason had prompted the invitation but he seems to have been genuinely taken aback when, during lunch, Gamelin told him that he was increasing the number of armoured divisions to four and had appointed de Gaulle to command the fourth. De Gaulle did not attempt to conceal his delight or apprehensions. "Whatever my general feelings about our perhaps irremediable lateness in respect of mechanised forces, I felt very proud at finding myself called upon, as a colonel, to command a division. I said so to General Gamelin. He replied simply: 'I understand your satisfaction. As for your misgivings, I don't believe they are justified!' "[13]

It was a tantalising moment. De Gaulle was achieving one of his most cherished ambitions in hopeless circumstances. Gamelin had a defensive plan worked out to the last detail. Provided he stuck to it he was supremely confident of winning. "It was with respect, but also with a certain uneasiness, that I took leave of this great leader, as he made ready in his cloister to assume all of a sudden an immense responsibility, staking everything for everything on a move I judged to be wrong."[14] His judgment was soon to be put to the test.

De Gaulle returned to Wangenbourg to await orders. His new armoured division was to come into existence on May 15, which gave him five weeks to prepare his command. Gamelin was as good as his word and on May 11 de Gaulle received orders to take over his division. He established his headquarters at Le Vésinet. But already the blow he dreaded had fallen. The day before, German troops crossed into Holland, Belgium and Luxembourg. The battle of the frontiers had begun. Almost everything that de Gaulle had feared happened. The resistance of the Dutch and Belgians was overcome in a matter of days; German armour came through the Ardennes exactly where Pétain had said it was impossible for them to do so, turned west, swept towards the sea and cut off the British and Northern French armies; the Germans were then in a position to take the Maginot Line in the rear.

At the end of ten days Gamelin's plans were in chaos and he was replaced by Weygand, while Pétain was summoned from Spain to become Vice-President of the Council. Within forty-eight hours both Pétain and Weygand were pressing the War Council to take France out of the war before the French armies were completely destroyed. Thereafter it was only a question of how soon the end would come and in what form.

But although de Gaulle was powerless to influence the main course of the battle his part in it was crucial both for himself and for France, for from his experience sprang his iron resolve never to admit defeat and the enhanced confidence which enabled him to play the part he was soon to cast for himself.

While his division was assembling de Gaulle was summoned to General Georges's headquarters. General Doumenc, one of the first French officers to propose the formation of armoured divisions, gave him his instructions. He was to cover the deployment of the 6th Army under General Touchon which was to bar the route to Paris. To do so he must operate alone to the north and east of Laon and so gain time for the deployment to take place. He then saw General Georges, the Field Commander of all the French armies, and found him "calm, cordial, but visibly overwhelmed." Nevertheless General Georges confirmed the orders and added, "There de Gaulle. For you who have so long held the ideas which the enemy is putting into practice, here is the chance to act."[15] That same afternoon of May 15 de Gaulle transferred his headquarters to Laon to await the last units of his division.

The next day, with his staff, he was able to reconnoitre the position and it was then that he first grasped the extent of the catastrophe. In his memoirs he wrote, "Miserable processions of refugees crowded along all the roads from the north. I saw, also, a good many soldiers who had lost their weapons. They belonged to the troops routed by the Panzers during the preceding day. Caught up, as they fled, by the enemy's mechanised detachments, they had been ordered to throw away their arms and make off to the south so as not to clutter up the roads. 'We haven't time,' they had been told, 'to take you prisoner!'

"Then, at the sight of those bewildered people and of those soldiers in rout, at the tale, too, of that contemptuous piece of insolence of the enemy's, I felt myself borne up by a limitless fury. 'Ah! It's too stupid! The war is beginning as badly as it could. Therefore it must go on. For this, the world is wide. If I live, I will fight, wherever I must, as long as I must, until the enemy is defeated and the national stain washed clean.' All I have managed to do since was resolved upon that day."[16]

For the moment at any rate he could fight the German Army which had come through the Ardennes, and instead of heading for Paris had swung westwards towards St. Quentin and the coast. De Gaulle decided to take it in the flank at once, with whatever units he could muster, and cut the main road by which it was advancing. He attacked the very next morning with three battalions of tanks and reached Mont Cornet, about 30 kilometres north-east of Laon. But having no mechanised infantry to consolidate his rear and finding that his battalions were being attacked by a Panzer division supported by an infantry division, he had to withdraw towards Laon. With reinforcements de Gaulle, now Brigadier-General as a result of his previous action, attacked again on both the next two days, this time due north as far as Crécy, the history of whose earlier battles he himself had written. Again his tanks were successful and having fulfilled their task and given time to the 6th Army to take up its position, were recalled for even larger tasks.

Gamelin had planned a pincer movement to cut off the extended German forces which had penetrated the allied front. The northern Anglo-French armies and the southern French armies were both to converge on Arras. De Gaulle was to lead the southern thrust. But Gamelin fell on May 19 and by the time Weygand had taken over, the breach between the allied armies was too wide for any chance of success. De Gaulle was therefore ordered to reduce the enemy breach-head over the Somme at Abbeville. He fought his way to the outskirts of the town and, attacking on May 29, pushed the Germans back 14 kilometres in twenty-four hours, captured 500 prisoners and much material. The 4th Armoured Division had not taken the Abbeville bridge-head but by the time it was relieved by General Fortune's newly disembarked 51st Highland Division, it had reduced it by a third.

A vivid picture of de Gaulle in action is given by his subordinates, both in the official journal of the 4th Divison and in individual accounts. "Always in the front line, often among the advance reconnaissance units, with his headquarters exposed to enemy fire; if it was a question of an attack he refused to listen to the slightest objection, even if it was well-founded. One saw his leather jacket, his helmet with the eternal cigarette underneath it, everywhere. Day and night did not count. He was not easy to approach or easy to live with. He was haughty and serious, spoke little. If one asked him a question one got a rebuke. As in the First World War he disdained the slightest precaution. Although he had no air support and his tanks were subject to constant attacks by Stukas, he always stood with the hatch of his own tank open and, if on his feet, refused to notice bombs and thundered at anyone who threw themselves on the ground."[17] Corroboration of the effectiveness of de Gaulle's leadership has since come from the other side. A German, Major Gehring, writing of the action at Abbeville, admitted that on May 28 his troops were thrown into confusion: "A profound terror of the tanks had got into the bones of our soldiers . . . Losses were heavy . . . there was, practically speaking, nobody who had not lost beloved comrades."[18]

De Gaulle's own summary of the part he and his division played was no less eulogistic: "It was true that the division included only a single battalion of infantry, and this transported in buses and therefore extremely vulnerable when on the move . . . It was true that the artillery had only just been formed out of detachments furnished by many different depots and that many officers were literally meeting their men for the first time on the field of battle. It was true that we had no radio network and that I could command only by despatching motor-cyclists to the subordinate echelons and—above all—by going to see them. It was true that all the units were badly short of the transport, replacements and victuals they should normally have included. And yet, already, an impression of general enthusiasm was emerging from this improvised body."[19]

Neither of these minor actions could have any permanent effect on the battle, but they gave an opportunity for de Gaulle to prove himself as a Divisional Tank Commander and were effective enough to show not only to de Gaulle but to his superiors what might have been done, even since the outbreak of war, had France's 3,000 modern tanks and 800 self-propelled machine guns been used as de Gaulle had urged. Poignantly de Gaulle pondered these lost opportunities in the intervals of fighting his own battles: "It is improbable that France could have won the battle, but she could have inflicted such losses on the Germans and so delayed them as to alter the whole course of the war."

For one fleeting moment it looked as if de Gaulle might be given a chance to retrieve something from the disaster. When the 4th Armoured Division was relieved at Abbeville on May 30 the battle of the frontiers was over. The German armies had reached the Channel coast, King Leopold had laid down his arms, the British had begun their evacuation at Dunkirk. France was isolated but there was a pause of a week while the Germans regrouped before turning south to begin the battle of France. On the first day of that week de Gaulle was summoned by Weygand to his headquarters at the Château de Montry. Although they had known each other on and off for twenty years they had never been friends. Weygand had remorselessly opposed de Gaulle's proposals for the reform of the army and was equally strenuously to oppose him in the days that were to come. At the moment, however, he needed his advice. The French Army still had some hundreds of tanks capable of fighting and, according to de Gaulle's later account, Weygand did not know what to do with them.

Weygand complimented de Gaulle on his recent action, about which he had already written a glowing citation, and then asked his opinion. De Gaulle at once said that the tanks should be divided into two groups and used to counter-attack the Germans when, having broken through the French lines on their southward march, they were at their most extended. Improvisation though it was, it was probably the only plan that had the slightest chance of delaying the German advance. But the flicker of determination which must have prompted Weygand to ask de Gaulle to visit him, died as he listened. In his heart Weygand had already given up hope. He thanked de Gaulle for his advice and said good-bye. De Gaulle left, knowing that his plans for the tanks would not be put into operation. When the two men met again a few days later it was already too late either for Weygand to muster the tanks or for de Gaulle to command them.

CHAPTER V

THE BOTTOM OF THE PIT

By all normal odds de Gaulle's life should have ended within a few days of his visit to General Weygand. His armoured division was resting, but it was only a few miles behind the line in the very sector where the Germans were to launch their first attacks in the great drive southwards through France. If they were to be stopped anywhere it had to be by the counter-attacks which de Gaulle would deliver— counter-attacks which he would certainly press home and from which, this time, there would be no withdrawal. De Gaulle was determined not to become a prisoner of war for a second time.

On June 5 the German 4th Army under General von Bock attacked in the Amiens-Abbeville sector. The Panzer divisions made rapid progress. In the early hours of June 6 de Gaulle was at his headquarters awaiting the orders which he knew might be his last. The telephone rang. But the call was entirely unexpected. General Delestraint, the commander of a neighbouring infantry division, had heard on the radio that Reynaud, the Prime Minister, had reshaped his Cabinet and had appointed de Gaulle Under Secretary of State at the Ministry of Defence. General Delestraint was ringing to congratulate him.

No false heroics clouded de Gaulle's pleasure at this promotion. He enjoyed commanding his division and was ready to give his life even in a hopeless action. But the prospect of being once more at the centre, of influencing events and perhaps helping to save something from the coming wreck outweighed all other considerations. When the official telegram of appointment arrived later that morning de Gaulle took immediate leave of his division and set off for Paris.

What had happened? How had Reynaud, who had not only been forced to reject de Gaulle a fortnight earlier but had since taken Pétain into his Cabinet, thrown off the shackles of the defeatists and re-asserted himself? How strong was his position? Had the United States or perhaps the Russians given some unexpected twist to the pattern of the war? These questions, which de Gaulle asked himself as he drove to the capital, were quickly answered. He was taken at once to the Prime

Minister. Reynaud had no comforting news. Defeat still stared him in the face. But he told de Gaulle that Pétain and Weygand had not only given up all hope but were doing their utmost to persuade the other members of the government of the necessity for an armistice. Reynaud, on the other hand, was determined to fight on even if it meant abandoning France and transferring the government, the fleet and as much of the army and air force as possible to North Africa. Although he had kept Pétain in the Cabinet because he thought it was safer to have him inside than out, he had dropped some of the Marshal's chief supporters and tried to reconstruct the government with a majority which shared his own views. Daladier had been moved to the Ministry of Foreign Affairs and Reynaud himself had taken over the Ministry of Defence. In spite of the objections of both Pétain and Weygand, who declared that he was "too young," Reynaud had appointed de Gaulle Under Secretary of State, personally responsible to himself.

De Gaulle saw at once that speed was the essence of Reynaud's policy. He told Reynaud that he thought he had made a mistake in retaining Pétain and that it would make it more difficult for him to carry his Cabinet. But everything hinged upon how quickly the arrangements for evacuation could be made and he asked at once if he could be put in charge of them. Reynaud agreed and told him to go to London as quickly as possible to arrange for shipping and all other necessary help. De Gaulle needed no further orders, but while waiting for clearance for his journey he took one other important step. Since every hour by which the German advance could be delayed meant more time in which to evacuate both government and military units to North Africa, he had to know Weygand's plans and gauge his capacity to fulfil them. That very evening, therefore, he paid another visit to the Commander in Chief at his headquarters in the Château de Montry.

It was a dramatic meeting. Instead of being summoned by General Weygand to give advice, de Gaulle now came as the Commander in Chief's immediate superior to demand information.

In a report written after the war Weygand said that the first three days he had been hopeful of stopping the German advance. That was not de Gaulle's impression. The first words Weygand spoke, which remained "graven" on de Gaulle's mind, were: "You see, I was not mistaken when I told you a few days ago that the Germans would attack on the Somme on June 6. They are, in fact, attacking. At this moment they are crossing the river. I can't stop them." De Gaulle pressed the General about his intentions.

"All right! They are crossing the Somme. And then?"

"Then? The Seine and the Marne."

"Yes. And then?"

"Then? But that's the end!"

"How do you mean? The end? And the world? And the Empire?"

General Weygand gave a despairing laugh. "The Empire? But that's childish! As for the world, when I've been beaten here, England won't wait a week before negotiating with the Reich."[1]

Among Weygand's staff, de Gaulle found the same spirit of defeatism. They were carrying out their duties automatically but talking and thinking only of how to bring the war to an end. If they had their way the Germans might overrun the country so quickly that even the government might be unable to move.

When de Gaulle returned to Paris he told Reynaud that Weygand ought to be relieved of his command immediately. Reynaud agreed but confessed that he was not in a strong enough position to give the necessary orders. If he did the government might collapse. However Reynaud was prepared to discuss who Weygand's successor should be and, with de Gaulle, eventually decided upon General Huntziger. For the moment no further action was taken.

Next day de Gaulle left for London. He was accompanied by Roland de Margerie, Reynaud's *Chef de Cabinet Diplomatique*, and a tall, fair-haired rather serious young man named Geoffroy de Courcel, a former member of the Foreign Service who had just returned from Syria and become his A.D.C. The sudden change in de Gaulle's status was emphasised by the first appointment which had been arranged for him. It was at "Number Ten."

"Mr. Churchill received me in Downing Street," wrote de Gaulle in his memoirs. "It was my first contact with him. The impression he gave me confirmed me in my conviction that Great Britain, led by such a fighter, would certainly not flinch. Mr. Churchill seemed to me to be equal to the rudest task, provided it had also grandeur. The assurance of his judgment, his great culture, the knowledge he had of most of the subjects, countries and men involved, and finally his passion for the problems proper to war, found in war their full scope. On top of everything he was fitted by his character to act, take risks, play the part out-and-out and without scruple. In short, I found him well in the saddle as guide and chief. Such were my first impressions."[2]

These grandiloquent reminiscences can bear little relation to de Gaulle's feelings at the time. He was in London as Reynaud's emissary, commissioned to make certain urgent arrangements. He saw Churchill, accompanied by officials, to get the British Prime Minister's general blessing for the plan of evacuation and to deliver certain messages from Reynaud. He can have had no time to plumb Churchill's general knowledge or his military expertise. The interview was short and made so little impression upon Churchill that when he came to write his account of these days he made no mention of it at all.

Nevertheless de Gaulle had a sympathetic reception. Churchill was as anxious as Reynaud that France should stay in the war if only to ensure that the French Fleet did not fall into German hands. When de Gaulle asked for ships for a general withdrawal across the Mediterranean to North Africa, he at once agreed. Although every ton of British shipping was being used to capacity the Admiralty, too, promised that, if the French did evacuate, they would somehow help them to do it. De Gaulle's second request was even more outrageous. On Reynaud's instructions he asked that all the troops evacuated at Dunkirk should be re-equipped as soon as possible and sent immediately back to France. Since the whole world knew that France was on the point of collapse de Gaulle must have expected a refusal. He got nothing of the kind. Suicidal though it seemed, the British were continuing to fulfil their programme of sending troops to France. Although the French front was in chaos and the French Commanders in Chief were pressing for an armistice, although the French Government was contemplating flight to North Africa, a British division was completing its disembarkation in Normandy at the very moment de Gaulle was making his request and the first Canadian division was to embark for Brittany the following day. These were the last properly equipped troops in the British Isles and they were to return within a week, minus much of their equipment, with what was left of the British Expeditionary Force in France. It was a smaller and lesser-known Dunkirk in which 156,000 men were evacuated from Brest, Cherbourg, St. Malo and St. Nazaire.

When de Gaulle asked for troops, therefore, Churchill was able to say with complete truth that he was already getting them and that he would continue to do so. It was only when, again on Reynaud's instructions, de Gaulle asked that the remaining British air squadrons be sent across the Channel that he met with a refusal. Because Churchill felt so keenly "that Britain, with her forty-eight million population, had not been able to make a greater contribution to the land war against Germany"[3] and that so much of the slaughter and suffering had fallen on France alone he had taken a fearful risk. He had sacrificed the British Army and risked much of the fleet. But he had promised Air Marshal Dowding, who led Britain's Fighter Command, that he would never part with the twenty-five squadrons considered the minimum necessary to deal with the Luftwaffe.*

* A week later, when de Gaulle was again in London, he repeated this request and

De Gaulle left England well satisfied with his mission. With the exception of the Fighter Squadrons, he had been promised everything he asked. Provided the French Government was firm in its resolve to move to North Africa there was no reason why France should not remain in the war. But during the forty-eight hours he had been away, a sickening change had taken place in his own country. When de Gaulle arrived back on the 9th, Paris was already threatened and Italy on the point of declaring war. Panic was spreading. On June 10, the last day that the French Government was to spend in Paris, General Weygand burst into the Prime Minister's room unannounced and laid a paper on the table formally demanding an armistice. Reynaud, taken aback, countered by saying that, if that was how the Commander in Chief felt, it was open to him to tell his troops to lay down their arms. Weygand indignantly refused, saying that any surrender must be the responsibility of the politicians. He would not dishonour the French Army. Eventually Reynaud ushered the Commander in Chief to the door and saw him out. When he came back into the room de Gaulle urged the Prime Minister once more to dismiss Weygand at once.

It was plain, he said, that the Commander in Chief was not only unwilling to continue the war, but was seeking to dictate to the government and to ensure that, whoever was ultimately blamed for the catastrophe, it should not be him.

This time Reynaud acquiesced and sent de Gaulle to see General Huntziger at Arcis-sur-Aube, the headquarters of the centre group of armies which were not at that moment being attacked. Huntziger agreed to take over if Weygand was dismissed, but when de Gaulle got back to Briare, where Reynaud and the government had made their first stop on the trek which was to lead to Bordeaux, he found the Prime Minister's resolution had once more evaporated.

At that moment probably half Reynaud's Cabinet was behind him in wishing to continue the war, and he had the additional support of M. Jeanneney, President of the Senate, and M. Herriot, President of the Chamber; but the influence of the defeatists and above all of Pétain was once again too strong for him. As de Gaulle left Reynaud's office he ran into Marshal Pétain whom he had not seen since 1938. "You're a General!" said Pétain to de Gaulle. "I don't congratulate you. What good are ranks in defeat?" "But you yourself, Monsieur le Maréchal," replied de Gaulle, "received your first star during the 1914 retreat. A

met with a second refusal. As he left the room he turned back to the Prime Minister and said in the English he so seldom used: "I think you are right."
Their Finest Hour. Winston Churchill. p.189.

few days later there was the Marne." "No comparison!" Pétain grunted, and passed into the Prime Minister's room.[4] The two men were never to speak to each other again.

But de Gaulle did not give up hope. He knew that the next day he would have fresh allies in his struggle to bolster Reynaud's determination. On June 11 Churchill and Eden came to Briare. It was a dismal conference at which Pétain made it plain that Paris would not be defended and Weygand not only hinted at an armistice but implied that Britain's turn to sue for one could not be long delayed. Churchill's reply that, although not a military expert, he was advised that the best way to deal with a German invasion was to drown as many as possible on the way and knock the others on the head as they crawled ashore, was met with supercilious disbelief. Nevertheless, Churchill by his very presence put new heart into Reynaud. For de Gaulle the visit had a further and special importance. For the first time he made an impression on Churchill. They sat next to each other at dinner and de Gaulle enthused Churchill with his ideas of carrying on guerrilla warfare even after France had been overrun. In reporting to the British War Cabinet next day Churchill mentioned de Gaulle as a young and energetic Minister who had made a very favourable impression upon him. "I thought it probable that if the present line collapsed Reynaud would turn to him to take command."[5]

On June 12 the French Government had to take another critical decision. The Germans were about to cross the Loire. Should the government go to Bordeaux or to Quimper in Brittany? De Gaulle favoured Quimper not because, like Churchill, he thought a stand in Brittany would have any military value but because, if once the French Government got to Quimper, it would be forced to put to sea so as to avoid capture. But Reynaud again gave way and decided on Bordeaux.

The sands were running out. Next day the government moved to Tours and Churchill came once more to France to meet them. It was to be his last visit for almost exactly four years. By now Pétain and Weygand had both openly declared for an armistice and Reynaud wanted to know what attitude the British Government would take if such a request were made. Would Churchill release France from the solemn undertakings they had given not to make a separate peace? Although Churchill refused he was so obviously and deeply distressed that the French Ministers came away from the meeting feeling that, so long as the French Fleet sailed to British ports, the British Prime Minister might relent.

De Gaulle only reached Tours when the conference was half over.

He had been summoned by de Margerie who feared that Pétain and Weygand might prevail upon Reynaud to take France out of the war that very day. Having heard what had passed he at once challenged Reynaud himself with being prepared to ask for an armistice. Reynaud indignantly denied it and excused his conduct on the extraordinary grounds that he wished to give the British a shock so as to get more help out of them. In despair at Churchill's indulgence and Reynaud's weakness de Gaulle wrote out his resignation that night. But before he could post the letter Georges Mandel, warned by de Gaulle's *Chef de Cabinet*, Jean Laurent, asked to see him. "Mandel spoke to me in a tone of gravity and resolution which impressed me," wrote de Gaulle later. "He was convinced, just as much as I was, that the independence and honour of France could only be safeguarded by continuing the war. But it was because of this national necessity that he recommended me to stay on in the post where I was. 'Who knows,' he said, 'whether we shall not get the government, after all, to go to Algiers?' He described to me what had happened in the Cabinet after the departure of the British; firmness had prevailed there in spite of the scene which Weygand had come to make. He gave me the news that, at that moment, the first German troops were entering Paris. Then, pointing to the future, he added: 'In any case we are only at the beginning of a world war. You will have great duties to fulfil, General! But with the advantage of being, in the midst of all of us, an untarnished man. Think only of what has to be done for France and consider that, in certain circumstances, your present position makes things easier for you.'"[6] Mandel prevailed and de Gaulle found himself next day at Bordeaux with the other members of the government.

Again he saw Reynaud and at last got a firm decision from him. Prodded by de Gaulle, who reproached him for his weakness, the Prime Minister said bluntly that he would take the government to Algiers. He agreed that de Gaulle should go to London to arrange transport and said that he would meet him in Algiers on his return. But that evening, at the Hotel Splendide, de Gaulle saw Jean Ybarnégaray, a deputy, who until that moment had seemed as resolute as any, and found that he had succumbed to Pétain. This was ominous. If Pétain could prevail over such a man Reynaud's prospects of retaining any following were slender, and without a following he might weaken again.

As Pétain happened to be dining in the same room, de Gaulle went over to his table and saluted. The Marshal rose, shook his hand, and without a word sat down. It was a silent prelude to victory. De

Gaulle, for once, had nothing to say. They were never to see each other again.

De Gaulle set off for London by car. On the way he stopped in Brittany to arrange for ships to evacuate as many French troops as possible and then boarded the destroyer *Milan*, which was taking a party of chemists and their "heavy water" to Plymouth. He arrived in London early on June 16. De Gaulle's official business was quickly finished and the necessary transport arranged. If the French Government really was prepared to leave France, the British were prepared to do everything possible to help it. As an earnest of the French Government's intentions, de Gaulle, on his own authority, diverted to a British port the cargo ship *Pasteur*, bound for Bordeaux and carrying a thousand 75 mm. cannon, many thousands of machine guns and much ammunition. But just as he was on the point of leaving for Bordeaux a sudden and dramatic proposal postponed his departure.

The idea of a union between France and Britain had emerged two days before at a meeting between Sir Robert Vansittart, Desmond Morton, Mr. Churchill's private secretary, M. Corbin, the French Ambassador in London, and M. Monnet and M. Pleven, members of the French Economic Mission. It had been put to Churchill who had demurred. M. Corbin and M. Monet now canvassed de Gaulle, telling him that it had been arranged for him to lunch with Churchill and, if he liked the plan, he must persuade Churchill to accept it. The plan was a desperate, last minute attempt to prevent the French Government from making peace. None of its details had been thought out nor could have been, but a further meeting between Reynaud and Churchill to discuss its implications had been tentatively arranged for the following day at Concarneau on the coast of Brittany. De Gaulle of all men was unlikely to agree to the fusion of France and Britain on a sudden impulse, but he felt that the grandeur of the idea might give Reynaud something fresh and dramatic with which to appeal to his faltering cabinet and he agreed to speak to Churchill. His approach was subtle and successful. He began by gently chiding the Prime Minister for his attitude at the Tours meeting. What the French Government needed at this crucial moment was not sympathy and understanding, not an attitude of resignation, but firmness and encouragement. He then raised the question of union.

Churchill agreed and has recorded his surprise when he proposed the union to the British Cabinet that afternoon to see "the staid, solid experienced politicians of all parties engage themselves so passionately in an immense design whose implications and consequences were in no way thought out."[7] The British Cabinet accepted the plan. Churchill had already instructed Campbell, his Ambassador at Bordeaux, to withdraw his conditional release of the French Government from its obligation not to make a separate peace and, after de Gaulle had given Reynaud the text of the union plan over the telephone, spoke himself and arranged to meet the French Prime Minister the next day. He then put an aeroplane at de Gaulle's disposal so that he could fly to Bordeaux with the text of the agreement in his pocket.

Within half an hour Reynaud laid the proposals for a Franco-British union before the French Cabinet. Its reception was very different from the one it had received in London. Weygand, who had managed to tap the telephones of those ministers who wished to continue the war, including Reynaud, had already warned many members of the cabinet what to expect. Not one voice was raised in favour. Reynaud's supporters were taken by surprise. The others treated it as a trap to humiliate France and as a means of stealing her empire and converting her into a British Dominion or as a simple ruse to persuade her to continue a hopeless fight. Ybarnégaray said bluntly, "better be a Nazi province. At least we know what that means."[8] Pétain was even more contemptuous. Believing that Britain would be subjugated within a few weeks of the end of French resistance, he said that the proposals meant fusion with a corpse. Reynaud had played his last card. An hour later Edward Ward of the B.B.C. and Virginia Cowles, an American war correspondent, who were waiting in the passage outside Reynaud's room, saw Georges Mandel come through the door, tears streaming down his face. "It is finished," he said, as he passed them. Reynaud had resigned.

Meanwhile de Gaulle was in the air. When he landed at 9.30 p.m. he was met by two of his staff, Colonels Humbert and Auburtin, and told of Reynaud's resignation and Lebrun's request that Pétain should form an administration. He went at once to Reynaud. It was no time for reproaches. Reynaud had been his champion and de Gaulle knew better than anyone that he had wanted desperately to continue the war from North Africa or wherever the French flag could still fly. The truth was simply that Reynaud had not proved equal to an occasion which demanded almost superhuman qualities. To succeed he would have had to become a dictator using emergency powers. If, on assuming office, he had sought such powers, as Pétain was to do on succeeding him, if he had ruthlessly pruned his government and the military High Command of those who were half-hearted or worse, if he had used de Gaulle as he originally meant to use him, he might conceivably have rallied support in the country and in the armed forces which could have slowed down the German advance and given him time to build up a strong position in North Africa. But Reynaud was neither ruthless nor confident enough. He was a lawyer and a parliamentarian who sought to gain his ends by persuasion and manoeuvre. Except in war such attributes are virtues; Reynaud was called to power when they were fatal weaknesses. Although de Gaulle did not share these weaknesses he was, and was to remain, generous to Reynaud. That night he urged him to come to London with him. Reynaud refused. But he approved de Gaulle's plan and gave him such cash as he had in his office belonging to the secret funds. It amounted to about £100.

By the time de Gaulle left Reynaud's room the journalists had gone and the house seemed empty. Only one half-hidden light was shining in the hall. Suddenly the door opened and he heard voices. He stood still by a pillar to see whose they were. De Gaulle was in luck. Reynaud's late visitors were not new Ministers whom he might wish to avoid but the very men whom he most wished to see, the British Ambassador, Sir Ronald Campbell, and Churchill's special liaison officer to Reynaud, General Spears.

When Churchill had sent de Gaulle back to Bordeaux in a British aircraft he had told him that it might stay overnight in France in case he needed it to return to London to continue the arrangements for evacuating the French Government to North Africa. However the orders to the pilot had to be given by the British Ambassador. If de Gaulle were to reach England he had to find Sir Ronald Campbell before the aircraft left next day. Now here the Ambassador was, groping his way through the same darkened hall as de Gaulle. De Gaulle stepped out of the shadows and told General Spears that he must see the Ambassador urgently. They arranged to meet later that night at the Hotel Montré where Sir Ronald was staying.

When de Gaulle saw Sir Ronald he asked if he might return to England in the aircraft which had been put at his disposal. But circumstances had changed so drastically that General Spears felt it necessary to telephone to No. 10 Downing Street to get permission. Churchill agreed and after some persuasion allowed Spears to accompany de Gaulle to London. The three men then concocted a plan which would allow de Gaulle to get away without arousing suspicion and agreed to meet at the hotel at 7 o'clock next morning.*

For the rest of that night de Gaulle hid—to this day no one knows where. He knew with what suspicion the new administration regarded him. While he was Under Secretary for Defence Weygand had said that he would like to shoot him, and Pétain must have felt

* The accounts of General Spears and General de Gaulle differ. See Special Note to Chapter V (p.476).

equally strongly. From what Campbell and Spears told him he was in serious danger of arrest if he returned to his hotel or was seen in public.[9] And while he sat, somewhere in Bordeaux, waiting for the dawn, Gaullism was born. It was an agonising labour. Of the thousands of French men and women who were in tears that night, none felt the humiliation of defeat more acutely than de Gaulle. His mystical vision of France as God's chosen country, his belief in the army as that country's finest expression, were alike shattered. Among the dregs of the cup he was draining was an additional sense of personal failure. Since the Polish campaign twenty years before he seemed to have failed in everything he had undertaken, above all in the one task that he had set himself in his short spell as a Minister—that of persuading the French Government and in particular Reynaud to leave France and carry on the war overseas.

One of de Gaulle's chief detractors has suggested that de Gaulle's real struggle that night was in deciding whether to leave France or not, and that it was only because Reynaud had seen Pétain's new list of Ministers and told de Gaulle that he was not among them that he finally decided to go to London. This is a gross calumny. To pretend that he would have served under Pétain is grotesque. De Gaulle was outraged, not by defeat but by Pétain's acceptance of it. Other armies had been defeated, other countries overrun, but rather than come to terms with Hitler the governments of Holland, Norway and Poland had gone into exile. Shadows though they were, these governments in exile, whose numbers were to increase as the war dragged on, were a symbol of the resistance of their people. Yet France, with vast territories overseas untouched and a ready-made haven across the Mediterranean, was giving up the struggle. For de Gaulle, like every thinking Frenchman, knew on June 16 that once armistice terms had been asked for they would be accepted however onerous.

It was the Armistice that was the great betrayal. For the rest of his life de Gaulle considered those who asked for it traitors and only those who refused to accept it true Frenchmen. His attitude towards Vichy was fixed before he ever left the shores of France. But what distinguished de Gaulle from other Frenchmen who decided to go on fighting was that, whereas they acted as individuals, he identified himself with France. He was not leaving France just to enlist in an allied army. Somehow, somewhere he was going to turn the facts upside down and assert that France had never agreed to an armistice, that she had been betrayed by a small clique of self-seeking defeatists and that he and anyone else who would join him were the true representatives of the French people rather than Pétain and his manipulators. In

Bordeaux this vision was still instinct and the means of achieving it unimaginable, but from that moment it inspired every move that de Gaulle made.

Luckily, during those numbing hours in Bordeaux, de Gaulle did not realise how preposterous his vision was. For Pétain had not yet asked for an armistice. Within forty-eight hours of Pétain's request, however, the vast majority of Frenchmen had accepted the terms with resignation and even relief. The people swallowed the anodyne of the Marshal's broadcast in grateful gulps. The French army had fought gallantly but had been overwhelmed by superior equipment. Defeat was total and must be accepted to save useless loss of life. The causes lay within the soul of France itself and must be expiated. The Marshal would lead the expiation. Taking its cue, the press immediately and almost unanimously began to portray the war as a ghastly mistake into which France had been led unprepared by her ally, Britain, and then deserted on the field of battle. Across the world the attitude of representative Frenchmen, with honourable exceptions, changed with a rapidity which was only to be emulated by the Russians when Hitler attacked them a year later. Governors-General, Generals, Ambassadors and officials who had been working in the greatest intimacy with their British counterparts suddenly became remote and inaccessible. Even men like René Massigli, then Ambassador in Turkey and later to become de Gaulle's Foreign Minister and a distinguished Ambassador in London, severed every connection with his British colleagues and even cut some of them in public.

As for the notion that the war might be carried on in North Africa, it was ridiculed by soldiers and politicians alike. Weygand, who had scoffed at it when de Gaulle had proposed it to him, led the argument against it. The army in North Africa was feeble, its weapons light and out of date. Such reinforcements as might have been evacuated from the mainland would have been almost as naked as the troops rescued from Dunkirk. The air force would have lacked reserves, spares and ammunition. The attitude of Spain was uncertain and in Libya the Italians had a well equipped army of a quarter of a million men. For the French Government to move to North Africa was simply to invite the Spaniards and Italians to carve up the French territories between them or, if they failed, to draw down upon North Africa a German occupation which the French would be powerless to prevent.

From the moment he had become a Minister de Gaulle had tried to expose these arguments as specious, inaccurate and defeatist. In council and in conversation he had argued that, if the French Government had moved to Algiers, not only might a large part of the air force, several hundred thousand soldiers and a good deal of equipment have been transported there but the entire French Fleet could have been stationed in North African ports. Algiers and Tunisia would have become an allied base comparable to the Canal Zone in Egypt, directly accessible to supplies from the United States. With the French Fleet in active operation, the Mediterranean sea lanes would have been kept open. The superiority of French over Italian troops had already been demonstrated in the Alpine fighting before the Armistice, and there can be little doubt that the Italian forces in Libya and Cyrenaica, attacked by the British in the East and the French in the West, could have been liquidated within a few weeks.

The Germans were not prepared for an invasion which presented formidable difficulties. The Norwegian campaign had already weakened the German Navy and what remained of the surface warships would have had to run the risk of a full-scale battle with the British in order to get into the Mediterranean. Submarines could and did get through the Straits of Gibraltar but were more vulnerable in the narrow seas than in the Atlantic. The British Fleet in Alexandria would have taken care of the Italians; the task of the French Fleet would have been to sink German transports and light escorting vessels while protecting themselves from submarines and concentrated attacks from the air. Certainly the French Air Force would have been much inferior to the German. Perhaps 500 aircraft in all could have been evacuated from France and, in the two months or so it would have taken the Germans to prepare for an invasion, these could have been reinforced from other parts of the French Empire and perhaps from the United States as well. But the French would have been operating close to their aerodromes in North Africa whereas the Germans would have been at extreme range—as the British were a year later when fighting over Crete from bases in Egypt.

There were immense risks, but on any calculation there was clearly enough hope of effective resistance to make the risk worth taking. From France's point of view the political gain would have been enormous. She would have remained a major combatant, controlling the Mediterranean, stabilising the Middle East, drawing upon her empire for men and supplies. In North Africa she would have been employing more troops than the British and, whatever course the war had taken, she would have continued to exercise a major influence in Allied councils. Collaboration with the enemy could never have become official French policy and a fratricidal schism within the French community would have been avoided. Any allied invasion of Sicily and Italy, even of France itself, would have been organised under French auspices in North Africa and very probably carried out under French command. The war might have ended sooner and without the Russian occupation of half Europe.

But Weygand prevailed. The plain fact was that most Frenchmen never had their hearts in the fight. The majority of fourteen to six in Reynaud's Cabinet in favour of an armistice may well have exaggerated the strength of those who wanted to continue the war. The reason why Reynaud never dared get rid of Pétain and Weygand was that he knew they represented French opinion far more closely than he did. By democratic standards, therefore, Pétain was not a traitor. He was expressing the will of France. The vote given him later by the Assembly was not a vote under duress. It was an acceptance of defeat for which most Frenchmen had been ready since 1936, certainly since Munich. Pétain had believed the country would turn to him and played a skilful waiting game. He had been ready to capitulate in 1916 and 1918. He was ready again in 1940. On each occasion he blamed the British and saw nothing shameful in accepting defeat.

Neither Pétain nor Weygand was capable of seeing their own hypocrisy when they blamed the politicians for France's unpreparedness. They believed themselves the victims of a political system they despised and, as Reynaud admitted, the higher ranks of the army were solidly behind them. Pétain was not a dreamer like de Gaulle. Out of disaster he genuinely hoped to bring regeneration. He saw himself as the saviour and redeemer of his country and in June, 1940, the French accepted him as such. Of course de Gaulle knew all this and it was because the knowledge was fatally discreditable to France that he determined never to admit it, even to himself.

A few hours earlier, when de Gaulle was in London, Churchill had commented that the young French general seemed to have a remarkable capacity for feeling pain. Traces of the suffering de Gaulle endured that night in Bordeaux lingered in his face for many months. Yet when dawn came he was ready for action. The evening before it had been arranged that de Gaulle was to go to the British Ambassador's hotel at seven o'clock, pick up General Spears and drive to the aerodrome ostensibly to see him off. On the way they were to call at two different offices belonging to the Ministry of Defence where de Gaulle was to tell officials to make a series of appointments for him later in the day. At each stop the engine of the car was to be kept running so that, if suspicion was aroused, they could make a dash for the aerodrome. De Gaulle arrived at the hotel in time and to start with all went according to plan. However, when they reached the aerodrome, the tarmac was so packed with French aircraft which had been assembled to fly to Morocco that it was difficult to get the car alongside the British machine. In the end they succeeded and the luggage, which had been covered with overcoats while in the back of the car, was stowed on board. The last handshakes were made and de Gaulle stood back as if to salute as the aircraft taxied away. Spears was standing in the open doorway. Then, as the aircraft slowly began to move, de Gaulle rushed forward followed by de Courcel, to the stupefaction of the chauffeur who was standing by. They were hauled on board and the door was slammed.

In this rather ignominious fashion the moment for which de Gaulle's whole life had been a half-conscious preparation had arrived. He had dreamed since he had been a boy of performing "some signal service" for his country. He had certainly never imagined that the opportunity would come in raising the standard of revolt. Yet this was what he was doing. All the emphasis he had laid throughout his life on discipline, on the traditions of the French Army, on the subordination of the civil to the military power, was being summarily discarded. He was defying not merely his military commanders but the government of his country. As the one Minister beyond the shores of France who had been appointed by the French Premier in freedom rather than in thraldom, he might persuade himself that he was the only "legitimate" representative of France. But how many Frenchmen or others would agree with him? Except for the young A.D.C. whom he had known less than ten days, he was alone. He had never been a lover of England and had no English friends. From his recent visits to London he knew that England had already given France up for lost, and knew too how unlikely it was that the handful of his countrymen who represented France in the British capital would follow his lead. His meetings with Mr. Churchill gave him reason to hope for some support from the British Prime Minister, but only as a fighting soldier willing to organise exiled Frenchmen into units to fight for the allies. Yet this was not his goal. It was the resurrection of France that he was contemplating, not the hands of alien liberators at the end of a long war, but beginning at the moment he would set foot on British soil. Not since Louis Napoleon had landed in England nearly a hundred years before to prepare for his descent upon Calais can a French Pretender have embarked with such grandiose and forlorn hopes.

General Spears records that de Gaulle seemed to him to be under a great strain; in the aeroplane he was mostly silent. It is not surprising. As de Gaulle writes in his memoirs: "I seemed to myself, alone as I was and deprived of everything, like a man on the shore of an ocean, proposing to swim across."[10]

CHAPTER VI

THE LONE REBEL

When de Gaulle arrived in London on the morning of June 17 he was alone and almost penniless. De Courcel had come with him but only in order that he might return to Syria. Although de Gaulle was still nominally a serving officer, he could expect no pay and had nothing but Reynaud's £100 and overnight clothes in a small suitcase. The armistice had not yet been demanded, but de Gaulle was already an outcast.

De Gaulle and de Courcel booked rooms at the Hotel Rubens in London and then, while de Courcel got in touch with the staff of the French Embassy, who were already cautious in their attitude, de Gaulle went to lunch with Spears at the Royal Automobile Club. He received welcome news. Churchill had agreed to see de Gaulle that same afternoon. After lunch General Spears took him along to No. 10 Downing Street, where they found Churchill sitting in the garden. Neither Churchill nor de Gaulle have left any account of the interview. On Churchill's part this is not surprising. He had already taken a measure of the man who, like others before him, he saw as the "Constable of France," and had made up his mind to help him rally such Frenchmen as he could to continue the fight. It is clear from Churchill's minutes to General Ismay that he was not then thinking of the political consequences.[1] But for de Gaulle the interview meant everything. "Washed up from a last shipwreck on the shores of England," he wrote later, "what could I have done without his help? He gave it me at once and put the B.B.C. at my disposal."[2] It was arranged that de Gaulle should broadcast as soon as it was announced that Pétain had asked for an armistice.

However de Gaulle made one last attempt to influence the course of events in Bordeaux. After leaving Downing Street he telegraphed to the Minister of War in France offering his services in carrying out the negotiations he had begun in London the day before about the transports for North Africa, the transfer of German prisoners to

England and the destination of war material coming from the United States. Some of de Gaulle's critics have suggested that this telegram and others he was to send in the next few days were no more than clever ruses designed to cloak his determination to make himself master of France. This is pure fantasy. De Gaulle's position was far too desperate for him to have formed any such clear purpose, and the position at Bordeaux was still fluid. When his telegram arrived Pétain had still not asked for an armistice and the Cabinet was still discussing whether to send a representative body to North Africa. The Marshal himself had already decided to stay in France but was considering sending Chautemps, Vice-President of the Council, to act in his name. President Lebrun and the presidents of the French Senate and Chamber were in favour of such a step; Weygand thought that it would prejudice the armistice negotiations and Laval saw all his plans for collaboration being ruined. Admiral Darlan seemed willing to collaborate and offered to transport all political figures of influence in the auxiliary cruiser *Massilia*. Many at once prepared to leave. It was quite conceivable that a renewed offer of British transport might have tipped the scales in favour of some sort of move to North Africa.

However it is doubtful if Pétain ever knew of de Gaulle's telegram. It was not mentioned in Cabinet and by six o'clock on that same afternoon Pétain had formally asked for an armistice. All that de Gaulle ever received in answer to his wire was a despatch which arrived two days later ordering him to return immediately to France.

It was not until the next evening that de Gaulle spoke on the radio and he spent much of the day, which happened to be the anniversary of the battle of Waterloo, preparing what he was to say. Since he had no secretary de Courcel rang up a French girl who worked for the French Blockade Mission in London, Elizabeth de Miribel, and asked her to type it. She became an ardent follower overnight. Legend has made this first broadcast more dramatic than it was. No doubt for some of the few Frenchmen who heard it, it lit a flame which burned brighter as the war went on and to de Gaulle and his followers it became a symbol of the revolution they gradually achieved; but when delivered the broadcast had a more immediate and limited aim. In his opening paragraphs de Gaulle was defiant. He called upon Frenchmen to reject the armistice and went on to say: "I, General de Gaulle, now in London, call on all French officers and men who are at present on British soil ... to get in touch with me." Next day he went further: "I realise that I now speak for France. In the name of France I make the following solemn declaration: It is the bounden duty of all Frenchmen who still bear arms to continue the struggle."[3] As a French general speaking in

London he was simply appealing to French servicemen everywhere—
and particularly in Britain—to continue the fight.

De Gaulle's enemies have fastened on his use of the first person
singular to accuse him of making a bid for leadership from the outset.
But at that moment a personal appeal was all that was open to him.
Neither de Gaulle nor anyone else then knew how many French politicians would leave France nor how many of her great Proconsuls
throughout the French Empire might reject the armistice. As de Gaulle
himself admitted, had General Noguès, Commander in Chief in
North Africa and Resident General in Morocco, acted upon his first
instinct and rejected the armistice, the whole of the French Empire
would have rallied to him at once; had Daladier, Mandel or Campinchi,
who were about to embark in the *Massilia*, succeeded in setting up a
provisional government in Casablanca or even in escaping to Britain,
they would undoubtedly have led Free France. As late as June 25
General Noguès reiterated to the French Cabinet his willingness to
continue the war in North Africa and on that day Churchill, with de
Gaulle's full knowledge, sent Duff Cooper and Lord Gort to Rabat
to establish contact with Daladier and his colleagues. But Noguès
wanted to act with Pétain and not against him, and Daladier and his
friends remained imprisoned in their ships. Had Paul Reynaud gone
to London he too could have become leader, but, as he explained to the
author a quarter of a century later, he was dissuaded by the thought
that, having accepted Churchill's plea for a union, he would have had
to serve under him, and this might have damaged him in the eyes of
Frenchmen. It was for this reason that, at the time, Reynaud felt that
de Gaulle was making a great mistake.

There can be no question therefore that, during his first few days
in London, de Gaulle did his utmost to find a superior to lead his
movement. He wrote to Weygand urging him to put himself at the
head of the Resistance, he telegraphed Noguès and the heads of all
the important French Colonies appealing to them to form a Committee
to continue the war and offering to serve under them. He appealed
to them through the B.B.C. But desperately though he needed it, de
Gaulle got no support. Only General Catroux, Governor of Indo-
China, and General Legentilhomme, commanding the troops in
Somalia, stood out against the armistice. Both were immediately relieved of their commands.

In Britain de Gaulle met with no better response. Only one member
of the staff of the French Embassy rejected the summons to return to
France. The Marquis de Castellane, an engaging and eccentric aristo-
crat who remained as Chargé d'Affaires, was loyal to Pétain. After

notifying de Gaulle of the order of the French Government to surrender himself at the Saint Michel prison in Toulouse to be tried by the War Council, he cut off all contact. The heads of the various French economic and military missions in London, René Mayer, later to be head of the European coal and steel authority, Jean Monnet, the post-war architect of the Common Market, returned to France or went to America. Monnet, in his letter to de Gaulle of June 23, echoed the feelings of many Frenchmen when he said it would be a great mistake "to set up in England an organisation which might appear in France as an authority abroad under British protection."[4] A week after de Gaulle's first broadcast only a few hundred volunteers were encamped in the famous Olympia Stadium which had been made over by the British for those who rallied to de Gaulle's banner. It was clear that no really prominent Frenchman would either lead or support him. If there was to be a French Resistance at all he must lead it alone.

On June 26 de Gaulle drew up a memorandum which he hoped might be the basis of an agreement with Churchill. On June 28 the British Government gave a preliminary answer by announcing that it had recognised General de Gaulle "as the chief of all the Free French, wherever they may be, who rally to him for the defence of the allied cause."[5] During the next six weeks an agreement was worked out, based on de Gaulle's memorandum, which became the charter of the Free French movement. Its terms were published on August 8.

Since de Gaulle's attempt to form a national committee composed of prominent Frenchmen throughout the empire had failed, he now undertook to form a French committee in Britain to unite all Frenchmen on British soil who wished to continue fighting and to serve and encourage any groups of Frenchmen anywhere, including Metropolitan France, who might wish to help the allies defeat the Germans. From de Gaulle's point of view the essence of the agreement was that the British Government recognised him as the Supreme Commander, acting under the general direction of the British High Command, and agreed that such forces should remain essentially French. Arms and equipment which had been bought by the previous French Government and were in British territory or ships should at once be given to de Gaulle and the British Government would, "as soon as practicable," provide additional equipment. Ships which the French could man and operate would be under de Gaulle's command, other French ships should be at the disposal of the British Admiralty until such time as the French could take them over. The British Government would pay the French forces broadly on the same basis as their own, but the payments would be regarded as a form of lend-lease, the ultimate balance to be settled by agreement when the war was over.

All orders to the French forces would be transmitted through General de Gaulle and no French force would be placed under British command except by mutual consent. A special clause, which was to become the subject of bitter recrimination between Frenchmen, ensured that "this force will never be required to take up arms against France." However in an exchange of secret letters with Churchill de Gaulle "took note" that, in the view of the British Government, this phrase must be interpreted as meaning "a France free to choose her course without being under direct or indirect duress from Germany."[6]

By this agreement Churchill made de Gaulle. Without it the latter would have had neither money nor base nor status. He could have become the commander of Free French units operating within the British Army like the Free Poles, Czechs, Dutch or Norwegians; he could no doubt have made his way to the New Hebrides, barren little islands off the northern coast of Australia, which had already rallied to him, and attempted to preserve an enclave of French territory free from German domination, but he would not have become the leader of the French Resistance and it is highly improbable that he would ever have become President of France.

De Gaulle owed his position to Churchill personally, but Churchill had not had matters all his own way. Neither Eden at the War Office nor Halifax at the Foreign Office liked the agreement and the heads of the fighting services were strongly opposed to it. All foresaw the difficulties that were to come. The Foreign Office pointed out that, although the agreement was military, the recognition of de Gaulle as leader of the Free French "anywhere" must have political consequences and might embarrass our relations with the United States. Eden, desperate for equipment with which to resist an invasion, was appalled at being asked to provide for yet another "allied" unit. When Chamberlain, in July, remarked that he was anxious to see de Gaulle "let loose somewhere," Eden replied that he could ask nothing better.[7] But Churchill overrode all objections. He loved France, he had been fired by de Gaulle's passion for the honour of his country, he had picked his man. In spite of the bitter quarrels Churchill was to have with de Gaulle, leading him more than once to consider disowning him, he sustained him until the end. De Gaulle had owed much to Pétain; from August, 1940, onwards he owed much more to Churchill. The second dramatic personal relationship in de Gaulle's life had begun.

Throughout June, July and August, 1940, the organisation of the rebellion which Churchill called "Free France" and de Gaulle later changed to "Fighting France," gradually took shape. Immediately after his first broadcast de Gaulle moved from the Rubens Hotel to a two-roomed flat in Seymour Place which he rented from Jean Laurent, a former member of the Bank of Indo-China whom he had appointed to his staff when in Bordeaux. Spears, who headed a small mission which Churchill assigned to de Gaulle, found him two rooms in St. Stephen's House, across the road from the House of Commons, for use as an office. The furniture consisted of a trestle table, a few hard chairs, naked electric light bulbs and, in the passage, a barrel of wine which Spears's secretary, Miss Morris, had thoughtfully bought so that those who signed on with de Gaulle could pledge their future. Life was hectic. De Courcel, who had abandoned his intention of going to Syria, was often alone in the office, while de Gaulle rushed from one government department to another trying to locate Frenchmen and equipment. In the first fortnight a fairly steady stream of volunteers came up in the lift. One, George Boris, a Jew and a left-wing journalist, asked de Courcel if he might enrol and, being at once accepted, was told to take over the office because de Gaulle had summoned de Courcel to go elsewhere. Boris, knowing nothing, was left in charge for several hours. Two of the team of Frenchmen who had been working for the B.B.C. and had heard the first broadcast, Jean Marin and Jean Oberlé, joined in the first few days and soon became members of the Free French radio team. Pierre Cot, a former Minister of Aviation under the *Front Populaire*, offered himself in any capacity, even that of floor sweeper, but was considered too unpopular and compromised a figure to be accepted.

Within a fortnight several of the names which have since become part of the Gaullist history were inscribed among the volunteers. Lapie, Palewski, Pleven, St. Denis, Maurice Schumann, Massip, Tissier, Hettier de Boislambert, all enrolled. Christian Fouchet flew in with some other pilots having escaped from a military aerodrome near Bordeaux. On June 29 de Gaulle was able to visit General Béthouart, the commander of the French Light Alpine Division which had fought at Narvik. Béthouart, de Gaulle's senior in rank, was at Trentham Park and although he wanted to continue fighting did not think London was the place to do it from. He thought he would be more useful in Morocco. Nevertheless Béthouart allowed de Gaulle to visit each of his units where he managed to persuade part of two battalions of the Foreign Legion with their leader, Lieutenant Colonel Magrin-Verneret, (who became known as Monclar) and his second in command, Captain Koenig, two hundred *chasseurs*, a few gunners, engineers and signalmen to join him. It was a meagre harvest, but it included André Dewavrin (later known as Passy) and Tissier, both of whom were to play an important part in the Free French movement.

Next day de Gaulle visited the camps at Aintree and Haydock where there were several thousand French sailors, but the British admiral in command refused to allow him to see them as he feared it might start quarrels among the men. At Harrow Park de Gaulle was luckier. With the help of four corvette commanders who had already enrolled, Captain d'Argenlieu, a Carmelite monk who had been on the naval reserve, and Captains Wietzel, Moulec and Jourden, he enlisted the officers and crew of two submarines and a patrol boat. At St. Athans, in South Wales, he found a number of airmen willing to join and they were later put under the command of Major Pigeaud who came up with a hundred or so more airmen from Gibraltar.

Of the 2,000 French wounded who had been evacuated at Dunkirk only 200 joined de Gaulle. On the other hand all the forty fishermen of the island of Sein, which lies off the coast of Brittany, took to their boats with their priest and sailed to England. A few Frenchmen living abroad managed to get to London, among them a young professor of ethnology who had been working in Canada, Jacques Soustelle. Most important, as it seemed at the time, Admiral Muselier, who like Béthouart was senior to de Gaulle, arrived in London by flying boat from Gibraltar on June 30 having persuaded the captains and crews of an armed merchantman and three smaller boats of the French merchant navy which were in the harbour of Gibraltar to follow him in due course.

Muselier, a former commander of the 11th French Cruiser Squadron, who had fallen foul of Darlan and had been put on the retired list, was a character worthy of one of Dumas's novels. Short, dark and sharp-featured, he had a fiery temper and a passion for women. Muselier had expected to find Reynaud in London and knew nothing of de Gaulle; but he had heard him broadcast and was prepared to take him on trust as "a man" because Reynaud had supported him. "I was struck immediately by the physique of the man," he wrote of his first meeting with de Gaulle. "His great height, with a small, rather ill-formed head and too low a forehead. His small grey eyes did not look squarely into one's own but always turned away when he was answering a precise question. The chin, of a very peculiar shape, did not suggest a strong will. The pronunciation was slow, as if he were listening to himself speaking; and his mouth, neither large nor small, sometimes opened in a complete circle over his irregular teeth. The nose was powerful, almost Bourbon. The ears, badly formed, stuck out widely."[8] But

Muselier was won over by de Gaulle's eloquence and determination to
continue to fight.

Next morning de Gaulle formally appointed Muselier commander
of all French naval forces which were prepared to continue the war and
provisionally commander of the air forces as well. Muselier at once
wrote an Order of the Day appealing to officers and men of all French
ships in British ports to rally to him, guaranteeing that those who did
not wish to do so would be returned to France. But before the order
could be communicated a blow fell which not only wrecked Muselier's
hopes but nearly put an end to the whole Free French movement. On
July 2 all officers and men of the French ships at Portsmouth and Plymouth were arrested by British troops and marched into prison camps
while the ships themselves were taken over by British sailors. On July
3 British warships under Admiral Somerville opened fire on the French
Fleet in the harbour of Mers-el-Kebir, close to the city of Oran.

De Gaulle's enemies have alleged that the British Government was
induced to take this action because of the misleading statements he
had made about the disposition of the French Navy under the terms
of the armistice. This is a wildly prejudiced accusation. Under Article 8
of the Armistice ships of the French Mediterranean fleet were obliged
to return to harbours in Metropolitan France to be disarmed under
German and Italian supervision. As drafted this meant that each ship
would return to the port where it had been fitted out and most of these
ports were in northern France which was under German occupation.
However, under an oral amendment obtained later by General Huntziger, it was agreed that all ships should go to ports in southern France
and remain under French control. In due course French warships left
Brest and other ports on the Atlantic coast and assembled at Toulon.

But this was all in the future and whether de Gaulle knew of this
oral amendment is beside the point. He did not recognise the armistice,
which he regarded as a betrayal of France and, like Churchill, he in no
way trusted the word of those who had concluded it. Even if de Gaulle
had brought the amendment to Churchill's notice it is absurd to pretend
that it would have had the slightest effect on the British Prime Minister.
As Churchill stated in the House of Commons on June 25, the neutralisation of the French Fleet was vital to Britain. If its units at Mers-el-
Kebir, which included the modern battle cruisers *Dunkerque* and
Strasbourg, built especially to out-gun the *Scharnhorst* and *Gneisenau*,
had fallen into German hands, the whole British position in the Middle
East would have been undermined and British capacity to continue the
war with any hope of success destroyed. Hitler's promise not to use
the French Fleet was worthless and Admiral Darlan's assurances that

he would never allow it to fall into German hands not much better. For Darlan had already changed his mind once and was soon to change it again. On June 17 he told General Georges that he was going to take the fleet to allied ports; on June 18, having become Minister of Marine under Pétain, he decided to observe the armistice and retain the fleet in France. Within a few months he was to sign secret protocols which gave the Germans the use of the French North African ports and it was only because Marshal Pétain himself refused to ratify his signature that Darlan did not carry out his bargain. It is now known that Darlan had already issued secret orders to his commanders that they were to scuttle their ships rather than allow them to fall into German hands and two years later, when the Germans occupied southern France, the orders were carried out. But even if Churchill had been aware of this it could not have altered his decision. No one in Britain, in July 1940, believed that the Germans would observe the armistice any further than it suited them or that Marshal Pétain's government would take effective action against any breach of its terms.

The truth was that if the British meant business they had to act, and Churchill not only meant business but was determined to show the world and his countrymen that under no circumstances would he surrender. The secret circular Churchill sent out before the action at Mers-el-Kebir shows that he sensed the critical state of British morale and the ovation he received in the House of Commons when he announced the news of the action and explained the reasons for it was a measure of the renewed will to fight that he had inspired among his countrymen. It was a tragedy that the first assertion of this will had to be taken against our recent French allies, but if Churchill had hesitated the determination of many of his followers might have faltered.

Nevertheless Mers-el-Kebir was a grave set-back for de Gaulle. It practically dried up the thin stream of volunteers and enabled Pétain to exploit all the latent jealousy of the British Navy among French mariners and to present de Gaulle nakedly as a British tool. Yet de Gaulle behaved with great courage. When he first heard the news he burst out in furious indignation calling the British fools and criminals. With Admiral Muselier he decided to ask to be sent to Pondicherry or some other part of the French Empire which had not submitted to the armistice, unless the action was broken off immediately. Fortunately the bombardment lasted only ten minutes and, although it was followed by air attack, all was over within two hours. Churchill spoke again in the Commons on July 4, and on July 5 Admiral Muselier visited the Admiralty. There was a stormy interview during which Muselier threatened to throw up his command and join the sailors who wanted to return to France. But the sympathy of everyone present was really with him and in the end an agreement was drawn up, later to be confirmed by de Gaulle, which assured the continuance of the Free French Navy. Surprisingly, in spite of Mers-el-Kebir, two submarines, one of which, the *Surcouf*, was later to be sunk after many brilliant exploits, several armed trawlers and corvettes and some hundreds of volunteers joined Muselier's force in the next few days. But, except for a few individual volunteers, they were the last to come forward in Britain.

When de Gaulle spoke to France over the radio on July 8 the immediate crisis had passed and he was able to give his considered views. After begging the British not to portray "this hateful tragedy" as a direct naval success he went on: "This being said, let me address a word to my compatriots, asking them to consider the whole affair fundamentally from the one point of view that matters in the end, that is to say, the point of view of ultimate victory and the deliverance of our country. By virtue of an agreement contrary to all honour, the government then established in Bordeaux agreed to place our ships at the mercy of the enemy. There cannot be the slightest doubt that, on principle and of necessity, the enemy would have used them either against Britain or against our own Empire. I therefore have no hesitation in saying that they are better destroyed."[9]

But although de Gaulle was courageous enough to support Churchill's reasons for destroying the French Fleet, few of his compatriots sympathised with him. Muselier's personal aide at once asked to be allowed to return to the prison camp where the French sailors were being held in Britain and Captain d'Argenlieu asked for four days' leave in order to consult his conscience. The vast majority of sailors decided to return to France. Many Frenchmen abroad, who were either on their way to Britain or making plans to join de Gaulle, changed their minds. In France Britain was called "the enemy" in the press for the first time. Unless de Gaulle could achieve some striking success his movement looked as if it would be strangled within a fortnight of its birth.

CHAPTER VII

A LUCKY THROW

"It all really began in Africa," remarked Gaston Palewski, one of de Gaulle's oldest and most loyal followers, when discussing the early days of the movement. What he meant was that if de Gaulle had not found some part of the French Empire to acknowledge his authority, he would have become a stateless exile, a tool to be used or discarded at the British Prime Minister's whim.

After the catastrophe of Mers-el-Kebir de Gaulle took stock of his position. In Britain about 7,000 volunteers had answered his appeal, the greater part of whom manned the few warships and merchantmen under Muselier's command. His soldiers were short of equipment, his airmen had no aircraft. He could expect no further recruits. With Muselier's support he turned once more to the empire. Was it possible to find a base on French soil? In the week before Mers-el-Kebir the Governor of the New Hebrides had declared his allegiance to de Gaulle but his islands were too insignificant and far away to be more than a refuge.

On the other hand reports had been reaching London from British and French sources since the beginning of July that French Equatorial Africa was far more favourable to Free France than the rest of the French Empire. This was not surprising. Countries like the French Congo, the Cameroons, Gabon and Ubangi were a long way from Vichy and even from North Africa and most of them were contiguous with British territories and largely dependent upon them for their trade. Educated black Africans had little to hope for from the defeated French régime which was already succumbing to Hitler's racial policies. In particular Félix Eboué, an African from the West Indies who had become Governor of Chad, and his army commander, Colonel Marchand, had made known their intention of defying the armistice. De Gaulle at once began exchanging cables and, in collaboration with the British, making plans to rally the French Equatorial territories.

Fortunately de Gaulle's desperate need fitted in with British thinking. Several members of the Cabinet had considered Churchill's recognition of de Gaulle to be impetuous and when they saw what small success he had had in attracting volunteers from among other Frenchmen their impatience grew. From the British point of view the French territories in Western and Equatorial Africa were important as they lay across the land-lines of communication with East Africa and Cairo and, if their harbours became bases for German submarines, they would add to the danger to our convoys. Churchill had tried and failed to win over Casablanca and his thoughts now turned to Dakar.

Helped by the Spears mission and a number of Churchill's personal staff de Gaulle proposed two plans. Since the populations of the equatorial territories were reported to be overwhelmingly in his favour and only a few officials stood in the way de Gaulle proposed that a mission should go to Lagos and, in collaboration with the British authorities there, try and win the territories over. This plan was quickly agreed and on August 13 Pleven, Parant, Boislambert, and Captain de Hautecloque—in future to be known as Leclerc—arrived in an aeroplane which had been put at their disposal by the British Minister of the Colonies, Lord Lloyd. They were joined by Colonel de Larminat who had made his way to the Belgian Congo from Egypt and Colonel d'Ornano from Chad.

West Africa was a different proposition. Boisson, the Governor General of the whole equatorial area, had moved to Dakar from Brazzaville and was already energetically opposing all those who had declared for de Gaulle. Several prominent officials had been arrested and the well-equipped fortress of Dakar put on the alert. The battleship *Richelieu*, damaged but still able to fire, lay in the harbour which was protected by a naval squadron, some submarines and several squadrons of aircraft. De Gaulle knew he could not take Dakar from the sea. He proposed to land at Conakry in Guinea with a small force, march inland collecting troops and rallying the population, and so gradually occupy Senegal from the rear and cut off Dakar from its food supplies. If the British blockaded the port from the sea the fortress would be bound to surrender. Such a plan demanded the help of the British Navy and towards the end of July de Gaulle consulted Churchill.

De Gaulle has described the sequel. Churchill wanted Dakar but as any operation would require a large naval force and as ships could not be spared long enough to impose a blockade, the action must be short and decisive. Striding up and down the Cabinet Room with maps spread out on the table, Churchill outlined his plan: "Dakar wakes up one morning, sad and uncertain. But behold, by the light of the rising sun, its inhabitants perceive the sea, to a great distance, covered with ships. An immense fleet! A hundred warships and transport vessels!

Cecil Beaton

7. General de Gaulle in London in 1940

8. General and Madame de Gaulle in England. *Below*: A meeting of the Free French National Committee, 1941. Seated round the table (left to right) General Valin, M. Pleven, General de Gaulle (President), M. Dejean, General de Gentilhomme, M. Diethelm

These approach slowly, addressing by radio messages of friendship to the town, to the navy, to the garrison. Some of them are flying the *Tricolore*. The others are sailing under the British, Dutch, Polish or Belgian colours. From this allied force there breaks away an inoffensive small ship bearing the white flag of parley. It enters the port and disembarks the envoys of General de Gaulle. These are brought to the Governor. Their job is to convince him that, if he lets you land, the allied fleet retires, that nothing remains but to settle, between him and you, the terms of his co-operation. On the contrary, if he wants a fight, he has every chance of being crushed."[1] De Gaulle realised that, as the British Fleet could not maintain a blockade, his own plan had little chance of success. He accepted Churchill's alternative. He agreed with Churchill that, even if the French at Dakar resisted, it was unlikely that Vichy would declare war on Britain and that there was enough hope of divisions among the French defenders to make it possible to take the town without a major battle. With Admirals John Cunningham and Muselier, de Gaulle set about making the detailed arrangements.

Meanwhile good news came from Equatorial Africa. On August 25 Governor Eboué declared the adherence of Chad to Free France. The same day General Sicé, the senior medical officer in the French Congo, secured control of Brazzaville, just across the river Congo from Leopoldville and the capital of French Equatorial Africa. Two days later Leclerc and Boislambert at the head of twenty-three men entered Duala and brought over the French Cameroons. Saint-Marc, Governor of Ubangi, followed Eboué's example, and Macon, Governor of Gabon, declared his allegiance on August 29 but withdrew it two days later under pressure from Vichy. However, Libreville, the capital of Gabon, was now isolated and within a few weeks was to fall to a combined Free French operation launched from the Cameroons. Before de Gaulle left with the Dakar expedition therefore he knew that the first part of his plan had succeeded and that a base for the Free French movement stretching from the basin of the Nile to the Atlantic had been established. Even if the attempt on Dakar failed he could go on to Equatorial Africa and attempt to consolidate his movement on French territory.

The Dakar expedition sailed on August 31. It comprised more than a hundred ships, led by Cunningham in the battleship *Barham*. On board were some 2,000 well-armed Free French troops under the personal command of de Gaulle and a much larger force of British troops under Major-General Irwin. In *Barham* the ship's company included a rather surprising emissary from the Prime Minister in the person of

Mr. Alistair Forbes, a young journalist who was then serving as a junior member of Churchill's staff. De Gaulle, accompanied by Spears, sailed in the Dutch liner *Westerland* with the French *Tricolore* flying alongside the Dutch flag.

The expedition was dogged by ill luck from the start. It was late in sailing and, owing to the slow speed of the cargo ships and a long detour in the Atlantic to avoid German submarines, lost several days on the journey. While it was at sea one of those incalculable accidents of war, about which de Gaulle had so often lectured in the past, occurred. Worried by the news of defection in Western Equatorial Africa the French Government suddenly decided to send a force of three heavy and three light cruisers to show the flag in the ports of the West African seaboard and stiffen the loyalties of the French commanders and administrators. Although the British had received warning of this from a French Intelligence officer at Tangier who had secretly defected to the Free French and by formal notification of the Vichy Government through the embassy in Madrid, an extraordinary series of mistakes, some of them due to the blitz on London, prevented the admiralty from hearing the news until the ships had passed the Straits of Gibraltar. By the time the Admiralty knew, the six cruisers had actually reached Dakar.

The British War Cabinet learned of the arrival of the cruisers in Dakar on September 16. It at once concluded that news had leaked and that the Vichy Government had sent these ships to help repulse the invasion. A message was at once sent to Admiral Cunningham cancelling the operation and recommending that the fleet should accompany de Gaulle's ships to Duala so that he could consolidate his position in Equatorial Africa.

The Dakar convoy reached Freetown, the capital of Sierra Leone which lies well to the south of Dakar, on the following day. All three commanders at once pronounced themselves against abandoning the enterprise, arguing that the presence of the cruisers, reported to be lying in harbour with awnings spread, did not alter the situation and provided an excellent bombing target. Heartened by this show of fight Churchill countermanded his previous order and left the decision to the men on the spot. Then events took a new turn.

On September 19 news was received in Freetown that the three heavy cruisers plus another from the Dakar squadron, had weighed anchor and were steaming south straight into the jaws of the vastly superior British Fleet. De Gaulle realised at once that they were heading for Libreville which was still in the hands of Vichy supporters, with the intention of recapturing Duala and Pointe Noire, the fort at the mouth of the river Congo, and restoring the authority of Vichy throughout Equatorial Africa. Admiral Cunningham decided that the French ships must be stopped and deployed his fleet to intercept them. When challenged by this totally unexpected force the French ships turned about and made off at full speed. Two, faster than the British ships, got safely back to Dakar; the *Primaguet* and the *Gloire*, both suffering from engine trouble, were escorted by British cruisers to Casablanca. Equatorial Africa had been saved and, from de Gaulle's point of view, this lucky accident had already made the Dakar expedition infinitely worthwhile. It is all the more surprising that he was so bent on pressing the attack on Dakar itself. No doubt his agents in Bathurst, so close to Dakar, were over-optimistic of the support he would get and the news which had come in while he was on the high seas that the French Polynesian Archipelago in the Pacific Ocean and the French Enclaves in India had declared their allegiance encouraged him; but Dakar had been alerted and the morale of its Vichy supporters had been strengthened by naval officers still smarting under the humiliation of Mers-el-Kebir. Certainly the French cruisers had turned round when challenged, but a desire to avoid committing suicide when caught in an ambush could scarcely be interpreted as a sign of lukewarm loyalty to Vichy. The risks were far greater than when the expedition left England; yet all three commanders decided to carry on.

Bad luck still dogged them, for when they arrived before Dakar on September 23, thick fog shrouded the whole coast. Any psychological effect which the sight of the British armada might have had on the defenders was obliterated. De Gaulle's first emissaries, who landed in an unarmed aircraft, were at once arrested. One of them had in his pocket a list of their chief supporters in the city and these were quickly rounded up. A small sea-borne party, led by d'Argenlieu, only avoided the same fate by turning and running back to their ships; but they were fired upon and d'Argenlieu and another officer severely wounded. Thereafter the shore batteries opened fire and although the British ships did not immediately retaliate, it was plain that all hope of peaceful surrender had vanished. De Gaulle made one attempt to land his troops in a little port out of range of the fort's guns, but the resistance was too great and he withdrew. In the native township of Dakar some Africans made a demonstration in favour of de Gaulle, but *Richelieu's* guns were turned inland to fire on them for a few moments and the rising quickly subsided. By the evening of September 24 de Gaulle, conferring with Cunningham and Irwin, decided that the action should be abandoned. Mr. Forbes sent the Prime Minister a signal supporting them.

However, during the night a cable from Churchill ordered Cunningham to "stop at nothing" to effect a landing, and next morning the ships again opened fire. Although a fort was destroyed, the *Richelieu* badly damaged, and a French destroyer and two ships sunk, the French kept on firing with great accuracy. A submarine torpedoed the submarine *Resolution* which had to be taken in tow; several other British ships were damaged. On the afternoon of September 25 Cunningham withdrew and the expedition returned to Freetown. It had been an abysmal failure.

The next few days were some of the worst in the whole of de Gaulle's career. "I went through what a man must feel when an earthquake shakes his house brutally and he receives on his head the rain of tiles falling from the roof," he wrote later.[2] The defeat had been absolute and de Gaulle's claim on the allegiance of fighting Frenchmen had been shown to be spurious. Vichy commanded far more loyalty than he did and Vichy was jubilant. Congratulations upon his victory were showered upon Boisson. "In London a tempest of anger, in Washington a hurricane of sarcasms" was let loose upon de Gaulle.[3] For of course de Gaulle was blamed. According to the British press it was he who had thought of the plan, he who had over-persuaded Churchill when the latter wanted to abandon the expedition after the French cruisers reached Dakar; it was due to leakages among the Free French that Vichy had been informed of the enterprise and the cruisers sent. Spears kept bringing de Gaulle reports from news correspondents suggesting that, as a result of the fiasco, he was about to resign and hand over to Admiral Muselier or General Catroux, who had just reached London from Indo-China, either of whom would conduct the Free French exercise on a more modest scale. Sitting alone and exhausted in his stifling cabin de Gaulle was overwhelmed by his sense of failure. For the second time in his life he seriously contemplated suicide.

At Freetown his spirits revived. The French contingent with him showed no signs of wavering and heartening telegrams came from de Larminat and Leclerc in Equatorial Africa. In spite of the tirade against the Free French no news of defection came from his headquarters in London. Gradually de Gaulle managed to see Dakar in perspective.

The balance was not wholly unfavourable. Of course Vichy had been strengthened. From now on de Gaulle realised that he could not hope for the voluntary defection of any French territory. Vichy officers and administrators would have to be overthrown by revolution fomented from within or by force from without. He saw too that Vichy had confirmed its usefulness in American eyes for, by successfully defending Dakar, Boisson had removed the excuse the Germans were openly seeking to occupy French North Africa on the grounds that the French could not hold it themselves. Roosevelt believed that the armistice had been inevitable and that Pétain was helping Britain by keeping Hitler from the Western Mediterranean; Dakar convinced him that de Gaulle was a dangerous nuisance who might throw away the advantages that the armistice had gained.

Although Churchill was to defend de Gaulle in the House of Commons, saying that "our opinion of him has been enhanced by everything we have seen of his conduct in circumstances of peculiar and perplexing difficulty,"[4] he was in reality defending himself. For he was under heavy criticism for having acceded to what it was believed were de Gaulle's wishes. Churchill did not tell the House that the plan for the assault on Dakar was really his own but described the operation as "primarily French."

In private he had expressed doubts about de Gaulle even before the defeat of Dakar. Now, equally privately, he began to look for a successor. General Catroux, who as Governor General had felt unable to bring Indo-China over to de Gaulle because he could see no prospect of defending it against the Japanese, had arrived in England on September 17, a week before the Dakar operation began. Before leaving, Catroux had come out openly in favour of de Gaulle. In London he found waiting for him two letters, one from de Gaulle telling him that he hoped he would be the Gaullist representative in the Middle East, and another from Churchill inviting him to visit the Prime Minister that very day.

Churchill came at once to the point, saying that he thought Catroux should stay in London and take charge of the Free French because the movement lacked leadership. Catroux declined, replying that de Gaulle had placed himself "above all hierarchies" by his appeal of June 18 and that he wished to serve under him. Later Lord Lloyd elaborated on Churchill's scheme, explaining to Catroux that, although Churchill had a great admiration for de Gaulle, it was clear that his personality repelled most Frenchmen, and that someone with greater standing and authority was plainly needed. Catroux's reply was to communicate with de Gaulle. Next day Churchill, changing his tactics, asked Catroux to go at once to the Levant to start a movement of resistance. Catroux again told de Gaulle what was happening. He went to the Middle East, but when he reached Cairo he obeyed de Gaulle's summons to join him in Equatorial Africa.

No one could blame Churchill for his misgivings and no one could have reproached him if he had persuaded Catroux to supersede de

Gaulle. Churchill was thinking entirely of Britain's lone and desperate struggle against Hitler and wanted the right Frenchman to lead the Free French. Generals, even Free French Generals, must be sacrificed if they could not do their job. But to de Gaulle in Freetown, aware that Churchill had entertained these doubts before Dakar, it now seemed that his whole position hung by a thread. Catroux had proved loyal— but what if Churchill found someone else? If Churchill revoked his agreement with de Gaulle even Equatorial Africa might fall away. But Churchill did not repudiate de Gaulle. Impressed by Catroux's firm allegiance and anxious to save something from the Dakar fiasco he instructed Cunningham to escort de Gaulle and his troops to Duala if he decided to go there. With such backing de Gaulle knew that he could capture Libreville and so deny Vichy the only port from which they could attempt a reconquest of Equatorial Africa. He at once accepted Cunningham's offer.

The convoy arrived at the mouth of the Houry on October 8. The British ships saluted and left. Five little French ships of war escorted the four cargo boats into the harbour to be greeted with acclamation by the mainly African population. For the next two months de Gaulle made a royal progress through Equatorial Africa. The people received him everywhere as the saviour of France and seemed determined to make good through enthusiasm what they lacked in resources. From Duala he went to Yaounde, a charming little town built on a cluster of conical hills in the middle of a forest, from Yaounde to Fort Lamy in the southern Sahara. It was on this journey that the engine of the Potez aircraft in which de Gaulle was travelling failed and a crash landing had to be made in a swamp. Luckily no one was hurt and de Gaulle was able to meet Félix Eboué, the gallant African governor who had been one of the first to declare for him. From Chad de Gaulle went to Brazzaville on the Congo, then to Ubangi and finally, after its capture, to Libreville, the capital and port of Gabon.

De Gaulle had given orders for the invasion of Gabon while he had been in Duala and during October his orders had been carried out. It was a combined operation, two small columns, one from the Cameroons under de Larminat, the other from the French Congo under Parant, advancing in a pincer movement overland, and a seaborne force under Leclerc, with Koenig commanding the assault troops, sailing directly upon Libreville from Duala. On Churchill's instructions Cunningham stationed himself across the sea-route from Dakar to prevent reinforcements being sent by Vichy from West Africa. There was little serious fighting except in Libreville itself where the sloop *Bougainville*, having opened fire on d'Argenlieu's ships, was set on fire. Vichy troops resisted in the streets and on the aerodrome. But within a fortnight the whole operation was over. Koenig occupied the town and Parant became Governor of Gabon. Twenty-three men had been killed. The former Governor, Macon, who had declared for de Gaulle and then reverted to Vichy, hanged himself in his cabin on the way back to Duala.

And so in six weeks and in spite of Dakar, de Gaulle had secured the future of the Free French movement. From now on it could not be said that he represented no one but himself and a handful of volunteers. He might remain dependent upon Britain and her allies for money and supplies but he controlled a large part of the French Empire which was strategically important for the conduct of the war. Above all, the Free French movement had acquired a constitution as well as a territorial base. In London de Gaulle had been unable to form any organisation which could even pretend to represent French interests. When he had spoken "in the name of France" it had been pure romanticism. During his tour of Equatorial Africa all this was changed. As his authority in each state was established he organised a Confederation of Free French Equatorial African states. He made Félix Eboue Governor General with his capital at Brazzaville and Marchand Commander in Chief. Monsieur Lapie, the former socialist deputy, was summoned from London to become Governor of Chad. Cournarie, a colonial administrator, became Governor of the Cameroons, Saint-Marc remained Governor of Ubangi, de Larminat was appointed High Commissioner and de Gaulle's representative. Pleven, who had been a member of the original French mission to Lagos, was appointed Secretary General with the task of organising trade and assuring supplies for the troops. Soon, under Pleven's guidance and with the help of neighbouring British Governors, these territories were transformed from being some of the poorest in Africa to a state of well-being they had never known.

But de Gaulle needed more than an efficient colonial administration. Frenchmen respect formality even in revolution. If he was to gain a wider acceptance for his movement he had to achieve a semblance of legality. Accordingly, on October 27, at Brazzaville, de Gaulle issued a manifesto, two ordinances and an "organic declaration" which constituted the "Charter" of the Free French movement. In the manifesto he formally denounced the Vichy Government as "unconstitutional," because it was in subjection to the invader. He undertook "the sacred duty" of directing the French war effort himself. "I shall exercise my powers," he stated, "in the name of France and solely in order to defend her and I solemnly undertake to render an account of my actions to the representatives of the French people as soon as it shall have been possible for it to designate such freely."[5] In the Ordinances he announced the formation of an Empire Defence Council composed of Catroux, Muselier, de Larminat, Eboué, Santot, Sicé, Cassin, d'Argenlieu and Leclerc to exercise "the general conduct of the war with a view to the liberation of the Fatherland . . ."[6] However he made it clear that the power of decision rested with himself "after consulting, if need be, the Defence Council."

In the Organic Declaration he sought to base "our taking of power and the creation of a French Empire Defence Council" on various laws from 1872 onwards dealing with the part to be played by General Councils in exceptional circumstances. For the first time and with all the arrogance of a revolutionary he used the phrase "We, General de Gaulle, leader of the Free French . . ."[7]

It is highly improbable that any national or international court would have entertained de Gaulle's claim to legitimacy, but this did not matter. What de Gaulle was doing was to say that the Republic was still in existence and that he and the Empire Defence Council were its trustees until such time as the French people were free to take their own decisions. He was appealing to the mass of Frenchmen over the heads of Pétain and his government because these were under the heel of the enemy. In Brazzaville de Gaulle ceased to be a general rallying soldiers to the allied cause and became a revolutionary political leader, a "Pretender" to the exercise of sovereignty not merely in Equatorial Africa but in France itself. From now on he spoke always in the name of France, not personally as on June 18, not even as the head of a government in exile, but as the head of a government of a considerable part of the French Empire claiming authority over the whole.

Although in the eyes of most Frenchmen this claim was still preposterous it was immediately strengthened by two events. In October, at Fort Lamy, Catroux had met de Gaulle and although himself a full general had formally acknowledged him as leader. "No one made any mistake about the weight of the example thus given," said de Gaulle later.[8] Among the Free French, at least, this was true. And then, on October 24, Pétain shook hands with Hitler when summoned to meet him at Montoire and committed France to a policy of collaboration. No amount of explanation could efface the shock which the news of that meeting caused Frenchmen everywhere. From then onwards those who genuinely wanted to fight the Germans turned away from Pétain and began to listen to de Gaulle.

CHAPTER VIII

FROM GAMBLER TO PROPHET

De Gaulle returned to London from Africa a prophet rather than a penitent. The humiliation of Dakar had been erased from his mind. The Commando General, who had lost a desperate gamble, was now the acknowledged leader of several million subjects, bursting with a desire to spread his gospel of resistance in any part of the world where the French flag flew. The Under-Secretary of State-in-exile, who had been so anxious to find some eminent Frenchman to be his sponsor, was now convinced that he and he alone could redeem the honour and restore the prestige of France. Compatriots like de Kerillis in New York or Robert Mengin, a junior embassy official in London, who accused him of seeking to establish his personal rule, were perfectly correct. What they failed to grasp and were incapable of sharing, was the vision that inspired his ambition. For de Gaulle was now not only sure of himself but sure of his goal. Vichy was the enemy, to be destroyed first in the empire and finally in France itself. Henceforth the war against Hitler was of secondary importance, a framework within which de Gaulle was to wage a civil war the full ferocity of which would only emerge when Hitler was defeated.

While de Gaulle had been in Africa his chances of winning this civil war had greatly improved. The Battle of Britain had been won and there were already rumours that Hitler was planning an attack upon Russia. De Gaulle knew already that the war would be long and that time was on his side. As the German yoke weighed more heavily upon France more Frenchmen would turn to him. His nightmare was that at some point in the struggle the men of Vichy would extricate themselves from their bondage and re-enter the struggle on the side of the allies.

This obsession inevitably changed de Gaulle's attitude towards his allies and particularly towards his protector. Before Dakar, de Gaulle had accepted Churchill's leadership, even over Mers-el-Kebir. After Brazzaville he began to speak as an equal and to stand up for what he considered his own rights. Because he was weak he was hypersensitive

and often impossible to deal with. But he had much to fear. From
Catroux he already knew that Churchill had wished to supersede him
as leader of the Free French. Even more dangerous, Churchill had been
in contact with Pétain.

The action at Mers-el-Kebir had put an end to all direct communication between the British Government and Vichy. Such contacts as
there were, were maintained through the Canadian Ambassador in
Madrid or through the Americans. The Americans not only welcomed
the armistice but had maintained full diplomatic relations with Vichy.
Roosevelt, still a neutral but committed to help Britain, took a more
global view of the war than Churchill. From the other side of the Atlantic the existence of Southern France governed by Frenchmen seemed
an inestimable advantage. Hitler had made a mistake and the democracies must profit by it. If, by strengthening Vichy, the Americans could
ensure that Darlan kept control of the French Fleet and that Pétain
and Weygand between them could prevent the Germans occupying the
French North African territories, then they would be doing Britain
a service. Nor did the Americans think it improbable that one day Pétain,
or at least Weygand, Governor General of North Africa since October
1940, would re-enter the war against Germany. They knew that the
small French metropolitan army permitted by the armistice, under
General Huntziger, was being trained as a nucleus for a larger force
and that arms and munitions were being hidden from the German and
Italian Armistice Commissions. Weygand, although bitter about the
British, was passionately anti-German and was doing his utmost to
make the French Army in North Africa capable of defending itself
should the Germans launch anything but an overwhelming attack.

Pressed by Roosevelt, Churchill also had second thoughts about
Vichy. Once it was clear that the vast majority of Frenchmen stood
behind the Marshal he realised that some form of understanding with
Pétain was in Britain's interest. When Professor Rougier, a historian
and friend of Professor Lionel Robbins of the London School of
Economics, came to London as an unofficial emissary from the Marshal
in October 1940, he returned to Vichy with a document annotated in
Churchill's own hand setting out the basis of an understanding between
the French and British Governments.

The agreement was not intended to be a formal treaty. It tacitly
recognised that the French Government must publicly maintain an
attitude of restrained hostility towards Britain in order to deny the
Germans any excuse for occupying the whole of France. But Rougier's
document was, as he described it, a "Gentlemen's Agreement" according to which matters of mutual interest might be regulated.

Broadly the terms stipulated that, so long as the Vichy Government prevented the Germans from occupying or using the French Colonial territories and kept control of the French Fleet, the British would not attack such colonies and would allow food and some other supplies from French North Africa to pass through the British blockade. The French Government undertook that the French Empire would re-enter the war as soon as the Allies were in a position to guarantee its protection, and to rearm the French Colonial Army. The British Government would refrain from attacking Marshal Pétain personally over the radio and Pétain undertook not to attempt to recapture the colonies that had already rallied to de Gaulle.

Obviously there were loopholes. Some of the supplies reaching French North Africa were bound to find their way into the hands of the Germans and Italians and it might be difficult to define just how much use the Germans and Italians, through their legitimate Armistice Commissions, were making of any French colony. But, since de Gaulle could not win French North Africa to his cause, it was a gain for Britain to know that Weygand would defend it and deny the use of its ports to the enemy. In the course of the war both the British Government and Vichy were to break the spirit and the letter of the agreement, but it offered sufficient mutual advantages to prevent them formally going to war.

De Gaulle had been informed of these negotiations while on the Dakar expedition. He understood the reason for them and was to some extent appeased by the clause stipulating that Vichy would not try to recapture the French Equatorial territories. But he saw at once that any firm understanding between the Anglo-Saxons and Vichy was a mortal danger to his own movement. Already he lived in constant fear of being supplanted as Free French leader by any outstanding Frenchman who might desert Pétain; to this danger was now added the possibility that Weygand or some other French leader in North Africa might, at a crucial moment, come over to the Allies with the Marshal's secret approval and play a far larger part in the ultimate liberation of France than any of which he might be capable. In that event the armistice and Vichy itself would be justified and the men he regarded as traitors end up as the saviours of their country.

From the moment that de Gaulle laid claim to French sovereignty at Brazzaville, therefore, he was forced to play a double game. He had to fight Hitler, for his capacity to do so on however small a scale was the one decisive advantage he had over Vichy; on the other hand, in order to destroy Vichy, he had to fight American policy and in particular to try to counteract Roosevelt's influence over Churchill. It was a game that made him devious and suspicious and led him into intrigue and violent quarrels with the Allies. Occasionally the hand he played would be illuminated by a flash of glory as his minuscule forces performed some military feat which showed the world that Frenchmen had not forgotten how to fight. More often he was at odds with everyone, particularly with Churchill.

Soon after de Gaulle's return from Africa a clash with Churchill was provoked by an episode which might have come straight from the pages of Jules Verne. On Churchill's orders Admiral Muselier, de Gaulle's senior military commander, was arrested as a traitor.

The trouble arose out of the nature of de Gaulle's staff. They were an odd collection. Almost all were young and, apart from a handful of regular officers, had received only elementary military training. There were journalists, lawyers, business men, artisans, all in uniform but with variegated political backgrounds. Some Free French pilots had fought for the Republic in Spain, some for Franco. Ardent supporters of the *Front Populaire* found themselves sharing a room with fascists and *cagoulards* who had manned the barricades in the uprising in Paris. Henri de Kerillis, a former Deputy, then supporting de Gaulle in New York, believed that some of the General's entourage were spies planted by Vichy and even by the Germans.

In this company Muselier was a gladiator among conspirators. He hated politics and wanted only to be left alone to get his ships back into the war as quickly as possible. Like all French sailors he regarded the navy as an independent branch of the armed forces and, as his ships and crews made by far the largest French contribution to the war effort, tended to set his authority against de Gaulle's. De Gaulle was well aware of this and before he embarked for Dakar had taken steps to limit Muselier's power. All civil affairs were placed under the control of a M. Antoine, a manufacturer of electrical goods who had come to England in August. Antoine, who like the other early conspirators took a false name and became known as Major Fontaine, remained in direct communication with de Gaulle on the high seas and took instructions from him. Dewavrin, now known as Colonel Passy, was appointed Chief-of-Staff with control over the ground forces and the Intelligence Service. Although Muselier was recognised as the Supreme Commander of all French Forces in Britain, he had to act in collaboration with these other men, both of whom could appeal directly to de Gaulle over his head.

Quarrels began as soon as de Gaulle left England. André Labarthe, the former Socialist Deputy who had been one of the first to join de Gaulle, was technical supervisor of armaments and scientific research.

Passy and Fontaine, both anti-republicans, had already tried once to remove him but were thwarted by Muselier's intervention with de Gaulle. With de Gaulle out of the country Fontaine sacked Labarthe and, in spite of Muselier's cabled protests, de Gaulle upheld Fontaine. Labarthe left the Free French movement taking with him several supporters and, backed by a large number of Frenchmen in England who had refused to join de Gaulle but were anti-German, founded the magazine *La France Libre* which was published in London and became a thorn in de Gaulle's side.

Labarthe's dismissal was the first move in a carefully planned campaign. One of the lasting handicaps which the failure at Dakar imposed upon the Free French was a profound mistrust of their security. The British Government and press were convinced that the expedition had been compromised by leakages from Carlton Gardens. In fact this suspicion was exaggerated. Security throughout Britain was almost non-existent in 1940, and although many Frenchmen talked more than they should have, so did the British. De Courcel, de Gaulle's A.D.C., was told by an English woman with whom he dined several days before sailing, that she knew where he was going and that she had been told by British officials. No attempt was made to prevent the Free French buying their tropical kit quite openly in London stores or to screen trains by which they left London for the coast. Literally hundreds of people knew that an expedition was being sent to Dakar. The miracle is that, as is now clear from German and Vichy documents, the information never reached either the German or French Governments.

However, the Free French were not blameless and Passy, in charge of intelligence, suspected some of his colleagues. He therefore suggested to Muselier that security be reorganised and proper liaison established with the British Security and Intelligence Services. Muselier approved but vigorously opposed Passy's choice of a man named Meffre as head of the new Security Organisation. Meffre, who had taken the name of Howard, had been promoted by Passy with de Gaulle's approval to the rank of Major. Muselier had made inquiries about Meffre and discovered that he had worked for the *Cinquième Bureau* as well as for foreign intelligence services in Paris, and that he had an unsavoury record which included minor peculations. In spite of Muselier's objections Passy insisted on the appointment and Meffre at once embarked on what purported to be a thorough "vetting" of all the senior members of the Free French movement. Officers and civilians alike found that their papers were being secretly searched, their blotting paper taken away and the imprints transcribed, their movements watched and reported upon. Resentment was intense and Muselier complained not only to Passy and Fontaine but also to the British. When de Gaulle returned from Dakar Muselier told him bluntly that Meffre's activities must cease and after much argument de Gaulle agreed that he should be dismissed after Christmas.

Meffre was given notice and at once planned his revenge. His work had always had the character more of a personal vendetta than of security and, perhaps because he knew that Muselier had opposed his appointment, he had concentrated particularly upon the navy and the merchant marine. Some of the men he employed were bad characters and one had already deserted from the Free French forces. Now he used a man named Colin to forge some letters which branded Muselier as a traitor. The letters were ostensibly from a General Rozoy who had been sent to London by Vichy after the armistice to wind up the French Air Commission and had since been repatriated. The letters bore the letter-heading of the French Consulate in London, which had remained loyal to Vichy, and they were supposed to have been sent to France through the Brazilian Embassy. In the letters General Rozoy said that Muselier had informed Vichy of the Dakar expedition, that he had planned to send the submarine *Surcouf* back to France, and that he had received £2,000 as a reward for dissuading French sailors from joining the Free French Navy.

Meffre made clever use of the letters. Instead of showing them to Passy, who might have been suspicious, he passed them to the British Intelligence Service. British Intelligence had had a good deal of trouble with Passy's embryonic organisation, which had begun to interfere with their own network of agents in France, and were predisposed to be suspicious of the Free French as a whole. Major Younger,* who was now in charge of the section dealing with the Free French, had only just taken over and knew nothing of the background of Free French intrigue. He was not convinced of the genuineness of the letters but, because of the serious nature of the charges, informed one of Churchill's personal assistants and said he was investigating further. Unfortunately the assistant told Churchill who, apparently without consulting anyone, gave orders that everyone mentioned in the letters must be under lock-and-key within twenty-four hours. It was a fantastic thing to do, but, with fears of invasion still alive, no one dared intervene. Younger protested but was powerless.

Meffre, meanwhile, had warned de Gaulle that serious charges were pending against Muselier. As de Gaulle had heard little else but

* Mr. Kenneth Younger, later Minister of State for Foreign Affairs in Mr. Attlee's Government and now Director of the Royal Institute of International Affairs at Chatham House.

charges and counter-charges from his staff since his return from the Dakar expedition, and as he had already dismissed Meffre, he ignored the story and went to join his wife whom he had not seen for many weeks.

Churchill's order had been given on December 31. There was some delay in executing it as Muselier and the others mentioned in the letters were celebrating the New Year and were not to be found in their usual lodgings; but on Thursday morning, January 2, Muselier, his chauffeur and batman, two other officers and two women, were all arrested by the British police.

Muselier has written amusingly and without rancour of his imprisonment. After being taken to Scotland Yard he was sent to Pentonville where he was treated as an ordinary criminal, forced to wear prison uniform and put in a bitterly cold cell. When he told the doctor, who came to examine him, that he was a French admiral the doctor justifiably replied, "If you were an admiral you wouldn't be here." From Pentonville he was moved to Brixton where he was a little more comfortable.

Meanwhile the British Admiralty, with which Muselier had been on excellent terms, had intervened and, on January 7, had persuaded Scotland Yard to allow them to take charge of the admiral until the inquiry was concluded. Muselier was therefore lodged in comfort at Greenwich with one of his own officers in attendance. By this time the truth about the letters had been established. On January 6 Muselier himself had been shown the letters and had pointed out in detail the evidence of their forgery. Members of his own staff had made a careful examination and presented a memorandum to General de Gaulle who passed it on to Eden and Vansittart.

The British Intelligence Service was also convinced and on January 10 Muselier and his colleagues were released. Next day the Admiral received a letter of profound apology from Mr. Eden and shortly afterwards was invited to lunch with the Churchills and received in audience by the King. As far as the British were concerned, Muselier was placated.

It was quite otherwise within the Free French movement. Muselier, contrary to all the evidence, was convinced that de Gaulle had tried to frame him and was determined to force a reorganisation of the system of committees which loosely administered Free French affairs. Soon after his release he put forward suggestions by which he hoped to prevent the political and intelligence committees from meddling in military affairs and so strengthen his own position. But de Gaulle was too clever for him. He accepted most of Muselier's suggestions

but managed to interpret them so as to confine Muselier's responsibilities even more narrowly to the navy. Had it not been for the
British Admiralty, Muselier would probably have resigned then and
there.

De Gaulle's position was strengthened in another and more para-
doxical way as the result of Muselier's arrest: in its embarrassment the
British Government went out of its way to please him. On January 6,
when it was known that Muselier was innocent, Churchill published a
letter he had written to de Gaulle on Christmas Eve acknowledging the
Council of Defence which he had set up in Brazzaville and stating that
His Majesty's Government would be "happy to treat with" de Gaulle
as leader of those Free Frenchmen in the overseas territories which
had recognised him. Churchill was careful not to endorse de Gaulle's
claim to legality as the true representative of France itself, but for the
first time de Gaulle had been acknowledged as a political leader. De
Gaulle was also able to establish military jurisdiction over the Free
French in Britain, making a repetition of the Muselier affair impossible.

Yet de Gaulle was not appeased. Churchill's high-handed action
had confirmed his worst suspicions about the British Government. He
believed, and no doubt believes still, that Muselier's arrest was deliberately engineered by British Intelligence to discredit the Free
French Movement. He was certain Meffre had been planted by the
British in Passy's organisation for this sole purpose.

In the absence of any documents, and after a lapse of twenty years,
it is not easy to piece together the evidence. However, the explanation
seems to be quite simple. It was not the Intelligence Service but
General Spears, then de Gaulle's most ardent advocate in London, who
had recommended Meffre to Passy. Spears did so because he had heard
a good account of him from Lord Howard, a member of the British
team working on heavy water in Paris. Although Meffre did confide
in a junior colleague in the British Intelligence Service, it is certain that
neither Major Younger nor any officer responsible for liaison with
the Free French knew anything about Meffre's activities until they
were confronted with the forgeries. They then reported all they knew.

But once de Gaulle adopted an idea it was not easy to dislodge it
from his mind. Churchill, in his view, had acted equivocally, first over
Catroux, then over Rougier, and now over Muselier. Henceforth he
would be permanently on his guard. "This lamentable incident," he
was to write later, "by setting in relief the element of precariousness
always present in our situation relative to our allies, did not fail to
influence my philosophy on the question of what should definitely
be our relations with the British State."[1] What he meant was that he

would hold Churchill to his agreement if he could, but that he would not hesitate to break it himself if it suited him or to find a new patron if the occasion demanded it or opportunity offered. He was to attempt both courses before the war was over.

However, all that lay in the future. For the moment de Gaulle and his family did their best to settle into war-time English life. From Shropshire his wife had moved to Berkhamsted with their invalid daughter Anne. Élisabeth, the elder girl, was at the College of the *Dames de Sion*, preparing to enter Oxford; Philippe, his only son, was serving in the Free French Navy. Thanks to General Spears the headquarters of the movement had migrated from St. Stephen's House to more spacious quarters in Carlton Gardens, whence it was gradually to spread into various other buildings; the Intelligence Services under Passy moving to Duke Street, the Marine and Air headquarters under Muselier, to Westminster House. Spears himself left the mission after returning from Dakar and was succeeded by Sommerville-Smith, a civil servant whose influence in Downing Street was in no way comparable. Until the appointment of Charles Peake in the autumn of 1941, de Gaulle's chief link with Churchill was Major Desmond Morton, one of the Prime Minister's special secretaries.

De Gaulle stayed several nights a week at the Connaught Hotel which, besides being central, was reputed to provide some of the best food in London. Official business crowded his day. Sitting under the portraits of Joan of Arc and Napoleon he would receive a stream of visitors and conduct the business of his unrecognised but active revolutionary movement. Except in West Africa it had no jurisdiction outside Britain; on the other hand, strong movements in favour of de Gaulle were developing in Madagascar, Eritrea, the islands of St. Pierre and Miquelon off the coast of Newfoundland, and in French Guiana. These had to be fostered. Contacts had to be maintained with the small but growing resistance movement in France itself.

In London, quite apart from the day to day dealings with the British authorities, there was the problem of the French colonies which remained outside the Gaullist movement, some of whom were loyal to Pétain. The existence of a Vichyite Consul-General in the former French Embassy to whom these "dissident" Frenchmen could report, was a constant threat to security. A trickle of recruits from overseas continued to arrive and their credentials had to be vetted. Friendly and tactful relations had to be maintained with the voluntary associations, like the committee of the "French in Great Britain Fund," presided over by Lady Crewe, or the "Friends of the Volunteers" under Lord de la Warr, who not only made gifts of all kinds but ran clubs, nursing homes and rest houses for the officers and men of the Free French forces. Above all there were the differences, intrigues and open quarrels among the haphazard collection of Frenchmen who had grouped themselves around de Gaulle, which demanded constant mediation or an assertion of authority.

De Gaulle had little time and less taste for social life. As an honorary member he would sometimes lunch at the Cavalry Club and occasionally entertain at the Connaught. Sometimes he and his wife would be invited to Chequers for the week-end, but he usually went alone because Madame de Gaulle did not like to leave their invalid daughter Anne. But he never really entered into war-time social life or appeared in the houses of the friends of the Free French movement. Whenever possible he went home in the evenings and, at week-ends, his life was as secluded as those of his suburban neighbours. He did not invite friends to his home. Senior members of the British mission attached to him never went to the house in Hampstead, to which he moved in 1941, or even knew exactly where it was.

The English who met him were impressed but often repelled by his absorption with his own affairs. He seldom spoke of the war and seemed little interested in its general progress. It did not take long for men like William Strang, who supervised Free French affairs at the Foreign Office, to realise that they were dealing with an exceptional man and to conclude that he and he alone was capable of leading the Free French movement; but it was difficult to persuade those who judged de Gaulle from a distance, particularly the Americans, to share this conviction.

Women found de Gaulle affable but irritating. The wife of one British Minister, who was often forced to sit next to him at meals, said that the only subject on which she could get him to expand was his childhood. Another lady, whose husband was for a time head of the British mission attached to him, said that whenever she met the General he invariably began the conversation by asking how many children she had. This infuriated her. Once he asked if she was doing any war work and nodded approvingly when she told him she was working as a nurse. To jolt him the lady went on: "If you really want to know, this morning I have been de-lousing the heads of the recruits to the Women's Royal Army Corps." The General made no reply. He seemed quite shocked.

Madame de Gaulle organised without dominating his life. While in England she remained severely unfashionable, wearing no make-up and setting an example of dowdiness which reflected the straitened circumstances in which most of the Free French lived. She was a retiring serving-officer's wife, arranging her life solely for her family and above all for the General. Lunching with the Churchills one day she was asked what time the General came home for dinner. "Oh, I can never tell," she replied. "Sometimes around nine o'clock, sometimes nearer midnight." "You are far too lenient," Lady Churchill rejoined. "If Winston isn't home by eight-fifteen p.m. he just doesn't get any dinner."[2]

De Gaulle's aloofness was natural to him, but it was enhanced by his position. London was his refuge but it was also, in a sense, his prison. He was a pensioner of the British Government, always supplicating one department after another, always under supervision or restraint; and from London there was little he could actively do. Muselier's ships could sail the seas, but for the army there was nothing but training and, for himself and his administrators, little but future plans. With every day that passed he became more acutely aware that, if he were to defeat Vichy and silence his detractors, he must somehow get the Free French back into the fight against the Germans.

At the beginning of 1941 this was not easy. For the British that winter and spring was perhaps the bleakest period of the whole war. The Battle of Britain had been won but the nightly air bombardment of British cities was continuing and, in place of the enthusiasm which had stimulated the whole people when they had found themselves alone, had come the grim realisation of the long struggle that lay ahead. A German invasion was still possible and in Eastern Europe one small ally after another was being overwhelmed. In the Far East the Japanese had taken advantage of the collapse of France to establish themselves in Indo-China, which they plainly intended to use as a base of operations against Singapore. Representatives of Vichy made no attempt to resist them and de Gaulle could only declare impotently that one day he would restore these dominions to France. The one bright spot had been Wavell's defeat of the Italians in Libya; but the calls made on his resources by the Greek campaign prevented him from consolidating his gains and allowed Rommel and the Afrika Korps to gain a foothold. Amongst all these troubles the claims of the Free French who, apart from the merchant marine under Muselier, could offer only the help of a few poorly armed and scattered units, were scarcely worth bothering about.

Yet de Gaulle persisted. When the British turned down his offer to send a token Free French contingent to Greece he turned his attention to the Near East and Africa, the only regions where British initiative still seemed possible. He knew that General Wavell was planning to open his campaign against the Italians in Abyssinia and Somalia and he was determined that French contingents should take part; with Rommel on the horizon, he saw an opportunity in Libya.

First, as a gesture of which he admitted he had little hope, de Gaulle wrote to Weygand urging him to unite with the Free French and bring the North African Army back into the war. Weygand did not reply. De Gaulle then looked towards the Sahara. In December a small detachment of French troops from Chad under Colonel Colonna d'Ornano, co-operating with a British and New Zealand unit from the Nile Valley, had made a spectacular raid across several hundred miles of swamp and desert against the Italian outpost of Murzug and, although unable to take the fort, had destroyed several aircraft on the ground. D'Ornano, a towering and glamorous figure in his Touareg cloak and black eyeglass had been killed and buried just outside the fort. Now de Gaulle ordered Leclerc to carry out the operation he had outlined on his first visit to Chad and to capture the oasis and airfield of Kufra, which lay 600 miles to the north of Fort Lamy. It turned out to be one of those minor epics with which the war in the Western Desert is studded, and which drew special praise from Churchill in the House of Commons. After a month's siege Kufra fell, 300 Italian prisoners were taken and the lines of communication between Libya and Ethiopia, for which Kufra was a refuelling station, were cut. Leclerc stayed in Kufra, planning an offensive on the southern part of Libya called the Fezzan which he hoped would coincide with Wavell's next thrust in the Western Desert.

While Leclerc was attacking Kufra, de Gaulle ordered Catroux in Cairo and de Larminat, his High Commissioner in Equatorial Africa, to organise a brigade to take part in the campaign in Ethiopia and Eritrea. The 3rd Battalion of the Chad Regiment and the 14th Battalion of the Foreign Legion, which were in Egypt, were combined into the *Brigade d'Orient* under Colonel Monclar and, with an air group under Major Astier de Villatte, fought with distinction alongside the British and Indian troops in the capture of the Keren Heights and were the first to enter the port and capital of Eritrea, Massawa.

All attempts, however, to seduce French Somaliland with its valuable port of Djibuti, which was also the terminus of the railway from Addis Ababa, failed. De Gaulle had originally hoped that General Legentilhomme, the former Commander of the French troops in Djibuti, would be able to win over the French garrison in a bloodless coup; but both Catroux and Wavell doubted this and an attempt was made to rally Djibuti by a mixture of propaganda and blockade. De Gaulle fulminated because the blockade was incomplete but Wavell, with a war on three fronts on his hands already, was unwilling to antagonise further the Vichy French, and tried to negotiate with M. Nouailhotas, the Governor. The Governor seemed willing to allow the British to use the port and railway but not the Free French. As this was contrary to Churchill's policy the desultory blockade dragged on, satisfying no one and convincing de Gaulle that the real aim of the British was to exclude France from East Africa altogether. Gaston Palewski, who was left in charge of Free French interests in Somalia, was to spend two frustrating years in Cairo, which ended only when the Americans landed in North Africa and Nouailhotas, obeying Darlan's orders, brought his little colony over to the allied camp.

Nevertheless, by the spring of 1941 the prophet of Free France was not without honour in the allied camp. His voice was heard, if not always with pleasure. Now, suddenly, it was to be raised in a tempest of recrimination not against Vichy or the Germans, but against the British. De Gaulle's private war was entering a new phase.

CHAPTER IX

AT WAR WITH WHOM?

It was over Syria that de Gaulle's smouldering suspicions burst into flame and brought about his first major clash with the British. At the time of the armistice General Mittelhauser, the French High Commissioner for Syria and the Lebanon, had opted for de Gaulle. Although he had changed his mind within a few days he had been dismissed and, from September, 1940 onwards, Vichy had been represented in Beirut by General Dentz, a firm supporter of the Marshal, who commanded some 30,000 French troops and a much larger number of local Levies.

Both de Gaulle and Catroux realised the immense importance of Syria to the Free French movement, but they could see no immediate way of gaining control. Then events played into their hands. As the Germans advanced through Eastern Europe Hitler's interest in the Levant grew. The occupation of Syria would not only outflank the British in the Canal Zone but isolate Turkey and open the back door into Russia. In February a German mission headed by two Intelligence experts, von Hintig and von Rosen, arrived in Syria and began at once to make overtures to Arab leaders and to encourage those who were anti-French. General Dentz was instructed by Vichy to be friendly to them. Then on April 1, after weeks of tension, a revolt broke out in Baghdad. Rashid Ali seized power and besieged the British forces on Habbaniya airfield. At the beginning of May Hitler began to put pressure on Vichy and on May 11 summoned Darlan to Berchtesgaden to sign an agreement by which not only Syrian but French North African ports and airfields were to be opened to German forces. Although both Pétain and Weygand later refused to ratify this agreement and were able to prevent its application to North Africa, they acquiesced in Syria. Throughout May German aircraft made use of Syrian aerodromes and the arms and munitions which had been collected by the Italian Armistice Commission were sent across the desert to Rashid Ali. General Dentz had orders to treat the Germans as allies and to resist the British if they tried to intervene.

From the moment that the German mission arrived in Beirut de Gaulle saw what was coming. He asked and was granted leave to go to Cairo and arrived there via Khartoum on April 1. The information he received from his agents in the Levant encouraged him to think that, if the Free French alone were to appear on the Syrian border, they might be welcomed as allies even by General Dentz, and he instructed Catroux and Legentilhomme to prepare to move. But General Wavell, the British Commander in Chief, anxious at all costs to avoid opening another front, was sceptical of de Gaulle's chances and clung to the hope that Dentz would resist the Germans. He continued to allow food supplies to enter Beirut. De Gaulle, furious that his plan had been turned down, left Cairo for Brazzaville. However, when it became clear that General Dentz was collaborating with the Germans, the British changed their minds. Churchill asked de Gaulle to go back to Cairo and to work out a plan for the conquest of Syria with General Wavell. De Gaulle was so pleased that for once he replied to Churchill's message in English.

It was a strange campaign. The Free French, with 6,000 men, eight guns and ten light tanks could not possibly undertake it alone; on the other hand Wavell, pressed by Rommel in the Western Desert, clinging on desperately to Crete, still fighting in Abyssinia and suppressing Rashid Ali's revolt, had the utmost difficulty in finding troops. Instead of the four divisions and large air force de Gaulle demanded, Wavell could muster barely two divisions and some sixty aircraft, many of which were manned by pilots straight from flying school. The allies were numerically weaker than the forces they were attacking.

The advance began on June 8. An Australian division moved up the coast road, the British through the centre and the Free French on the right flank heading for Damascus. Hoping to avoid fighting, bands played the "Marseillaise" in front of the troops and a white flag of truce was carried alongside the *Tricolore*. Aircraft flying ahead dropped leaflets promising independence to Syria and appealing to the people to join Free France. But these hopes were soon dispelled. As soon as General Dentz realised how weak the attack was, he ordered a strenuous resistance. The whole advance was held up. A British battalion was overrun by French tanks at Kuneitra. General Legentilhomme was wounded by fire from a French aircraft and the Free French were stopped ten miles short of Damascus. The Australians made no headway.

The fighting had often been bizarre. In some engagements the Vichy French had fired on the flag of truce, maltreated prisoners and met appeals to join the Free French with violent abuse; on the other hand one Free French unit captured a hill by advancing with their rifles slung over their shoulders; the Frenchmen opposed to them refusing to fire. During one battle, two men, their hands raised to hurl grenades at each other, suddenly saw that they were brothers. When a detachment of Free French Circassians met some of their own people on the other side they fell on each other's necks with shouts of joy. More serious, a Free French battalion of the Foreign Legion refused to fire on other Frenchmen and had to be withdrawn.

However, with the collapse of Rashid Ali's rebellion in Iraq, Wavell was able to send reinforcements to Syria. Two columns of British troops moved across the desert from the east and south and this proved decisive. On July 8 General Dentz was allowed by Vichy to ask for the armistice he had been urging for many days. The Cease Fire came on July 11.

But with the end of the fighting de Gaulle's real battle began. Somehow he had to persuade the British to disgorge their prey. For the British were in overall command in the area and although both Churchill and Eden were undoubtedly sincere in their repeated declarations that the British Government had no desire to take advantage of the weakness of France or to annexe any part of her empire, there was a very real danger that the men on the spot might wish to retain British control while the war lasted and leave the question of France's participation to be decided at the Peace Treaty.

In Cairo General Wavell, who had been on good terms with de Gaulle, had just been replaced by General Auchinleck, whose main concern was to settle the Syrian problem as quickly as possible and regroup his forces to deal with Rommel. General Sir Henry Wilson, the British Commander in the Syrian campaign, was positively hostile to the Free French. General Catroux's punctiliousness irritated him and the two men were hardly on speaking terms. More serious, in the course of the fighting Wilson had come to regard Free French troops as a liability. He now felt that their continued presence in the Levant would perpetuate the bitterness between Frenchmen and provoke disturbances among the Arabs. Wilson had powerful support. In Palestine, Jordan and Iraq there were Englishmen in important positions whose memories went back to the "treasonable" and secret Sykes-Picot agreement of the First World War and who devoutly wished to see the French excluded altogether from the Levant. Among the Arabs the Emir Abdullah of Jordan, the master of Glubb Pasha, whose Jordanian Frontier Force had played some part in the campaign, was himself hoping to become King of Syria and avenge his brother Feisal's treatment by the French in 1919.

Everything hinged upon the terms of the armistice which, in their turn, hinged upon the question of independence for the Syrian and Lebanese people. In 1936 the French had concluded treaties with the Syrians and Lebanese bringing the League of Nations mandate to an end and granting them independence in close alliance with France much in the same way as Britain had granted independence to Iraq. But the French Parliament had not ratified these treaties. This in itself was a difficulty for de Gaulle. He knew that if he wished to win the allegiance of the Syrians and Lebanese he must make some declaration in the spirit of the 1936 treaties, but at the same time he realised that Vichy would make political capital out of any offer of independence and accuse him of surrendering a part of the French Empire.

Nevertheless de Gaulle had decided to make the offer before the campaign began and had informed the British. Churchill and Eden were delighted and secretly surprised because they had come to believe that no Frenchman would ever surrender control of the Levant. They at once asked that the declaration should be a joint one. Historians have questioned their right to do this, but it was a natural enough reaction. Churchill and Eden knew that British troops would have to conquer Syria and they felt that a French guarantee backed by the British would carry more weight with the local population. They also suspected, as emerges from Churchill's letters to de Gaulle before the campaign began, that once de Gaulle was in control of Syria he might have second thoughts and defer independence to the Greek Kalends. It was in British interests that Anglo-French policy towards the Arab people should run in parallel.

De Gaulle was at once suspicious. He saw the British guarantee as an effort to convey to the Arabs and to the world that independence would come as a British rather than a French gift and he feared that it might be used as a pretext for future interference in Syrian and Lebanese affairs. He therefore refused and, on the day the campaign began, instructed Catroux to declare in the name of France, by radio and leaflet, that the Free French were coming to offer independence to Syria and the Lebanon and to negotiate treaties of alliance with France. The British countered by publishing their own independent guarantee of this declaration the following day.

A clash was inevitable. The British were determined that independence should be granted to the Syrians and Lebanese and had kept their hands free to implement this guarantee themselves should the French fail in their undertaking. De Gaulle, on the other hand, was determined to assert Free French sovereignty. Apart from the honour of France, he saw clearly that if, after pitting Frenchmen against French-

men in a fractricidal struggle, he failed to win control of the Levant,
not only might his whole movement disintegrate but his own position
as leader be in danger.

To try and forestall the clash de Gaulle let Churchill know, during
the first week of the campaign, the sort of terms he thought suitable
for an armistice. It must include a British guarantee that French interests in the Levant would be maintained and that the Free French
would represent those interests. On June 19, at a meeting in Cairo with
the British Ambassador to Egypt, Sir Miles Lampson, General Wavell
and General Catroux, he drew up a written text embodying these ideas.
But the text was rejected in London. The British feared that such open
support for de Gaulle would drive Vichy further into the arms of the
Germans. A different text was drawn up and forwarded to Beirut.

De Gaulle got wind of the new text and said at once that it was
unacceptable. He again warned Churchill and Eden of the effect on
their relations any such settlement would have. Damascus fell on June
21 and on June 23 de Gaulle flew there to be received by General
Legentilhomme, Military Governor, to meet the Arab notables and,
in defiance of Churchill's express wishes, to instal General Catroux
as "Delegate-General and Plenipotentiary in the Levant." Catroux's
instructions were to negotiate treaties of independence and alliance
"with Governments approved by assemblies really representative of
the people as a whole and called together as soon as possible."[1] De
Gaulle then removed himself. Expecting an armistice to be demanded
at any moment and not wishing to be involved in negotiations of
which he disapproved, he decided "to gain space and height, to reach
some cloud and from there swoop down upon a convention which
would not bind me and which I would tear up as soon as I could."
The cloud was Brazzaville.

The armistice was signed at Acre, the little fortress on the coast
just north of Jaffa which Richard Coeur de Lion had once captured and
Sidney Smith had held against Napoleon. In spite of Vichy's objections,
de Gaulle had ensured that Catroux should at least be present; but the
agreement was signed only by General de Verdilhac, who had commanded the Vichy forces, and General Wilson. Its terms confirmed de
Gaulle's worst fears. Vichy surrendered to the British. General Dentz
and his 30,000 French troops were to leave Syria for France with all
the honours of war and hand over supplies and war materials to General
Wilson. The British were to assume command of the Syrian and Lebanese Levies. It was stipulated that any Frenchman, soldier or civilian,
who wished to rally "to the allied cause" could do so, but a secret
agreement between Verdilhac and Wilson had stipulated that no Free

French should be allowed to make contact with General Dentz's troops in order to persuade them to join de Gaulle. "Allied" prisoners were to be set free and those sent to France brought back. The British retained the right to imprison Vichy French of the same rank and numbers if this clause was not fulfilled. Not once in the whole twenty-two clauses were the Free French mentioned.

De Gaulle first heard an outline of the armistice over the radio. He at once repudiated it without knowing the details. Then he flew by stages to Cairo, heralding his arrival by measured protests to each British representative who met him on the way. On July 21 he met Oliver Lyttleton, the new British Minister in the Middle East and a member of the War Cabinet, who had arrived only ten days before. This was the crunch. Unless de Gaulle could persuade Lyttleton to amend the terms of the armistice all the fruits of his Syrian campaign would be thrown away. The drama was heightened by Lyttleton's character. In many ways he was a match for de Gaulle. He was not quite as tall but of an equally powerful build. He had a disarming smile, but there was a good deal of the bulldog in his face and in the way his head was set upon his shoulders. Like his forbears, Lyttleton was an athlete and a scholar, a scratch golfer who could quote Greek and speak French almost perfectly. Big business had taught him to negotiate.

Both men have left revealing accounts of their conversations. "Casing himself in ice" to avoid explosions, de Gaulle told Lyttleton that authority in Syria and the Lebanon must be given to Free France.[2] He insisted that the Syrian and the Lebanese Levies must come under Free French command and that his representatives be given the opportunity immediately to recruit as many of Dentz's men as possible.

Lyttleton replied that Britain had no interest in usurping the French position in the Levant but that it was essential that Syrians and Lebanese should settle down peacefully. Independence, which Britain had guaranteed and de Gaulle promised, must be granted and so long as the war lasted British commanders must have overriding control over both countries. De Gaulle stood his ground. He recognised British command over the Free French forces only "in strategic matters and against the common enemy"; internal order was his responsibility. He then delivered an ultimatum. As from July 24, in three days' time, he was withdrawing the Free French forces from the British Command. Catroux was to assume complete authority and his forces would take control of both countries whatever opposition from any quarter they might encounter. He would make every effort to bring over General Dentz to the Free French cause.[3]

From de Gaulle's account one would derive the impression that

these exchanges took place in an atmosphere of restrained formality;
Lyttleton, however, records that de Gaulle, after handing him a type-
written copy of the ultimatum, which he refused to accept and there
and then tore up, broke into a violent tirade. They had a "scene" which
lasted until 12.30 p.m. Lyttleton then remarked that it was time for
luncheon and that afterwards he would take his usual siesta. He suggested meeting again at five o'clock when both the day and they themselves would be cooler.

When de Gaulle returned Lyttleton thought him in a different mood,
perhaps because his staff had pointed out to him the dangers of breaking
with the British. This could have been true, for in London Muselier,
Cassin and d'Argenlieu, all three members of the Empire Defence
Council, had cabled protests to de Gaulle about his threats to break
with the British. However, de Gaulle thought it was Lyttleton who
had become conciliatory and the result bears him out.

For Lyttleton not only admired de Gaulle, but realised that the
way the armistice had been drawn up was a mistake. He was furious
at not having been informed of the secret clause. By July 24 he had
agreed with de Gaulle an "interpretation" of the armistice under which
most of the clauses to which de Gaulle objected were reversed. War
materials were to be handed over to the Free French; the Free French
were to take command of the Syrian and Lebanese Levies and, although
Lyttleton did not feel able to cancel the secret clause outright, he held
himself free to denounce it and any other clauses if the armistice was not
rigorously observed.

Breaches were soon reported. A bridge was blown up by Dentz's
men and, even more serious, British prisoners of war had been shipped
to France where they would unquestionably be handed over to the
Germans. These things occurred without, apparently, any steps being
taken by the British Armistice Commission to prevent them. Lyttleton
flew to Beirut and found, to his amazement, that the British seemed
more in sympathy with Vichy than with the Free French who had
fought alongside them. Incensed at this attitude he had what he described as a "memorable" interview with General Wilson and General
Chrystall who was head of the Armistice Commission, at the end of
which he ordered General Dentz's arrest for breaches of the armistice.
The change was immediate. The British prisoners were at once sent
back, de Larminat and his staff were able to visit those of General
Dentz's troops who had not already embarked and persuaded 127
officers and 6,000 N.C.O.s and men—one fifth of the French troops
in the Levant—to join de Gaulle. Catroux assumed full responsibility
for the administration of the territories.

So de Gaulle had won. It was a great personal triumph and it might easily have gone the other way. For neither Catroux, who had not objected to the armistice, nor de Gaulle's colleagues in London or the empire would have stood out against the armistice terms. In that case the British would almost certainly have taken over the whole of the Levant, granted independence to Syria and the Lebanon, and left France to make what arrangements she could when the war was over. Now, however, de Gaulle could rightly claim that it was Vichy who had surrendered French sovereignty and he who had saved it. He had a base in the Mediterranean and enough troops and arms to garrison Syria and the Lebanon and field two well-equipped divisions for service elsewhere. When he returned to Cairo he told General Auchinleck that he would put them under his command as soon as they were ready, provided they were to fight. Auchinleck replied that Rommel would see to it that they did.

But above all de Gaulle had stood up publicly to Britain and come out on top. As Lyttleton remarked, this unknown man, a pensioner of the British, had raised himself within a few months to an international position almost within sight of the statesmen at the summit, Roosevelt, Stalin and Churchill. De Gaulle still had a long way to go before he and his revolutionary movement were recognised even as the provisional representatives of France and his intransigence was to jeopardise his position unnecessarily more than once in the coming years. But after the summer of 1941 the Free French movement could no longer be ignored and it became increasingly difficult to replace de Gaulle as its leader. Syria and the Lebanon remained a bone of political contention, the British pressing for elections and the granting of full independence, the Free French, as anticipated, using the war as an excuse for procrastination. In the end the Arabs revolted and in 1945 de Gaulle was forced to withdraw altogether. But by then he was undisputed master of France and could shed the Levant as he was later to shed Algeria. His bold stand in Cairo had served its purpose.

CHAPTER X

FLIRTING WITH THE BEAR

When de Gaulle returned to London on September 1, 1941, the world was very different from the one he had surveyed with Churchill that week-end in March before leaving for Africa. The whole of Western and Central Europe except the British Isles and the Iberian Peninsula was now under Nazi control and, on June 22, the day after the fall of Damascus, the Germans had delivered the attack on the Soviet Union which everybody except the Russians had been expecting. The German Armies were deep in the Ukraine, at the gates of Leningrad and driving towards Moscow. While Stalin demanded an immediate invasion of France, Britain watched the titanic struggle with increasing anxiety. Churchill had been to Moscow and believed that Stalin would be as good as his word and hold both his capital, which he was on the point of evacuating, and the line of the Caucasus; but Churchill's military advisers took a more gloomy view. In the Mediterranean there was a pause while the Germans tried to break the British blockade and get enough supplies across to Rommel to enable him to capture Tobruk and Auchinleck, to Churchill's dismay, waited for reinforcements before launching an attack. In the Far East Japan had completed the occupation of Indo-China and was preparing an onslaught on the British and Dutch Empires. Roosevelt had imposed an embargo on trade with Japan and had warned her government that, if she continued her aggression in the Pacific, it would bring her into conflict with the United States. There was hardly a corner of the globe which was not now involved in some way in the struggle.

Of all these events the most important was the entry of Russia into the war. In Cairo de Gaulle had formed a poor view of the British Army which, he said, rather patronisingly, was only just beginning to learn how to use armour; he had concluded that the British alone could never beat the Germans. Now this no longer mattered. The centre of gravity of the war had shifted to the Eastern Front and, in de Gaulle's view, would remain there. In spite of the speed of the German advance into the Ukraine his instinct told him that the Russians would survive and he was for the first time convinced that in the end the allies would win the war. For Free France, therefore, it was no longer a question of living on hope; the future must be planned within the framework of victory. Above all, with Russia as an ally, de Gaulle saw the opportunity of reducing his dependence upon Britain.

In his own memoirs the General makes careful selection of his exchanges with Stalin, but the Russian documents on Soviet-French relations published in 1959, show that, from the moment of the German attack, de Gaulle was in constant communication with Moscow; that he cultivated a far closer understanding with the Soviet leaders than his western allies suspected and that he used this understanding not only to strengthen his position in Metropolitan France but to counterbalance Anglo-Saxon threats to supersede him.

Two days after the German attack upon Russia de Gaulle, from Damascus, instructed his colleagues in London to see Maisky, the Soviet Ambassador, and convey to him that the French people "were with the Russians against Germany" and that the Free French wanted to organise "military relations" with Moscow. He followed this up by asking, through Maisky, whether the Russians would enter into direct relations with the Free French. In August, while still in Beirut, he sent Jouve to see Vinogradov, the Russian Ambassador in Ankara, with a proposal that the Free French should send two or three representatives to Moscow so that they could have direct relations instead of communicating through the British. He did not at this stage ask for diplomatic recognition, but intimated that he was considering transferring Free French headquarters from Brazzaville to Beirut in order to be closer to the Russians. To these advances the Russians gave courteous but cautious replies. They had just concluded their alliance with Britain, they were uncertain of de Gaulle, whose movement seemed to be a one-man show, and they wanted to feel their way.

This rebuff made an impression on de Gaulle and prompted him to carry out a reform which had been pressed upon him for some time. Ever since the formation of the Empire Defence Council in October, 1940 de Gaulle had been issuing ordinances, decrees, "organic texts," military orders, resolutions, circulars, memoranda and a mass of administrative documents dealing with subjects as diverse as rationing, promotion, travel documents and treaties with foreign powers, all of which were published in the official journal of the Free French, first issued in London on January 20, 1941.[1] The ordinances and decrees began with the words "We, General de Gaulle, leader of the Free French . . ." and were signed by de Gaulle alone. Many, even those dealing with parts of the empire, had been issued on his sole authority without either the Council of Defence or even the committees in London being consulted.

De Gaulle could justifiably argue that the very nature of the Free French movement, scattered as it was across the globe, had made some such loose form of personal rule the only one possible. The Empire Defence Council had been an acknowledgment of the federal nature of Free France, and it was not de Gaulle's fault that it could seldom be convened. The truth was, however, that the Council had become simply a façade. Three or four members were sometimes in London together and held informal discussions, but its records show that it was only formally consulted twice in its existence, both times by letter and both times in order that de Gaulle might get backing for an extreme course of action. The Council exercised no effective power whatever.

This total disregard by de Gaulle of his colleagues was causing increasing resentment. Most Americans said bluntly that he was no democrat but out to make himself master of France. In Britain this view was shared by the Liberal-Socialist faction who rallied to "dissident" Frenchmen like André Labarthe. Among his own supporters not only Muselier but Cassin, his legal adviser, Dejean, who was in charge of foreign relations, and Leclerc were openly critical. Now that the Russians had also shown apprehension de Gaulle realised that, if his movement was ever to gain even limited diplomatic recognition, he must give it an organisation capable, in appearance at least, of becoming a provisional government rather than a dictatorship.

Back in London, therefore, de Gaulle decided to accept the plan for a national committee which was being pressed upon him by his colleagues and about which he had originally spoken to Churchill. The negotiations were critical. In the past year de Gaulle's belief in himself as the sole champion of France's honour had reached almost religious proportions. He was less than ever prepared to share the role of leader. He also saw more clearly than his colleagues that the Free French movement could never acquire a truly democratic basis so long as the war lasted. Now that Free France had attained the status of a minor power he clearly had to form an administration whose character and responsibilities would command the respect of his allies. Yet in his absence opposition to his leadership had grown. Muselier wished more than ever to make de Gaulle a mere titular head and to take the military command himself; Cassin and Dejean were urging something like joint cabinet responsibility. The arguments were long and heated and in the end Muselier was only persuaded to accept de Gaulle's draft at the insistence of his British friends.

But the national committee which came into existence in September,

1941, was an advance on anything that had gone before. With one exception, Diethelm who had just arrived from France and was given the Commissary of Labour and Information, it was formed by the men who had stood by de Gaulle and Free France since its foundation. Each had the title of Commissioner and each enjoyed clearly defined responsibilities; Pleven (Finance and Colonies), Cassin (Justice and Education), Dejean (Foreign Affairs), Legentilhomme (War), Valin (Air), Muselier (Navy and Merchant Marine), Catroux (High Commissioner in Syria) and D'Argenlieu (High Commissioner in the Pacific).* The Committee met weekly and although de Gaulle still retained the power, for no votes were taken and the Committee's decisions were circulated in writing only after de Gaulle had approved them, at least he had to listen to the reports which were presented and to let his views be known. However cavalierly de Gaulle might sometimes treat it, the Commission was to grow in stature as the war went on.

The announcement of the National Committee had an instant effect. The Russians at once recognised de Gaulle as leader of the Free French and said they were ready to enter into relations with the Empire Defence Council, which remained in being, and to promote collaboration in the overseas territories which had rallied to de Gaulle. Moscow accredited Bogomolov, who had come straight from Vichy, Ambassador to the refugee governments in Britain and to the Free French National Committee. The British Government welcomed the National Committee as the fulfilment of de Gaulle's early intention and British recognition was followed by that of the refugee governments in London. Only the United States held aloof, contenting itself with expressing "appreciation" of the fact that it had been informed of the Committee's existence. Even this was an advance on its previous attitude of ignoring the Free French altogether.

But American aloofness could not last much longer. Ever since the introduction of Lend-Lease in March, the United States had been drawing closer to war. She had already become the "Arsenal of Democracy," which meant effectively Britain, and had taken the most unneutral step of agreeing to convoy supplies half-way across the Atlantic. In May Roosevelt had declared a state of "unlimited national emergency" and, throughout the summer, secret staff talks between the British and American military chiefs proceeded. As Japan began to take advantage of Russia's struggle for survival and to spread the war in the Pacific, Roosevelt and his advisers realised that America must soon be directly threatened.

* Of the earlier committee Antoine had taken a subordinate position and Palewski was watching over Djibuti.

De Gaulle was uneasily conscious of how the entry of the United States into the war might affect his own position and with more finesse than usual had been trying throughout the summer to reach some sort of understanding with the Americans. Across the Atlantic the Free French movement was still weak. Eugène Houdry, a French industrial chemist and a man of great energy, had come out in de Gaulle's favour but had made little headway. He had a committee and enough money to continue the publication of a magazine, *France For Ever*, which supported de Gaulle. But the majority of Frenchmen in the United States were pro-Vichy or took the view of Jean Monnet and André Maurois that the best way to help France was simply to help the Allies. Jacques Sièyes, the former socialist deputy and a contemporary of de Gaulle's at St. Cyr, was his first official spokesman, but the bitterness between the different French groups was far greater than in Britain and as the State Department came down firmly on the side of Vichy and American law forbade United States citizens to encourage foreign political movements in opposition to their government, progress was difficult. A few liberal papers and magazines took up the Gaullist cause but the press as a whole had followed the government's lead.

However, in June de Gaulle himself began to intervene. On the eve of the Syrian campaign, when as a result of Darlan's meeting with Hitler de Gaulle feared that Vichy might attempt to reconquer the Free French colonies in Equatorial Africa, he handed the American Minister in Cairo a note pointing out that Africa could one day become a base from which the Americans could liberate Europe and offering facilities for the United States Air Force in the Cameroons, Chad and the French Congo. At the same time he sent René Pleven to New York to press his offer and try to establish relations with the State Department. Pleven had some success. The Americans sent a military inspection team to the Free French Colonies—which they later withdrew after protests from Vichy—and began discussions on extending Lend-Lease to Free France; but it was not until October that Pleven was coldly but officially received by Sumner Welles at the State Department and not until November 11 that a Lend-Lease agreement was reached.

However, these were important steps and events now began to tip the scales in de Gaulle's favour. On November 18 Pétain, on German insistence, dismissed Weygand from his post as Governor-General of North Africa. Since the Americans had based their support of Vichy largely on Weygand's known hatred of the Germans and his secret assurances that, if the Allies landed in sufficient force in North Africa, he would join them, this was a severe blow to their hopes. Admiral Leahy, the United States Ambassador in Vichy, advised a complete change of policy and asked to come home. Pétain retaliated by saying that, if the Americans abandoned him, he would have to rely entirely on the Germans, and Roosevelt, succumbing to blackmail, told Leahy to stay. Then on December 7 the Japanese attacked Pearl Harbour and the United States was in the war.

"One might have thought," wrote de Gaulle in his memoirs, "that from that moment American policy would treat the Free French, who were fighting its own enemies, as allies."[2] One might also have thought that de Gaulle, realising his opportunity, would have gone out of his way not to hurt American susceptibilities and to have made it possible for Roosevelt to reverse his policy towards him with as little loss of face as possible. Instead he did exactly the opposite.

For some time de Gaulle had wanted to rally the small group of islands off the coast of Newfoundland known as St. Pierre et Miquelon. The population was known to be overwhelmingly pro-de Gaulle but the Governor had held the islands for Vichy and the Americans hoped they would be included in an agreement they were negotiating with the French Admiral Robert in Martinique for the neutralisation of all French possessions in the American hemisphere. It is true that there was a radio station on St. Pierre, but there was no evidence that it had been used either for Vichy propaganda or to give help to German submarines. On the other hand the Canadians were nervous that it might be so used and were discussing with the Americans the possibility of taking it over themselves as a precaution once the agreement with Robert was signed.

De Gaulle, hypersensitive about French sovereignty and anxious to add even the smallest island to his empire, decided to act. The occasion presented itself in a visit Muselier was paying to the submarine *Surcouf* then operating from Halifax. De Gaulle ordered him to take the islands. Muselier did not like the order and on his own initiative consulted the Canadians and the Americans. The answer in both cases was a firm "No." Now that the secret was out the British Government asked de Gaulle to postpone the operation. This he agreed to do. De Gaulle says that he then heard that the Canadians were definitely going to take over the radio station on St. Pierre and that he changed his mind. If so he was misinformed. The Canadian Government had in fact abandoned its plan. Nevertheless, on December 18, de Gaulle sent Muselier a message in the French naval code ordering him peremptorily "to proceed to rally St. Pierre et Miquelon with your own means and without saying anything to the foreigners." He added, "I take entire responsibility for this operation which has become indispensable to keep French possessions for France."

Muselier was in a dilemma. He either had to do something which he knew would outrage the allies and perhaps lose him the goodwill he had so carefully fostered among their admirals, or "rat" on his own committee and its leader. Both he and the officers who deciphered the cable thought de Gaulle had gone mad, but Muselier decided to obey. He was delayed by ice and storm, but on Christmas Eve he and his small flotilla entered the harbour of St. Pierre unopposed and within a few hours had captured the island. The Governor had been taken by surprise and the inhabitants were enthusiastic. Muselier was soon able to establish complete control.

But although the operation was successful the diplomatic effects were disastrous. Cordell Hull was furious and took de Gaulle's breach of his agreement as a personal affront. He was convinced that his policy towards Vichy had kept the French Fleet out of German hands and, even more important in view of the invasion now being planned, had prevented the Germans from occupying French North Africa. Everything was being jeopardised by de Gaulle's vanity and ambition. It was the Dakar argument over again. Hull felt that neither the British nor the Free French appreciated that, if Vichy could not protect its overseas possessions, the Germans would simply occupy the whole of France and take charge of the French Empire as well. He did not believe that preoccupation with the Russian Front would hinder them and in two interviews with Halifax and a "blunt" conversation with Churchill, who had arrived in Washington the day Muselier's operation began, demanded that the British Government force the "so-called" Free French to withdraw from St. Pierre and allow the Americans and the Canadians to supervise the radio station.

But Hull had miscalculated. Mackenzie King, the Canadian Prime Minister, resented American interference in what he considered a Canadian concern and refused to take any action. Churchill also demurred. He had a great respect for Hull but thought he misread recent developments in France. With Weygand dismissed, Darlan was in complete control at Vichy and seemed only too willing to do as the Germans told him. Churchill agreed with de Gaulle that the American attitude to Vichy might halt the rebirth of a fighting spirit in France itself and although embarrassed by de Gaulle's chicanery he stood up for him.

On December 30, in Ottawa, Churchill delivered a blistering attack on Vichy. Next day he sent de Gaulle a telegram in which he said, "I pleaded your case strongly to our friends in the United States. Your having broken away from the agreement about St. Pierre et Miquelon raised a storm which might have been serious had I not been on the spot to speak to the President. Undoubtedly, the result of your activities there has been to make things more difficult with the United States and has in fact prevented some favourable development from occurring. I am always doing my best in all our interests."[3]

Churchill's defence of de Gaulle closed the incident. Roosevelt had begun by supporting his Secretary of State but he soon saw that a trivial affair was being blown up into a diplomatic rumpus and he was conscious that many Americans resented Hull's slighting reference to "the so-called Free French." Newspaper editors had begun to talk of the "so-called State Department" and the "so-called Secretary of State." Although Hull fulminated and even threatened to resign, Roosevelt decided to shrug off the whole affair. In the end Hull had to climb down and de Gaulle could claim that he had now successfully defied two of his most powerful allies.

But the price he had to pay nearly wrecked the Free French movement. Instead of paving the way for an American-Free French alliance he had angered Roosevelt by making him look foolish and had earned Hull's implacable hatred; he had annoyed the Canadians and embarrassed Churchill at a critical moment in his relations with the American President. Also, as Churchill learned when he returned to London, for the first time de Gaulle had been caught telling a deliberate lie. When the Admiralty first confronted him with the news of Muselier's action, de Gaulle denied that he had any part in it and blamed Muselier who, he said, had disobeyed his orders. De Gaulle had forgotten—or did not know—that the British had the French naval code and had intercepted all his messages. The Admiralty officials had in front of them the telegram ordering Muselier to take the island. Later de Gaulle accepted responsibility, but the impression made by his denial could not be effaced. The knight in armour who stood for the honour of France had tarnished his reputation.

The effects of de Gaulle's duplicity were immediate. One of the first tasks which Churchill and Roosevelt had completed in Washington was the drawing up of the United Nations Declaration which was to guide the conduct of the allies after the war. Churchill proposed that the Free French should sign. Roosevelt was prepared to agree but Hull objected strenuously on the grounds that the Free French were not a nation and, therefore, were not qualified. Hull won. The declaration was signed on January 1. De Gaulle was not invited to add his signature until January, 1945. Apart from the Pacific, the main discussion in Washington had been about a possible allied invasion of North

Africa which might take place in the autumn of that year. The American determination that the Free French should play no part was now absolute and Churchill acquiesced. De Gaulle was not even to be told about it. Even in Equatorial Africa and the Pacific, where the Americans had accepted the Free French offer of bases, mistrust delayed negotiations; in Nouméa American troops and the Free French almost came to blows.

But from de Gaulle's point of view the most serious aspect was the effect that it had upon his relations with Churchill. These had always been mercurial, but had been saved by a personal bond which sprang from the mixture of patriot, adventurer and romanticist of which both men were made. There is a story told by one of Churchill's private secretaries of a meeting that occurred after de Gaulle had returned from one of his trips to Syria. Churchill was angry that de Gaulle kept putting off the elections he had promised and decided to put him on the mat. The meeting was to be formal. De Gaulle was to sit opposite Churchill across the wide table in the Cabinet Room, and the secretary was to translate exactly what Churchill said. The meeting began with Churchill at his most biting and the secretary did his best, but it was not good enough. Churchill turned on him, accused him of toning down his remarks, and told him to get out and send over a member of the Foreign Office who was bilingual. The secretary went, his colleague came across from the other side of Downing Street and the secretary then sat outside the door. After about ten minutes the door of the Cabinet Room opened and his colleague from the Foreign Office appeared, red in the face and protesting that he thought both men were mad. De Gaulle and Churchill were left alone shouting at each other. The meeting dragged on and as Churchill had other engagements the private secretary at last summoned up his courage to interrupt. Nervously he opened the door. Instead of glowering at each other across the table the two men were sitting side by side, Churchill laughing and joking in his execrable French and de Gaulle in the best of humours.

This bond was never to break completely because Churchill was too warm and impulsive ever to be proof against an appeal to the memories of 1940 and de Gaulle had a grudging but genuine admiration for Churchill. But from the beginning of 1942 Churchill's impulses were rarer, his doubts and irritations over de Gaulle more frequent and more substantial. Now that America was in the war he was often to carry his loyalty to Roosevelt to the point of servility so determined was he that nothing should hinder the smooth working of the alliance. He had robustly defended de Gaulle in Washington, but had nonetheless resented being brought into conflict with Roosevelt and Hull.

He had always regarded de Gaulle as expendable if some more eminent Frenchman emerged to take his place; now he realised that de Gaulle could become a liability and might have to be jettisoned. In future this fear was always present in his mind to balance any advantages the Free French might have to offer in the alliance. De Gaulle sensed this and more than once protested to Churchill that, in spite of the burden Britain had carried, he had allowed himself to become subservient to Roosevelt. In future it was to Eden rather than Churchill that de Gaulle looked for support and yet, as he himself admitted, in the last resort everything depended on the Prime Minister.

De Gaulle's first meeting with Churchill after his return from Washington was amicable; the St. Pierre episode was buried. But signs of a change in the attitude of the British Government were soon evident. In March, 1942, Admiral Muselier returned to England from St. Pierre and, after being congratulated by de Gaulle on his successful operation, carried through the determination he had formed in Halifax and resigned from the National Committee. He expressed his intention of retaining command of the Free French Navy and continuing the war "at the side of the allies." This, in effect, was a bid to set himself up as an independent rival to de Gaulle. The General at once dismissed Muselier and appointed Captain Auboyneau in his place.

At this point, however, on the instigation of A. V. Alexander, the First Lord of the Admiralty, the British Government intervened with a request to de Gaulle, delivered by Eden and Alexander in person, that he retain Muselier in command of the Free French Fleet. De Gaulle refused point-blank, suspended all communications with the British Government and went into the country leaving a "sort of secret testament" behind with Pleven, Diethelm and Coulet which instructed them to explain to the people of France what had happened in the event of his being unable to do so himself. He plainly expected that his agreement with Churchill would be torn up and thought that he might even be arrested.

Meanwhile, however, the British had learned that Muselier greatly over-estimated his personal following among the Free French sailors, the majority of whom accepted Auboyneau and remained loyal to de Gaulle. The British Government climbed down and Muselier, having refused the office of Inspector-General of Naval Forces Overseas, left the Free French movement altogether. A year later he re-emerged under a different leader in a very different post.

But although Churchill had not denounced his agreement with de Gaulle he had already decided on a serious breach of it. Ever since Pearl Harbour de Gaulle had been stressing to both the British and the

Americans the importance of Madagascar. This huge island, nearly a thousand miles long, which lies off the east coast of Africa had remained loyal to Vichy and was garrisoned by a considerable number of French troops. Now that Japan had entered the war there was a danger that the French might allow it to become a base for Japanese submarines, or that the Japanese would conquer it. It was important that the allies should forestall either possibility and de Gaulle suggested a Free French expedition supported by British ships. At first Churchill favoured it. Now, he changed his mind and decided not only that it should be a purely British operation but that de Gaulle should not even be told about it. It was from a press agency, therefore, that de Gaulle learned in the early hours of May 5, 1942, that a British force was landing at Diego Suarez, the port on the northern tip of the island. He was even more enraged by a communiqué, issued later that day from Washington, which intimated that, although the island would be restored to France after the war, allied occupation would continue as long as it was essential to the common cause of the United Nations.

Churchill had hoped that, by excluding the Free French, the Vichy troops in Madagascar would put up only a token resistance. However, Darlan had sent a message reminding them how the British had betrayed them in Flanders, fought them in Mers-el-Kebir, Dakar and Syria, were bombing their relations in France and starving their compatriots in Djibuti, and ordered the fiercest resistance. His orders were obeyed. By the time de Gaulle saw Eden, therefore, the British realised they had taken on more than they had bargained for and that they might need the Free French after all. Eden met de Gaulle's protests by saying that His Majesty's Government intended that the Free French should administer the territory when it was liberated. De Gaulle was sufficiently placated to speak to the French people on the radio next day and to announce Eden's assurance. But the conquest of Madagascar took many months and it was not until November that de Gaulle was able to install Legentilhomme as Governor-General.

De Gaulle did not accept these changes in the attitude of the British Government passively. Ever since the Germans had invaded Russia he had seen the possibility of using the Soviet Government as a counterweight in his struggle with the Anglo-Saxons and since his return from Syria had cultivated the Russians assiduously. When Auchinleck made no use of the two Free French Divisions in the Middle East in the early stages of his winter attack, de Gaulle suggested through Bogomolov in London that they be sent to the Russian Front. Auchinleck objected and the Divisions remained where they were. However, de Gaulle was in constant communication with Molotov, the Soviet

Foreign Minister, through his representative in Moscow, Garreau. Most of the communications were complaints about the treatment he was receiving at the hands of the British and Americans. He complained over Syria, over St. Pierre, over Madagascar. He praised the Russian Armies and said that the French people wanted to give them the fullest possible support. He openly supported Russian demands for a second front. When Molotov visited London in May, 1942, de Gaulle had a long talk with him and tried to enlist his sympathy by stressing the part Free France could play in an invasion of the Continent through its contacts with the Resistance in France itself.

As the summer wore on and de Gaulle realised that Africa was definitely the target for the Anglo-American campaign of that year, he became almost hysterical. On June 6 he cabled the members of the Empire Defence Council that he had reason for thinking the British and Americans were planning attacks on Senegal and Niger and that, in such an event, he would break with the Anglo-Saxons altogether. That same day Bogomolov sent a despatch to Moscow saying that he had seen de Gaulle who had asked him whether, if he denounced his agreement with Britain, the Russians would admit him and his forces to their territory.

De Gaulle was not bluffing. He had simply lost his head. The British were putting constant pressure on Catroux to hold elections in Syria and, in de Gaulle's opinion, General Spears, now British Minister to the Levant, was deliberately working to bring an end to the Free French administrations. If the Anglo-American invasion of North Africa succeeded without his playing any part he could foresee the end of his whole movement. In this desperate situation his one hope seemed to be the Russians who, he was convinced, would break the German Army and have a dominating influence in Europe when the war was over.

Yet had de Gaulle been capable of calm deliberation or listened to cool-headed colleagues, like Dejean, he would have seen that if the Russians had granted his request he would have been finished. Either he would have become Stalin's tool, in which case the majority of his own countrymen would have rejected him, or he would have been discarded by Stalin as soon as he failed to do his bidding. For, as de Gaulle was to learn later, Stalin judged statesmen not by what they said but by the number of divisions they could put into the field.

Ironically it was the conduct of one of his only two divisions, fighting its first major engagement alongside the British, that rescued de Gaulle from his dilemma. When the British armour broke in face of

Rommel's attacks at the end of May and abandoned the Gazala position, General Koenig and his Free French Brigade found themselves surrounded by the Germans and Italians at Bir Hakim on the British southern flank. Rommel expected swift surrender and several times sent officers under a white flag asking General Koenig to lay down his arms. Koenig scornfully rejected all offers and for sixteen days held the enemy at bay, finally breaking out at night with 2,700 of the 3,600 men with which he had begun the battle, and making a rendezvous with the British transport column which had been sent to fetch them. It was a brilliant feat of arms and the world rang with the praises of the Free French troops. De Gaulle, on hearing the news, shut himself alone in his room and wept. In Britain, in particular, Koenig's action silenced many voices which had been proclaiming that the French were finished as a fighting race; the contrast with the tame surrender of 35,000 British troops at Tobruk a few days later went home.

Bir Hakim softened the atmosphere. On June 10, the day that Koenig was planning to break out, Churchill invited de Gaulle to come and discuss Madagascar. It was one of those days when their spirits met. According to de Gaulle's account, Churchill began with warm praise of Koenig and his troops and went on to admit that de Gaulle had reason to feel offended at the way he had been treated over Madagascar. Churchill said he could not employ Free French troops because he felt they would only stiffen resistance, but he again pledged himself to establish a Free French administration once the fighting was over. When de Gaulle pressed him, Churchill suddenly jumped to his feet and cried out, "I am the friend of France! I have always wanted, and I want, a great France with a great army. It is necessary for the peace, order and security of Europe. I have never had any other policy!"

"That's true!" replied de Gaulle. "You even had the merit, after Vichy's Armistice, of continuing to play the card of France. That card is called de Gaulle: don't lose it now!"

The conversation turned to Roosevelt and Churchill told de Gaulle not to rush things. "Look at the way I yield and rise up again, turn and turn about," he said. "You can," replied de Gaulle, "because you are seated on a solid state, an assembled nation, a united empire, large armies. But I! What are my resources? Yet I, as you know, am responsible for the interests and destiny of France. It is too heavy a burden and I am too poor to be able to bow." They talked for an hour and as de Gaulle got up to leave Churchill became warm and expansive. "We still have some stiff obstacles to get over but one day we shall be in France; perhaps next year. In any case we shall be there together."[4]

In such a mood Churchill was irresistible; de Gaulle succumbed and a week later when Dejean, the member of his national committee responsible for Foreign Affairs, saw Bogolomov he forestalled any answer to his previous request for asylum by saying at once that de Gaulle had unwittingly exaggerated his differences with the British Government and had unnecessarily raised the question of moving the Free French to the Soviet Union. For better or for worse de Gaulle had realised that he had to fight the Anglo-Saxons alone without Russian help.

In Washington Bir Hakim also produced its effect. During April and May, while the possibility of a direct autumn assault upon France rather than North Africa was being canvassed, there were some minor breaches in the official ostracism of the Free French. It appeared that de Gaulle really was gaining influence over the little pockets of underground resistance in France itself and might be useful in saving American lives if an invasion took place. In May the War Department accepted a Free French mission to deal with military problems and the American Ambassador in London held friendly conversations with de Gaulle. Roosevelt talked for the first time of inviting de Gaulle to Washington and, although the invitation was postponed, he agreed to a visit from Emanuel d'Astier de la Vigerie, one of the resistance leaders, who had come to London to discuss the organisation of the underground movement in France. Then in July it was announced that America would accredit representatives to de Gaulle's National Committee in London and make Free France directly eligible for Lend-Lease instead of being supplied through the British. On July 14 both General Eisenhower and Admiral Stark, who had become the United States representative to Free France, attended the parade in London at which de Gaulle reviewed Free French troops. De Gaulle was elated and told Adrien Tixier, who had succeeded Pleven as his representative in Washington, that full recognition must follow.

But de Gaulle was over-optimistic. Neither the State Department nor Roosevelt had really changed their opinions. They were prepared to make use of de Gaulle but not to give him diplomatic recognition. This, they still believed, would exasperate French public opinion and perhaps drive Pétain to make war on the allies. Sumner Welles, Hull's Under-Secretary of State, told Halifax that, in his opinion, the only hope for the Free French was the reconstitution of the National Committee and the total exclusion of de Gaulle. Nor, in spite of his impulsive gesture, had Churchill's attitude really altered. When, towards the end of July, the decision to launch "Torch," the code name for the North African invasion, was finally taken, no voice was raised on behalf of de Gaulle. He was to be kept in ignorance of the whole affair and the Free French totally excluded.

De Gaulle, naturally, was not told of this decision, but he sensed it because of the evasiveness and even embarrassment of the British and American leaders whom he was constantly meeting. He knew that a fresh crisis in his career was approaching. He did not doubt that the allied invasion of North Africa would succeed and that whatever resistance French troops might offer it would be overcome and some, if not all, of the French North African Army would then join the allies against the Germans. In that case a new French leader would emerge, selected by the allies, who would have at his command far larger forces than de Gaulle and would be in a position to play the dominant role in future operations against the continent of Europe and in the ultimate invasion of France itself. Whatever accommodation might be reached between such a leader and de Gaulle himself, de Gaulle was likely to be forced into second place and the Free French movement to be threatened with absorption or extinction. The end of his dream seemed near. To avoid humiliation, to prepare those who had been loyal to him for the coming struggle and to keep himself occupied during the weeks of apprehension which he knew must now follow, de Gaulle decided to leave London and go on a prolonged tour of the Middle East and Equatorial Africa. He left London on August 5 for Cairo. He was not to return until the allied invasion of North Africa was on the point of departure. By then his fate was apparently sealed.

CHAPTER XI

OUT IN THE COLD

Since de Gaulle has returned to power in France it has become fashionable to criticise American war-time policy towards Vichy and, in particular, to ridicule the tactics employed in the invasion of North Africa. The implication is that if Hull had accepted Churchill's advice to use de Gaulle and the Free French as his agents in 1942, French resistance in North Africa might have been neutralised, the campaign shortened and an invasion of Europe have been possible in 1943. It is extremely difficult to make the facts fit such a theory.

In the memorandum Churchill prepared for his talks with Roosevelt at the beginning of the year, he had written: "If Vichy were to act as we desire about French North Africa, the United States and Great Britain must labour to bring about a reconciliation between the Free French (de Gaullists) and those other Frenchmen who will have taken up arms once more against Germany. If, on the other hand, Vichy persists in collaboration with Germany, and if we have to fight our way into French North and West Africa, then the de Gaullist movement must be aided and used to the full."[1] But when, in the summer, the campaign in North Africa was finally decided upon, Churchill acquiesced completely in the American view that it should be planned on the assumption that French troops would put up only token resistance and that the employment of the Free French would harden rather than soften their hearts.

The truth was that Churchill was as anxious as Roosevelt to find a successor to de Gaulle and did not care whether he came from Vichy provided he could command the allegiance of the French troops in North Africa. The attitude adopted towards the rival French factions by the Allies, therefore, was not the policy of the Americans alone. Churchill could justify it on military grounds as he had justified the alliance with Russia, yet it led to a political defeat almost as great as that which he was later to suffer at the hands of Stalin.

America's agent in Vichy was Admiral Leahy, whom Roosevelt appointed Ambassador at the end of 1940 with instructions to gain the confidence of Marshal Pétain. Leahy was a clever choice. He was a man of medium height, spare, balding, bushy eyebrowed, who spoke deliberately but bluntly. He had already been Chief of Naval Operations and was America's senior serving Admiral. In politics he was deeply conservative, less likely, if one may judge from his reminiscences, to be shocked by the racial policies and authoritarianism of the Vichy régime than some others of the President's advisers. Like Marshal Pétain, he despised the British, particularly the Royal Air Force. In his reminiscences, which are based on notes he made throughout the war, every British mistake or failure is carefully recorded and he even finds room for a graceless comment on the distress of Admiral Cunningham's wife at her husband's departure from Washington for a dangerous command of the Mediterranean fleet. With such credentials, Leahy was soon on intimate terms with Marshal Pétain. But although an Englishman may regret Leahy's qualifications, there can be no question that he did the Allied cause great service.

From the time of the announcement of Lend-Lease in March, 1941, he was convinced that the Americans would come into the war and his constant warnings to Pétain of the harm that collaboration would do to French interests throughout the world when the allies had won stiffened the old man's resistance. Because of his influence Leahy was detested by both the Germans and French collaborationists and constantly vilified in the press; but for his prescience it is possible that the Darlan-Warlimont agreements would have been fulfilled and all the French African ports have come under German control. It was the presence of the American diplomatic mission in Vichy which made it possible for Murphy to go to North Africa. It can be argued that the whole North African campaign was a mistake; that if General Marshall's plan of a cross-Channel invasion in 1943 had been followed, Anglo-American troops could have entered Germany two years before they did and long before a single Russian soldier had crossed into Poland or Rumania; it is not possible to argue that, once the North African campaign was launched, it would have been carried through as speedily and bloodlessly as it was without Murphy's presence in Algiers or the relationship he had established with French leaders.

Militarily, therefore, the North African campaign was a success. Politically, it was a disaster. The object of Roosevelt and Churchill was not only to occupy the whole North African coast and use it as a spring-board for the invasion of Italy and southern France, but to rally the whole of French North and West Africa to the allied cause under a leader who would command the allegiance of the French civil and military authorities, and who would accept the allied formula that the people of France must be free to choose their own government after the war. As is clear from Churchill's first memorandum, it did not matter to the Allies—indeed it would be an advantage—if that leader had served Vichy. By the end of November, 1942, the vast majority of men and women in France had recovered from the shock of the armistice. They hated the Germans and longed to see them defeated. Within the ranks of the Vichy hierarchy there were many who, although still loyal to Pétain, wanted to bring France back into the war. Some such men could surely be induced to come forward. There is clear evidence that at times Pétain himself entertained such a hope, for he not only knew that arms and equipment had been hidden from the German Armistice Commission, but had regarded the Metropolitan Army, 100,000 strong, permitted under the armistice, as the nucleus of a larger force which might one day play its part in the liberation of France. It seemed to both Roosevelt and Churchill that, once it was understood that the Americans were invading North Africa in force, even Pétain must see that this was the first step to the liberation of France and give it his secret if not his official blessing.

Nevertheless, they did not approach Pétain. Both Churchill and Roosevelt accepted Leahy's view that this aged and frightened man "had neither the will nor the stamina to resist the pressure of the conquerors of his people,"[2] and might well warn the Germans of their plan. They had then returned to Weygand, living in retirement at Cannes in the south of France since his recall from North Africa. Weygand had been visited by Douglas MacArthur Jr., a nephew of the American General and a secretary at the Embassy at Vichy, in January, 1942. MacArthur bore a personal letter from Roosevelt conveying New Year greetings and a verbal message intimating that the United States was considering forestalling a German occupation of North Africa and that Roosevelt would like Weygand to be in Africa to represent France in such an eventuality. But Weygand not only declined, he insisted on informing Pétain privately of MacArthur's visit. From then onwards, therefore, Pétain had no doubt what was in Roosevelt's mind and when Leahy sounded him out Pétain made it very plain that he would defend French North Africa against any invader including the Americans.

The search for a French leader for North Africa now seemed more important than ever. Leahy approached Herriot, the former President of the Assembly, who promptly recommended de Gaulle. Leahy vetted Generals de la Laurencie and Odic, but concluded neither were of sufficient standing. Then suddenly, on April 17, Henri Giraud, a five-star general who had been taken prisoner during the Battle of

France, repeated his exploit of the First World War and escaped from the fortress of Koenigstein. He arrived in Vichy a few days later. At once both Churchill and Roosevelt felt they had found their man. It was disconcerting that, at Laval's insistence, Giraud had signed an oath of loyalty to Pétain; unfortunate that he seemed interested in organising Unoccupied France as the spearhead of an American invasion of the Mediterranean coast. The Allies persevered. Giraud was visited many times and eventually persuaded to join the North African expedition.

But the Allies had miscalculated. As things turned out it was de Gaulle, who had never compromised with the Germans and for whom Vichy had always been the chief enemy, who triumphed. He was able to use the campaign from which he was excluded to wipe the last traces of the régime he hated from the map and, in the teeth of Anglo-Saxon opposition, impose himself and his revolution first upon North Africa and then upon France itself.

*   *   *

The preparations for the North African assault really began when Roosevelt appointed Robert Murphy as his special representative in Algiers at the end of 1940. Murphy, a comparatively junior career diplomat who had acted as Chargé d'Affaires in Vichy in Ambassador Bullitt's absence, was a Roman Catholic who had already served in both Germany and France between the wars. Walter Lippmann described him as "a most agreeable and ingratiating man whose warm heart causes him to form personal and passionate attachments rather than cool and detached judgments."[3] Harold Macmillan, on the other hand, who was to be his opposite number in the later period of the North African campaign, found him easy to work with and thought he made a valiant attempt to carry out what became an impossible policy.

Murphy's original assignment from Roosevelt had been to survey North and West Africa and advise whether it was a suitable base from which France could be brought back into the war. It soon turned into the mission of a secret agent whose job was to provide intelligence and organise underground collaboration for an allied invasion. Murphy's first step was to make an agreement with Weygand, Vichy's Delegate-General in North Africa, under which the Americans, with British consent, undertook to send certain supplies into North Africa. In the first few months after the armistice North Africa had seemed like a paradise to those who had fled from France, with food and clothes at reasonable prices and a life which seemed unaffected by the war. All this soon changed. German business men, in the guise of tourists, the German and Italian Armistice Commissions and French collaboration-ists led by the *Banque Worms*, descended on North Africa and bought up everything they could lay their hands on for shipment to France and Italy. Money became almost worthless and barter and the black market the normal means of survival. There was serious risk of the indigenous people rising in rebellion and providing the Germans with an excuse for occupying the whole area. On paper, therefore, Weygand and Vichy had much to gain from the agreement and the only stipulation the Americans made was that their five consulates in French North African cities, each of which had a staff of some twelve officers, should be reinforced by twelve Vice-Consuls whose duty it would be to super-vise the distribution of supplies and see that they did not fall into German and Italian hands.

But the agreement was not all that it seemed. The Vice-Consuls were really intelligence officers and, by a secret clause, Weygand granted them and the Consulates the privilege of using secret codes and diplomatic bags. The supplies, mainly sugar, tea, petrol and cotton goods, never amounted to more than a trickle and were constantly suspended or delayed according to whether Washington felt that Vichy was proving more or less collaborationist. Nothing the Vice-Consuls could do could prevent a large proportion even of what did arrive from finding its way into the hands of the enemy. Yet although Pétain, Weygand and the Germans knew much of what was happening, the agreement suited each of them just well enough for it to be allowed to stand.

From the summer of 1941 onwards, therefore, the French North African cities became as much a cloak and dagger paradise as the neutral capitals of Istanbul, Berne, Lisbon or Dublin. American Vice-Consuls sat opposite German and Italian officers of the Armistice Commission at the roulette tables in the Casino or watched them drink-ing in cafés on opposite sides of the street. All used the same secret methods of meeting their "contacts" who were often the same people. Double agents thrived. The *Légion des Combattants*, the Vichy version of the National Socialist movement, developed into a mixture of racketeer and security police, controlling the black market, spying upon and denouncing those who supported the allies. Resistance groups sprang up in opposition and waged clandestine war. Meanwhile Murphy's preparations went ahead.

While Weygand remained Delegate-General American hopes were

pinned upon him, but as none of his demands for military equipment were ever met and as he made it plain to Murphy that he would never take action independently of Vichy, it must always remain doubtful whether he would have co-operated with an allied invasion. When Weygand was recalled in November, 1941, as a result of German pressure upon Pétain, the prospect of any French high official in North Africa being willing to collaborate with the Allies became remote. General Noguès, the Resident General in Morocco, General Juin, the Commander in Chief in North Africa, and M. Boisson, Governor-General of West Africa whose Headquarters was in Dakar, had all at some time seemed dissatisfied with the armistice, but none were trustworthy enough in Murphy's opinion to be approached. Murphy had to look elsewhere.

He turned to the Resistance. The small isolated resistance groups which had sprung up in North African cities were very different from those in Metropolitan France. Most of the leading citizens of French North Africa, and particularly the officers of the three services, were not only loyal to Pétain but far more in sympathy with the Fascist spirit of his "National Revolution" than their compatriots on the mainland. Some were making a lot of money selling African produce to the Armistice Commissions and other procurators. There were few communists or socialists in North Africa and many of the resistance groups were imbued with the spirit of the *Colons* who regarded French domination of the Moslem population as the essence of sovereignty. One small group, headed by Henri d'Astier de la Vigerie, brother of Emanuel, the left-wing resistance leader in France, consisted of royalists working for the return of the Comte de Paris to the throne of France. The Comte himself was in Tangiers. Almost all hoped that, in the event of an Allied invasion of North Africa, Vichy would declare itself in favour of the Allies and that Marshal Pétain or his chosen representative would cross the Mediterranean and bring France formally back into the war. On the other hand, these men hated the Germans and, if Vichy failed, were prepared to act independently provided the Allies guaranteed French sovereignty in Africa.

By the spring of 1942, Murphy had managed to bring together this odd collection into some sort of organisation. In Algeria they formed a committee of five, of whom the most important were Jacques Lemaigre-Dubreuil, president of one of the leading French vegetable-oil firms, Huiles Lesueur, General Mast, the commander of the 19th Army Corps stationed in Algiers, and Colonel Van Heck who could guarantee the ardent support of fifteen hundred members of the *Chantiers de la Jeunesse*, of which he was commandant. In Casablanca the

divisional commander, General Béthouart, who had led the French
Light Brigade in Narvik but refused to join de Gaulle on his return to
England, undertook to immobilise the Resident General in Morocco,
General Noguès, and to silence the shore batteries if a landing took
place.

American Intelligence estimated the strength of these resistance
groups and the forces they could count upon at some 16,000 Frenchmen, many of whom were recently demobilised officers, and perhaps
20,000 African regulars. Their plans were carefully laid. In face of the
French North African Army which, though scattered, amounted to
more than 100,000 men, surprise was essential. The resistance could not
hope to overcome the French Army, still less the Germans if they
landed, but it could dislocate communications and hold vital points
during the crucial first stages of an Allied invasion. In Casablanca and
Algiers resistance leaders counted upon being able to neutralise French
defences for at least twenty-four hours and perhaps be able to hold the
province of Oran for a whole week. Provided the timing was correct
such an effort could make all the difference between an opposed and a
virtually unopposed landing.

Murphy's greatest difficulty, however, was to keep the Resistance
in being in face of constant discouragement. When Laval returned to
power in April, 1942, Vichy policy towards North Africa changed
abruptly. The virtual independence which Weygand had established
and Noguès and Juin sought to perpetuate, was brought to an end.
Officers of doubtful loyalty in the forces were systematically replaced.
The *Légion des Combattants* was strengthened and encouraged to hunt
down "dissidents." One whole resistance network in Morocco was
betrayed and annihilated that summer.

Unfortunately the military equipment with which Murphy hoped
to be able to counteract these set-backs was never forthcoming. From
the moment the United States came into the war prospects of an
invasion of North Africa had been discussed almost as much in Berlin
as in Washington, London and Algiers. The nightmare which haunted
the Resistance was that the Germans would beat the Allies to it. What
they wanted above all, therefore, was a supply of modern arms and
explosives; if they could not hold off the Germans, at least they could
make their occupation a costly drain on their resources. But in Washington Murphy's repeated pleas for arms fell upon deaf ears, even when
supported by General Bill Donovan, the powerful head of the O.S.S.
The only modern arms ever to reach North Africa before the end of
1942 came from the British through Gibraltar.

It was in these circumstances that Giraud's sudden appearance on the scene became so important. Looking back it seems odd that Giraud's name carried the weight it did. He had distinguished himself as a young officer, but as de Gaulle was to write sarcastically later on, his command in the Battle of France had been entirely unsuccessful and he had no reputation as a staff officer. Yet when Giraud escaped, not merely Roosevelt but Churchill and even de Gaulle himself became intensely excited. De Gaulle at once said that Giraud, his old commander at Metz, was the one Frenchman under whom he would be prepared to serve and through Passy tried to get a message to him in Switzerland warning him not to go to Vichy, where he might be handed back to the Germans, but to come to England. Giraud ignored the message, treating de Gaulle as a "dissident"; yet de Gaulle's fears were justified and it was only with difficulty that Giraud resisted Laval's demand that he should return voluntarily into captivity. Roosevelt, on the other hand, saw in Giraud the longed-for substitute for de Gaulle as leader of all Frenchmen who wished to re-enter the fight, the obvious man to command the French in North Africa in the event of an Allied invasion. Churchill was inclined to agree with him. And so Murphy was instructed to contact Giraud.

Murphy chose as his intermediary Lemaigre-Dubreuil, one of the most curious figures in the whole story. His police dossier, which Lemaigre-Dubreuil told Murphy he had specially planted in the files, showed that he had been a Nazi collaborator before the war. His business was flourishing and his contacts with both the Germans and Laval were so good that he had freedom of movement from Dakar to Dunkirk, in both of which ports he had factories. If the Germans had won he would have been well placed. Yet there seems no doubt that he genuinely hated the Germans and wanted to bring France back into the war under any auspices except de Gaulle's, whom he considered a dangerous revolutionary. Murphy grew not only to trust Lemaigre-Dubreuil but to find in him a source of "inspiration and comfort."[4]

Lemaigre-Dubreuil was successful. He found Giraud living at a villa near Lyons, obsessed with plans to reorganise the "Armistice" army so as to resist further German encroachments in France and facilitate an allied landing on the Mediterranean coast. After many meetings Giraud agreed to co-operate with the Americans in an invasion of North Africa, but on the understanding, which he always maintained had been given, that once the invasion had taken place he was to be the overall commander. There seems little doubt that, once in command, he intended to redirect the whole operation on to the southern coast of France. Giraud appointed General Mast, who had been a fellow prisoner at Koenigstein, as his representative in North Africa.

But while Lemaigre-Dubreuil was persuading Giraud, a new figure came upon the scene. Admiral Darlan, supplanted by Laval as head of the Vichy Government but remaining Commander in Chief of all French forces, let Murphy know, through Admiral Fernand in Algiers, that he now considered an Allied victory inevitable and was ready to take command of all French forces in Africa independently of Vichy if the Americans could assure him they would invade with sufficient force. The Admiral's son, Alain, a young naval officer also in Algiers, reinforced Fernand's approaches with personal assurances of his father's intentions. For many months no reply came from Washington or London to Murphy's reports of Darlan's proposals. It was not because either Roosevelt or Churchill flinched from using Darlan. As Eisenhower records, Churchill told him that, much as he hated Darlan, he would cheerfully crawl on his hands and knees for a mile if by so doing he could win over the French Fleet. But neither statesman trusted Darlan and having just made an agreement with Giraud they were in a quandary. Eventually Eisenhower, who had been selected to command the North African invasion, which had been given the code name Torch, suggested that Darlan and Giraud should divide the command.

An attempt to resolve this difficulty was made at a clandestine conference between American and French generals which took place at Cherchell, a village on the North African coast a few miles west of Algiers, when the armada carrying the invasion forces was already on the high seas. General Mast, ignorant of the imminence of invasion, had, on Giraud's behalf, asked for staff talks to settle the plan of campaign. The Americans agreed and sent General Mark Clark, Eisenhower's deputy, with General Lemnitzer and Captain Gerauld Wright. It was a fantastic episode. The Americans arrived by night in a submarine and were taken to a villa belonging to a Mr. Knight, who was one of Murphy's Vice-Consuls. There they met Mast and Béthouart. Murphy was present as Roosevelt's representative.

At one point the French police broke in, tipped off by Knight's Arab servants who thought the Americans were smugglers. Clark and his colleagues had to hide in the cellar while Murphy and his friends pretended to be having a drunken evening. If Clark had been found, the whole secret of the invasion would have been disclosed and the Allied landings have ended in disaster. Yet, in spite of the risks taken, the conference was abortive. Since neither Murphy nor Clark could tell the French the invasion was on its way the plans discussed were futile. According to Murphy, Clark said that Giraud would be given "overall command" as soon as possible, and thus confirmed in the minds of Giraud's representatives an undertaking to which neither the American nor British Governments had ever subscribed. Mast objected so strongly to Darlan's inclusion in the plan that his role was left in abeyance. The Americans departed and the French were soon to consider themselves "outrageously deceived."

The truth was that, although the invasion would take place within a fortnight, allied plans were in a muddle. Roosevelt, who laboured under the illusion that American troops would be welcomed with open arms by Frenchmen wherever they might be, believed that the landings would be almost unopposed. Murphy may have contributed indirectly to this belief because, when in Washington, he had been advised to over-emphasise French support for an American invasion in order to get the idea accepted at all. But Murphy had also stressed the need to arm and organise resistance and in this he had the backing of the British and of Eisenhower. Churchill, while hoping that Roosevelt might prove right, wanted no repetition of Dakar and Eisenhower, who regarded the whole venture with apprehension, believed that the elimination of the coastal batteries at Casablanca was a better guarantee of an unopposed landing than walking up the beaches with a white flag.

Yet, vital though the role of the resistance must be, Roosevelt would not allow Murphy to inform its leaders of the landings until twenty-four hours before they took place—far too short a time for Mast and Béthouart to put their plans into operation. Confusion went further. Up to the moment of the landing Giraud believed that he was to take overall command and Darlan that his offer of collaboration was still open. The only things certain were that the invasion was at sea, de Gaulle and his followers had been totally excluded and that, although most of the ships and aircraft and one army were British, no mention of British participation was to be made. Eisenhower's apprehension had ample foundation.

And yet, thanks to Murphy the Allies muddled through. There was a last minute scare that the Germans knew of the invasion and were going to land first, but it proved a false alarm. Both Vichy and the Germans remained convinced that the ships coming through the Straits of Gibraltar and the massive preparations in Gibraltar itself were for the relief of Malta. Although Giraud was furious at having been kept in the dark about the date of the landing and refused to co-operate unless given overall command, his absence was unimportant. When he did arrive he was treated as a traitor by his brother officers and had no influence whatever. Mast and Béthouart were equally enraged when they discovered how they had been deceived, but nevertheless did their utmost. Béthouart took over army headquarters in Casablanca and had Noguès put under house arrest in Rabat; but the American troops landed later than he expected and as he had failed to have Noguès's secret telephone cut the Resident General was able to tell the shore batteries to fire. Soon Béthouart himself was under detention. In Oran the resistance leaders lost their nerve and the allied landings were opposed from the outset.

But Algiers was the key and in Algiers Murphy's plotting paid off. General Mast's 19th Division and the Cadets of the *Chantiers de la Jeunesse* occupied the main buildings of the city and cut all telephone wires; irregulars surrounded the house of General Juin, the Commander in Chief of all North African land forces, and put him under arrest. Murphy at once visited Juin and told him, with tactical exaggeration, that the Americans were landing with half a million men. Juin apparently accepted the position at once; but he was in a difficulty. A few days previously Darlan's son, Alain, had been stricken with infantile paralysis and his father had come over to see him. He had arrived unannounced and stayed with Admiral Fernand in the city. Murphy heard of his arrival and immediately cabled Roosevelt saying that it was believed Darlan would have returned to France before the landings started. But, unknown to Murphy, Darlan had stayed and, as he was Supreme Commander of the French armed forces, Juin knew that it would be useless for him to give orders which Darlan might countermand. Juin, therefore, telephoned to Darlan who came round at once with Fernand.

It was then two o'clock in the morning and for the next twelve hours the roles played by all the chief actors were reduced almost to farce. When Murphy told Darlan that American troops were landing, the Admiral went puce in the face and blurted out that he had always known that the British were stupid but he had believed the Americans were more intelligent; now he saw they had the same genius for making massive blunders. Murphy, striding up and down Juin's sitting-room, failed to persuade Darlan to throw in his lot with the Allies, but did persuade him to send a message to Pétain asking for a free hand to deal with the situation. However, when they all went out to send the message, the irregulars in the garden barred their passage. Murphy managed to get one of his vice-consuls, who was waiting in a car on the road beyond the garden, to take it to Naval Headquarters; but it was never sent, Vichy was simply informed that Darlan and Juin were prisoners of the Americans.

Meanwhile, Murphy and his French "hosts" returned to Juin's villa. The atmosphere was icy. The French realised they were prisoners, and Murphy was on tenterhooks, waiting for American troops which should have arrived hours before. When dawn came there was shouting outside and Murphy went out to find that the *Garde Mobile* and some of Juin's regular troops were driving away the irregulars and surrounding the house. He himself was arrested at machine-gun point and, although Darlan made himself responsible for his safety and left Fernand with him, Murphy was unable to leave Juin's villa until the afternoon. By then Darlan knew that the landings had taken place and asked Murphy to get in touch with the American General Ryder. Murphy drove off, ran into Randolph Churchill on the beach who took him to Ryder, who at once agreed to come back with him to the villa.

As American troops were then in the outskirts of the city, Juin ordered his own troops to withdraw and Darlan agreed to a Cease Fire in Algeria. But he still prevaricated over a Cease Fire for the whole of North Africa. Pétain had ordered all-out resistance and, although the feelings of most French officers changed dramatically when they heard that the Germans had already invaded Unoccupied France, French sailors were still fiercely resisting in the harbours and Noguès was fighting in Casablanca. It was not until General Mark Clark flew over from Gibraltar and threatened Darlan with imprisonment that the Admiral gave way. The "Darlan Deal" was signed on November 12 and the French troops in North Africa not only ceased fighting the Americans but, under Darlan's leadership and in the belief that he had the secret blessing of Pétain, joined the Allies to fight the Germans.

In spite of all the difficulties, Murphy's mission had succeeded. He had not prevented the French from fighting the Americans, nor had his underground movement been able to neutralise the French defences as they might have if he had been able to give them sufficient warning, but the occupation of Algiers by Mast's irregulars had enabled him to win over Juin, and through Juin to contact Darlan at the crucial moment.

Had Darlan committed the French in North Africa to all-out resistance, as he might well have done but for Murphy's presence in those first few hours, the invasion would have taken on a very different character. It is possible that casualties would not have been much greater, for French resistance was almost exhausted by the time that Darlan ordered a Cease Fire, but instead of dealing with an ally, however difficult, the Allies would have found themselves in the position of an occupying power with a hostile French administration and the French Army at best sullenly neutral. The whole campaign might have lasted an extra year, postponing the invasion of France into 1945, giving Hitler time to bring his V.2s into full operation and the Russians the opportunity to overrun Europe. It was not the four days of Darlan's hesitation so much as the American refusal to follow Churchill's advice and land their troops at Bône, which enabled the Germans to get a foothold in Tunisia; and it was the advance of Juin's French troops into Tunisia which confined that foothold to a comparatively narrow bridgehead and ensured a German defeat.

CHAPTER XII

A WAITING GAME

De Gaulle impotently watched these events from London. He had been fully aware, since the end of July, of the Allied decision both to invade North Africa and to exclude him entirely from the operation. He knew also of the attempts which were being made to find a man to supplant him as leader of the French who wished to re-enter the war. But except for the small group under René Capitant and Louis Joxe, who attempted to extend the resistance movement *Combat* from Southern France across the Mediterranean, he had no links in North Africa, and received little information.

But he was not idle. The resistance movement in France was not founded by de Gaulle. During the first two years after the armistice the majority of those in Occupied and Unoccupied France who supplied information to the allies, organised sabotage or published and distributed clandestine newspapers, had never heard of him. Until 1943 the British Secret Service had far more contacts and was far more active in France than the Free French organisation under Passy. But from the beginning de Gaulle had understood the importance of the resistance in France and, true to his principle that all action undertaken by Frenchmen anywhere must be done in the name of the Free French, he set out first to co-ordinate the work of the various resistance groups within France itself and then to bring them under his own control.

As always, the British were the main obstacle. The British Secret Services under General Stewart Menzies, and S.O.E. (Secret Operations Executive) under Colonel John Buckmaster, were always prepared to collaborate with the Free French, to exchange information, arrange parachute drops and supply equipment to Free French agents; they were unwilling to become the tools of de Gaulle's political ambition or to be involved in the struggle for political power which became inevitable from the moment the Communists entered the field. If the British had become wholly dependent upon the Free French for intelligence and for the execution of sabotage, valuable information might have been withheld and operations undertaken for reasons which suited de Gaulle but had nothing to do with the struggle against the Germans. Throughout the war, therefore, the British had a network of agents in France wholly under their control and competed with the Free French in recruiting them. To a certain extent this undermined de Gaulle's authority.

Until the last year of the war, when even *collaborateurs* thought it politic to play some part, the numbers engaged in resistance were small. Both Colonel Rémy and Emanuel d'Astier de la Vigerie, two of the most brilliant leaders, put the figure at around 10,000. However—and in this lay their importance to de Gaulle—they were 10,000 of the most courageous and determined people in France. Even to-day a glance through the roneoed bulletins and news-sheets, which were distributed in the early years and are now preserved in the Bibliothèque Nationale, conveys something of the danger of their lives. Operating in isolation, the groups were very vulnerable. Leader after leader was caught and often whole networks were liquidated. Gradually, however, contact between groups was established and at the end of 1941 Jean Moulin, who had visited most of the leaders, came over to London and suggested to de Gaulle that the whole resistance movement should place itself under Free France. This was exactly what de Gaulle had been waiting for. On New Year's Day, 1942, Jean Moulin returned to France.

By the time of the invasion of North Africa a good deal of progress had been made. The three main resistance movements in Occupied France had declared for de Gaulle under the slogan "*Un seul combat, un seul Chef*," and in the north Rémy had established a general staff to control all para-military operations. It would still be some months before de Gaulle could appoint General Delestraint commander of the secret army in France, and more than a year and a half before the General had established effective control; but by November, 1942, it was clearly recognised in London and beginning to be understood in Washington that the French Resistance Movement had adopted de Gaulle as their "Symbol" and that effective liaison with it could only be established through him. Whatever might happen in North Africa, therefore, de Gaulle could no longer be brushed aside. The nearer the allied invasion of the Continent came, the more de Gaulle had to offer. Whomsoever the allies might eventually establish as the French leader in North Africa would one day have to come to terms with him.

Nevertheless the actual landings in North Africa came to de Gaulle as a shock. He was informed of them in the small hours of November 8 by Colonel Billotte, his Chief of Staff, who had himself been told at 4.30 in the morning by a member of the British Cabinet. De Gaulle, whose yellow pyjamas seemed to Billotte to enhance his indignation, burst out: "Very well, I hope that the Vichyites throw them back into the sea."[1] But the British Chief of Staff, Sir Alan Brooke, was sympathetic, explaining that the Americans had insisted on the date of the landings being withheld from de Gaulle and adding, "I understand your bitterness; now overcome it."[2] This de Gaulle did.

To Churchill he expressed surprise that the British, who had hitherto borne the brunt of the war, should allow themselves to be dictated to by the Americans in a theatre where they were still playing a major part, but his elation at the thought of the liberation of North Africa was genuine and although, for once, he did not trust himself to compose his own speech for the radio, by eleven o'clock, when he delivered it, he was enthusiastic. "Rise up," he said. "Help the Allies. Join them without reserve. Fighting France demands it of you. Do not worry about names or formulas. One thing only counts, the safety of the country . . . This is the great moment, this is the hour for common sense and courage. Everywhere the enemy is wavering and yielding. Frenchmen of North Africa, let it be through you that we re-enter the front line, from one end of the Mediterranean to the other, and thus the war will be won thanks to France."[3]

At the same time, true to the resolution the National Committee had passed advocating an understanding with whatever French commander the Allies selected in North Africa, de Gaulle planned to send a mission to discuss means of co-operation with Giraud. De Gaulle blamed Giraud for accepting his command at the hands of the Americans, which he thought "inadmissible" for any Frenchman, but felt that, as things settled down, Fighting France would emerge as "the only worthwhile organisation" and that he would be able to assume control.

But when the news of the Darlan deal reached de Gaulle his whole attitude changed. In a rage he called on Admiral Stark, Roosevelt's personal liaison officer with the Free French, and handed him a note which read simply "The United States can pay traitors, but not with the honour of France."[4] Later he withdrew the note but allowed its contents to leak to the press. The weekly Gaullist magazine, *La Marseillaise*, published in London, exploded with rage, calling the invasion "an occupation" of North Africa by the Americans, and saying that it had done an even greater injury than the occupation of France by the Germans because it affected French honour.[4] The proposed mission was cancelled and de Gaulle refused to have anything to do with Darlan's régime at all.

Of course de Gaulle was right. Long before the Germans occupied southern France without any token of French resistance, Vichy had become utterly discredited. Laval's government had not only just collaborated, it had Nazified France. Tens of thousands of Frenchmen had been press-ganged to go and work in German labour camps; the persecution of the Jews had been intensified, all personal freedom suppressed and, through the French Legion, a system of terror established in every French village. To this apparatus a French S.S. was now to be added in the form of Darnand's Militia. And, in North Africa, the same pattern of tyranny reigned. If this was to be perpetuated under Darlan's rule the whole purpose of the war would be betrayed. So long as any corner of France remained under Pétain's control he could claim that his régime was of value to the Allies. Now he himself had become virtually a prisoner and his "government" simply the tool of the German occupation. It is possible to understand and even approve Pétain's refusal to leave France; by doing so he may have prevented Laval and his colleagues from declaring war upon the Allies. What was not possible, for any Frenchman outside North Africa, was to envisage a rump of the Vichy régime, sustained in power in Algiers by Allied bayonets, returning to France with the liberating armies and claiming to be the legitimate government.

De Gaulle was not alone in his revulsion. Liberal opinion everywhere was outraged. The press, usually so docile in war, was shrill with indignation. Churchill was acutely embarrassed. Instead of taking a bold stand on military necessity he tried to laugh off Darlan to the House of Commons by poking fun at the French nation. When he saw de Gaulle on November 16, four days after Darlan had assumed power, he lamely excused the British part in the whole affair by saying that England gave her consent only on condition that the move was "an expedient." He showed de Gaulle the telegrams he and Roosevelt had exchanged.

De Gaulle was not the man to resist such an opportunity. Speaking almost as much for Britain as himself, he upbraided Churchill for being so subservient to the Americans. He reminded him that, but for the 8th Army's defeat of Rommel, there would not have been a single American soldier on the soil of Africa. He went on to warn the British Prime Minister that, if France woke up to find that liberation consisted of Darlan, morally the Allies would lose the war.

But Churchill was in an even more humiliating position than de Gaulle knew. So desperately anxious had he been to ensure that the invasion of North Africa took place that he had agreed to allow nothing to be broadcast from Britain while the action was in progress without the approval of the American President. Realising in what an impossible position he had put de Gaulle, he cabled at once to Roosevelt insisting that the general be allowed to make his own position clear. That evening a special bulletin was broadcast to France saying that de Gaulle and the National Committee "took no share and assumed no responsibility in negotiations in progress in Algiers."[5] But when the resistance movements in France addressed a joint note to the Allied Governments a few days later pledging support for de Gaulle and refusing categorically to accept the authority of any Vichy minister in Algiers, the British Cabinet, on American instructions, refused to allow it to be broadcast. On November 21 an address which de Gaulle himself was to have delivered was postponed. Eden defended the delay in the House of Commons as if it had been entirely a British decision.

However, neither de Gaulle's protests nor the public outcry had much effect. On the day that de Gaulle saw Churchill, Roosevelt wrote a statement to the press acknowledging that no permanent arrangement could be made with Admiral Darlan and describing the arrangement as "a temporary expedient justified solely by the stress of battle."[6] He also informed Eisenhower that Darlan was not to remain in control of the civil power longer than was absolutely necessary. But Darlan stayed and in spite of Roosevelt's declaration consolidated his position. The ordinances he issued began with the words "We, Admiral of the Fleet, High Commissioner of French Africa acting in virtue of powers conferred upon us by the Marshal of France, Head of State, order . . ."[7] and in Africa were everywhere obeyed. Although the French Fleet in Toulon refused to answer his call to sail to North Africa and obeyed his original orders to scuttle itself, at the end of November Boisson, the Governor-General of Dakar, who had repulsed de Gaulle two years before, brought West Africa under Darlan's rule and with it an army of 50,000 men.

In spite of Darlan's assurances to Eisenhower that his rule would be liberal and enlightened, the Vichy laws remained in force. Arrest was arbitrary and imprisonment usually without trial. Hundreds of soldiers and civilians who had helped the Allies in their landing, General Béthouart among them, remained in gaol. Gaullists were persecuted, well-known German sympathisers reinstated in their jobs. At the end of November, with Murphy's support, Darlan further strengthened his hand by making Marcel Peyrouton, a former member of the Vichy Cabinet who had been active in crushing the resistance in France, Governor of Algiers. It looked as though Vichy was winning after all.

And then, on Christmas Eve, Darlan was assassinated. Fernand Bonnier de la Chapelle, the young man who fired the shots at point-blank range outside Darlan's office, had been one of the irregulars who took charge of Algiers the night that the Americans landed. There can be no question that he acted as the instrument of an important group in Algiers. His first confession, made in writing and signed that same day, was burned by Commissioner Garinacci who received it. No one has been able to discover whom it incriminated. Thereafter the young man would say little until just before he died when he is believed to have repeated his story to the priest who confessed him. But until the last moment Bonnier de la Chapelle confidently believed that important people would come forward to save him. None did. He was tried by a Military Tribunal on Christmas Day and in spite of strong pleas from Henri d'Astier de la Vigerie and others, Giraud, as Commander in Chief, refused to alter the sentence.

In great secrecy, and without even his name being published, Bonnier de la Chapelle was executed next day. The British accused the Axis of complicity in Darlan's murder; the Americans thought de Gaulle responsible. Many Frenchmen have called it a monarchist plot because Bonnier de la Chapelle was one of a group of young men who wanted to restore the monarchy. Their representative, the Comte de Paris, was in North Africa at the time offering his services to the Allies as a successor to Darlan in the interests of French unity. De Gaulle hints in his memoirs that Giraud was involved, because of the speed and secrecy of the trial and execution. Giraud thought it was a Gaullist conspiracy and feared for his own life and even for that of Murphy. Some facts suggest that he was right.

Although Henri d'Astier de la Vigerie was a monarchist, two of his brothers were ardent Gaullists and one had completed a mission to Algiers on behalf of de Gaulle the day before Darlan died. He had, in fact, been ordered to leave. The Abbé Cordier, a fanatical Gaullist priest, was Bonnier de la Chapelle's confessor and provided him with the false identity card in the name of Moraud with which la Chapelle gained admission to Henri de la Vigerie's office. It is probable that it was by this means that the young man broke through the security cordon guarding Darlan.

More significant still, the plot to kill Darlan was known and discussed in Gaullist circles in London some days before the crime took place. A dinner given by an intelligence officer from Combined Operations to a prominent member of de Gaulle's staff was attended by a young American, Miss Virginia Cowles, acting as personal assistant to Ambassador Winant. During dinner the Frenchman inveighed against Darlan and the stupidity of the Americans in supporting him. Miss Cowles, irritated by his persistence, finally exclaimed: "Why do you go on about the Americans? Darlan is a Frenchman and it seems

to me that the French ought to be able to deal with him themselves."
A few days later, Miss Cowles received a telephone call from a Frenchman who refused to disclose his name but said that he was a member
of the Resistance and had heard about her conversation at dinner; if
she would watch the papers she would soon see that her advice had
been taken. She was appalled a day or two later when news of the
assassination came through. It does not follow, of course, that de Gaulle
himself was in any way implicated. It does seem probable that individual
Gaullists were prominent members of the group behind Bonnier de la
Chapelle.

But whatever hopes some of de Gaulle's followers may have en-
tertained, the removal of Darlan did not immediately help their cause.
While Darlan lived the sense of guilt which both Roosevelt and
Churchill felt had begun to ease de Gaulle's path. On November 20
Roosevelt had agreed to receive Adrien Tixier and André Philippe, de
Gaulle's emissaries, and although the meeting was a failure, Roosevelt
speaking of the United States as the "occupying power" in North
Africa and the two Frenchmen furiously repudiating the right of any
foreigner to administer an inch of French territory, Roosevelt persisted
in his wish to meet de Gaulle personally. A visit to Washington was
arranged for early in the New Year.

In London the long dispute over the administration of Madagascar
was finally decided in de Gaulle's favour. Churchill says in his memoirs
that he had deliberately timed this concession so as to sweeten the
pill of his exclusion from North Africa; it was also true, however, that
the British were having increasing difficulty with the Vichy representatives in the island. When the agreement was signed on December 14
de Gaulle, in a broadcast, paid tribute to "the complete loyalty which
our splendid and traditional ally, England, had manifested once again."
At the same time Churchill at last agreed that the Free French forces
which had been waiting on the borders of Somaliland for two years
should be allowed to move. Before the end of the month they had
entered Djibuti without a shot being fired.

Even in North Africa itself de Gaulle had been granted an opening.
Eisenhower, who got on with him better than most Americans,
suddenly agreed to let de Gaulle send a mission to Algiers in the hope
of promoting unity between the Fighting French and Darlan's government. The mission failed because General François de la Vigerie, de
Gaulle's Commissioner for the Interior and brother of both the resistance leader and Henri, bluntly told Darlan that he himself was the
chief obstacle to unity. But before the general was ordered to depart
he had been able to meet most of the leading Gaullists, give them

money and spur them to further activity. He had also met Giraud whom he found far less antagonistic to de Gaulle than his colleagues.

Darlan's death changed the whole atmosphere. The pangs of conscience which had troubled Roosevelt were immediately assuaged by a strong suspicion that de Gaulle had been responsible for the assassination. Instead of feeling under an obligation to appease him, Roosevelt and his advisers seized what they believed to be a heaven-sent opportunity finally to exclude de Gaulle from leadership. General Giraud might have proved a disappointment, but he was Roosevelt's man, he wanted to fight the Germans and had no ambition to rule France. By quickly appointing Giraud as Darlan's successor Roosevelt believed he would not only assure the maximum French contribution to the war but enable France to be liberated without any faction claiming the right to impose a government on the country. As soon as Roosevelt heard the news of Darlan's death de Gaulle's visit to Washington was cancelled and instructions sent to Eisenhower, without consultation with the British, that Giraud must succeed to the leadership. Within a few days the Council of the Empire, consisting of Darlan's nominees, carried out the President's wishes. Giraud was appointed Civil and Military Governor of French Africa.

The assassination, therefore, had produced the one thing that de Gaulle had been trying to avoid. Instead of being able to talk to Giraud as an equal he was suddenly faced with Giraud as head of a rival French Government-in-exile, controlling the most important French territory overseas, backed by the Americans and supported by a French army ten times larger than his own. De Gaulle's hopes of becoming the liberator of France seemed more remote than ever.

But de Gaulle knew Giraud. He had been deeply despondent while Darlan was in command in North Africa and, only a few days before the admiral's death, had told Charles Peake, the Foreign Office representative attached to him, that he was considering disbanding his whole organisation. It seemed, he said, that it was not Darlan and the things for which he stood but de Gaulle and the things for which he stood which was impeding the unity of the Allies. With Darlan out of the way, he felt his chance had come.

De Gaulle had always said he was prepared to serve under Giraud and on Christmas Day had cabled him pointing out that Darlan's murder was "a symbol and a warning" and suggesting that they meet as soon as possible on French territory to try and establish a unified national authority to control all French forces within and without Metropolitan France. But Giraud refused. He was not averse to collaborating with de Gaulle, but as he remarked in his memoirs, on terms which reflected their mutual strength. As the Americans had under-taken to re-equip up to eleven divisions in North Africa, this strength, in Giraud's eyes, amounted to eleven to two. Giraud suggested that de Gaulle send a representative to North Africa to help unite the Free French forces, which were advancing westwards under de Larminat and Leclerc, with his own which were facing eastwards in Tunisia. All, naturally, were to come under Giraud's command.

De Gaulle was furious and from that moment set out to destroy Giraud. Although he admired Giraud's fighting spirit he had no opinion of his political or administrative ability, and was supremely confident that in the end he could out-manoeuvre him. While the war rolled across the Mediterranean de Gaulle had only one preoccupa-tion—to wrest the command of the French armies in North Africa from Giraud and to set up a provisional government for France. It did not matter to him that his actions would embarrass the allies or weaken the contribution that France could make to the fighting. That contribution, he knew, would be minimal in any case. All that he cared about was the reassertion of French sovereignty, the reinclusion of the representative of France in the highest councils of the Allies. He was sure at last that this representative must be himself.

De Gaulle began by issuing a communiqué in London setting out the need for "a central power founded on national union"[8] to take charge of French affairs until such time as the nation could decide upon its future government. He then publicly reiterated his demand for a meeting with Giraud and publicly upbraided him for postponing it. He extended his internecine warfare to every quarter of the globe where Frenchmen lived or where French ships sailed. He began with a victory, his supporters capturing the island of Réunion in the Indian Ocean and bringing him the first addition to his empire since St. Pierre et Miquelon. He suffered a defeat in March, when French Guiana threw off its allegiance to Vichy, because, to Admiral Leahy's delight, the Americans were able to prevent the Gaullist representative from reaching the colony and to secure it for Giraud. He fought a drawn battle in Martinique where the population wished to join him but Admiral Robert was unable to make up his mind to declare for either general.

Gaullist recruiting officers, however, were almost universally successful. Once the Vichy Government became a puppet of the Ger-mans the Allies ceased to respect the neutrality of French ships in-terned in their ports and began to prepare them for war under Giraud's banner. By encouraging desertion de Gaulle prevented many of these ships sailing or contrived that they sailed only under the Cross of

Lorraine. The battleship *Richelieu* and several merchantmen were immobilised in New York harbour. Six merchantmen at Greenock were left practically without crews. In North Africa desertion threatened the whole structure of Giraud's army. The higher ranks were still loyal not so much to Giraud as to Vichy, but when the Germans were finally driven out of Tunisia in May and the troops of de Larminat and Leclerc joined hands with Juin's men, desertions took place in hundreds at a time.

Neither the allies nor Giraud took this onslaught lying down. The Americans arrested many deserters and often boarded French ships. Giraud not only protested personally to de Gaulle but issued ordinances imposing heavy penalties for desertion. Much of the Anglo-American press and many of the magazines published by the French in exile took Giraud's side and attacked de Gaulle violently. Roosevelt's attitude hardened into a determination to prevent de Gaulle from supplanting Giraud even if it meant Eisenhower taking over the administration of North Africa. Churchill sought a compromise. He was still looking for a Frenchman to supersede both de Gaulle and Giraud; he now hoped, rather pathetically, that the man might be his old friend General Georges. He, therefore, proposed to de Gaulle and Roosevelt the formation of a wider French National Committee of which both Giraud and de Gaulle should be members but in which, as he intended, other men such as Georges, Massigli and Monnet should wield the true authority.

When Roosevelt and Churchill met at Casablanca towards the end of January, 1943, Churchill's suggestion was still in the air. Most of the conference was devoted to the more important questions concerning the invasion of the Continent but, since the conference was held in North Africa, the French question inevitably cropped up. Roosevelt, believing in personal contact and the power of his own charm, suggested that they try and settle it by bringing de Gaulle and Giraud together while they were there. "If you will produce the bride," he said to Churchill, "I will produce the bridegroom and we will have a shotgun marriage."[9]

But the bride would not walk up the aisle. Eden, whose views were far closer to de Gaulle's than Churchill's, pleaded with him to accept the invitation to Casablanca. De Gaulle was adamant. He was still willing to meet Giraud independently on French soil and suggested Fort Lamy in the Chad. He refused to go to Casablanca, first because the invitation had only come from Churchill and second because he denied the right of the Allies to invite any one Frenchman to meet another on French soil. Exasperated, Churchill sent an ultimatum that unless de Gaulle came the British Government would withdraw all support from him. Eden watered down the ultimatum and, with the help of other members of the French National Committee, finally persuaded de Gaulle to go.

But for Churchill it was a Pyrrhic victory. The meetings at Anfa, the heavily guarded suburb outside Casablanca where the conference was held, were a fiasco. De Gaulle lunched with Giraud the day of his arrival; his first words were scarcely emollient: "What is this? I ask you for an interview four times over and we have to meet in a barbed-wire encampment among foreign powers."[10] De Gaulle not only reproached Giraud for pledging his loyalty to Pétain but told him bluntly that he was no administrator and understood nothing about politics. "Buonaparte," he said, "came forward as a leader who had showered France with great victories . . . I hope with all my heart that you will do as much, but at the moment where are your triumphs?"[11] Giraud, however, was conciliatory and at least they parted on terms which allowed them to meet again.

The impression which de Gaulle made upon Roosevelt, on the other hand, was disastrous. This was partly bad luck. Admiral Stark, the officer Roosevelt had accredited to de Gaulle in London, had fallen completely under the General's spell. With the best of intentions Stark urged de Gaulle to give the President his well-known interpretation of French history which the admiral found so captivating. Accordingly, at his very first meeting with the President, de Gaulle let himself go. He expatiated upon the greatness of France, emphasising in particular that the capacity for leadership was so widely diffused among the French people that someone had always been thrown up from the masses to give inspiration in times of misfortune. This had been true since the days of Charlemagne, and he instanced among others Joan of Arc, Napoleon, Poincaré and Clemenceau. "Perhaps this time," he added, "I am one of those thrust into leadership by circumstances and by the failure of others."[12] Nothing could have been more unfortunate. Roosevelt saw in the allusions only *folie de grandeur* and made up his mind then and there to abandon the "marriage" and back Giraud. Maliciously, he enlarged upon the story of his meeting which became so twisted that de Gaulle was supposed to have said that he saw himself as Joan of Arc. Roosevelt won his laughs but his gibes were inevitably repeated and de Gaulle never forgave him.

Between Giraud and de Gaulle there was soon complete deadlock. Giraud maintained that de Gaulle's duty was to merge his forces with the French North African Army and come to North Africa in a subordinate position. De Gaulle answered that any French command must be responsible to a French authority, that his own organisation was the only one capable of fulfilling this function and that Giraud would have his place in it, but subject to de Gaulle's political control. Cynically, Roosevelt contrived to have the two French generals photographed standing and shaking hands in front of himself and Churchill, both of whom remained seated. The world may have thought that a marriage had been consummated, but Roosevelt himself had no such illusions. He now proceeded to take matters into his own hands.

After Churchill had left Casablanca for Turkey, Roosevelt saw Giraud alone. Giraud presented him with two memoranda. The first set out the terms for the rearmament of the French forces in North Africa. Although this was essentially a matter for the Joint Chiefs of Staff Roosevelt accepted it. The second went much wider. It was a document which bound the British and American Governments to recognise in Giraud "the Civil and Military Commander in Chief, with his headquarters in Algiers, the right and duty of preserving all French interests in the military, economic, financial and moral plane."[13] This sweeping declaration, which gave away all that de Gaulle had been seeking and made Giraud the trustee of French sovereignty until such time as France was liberated, must have meant the end of Churchill's relationship with de Gaulle. Yet, without consulting Churchill, Roosevelt signed it.

Roosevelt's action was too frivolous to pass unchallenged. Churchill was considering a break with de Gaulle, but it was a serious step and needed careful preparation. He was still in Turkey when he heard from Macmillan what had happened and decided to intervene when he passed through Algiers on his way home. His chief concern was with the first memorandum. He feared that French rearmament might interfere with supplies to the British forces and had it amended so that the priorities were clear. To keep the door open for de Gaulle, he also changed the second memorandum, limiting Giraud's trusteeship to North and West Africa. Roosevelt acquiesced, admitting that he had signed it "over a drink." Churchill then returned to London.

Once more de Gaulle's fate lay in Churchill's hands. In spite of all the progress de Gaulle had made, if Churchill repudiated him now he was lost. He could exile himself to Syria or Central Africa and lead a dissident colonial movement; he could go to France and lead the resistance; he could be a nuisance to the Allies in many ways. But he could not return as the liberator of his country unless he could command the French forces in North Africa, and of that he had no hope unless Churchill continued to honour his agreement. And Churchill was still undecided.

Shortly after he returned to London the Prime Minister sat down and wrote a long memorandum on his relations with de Gaulle. In it he set out all the arguments for a rupture. De Gaulle's anglophobia, his dictatorial tendencies, his recalcitrance over Syria, his attempts to play off Britain against Russia and, paradoxically, his acceptance of communist support in France were all set out as proof of his undependability. It was a damning document and if Churchill had presented it to the Cabinet he might well have carried it with him. But still he hesitated. Churchill was not primarily concerned, as many American writers have suggested, with British prestige; in the North African campaign which was just drawing to its close British troops had outnumbered American by three to one and British prestige had never stood higher. He was looking further ahead. The spectre of a communist-dominated Europe after the war was already haunting him, and he was beginning to realise that Roosevelt was incapable of appreciating the danger. For Churchill, therefore, a strong post-war France was doubly essential. Whatever difficulties de Gaulle might create, he dared not jettison him until a suitable successor had been found. Giraud, he was sure, was not the man. Churchill, therefore, put his memorandum on one side.

Nevertheless in the days following Casablanca de Gaulle was made to feel his dependence upon the British more acutely than ever. Knowing all that had happened between Roosevelt and Giraud, de Gaulle asked Churchill if he might go to Syria. Churchill refused. De Gaulle then applied to go to Brazzaville. Churchill again refused and added that he would provide an aircraft only to take de Gaulle back to London. As Giraud controlled all French aircraft in North Africa de Gaulle had no option. To London he went.

De Gaulle bore these humiliations with unusual calm. He knew that, as the North African campaign drew to its close, the attention of the Allies would be focused upon the invasion of the Continent. Although Churchill and the Foreign Office might prevent him broadcasting, they were not going to interrupt Free French communications with France on which so much might depend. Throughout the first five months of 1943, while Giraud was struggling to establish himself in North Africa, de Gaulle from London consolidated his hold over the resistance in Metropolitan France.

Clandestine traffic between France and England steadily increased; literally hundreds of agents went back and forth, and although many were working directly for the British, liaison between the various

British Secret Services and Free French improved. Those in command of S.O.E. in particular were by now convinced that only de Gaulle could unite the French resistance movements and mobilise France to help the Allies when the invasion took place. Until now the communists in France had operated more independently than other groups, but in these months Fernand Grenier came to London to work with Soustelle on propaganda and Louis Saillant, a trade unionist who was to play a leading communist role for the next two decades, paid a visit as a result of which the communist trade unions ranged themselves under de Gaulle's banner.

In March Jean Moulin and General Delestraint returned to France, the former to organise the National Council of Resistance, the latter to prepare the secret army for co-operation with the allies. However anxious Churchill and Roosevelt might be to muzzle de Gaulle, their military advisers were fully alive to the importance of Delestraint's mission. Sir Alan Brooke, General Ismay and Admiral Stark briefed General Delestraint and kept in close touch with him after his return. When Delestraint was captured and executed by the Germans they did the same with his successor, General Koenig.

At the same time de Gaulle was busy mobilising political support. Considering how bitterly he had railed against the old party system, this was a strange somersault, but he already foresaw the danger of the communists gaining control through the resistance and needed a political counterweight. André Philip, therefore, was given the task of rallying the rump of the old political parties to de Gaulle's standard.

Throughout the early months of 1943 men whose names were already well known in France and others whose names were to become known declared themselves for de Gaulle: Herriot and Jeanneney, former Presidents of the Chamber of Deputies and Senate respectively, Jules Moch, Queuille, Gouin, Farjon, Hymans, Paul-Boncour, Blum and Mandel (both of whom were in prison), trade unionists like Buisson, Poimboeuf and Hauck, Generals Beynet and de Lavalade. Massigli, a diplomat who had served Pétain up to Laval's return to power but left him in disgust when told personally by the Marshal that he hoped the Germans would win the war, also defected and came to London. He was appointed National Commissioner for Foreign Affairs by de Gaulle almost immediately. By the end of May, 1943, William Strang, who headed the French section of the British Foreign Office, was convinced that all political factions in France opposed to Vichy accepted de Gaulle as the only political leader. This did not mean that the British Government was as yet prepared to recognise the National Committee as a provisional government; it did mean that de Gaulle could no longer be set aside in favour of Giraud or anyone else without disastrous effects upon allied strategy.

More confidently than ever, therefore, de Gaulle continued to resist pressure to come to terms with Giraud. He had not broken off relations entirely and, shortly after the meeting at Anfa, sent Catroux to North Africa at the head of a mission whose other members remained when Catroux returned to the Middle East. General Bouscat was accredited to de Gaulle in London by Giraud. But these missions did no more than liaise. Until Giraud accepted his terms, de Gaulle would make no further move.

It was the Allies who became nervous. While at Casablanca Harry Hopkins, who was at this time closer to the President than anyone else, had been disturbed by the reports he had received from Eisenhower about the unsatisfactory nature of Giraud's administration. Giraud's obsession with the re-equipment of the French Army, his contempt for all politics, had led him to assume the mantle of Darlan. After Darlan's murder he had arrested twelve of the most prominent "conspirators," including Henri d'Astier de la Vigerie, with no better evidence than the advice of Darlan's officials. He maintained Vichyites and collaborators at their posts and enacted Vichy laws. Hopkins realised that, so long as Giraud maintained his attitude, any hope of persuading the Free French to unite under Giraud was doomed.

On his return to the United States Hopkins managed to persuade Roosevelt to release Jean Monnet, who, having refused to join de Gaulle in 1940, had gone to America to work on the Combined Munitions Assignment Board, and send him to North Africa as Giraud's adviser. Monnet, a manufacturer of cognac who was later to become famous as the architect of the Common Market, was an able economist and a most persuasive man. He was also a democrat. Helped by Murphy and Macmillan, now a member of the War Cabinet and Churchill's representative in North Africa, Monnet proposed to Giraud a radical change of policy. Churchill's intervention had already slowed down the rearmament of the French Army and Giraud, afraid that it might stop altogether, agreed to co-operate. If Paris had been worth a Mass, he said jejunely, armaments were worth a speech.

On March 14, therefore, Giraud made a formal pronouncement in which he not only gave generous praise to the part de Gaulle's forces had played in the fighting in North Africa but annulled much Vichy legislation and promised a return to the Third Republic once France was liberated. Next day Lemaigre-Dubreuil, Bergeret and Rigault resigned from his administration to be replaced by Monnet himself, Couve de Murville, who had recently escaped from France and was now openly in sympathy with de Gaulle and Dr. Jules Abadie, a North African Jew. René Mayer, another Jew, who had been administrator of the French National Railways before the war, was appointed Secretary of Commerce shortly afterwards.

In North Africa the speech had a mixed reception. One ardent Vichy general explained it to his officers as a clever bluff intended to deceive the Anglo-Saxons. But the speech was enthusiastically received in the American and British press and both Churchill and Cordell Hull gave it public support. In Algiers Macmillan told a member of de Gaulle's mission that, now that the Civil and Military Commander in Chief had proclaimed the principles upon which Fighting France insisted, there was nothing to prevent a union of the rival French movements "around Giraud." The heaviest possible pressure was put upon de Gaulle to accept the speech as a basis of an understanding and to go to North Africa and range himself at the side of Giraud.

De Gaulle still resisted. He had already welcomed the speech and announced over the radio his intention of going to North Africa, but he would still only go on his own terms. These had just been published by the National Committee and included, as a prerequisite of any negotiations, the removal of Peyrouton, Boisson and Noguès. In addition de Gaulle still demanded that any committee which he and Giraud might form must be a genuine central authority to which all French military commanders must be subordinate. Despite Giraud's speech the two Generals were really no closer to an understanding. Without previous acceptance of Giraud's terms Churchill would not make an aeroplane available for de Gaulle; without acceptance of his own terms, de Gaulle would not climb aboard. So de Gaulle stayed in London.

But his long sojourn in England was drawing to its close. In North Africa, as in France, events were working in his favour. Paradoxically, as Giraud's reforms gradually took effect, it was de Gaulle who reaped the benefit. When the anti-Jewish laws were repealed the credit was given to de Gaulle. When the *Légion des Combattants* was disbanded and political prisoners were released, it was the Gaullists who rose in popular esteem. Desertions from Giraud's army to the forces of de Larminat and Leclerc were only a sympton of the prevailing mood. By the time General von Armin surrendered at Cap Bon on May 12 the Cross of Lorraine was appearing everywhere in North Africa and even Giraud himself was sometimes greeted with cries of "*Vive de Gaulle.*"

Three days after the German surrender de Gaulle received a telegram from Jean Moulin in Paris announcing that the National Committee of Resistance had been formed and that it demanded the formation of a provincial government in Algiers of which de Gaulle should be President and Giraud the subordinate military commander. When this telegram was broadcast to the world every embassy could draw the inevitable conclusions. "I was immediately the stronger for it," wrote de Gaulle in his memoirs, "while Washington and London weighed gloomily, but not without lucidity, the significance of the event."[14] On May 17 Giraud asked de Gaulle to come to Algiers at once to form a central authority with him. On May 25 de Gaulle replied that he was arriving in Algiers "at the end of this week." At noon on May 30 de Gaulle landed in a French military aircraft at Bufarik, to be greeted on the airfield by Giraud and Catroux with Macmillan and Murphy in attendance.

It was a moment of triumph. Almost exactly three years before he had landed in London alone with de Courcel. At Bufarik he had with him a small retinue, Massigli, Philip, Palewski, Billotte, Teyssot and Charles-Roux; but in Algiers as formerly in London he had neither troops nor police nor means of communication nor funds of his own. The whole weight of the allies was behind Giraud. Yet when thirty men, according to that "splendid French habit,"[15] sat down to a sumptuous luncheon in the Summer Palace, each one knew what was happening. De Gaulle had come to Algiers to consummate a victory, not only over Giraud but over the Allies as well.

THE DUEL

From the day de Gaulle landed in Algiers it took him just under six months to conquer Giraud, just over a year to humiliate Roosevelt and bring Churchill to a scarcely less grudging acceptance of his leadership of France. Considering the odds against him it was a stupendous achievement. Roosevelt's sneers about Joan of Arc were to turn sour in his mouth.

The negotiations opened with an exhibition of staged Gaullist petulance. De Gaulle had come to Algiers to set up a National Committee of which he and Giraud would be co-Presidents. At the very first meeting, however, he denounced the idea of a co-Presidency and urged Giraud, as Commander in Chief, to place himself under the new Committee which would wield the sovereignty of France. According to de Gaulle, Giraud not only refused but lost his temper. At the end of a long and heated argument de Gaulle rose from the table and left the room, slamming the door as he went out. It was a rough but carefully calculated beginning.

The following morning Giraud retaliated. For some days several thousands of de Larminat's victorious Free French troops had been moving on Algiers from their camp near Tripoli. Eisenhower had already given the order for these units to withdraw, but they had not done so and their presence was encouraging many of the Algerian garrison to desert. Giraud professed to believe that de Gaulle was planning a "putsch" and appointed Admiral Muselier, de Gaulle's most implacable enemy, as emergency commissioner for security. Muselier at once put Algiers in a state of siege, forbade all meetings and parades, and confined all troops to their barracks.

However, Muselier's action had an unexpected and, for Giraud, an unpleasant sequel. Marcel Peyrouton, the Governor-General of Algiers, suddenly sent in his resignation in two identical letters to Giraud and de Gaulle as joint Presidents of the National Committee. While Giraud tried to persuade him to withdraw it, de Gaulle, who as yet had no legal standing whatever in Algiers, accepted it and announced his acceptance to the press. Next morning Giraud was faced with a *fait accompli*. Had Giraud then and there ordered de Gaulle's arrest he would have been well within his rights and might have rallied considerable support. Even Catroux, one of de Gaulle's firmest supporters, was so angry that he demanded an interview with de Gaulle, told him that he was mad to have usurped Giraud's authority and left the room slamming the door as de Gaulle had done the previous morning. Catroux then wrote a letter to de Gaulle resigning from the committee.

But the crisis passed as suddenly as it had blown up. Giraud had not got it in him to carry through a political coup and both de Gaulle and Catroux were bluffing. Before the evening was out Catroux received and accepted an invitation to a further meeting of the Committee next morning. De Gaulle gave a press conference in which he stated baldly that he had come to Algiers to set up a central authority to exercise French sovereignty. De Larminat, on de Gaulle's instructions, ordered his troops to withdraw to Tripoli. It was plain that de Gaulle was not really contemplating a rupture.

On June 3 the French National Committee of Liberation came into existence. Both Giraud and de Gaulle gave something away. De Gaulle accepted the co-Presidency and from then on added his signature to Giraud's under the various decrees and ordinances. Giraud acquiesced in the statement that the committee was "the central French power" directing the French war effort "in all its forms and places" and exercising French sovereignty. The other five members of the committee each assumed various responsibilities. Massigli became Commissioner for Foreign Affairs; André Philip, Commissioner for the Interior, which included Metropolitan France; Jean Monnet, Commissioner for Armament. Besides being Commissioner for Muslim Affairs, Catroux was also appointed to succeed Peyrouton as Governor-General of Algiers. General Georges who, at Churchill's insistence, had come over from France to strengthen Giraud's hand, was Commissioner without Portfolio. As its first act the committee dismissed Noguès and Bergeret, the Secretary General of the Administration, and agreed that Boisson be relieved of his post as Governor-General of Dakar as soon as a Commissioner for the Colony was appointed.

De Gaulle had won the first round. Within four days of his arrival in Algiers he had launched the National Committee as a government wielding French sovereignty and persuaded it to dismiss the objectionable "Vichy proconsuls" whom Giraud had so long defended. Acceptance of the co-Presidency was a concession, but he excused it to the remaining members of the old National Committee in London as a compromise necessary in the interest of unity. It soon became apparent that he had not the slightest intention of abiding by it.

By his very next act de Gaulle showed how completely he already dominated his colleagues. On June 7, at de Gaulle's instigation and in complete secrecy, the committee voted to double its size. Three of de Gaulle's oldest followers, Pleven, Diethelm and Tixier were appointed Commissioners for Colonies, Economic Affairs and Labour respectively and three reputed supporters of Giraud, René Mayer, Jules Abadie and Couve de Murville, took over Transport, Justice and Finance. Henri Bonnet, as a neutral, was put in charge of Information. Technically Giraud still had a majority, but the truth was that de Gaulle's position was now unassailable—or would be as soon as the new members of the Committee arrived in Algiers. Monnet had long since realised that Giraud was incapable of exercising any political power; Couve de Murville, in spite of his having worked in the Ministry of Finance under Vichy, had already swung over to de Gaulle and Bonnet was to follow suit. The only man on whom Giraud could count was General Georges who had no influence at all. Churchill's dream of a committee strong and independent enough to wrest the real power from de Gaulle was already a delusion.

But de Gaulle was taking no chances. Knowing that it would take some days for the new members of the committee to arrive, he decided to stop it doing any business until they did. On June 8, therefore, he once more hotly demanded not only that Giraud resign either from the co-Presidency or as Commander in Chief, but that he himself should fill the office of Commissioner of Defence. When Giraud again refused, de Gaulle wrote a letter to the committee announcing that he would attend no more meetings unless the "structure of the committee was made to conform to the responsibilities he must carry on behalf of France by virtue of the confidence of a large number of Frenchmen."[1] Privately he let it be known that he was thinking of going to Brazzaville. Washington was delighted and naïvely kept asking Murphy for confirmation of de Gaulle's "resignation." Then on June 12, when the new members had arrived in Algiers, de Gaulle, without consulting anyone, published their names and suggested a meeting of the full committee for June 14.

This piece of calculated blackmail had an electrifying effect. Both Murphy and Macmillan cabled their governments that de Gaulle was trying to make himself master of the committee and between them managed to get the meeting postponed. Roosevelt cabled Eisenhower that, if de Gaulle made himself head of the French Army, the United States would have to consider "occupying" West and perhaps North

Africa as well and empowering him to do anything he felt necessary
to prevent de Gaulle seizing power. Churchill announced that his
government supported American policy.

But Churchill was in a difficult position. Only three weeks earlier,
while in Washington, he had come into conflict with his Cabinet over
de Gaulle. The desertions from the *Richelieu* and other French ships
in American harbours, fomented by Gaullists, were at their height and
some Americans began hinting that Churchill was using American
money, which he obtained through Lend-Lease, to frustrate agreed
policy towards France. Churchill was so exasperated that he cabled
to London formally proposing that the British Government cut
off all connection with de Gaulle. Under Attlee's leadership this
proposal was turned down by the Cabinet. Churchill could not be sure,
therefore, that in supporting Roosevelt he could carry his Cabinet
with him.

Also, up to a point, he had already condoned de Gaulle's behaviour.
From Washington Churchill had flown straight to Algiers to see Eisenhower and had actually been in the city when de Gaulle landed.
Churchill had sent for Eden as someone "better fitted to be present
at the Giraud-de Gaulle wedding" than he was.[2] However, no invitation was forthcoming. De Gaulle, who resented what he considered
Churchill's intrusion into a purely French affair, ignored his self-
invited guest. But when, three days after the committee had been
formed, Churchill invited all its members to a "country dinner," de
Gaulle relented. The meeting had been quite friendly. Churchill, who
had been kept informed by his old friend General Georges, had denied
any intention of meddling in French affairs and merely observed that
he would have had to take some action "if too brutal a shock had been
delivered" and de Gaulle had devoured Giraud "in one mouthful."[3]
Since Giraud was still co-President, de Gaulle could reasonably claim
that he had only begun to nibble.

By the time the new and larger committee was announced Churchill
was back in London. Pulling from his drawer the paper which he had
written three months earlier listing all the reasons for discarding de
Gaulle, he gave it to Brendan Bracken, his Minister of Information, to
brief the press confidentially. But the briefing backfired. In view of the
National Council of French Resistance's declaration in favour of de
Gaulle the British press had made up its mind that de Gaulle was
Britain's best bet. The document had little more effect when, a month
later, it was leaked to the press in Washington during Giraud's visit
to the United States. In answer to a question in the House of Commons
Churchill admitted that he alone was the author, but refused to discuss

the document except in secret session. Nobody felt it worthwhile to hold one for such a purpose. All that the document really showed was that Churchill was losing his grip. He could not abandon de Gaulle in face of British opinion yet he dared not back him openly for fear of antagonising Roosevelt. It was a bad omen for the future conduct of the war.

De Gaulle was quite unmoved. Eisenhower had been away from Algiers when Roosevelt's instructions arrived; on his return he invited de Gaulle and Giraud to meet him. De Gaulle liked Eisenhower and always felt that if Roosevelt had left him a free hand he could have come to an immediate understanding with him. But on June 19 he was at his most uncompromising. "I purposely arrived last and spoke first," he says in his memoirs,[4] and he proceeded to tell Eisenhower that he, de Gaulle, had come in his capacity as President of the French Government "because it is customary that during operations the Chiefs of State should come in person to the Headquarters of the officers in command of the armies they have entrusted to their charge."

Eisenhower kept his temper and repeated Roosevelt's demand for an undertaking that Giraud should take command of the French Army. After a long harangue de Gaulle refused, saying that the command of the French Army was a matter entirely for the French National Committee. When Giraud intervened to point out that the army could not exist except "within the framework of the allied command," de Gaulle got up and left, asking Eisenhower to put his request in writing.[5]

Two days later the full National Committee met to consider Eisenhower's message. It sat late into the night and finally proposed a compromise; Giraud was to keep command of the North African forces and de Gaulle of all other forces within the French Empire. Instead of de Gaulle being appointed Commissioner of Defence, a military committee was formed of which both he and Giraud were members. It was an absurd arrangement to which de Gaulle agreed knowing it would not work.

Meanwhile Giraud had accepted an invitation to visit the United States where he hoped to make his position impregnable by completing arrangements for the equipment of the eleven divisions Roosevelt had promised him at Anfa. While he was away de Gaulle planned to assert his sole authority over the National Committee and to set it to work as a provisional government. This he proceeded to do with such effect that within a few weeks allied military and civil representatives were forced to admit that the new committee was more efficient and effective than any government France had had for many years.

The Gaullist revolution now really began. De Gaulle himself toured North Africa proclaiming the renaissance of France and the arrival of a government representing not only French unity but a new revolutionary spirit. Everywhere he went he received a tremendous ovation. Meanwhile he purged all those who had been most ardent in the support of Vichy. De Gaulle was quite prepared to make arbitrary distinctions. Generals like Juin were acceptable because, although they had loyally served Vichy and Darlan, they had also fought the Germans and tended to support de Gaulle rather than Giraud. Couve de Murville and Massigli had served Vichy but had left when the Germans occupied Southern France and become ardent Gaullists. Men like General Priaux or Admiral Esteva, on the other hand, who had maintained their loyalty to the Marshal even if it meant collaboration with the enemy, were eliminated. With Giraud away, de Gaulle listed 400 officers who must be dismissed and on July 21 the committee duly approved his actions. But the purge went further. Concentration camps were set up and officers and officials who had been zealous Pétainists or members of the *Légion des Combattants* and civilians who had made money out of collaborating with the Germans suddenly found themselves behind barbed wire or exiled to the Sahara. The Gaullist press became more and more violent and openly attacked Giraud who was described as "a puppet of the Americans." The French in North Africa were being given a taste of what was to come in France itself eighteen months later. The allies were powerless to intervene.

When Giraud returned on July 25 his position had been completely undermined. De Gaulle was in the saddle and the committee had become his obedient tool. On July 31 he emphasised his supremacy. The committee decided, with Giraud's consent, that de Gaulle should preside over all its sessions. This meant that, although Giraud was to remain nominally co-President, de Gaulle alone would wield political power. In return the committee confirmed Giraud in his post as Commander in Chief and decreed that the Gaullist forces should be brought under his command. Giraud, delighted that at last the armies throughout the French Empire were to be united, signed the decree, upon which de Gaulle was moved suddenly to rise and embrace him. No doubt the impulse was genuine, nevertheless it was the kiss of Judas. For what Giraud had failed to appreciate was that in signing the decree he acknowledged the committee's authority over himself. He was no longer the independent military commander installed by the allies and supported by Roosevelt and Eisenhower; what the National Committee gave it could take away, and as, at this same meeting, the military committee was transformed into the Committee for National

Defence of which de Gaulle was chairman, it was not difficult to guess what would eventually happen.

For the moment, however, de Gaulle was satisfied. If Giraud would accept subordination they might yet work together. And there were important things to do. On the day that Giraud returned, Mussolini had fallen and Marshal Badoglio had secretly begun to seek an armistice. A new phase of the war was opening. Already in his speeches de Gaulle had warned the Allies, whom he sarcastically called "realist," that Frenchmen were fighting for France and that any plans to make use of the French effort while leaving France out of account were absurd. Now he reiterated his warning and began to press Eisenhower to include the French North African Army in the coming Italian campaign. Sicily was already being overrun and Eisenhower was planning to leave all French troops in North Africa to prevent any possibility of an Arab uprising. In the end Eisenhower gave way and Giraud began to look forward to the greatest command of his career.

Meanwhile the strength of Fighting France grew. Admiral Godfroy had declared his allegiance to the National Committee and brought his ships, which had lain for three years in the harbour at Alexandria, round the Cape to North African ports, in spite of American attempts to dissuade him. Admiral Robert, in Martinique, did the same. The committee despatched Henri Hoppenot, its representative in Washington, to take over the Antilles. Except for Indo-China, which was under Japanese occupation, every French overseas possession had now declared its allegiance. De Gaulle was the virtual ruler of all Frenchmen outside France.

But Giraud was incapable of accepting the subordination to which he had agreed or of realising the danger of his own position. Ironically it was the liberation of the first department of France which proved his undoing. The people of Corsica traditionally regard any form of government with suspicion; resistance to occupation was therefore natural to a large proportion of the population. De Gaulle had early sent a representative there who successfully organised a "National Front." But Captain Scamaroni had been captured and tortured to death by the Italians at the end of 1942 and direction from then on fell into the hands of the communists. Unknown to de Gaulle Giraud had been in touch with them since the spring of 1943 and was organising the whole resistance movement through the Military Secret Service he had inherited from the Darlan régime. Preparations were thorough and included considerable shipments of arms brought by British submarines. At the beginning of September, the day after Marshal Badoglio signed the Italian Armistice, Giovanni, the communist leader, secretly visited Giraud to discuss final plans for the capture of Ajaccio, the Corsican capital, and the neutralisation of the Italian occupying forces. These plans were successfully carried out on September 9 and Ajaccio was occupied without Italian opposition. It was only then that Giraud told de Gaulle what he had been doing.

De Gaulle at once reproached him for having acted independently of the National Committee, but as a small force of Germans was still occupying the north of the island and could be reinforced from Sardinia, said no more and arranged for troops to be sent at once. The operation was brilliantly successful and, although the Germans escaped, the island was securely in French hands by October 4. However, André Philip who, as Commissioner of the Interior, visited Corsica while the fighting was still going on, found that the communists, through the resistance, were appointing local councils of their own choosing and taking control of the radio and press. Since French troops were now in command de Gaulle was soon able to change this and by the middle of the month the Prefect and Military Governor who had been despatched by the National Committee were in command. But the warning had been taken to heart as much by the National Committee as by de Gaulle himself. If the pattern of events in Corsica were to be repeated in the other departments of France where the liberating forces would be not French but Anglo-Saxon, the embryo of Gaullism might be strangled at the moment when it should be given birth. The Americans might even decide to use the remnants of the Vichy régime to repress communism rather than the Gaullists whose authority in France they disputed. Giraud could not be permitted to blunder again.

On September 25, therefore, while the fighting in Corsica was still in progress, de Gaulle proposed to the National Committee that the co-Presidency should be abolished. In spite of Giraud's protests the committee not only approved the proposal but decreed a military re-organisation which left the Commander in Chief little but a nominal role. In the end, Giraud, who was still dreaming of being offered the Supreme Allied Command in Italy, co-signed the ordinances. In so doing he virtually acquiesced in his own eventual dismissal.

A month later de Gaulle took his next step. The Consultative Assembly, which had been foreshadowed two years earlier in the London Committee's first declaration, had just been convened in Algiers, bringing many former parliamentarians and resistance leaders to the North African capital. De Gaulle decided to use their presence to broaden the basis of the committee. He asked for the resignation of all its members and when the new committee was announced it was seen that not only General Georges, Jules Abadie and Couve de

Murville, all of them Giraud's nominees, had been left out but that Giraud himself was no longer a member. The writing was now plainly on the wall. Either Giraud complied promptly and unquestioningly with de Gaulle's orders, transmitted by the committee, or he faced dismissal. Giraud threatened to resign and appealed to Murphy for American support. If he had received it de Gaulle would certainly have dismissed him. But the Americans were at last becoming disillusioned.

Giraud's demands over the past year for the rearming of eleven French divisions had become so unrealistic that Roosevelt's military advisers had ceased to take him seriously. Eisenhower insisted that any division which was to form part of the Allied Expeditionary Forces must be fully officered and manned not only for combat but in all the auxiliary and technical administrative services. The shortage of French officers and technicians in North Africa, intensified by de Gaulle's purges which Giraud had been quite unable to prevent, made this impossible. Eight divisions were the most the French could ever muster by D Day. Although Roosevelt bitterly resented de Gaulle's success, he decided not to intervene.

The end came inexorably. Giraud had always kept the North African Army Intelligence Service, which he inherited from Vichy, under his own command. But as preparations for the invasion of France went ahead it became necessary to amalgamate this service with the Free French organisation under Passy. Giraud resisted every persuasion. At the beginning of April, therefore, the National Committee issued an ordinance designating de Gaulle head of the French Army with General Béthouart as his Chief of Staff. Giraud was offered the post of Inspector-General which he indignantly refused saying that he would be Commander in Chief or nothing. His efforts to find backing within the committee and the Allied Commands were in vain. By now the Americans placed more trust in Juin and de Lattre de Tassigny who had become the French commanders in the field. No one protested. On April 14, 1944 a decree appeared in the *Journal Officiel* placing Giraud on the retired list.

The long duel was over. De Gaulle was now not only head of the National Committee but Commander in Chief as well. Yet there is reason to believe that de Gaulle genuinely regretted Giraud's retirement. In de Gaulle's eyes Giraud had done France a service. Both under Darlan and as Civil and Military Commander in Chief he had infused the army with an enthusiasm which it never lost. In Tunisia his troops had been badly equipped and had often been forced to give way; the British General Anderson, under whose command they came, was constantly called upon to "plug the leaks" their withdrawals caused.

But no one had anything but praise for the fighting spirit the men showed. Militarily, the Corsican operations had been a miniature triumph. Since de Gaulle also knew from men who had recently left France that Giraud's family had been arrested and were being abominably treated by the Germans, he genuinely wished to spare his old commander any further humiliation. He had hoped that the allies might offer Giraud command of the Anvil Operation. When that hope died with the appointment of the American General Patch, he hesitated long before taking the final step. Perhaps the most apt comment is Giraud's own. Remarking in his memoirs that within eleven months of landing in North Africa de Gaulle had driven him from office he goes on: "This proves simply that neither my intelligence nor my character were equal to the circumstances."[6]

The indomitable old soldier retired to a villa at Mostaganem near Oran where within a few months he was severely wounded in the jaw by a lone Muslim gunman. The man was caught but to all questions replied that he had been obeying the will of Allah and that his ooly regret was at not having succeeded. No one ever discovered who supplied him with transport and arms. Although Giraud exonerated de Gaulle he suspected the Gaullists and, when the man was condemned, pleaded for his life on the grounds that he was merely a tool of others. His plea was never answered and he refused to become Grand Chancellor of the Legion of Honour, which he thought de Gaulle offered him as compensation for his broken jaw.

But Giraud never harboured resentment. More than a year later, when de Gaulle was ruling France, the two men met again at Lille and Giraud generously offered to serve once more in any capacity de Gaulle might choose. He was given an administrative post in Northern France which he held until his death in 1949. It was a fitting epitaph that he was able to forget his failure in the service of France.

CHAPTER XIV

PLANNING A TAKE-OVER

De Gaulle was now in a tantalising position. He was the acknowledged ruler of all Frenchmen outside France and Commander in Chief of armies numbering nearly a quarter of a million men. He was the only leader whom the resistance fighters within France itself would recognise as exercising French sovereignty. Yet he could still be prevented from doing so either by his western allies, who were planning to put his country under their own military government as they liberated it, or by a rival political movement rising from the ashes of Vichy or spawning from the resistance and establishing its authority before he had a chance to make his influence felt. Either, therefore, de Gaulle had to win recognition for the National Liberation Committee as the provisional government of France before the invasion took place, or somehow to install his own administration in the wake of the Allied armies, perhaps in the teeth of Anglo-American opposition and of a competing French authority as well. In the early months of 1944 it seemed most unlikely that he would succeed.

For while de Gaulle was fighting his long duel with Giraud, the very threat he most feared began to appear in France itself. The whole organisation which he had so laboriously constructed to unify the many resistance groups was suddenly wiped out. Almost certainly as the result of treachery, Jean Moulin and all but one member of the Committee of National Resistance were arrested within a few days. Shortly afterwards General Delestraint, the Commander of all paramilitary forces, was also caught, perhaps through his own carelessness. All through the summer and autumn arrests continued. The unity and with it the efficacy of the whole resistance movement was threatened.

The Allies were as concerned as de Gaulle. Preparations for the invasion of France were already under way and, if the resistance was to play the part expected of it, it was essential to restore a central command. A special joint mission consisting of Passy, the head of de Gaulle's intelligence in London, and Captain Yeo Thomas, representing the Special Operations Executive in Europe, were sent over

secretly to France to investigate. But they were never able fully to restore the position. The Committee of National Resistance was recon-
structed and Georges Bidault, a political journalist later to become
Prime Minister, was elected chairman. But whereas Moulin had been a
natural leader, sometimes described as the only member of the Gaullist
movement who could ever have succeeded de Gaulle himself, Bidault
was of an altogether different stamp. Although brave and intelligent,
this dapper little man could never dominate the committee like his
predecessors. Even worse from de Gaulle's point of view, he was not a
Gaullist but, at this stage of his career, a liberal-minded Christian
Democrat who regarded the National Committee of Resistance more
as an embryonic government than a tool of de Gaulle or the Allies.
Inevitably resistance leaders with party or personal ambitions, and in
particular certain communists, began to assert themselves and to plan
a revolution of their own.

The French Communist Party had begun to disintegrate even
before the collapse of France. When Stalin signed his pact with Hitler
in 1939 many communists denounced the war and were arrested.
Maurice Thorez, their leader, fled to Moscow. Under Pétain the party
was dissolved, along with all the other political organisations of the
Third Republic, and went underground. It came to life after Hitler's
attack on Russia when communist cells began to organise sabotage in
mines, factories, power stations and on the railways. In spite of the
difficulties of communication the cells kept in touch and by the middle
of 1943 communist groups in Paris and South Western France were
planning to take control of their districts and proclaim the revolution
of the Soviets as soon as the Germans were driven out. This was de
Gaulle's great danger. The main communist groups were represented
on the National Committee of Resistance and, if they co-ordinated
their plans, de Gaulle might find himself faced with a rival movement
in control of large areas of France which could only be dislodged by
waging civil war. In that case the Anglo-Saxons would certainly step
in and install military government. De Gaulle's hope of entering France
as its liberator and of leading his country in the final stages of the war
would be doomed.

In the autumn of 1943, therefore, de Gaulle embarked upon perhaps
the boldest and most difficult operation of his whole career. It was
nothing less than a take-over of the whole French administration from
the highest civil servant to the most junior sub-prefect. And it had
to be planned in secrecy not only from the Allies and the Germans but
from sections of the resistance as well. He began as soon as he was
able to establish his ascendancy over the National Committee of Liber-

ation. The men he chose for the task were his Commissioner for the Interior, André Le Troquer, and the Commissioner for Justice, Jules Abadie. Working together these men produced a series of ordinances, most of which were kept secret for many months, setting out how the Vichy régime was to be swept aside and what was to be put in its place. Regional Prefects were to be replaced by "*Commissaires de la République*" invested with powers extensive enough to enable them to govern their districts even if cut off from the rest of France by the battle. The *Commissaires* need not be members of the Civil Service or have previous experience. They would be assisted by Liberation Committees to keep them in touch with the views of the various resistance groups. Local councils appointed by "the *de facto* organisation posing as the French State" (de Gaulle's way of describing the Vichy government) were to be dissolved and the old municipal councils of 1939 restored. No one who had served in any Vichy organisation was eligible for any office. All municipal magistrates who had "directly assisted the enemy or the usurper" were to be dismissed. New courts were to be set up. At the departmental level—the departments of France being roughly equivalent to English counties—the old *Conseilles Généraux* were to be re-established, the Prefect being empowered to appoint delegates and to fill the gaps caused by death or disqualification. At the centre a similar purge of civil servants was to be carried out in all Ministries. All these provisional bodies and appointments were to be revised as soon as it was possible to hold elections and establish government on a truly democratic basis, but no one even suspected of sympathy with Vichy was to be allowed to vote.

However, it was one thing to pass ordinances and another to carry them out when liberation came. An administrative revolution on such a scale would have bristled with difficulties even in the hands of an established and recognised government; during the chaos which could be expected at the time of liberation everything depended upon men being available to take control on the spot. Undaunted, the National Committee embarked on an intensive recruiting campaign so that all the key jobs could be filled in advance and some at least of the candidates trained for their duties. For the vital posts of *Commissaires*, on whom the whole success of the scheme would depend, a special commission was set up in France consisting of Henri Teitgen, an eccentric lawyer endowed with an endless flow of oratory, and Michel Debré, later to be one of de Gaulle's Prime Ministers, who was at the time *Maître des Requêtes* to the Vichy *Conseil d'État.* Although a Vichy official, Debré was already a trusted Gaullist. Through his office he was able not only to compile lists of all Prefects and Sub-Prefects considered reliable by Vichy and those suspected of favouring the resistance, but to visit the officials he trusted under the very eyes of the Germans. In a room in the Rue Garancière, belonging to Francisque Gay, a final list was compiled.

Reliable Gaullists were to be confirmed in their posts or promoted. Literally thousands of new names appeared to take the place of officials who had served both the Third Republic and Vichy. By D Day Debré's lists had been matched with those drawn up in Algiers and London and everything was ready. So long as de Gaulle and enough of his agents could actually get to France on the heels of the Allied armies they at least had a chance of seizing power. Would the Allies let them?

It did not seem likely. In the months before D Day the attitude of Roosevelt and Churchill towards de Gaulle became almost pathological. Most of their subordinates had now conceded that he was the only man capable of imposing order in France during the process of liberation. Eisenhower and his staff were prepared to reach a firm understanding with him. The British Foreign Office and most of the British and American press had swung round in de Gaulle's favour. By the beginning of 1944 no fewer than twenty-six governments, including the Soviet Union, had recognised his National Committee of Liberation as in some sense representing French sovereignty. Stalin had stated bluntly that it represented "the interests of State of the French Republic."[1] Yet Roosevelt continued to treat de Gaulle as if he were an impostor and Churchill to acquiesce.

At Quebec Churchill, under pressure from Eden, had tried to bring Roosevelt round to the idea of "recognising" the French Committee; but Roosevelt, smarting under the treatment accorded to Giraud and obsessed with the fear of giving de Gaulle "a white horse on which he could ride into France and make himself master of the government there,"[2] refused. Churchill was as afraid as ever of annoying Roosevelt. The two governments, therefore, issued different statements both of which were so hedged with qualifications that it was plain that they reserved the right to withdraw their support from the National Committee at any time.

The treatment of de Gaulle throughout the negotiations for an Italian Armistice was even more equivocal. As soon as Mussolini fell de Gaulle, speaking in Casablanca, had emphasised that no general settlement of the Italian question would be valid unless France was consulted. This was sufficiently obvious and, since French Divisions were fighting with great gallantry in Italy, the Allies acknowledged the National Committee's interest by asking whether Eisenhower could sign an Armistice on behalf of the Committee as of other allied governments. To this de Gaulle agreed provided he was immediately informed of the armistice terms. Yet only a week later the Italian surrender was accepted and the armistice signed not only without the French being informed of its terms but without their even being mentioned in the document.

De Gaulle, understandably exasperated, decided to play the Anglo-Saxons at their own game. He at once made overtures to the Russians. Several weeks earlier Stalin had accredited Bogomolov, the Russian Ambassador in London, to the Committee in Algiers. But Bogomolov was still in London and de Gaulle suspected that the British were preventing him from leaving. On October 8, at Ajaccio, he made a speech in which he referred to France's "natural friend and ally, dear and powerful Russia."[3] Significantly, Bogomolov landed in Algiers next day. Seeing the effect of de Gaulle's speech Stalin quickly exploited it. Although the Russians had been informed of the armistice terms, the Anglo-Saxons did not propose to include them in the Italian Armistice Commission since no Russian troops had fought in Italy. Stalin now proposed a permanent Anglo-Soviet-American Commission to deal generally with the Mediterranean and suggested that a representative of the French National Committee be included. Roosevelt and Churchill wanted neither the Russians nor the French interfering in the Italian theatre of war, and at the Moscow Conference at the end of the month, whittled down Stalin's proposal to an Advisory Committee. All the important decisions regarding Italy were to be taken by the Armistice Commission on which neither France nor Russia were represented. However, the existence of the Advisory Committee, with headquarters in Algiers, enabled the Russians to send to North Africa, not only Bogomolov, but Vyshinsky as well, both with large staffs all of whom were warmly received by de Gaulle as host. It was an example of allied diplomacy at its most inept and its immediate results were limited only by de Gaulle's fear of increasing the prestige of the communist resistance.

With the Russians at his side de Gaulle began to assert the authority which his Western Allies refused to recognise in the most aggressive manner. His opportunity came in the Lebanon. In August the long-awaited elections had been held and the Nationalists had won, defeating the pro-French candidate. A new government had been formed under Bachara Khury, who at the end of October demanded that the French *Délégation Générale*, headed by Catroux's deputy, Jean Helleu, convert itself into an ordinary diplomatic mission in recognition of Lebanese sovereignty. Helleu at once went to Algiers for consultations and was told by de Gaulle that no change could be made in the constitution until a new treaty had been negotiated with France. However, on his return to Beirut on November 9, he found that the National Assembly had already approved the new constitution. He promptly arrested the President and all members of the government.

Since it was de Gaulle himself who, through Catroux, had promised the Syrians and Lebanese independence, and since the British Government had guaranteed that the promise would be kept, the good faith not only of de Gaulle but of the ally who had made his entry into the Lebanon possible, was at stake. The British reacted violently. Churchill fully supported by Roosevelt, ordered General Wilson to prepare for the introduction of martial law if the prisoners were not released. De Gaulle stood by Helleu. Finally Catroux was sent to Beirut to mediate. Realising that the country was on the verge of civil war, he persuaded de Gaulle to recall Helleu and himself released the prisoners. He did not, however, concede independence and negotiations were to drag on for another two years. De Gaulle had once more gained his point.

But although de Gaulle had been deliberately high-handed over Syria, in the general conduct of his administration of Algiers he was going out of his way to satisfy the democratic sensibilities of his critics. He had declared, in one of his earliest statements on behalf of Free France, that he intended to call the Consultative Assembly as soon as conditions permitted. He now summoned one to North Africa. Fifty representatives from the resistance groups in France and twenty from the empire, twelve communists, mainly from the Department of the Seine, ten general advisers from Algiers and twenty-four Members of Parliament from among those who had voted against the acceptance of the armistice in 1940, arrived in Algiers at the end of October, 1943. They remained in continuous session until long after the liberation of France.

De Gaulle made brilliant use of the Assembly, not only to win support for his movement in France but to answer the charges levelled at him by Roosevelt and Stalin that he intended to set himself up as a dictator. Considering how scathing he had been about the role of parliamentarians between the wars his treatment of the delegates was exemplary. He spent long hours on the benches among his ministers listening to and intervening in debates; he was respectful to the Assembly as a whole and affable to its members; he gave them serious work to do. Under the Presidency of Félix Gouin the Assembly was divided into working groups each under a Commissioner who was a Minister in all but name. In more than fifty sessions, twenty of which were addressed by de Gaulle, it examined in detail the Committee's plans for the rejuvenation of France. Delegates discussed the evolution of the

French Empire into a French Union, the future constitution of Metropolitan France, France's future role in the world, retribution against the supporters of Vichy and the ordinances dealing with the establishment of law and order as the Germans were driven out of France.

Although the Assembly was purely advisory it was soon apparent that de Gaulle was genuinely seeking its support, that he was prepared to listen and sometimes to take advice. The delegates were by no means always docile. In the discussion on the future constitution of the Republic de Gaulle ran into serious opposition. He was anxious above all to avoid the ineffectualness which had plagued French politics between the wars due to the excessive power wielded by the Assembly over the executive. He, therefore, proposed a constitution in which the executive should be largely independent of the legislature with a Head of State able to act as "national arbiter" with powers to override the Assembly in an emergency or through the device of a mass referendum.

But the journalists, lawyers, trade unionists, civil servants and business men who sat around him had had a taste of authoritarianism under Vichy or the Germans and they wanted no more of it. To them the days of the Third Republic now seemed a halcyon period of liberty. They spoke overwhelmingly in favour of a return to that form of sovereign assembly which had played such a large part in the downfall of their country. "I reached a point," de Gaulle was to write later, "when I asked myself if, among all those who spoke of revolution I was not, in truth, the only revolutionary."[4] It was an omen of a struggle which de Gaulle was to wage for twenty years.

However, the Assembly did propose some changes. A communist delegate suggested that the elections of the first Assembly after liberation should be carried out by a show of hands in public squares of French cities and villages under the eye of the resistance fighters. The opportunity for intimidation was too obvious and the suggestion was not adopted. On the other hand it was agreed, for the first time in French history, that women should have the right to vote and to hold office.

When it came to vengeance the delegates were more extreme than de Gaulle and forced his hand. In the first days of its existence the Committee of National Liberation had passed a resolution to bring Pétain and the other leading Vichy "traitors" to justice as soon as possible. The Assembly endorsed this, but several members were disturbed at the number of Vichy officials who were now serving de Gaulle and demanded far more sweeping retribution. Wishing to limit retribution to those who played prominent roles in Vichy politics and to the men who had made themselves the direct accomplices of the enemy, de Gaulle decided to make an example. On December 21 he arrested Peyrouton, Boisson and Flandin. Like the arrests in Syria, this was another brutal slap in the face for the Allies. All three men had held high office under Pétain and had been steadfast opponents of Gaullism; on the other hand all had rendered considerable services to the British and Americans. Roosevelt took equally high-handed action. "Please inform the French Committee," he cabled Eisenhower, "in view of the assistance given to the allied armies during the campaign in Africa by Boisson, Peyrouton and Flandin, you are directed to take no action against these three individuals at the present time."[5] But Eisenhower refused to deliver the message and, although Churchill had written to Roosevelt of the danger of civil war being precipitated in France by de Gaulle's actions, he did not press his point when he saw de Gaulle a fortnight later while convalescing from pneumonia in Marrakesh. The Assembly supported de Gaulle. In the end he postponed the trial but kept the three men in prison.

In spite of these brushes with his principal allies, by the beginning of 1944 de Gaulle had convinced most of those who paced the corridors of power in the free and neutral world that his intentions towards France were honourable. The Assembly's debates had been regularly attended by foreign diplomats and covered in the world's press. The respect that de Gaulle had shown towards the delegates, his constant attendance, the patience with which he expounded his views, the complete freedom of expression he had encouraged in debate had all been widely reported. Of course de Gaulle was playing a part but it was legitimate and convincing theatre. Certainly no one who studied the Assembly's proceedings could doubt that de Gaulle was the only man whom the delegates would accept as leader of France until liberation, or that his leadership would end or be endorsed as soon as elections could be held. For, at de Gaulle's suggestion, the Assembly decided that it would move to France at the first opportunity and that, after its membership had been increased by further representatives of the resistance, elections would be held under its auspices. The proof of de Gaulle's success was shown in the respect he was paid at all levels below the summit. In every Allied and neutral capital he was treated like a prime minister and his National Committee like a government. In matters of finance the British administration transferred all the undertakings which it had previously concluded with de Gaulle to the National Committee. The old financial agreement was wound up, the French paying their debts from the gold reserve of the Bank of France of which they had at last got possession, and a new agreement entered into under which, during the coming months, millions of pounds worth of supplies were dropped by parachute into France. The American Government accorded the National Committee the full benefits of Lend-Lease and was re-equipping French troops in North Africa which were under de Gaulle's command. French Diplomatic Missions were received in London, Washington and Moscow. In Algiers Murphy was replaced by a regular diplomat, Edward Wilson, and a little later Harold Macmillan by Duff Cooper, who had the title of Ambassador. Bogomolov and his large staff were accredited to the National Committee and Garreau went to Moscow as de Gaulle's representative. Through their good offices de Gaulle was soon able to send an air group to fight in Russia until the end of the war.

Yet Roosevelt continued to insist that de Gaulle was without legitimate authority, that "no handful of émigrés," to use Churchill's phrase,[6] should be allowed to impose their authority on France with the help of Allied arms, and that means must be found for the French people to express their views after liberation free from the influence of de Gaulle or his committee. As D Day drew closer Roosevelt's obduracy and Churchill's ambivalence began to endanger the most critical operation of the whole war.

For although every detail of the invasion of France concerned Frenchmen, both Anglo-American leaders continued to take their decisions without consulting de Gaulle or his Ministers. First the Foreign Ministers' conference, at which there was no French representative, decided that if an invasion of southern France were to take place, French troops from Italy would bear the brunt. Then, at Teheran, Roosevelt, Churchill and Stalin formally agreed that Overlord and Anvil, the invasions across the Channel and Mediterranean respectively, should take place simultaneously in May, 1944. Neither decision was communicated to de Gaulle or the National Committee of Liberation.

In Cairo, where Roosevelt met Chiang Kai-Shek, and at Teheran the President became almost paranoiac. He had begun to see the organisation of the post-war world as a matter to be settled only by the United States and the Soviet Union with China as a possible third. Without consulting the allies he agreed with Chiang Kai-Shek that it would be better if French Indo-China were put under United Nations' trusteeship rather than returned to France. At Teheran he readily accepted Stalin's assurances that Russia had no plans for aggrandisement and discussed ideas for putting all forms of "imperialism" under international supervision. When he found Stalin contemptuous of the French he was inclined to sympathise.

De Gaulle, who knew nothing of these discussions, was being more practical. Understanding the vital role that the French would play in the invasion he submitted a detailed scheme for providing the Allied forces with supplies, billets, transport, harbour facilities and for ensuring an orderly civil life behind the front line, insisting only that this vital co-operation be given under French sovereignty. The Allied Staffs found the plans sensible and workable, but, instead of being able to settle them they were blocked by Roosevelt, who submitted counter-proposals based on the premise that the French would not need a government during her liberation and the Allied commanders could make any necessary arrangement with whatever local authorities they found in being. What he really meant was that France should be put under military occupation until the Germans had been finally defeated.

Inevitably de Gaulle retaliated by reasserting his authority. The battle for Italy was at its height, and the first two French Divisions which had been sent there fought so well that General Clark called for more. Giraud, who was still in command, assigned the famous First Free French Division which, under Leclerc, had crossed the Sahara in the summer to link up with the British 8th Army. As the Division had British equipment the Americans felt it would complicate supply and asked for another. Without consulting the National Committee Giraud substituted the 9th Colonial. Next day the Committee, sitting under de Gaulle's presidency, countermanded Giraud's order, restored the First Division to the schedule and suspended all departures to Italy until the authority of the Committee over its own army was recognised.

For once Eisenhower was angry, believing that the Committee's action was a breach of the understanding reached at Anfa that in return for equipment the French Army would comply with his orders. He wrote demanding an assurance that the use of French forces should be governed solely by military considerations. The Committee responded by passing a decree that all decisions concerning the use of French troops must be taken by the National Defence Council and de Gaulle summoned Macmillan and Wilson to tell them, as head of the French Government, that he could not negotiate with Eisenhower but would deal with such matters only at governmental level.

At a subsequent conference a compromise was worked out which not only gave de Gaulle most of what he was asking but brought him into the strategic counsels of the Allies for the first time. Now at last he was told of the decisions taken at Moscow and Teheran to use French troops in the invasion of Southern France and he was able to insist that consultation should take place between the French and Allied Commands. De Gaulle also raised the question of Leclerc's division going to England to take part in the cross-Channel invasion and received a sympathetic hearing. Eisenhower went further and in a private conversation which Captain Butcher, his aide, described as a "love-fest,"[7] told de Gaulle that in the past he had done him an injustice, that he would need his help and that, whatever official relationship the American government might prescribe for them, he himself would recognise no other authority in France. Once more de Gaulle came out on top.

Next day Eisenhower left for Washington and his new command. But in Washington all the good work done in Algiers was once again sabotaged. Although isolated in his Cabinet—even Leahy felt it was now necessary to recognise de Gaulle—Roosevelt refused absolutely to negotiate with the National Committee as a government. Eisenhower, he said, might have conversations with de Gaulle but he was to sign no agreements and surrender none of his authority as Commander in Chief of an occupying power. On March 15 Roosevelt issued a directive to Eisenhower as Supreme Commander confirming this; the only change in his attitude was contained in a clause which forbade Eisenhower to have any relations with the Vichy régime except for purposes of abolishing it. "It does seem intolerable," wrote Duff Cooper, "that one obstinate old man should hold up everything in this way."[8]

It was now two months to D Day and major decisions about Allied collaboration with the French remained in abeyance. Eisenhower knew that if he attempted to carry out Roosevelt's instructions he would meet at best with passive resistance from the French behind the front line and possibly with hostility which would endanger the campaign. De Gaulle knew that unless his plans were cut and dried there was a serious risk of communist uprisings and civil war. He could wait for the Allies no longer.

On March 18 de Gaulle delivered a speech to the Consultative Assembly stating his position. He once again warned the allies that the French forces of the Interior would take orders only from the National Committee and that any attempt to deal with Vichy or to impose American military government would be disastrous. He then made an impassioned bid for unity among Frenchmen, stressing the need not only for a purge but for radical social and economic reform and ending with an appeal to the communists to join his government. He was not yet aligning himself with the Soviet Union but the hint was plain.

Since the only Allied response was the publication of Roosevelt's directive to Eisenhower, de Gaulle went further. First he included two communists, Billoux and Tillon, in his government; then published in the *Journal Officiel* the ordinances setting out the Committee's plans for the civil administration of France during liberation. This had been revised since it was drafted in September and the Committee now designated the Socialist, André le Troquer, as its Civil Delegate in France, and General Koenig as Military Delegate, both with plenary powers.

Roosevelt refused to recognise either appointment and continued with his plans for an occupation of France. In April, 1944 he insisted that no information whatever about Overlord should be given to de Gaulle. Churchill agreed. As a measure of general security, all foreign coded messages in or out of Britain were prohibited. De Gaulle was left without the means of communicating with those in London, like Generals Leclerc and Koenig, who were to play a vital role in the coming campaign. Then the American Government, without the agreement of the French, printed and issued five and a half billion "supplementary francs" for the use of the invading forces. In defiance of the arrangements de Gaulle had already made public, a large team of Anglo-American officers was being hurriedly trained to take over the civil administration of liberated French Departments. Finally the date for Anvil, the invasion of Southern France in which French troops were to play the major part, was unilaterally postponed by the Anglo-Saxons.

De Gaulle continued to assert his power. Since neither Roosevelt nor Churchill would recognise his government, he denounced the Clark-Darlan agreement under which the French had co-operated with the Allies in the administration of North Africa and proceeded to govern the French territories alone. In response to a unanimous vote in the Consultative Assembly he formally declared that the National Committee of Liberation was the provisional government of France, reiterated to the Allies the great danger of ignoring its authority and spoke once more of post-war France as a centre of "direct and practical co-operation" with "dear and powerful Russia, a permanent Ally."[9] The allies could never complain that they had not been warned.

Fortunately some common sense continued to prevail at lower levels. Both Cordell Hull and Eden assured the French that the allies had no intention of exercising military government in France. Although they were defying Roosevelt the Allied commanders began to arrange matters among themselves. Eisenhower had been empowered by Roosevelt to use any French agency he thought fit to further his military plans; he proceeded to use these powers in the way he had promised de Gaulle before he left North Africa. General Koenig, who was de Gaulle's Commander in Chief designate of the French forces of the Interior, was allowed to make reasonably satisfactory plans with his opposite numbers in S.H.A.E.F., although he too remained in

9. Mr. Churchill between General Sikorski and General de Gaulle

10. De Gaulle's first speech in liberated France in the square at Bayeux on June 14 1944. (*See page 230*)

ignorance of the date of the invasion. Soustelle, now controlling the French Intelligence Services, was allowed to communicate with Special Force Headquarters through British channels. Colonel de Boislambert arrived in England to train some 180 French liaison officers to act with the Allied forces. There was, therefore, at least a rough and ready co-operation among those who were to do the fighting.

Yet, a week before D Day, Eisenhower was facing the absurd prospect of having the territories he was to liberate administered by a provisional government which he could not recognise and with whose civilian officials he could not negotiate. Churchill at last became worried that this situation might seriously hamper military operations. He, therefore, invited de Gaulle to London. Roosevelt objected even to this and insisted that, if de Gaulle came, he must stay until after D Day to avoid any possibility of a "leak." Insult could bite no deeper; de Gaulle refused to come. This time, however, his own colleagues intervened.

However much the members of the National Committee of Liberation shared de Gaulle's indignation at the way he was being treated, they realised that the success of all their plans depended upon his giving at least the appearance of being a partner with the Allies. The French people must believe that he was at one with the invading armies. At any sign of a rift support among the resistance might fall away just when it was most critical. To give this appearance de Gaulle must be in London. Massigli and several other members of the National Committee threatened to resign unless he accepted Churchill's invitation. On June 3 de Gaulle left Algiers in an aeroplane, once more provided by Churchill, taking with him Palewski, Béthouart, Teyssot and—with what nostalgic memories—Geoffroy de Courcel, his sole French companion almost exactly four years before. He landed in England on the morning of June 4, still ignorant of the fact that the forces which were to liberate his country were already at sea.

CHAPTER XV

THE RETURN TO FRANCE

The moment for which every battle in the Western hemisphere for the past four years had been preparing was now approaching. One hundred and fifty thousand British and American troops were cruising off the South Coast of England waiting for the order which was to hurl them on to the Normandy beaches. Thousands of French men and women were listening anxiously for the code word from the B.B.C. which would tell them that the invasion had begun and launch them into open guerrilla warfare. Yet de Gaulle, for whom these should have been days of supreme elation, felt nothing but isolation and bitterness. He had been unable to communicate with London for several weeks. As he drove down to the train near Widewing which Churchill had made his Overlord Headquarters, he did not know that the armada had sailed nor against which beaches it was to be directed. On the other hand he was only too well aware that both Roosevelt and Churchill were refusing to treat with him as the head of a provisional government and that, in all their dispositions, they had kept open the option to use him if it suited them and to discard him if they could find other means of securing the co-operation of the French people. Everything for which he had worked for four years still hung in the balance. With de Gaulle in such a mood a meeting with Churchill was bound to be stormy; it turned out to be one that de Gaulle never forgave nor forgot.

Churchill greeted de Gaulle cordially enough. The Prime Minister began by explaining the overriding need for security which had prevented him from communicating with Algiers and went on to describe the scope of the vast Overlord operation. De Gaulle congratulated him on the part that Great Britain was playing. However, when Eden intervened and suggested that in order to reach a political understanding it would be desirable for de Gaulle to visit Roosevelt as soon as possible, the General took immediate offence. He said curtly that he needed neither American nor British sanction for his authority in France. His government existed and none other was possible. What concerned him were the arrangements for the administration of liberated France.

Both Churchill and Eden knew perfectly well that for de Gaulle this was the cardinal question. Yet both flared up. Churchill launched into a diatribe about the risks that the British and Americans were running in order to liberate France and added that, if there was a split between the National Committee of Liberation and the United States, he would always side with the United States. Neither he nor Roosevelt were prepared to present de Gaulle with "the title deeds of France."[1] De Gaulle replied icily that he was well aware that in any dispute between France and the United States Britain would align herself with the latter, and there the conversation ended.

In moments of such tension men often say more than they mean, but de Gaulle felt that, when Churchill said that he would always side with the United States, he was speaking from his heart. He was to refer to this phrase over and over again in the coming years. Yet it was a gratuitous insult on Churchill's part. Churchill felt that de Gaulle was behaving abominably. Here was the moment for which he above all had been waiting for four long years; but instead of going on his knees in gratitude to his allies he was raising questions which could only be settled when the battle was won. It seemed almost as if he resented the coming Anglo-Saxon landings on the shores of his country as much as he had the invasion by the Germans. On this occasion most of Churchill's colleagues agreed with him.

De Gaulle, on the other hand, could think only of France. It was France that was to be liberated and most of the governments of the free world had already recognised him as the representative of France. Thousands of Frenchmen in the resistance who acknowledged him as their leader had already died paving the way for the Allies. Thousands more were to do so in the coming weeks. The French Army was waiting to invade Southern France. Yet de Gaulle had hardly been consulted and vital decisions concerning the future of his country were being taken without his knowledge. It was not merely the future of Gaullism that was at stake; by ignoring him the Allies risked plunging France into civil war. How could he be other than "bristling"?

Eisenhower, to whose headquarters Churchill accompanied de Gaulle, did his best to restore harmony. The Supreme Commander shared none of Churchill's political inhibitions. He knew that de Gaulle's help would be vital in the coming campaign, he had given him his word that he would deal with no other French authority and he meant to keep it. When de Gaulle reached his hut in the woods near Churchill's train, Eisenhower showed that he was genuinely pleased to see him. Standing in front of the maps which covered the walls he explained his plan of attack in detail. Then, with a grace which had been lacking in every other Allied leader, he asked de Gaulle's advice. Eisenhower was facing his gravest decision. The armada was already at sea and the landings had just been postponed for twenty-four hours; but the weather in the Channel was still so bad that there was serious risk to the landing craft. Should he postpone the invasion again? De Gaulle made it quite plain that he would support whatever decision Eisenhower might take but added that in his place he would not delay. The risks to security and morale of a postponement were, he thought, even greater than the weather. But not even Eisenhower could avoid giving offence. Before de Gaulle left Eisenhower handed him a copy of the proclamation that he was to broadcast on D Day. De Gaulle read it quickly and at once objected to its tone. De Gaulle was not mentioned and the people of France were called upon to obey Eisenhower's orders rather than those of their own government. Thinking that the copy he had read was a draft, de Gaulle took it away to suggest some amendments. However, before he could make them he learned that the proclamation had already been printed for a week and that millions of copies were soon to be rained down upon France from the air.

This was the last straw. De Gaulle realised that neither the British nor American Governments were going to do anything to help him and that if he was to establish his authority in France he must do so in spite of them, working through Frenchmen alone. In his interview with Churchill de Gaulle had agreed to speak to the French people once the assault on the beaches was under way. But when Charles Peake, an old friend who had again been assigned as liaison officer to de Gaulle by Churchill, came that same afternoon to make arrangements for the D Day broadcasts, he found the General in a most difficult mood. It had been arranged that de Gaulle should speak immediately after Eisenhower. This he refused to do because it would imply that he was endorsing what Eisenhower said. Eventually de Gaulle got his way and arranged to speak alone at six o'clock in the evening. When he did so he flatly contradicted the Supreme Commander, telling the French people on the one hand to fight the enemy by every means in their power—whereas Eisenhower had told them to be patient and to prepare—on the other to give strict obedience to the orders of the French Government. Eisenhower, in his turn, was not mentioned.

But the battle of words was drawing to an end. At last de Gaulle's claims were being put to the test. They seemed well founded. As a result of his broadcast the resistance came out into the open next day and fought several pitched battles with the Germans. Militarily their effort was mistimed, but it had an electric effect on French morale. Nevertheless, if de Gaulle was to triumph it was essential that he in person should catch the French imagination. He was still only a name to the forty million Frenchmen who had been living under the Germans; a name with a familiar voice but whose face, as he was soon to discover, scarcely a man or woman in any French street would recognise. If his *Commissaires* were to be accepted, he himself must be acclaimed by the French people at the earliest possible moment. De Gaulle had already obtained permission in principle to visit the bridgeheads and, as soon as the first sub-prefecture had been liberated, he applied to the allied commanders for leave to go to France. Even then, in deference to Roosevelt, Churchill tried to delay his visit. But the Cabinet in London held to the arrangements that had been made and on June 13, in the French destroyer *La Combattante*, de Gaulle crossed the Channel.

Montgomery's troops had had an easy landing on the beaches near Bayeux and it was for Bayeux that de Gaulle was heading. The sea was rough and the DUKWs which took de Gaulle and his companions to the shore had to make two journeys. De Gaulle had with him Viénot, his Ambassador in Britain, D'Argenlieu, the fiery admiral-priest, Béthouart, Palewski, Billotte, Chevigné, Boislambert, Teyssot, the faithful de Courcel and François Coulet, one of the *Commissaires* who spent the journey sitting on a trunk containing twenty-five million French francs.

Montgomery correctly sent a guard of honour under a Captain to meet de Gaulle. After he had inspected the men de Gaulle went straight to see the British Commander in Chief. Montgomery received him in his famous trailer which had a picture of Rommel on the wall. "I missed him in Africa," he said pointing to the picture, "but I hope to get him this time."[2] The two men got on well and after Montgomery had explained the battle of Caen, which was about to begin, he asked de Gaulle to address his staff. Before leaving de Gaulle mentioned casually that he was instructing François Coulet to take over the administration of Bayeux. It is doubtful whether Montgomery took in the importance of this observation although under Eisenhower he was technically responsible for selecting the Frenchmen with whom he would deal in civil affairs. Nevertheless, de Gaulle could claim to have satisfied the proprieties. Refusing lunch, he set off at once for the town in a jeep.

Bayeux was not unprepared. Maurice Schumann, de Gaulle's

mouthpiece on the B.B.C., had been in the town for several days with an advance guard. That morning he had toured the streets with a loud speaker telling the people to assemble at four o'clock round the fountain in the Place du Château to hear General de Gaulle speak. However de Gaulle did not hurry. He could not be sure that the news of his arrival had reached the town, nor how the people would receive it. While he had been talking to Montgomery his companions had gone on ahead of him and he wanted to give them time. On the way he met two policemen on bicycles. He stopped the car and spoke to them. They had not the slightest idea who he was and, when he told them, were speechless with surprise. Then he asked them to do him a favour and ride back into Bayeux to tell the townsfolk he was coming. "I shall not move from here for a quarter of an hour," he said.[3] They saluted and rode away. Half an hour later de Gaulle reached Bayeux to find that the streets were empty. Still uncertain of his reception he drove straight to the *sous-préfecture* where he met and shook hands with Rochat, the *sous-préfet* who had served Vichy during the war and for the last eight days had stoutly maintained his official position in face of the Allied Armies. After a quarter of an hour's rather frigid conversation under the portrait of Marshal Pétain, which still hung in Rochat's room, de Gaulle went on to the Square.

It was the first of many similar scenes. Every man, woman and child in the town had assembled to greet him. Many of them wept tears of joy, threw flowers, crowded round to touch the long overcoat of the tall, haggard man whose voice they knew so well. De Gaulle could scarcely speak as he shook hands with those nearest him. When he mounted the platform, which had been hastily erected and decorated with the *Tricolore*, flanked by British and American flags, he said very little: "We are all moved to find ourselves together again in one of the first metropolitan French towns to be liberated; but this is not the moment to talk of emotion. What the country expects of you here behind the front is to continue the fight to-day as you have never ceased from fighting since the beginning of the war . . . I promise you that we shall continue to fight until sovereignty is re-established over every inch of our soil. No one shall prevent our doing that. We shall fight beside the Allies, with the Allies and as an ally and the victory we shall win will be the victory of liberty and the victory of France."[4] In an unhesitating, loud and not very tuneful voice he then led the crowd in the first part of the "Marseillaise."

De Gaulle had chosen his words carefully. They were directed first at the French and then at the Allies. The people had not, in fact, seen any fighting since 1940, for Bayeux was in a closely guarded coastal zone where the resistance had little scope. Nor had they suffered physically. To their surprise Allied troops were offered abundant food and wine. But the whole thesis of Gaullism was that the French people had never ceased to resist, that they had been betrayed by Vichy in 1940 and that now, under de Gaulle, they would rise and themselves drive the Germans out. A belief in themselves was an essential part of their renaissance. As for the Allies, they were being given notice that any attempt to interfere with de Gaulle's administration would be defied. His words were faithfully reported and echoed loudly in every Chancellery. De Gaulle had declared himself the ruler of France and received a tumultuous reception. The hope that still lingered in the White House that another might supplant him had been reduced to a phantom.

Next day François Coulet installed himself in Rochat's office and issued his first proclamation as *Commissaire*. Rochat himself had removed the Marshal's picture and retired with such good grace that he gave his successor his uniform, reminding him only to change the Vichy buttons. British and American officers, once they had recovered from the shock of finding a Gaullist in charge of the town, established excellent relations. The Gaullist revolution was in progress.

De Gaulle returned to England on June 15, more sure of himself than he had been at any time since the lonely days in 1940. He had tested his reception at the hands of the French people and found it overwhelming. He was certain at last that unless the Allies physically prevented him, he could make himself master of France. In London he sensed at once the effect of his visit to Bayeux. Although no one spoke of formal recognition, Eden suggested that negotiations for an Anglo-French treaty begin. Since this meant in fact that the National Committee was to be treated as a government de Gaulle agreed. He also received a formal invitation from Roosevelt to visit Washington, but to this he made no immediate reply.

For de Gaulle was needed elsewhere. Now that the Allies were firmly established in their Normandy bridgeheads his immediate concern was for Anvil, the planned invasion of the South of France. No date had been settled but de Gaulle wanted to make sure that he was consulted and that the major role that French troops were to play was in no way whittled down. On June 18 he flew to Algiers.

In Algiers good news greeted him. A breakthrough had at last been achieved in Italy, where the French troops under Juin had greatly distinguished themselves. Rome had been taken, Victor Emmanuel had abdicated and a new government had been formed. As a *bonne bouche* a French detachment completed the conquest of the island of Elba.

However, success had whetted General Alexander's appetite and he was once more pressing the Allied High Command to allow him to exploit his victory by driving on through the Brenner Pass to the Danube and so bring the war to an end that year. But for this he needed reinforcements which could only be met at the expense of Anvil. De Gaulle, therefore, went to Rome.

Militarily he approved of Alexander's strategy and his sympathy was deepened by an audience with Pope Pius XII who expressed profound concern at the coming ordeal of those Christians who would be subject to communist rule. But Anvil was vital for the prestige of France, and although de Gaulle allowed French troops to continue fighting in Italy until the last moment, he stipulated to Alexander that they must be free to move from July 25 onwards. Shorn of his sea transport and the French troops, Alexander had to resign himself to a purely Italian campaign and so miss the first of several opportunities to win the peace as well as the war. But this was not de Gaulle's concern. While he was in Italy, the date of the landing in the South of France was fixed for August 15.

Back in Algiers at the beginning of July de Gaulle was at last forced to make up his mind to visit Washington. Allied offensives in Normandy and Provence were to begin in a month's time and if there was to be any improvement in his relations with the United States the visit could not be postponed. After consulting the National Committee, de Gaulle accepted Roosevelt's invitation. On July 6, in an aeroplane the President had sent specially for him, he left Algiers for Washington.

But what should have been one of the dramatic moments of de Gaulle's life was an anti-climax. De Gaulle had, of course, already met Roosevelt at Anfa. Since that stilted encounter the two men had fought a strenuous political duel. The President of the most powerful nation on earth had been beaten in every *reprise* by a two-star general with hardly any troops who, although he claimed to be the head of a provisional government, had neither capital nor country nor constitution. Now the upstart was on his way to receive the acknowledgments of the war lord.

But there was neither clash not contrition. To the surprise of the Americans de Gaulle made himself agreeable. Even Admiral Leahy condescended to remark that he found him "less formidable in manner and appearance" than he had expected.[5] The President was urbane. De Gaulle had made it known before he left Algiers that he had nothing to ask or to negotiate; the President on his side talked in generalities.

He enlarged on his vision of a post-war world run nominally by the United States, Russia, China and Great Britain, but in reality by the first two powers. He talked of the self-determination of colonial peoples. He spoke of his affection for, but disillusionment with, France and gave de Gaulle clearly to understand that his country could never be a prominent power again.

De Gaulle agreed that empires must change into partnerships but stressed the dangers of too rapid a change. He stated the case for a strong Europe and a strong France. Roosevelt promised material help, which indeed was already being delivered on a massive scale, but smiled his disbelief in its efficacy. "We shall do what we can," he ended cryptically, "but it is true that in helping France no one can replace the French people."[6] No immediate problems were discussed, nothing was settled; the two men sparred gently and parted without coming one whit closer together. After de Gaulle had spoken to the Canadian Parliament, received a mass ovation in Montreal and returned to Algiers, a declaration was made by the American Government recognising the French Committee of Liberation as "qualified to exercise the administration of France."[7] It was an ambiguous phrase and, as de Gaulle was soon to learn, was meant to be; but it at least allowed Eisenhower to enter more formal relations with Generals Koenig and Leclerc.

From America de Gaulle returned to Algiers. He was needed at the seat of government. Montgomery's offensive at Caen, the hinge which was to open the door to the American breakthrough at Avranches, was just about to begin. Alexander in Italy was pushing the Germans back to the Po and, supported by the American Mark Clark, was once more pressing for the cancellation of the landing in the South of France and the retention of the French forces in Italy. This time his objective was a drive through the Lubljana Gap into Hungary or eastwards through Trieste into Yugoslavia. Again, had his advice been accepted the war might have been won in 1944, for a successful thrust through the north of Yugoslavia would have cut off Hitler from mineral resources without which Speer's production programme would have come rapidly to a halt. But for once de Gaulle and the American Government were on the same side. Roosevelt's faith in Stalin's good intentions and General Marshall's inflexibility in face of changing circumstances exactly suited de Gaulle's wishes. For it was of supreme importance to de Gaulle that the French Army should fight on French soil. It was necessary for morale. He needed the army in France to maintain internal security. He was determined that it should take part in the final assault across the Rhine and carve out a French zone of occupation in Germany. De Gaulle, therefore, threw his weight behind Marshall and the plans for Anvil were confirmed. He could now turn his whole attention upon France.

In France the work of the resistance had exceeded the most sanguine expectations. For a month before and after D Day a campaign of sabotage played havoc with German communications. During June and July 600 trains were derailed, 1,800 locomotives and 6,000 wagons put out of action. Cable wires and telephone communications behind the German front line were paralysed for days at a time. A flood of accurate information about German dispositions and troop movements reached London every day. The S.S. Panzer Division which was summoned from Toulouse to take part in the Normandy battle was delayed seventeen days on its journey; the armoured division which travelled swiftly from the Russian front to Strasbourg took twenty-three days to fight its way through to Normandy.

On D Day itself, in obedience to de Gaulle's orders, a general uprising took place throughout France. There were several pitched battles, some of which ended in defeat for the resistance. The gallant defence of the Vercors Plateau in the foothills of the Alps, where some 2,000 Maquisards lost their lives, was the most dramatic; but in Ain and Corrèze, at Le Monchet, in the Rhône Valley, at Grenoble, Quercey and Périgord there were serious engagements in which both sides lost many thousands of men. When the American Fifth Army broke out across Brittany they found the entire province in the hands of the resistance who had buried 1,800 Germans and taken 3,000 prisoners. By the end of July the Allied Command valued the French underground army at six divisions and reckoned that eight German divisions were being used to hold it down. Add to this the devastating effect of chronic insecurity upon German morale, the sabotage of factories producing war material and the havoc among communications, and one begins to get an idea of the contribution the French were making. Statistics suggest that the resistance, armed by S.O.E., did damage to the German war effort comparable to that inflicted by Bomber Command at a fraction of the cost and with no greater loss of life.[8] Eisenhower paid generous tribute to this achievement when Special Forces Headquarters was disbanded in May, 1945.

But the very effectiveness of the resistance was a danger to de Gaulle. For the more completely French guerrilla troops dominated an area the more likely they were to set up their own administration. In the wake of the allied armies de Gaulle's plans had been working well. Close behind the front line, in Normandy and Brittany and later on the roads to Paris, small caravans, each of two jeeps and perhaps a couple of lorries, would thread their way between the supply columns along the roads, stopping at each major village or town. As soon as the little convoy reached the main square out would get one or two civilians and some officers who immediately scattered to find the Mayor, the local resistance leaders and the Chief of Police. These agents of the *Commissaire* would then take over the local administration. If the local officials were approved by the resistance leaders or had been sanctioned in advance by Debré's Commission, they would be confirmed in their posts. If not, others were appointed. Innumerable forms dealing with every kind of emergency likely to arise during liberation—forms for enlistment in the forces, forms for ration cards, log-books for motor vehicles and petrol, movement permits—had been prepared in advance and were distributed around the offices. A special rubber stamp to overprint the Marshal's portrait on all official documents had been specially made at Coulet's request and was soon in general use. Within a few hours the convoy would have done its work and passed on.

Sometimes the Gaullists who were to take over arrived ahead of the allied troops and toured their districts clandestinely, preparing officials and people for the changes to come. Usually the Vichy officials who were to be superseded accepted the inevitable, kept their mouths shut and stayed at their posts until Allied troops arrived. Occasionally a Vichy fanatic would betray de Gaulle's agents and a few were arrested by the Germans and shot. More frequently members of the resistance wreaked summary vengeance upon compatriots who had persecuted them before the new administration could impose its will. But a month after D Day no Allied commander questioned for a moment that de Gaulle was the *de facto* ruler of France and, in the absence of inter-governmental treaties, the allied generals made their own arrangements with de Gaulle's representatives. General Koenig was confirmed by Eisenhower as Commander in Chief of the French Forces of the Interior and was given equal status with the other Allied Commanders in Chief.

The Allied officers who had been specially trained to become military governors of liberated areas, finding Frenchmen already installed in the places they had expected to occupy, usually put a brave face on their disappointment and acted instead as liaison officers between the armies and the civil power. In return, de Gaulle allowed 200 French liaison officers, who had been trained in England to work with the allied forces, to go to France and play their proper part. When Emanuel d'Astier, de Gaulle's Minister of the Interior, toured the northern part of France in September he found relations between the French and the Allies excellent. British officials, he said, had distinguished themselves by their scrupulous respect for French sovereignty.

The situation was very different in the south-west of France and in some of the big cities which the resistance was liberating on its own. With no Allied armies to restrain them resistance leaders were taking the law into their own hands, arresting or killing Vichy officials and supporters and installing themselves as mob rulers. In Paris in particular, where the communists dominated the resistance, the situation was critical. By the middle of August the Allied armies had crossed the Seine on both sides of Paris. However, Eisenhower saw no reason to enter the city and intended to by-pass it and drive straight for the Rhine. This was the communists' opportunity. With Paris cut off from the rest of France they could stage an insurrection against the German garrison, free the city from within and set up their own administration. As de Gaulle well knew, their plans had been carefully laid, and he feared that if they gained control he might find himself facing a repetition of the situation of 1871 when the *Commune* took command of the capital and had to be dislodged by force. To forestall them he had to get to France himself and stay there.

The full absurdity of de Gaulle's position now became apparent. Both Roosevelt and Churchill had recognised the National Committee of Liberation as the *de facto* government for all the liberated areas of France. In those areas de Gaulle's administrators were proving effective and helpful to the Allies. Instead of the chaos and strife which Roosevelt had prophesied, order was most quickly restored wherever de Gaulle's writ ran. Political support for Pétain was non-existent. The franc remained reasonably stable. The danger of famine was being averted partly by the surplus rations of the Allied troops but also by the food supplies that the National Committee had laid in store. The only danger to Eisenhower's communications came from the zones outside de Gaulle's control, of which the capital was one. Yet Roosevelt and Churchill were still bent on preventing de Gaulle from reaching Paris. At that very moment Roosevelt was entertaining the futile hope that Laval's plan to induce Herriot to recall the Assembly of 1940 might succeed and a civil authority other than de Gaulle be set up. And since de Gaulle, still in Algiers, had to apply to the Allied High Command for permission to visit France, the Allied leaders had the means of imposing their will.

De Gaulle was forced, therefore, deliberately to deceive them. On August 16 he asked Sir Henry Maitland Wilson, the Commander in Chief of the Mediterranean, for permission to visit the liberated areas and, if necessary, to go to Paris. Wilson cabled S.H.A.E.F. in London and S.H.A.E.F. talked to Washington where McCloy, the Assistant

Secretary for War, asked for an assurance that de Gaulle was only paying a visit and did not intend to stay. De Gaulle gave the assurance and permission was granted.

An extraordinary series of incidents then punctuated de Gaulle's trip. Knowing that de Gaulle's own Lodestar had not the range to fly from Gibraltar to Cherbourg, the United States command put a Flying Fortress with an American air crew at his disposal. De Gaulle accepted the aircraft with reluctance. But, on landing in Algiers to pick him up, it overshot the runway and broke its undercarriage. No pilot would do such a thing deliberately, but de Gaulle was convinced that the action was part of a plot to delay his landing in France. He therefore flew in the Lodestar to Casablanca while another Fortress brought General Juin after him. De Gaulle had intended to leave Casablanca that same night for Maupertuis, near St. Lo, but minor defects delayed the second Fortress and he lost a day. On August 19 he took off again, this time in the Fortress with the Lodestar following, but the allies insisted on his landing in Gibraltar. At Gibraltar the Fortress burst a tyre and de Gaulle was told it would take twenty-four hours to provide a new one. The Governor, Sir Mason Macfarlane, strongly urged him not to fly on in an unescorted, unarmed aeroplane which, if the winds were contrary, might not have the fuel to reach Maupertuis. Having consulted the pilot, Colonel Lionel de Marmier, de Gaulle decided to take the risk. Carrying every ounce of fuel the Lodestar could hold, de Marmier just managed to get off the Gibraltar runway that night and headed north. De Gaulle, who hated flying, smoked throughout the trip and said nothing. The weather worsened the farther north they got, but with half an hour's fuel left de Marmier sighted the English coast. He told de Gaulle that he would have to land there. De Gaulle refused absolutely to land in England and ordered him to head for France. With the tanks almost empty and in very poor visibility they crossed the French coast at a point de Marmier did not recognise. He handed the map to de Gaulle who looked out and, after a moment's hesitation, said they were just east of Cherbourg. De Marmier got his bearings and, seeing an improvised fighter strip before him, landed. They were near Maupertuis, although not on the aerodrome at which they were expected. No one was there to meet them. The party drove into Cherbourg where an officer was sent to summon General Koenig and to arrange for de Gaulle to see Eisenhower. De Gaulle meanwhile had breakfast and a shave. It was August 20.

When Koenig arrived later in the morning he brought alarming news. The general uprising in Paris had begun. Nominally all sections

of the resistance acknowledged de Gaulle's leadership and his representatives, Parodi, Minister delegate for the territories as yet unliber-
ated, Chaban-Delmas, the Wimbledon tennis player now a military
delegate, Charles Luizet, Prefect-Delegate of the Police, and General
Hary, who was to take charge of the *Garde Républicaine*, the *Garde
Mobile* and Fire Service, had been living in Paris clandestinely for some
days. But in every factory and throughout the public services there
were factions who looked, not to de Gaulle, but to the communist
Rol-Tanguy as their leader, and for the past ten days a fierce struggle
for power had been going on. Parodi had been trying to prevent a
general uprising until the Allied troops were in the outskirts of the
city; Tanguy had been trying to provoke one.

Rol-Tanguy's first success came on August 10 when the railwaymen
stopped work, forcing the Germans to send in slave labour to move
essential traffic. On August 15 Rol-Tanguy managed to bring out the
police force who struck to a man and put on civilian clothes. This
cleared the way for an uprising, for without the police the resistance
could do as it pleased. Parodi and his colleagues were desperate. They
knew that the Germans had orders to defend Paris to the last man and
that, if the population rose, there would be a massacre in which hundreds of thousands of civilians would lose their lives and the city be
reduced to ruins. They also knew that if the rising succeeded their
authority, and perhaps de Gaulle's as well, would be at an end. In vain
they pleaded with Rol-Tanguy and his colleagues to hold their hand
until contact had been made with the Allies. "Paris," said Rol-Tanguy,
"is worth 200,000 dead."[9]

On August 18, while de Gaulle was on his way, Parodi decided to
change his tactics. If he could not stop the uprising he would try to
control it. Sending his girl courier out on her bicycle, he secretly
summoned the Gaullist sections of the police to storm the Prefecture
next day. They were to inform their communist colleagues only when
the action was over. As all German and Vichy police had already left
the city the Prefecture was quickly occupied, but Tanguy, furious at
being outdone, at once ordered the general uprising. During the
afternoon of August 19 hundreds of barricades sprang up in the streets
of Paris. Since the German garrison still held many strongpoints in the
city and had enough troops around the perimeter to crush a revolt,
there seemed little hope of avoiding a massacre.

After listening to Koenig de Gaulle went straight to Eisenhower.
If he could not persuade Eisenhower to alter his plan and order
Leclerc's division to march on Paris, he intended to issue the orders
himself and then go into Paris alone ahead of the army. Chaban-

Delmas, his military delegate, at once made arrangements for him to do this if necessary. But although de Gaulle used all his powers of persuasion Eisenhower would not give him an immediate answer. De Gaulle was faced with an excruciating decision. Either he must risk antagonising the Supreme Commander and perhaps forfeit the role he intended the French Army to play or he must risk Paris. Warning Eisenhower that if he delayed too long he would himself order Leclerc to move, de Gaulle waited.

The fate of Paris now depended upon one man, Dietrich von Choltitz, the German garrison commander. If he obeyed his orders, Paris would become a battlefield and the centre of the city be reduced to ruins before the Allies could arrive. Von Choltitz, who had led the parachute attack on Rotterdam in 1940 and stormed the great fortress of Sebastopol in 1942, had been sent to Paris at the beginning of August with explicit instructions to defend the city to the last man. If the people rose he was to crush them ruthlessly. If he had to leave Paris, he must leave it in ruins.

However, von Choltitz already knew that he could not hold Paris against the Allies, for General Model, the Commander in Chief of the Western Front, was in such despair that he was already planning to withdraw. Von Choltitz, therefore, was on his own with 22,000 second-class troops, a hundred tanks and about ninety aircraft. In addition he had been sent a special squad of demolition experts to ensure the destruction of key points. By pure chance Captain Ebenech, their commander, had discovered a store of 300 torpedoes stacked in a road tunnel at St. Cloud. With the help of these he systematically mined all the forty-five bridges across the Seine, all the power stations and communication centres, the Luxembourg Palace, the Eiffel Tower and 200 factories. While de Gaulle was talking to Eisenhower von Choltitz was poised to crush the resistance and leave Paris in the state which Hitler demanded.

Yet von Choltitz hesitated. Whether because of the impression of madness which Hitler had given him when he last saw him or because Model would give him no help, he was no longer a fanatical Nazi. The idea of leading his garrison to extermination did not appeal to him. When the insurrection began on August 19 von Choltitz made no immediate move but ordered his tanks and aircraft to be ready for action next day. But that evening he received an unexpected visitor. The Swedish Consul, General Raoul Nordling, knowing that a German attack on the Prefecture and the barricades was imminent, had sought out the German commander to make a personal appeal for a Cease Fire. Von Choltitz agreed to give it a trial. To Jodl, who telephoned soon afterwards from Hitler's headquarters in East Prussia to know why demolitions had not begun, von Choltitz replied that he was carrying out his orders to defend Paris and not to destroy it. He would do this only if defence became impossible.

Nordling went off to see Parodi who managed to persuade the National Committee of Resistance to accept the truce. Notices were rushed out to all corners of the city and a German military policeman, flanked by two gendarmes, patrolled the streets with a loud-speaker ordering a Cease Fire. Parisians began to breathe a sigh of relief.

However, their respite was short lived. The communists, out-voted in the Committee of National Resistance, had no intention of observing the truce. Rol-Tanguy countermanded Parodi's orders the next day and fighting began again. Still von Choltitz waited. He had learned that Model was withdrawing the German divisions to the south of the city and leaving the approaches open to the Allies. Now he hoped the Allies would come. If the insurrection seriously threatened the safety of his troops he would suppress it and give orders for demolition; but he was playing for time. When Nordling and Parodi came to see him they confessed that they could not control all the forces of the resistance; but when they asked permission to send a party through the German lines to contact the Allies, von Choltitz consented. He gave them forty-eight hours. If he received no news of an Allied advance within that time he would stamp out the revolt and destroy Paris.

This was the position which had been reached while de Gaulle was waiting for Eisenhower's decision. On August 21, he received no word, but by the 22nd not only Nordling's cabled messages but a lone Gaullist named appropriately Gallois had come through the German lines and reached Bradley's headquarters. He convinced Bradley that the allies must enter Paris and Bradley convinced Eisenhower. In the afternoon not only Leclerc's Second Armoured Division but Gerow's Fourth Division were ordered to get into Paris as fast as they could.

By now de Gaulle had moved from Rennes to Laval and from Laval to the old Royal Palace of Rambouillet, which had been the peace-time residence of French Presidents. The furniture was still intact but it was only at the last moment that the intendant accompanying de Gaulle could get a supply of electricity. The former President's bedroom had been prepared for de Gaulle; tactfully he refused to occupy it and installed himself elsewhere. Then he sent for Leclerc, who explained his plans for the attack on Paris next day. Having approved the plans, de Gaulle made a rendezvous with Leclerc at the Gare Montparnasse and wished him Godspeed. "How lucky you are!" he said as they shook hands. "Go quickly. We cannot afford another *Commune*."[10]

For the next two days de Gaulle waited at Rambouillet, once more alone with de Courcel. From the bookshelves de Gaulle had taken down Molière's *Le Bourgeois Gentilhomme* which he occasionally scanned; he read the resistance newspapers which for the last two days had been appearing openly in Paris; but for most of the time he paced up and down the garden smoking endless English cigarettes and saying nothing.

What obsessed him was the fear that Paris would have passed beyond his control before he could enter it. He knew that conditions were desperate. Food had almost run out; water was scarce; there was no gas, and electric power only for half an hour a day. The normal public services were at a standstill. Looting of what little remained in the shops had begun. If anarchy reigned when the Allies entered, Eisenhower might declare martial law. Even worse, if the men at the barricades overcame a half-hearted German attack, Rol-Tanguy might be in charge of the city with a government of the resistance already formed. This was the fear which governed his every action in the next few days.

On August 23 a Doctor Favreau, who had left Paris that morning, reached Rambouillet with messages from Luizet, Prefect of the Police, giving favourable news of the general uprising. The Germans had not attacked anywhere in force. In the evening the B.B.C. prematurely broadcast that the resistance had liberated Paris. The news infuriated the men and women fighting at the barricades, but drew a telegram of congratulations from King George to de Gaulle next morning. In the afternoon of August 24 Nordling's emissaries, one of whom, Poch-Pastor was both a member of von Choltitz's staff and an Allied secret agent, visited de Gaulle. They came to press him to convene the old National Assembly on his entry into Paris so as to give his régime an appearance of legality. De Gaulle indignantly refused.

By that evening both Leclerc's and Gerow's divisions were in the outskirts of the city. While the bells of every church rang, the radio played the "Marseillaise" which was relayed through the streets by loud speakers. When General Speidel rang von Choltitz from Model's headquarters the latter held the receiver towards the open window of the Hotel Meurice so that Army Group B's Chief of Staff could hear the mingled noises. The allies had beaten the German Panzer Divisions in the race for the capital and Paris would not now be destroyed. When Hitler, far away in Rastenburg, shrieked at Jodl that same evening, "Is Paris burning?" he received no reply. The time had come at last for de Gaulle to prepare for his own entry into the city.

Hitherto the liberation of France had been a disappointment for many Allied soldiers. When their turn came the Dutch and Belgians went mad with joy and overwhelmed the troops with kindness. The French often seemed aloof. However, in Paris on August 25 there was no lack of enthusiasm. The first troops to enter the town the night before were mobbed with kisses and had wine and what little else the people had to eat or drink pressed into their hands. And, although fighting was still going on all over the city, huge crowds turned out to welcome de Gaulle.

"Gripped with emotion and filled with serenity"[11] he drove through Longjumeau, passed Cour-la-Reine, and on to the Porte d'Orléans, beyond which the avenue was black with people. Their cheers drowned the shots which had split the silence before de Gaulle's little caravan arrived. But emotion never dulled de Gaulle's brain. The manner of his entry had supreme political significance. He had been asked by Luizet, and the crowd expected him, to go to the Hôtel de Ville to meet the National Committee of Resistance and the Paris Committee of Liberation. He had already sent a message that this was not his intention. At the Avenue de Maine, therefore, his car suddenly forked left into streets which were practically deserted and a little before four o'clock in the afternoon he arrived at the Gare Montparnasse to keep his rendezvous with Leclerc. There he learned of von Choltitz's surrender and had the pleasure of seeing his son, Philippe, with a German Major by his side, leave the station in the marine tank in which he had fought his way into the city to receive the garrison's capitulation.

Both Leclerc and Rol-Tanguy were at the station of Montparnasse, and, having congratulated them warmly on their achievements, de Gaulle then read the text of the surrender. To his surprise he found that Rol-Tanguy's name was included with Leclerc's as one to whom the surrender had been made. He at once reproached Leclerc for allowing a resistance leader to assume such a standing and became even more determined to show Tanguy and his colleagues their place. Without hurrying, therefore, de Gaulle went from Montparnasse to the centre of government in war, that same Ministry of Defence which he had briefly occupied as Under Secretary of State four years before.

"I was immediately struck," he wrote in his memoirs, "by the impression that nothing had changed inside these venerable halls. Gigantic events had overturned the world. Our army was annihilated. France had virtually collapsed. But at the Ministry of War the look of things remained immutable. In the courtyard, a unit of the *Garde Républicaine* presented arms as in the past. The vestibule, the staircase, the arms hanging on the walls—all as they had been. Here, in person, were the same stewards and ushers. I entered the Minister's Office which Monsieur Paul Reynaud and I had left together on the night of June 10, 1940. Not a piece of furniture, not a rug, not a curtain had been disturbed. On the desk, the telephone was in the same place, and exactly the same names on the call buttons. Soon I was to learn that this was the case in all the other buildings in which the Republic housed itself. Nothing was missing except the State. It was my duty to restore it: I installed my staff at once and got down to work."[12]

First Parodi came to make his report and de Gaulle learned of the annoyance of the Committee of National Resistance and the Paris Committee of Liberation that he had not made the Hôtel de Ville his first port of call. He was quite unmoved and went on to reproach Parodi for allowing the Committee of National Resistance to make a proclamation the night before in which it claimed to speak for "the French nation." Parodi, knowing the resentment it would cause if de Gaulle refused to go to the Hôtel de Ville, tried to persuade him. De Gaulle remained adamant and said that, if he was to meet the resistance leaders at all, it should be in a government office. Only after Luizet had been called in and reinforced Parodi's plea did he relent. Even then he was in no hurry. He told both men of his plans for a splendid parade the next day at which he would make his "official entry" and asked them to make the necessary arrangements. Then he announced that he would next visit the Prefecture, since the police were the symbol of authority and by their strike and subsequent action had not only begun but set the seal of authority on the insurrection. Luizet and Parodi followed meekly.

This was an act of deliberate provocation. Even Bidault, when he heard that de Gaulle was on his way to the Prefecture, angrily exclaimed that no one had ever kept him waiting for so long before. "This is where the people of Paris are," he cried, "not at the *Maison des Flics*."[13] (House of Cops.) One of his colleagues was heard to murmur: "Those sons of bitches have been arresting us for four years and now de Gaulle goes and pays tribute to them." But de Gaulle still took his time. He reviewed the police, spoke to them, thanked them for the example they had set and then, with their cheers ringing in his ears, walked slowly through the crowds with Parodi, Le Troquer, Juin and Luizet to the Hôtel de Ville. It was a tense moment. As he approached the building he saw Bidault waiting for him at the bottom of the great staircase. As they slowly walked up the steps resistance guards presented arms. Side by side they walked to the centre of the Great Salon where the resistance leaders had waited for so long to be greeted, according to de Gaulle, by a "salvo" of cheers.

The speeches of welcome were short and moving. De Gaulle replied with great eloquence, making no attempt to hide "the sacred emotion that grips all of us, men and women alike, in these moments that transcend each of our poor private lives."[14] He acknowledged that Paris had been liberated by her people with the help of the army and of all France; he paid tribute to the allied troops now advancing up the Rhône valley; but never once did he mention the resistance and its leaders. When Bidault excitedly drew a prepared proclamation from his pocket and cried out: "General! Here around you are the National Committee of Resistance and the Paris Committee of Liberation. Will you go out on to the balcony and formally proclaim the Republic assembled here?", de Gaulle looked down at him and coldly replied: "No. The Republic has never ceased to exist. I myself am President of the government of the Republic. Why should I proclaim it now?"[15]

But he went out on to the balcony and spoke to the people, presenting such a target for a sniper that his aide-de-camp, Captain Guy, held on to the belt of his Sam Browne to prevent him falling on to the crowd below if he was hit. The cheers that greeted him, the chanting in unison of "de Gaulle, de Gaulle, de Gaulle," that echoed across the Seine, were the answer to the men behind him. In the few hours he had been in Paris de Gaulle had proved that, in the eyes of the people, it was he and not the resistance who was the Saviour of France. That was why he had kept its leaders waiting, why he had refused to read their proclamation or to allow them any political role. He had demonstrated brutally that the leaders of the resistance were his servants not his sponsors. As he turned and walked back through the salon without waiting to drink the toast that had been prepared for him, a communist member of the Committee of National Resistance was heard to murmur: "It is simple. We have been had."[16]

Next day, August 26, set the seal on de Gaulle's triumph. Militarily the parade that de Gaulle had organised, a march from the Étoile to Notre Dame, was mad. German snipers were still scattered through the city, the German rearguard was in its eastern suburbs, reinforcements were pressing in from the north. The Luftwaffe had ninety bombers still on the airfield at Le Bourget ready to attack. It was known that Hitler had ordered them to do so in conjunction with all the V.1 and V.2 rockets that could be trained on Paris. Yet de Gaulle planned to bring a million people into the streets to watch a Victory March.

Once more his decision brought him into conflict with the allies. The German 47th Division, which Model had ordered to go to von Choltitz's aid, had reached Le Bourget and St. Denis. General Gerow ordered Leclerc to move his division out of Paris to bar their passage.

De Gaulle countermanded the order, upon which Gerow, through his liaison officer, Major Levey, sent Leclerc a message that if his division took part in the parade he would regard it as a formal breach of military discipline. Leclerc took Levey to de Gaulle, who had the grace to say that militarily Gerow was right. "But," he added, "I loaned you Leclerc, I can certainly borrow him back for a few moments. We must have this parade. It is going to give France political unity."[17]

So, at three in the afternoon of Saturday, August 26, de Gaulle stood under the Arc de Triomphe and relit the flame over the tomb of the unknown soldier. Before him in the Place d'Étoile, down the Champs-Élysées all the way to Notre Dame, Paris had assembled. Warned by the radio, the people had come on foot through the night and early morning, for there were neither buses nor metros. Except for a few photographers and reporters and one hospital unit, there were none but French men and women. A police car announced to the crowd that de Gaulle "was confiding his safety to the people of Paris." Then, preceded by four of Leclerc's tanks and followed one pace behind, as he requested, by the members of his government, the generals and resistance leaders in a haphazard group, de Gaulle began his walk down the Champs-Élysées.

A single flight of German aircraft could have turned triumph into disaster, but no aircraft came. Had the crowds stampeded, the police and resistance soldiers lining the route would have been powerless to hold them. But the crowd held its ranks while the lone tall figure passed and then fell in behind him, flowing down the great avenue in a solid mass. As he had planned it, de Gaulle was borne along by the people. In his memoirs de Gaulle has described how, as he passed each monument, the heroes of the past rose up before him. He saluted Clemenceau's statue, thought of Henri IV dying under an assassin's knife close to where he walked, pictured in his mind the Grand Monarch walking in front of the Louvre, saw Joan of Arc repulsed at the Porte St. Honoré by the city she had just restored to France. Yet even then de Gaulle did not allow the moment to carry him away. At one point on the march he noticed a small group of women in uniforms he did not recognise. He asked who they were. "The ambulance unit of Lady Spears," came the reply. Syria still rankled, and that evening Lady Spears and her unit were ordered out of France.[18]

In the Rue de Rivoli, beyond the Place de la Concorde, de Gaulle got into an open car to drive to Notre Dame. Although no one knew it at the time, a German sniper held him in the sights of his sub-machine gun as he entered the cathedral square, but refrained from firing because he had no means of escape and knew that the crowd would lynch him. Nevertheless, as de Gaulle got out of the car, shots rang out. Apparently three men were firing from one of the towers of Notre Dame. They were answered at once, first by the police, then by the men of the resistance until everyone with a gun seemed to be shooting. De Gaulle, missing the whine of the bullets, realised that even from the towers the men were firing into the air. He concluded at once that those doing the shooting were communist members of the resistance who wanted to create pandemonium and prevent the service from taking place. The crowd began to panic. Without showing the least concern de Gaulle got out of the car and walked slowly to the cathedral. Watching him the crowd rallied. As he walked up the aisle shots rang out from the roof of the nave. De Gaulle never hesitated but, with Parodi and Le Troquer behind him, advanced towards the altar to be received by the priests while the congregation ducked below their seats. After de Gaulle had reached his place of honour at the head of the nave, General Koenig, standing behind him, looked back down the rows of apparently empty chairs and shouted, "Have you no pride, stand up."[19] The choir then broke into the Magnificat and de Gaulle, prayer book in hand, loudly led the responses. But the shooting went on and several people were hurt, more by splinters than by bullets. Therefore, when the singing was over, de Gaulle abbreviated the ceremony and slowly walked back down the aisle and out to his car. Even his enemies now knew that spiritually de Gaulle was master of France.

CHAPTER XVI

POWER & GLORY

Although Paris had acclaimed him, de Gaulle's authority hung by a thread. Neither Britain nor America had formally recognised him as head of a provisional government. Officially he was only paying France a visit and, at the slightest sign that his authority was being resisted, his enemies in Washington and London would demand his recall. The agreement with Eisenhower under which General Koenig was organising French co-operation in the field had not been signed and it was still open to the Supreme Commander to change his mind. In France, the National Committee of Resistance, smarting under the treatment it had received the day before, was still demanding that the Charter it had proclaimed be acknowledged as the basis of de Gaulle's policy, that a national palace be put at its disposal, that C.O.M.A.C., its para-military command, be recognised as the authority over the French Forces of the Interior and the Committee itself become a permanent body exercising authority alongside de Gaulle. Unless de Gaulle could show that he had more Allied support than had been officially granted there was still a danger that a rival authority, stemming from the resistance, would be set up in Paris and in those parts of western and southern France which were in the process of liberating themselves. If that happened de Gaulle could assert his authority only by waging civil war. The Allies would step in and all that he had struggled for would be lost.

But now de Gaulle had a piece of luck. Surprising though it may seem, the Supreme Commander had not been informed of the row between Leclerc and Gerow or of Saturday's triumphal march, and had spent the day trying to locate de Gaulle to congratulate him on the liberation of the city. On Sunday he visited de Gaulle at the Ministry of War. It was a deliberate gesture of support. What mattered to Eisenhower was that Paris should be secure behind his front line and he believed that de Gaulle alone could assure this. He came to pay his respects and to tell de Gaulle that he himself proposed to set up his headquarters in Versailles, a choice which de Gaulle approved.

De Gaulle at once saw the importance of the visit and took advantage of it. The shooting at Notre Dame had alarmed him, not for his personal safety, but as a sign that the communists of the French Forces of the Interior might want to continue the insurrection in the hope of dislodging him and gaining power. On his instructions General Koenig had already obtained a large supply of American small arms for the Paris police. He now told Eisenhower that for security he felt impelled to keep Leclerc's 2nd Armoured Division in and around the city and asked him further to lend him temporarily two American divisions "to use as a show of force and to establish his position firmly . . ."[1] Eisenhower had no divisions to spare but, two days later, arranged that the American 28th Infantry Division should march in full battle array through the streets of Paris on its way to the front. De Gaulle took the salute. Although de Gaulle does not even mention the American parade in his memoirs its importance at the time cannot be exaggerated. In the eyes of Parisians de Gaulle was now the equal of Eisenhower.

Next morning de Gaulle struck at the resistance. He summoned the leaders of the Paris Liberation Committee and the members of the Committee of National Resistance to the Ministry of War and, having warmly congratulated them on their part in liberating the capital, told them bluntly that their role was over. Some members of the council, he said, might be included in his government and the council itself would be incorporated in an enlarged Consultative Assembly as soon as that body arrived from Algiers. The resistance forces would be either incorporated into the regular army or dissolved. He did not add that he had already received a promise from Eisenhower of several thousand Allied uniforms to make the assimilation of the French forces easier. There were expressions of dissent on many faces but no voice was raised. Under the arc-light of de Gaulle's authority the claims of the National Council of Resistance evaporated and its leaders dispersed. Only Bidault was to be invited to accept a government post.

De Gaulle now had to assert his authority in those areas of France which had liberated themselves. In many ways this was more difficult. The whole of the huge quadrilateral from the Pyrenees to the Loire and the Atlantic to the river Rhône was in the hands of the resistance with the exception of a few German garrisons in some of the Atlantic ports. In almost every town and Prefecture resistance committees had taken charge of the local administration. Communications were almost non-existent. Each resistance group, therefore, was able to operate without interference.

The French communist party had foreseen this and planned to take advantage of it to bring about a national revolution. They had quickly taken control of all radio stations in the south and, wherever possible the distribution of food. A secret instruction to the *Francs Tireurs Partisans*, the shock troops of the resistance on whom the communists were relying, which fell into the hands of some French regular officers, disclosed that once the communists had gained control over Limoges and Toulouse they intended to proclaim the Republic of the Soviets of the South of France.

Against this organised attempt at revolution de Gaulle could only rely on the non-communist elements of the resistance and the slender authority of the *Commissaires de la République* who had been able to make their way into the area in his name. And yet within a few weeks de Gaulle's authority had been asserted everywhere and within a few months the danger of a communist uprising averted. This remarkable success was due partly to quarrels within the communist party itself but mainly to de Gaulle's own firmness and the magic of his name.

The executive committee of the communist party was divided. Two of its four members, Le Coeur and Tillon, both resistance fighters, wanted to use the *Francs Tireurs* as the spearhead of the armed revolution and make an immediate bid for power. The other two, Duclos and Frachon, more orthodox politicians, believed in continuing the war in obedience to Moscow and infiltrating the administration at the same time. De Gaulle at once exploited this division. In the government of "National Unanimity" he formed on September 9 he invited François Billoux, a communist trade unionist, to become Minister of Health, and Tillon himself to become Minister for Air. Both accepted and other communists were appointed to high administrative positions. From that moment onwards many members of the party felt that it was already taking part in the work of national reconstruction and that loyalty to de Gaulle had become a duty. The revolution, therefore, was only half-heartedly carried out. The *Francs Tireurs* themselves had divided loyalties. Some pursued revolution, others were more interested in fighting the Germans still holding out in the Atlantic ports. On the other hand many of de Gaulle's supporters in the resistance were energetic and able men who beat the communists in the race for the control of the areas in which they had been operating. De Gaulle's name alone was often enough to thwart men to whom lawlessness had become second nature.

In the middle of September de Gaulle himself began a series of trips through the country which were to last on and off for two months. In the north and as far south as Lyons, where the French or Allied Armies had passed, all was comparatively orderly. In Toulouse his Commissioner, Bertaux, although in office, was finding difficulty in controlling "something like a Soviet" under a communist known as Ravanel. An English agent known as "Colonel Hilary" who commanded 700 men and claimed to rule the area in the name of de Gaulle and of the British Government, and a force of some 6,000 Spanish Republicans who had fought gallantly against the Germans and now wanted either to support a communist government or to mount an expedition against Barcelona, also contested Bertaux's authority. When de Gaulle reached Toulouse he at once reviewed all the resistance fighters, to whatever faction they belonged, praised them for the way they had fought and then gave them orders. Although "Colonel Hilary" had fought valiantly under de Gaulle's banner for two years, de Gaulle refused to attend an official lunch to which the Colonel had been invited and, after a stormy interview, ordered him to leave France within twenty-four hours. He addressed the self-styled "Colonel Ravanel" by his real name, "Second Lieutenant Asher" and posted him to a regular unit. To the Spaniards he offered mobilisation in the French forces, dissolution or arrest. Toulouse was pacified.

At Bordeaux, where the Germans were still occupying the north bank of the river, he addressed a huge meeting from the same balcony from which Gambetta had spoken in 1870. He then drove round the city which he had not seen since his escape in 1940 and met the resistance leaders. To those who seemed hostile he offered the alternative of incorporation into the regular forces or prison. They chose the former. Only in Marseilles did he feel real anxiety. Raymond Aubrac, his commissioner, had communist sympathies himself and was unequal to an almost impossible task. The communists were virtually in control. Nevertheless de Gaulle adopted the same tactics. Reviewing the resistance forces, offering them the alternative of the army or dissolution and, this time backing his offer by sending a regiment from Algiers to garrison the city, he quelled the *Commune*. By the beginning of November, when de Gaulle finally returned to Paris, there was no longer any question of another authority than his being established in any quarter of liberated France.

Back in Paris de Gaulle found a new and important ally. In March, 1940, Maurice Thorez, then secretary general of the French communist party, deserted from the French Army and made his way to Moscow. After the Stalin-Hitler pact and under his leadership the French communists openly denounced the "Imperialist" war and did all they could to undermine the army's already shaky morale. Many were arrested. Thorez thought he could serve the party better by escaping and leading it in exile from Moscow. As a result he had been condemned to death for desertion. Now, in November, 1944, de Gaulle decided to take a gamble. He sensed that Stalin was more interested in finishing the war than in fomenting revolution in France and he believed that Thorez would be obedient to Moscow. He, therefore, granted Thorez an amnesty and invited him to return to Paris. De Gaulle was amply rewarded.

Thorez arrived back in France that same month and on November 30 made a speech in Paris in which he not only proclaimed that for the moment the war was all that mattered but called upon all Frenchmen to unite, to create a powerful French Army, work hard and recreate French industry.[2] At the meeting of the Central Committee of the Communist Party in January Thorez went even further and approved the disbanding of the "Patriotic Militia," which the communists had been busily recruiting as a more reliable spearhead than the *Francs Tireurs*, and which de Gaulle had banned in October. There was no need for Stalin to urge de Gaulle, when he received him in Moscow in December, not to put Thorez in prison. His very orthodoxy made him de Gaulle's surest ally.

But although de Gaulle had established his authority in the towns and the prefectures he had still to restore order. For, in the first few weeks of liberation, the fires of retribution burned fiercely throughout France. The collapse of the Vichy régime after the allied landing in North Africa, and the subsequent extension of the German occupation over the whole country, had produced a state of suppressed civil war. The Germans bled France not only for food and the necessities of life but of man power. Nearly one and a half million French soldiers were kept in the Reich throughout the war and to these were later added two hundred thousand civilians deported as forced labour by Laval's government. Some 43,000 died in concentration camps or as the result of captivity. In France itself reprisals became more ruthless as resistance increased. The very nature of the civil war prevented any exact records being kept, but it is estimated that 24,000 men and women died fighting in the resistance and between 30,000 and 40,000 were killed by the Germans and French Nazis.

The horrors followed the usual pattern. The inhabitants of whole villages were massacred and the village burned over their bodies. The entire population lived in fear of the knock on the door and thousands of individuals simply disappeared. Towards the end of the war German reprisals were not only brutal but capricious. For example, when a German armoured vehicle blew a tyre in a street, the crew went into the nearest café, hauled out five men and shot them on the spot. In Paris alone there were twelve official torture chambers equipped with everything from the most modern electrical devices to the medieval ordeal of the bath. When one mass grave was disinterred every corpse was found without finger or toe-nails. And since a minority of Frenchmen believed in the German cause, collaborators had helped promote this terror in every walk of life. Ministers, government officials, police and the young men who had joined Darnand's militia to stamp out the resistance, had all denounced or hunted down their fellow countrymen.

Those who accuse de Gaulle of having inflicted upon France the worst massacre in her history forget what had gone on before he ever returned to French soil. Of course, it is true that by condemning the armistice and dubbing all those who supported Vichy as traitors he intensified hatred between Frenchmen; but this attitude was fundamental to the whole Gaullist movement. It is also true that retribution was planned and advertised. Lists of those who had been guilty of persecuting Frenchmen and of the most flagrant collaborators were drawn up by the resistance and forwarded to North Africa. Pucheu's execution in 1944 was hailed as an example to all other prominent Vichyites by the Fighting French Radio in both London and Algiers. "Look out, we have got your names," intoned the Fighting French commentators, and their threats were sometimes followed by a recording of the song *"Collaborateur, mon p'tit homme."*[3] But de Gaulle had already shown in North Africa that he intended only to make an example of the most prominent and ardent of collaborators. The explosion of vengeance which occurred when the German troops began to withdraw from France was not of his making.

Once armed men realised that they were suddenly and unbelievably free, they took the law into their own hands. The worst traitors, and in particular Darnand's militia, were hunted down and killed. Some were tortured. Hundreds of thousands of men and women were arrested on the unverified word of individuals. Most were released within a short time. The houses of the pro-German profiteers were looted. Women who had fraternised with the Germans had their heads shaved and their bodies daubed with tar and were paraded through the streets. Every kind of private score was paid off.

It was vital for de Gaulle to bring this lawlessness to an end. The Allies would not be slow to step in if disorder threatened communications nor the communists hesitate to assert their own form of control if he failed. While he was touring the country the emergency courts which had been decreed in Algiers began to sit. Those for minor offences were composed of two assessors chosen by the local liberation committees sitting beside a judge. Fear of intimidation or reprisal prevented many witnesses from coming forward and sometimes local resistance groups interfered directly in the proceedings or raided the prisons in an attempt to lynch the prisoners. The police, who had so often been the tools of Vichy, had been weakened by desertion or dismissal and were not always able to keep control. Sometimes they themselves were the targets of the resistance fighters. But gradually the sense of law was restored. In June, ten months after liberation, Adrien Tixier informed the Minister of Justice that the police were still having difficulty "in face of a popular and spontaneous movement of revenge."[4] But by the end of 1945 summary executions had ceased and although the purge continued intermittently in the courts until a general amnesty was proclaimed eleven years later, it had lost its savagery. Of the 2,071 people condemned to death by the court, de Gaulle personally pardoned 1,303, including all women. Thirty-nine thousand people were sentenced to imprisonment for "national unworthiness" which meant the loss of the right to vote, exclusion from public employment and, at its worst, exile. Eighteen thousand men and women were acquitted.

It is hard to distinguish between justice and terror at the Liberation. Since 1945 there have been no less than fourteen debates on the subject in the National Assembly and several investigations, official and unofficial, have been held to try and establish the facts. But it was in the interests of departmental officials to refuse information and no one will ever know the whole truth. When the official figures of those executed summarily and by the courts was given in answer to a parliamentary question put by Maître Isorni, Pétain's defence counsel in 1951, they were so low that Debré, one of de Gaulle's *Commissaires* at the time, described them as absurd. He added that a greater number had died in the departments of south-west France alone. Robert Aron, himself a member of the resistance, carried out an investigation of his own and put the number of summary executions after liberation at between thirty and forty thousand. On the other hand Adrien Tixier, Minister of the Interior at the time, told Colonel Dewavrin that 105,000 people had died in the purge. One of the most faithful members of de Gaulle's staff told the author of this book that he accepted that figure. All that one can say with certainty is that, as a result of German occupation, the Vichy oppression and the liberation, more Frenchmen were killed by Frenchmen than at any other time in French history since the Hundred Years' War. Had it not been for de Gaulle's authority the slaughter at the liberation would certainly have been greater and anarchy might have developed into open civil war.

*   *   *

Among those condemned but reprieved, was Marshal Pétain. De Gaulle had hoped that Pétain would stay in Switzerland after his release from German captivity and privately let the Swiss Government know that he would be pleased if it did not exercise the right of extradition. But Pétain insisted on returning to France to stand his trial. He still considered himself Head of State until a new Assembly had elected his successor and intended to use the trial to render his account to the nation.

Judicially the trial was grotesque. The judge had served Vichy and himself been responsible for implementing many of the laws for which Pétain was now arraigned. The jury were members of the resistance, many of them communists. But since thousands of smaller Vichy fry were being prosecuted it was a political necessity that the chief actor should be brought to book.

From the start the trial had an air of unreality. When the President of the Court, Monsieur Montgibeaux, ordered the accused to be brought in, the Marshal, in khaki and wearing white gloves, appeared in the doorway and saluted. Instinctively the entire court rose to its feet and stood in silence while he took his seat. Pétain had disdainfully rejected the advice of his counsel to plead mental incapacity and prepared his statement with minute care. He did not recognise the court's jurisdiction but spoke from the court directly to the people of France. Although he was eighty-nine he delivered his speech standing and without spectacles. It was a short and dignified defence of his conduct. He had not sought power but had been begged to assume it. He had inherited a catastrophe for which he was not responsible. The armistice had saved France and thereafter everything he had done had been designed to shield his countrymen from the worst effects of defeat. "Let those who accuse me and pretend to judge me ask from the depths of their consciences what, perhaps, they would have done without me."

"While General de Gaulle pursued the struggle beyond our frontiers I prepared the way to liberation by preserving a France stricken but alive."

He ended with a plea. "If you wish to condemn me, let my condemnation be the last. Let no other Frenchmen be condemned or detained for having obeyed the orders of his lawful chief."[5]

Once he had delivered his statement Pétain refused to answer questions or give further evidence. He spoke only twice more during the trial which lasted many months, once to deny that he had approved the broadcast in which Laval said he hoped for a German victory, and once when the aged General Lannurien, blinded at Verdun, was testifying in his favour. "I wish to speak," he said rising to his feet, "just for once, to say that I am as nothing in the presence of General Lannurien." And he clasped the old man's hand as he went out.[6]

All the chief actors in the great drama of the Third Republic, Reynaud, Daladier, Blum, Herriot, Jeanneney, Lebrun and Weygand came to the tribune. Each tried to justify the part he had played and many showed up poorly under cross-examination, especially at the hands of Maître Isorni, Pétain's Junior Counsel. It was an unedifying scene and it did little good to France or the witnesses to rake over again the harrowing controversies which had led to capitulation. De Gaulle realised this and ordered the judge to bring the trial to an end.

De Gaulle, through his ministers, learned that the judge intended to recommend that the Marshal be banished for five years—a sentence that would have been a political disaster. But the jury, after many hours of deliberation, voted fourteen to thirteen in favour of the death penalty, with a recommendation to mercy to which de Gaulle acceded at once. After being confined for three months at Portarlier, Pétain was taken with his wife to the Île d'Yeu, an Atlantic island off the rocky coast of La Vendée.

De Gaulle was disappointed in the trial. He had hoped that the prosecution would fasten upon the surrender of 1940 as the cardinal crime; instead the Court had been far more interested in bringing to light the way the Vichy régime had oppressed French citizens. Of course the court was right. If there is any validity in political trials, other than as acts of vengeance, it lies in the crimes against humanity which rulers allow to be perpetrated in their names. At a distance of a quarter of a century it is possible to say that, until 1942, Pétain's régime served the cause of the Allies. Thereafter his case falls to the ground. Pétain had not only told Massigli—and presumably he told others— that he hoped the Germans would win the war, but by accepting the nazification of France under Laval's second government he condoned the torture and terrorisation of his own people. It was for that that he was condemned.

De Gaulle had despised the Nazis, whether German or French, but politically they mattered less to him than those Frenchmen who had agreed to surrender. The "legitimacy" of his own movement as well as the honour of France was bound up with the repudiation of the armistice. If the French government capitulated then Frenchmen could only continue the war as volunteers in other people's armies. France was dishonoured and could only receive back her freedom at the hands of the conquerors—a prostrate humiliated nation. Pétain's trial showed how few people understood de Gaulle's attitude or really shared his view.

As for the Marshal, de Gaulle in his own mind had long since excused him on the grounds of his age. It was as "a drama of senility" that he described the trial in his memoirs. De Gaulle has frequently been capable of magnanimity but for the hollow shell that was now the Marshal he scarcely had any feelings at all. The reprieve was as much a political necessity as the trial. But de Gaulle refused constant appeals to ameliorate the old man's imprisonment and when, six years later, Pétain died at the age of ninety-five, insisted that he be buried without honours on the Île d'Yeu. Nevertheless Pétain had the last word. "De Gaulle and I are quits," he said to Maître Isorni who was visiting him in prison, "we have each condemned the other to death."

No doubt one day, when de Gaulle is dead, Pétain's body will be taken from the cemetery on the Île d'Yeu and reburied at Douaumont on the battlefield of Verdun where he wished to lie. It will then be possible to say that the scars inflicted upon France by the war against Hitler have been finally healed.

*　　*　　*

While de Gaulle was establishing his authority and restoring order, he also waged war. It would have been easy, and many people inside and outside France thought it would have been right, to do so passively. The small French army was short of equipment and had been fighting hard for many months in Italy. It needed a rest. The North African troops in particular required a period in the sunshine to regain their morale. The wave of disorder and reprisal that was sweeping France would have been more quickly mastered if regular units had been available for garrison duties. The British and Americans, who were using every ton of shipping to keep their own forces supplied, were reluctant to divert precious tanks or armoured vehicles to enable French forces to stay in the front line. Both Eisenhower and the combined Chiefs of Staff felt that the French Army could contribute most to the Allied cause by keeping open lines of communication, main-

11. De Gaulle leaving Notre Dame after the service to commemorate the Liberation. Bullets were whistling overhead at the time. (*See page 246*)

12. De Gaulle with Field Marshal Montgomery

taining order and mopping up the isolated pockets of Germans still holding out on the Atlantic coast. From a military point of view they were right, but the merest hint of their views touched de Gaulle on the raw and made him accuse them of wishing to keep France in a subordinate position.

Now that he was leading France, de Gaulle's whole ethos demanded that the French Army play a spectacular part in what was left of the fighting. It did not matter to him that logistically the French contribution would be minimal, nor did he ever admit the element of sham in the "glory" he was seeking. He was obsessed with the idea that if French honour was to be retrieved, French troops, well or ill-equipped must be in the front line. He believed that in no other way could France regain her status as a world power. In spite of the exhaustion of the people and the misery in which they were living, he was determined to enlarge both the size and role of the army.

On September 12, de Lattre de Tassigny's 1st Army, having advanced seven hundred kilometres in three weeks up the Rhône valley with the Americans, joined forces with Leclerc's division which de Gaulle had released from Paris a week before. All seven regular divisions were now in eastern France facing the enemy. However, many units needed relieving. To replace them de Gaulle proceeded to incorporate volunteers from the resistance forces, which were then estimated at four hundred thousand men. Not all were genuine "Resisters" but that no longer mattered. Two hundred thousand were kept in central and southern France for training and for formation into new divisions; a few more thousand were allocated to the *Gendarmerie* and *Garde Mobile*; forty thousand were transferred to the navy and air force and a hundred thousand sent to de Lattre. This "huge inchoate group"[7] comprised the young adventurers of France. Having been given arms they at least wanted action. It was a feat on the part of the Generals Chavance-Bertin and Schneider to have mobilised them in their local strongholds and then led so many of them, without incident, across south and central France to join the 1st Army.

But it was one thing to mobilise men and quite another to equip them. In his memoirs de Gaulle says that, from the day of the landing in Normandy to the German capitulation, the Allies failed to re-equip a single French division. This is inaccurate. During the last few months of the war the British rearmed the equivalent of three new French divisions and Churchill, at last shaking himself free of Roosevelt's tutelage, vigorously supported de Gaulle's attempt to re-establish France's position in Europe. It is true, however, that Allied commanders in the field gave French rearmament a low priority. They felt, with justification, that it would take time to mould raw resistance levies into regular soldiers and that meanwhile the limited supplies would best be used by Anglo-American forces. The French commanders, therefore, had to do the best they could with the equipment they had brought from North Africa and with arms captured from the Germans. They also managed to "adopt"—to use de Gaulle's phrase— a great deal more from Allied arms depots than the allies meant them to have. By the end of the war de Gaulle was able to put fifteen divisions in the line—in manpower roughly a quarter of the whole Allied force in France and Flanders.

De Gaulle did not create his army to help the Allies but to re-assert the prestige of France. This brought him once more into conflict with his Allies. In September, Eisenhower had told de Gaulle that he intended to incorporate the French 1st Army with the American 7th under General Devers to form the Southern Army Group under General Patch. The French were to be on the right wing covering the front from the Swiss frontier to Colmar. De Gaulle accepted the plan because he felt it right that the French, like the other Allies, should have their own zone of operation. Eisenhower refrained from telling de Gaulle that he did not intend the French to cross the Rhine except in the rear of the Americans; de Gaulle did not tell Eisenhower that he was determined that his troops should be among the first to do so.

The battle was much harder than most Frenchmen anticipated. Eisenhower rejected Montgomery's appeal for a concentrated drive in the north to take the Ruhr and in September launched an offensive along his whole front which he hoped would carry the Allies across the Rhine. Within a month his armies had been stopped everywhere by the Germans. Only the French had actually reached the river to the east of Mulhouse. Elsewhere they too had been halted. Leclerc had taken Strasbourg on November 23, but the Germans still held Colmar and neither there nor farther south could de Lattre or Béthouart make any progress.

It was not only the Germans that held them back. The French equipment was inferior, the winter was hard and there were not nearly enough reserves to give the troops the rest they needed. Resistance officers, confirmed in their ranks, were often unfitted for the commands they now had to undertake. The N.C.O.s lacked training. When de Gaulle visited the army in mid-December, he found a real crisis in morale. Both Generals de Lattre and Béthouart told him that, with things as they were, they could no longer attack the Germans. The troops had fought well but were discouraged by lack of support from the French people. The newspapers scarcely mentioned the fighting and were far more interested in the trials of collaborators or the shortage of food. Public opinion seemed to feel that the part being played by the French Army was so insignificant that it could be ignored.

Another man than de Gaulle might have taken this collapse of morale as a warning that France was neither morally nor materially equipped to support his policy of "grandeur." The truth was that the French people had assumed that peace had come with liberation. The presence of allied armies seemed to confirm their hopes. The spectacle of American military might with its vast supply services and abundance of everything which the French had been denied for so long, was intoxicating. The British in the north were scarcely less well-endowed. Plainly nothing could resist such armies and the French rightly deduced that the war was as good as won. What need, therefore, for them to take up arms or to worry about any enemy except the one at home?

De Gaulle was incapable of acquiescing in such a mood. It was only through ordeal by battle that France could obtain absolution. Instead of accepting a more humble role, as his generals advocated, he at once sought to extend their operations. He approved de Lattre's appeal to the Americans for reinforcements to take Colmar, and himself drafted in a half-hearted division from the resistance and ten thousand young men training in the military depots. On his return to Paris he called together the editors of the newspapers and asked for their support. He received only lukewarm replies, the editors pointing out that they had to establish their circulations and that their readers were not greatly interested in a war which they considered already won.

But Colmar was soon to be of secondary importance. While de Gaulle had been visiting the troops the Germans had launched their surprise offensive on the Ardennes, and by Christmas Day had nearly reached the Meuse. Eisenhower's thinly-held line seemed on the point of being broken and Hitler's goal, the recapture of Antwerp and Brussels, of being attained. To prevent a breakthrough, Eisenhower ordered the evacuation of Alsace. As de Gaulle at once admitted, militarily the retreat was justifiable; but for France there were other considerations. Alsace-Lorraine had been the shuttle-cock of Franco-German enmities since Bismarck had annexed them in 1871. Under Hitler the two provinces became once more Elsas and Lothringen and were incorporated into the Reich. Young Alsatians and Lorrainers were mobilised into the German Army and the full rigours of Nazi rule were imposed upon the population. If these unfortunate people were once more abandoned by the Allies not only would many of them be subjected to savage reprisals but their faith in France would be shattered. De Gaulle feared that his government might fall.

On his own initiative, therefore, de Gaulle countermanded the orders of General Devers, the American under whom de Lattre was serving, and instructed the French Army to hold Strasbourg at all costs. He then went to see Eisenhower at Versailles and, supported by Churchill who had come over specially from London, managed to persuade the Supreme Commander to modify his order. Although the Germans crossed the Rhine north and south of the city, Strasbourg was held. Shortage of fuel and a remarkable recovery by the Americans brought the German advance to a halt. By the end of January all the ground lost had been recovered and the French were able to take the offensive. By the middle of February Colmar had been taken and the whole of Alsace cleared.

De Gaulle's defiance over the defence of Strasbourg had been justified by success and the citizens of Alsace had given him a rapturous welcome when the battle was over. His next essays in search of glory had no military justification whatever, and were unquestionably in breach of the agreements he had signed with the Allies. "I wanted our army to enter enemy territories, to have its own sector of operations there, to conquer cities, land and trophies and to receive the surrender of the vanquished. This was, of course, a condition dictated by concern for our prestige," he wrote in his memoirs.[8] And for the sake of this prestige he was prepared, this time without the agreement of Eisenhower, to order his Generals to disobey their superior commanders and disrupt Allied strategy.

"Operation Eclipse," as the final plan for the crossing of the Rhine and the Allied advance into Germany was called, gave the French Army a supporting role only. De Lattre's troops were to cross the Rhine after the American 7th Army and help in the occupation of Württemberg. This meant that the French would penetrate Germany at the most as far as Karlsruhe—a distance of about sixty miles.

On March 4, de Gaulle summoned de Lattre to Paris and told him that at all costs the French Army must make an independent crossing of the Rhine and push on as far and as fast into Germany as they could. He knew that this meant crossing General Devers's line of advance but he ordered de Lattre to refer all American objections directly to him. De Lattre had established excellent relations with his American colleagues and, as a professional soldier, was embarrassed by being forced to disobey orders. But at de Gaulle's insistence he gave way. He pointed out, however, that his army stood opposite the steepest part of the Black Forest and one of the strongest sectors of the Siegfried Line.

He suggested, therefore, that he try and extend his line northwards to Speyer and, using the city as a base, drive to the north of the Black Forest towards Pforzheim and Stuttgart. De Gaulle agreed.

Before the main offensive began the Saar salient had to be reduced. Since this was too heavily defended, General Devers was glad of de Lattre's offer to take part in the battle and the French were able to penetrate German territory for the first time, force the Siegfried Line north of Lauterburg and reach Leimersheim. They were now close to Speyer. Since the American Army was to cross the Rhine at Worms and had no use for Speyer, neither Eisenhower nor Devers needed a great deal of persuasion in allowing de Lattre to extend his line a little farther north and include the city. The Allied command had already withdrawn the bridge crews from the French sector and had no reason to believe that the French intended, or would be able, to cross the river except in the rear of the 7th Army.

But de Gaulle had foreseen this. A motley collection of boats and bridging material for a ten-ton "pontoon" had been assembled already. As the British and Americans crossed the river farther north in the last days of March, de Gaulle sent de Lattre a telegram saying: "My dear General. You must cross the Rhine even if the Americans do not help you and you are obliged to use boats . . . Karlsruhe and Stuttgart expect, even if they do not desire you . . ."[9]

Accordingly on March 30, de Lattre's troops began to cross the river. Next day the bridge at Speyer was opened and, by April 4, one hundred and twenty thousand French troops were on the right bank of the Rhine. Since this fact could no longer be hidden, de Gaulle proclaimed in Paris that the French Army would conquer enough of Germany to assert itself in the decisions that would be taken by the allies about the fate of the defeated enemy. On April 7 he entered Karlsruhe in triumph.

By now the Allied command had become aware of what was happening and General Devers warned de Lattre against "a premature advance." It was the American 7th Army that was to take Stuttgart and go on down to the Swiss frontier; the French were to clean up the Black Forest. Once again de Gaulle countermanded the American orders and on April 15 instructed de Lattre to turn north and take Stuttgart, the capital of Württemberg, as they had planned. De Lattre turned north and on April 20 occupied the city. In his own account of what followed de Gaulle is disingenuous. He admits that General Devers told de Lattre that Stuttgart was vital to the 7th Army as a centre of communications, and that he ordered de Lattre to evacuate it. But de Gaulle implies that although the French allowed the Americans to pass through the city, they stayed in occupation. What in fact happened was that the new President of the United States sent a sharply worded note of protest to the French Government and, when de Gaulle refused to withdraw, announced that all supplies to the French Army would cease forthwith. The French Army then pulled out of the city, leaving behind a small garrison and a military governor. In this Eisenhower acquiesced, but he informed de Gaulle that in his view the French had broken the undertakings by which their army was receiving supplies. De Gaulle brushed aside the protest. All German resistance had now ceased and, having cleaned up the Black Forest, the French pushed on into Austria until on May 6, the *Tricolore* flew over the Arlberg Pass. They had taken more than a hundred thousand prisoners. For the moment honour was satisfied.

However, de Gaulle had more blows to strike for French prestige before the fighting subsided. As he had withdrawn his troops from the Italian theatre in order to take part in the invasion of Southern France, de Gaulle was not represented on the staff of General Alexander. He had not, therefore, been consulted about the arrangements for the military government of Italy. Nevertheless, Mussolini's cowardly attack on the French in 1940 and the subsequent Italian occupation of Nice had incurred de Gaulle's deep resentment and he determined to be revenged. A few formerly Savoyard Cantons on the Italian side of the Alps had partly French-speaking inhabitants and these de Gaulle decided to annexe. After driving the Germans out of the foothills of the Alps, General Doyen's troops had, therefore, crossed the Alps into northern Italy, occupied the Cantons and advanced down the Val d'Aosta as far as Ivrea to the east of Turin.

When the Germans in Italy surrendered, General Alexander asked the French to withdraw and allow military government to establish itself. On de Gaulle's instructions General Doyen not only refused to move, but intimated that he would resist if any attempt was made to force him to do so. Having already strained relations with the Americans almost to breaking point by his advance into Germany, such provocation in an area where de Gaulle could not hope to establish himself was almost incomprehensible. Glory had gone to his head. Churchill, who had supported him so stoutly over Strasbourg, was indignant and cabled to Truman that de Gaulle was "an enemy of the Allies." Truman once more bluntly told de Gaulle that, unless he complied with the Allied demands, supplies to his troops would be cut off. Alexander made it plain that if necessary he would evict the French by force. De Gaulle climbed down. General Doyen and his troops were ordered to withdraw. Later, at the Italian Peace Treaty, Count Sforza, the

Italian Prime Minister, willingly conceded the Cantons to France—a gesture he would almost certainly have made whether de Gaulle's troops had entered the Val d'Aosta or not.

Undaunted, de Gaulle courted one further rebuff, this time in Syria. Although a wide degree of self government had been granted to the Syrians after Helleu's disastrous intervention in November, 1943, French troops were still in occupation and no new treaty had been concluded with France guaranteeing Syrian independence. As the war in Europe drew to a close, the Syrians began agitating for the command of their own levies and the removal of all foreign troops. Choukri Kouatly, the Syrian President, had been unwilling to re-open negotiations with France, not wishing to grant her any special privileges after the way he and his ministers had been treated. But Churchill, who wished to see France's special relationship with Syria put on the same basis as the British with Iraq, called on Kouatly on his way back from Yalta in February, 1945, and over-persuaded him. However, instead of negotiating, de Gaulle chose this moment to reinforce French troops in the Levant. It was a provocative and futile gesture because, on de Gaulle's own admission, the French had enough troops to maintain order if the Syrian Levies remained loyal and not enough, even with reinforcements, if they did not. The British, who had a large army in Syria and Palestine, sensed trouble and asked de Gaulle to divert his troopships. De Gaulle refused. On May 17 the small French detachment landed.

At once the Syrians rebelled and for the next fortnight pitched battles were fought in the chief cities between French troops and Syrian insurgents. In Damascus, where the main public buildings were shelled and bombed by the French, the Syrians suffered two thousand casualities in two days. The Syrians appealed to the British to intervene and, on May 30, Churchill summoned Massigli, the French Ambassador in London, and told him that unless the French Government ordered a Cease Fire at once, British troops would go into action. De Gaulle, who had been informed by General Beynet, his commander in Syria, that the French had the situation under control, ordered a Cease Fire that night.

But the situation had become too inflamed for the British to trust the French to deal with it alone any longer. Next day Eden told the House of Commons that Sir Bernard Paget, the Commander in Chief in the Middle East, had been instructed to restore order and that French troops in Syria were to be confined to barracks. By design or mistake this announcement was made an hour before it was com-municated to de Gaulle. De Gaulle at once issued a statement from

Paris protesting that the British action was unwarranted and at a Press Conference on June 2 tried to convince the world that the whole affair was instigated by the British whose one desire was to drive the French from the Levant and establish a monopoly of power in the Middle East. But, as he himself later admitted, not even his own countrymen were convinced. He was forced to give way and within a few days British troops occupied Damascus and the other chief cities. The French troops withdrew to their barracks. Thereafter an uneasy peace was maintained until, in 1946, both Syria and the Lebanon obtained full independence.

Before then, however, de Gaulle's pursuit of glory had come to an unexpected end.

CHAPTER XVII

THE DIZZY HEIGHTS

When the Germans surrendered in Europe in May, 1945, de Gaulle stood at the very pinnacle of power. He was the undisputed leader of a French Government which, although it had not been elected and consisted only of his nominees, had won recognition from the entire world. He spoke on terms of equality with the statesmen at the summit. He was head of a great empire to which only Indo-China remained to be restored. The French Armies stretched out across Germany into Austria. The French people looked to him as the saviour of their country. Yet within less than a year he had stepped down from the heights and surrendered his position. How did it happen, and why?

De Gaulle in power had three ambitions: to redeem the honour of France, to set his country on the road to recovery and to give it a constitution which would enable him to lead it firmly into the post-war world. He succeeded beyond all reasonable expectation in achieving the first two, but failed in the third; yet it was partly the nature of his successes which made his failure so decisive. For as de Gaulle struggled to assert the grandeur of France, as he constructed the long-term framework of rehabilitation, he became more and more isolated from the French people. His vision and their experience were so far apart that, in the end, they would no longer follow him.

De Gaulle's isolation began the moment he launched the French Army so spectacularly into the fighting. He could justly claim that his stand for Strasbourg had saved Alsace and that the eruption of the French Army into defeated Germany had enabled him to demand a larger zone of occupation. But to a population living near or below the bread line such gains seemed derisory compared with the risk of alienating allies who had just liberated and were now feeding France. The re-equipment of the French Army and the fighting itself cost almost as much as the German occupation. The French press was accurately reflecting public opinion when it suggested the money would be better spent on rebuilding the country. Politicians, beginning to reform their parties and take the pulse of opinion, soon found the adulation of the days of liberation giving way to doubt. In particular, de Gaulle's behaviour over Syria struck even his supporters as inept. De Gaulle might speak darkly of Churchill having spoilt "perhaps for ever" the foundation of the alliance, but neither the Consultative Assembly, nor the press, nor many of de Gaulle's highest officials agreed with him. To thinking Frenchmen it was not Churchill but de Gaulle who was endangering the alliance, for it had already become clear that his military adventures were unnecessary.

By the time the war in Europe was over France had already been restored to her position among the world's leading nations, not because of her leader's military pretensions but because, geographically and politically, she was vital to the reconstruction of Europe. Knowing how anxious the people of the United States would be to bring their troops home once the fighting was over, Churchill foresaw the possibility that Britain might be left to bear the main burden of policing Germany and confronting the Russian Army stretched across Europe. The larger the part that France could play in containing Germany the better for Britain. Churchill's dislike of de Gaulle was tempered by these considerations. Once it was clear that de Gaulle was in undisputed control of France, Churchill made every effort to strengthen his internal position.

The real turning point in the political rehabilitation of France had come as far back as October, 1944. Towards the end of that month Eisenhower had agreed that the zones of France which were free of military operations should be handed over to de Gaulle's administration. In fact the "handover" was a formality. De Gaulle already administered three-quarters of France and from then onwards the whole of the country south of the Seine was declared a "Zone of the Interior" subject to French authority with the sole proviso that the French Government guaranteed Allied lines of communication. The message in which Eisenhower informed President Roosevelt of this arrangement contained a strong plea for recognition of de Gaulle's National Committee as the provisional government of France. But although the plea was backed by the whole of Roosevelt's Cabinet, including Leahy, the President still resisted. Then suddenly on October 23, as he was setting out for a speaking tour in preparation for the elections at which he was to stand for a fourth term, Roosevelt changed his mind. It was not that he felt differently towards de Gaulle; he simply bowed to American public opinion. This "very sharp turn" embarrassed Churchill, then in Moscow, because he feared that the Russians, who had withheld recognition only on Anglo-Saxon insistence, might be offended.[1] But the Russians shrugged their shoulders and all three Allied governments announced their recognition that same day.

From then onwards the status of France steadily improved. When Churchill and Eden paid a formal visit to France for the old Armistice Day celebrations on November 11—long before a single French soldier had set foot on German soil—they agreed that France should have a zone of occupation in Germany. The British next did their utmost to have France invited to the meeting of the Big Three to be held at Yalta in the Crimea in February. Both Roosevelt and Stalin refused but, when Yalta came, even de Gaulle was forced to admit that France had come well out of the conference. Although Stalin saw no reason why France should occupy a zone of Germany other than as an act of kindness, he confirmed the agreement. France was to be a member both of the Commission which was to determine the boundaries of the zones and of the Allied Control Commission of Germany. France was also invited to become joint sponsor with the four "Great Powers" of the meeting in San Francisco at which the United Nations was to be launched. While the conference was sitting in Yalta, Jean Monnet, in Washington, concluded a lend-lease agreement under which France was to receive nearly three thousand million dollars' worth of equipment of all kinds in return for supplying American military needs on her soil.

De Gaulle refused to be a sponsor of the San Francisco Conference on the grounds that France should not underwrite what she had not helped to prepare. But when the conference met at the end of April, 1945, the French delegation under Bidault, the Foreign Minister, played a prominent part. France not only obtained a seat on the Security Council but ensured that French became one of the four official languages of the new world organisation. When the Germans surrendered in Europe, General François Sevez, the French Chief-of-Staff, stood beside Montgomery, Zukhov and Eisenhower in the small schoolroom in Rheims to witness the ceremony and countersign the document. Later in the year General Leclerc represented France at the surrender of Japan. Within nine months from the day of liberation France had risen to her accustomed place among the nations of the world. Since it was de Gaulle who had inspired and guided her resurrection, to de Gaulle belonged the credit. Yet he proved incapable of using it.

For when de Gaulle came to express himself on the settlement of the post-war world his ideas turned out to be strangely old-fashioned. Certainly he knew nothing of the experiments in nuclear fission; but even when the atom bombs exploded over Japan it made no difference to his thinking. The dangers he foresaw were the dangers which had threatened France since 1870. He had set his heart on two things, the dismemberment of Germany and the establishment of France as the leader of a Western European block. As he watched the great Allied armies crossing France and sweeping towards the Rhine, the spectre of German armour once again streaming through the indefensible gaps in France's northern frontiers, which he had described so vividly twenty years before, rose up before him. This time, at least, Germany must be contained. There must be no fourth Reich. A loose federation of old pre-Bismarck German states, an autonomous republic west of the Rhine and international control of the Ruhr were the minimum that he demanded. Above all, when the war was over, France must have an army large and mobile enough to take the offensive instantly at the slightest sign of a recrudescence of German militarism.

De Gaulle first turned to Churchill. The hospitality de Gaulle had offered Churchill and Eden on Armistice Day, 1944, had been intended as a grateful acknowledgment of what they had done for him in 1940. No pains were spared, therefore, to make his guests welcome. Churchill, his wife and daughter Mary were lodged in state at the Quai d'Orsay and lavishly entertained. It may well be true that, as he accompanied Churchill down the famous half-mile of the Champs-Élysées, a minister within earshot heard de Gaulle growl at the mob for acclaiming "the old bandit."[2] But when de Gaulle ordered the band to play "*Le Père de la Victoire*" as Churchill placed a wreath beneath Clemenceau's statue, he was paying a tribute he genuinely felt.

Nevertheless, in his long and intimate conversations with Churchill, de Gaulle had a serious purpose. Throughout the cold, arduous day spent visiting French troops at the front de Gaulle sketched his plan for an Anglo-French alliance as the foundation of a Western European block. In essence he was proposing a Third Force independent of both Russia and the United States but capable of defending itself against either and above all of containing Germany. It was a theme he had often touched upon in the past and was to return to throughout his political life. Remembering the 1930s de Gaulle was afraid that after the war the British would return to their island and leave France with the responsibility of containing Germany. He knew that the task would be beyond French capabilities.

Yet although Churchill shared de Gaulle's fears he could not entertain any form of alliance which excluded the Americans from Western Europe. Churchill in 1944 was being asked to accept the proposition which de Gaulle tried to impose more than twenty years later when he withdrew from the North Atlantic Treaty Organisation—the substitution of France for the United States as the guarantor of Western Europe's independence. The idea was unacceptable in 1966; in 1944 it was preposterous. The hardest battle of the war still lay ahead and the Americans were to bear the brunt of it. France would play only a minor part. De Gaulle was the head of a provisional government and no one could tell how long he would remain in power or what military burdens the French would prove capable of shouldering. Churchill wanted to strengthen France, but he tried to impress upon de Gaulle that the army France would need to police Germany was quite different from the sort of army that would fight the coming battle.

De Gaulle at once took offence. He brushed aside Churchill's advice as an attempt to relegate France to the role of guarding allied lines of communication. If Britain would not collaborate in the way he desired he would find others who would. In this mood of resentment he turned to Russia and arranged to visit Moscow early in December. To the Russians de Gaulle put his proposition in a different form. He suggested that, in order to guarantee the dismemberment of Germany, the French frontier should be extended to the Rhine. This would be an additional security to the Russians and would make it unnecessary for the Americans to stay in Europe. De Gaulle felt that if he could persuade Stalin to guarantee this new frontier he might force the Anglo-Saxons to accept it as well or, in default, do without their assistance altogether. It was the old idea of a Franco-Russian containment of Germany in a new and more promising form.

But de Gaulle had even less success with Stalin than with Churchill. Stalin had already warned both Churchill and Roosevelt of de Gaulle's desire to visit him and of the subjects that were to be discussed. He kept them fully informed while the conversations were in progress. Stalin was apt to judge states by their military strength and cross-examined de Gaulle rather brutally:

Stalin: How is the restoration of French industry progressing?

De Gaulle: It is being restored, but very, very slowly. There are terrible transport difficulties and a coal shortage. In order to equip her army, France has to appeal for arms from the Americans and, for the moment, they won't give her any. It will take France two years to restore her industries.

Stalin: I find this rather surprising. Russia is not finding the restoration of industry such an insuperable problem. The south of France was liberated without much difficulty and there was not much fighting in Paris. So what's the trouble?

De Gaulle: Most of the French rolling stock was destroyed . . . and what is left is mostly used by the British and Americans.

Stalin later asked how the French stood for airmen.

De Gaulle: We have very few airmen and even those we have need complete retraining, as they are unfamiliar with modern aeroplanes.

Stalin: Now the French airmen of the *Normandie* squadron are doing very well on the Russian front; so if you are so hard up for airmen, we could perhaps send them back to France?

De Gaulle: No, no, this is quite unnecessary. They are contributing nobly to the common cause.[3]

Stalin quickly concluded that de Gaulle was a simple man with an exaggerated idea of the importance of France. When de Gaulle proposed that the Rhine should become the French frontier just as the Oder-Neisse rivers were to form the new western frontiers of Poland, Stalin replied that such matters would have to be discussed with the British and Americans who were at that moment fighting the battles that were to complete the liberation of France. He did, however, suggest that a Franco-Russian pact be studied, demanding in return that de Gaulle recognise the Lublin Committee as the Government of Poland. Where his own interests were concerned Stalin cared as little about the susceptibilities of his allies as de Gaulle. Having been refused the Rhineland, de Gaulle rejected the Lublin Committee and prepared to leave Moscow. On this the Russians relented and signed the pact to which they attached little importance, but which saved de Gaulle's face.

Baulked by Churchill and Stalin, de Gaulle cynically turned to the United States. In spite of Roosevelt's hostility to de Gaulle, France was already receiving massive American aid. Besides $700,000,000 worth of military equipment, 125,000 tons of rails, 130,000 tons of materials for bridges, 1,000,000 tons of construction materials including 4,000 tractors and 500 cranes, 1,150 locomotives and 13,600 railway wagons, 175,000 tons of food, clothing and medical supplies had been shipped across the Atlantic by February, 1945. Of course, much of this was used by the Allied forces but it was also the foundation of French recovery.

On the other hand, the Americans had been in no hurry to equip further French divisions. The German thrust through the Ardennes changed the American attitude. Eisenhower realised that the war might drag on for many months and that, if he were to maintain his strategy of attacking on a broad front, he would need more troops. At the end of December he cabled Washington asking that arrangements be made to equip eight more French divisions as quickly as possible. Within three days the Combined Chiefs of Staff approved his request.

De Gaulle, sensing the change of atmosphere, saw a chance of getting the sort of army he wanted, and appealed to Washington not for eight but for fifty more divisions. Considering the state of France it was a wildly impracticable suggestion, but de Gaulle was dazzled by the vision of France emerging once more as the strongest military power in Western Europe, able to impose her policy on the Germans. However, no sooner had the appeal been made than de Gaulle committed a flagrant blunder.

At the end of the Yalta Conference Roosevelt sent a warm message through his Ambassador in Paris, Jefferson Caffery, inviting de Gaulle to meet him on his way home. As the whole world knew, Roosevelt was very ill. The President apologised for not being able to come to Paris, but expressed the hope that Algiers would not be disagreeable as an alternative. De Gaulle had everything to gain from such a meeting. Yalta had put France back on the political map but left open many questions, particularly the future of Germany. If he wanted France to be included in the final Allied discussions, Roosevelt was the man to persuade.

But pique blinded him. Roosevelt, who had excluded France from the Yalta Conference and twice refused to come to Paris, now had the impertinence to invite de Gaulle to meet him on French soil. Although every report indicated that Roosevelt was dying, de Gaulle would make no allowances. On a pretext that a meeting might imply French ratification of the decisions at Yalta, he refused to go to Algiers. The Americans at once publicised de Gaulle's refusal and, although his Council of Ministers supported him, almost the entire French and allied press and most of the French Assembly were critical. To most Frenchmen de Gaulle seemed bent on antagonising the one power which was helping to resuscitate France and on whom she must depend for her security for many years. He scorned the "servility" of his critics; they feared the retribution which his arrogance incurred. It was not long in coming.

When Roosevelt reached Washington and was confronted with de Gaulle's request for the re-equipment of fifty divisions he minuted dryly that it would interfere with the prosecution of the war. It was the last decision he was to make regarding France. Three weeks later, on April 18, President Roosevelt died.

However, de Gaulle's German policy was finally scotched not by the Western Powers but by Russia. Stalin, already sure of Eastern Europe, was turning his attention to the west. On the morrow of V.E. Day he reiterated that it was Hitler and not the German people that Russia had been fighting and added that he had no intention of dismembering Germany. Stalin was bidding for communist control of the whole country. In face of this threat the Anglo-Saxon attitude towards Germany suddenly altered. When, in Washington, de Gaulle tried to persuade Truman to internationalise the Ruhr, the new American President replied that to attempt to divide Western Germany would be simply to throw the German people into the arms of Russia. It was agreed, more out of kindness than conviction, that de Gaulle's plans should be laid before the Foreign Ministers in conference in London; but when the Russians supported them and claimed the right to contribute to any international force which might control the Ruhr, the worst fears of the Allies were confirmed. To forestall Russian expansion it was decided that each power should administer its zone independently. It was not long before the three Western Zones, including the French, were amalgamated and a new centralised German Government was born. De Gaulle's twenty-year-old dream of protecting France by controlling the Rhineland was at an end.

*　　*　　*

Although de Gaulle and the French were becoming slowly and mutually disenchanted with each other, de Gaulle still had enormous reserves of political capital. If he could convince the people that he cared about their misery as deeply as he believed in their genius he was still in a position to win their confidence and be chosen as the man to lead them into the future.

And de Gaulle did care. When he began to govern, life in France was literally almost at a standstill. Out of 17,000 locomotives possessed by the French railways at the beginning of the war only 2,900 were serviceable; of nearly half a million goods and passenger wagons, less than half could run. More than 3,000 rail, road and canal bridges had been destroyed by the Germans or by allied bombing. Two thousand miles of railway and 25,000 miles of inland waterway were unusable. Many of the chief repair and marshalling yards had been destroyed. Power stations had been blown up, electrified lines, including the Paris Metro, were out of action. As de Gaulle himself put it "no train from Paris could reach Lyons, Marseilles, Toulouse, Bordeaux, Nantes, or Nancy. None could cross the Loire between Nevers and the Atlantic, or the Seine between Nantes and the Channel, or the Rhône between Lyons and the Mediterranean."[4] Road transport was in no better state. Even if bridges had been standing, only some 200,000 lorries were left to cross them and many of these suffered constant breakdowns. There was an acute shortage of petrol. Not a single port was available. Cherbourg was monopolised by the allies, such

Atlantic ports as had not been destroyed were in the hands of the Germans, who were still holding out in isolated pockets. Marseilles and Toulon were a mass of rubble. France had become a country of the horse or ox-drawn cart, the perambulator and above all the bicycle.

In the big cities people were cold and hungry. Most of them wore threadbare clothes and clogs were in fashion. The official ration was down to a thousand calories a day, which itself meant slow death, and even this was often not available. Paris and many other towns were without electricity. Coal production was only a million tons and most of it was used by the allied armies or what was left of industry. Nearly half a million houses had been destroyed and a million and a half badly damaged. The franc was worth only a quarter of what it had been in 1940. Rationing had completely broken down and men and women lived by barter and on the black market. Miners bartered coal, fishermen and lorry-drivers petrol for food. Townsfolk foraged by bicycle. Every Parisian knew that in the countryside they could get butter, eggs, sometimes even poultry; every evening and particularly at the week-end, hundreds of cyclists would converge on the cities, their machines festooned with packages.

Any attempt to establish orderly distribution was made doubly difficult by the attitude towards government which had grown up during the occupation. The French have always been allergic to direct taxation; under the Germans this allergy spread to every form of regulation and was developed into a science of evasion. Even officials vied with each other in defrauding the government for the benefit of their districts.

A desperate shortage of manpower aggravated the general misery. Although France was liberated French prisoners remained in Germany for many weeks after the end of the war. More than 400,000 soldiers and civilians had been killed fighting or by bombardment, another 300,000 civilians had been deported. Nearly 750,000 men were in the army. The labour force that remained was elderly, under-nourished and disorganised by a mass-movement of population. For, in the first winter after liberation, refugees of all kinds began to return home. Jews who had been in hiding, children who had been farmed out among relations in the country, tens of thousands of citizens who had fled from the occupied into the unoccupied zone, set out on the journey back to their own towns and villages. It was 1940 in reverse and the problems of feeding, transporting and eventually housing them were colossal.

Yet, miraculously, within eighteen months of de Gaulle's assump-

tion of power France was well on the road to recovery. Although the
French went cold and hungry through the first winter of freedom there
was no famine. The six months' emergency food programme which de
Gaulle's representatives had concluded with the United States, staved
off disaster. As communications were restored the country once again
became able to feed itself. The August, 1944, production was only a
quarter of its pre-war volume; during de Gaulle's second provisional
administration it rose nearly to the level of 1939. In spite of hardship
and poverty and the immensity of the task which faced them, the French
workers did not strike.

Once again the lion's share of the credit must go to de Gaulle.
Political opponents who argued that these things would have happened whether he had been there or not were forgetting the immense
prestige his name still carried and the inspiration he gave. But for de
Gaulle it is most improbable that Thorez would have co-operated with
the government, in which case there would have been wide-spread
industrial unrest. It was de Gaulle who insisted on the programme of
nationalisation which, in part at least, placated the revolutionary
ardour of the resistance and made the re-equipment of basic industries
possible, for the destruction had been so great that private capital was
quite inadequate. It was he who chose the architects of economic
recovery; he who launched the plans which, in essence, have been
followed ever since.

De Gaulle began by reconstructing his ministries. In the early days
after his triumphal entry into Paris his Commissioners-General came
over from Algiers to take charge of the administration. But he soon
saw that both government and Assembly needed broadening to include
the men who by their part in the resistance had earned the right to
be consulted, and some members of the main political parties which
had lain dormant under the Germans but were beginning to revive.
On September 9, 1944, he announced his first provisional government.
Bidault, President of the Committee of National Resistance, became
Minister of Foreign Affairs. De Gaulle resisted communist demands
for the key Ministries of Defence and the Interior, but persuaded Dion,
chief of the *Francs Tireurs*, and Billoux, Secretary-General of the
C.G.T., to accept the minor portfolios of Air and Health. Most of the
other ministers were re-shuffled. Pleven took the Colonies; René
Capitant, who had unfurled the unpopular Gaullist banner in North
Africa, Education; Pierre Henri Teitgen, the difficult post of Information with responsibility for revitalising the French press. The most
interesting new appointment was that of Mendès-France, who had
been a pilot in the French Air Force at the beginning of the war and in

Algiers had been preparing the measures necessary to restore the French finances. He became Minister of National Economy.

Of course, the new administration received massive help from outside, but this does not detract from de Gaulle's own performance. Rehabilitation had been carefully planned, and the core of the plan was his. He had outlined it in his speeches and proclamations in Algiers and now, before a picked audience of eight thousand people, he restated his aims at the Palais de Chaillot. After setting the plight of France in the context of the world struggle, after stressing the right of France to be consulted in all projected post-war settlements, he turned to the home scene. Once more he disclaimed all intention of becoming a dictator. As soon as the entire country was liberated and prisoners and deportees had returned home, elections for a new National Assembly would be held through universal adult suffrage which, for the first time, would include women. Until then the Consultative Assembly, transferred from Algiers and enlarged by members of the resistance, would remain consultative. He would govern and his Ministers would carry out his plans which would be subject to change or confirmation as soon as a properly constituted government came into being.

In the past, when speaking on his ideas for rehabilitation, de Gaulle had used the word "revolution"; at Chaillot he spoke of "renovation." But his ideas were still the same. Although assuring the people of as much liberty as possible and favouring the spirit of free enterprise, he went on to say that private interests must always be subordinated to public, that the main sources of wealth must be exploited and directed in the common interest rather than for any private advantage, and that great private monopolies must be abolished once and for all. In case these should be taken for mere words he announced that certain public services and some great enterprises would at once be placed under state control, till such time as proper methods of nationalisation could be worked out. Illicit profits through collaboration were to be confiscated and prices, wages and distribution regulated until production could meet demand. Most important of all, as it turned out, he outlined his scheme for a great "coalition" of committees consisting of qualified men from government, industry and trade unions and the academic world to gather information and plan the best use of all French resources whether publicly or privately owned.

Many of de Gaulle's critics have classified the Chaillot speech as a mass of vague generalities. Certainly it was not "revolutionary" in the classical sense. He did not seek to tear down the entire structure of the French state; on the contrary he reasserted the rule of law. He did not abolish private property, but he went much farther along the road of evolutionary socialism than the Labour Government that was shortly to be elected in Britain with an overwhelming majority.

By ordinance the coal mines of northern France which produced sixty per cent of French coal were taken over by the state that winter, and the rest of the mines followed in due course. Although the final acts were not passed until after de Gaulle had left office, all the preparatory work for the nationalisation of gas and electricity, the banks and insurance companies, were completed under his rule. The Renault and Berliet motor works, the Gnome and Rhône aircraft-engine works and the Societé d'Enterprises de Presse were transferred to public ownership because each of these concerns had forfeited their rights by assisting the enemy.

De Gaulle's programme of "renovation" did not stop at nationalisation. When he spoke at Chaillot of all French men and women working in dignity and security he was announcing the introduction of a welfare state. Under his governments the foundations were laid of a system of family allowances, sickness and unemployment pay, the right to appeal against dismissal, and worker participation in the direction of industry, which was to carry France ahead of other European countries in social security and industrial relations. When the public corporations were formed provision was made for trade unionists' and consumers' representatives to sit on the boards of directors. Works' councils were made obligatory in all concerns employing a hundred or more people and they were given the right not only to supervise all welfare but to be informed of the profits and suggest how they might be used.

In this great wave of reform the peasants were not forgotten. Not even the communist party had ever proposed to nationalise the land in France. De Gaulle took a step in the opposite direction. A new agricultural act gave every peasant first refusal of the land he occupied. Only if the landlord wished to take the land back and farm it himself could he terminate the lease, and then only if the tenant died. By making it worthwhile for the peasants to invest their savings without fear of being evicted this act did more than any of its predecessors to modernise French agriculture.

De Gaulle applied himself personally to the reform and reconstruction of the Civil Service. The old School of Political Science, damned as the cradle of old-fashioned liberalism and *laissez-faire* economics, was reformed into the Institute of Political Studies, to which was added a research and information centre known as The National Foundation of Political Science. He next founded the new

School of National Administration. Both these institutions prospered and exist in France to-day. Because of them candidates for the Civil Service receive a much broader training than in most other countries. Officials at all levels are given refresher courses and their interchange between different ministries and between industries and ministries has been made easier. Promotion is more by merit than it used to be. It is true to say that the close co-operation between the Civil Service, industry, the trade unions and the universities has been the foundation of France's economic recovery. Even some of de Gaulle's fiercest critics have admitted that, if he were remembered only for founding the National School of Administration, he would hold an honoured place among French reformers.

Finally de Gaulle established "*Le Plan.*" As almost his last act as head of the provisional government, de Gaulle set out the aims of the Planning Council with Jean Monnet as chairman. The council was to give the government the facts of the economic situation, to inform the country in a way which could be widely understood, to set up expert committees to guide the future development of France's industrial and agricultural life and to modernise it. Under the Council the General Commissariat co-ordinated the work of the committees and, within a few months, produced the first four-year plan. Not all the targets were achieved and the planning organisation was to undergo many changes, but its aims have remained the same and over the years it has become the envy of other countries.

"The forgotten years," as one writer has called the period of provisional government,[5] were, therefore, years of prodigious achievement. De Gaulle had not only restored the honour of France but catapulted her on to the road to recovery. Yet his hold over the French people slipped with every week that passed. De Gaulle saw that it was happening but never fully understood the reasons. It seemed to him that the French were not prepared to make the effort that was required. He warned the people constantly that recovery would be slow and arduous and entail great sacrifices. He thought them feckless. But de Gaulle was being unjust. The irony of his position, which he never perceived, was that he himself had crushed the very people who might have risen to the heights of his vision. At the moment of liberation most of the resistance leaders, whatever their origin, did share his desire to create a new France. Behind the hackneyed phrases of the Resistance Charter lay the hope of a clean sweep of the men and interests who had led France to her downfall: capitalists who had held money to be more important than liberty and humanity, men who had taken bribes to propagate Hitler's policies, politicians who had ceased to represent the people, fascists who had dishonoured France by be-coming Nazis. There was a longing for a "clean" society and an ardent hope that de Gaulle, as the symbol of the resistance, might somehow bind the people to him and build the new world. De Gaulle shared that longing. When he spoke in Algiers of his movement as the greatest revolution in the history of France he was still burning with the fire which he hoped would cleanse society of all that had led to the Vichy betrayal.

Had de Gaulle come to France in the same mood he might conceiv-ably have inspired the unity he had always longed for. For although he was not a true revolutionary his political philosophy was broad enough to attract many of those who were. He was not a fascist and, except for one short period later on, never stooped to the concept of a one-party state. He had many socialist beliefs but deplored class warfare. He mis-trusted the bourgeoisie and the peasantry because he thought they had put property before honour, yet he believed in the rule of law and the sense of order which these traditional sections of the French com-munity represented. What de Gaulle offered France in 1945 was what he found himself practising—a sort of "accidental monarchy." If Jean Moulin had lived and de Gaulle had been able to trust the resistance to follow him, he might have been able to persuade Frenchmen to keep him on his unorthodox throne.

But the moment de Gaulle decided to crush the resistance, long before he set foot on French soil, he destroyed the foundations of the régime at which he aimed. For the decision meant breaking the spirit of the men who might have followed him. It was a dilemma from which he could not escape. He knew that some communists intended to use the resistance to seize power; he could not tell what following they had or how well they would use it. As it turned out many leading communists were anxious to collaborate with him and several did. If, on the day that he entered Paris, he had appealed to Rol-Tanguy and his followers instead of humiliating them, if he had gone straight to the National Committee of Resistance at the Hôtel de Ville instead of insulting it by going to the Prefecture, he might have won the alleg-iance of all who put France before party and created then the *rassemble-ment* which he needed. But de Gaulle was afraid not only of the com-munists but of the resistance itself. He dare not take the gamble.

Although by his legislation de Gaulle fulfilled nine-tenths of the Resistance Charter, many of the men whom he most respected turned against him because they felt that he had betrayed its spirit. Albert Camus and Albert Olivier, who were then editing *Combat*, Emanuel d'Astier in *Libération*, attacked him constantly for taking Vichy officials into his reformed Civil Service and Vichy soldiers into his army. Socialist and even moderate politicians began to speak of de Gaulle's Buonapartist tendencies. Léon Blum, who had supported him throughout his stay in prison and had looked forward to the regeneration of France through the resistance, found on regaining his freedom only a collapse of morale and a descent into mediocrity.

Instead of leading a crusade, de Gaulle, therefore, found himself face to face with a demoralised population. The local leaders who might have inspired men to follow him were either in official positions or had turned sullen. The people were hungry. De Gaulle's reforms, even the achievements of his ministers, remarkable as they were, went unnoticed. As the prisoners of war and deportees returned in the spring and summer of 1945, disillusion deepened. The minister in charge of their rehabilitation probably did as well as a man could in the circumstances, but there was still a shortage of food and clothes, and houses were in bad condition or simply not available so that thousands of families had to live in temporary camps where they found life much as they had left it under the Germans. The occupation had made a virtue of cheating, lying, stealing and law-breaking and the bad habits stuck. The black market had developed into big business. Instead of selling their food to the army of cyclists who had been regularly buying for their families, the peasants were now reserving their stocks for the big operators who bought butter by the ton, transported it in lorries and stored it so as to supply smart restaurants. Insurance companies covered these illicit stocks against theft and damage. The sight of the extremes of wealth and poverty, the corruption which seemed the normal way of life reminded the home-comers of all they had hoped to get away from in prison. "Only fools work," wrote one of the more articulate ex-prisoners of war, "the others do their black marketing and eat . . ."[6]

De Gaulle knew that inflation was at the roots of the growing disillusionment, and that, if he was to halt the decline in his popularity, he must cure it and cure it fast. The crucial question was how. The franc had not collapsed but, as Vichy had simply printed paper to pay the cost of the German occupation, it was steadily buying less and less. Five times as much money was in circulation as in 1940 to buy a quarter of the goods. Everything went on to the black market. Ration cards could not be honoured, wages did not provide a bare living. The supply of money had to be reduced.

Mendès-France suggested Draconian measures. He proposed first to call in all bank notes, exchange them for new ones, cancelling all that were not surrendered, and then to block all bank accounts and deposits, releasing them only gradually as production rose. In this way, Mendès claimed, the money which financed the black market would disappear and those who had hoarded profits made from collaboration would be forced to declare or lose them, prices would tumble and wages once again be high enough to buy a full ration. Rough justice would be done at the expense of those who could best afford it.

The puritan in de Gaulle was attracted to the scheme, but his Cabinet was divided and in economic affairs he did not feel sure enough of himself to override it. It was the classical argument of austerity or expansion, of incentives to production or equality of sacrifice. The opponents of Mendès-France maintained that what France needed was a restoration of confidence rather than a shock and that, unless prices remained high enough to induce farmers and industrialists to produce more, the gap between money and goods would widen still farther. The people would suffer less if inflation were brought gradually under control.

Probably the decisive influence was the attitude of the eighteen million French peasants, who were soon to determine the general election. Most of them had made money out of the black market and hoarded it. Under Mendès-France's scheme they would lose their savings and perhaps barely get enough for their crops to buy their equipment. Yet France had to be fed. The communist party, for which most of the peasants voted, and many socialists therefore supported the bankers. When Mendès-France finally demanded a vote in the Cabinet only one Minister, Augustine Laurent, the Postmaster General, supported him. Mendès-France resigned, to be succeeded by Pleven.

Although the Consultative Assembly approved the Cabinet's decision almost unanimously, de Gaulle never felt happy about accepting Mendès-France's resignation. He continued to respect him more than any other French politician. His misgivings were probably sound. Had he followed Mendès-France's advice and overridden the Cabinet, the shock might have convinced the people that de Gaulle was on their side against all the vested interests. Recovery would, perhaps, have been slower but the political parties might have found it impossible to oppose de Gaulle in the coming elections and, therefore, in the constitutional debates which were to follow. It was one more gamble which the accidental monarch refused to take and which helped to lose him his throne.

As it was, and as de Gaulle himself admitted, the measures he approved, being a compromise, pleased no one. First he decreed a general rise in wages of approximately forty per cent with corresponding increases in pensions and family allowances. Since this must increase rather than diminish the money in circulation, he next launched a "liberation loan" at fixed interest of three per cent. This was fully subscribed after a good deal of persuasion, but as rather less than half the money was paid in notes it did no more than check the rise in their circulation. Prices continued to mount, the black market to flourish; further measures were soon necessary. Indirect taxation, particularly on spirits and tobacco, was increased, and Pleven introduced two moderate capital levies, one spread over four years. Lastly, only notes above fifty francs in value were called in to be exchanged for new notes. Although all large notes not surrendered became null and void this still left a lot of money in the pockets of collaborators and black marketeers. In all, perhaps half the money that Vichy had printed was taken out of circulation. It was a reasonable beginning, largely justified by its economic results, but it made little political impact. Protests turned into demonstrations and demonstrations into riots which had to be suppressed by the police. For thousands liberation seemed little better than life under the Germans. De Gaulle himself began to be blamed.

De Gaulle's personality did not help him bridge the gulf that was opening between himself and the people. Lucie Aubrac, the wife of his Commissioner-General in Marseilles, describes how, when de Gaulle visited the city, the *Maquisards* staged a hilarious parade. They wore all kinds of tattered clothes, had flowers on their rifles and dragged along an old German armoured car on which rode scantily dressed young women waving flags and screaming for joy. Although liberation was barely complete, de Gaulle was not amused, but sat glumly watching, muttering "quelle mascarade." The Marseillais concluded that he was a cold fish and a snob.[7]

But de Gaulle was just as withdrawn in distinguished company as among the *Francs Tireurs*. He believed that a leader should be remote and for four years had practised his belief until it had become second nature. His life followed a regular and austere pattern. Every day he commuted from his home in Neuilly to his office in the Rue St. Dominique. His wife and daughters were at home but he left early, got back late and saw little of them. In the office he exacted the most rigorous discipline. The agenda for Cabinet meetings, which were held at least twice a week, was prepared in great detail, under the guidance of the Secretary-General, Louis Joxe. The meetings were held in a room at the Hôtel Matignon, whose walls were left deliberately bare to avoid distractions. Ministers presented their reports, de Gaulle asked questions. If a discussion arose he seldom took part, but later recorded deprecatingly that the exchanges became most lively when questions of personality were involved. At the end he would sum up and, in case of disagreement, give his verdict which automatically became the decision of the Cabinet as a whole.

In any Cabinet the Prime Minister has the last word. De Gaulle's methods may not have been unlike those of an Attlee or a Chamberlain, but the spirit was utterly different. All his colleagues were his nominees and none was on anything approaching intimate terms with him. There was no inner caucus which met informally in the evenings to thrash things out. Not even Joxe, who as Secretary-General probably saw de Gaulle most often, could ring him up at short notice to discuss an urgent question. In foreign and military affairs de Gaulle took all the major decisions himself; his Chief of Staff and Ministers were there to take orders. "Juin," he wrote, "carried out my decisions . . . It was my duty to settle the most important matters, which I did in the Committee of Defence in the presence of the three Ministers and their Under-Secretaries. After this they went to their offices and their telephones to iron out the difficulties."[8]

This Cromwellian style of government, the distance de Gaulle kept between himself and other men, gradually made itself felt throughout the country. As his speeches show, de Gaulle was aware of the miseries which the French people were suffering. He warned them over and over again of the tribulations in store for them. In his own way he felt at one with them: "In the heart of the multitude, I was imbued with its joys and its cares."[9] But it was always from a mountain that he descended among them. He could not laugh with them or let them see that he suffered. Inevitably people came to feel that he neither understood nor greatly cared about their lives, that it was only the army and France's position in the world which really mattered to him.

It was in the knowledge of this declining popularity that de Gaulle faced the most important and difficult of all the tasks he had set himself, that of persuading the people to adopt the type of constitution he believed necessary for France. All his life he had thought about this. If France were to escape from the weaknesses of parliamentary government which had plagued it between the wars, the Head of State must have reserve powers in case of emergency and be able both to control his executive and appeal to the electorate over the head of the Assembly. Yet the opposition to his views was already so strong among the political parties that de Gaulle seriously considered imposing his will by force. He believed he could count upon the army and had enough support among the masses to succeed. But, as always when he contemplated dictatorship, his sense of history convinced him that such a course would be disastrous in the long run. He had promised repeatedly to surrender to the people the power which had come to him through the accidents of war; he realised that his political credit would be destroyed forever if he went back on his word.

Nevertheless de Gaulle was determined to make his appeal to the country in his own way. During the summer of 1945 all the five main political groups had held conferences, the communists, socialists and a new moderate catholic-socialist party known as the *Mouvement Républicain Populaire* (M.R.P.), the radicals and splinter parties of the right. All except the last had based their programmes on the Resistance Charter. All, with the same exception, had made it plain that they wanted to break away from the Constitution of 1875 and found their new democracy on the sovereignty of a single elected chamber. De Gaulle was convinced that if they had their way government would again be at the mercy of successive combinations of party groups and under a constant threat from the communists who, as the largest of them, might succeed in gaining control. De Gaulle, therefore, took several decisions. Since the only means of restraining the parties lay through the people he would appeal to them by referendum. The people must decide whether France should return to the 1875 Constitution or establish a Fourth Republic with a new one. The people must also decide whether the new Assembly was to be sovereign or should sit for a limited period with limited powers, its main task being to draft whatever constitution was decided upon. And when a new constitution was finally presented the people should decide whether or not they accepted it.

To strengthen his hand de Gaulle appealed to three elder statesmen and invited them to join his government. All refused. Léon Blum, who in prison had favoured an American presidential system, had changed his mind within a fortnight of his release. Édouard Herriot, former President of the Assembly, indignant at not being allowed to occupy his old official mansion was truculent and unco-operative. Louis Marin, one of the moderate party leaders in Lorraine, wanted a return to the old two-chamber system. Of the old guard, only Jules Jeanneney, former President of the Senate who had joined the provisional government in September, stood by him. It was he who prepared the ordinance under which the referendum and elections were to be held.

Each of the parties and the dying resistance movement, which held its last conference in the summer, pronounced against any form of plebiscite. De Gaulle ignored them. He shuffled his Cabinet so that those Ministers who had come in for the severest criticism were in less exposed positions, and went calmly ahead. On July 9 he presented the Electoral Statute to his government, telling its members that he accepted in advance any resignation which might be offered. None was forthcoming.

In case the referendum should restore the Constitution of the Third Republic, the Statute included provisions for the election of the old cantonal General Councils, whose duty it would then be to elect a Senate. Elections for the Assembly and the referendum were fixed for October 21 and the method of balloting laid down. This too had been the subject of heated discussion. De Gaulle had always envied the British their electoral system and, if the parties had been differently constituted, might have plumped for the single ballot. But with four main parties, a number of splinter groups and an even larger number of independent candidates, this would almost certainly have resulted in a communist victory, quite certainly in an overwhelming majority for a communist-socialist alliance. De Gaulle rejected proportional representation on a nation-wide basis as too impersonal, and finally decided upon proportional representation by departments. This meant that no overspill of losing votes could be transferred from one department to another. Constituencies were redrawn to meet changes in population. On July 12, de Gaulle broadcast to the nation. He sketched the history and weaknesses of the Third Republic and suggested that, by the referendum, the country would decide not to return to a system which had produced such "paralysis." He then explained clearly what the second question meant. If the people voted "No" they would elect an "omnipotent" Assembly which could exercise "dictatorship" over France for an unlimited period, an experiment which had almost always proved unsatisfactory. If they voted "Yes" the Assembly would be constituent and last for seven months at longest, during which time it would pass the budget, ratify or reject treaties and propose a constitution on which a further referendum would be held. He appealed for a "Yes" to both questions.

When the Statute was presented to the Consultative Assembly a few days later, opposition came to a head. The communists, supported by many socialists and some moderates, rejected it, accusing de Gaulle of trying to establish personal rule as Buonaparte and Louis Napoleon had before him. The M.R.P. and the rest of the socialist and moderate deputies accepted the plebiscite but demanded a sovereign Assembly. De Gaulle spoke last. He reminded his audience that, between 1875 and 1940, France had had one hundred and two governments compared with twenty in Great Britain and fourteen in the United States. He quoted Roosevelt's disparaging observation that even he, the President of the United States, sometimes found himself unable to remember the name of the current head of the French Government.

He begged his audience not to return to such a system. It was all in vain. The Assembly rejected the government's proposals outright by two hundred votes to nineteen, and later rejected a compromise put forward by Vincent Auriol. On this de Gaulle published the Statute on his own authority and announced that it would be submitted to the electorate.

De Gaulle already knew broadly how the elections would go. When the municipal councils had been chosen in April the results showed a marked swing to the left. Communists and socialists were bound to dominate the new Assembly, and to draft a constitution of which he would disapprove. His hopes lay in the referendum. If he could win enough support, then the politicians in the Assembly might hesitate to oppose him; if they carried a constitution against his will the people might throw them out when it was finally presented to them.

Since V.E. Day de Gaulle had been touring the country warning the people of the great decisions they were about to take. Now he held aloof while over the radio and on the hustings the party politicians plunged into the struggle. The campaign lasted two months. On October 17 de Gaulle made one last appeal over the radio. On October 21 the people went to the polls. The results were much as expected but gratifying to de Gaulle all the same. In the referendum the country overwhelmingly rejected a return to the constitution of 1875. Less enthusiastically but decisively it opted for a Constituent Assembly of limited duration with limited powers.

De Gaulle had won the first round in the constitutional battle. But statesmen and journalists who hailed it as a great victory and drew the conclusion that France was satisfied and wanted de Gaulle to continue were over-simplifying the position. Certainly the Assembly was as favourably constituted as de Gaulle had any right to expect. The communists had done well but were not in a position to dominate. The socialists, whose hierarchy in the end came out in qualified support of his electoral Statute, and the M.R.P. who contained most of de Gaulle's personal supporters, had a majority between them. The conservatives and radicals, discredited by their association with Vichy and their prewar record, had been defeated. Yet there was no sign that any party had come closer to de Gaulle's view of what the constitution should be, no guarantee even that the Assembly would elect him head of the second provisional government. A clash seemed inevitable.

The Assembly met on November 6, and once more chose Félix Gouin as its President. It then proceeded to the business of electing the head of the provisional government. For a whole week the parties held meetings without reaching an agreement. Although de Gaulle admitted that he found their deliberations "trying," he made no move, but continued to exercise his function as President. On November 11 he attended a great armistice celebration at the Arc de Triomphe, on the 13th he gave a dinner for Churchill, who was passing through Paris. Then at last, on November 14, the Assembly unanimously elected him President of the government of the French Republic and passed a resolution that "Charles de Gaulle deserved well of his country," a citation which despite the modesty of its wording put him among the ranks of France's heroes from Joan of Arc to Foch and Clemenceau. "Plutarch lied!" wrote Churchill. Ingratitude towards men was not always the sign of a strong people.

Yet for months de Gaulle felt a growing reserve on the part of the political leaders towards him. The nuances of applause when he spoke in the Assembly, the looks exchanged, the gossip repeated, all told him that although the politicians were genuinely grateful for the part he had played, most of them thought his role was finished. When he came to form his government their true feelings became clear. The radicals, under Herriot, refused point-blank to serve. Thorez, on behalf of the communists, demanded one of the key ministries, Defence, the Interior, or Foreign Affairs; the socialists stipulated that they would not serve in any government unless the communists were included. De Gaulle stood firm. He refused the ministries Thorez demanded and told the communists they would either enter the government on his terms or not at all. Next day he spoke over the radio and explained to the French people that he would not put the communists in a position to dominate French policy by surrendering to them "the diplomacy which expresses it, the army which sustains it or the police which protects it." He then wrote to Félix Gouin that, as he could not form a unified government, he was restoring his mandate to the Assembly.

It was a bold move. The flood of abuse which the communists poured on his head was mingled with cries of alarm from socialists and popular republicans, who feared that the very birth of the Fourth Republic might take place in political deadlock. All urged de Gaulle to give way. When he refused, the majority rallied to him. On November 19, the Assembly again debated the Presidency and again elected de Gaulle with every vote except that of the communists. Next day the communists capitulated and Thorez, quite unabashed, came to tell de Gaulle that not only would his party enter the government without conditions but that the President would find no more loyal supporters. De Gaulle had won another round.

De Gaulle now proceeded to form his second provisional government. He had no illusions about the intentions of the communist party, but for the moment he needed it. If recovery was to continue it was essential that men and women stay at work. Only the communists could ensure industrial peace. In the new government, which he announced on November 21, Thorez became one of the four Secretaries of State and four out of six economic ministries went to members of his party. The rest were divided between socialists, popular republicans and prominent resistance leaders. One radical, Giacobbi, defied his party and took a portfolio. It began to look as if a real sense of national unity was emerging and when de Gaulle introduced his promised legislation nationalising the banks, insurance companies and public utilities, the new Assembly willingly got down to work.

Yet cracks in this shining surface soon began to appear. On December 15, the Civil Service trade unions met at the *Vélodrome d'Hiver* in Paris and denounced the government's wages increases as absurdly inadequate. They called for a general strike. Within the Cabinet the socialists at once supported them and threatened to resign if the demands of the unions were not met. Once again it was Thorez, true to the words he had spoken on joining the government, who came to de Gaulle's rescue. Declaring that under no circumstances must the government yield to such intolerable pressure, he instructed his representatives at the *Vélodrome* to say that for the civil servants to go on strike at that moment would be "a crime against the country." Since no strike could succeed without the support of the communist party, the movement collapsed.

But the split in the Cabinet was soon to reappear. The debate on the budget began just after Christmas and on New Year's Eve the army estimates came up for discussion. It was clear that the Assembly as a whole was opposed to the idea of building up a large army when the needs of civil reconstruction were so great. When a little-known socialist deputy suddenly proposed an amendment cutting military expenditure by twenty per cent, both communists and socialists supported him, postponing a vote only until de Gaulle himself could take part in the discussion. This he did on the following day.

De Gaulle was furious. The communist and socialist leaders were members of his administration. If they could not control their deputies on a matter as important as the budget, government was plainly impossible. When he rose to speak he issued an ultimatum; if the credits for the army were not voted that same evening the government would resign. He then went on to deliver a solemn warning. "I should like to add a word," he said, "which is not for the present, but even now, for the future. The point that divides us is a general conception of government and its relations with the national representatives. We have begun to reconstruct the Republic. After me you will continue to do so. I must tell you in all conscience—and no doubt this is the last time I shall be speaking to you from this place—that if you do not take into account the absolute necessities of governmental authority, dignity and responsibility, you will find yourselves in a situation which I predict will cause you bitter regret for having taken the way you have chosen."[10] The delegates fell silent. Opposition collapsed and the budget was passed with the face-saving condition that the government introduce proposals for the reform of the army within six weeks' time.

However, the writing was on the wall. The real issue had not been the budget but the power of the Assembly to control the Government. Since the Assembly had the duty of passing the budget it was acting within its rights in voting any reduction it pleased; but by threatening a reduction so impulsively and then changing its mind, it showed that, from the moment it became truly sovereign, France would once again be exposed to all the vagaries of coalition rule. This was the one thing de Gaulle was trying to avoid. As he had already been told privately of the proposals the Constitutional Commission was going to make to the Assembly, and as he had also been informed that he would not be allowed to take part in the debate since he was not a member of the Commission, he knew what the future held.

De Gaulle made up his mind to resign that same evening. He then exercised his flair for the unexpected and went to the Côte d'Azur. "Antibes offered me the refuge of Eden Roc and for the first time for seven years I took a few days' rest," he recorded in his memoirs.[11] For a week he meditated by the sea and enjoyed the sunshine. Then on Monday, January 14 he returned to Paris. At the station de Gaulle was met by Jules Moch, the socialist Minister of Transport, to whom he confided his decision as they drove away from the station. Moch protested vigorously; de Gaulle was silent. Then suddenly he turned and said, "Really, one can scarcely imagine Joan of Arc, married, the mother of a family and—who knows—with a husband unfaithful to her."[12] Roosevelt's ghost must have smiled. In order that they should take precautions in case there were demonstrations, de Gaulle also informed the Ministers of the Interior, of Justice and the Army that he was resigning from the Presidency the following Sunday. He summoned the *Commissionaires de la République* to Paris for the same reason. For the rest of the week he behaved as if nothing had happened. He signed decrees and the Acts of Parliament which had accumulated in his absence. He attended functions, held Cabinets and went to the Assembly.

Here at least there was drama. Hitherto de Gaulle's opponents had refrained from attacking him by name. Their criticisms had been direc- to his policies and to the dangers of personal rule. On this Wednesday, however, Herriot, who had come out so strongly in de Gaulle's favour when approached by the allies in 1940, but who was now burning with resentment at the failure of the Radical Party and his own eclipse, could contain himself no longer. Seizing on the citations for gallantry of men killed and wounded when fighting the Americans in North Africa and brandishing the official journal in which their names had been gazetted the day before, he arraigned de Gaulle to his face, de- manding that he cancel the decorations which were an insult to the allies. Herriot was greeted with loud applause.

Perhaps de Gaulle had intended such an insult, for at that moment French troops were being finally expelled from Syria under an agree- ment which he claimed the British were deliberately misinterpreting. But Herriot was on dangerous ground. De Gaulle began his reply calmly, saying that there was no question of "snatching from the coffins of the lamented dead and from the breasts of the wounded" the crosses which had been awarded them for obeying courageously orders which had been wrongly given. Then, turning on Herriot, he remarked scathingly that he was a better judge of such matters because he, at least, had "never had dealings with Vichy or with the enemy save by gunfire."[13] Herriot was silent and the citations stood.

On Saturday evening, de Gaulle summoned his Ministers to meet him the following morning in the Hall of Arms at the Rue St. Dom- inique. Since Cabinets were unusual on a Sunday, most of them had guessed what was coming. Only Auriol, Bidault and Soustelle were absent abroad. When all were present de Gaulle entered, shook hands all round, and then, before anybody had time to sit down, said: "The exclusive régime of parties has reappeared. I disapprove of it. But aside from establishing by force a dictatorship, which I do not desire and which would certainly end in disaster, I have no means of preventing this experiment. I must therefore withdraw. To-day, in fact, I shall send the President of the National Assembly a letter informing him of the Government's resignation. I sincerely thank each of you for the sup- port you have given me and urge you to remain at your posts in order to assure the conduct of business until your successors are ap- pointed."[14]

There was complete silence. While de Gaulle was in the room not a Minister dared trust himself to speak. He bade a collective good-bye and returned to his office to write the letter of resignation to the President of the Assembly. In it he made no mention of political parties but seemed to be excusing his resignation on the grounds that France, in spite of all her difficulties, was well on the way to recovery and had no further need of him. He had already sorted out his papers and prepared his office for his successor. He went home to Neuilly.

CHAPTER XVIII

DISILLUSION & DEFIANCE

De Gaulle had miscalculated. He did not resign to escape into solitude and lament the folly of his countrymen. He expected that the news of his resignation would so shatter the hopes of the French people that there would be a national uprising to force the government to recall him. Adrien Tixier, the Minister for the Interior, feared that de Gaulle might be right and, having briefed the *Commissaires de la République* who had been summoned to Paris for the purpose, sent them hurriedly back to their posts in the Provinces. In Paris a rumour spread that de Gaulle had sent for Leclerc from Indo-China to lead the army in a *coup d'état* and Vincent Auriol, hearing that de Gaulle intended to appeal to the French people over the radio, rushed back from London to dissuade him. Rumours, hopes and fears were false. The streets of Paris were as quiet as on any other Sunday afternoon; throughout the country no one stirred.

De Gaulle's Cabinet colleagues were more relieved than alarmed at his departure. Their pent-up feelings burst out as soon as the door of the Hall of Arms in the Rue St. Dominique closed behind him. Jules Moch, to whom de Gaulle had first confided his decision, remarked dryly that good might come out of evil for de Gaulle's personality had stifled the Assembly which might now come into its own. Francisque Gay and Henri Teitgen reflected sententiously that they were now all under the heavy obligation of succeeding de Gaulle and must try to be worthy of the task. Thorez retorted that, as they had not been worthy of it while the General was with them, what made them think they would be now? De Gaulle's departure, he added, was not without grandeur. The regret expressed by foreign governments was perfunctory. British Labour leaders had been even less at ease with de Gaulle than Churchill, and although Truman had felt some sympathy for him he had also recognised that de Gaulle's views on Germany were creating divisions among the Western Allies. The Russians were indifferent.

To de Gaulle this indifference came as such a shock that he could not really believe it. In his memoirs, written a decade later, he says that he contemplated going to some distant country "to wait in peace," but that "such a tide of insult and invective" rolled over him that he decided to stay in France and face it.[1] But de Gaulle was romanticising. For weeks left-wing writers had been accusing him of Buonapartism and more moderate critics of destroying the unity he desired by bidding for personal rule. Now, except for an occasional article, the press ignored him. By Tuesday the banner headlines were devoted to his successor, Félix Gouin, and by the end of the week his name had disappeared from the front pages. L'Humanité, the communist daily newspaper, reminded its readers that de Gaulle was only a temporary General and that his substantive rank was that of full Colonel. In many papers he was not mentioned at all.

Still de Gaulle did not give up hope. He was convinced that the people were with him and that a crisis would soon arise, probably through a clash with the Soviet Union, which would enable them to call him back. Since the war damage at La Boisserie, his house at Colombey-les-Deux-Églises, was being repaired, he must find somewhere to go so as to be near at hand. The government offered him any one of the many châteaux at its disposal and he chose the Pavillon de Marly, a hunting-lodge built by Louis XIV on the outskirts of Paris. He rented it for a nominal sum from the Service des Beaux Arts and moved from Neuilly with his wife and family. Still wondering why no demonstrations were being made in his favour he sent an officer to tour Paris and see if the police were cordoning the roads to prevent the people reaching him. But there were no cordons and shortly afterwards a Gallup Poll was published which showed that more people were glad than sorry that he had gone and that few expected him ever to return. De Gaulle began once more to taste the bitterness of failure.

Meanwhile, liberated for a second time by de Gaulle's departure, his former colleagues settled down to enjoy normal political life. After a bid by Thorez to become head of a Communist-Socialist coalition had been rejected by the Socialists, Félix Gouin, President of the Assembly, was elected head of the government. He was a jovial, small-town socialist who benefited both from his previous alliance with de Gaulle and from Léon Blum's recommendation that he was the Frenchman most like Attlee, then British Prime Minister. Except that André Philip, disciple of Mendès-France, replaced Pleven as Minister of National Economy, no important changes were made in the government. The few Radicals who had agreed to serve under de Gaulle dropped out. Mendès-France declined to serve on the grounds that it was now too late to carry out his policy, and the Communists were again denied any of the three key ministries. With a Declaration of

Intent which the leaders elevated into a Charter, and in which they pledged themselves to avoid personal recrimination, tripartite government began.

It lasted less than three months. One thing alone mattered, the drafting of the Constitution which had to be completed before the end of April. De Gaulle's departure made little difference to the debates of the Constitutional Commission. All were agreed that the Assembly elected by universal suffrage should exercise power and that the President of the Republic should be a figurehead; but whereas the Communists wanted this power to be untrammelled by constitutional checks of any kind, the Popular Republicans and some Moderate Socialists wanted the Council of the Republic, in which the overseas states of the French union would be represented, to exercise some of the restraints of a second chamber. In the end the Socialists sided with the Communists in rejecting the Popular Republican amendments and on April 19 the Communist-Socialist majority voted a draft which gave absolute power to the elected Assembly. The Popular Republicans voted with the Opposition. On May 5 the referendum to approve the Constitution was held. It was rejected by approximately ten million to nine million votes with a fifth of the electorate abstaining. Elections for a new Constituent Assembly were at once announced for June 2.

By now de Gaulle had moved to Colombey and to a life of retirement. It was not easy for him. The aeroplane which the President of the United States had put at his disposal had been returned to the Air Force and his large American car exchanged for a small French one. Madame de Gaulle now learned to drive so as to be able to shop in the local town. Money was tight. The family drank water or beer, wine being reserved for the faithful few guests who came regularly to see him. De Gaulle was a large eater and fortunately liked vegetables and good peasant dishes like tripe and pigs' feet; but sometimes the guests went away hungry and made jokes among themselves about the fare. And de Gaulle was bored. It was not that he was idle. He had already begun to re-edit the books he had written between the wars which he hoped would earn him some money; he read voraciously, went for long walks and talked to whomsoever would listen. But inaction drove him to fury. Every day he listened punctually to the one o'clock news and afterwards burst into indignant comment at what he heard. The French people were "cattle" or "slackers," the politicians imbeciles, drivellers, slobberers, whiners, cheats or cowards, their policies soup, vomit, or, in good barrack-room style, cold piss. Occasionally the beauty of a spring day with the quietness of the countryside would soothe him into philosophising; more often he would ejaculate, "If only I were in power," and launch into a diatribe on the subject of the hour.

Soustelle, Malraux, Pompidou, Guichard, Foccard, Debré, Palewski, Capitant and other old faithfuls came and went or met him in Paris where he stayed at the Hôtel Lapérouse. They knew his moods and let him rant, although Malraux, after a particularly bitter outburst at the stupidity of the human race, did once remark that, however true, some things were better left unsaid. Sometimes after his rage had subsided de Gaulle would feel remorse and say that it was wrong to complain and swear he enjoyed being alone. His friends were not taken in.

Momentarily the rejection of the out-dated Constitution revived him. Perhaps, after all, the people were not such fools. Could he even now persuade them to turn against the political parties and adopt his own plan? Should he intervene in the elections? He consulted his friends, some of whom went so far as to suggest that he not only intervene but himself become a candidate—a grotesque proposal which de Gaulle ignored. His difficulty was that in advocating Presidential rule he must again lay himself open to the Buonapartist charge. He decided neither to speak nor vote.

The result of the elections seemed to justify his silence. The Popular Republicans gained a million votes and became the strongest party in the Assembly. The Communists and Socialists no longer had an absolute majority. The cry *"Thorez au pouvoir"* had not rallied the people. Even more encouraging, after the elections the country itself seemed to turn against the political parties. From the moment the results were known leader-writers and political commentators began inveighing against the rigid discipline of the party machines. It was an absurd criticism because it was a lack rather than an excess of discipline which was endangering the coalition. What was really happening was something quite different. The bourgeoisie was re-asserting itself. Now that the danger of communist rule had passed, the owners of property were regaining their confidence and attacking the *dirigisme* under which they had suffered both during and since the war. It was a revolt against the memories of Vichy, of what was left of the Resistance and even of de Gaulle's own rule.

De Gaulle, however, saw an opportunity. If he could reinforce the resentment against the parties he might force the Popular Republicans to throw out any Constitution of which he disapproved. This time he did not hesitate. In May he had scornfully declined Félix Gouin's invitation to take part in the V.E. Day ceremonies in Paris. Now he arranged to hold a ceremony in Bayeux on June 16 to commemorate his entry into the town two years before. It was an ideal occasion to remind the country both of his services and of the prestige he still enjoyed.

The platform, draped with the *Tricolore*, was set in the square where he had addressed the crowd in the hectic days of liberation. On it sat the most glamorous figures of the Free French Movement, Admiral d'Argenlieu, now High Commissioner in Indo-China, General Koenig, Commander in Chief of the French Forces in Germany, Marshal Juin, the Chief of the French General Staff, Maurice Schumann, once his "voice" on the B.B.C., Palewski, Capitant and Soustelle. There was an immense crowd and as de Gaulle entered the square, preceded by police outriders which the State still accorded him, there were cries of *"au pouvoir, au pouvoir."*

De Gaulle began by echoing his speech of liberation. He reminded his audience that it was at Bayeux, in that very square, that the true French State had reappeared after four years of servitude; true and legitimate because it was founded in the hearts of the people who had never ceased to regard the enemy as the enemy. Anticipating the accusations his opponents might level against him, he stressed that régimes weakened by party rivalries too often paved the way for dictatorship. It had happened in France, it had happened between the wars in Germany, Italy and Spain. At all costs it must be prevented from happening in France again.

Then, turning to the work of the Second Constituent Assembly, he sketched in some details of the sort of Constitution he hoped it would adopt; a parliament of two chambers, the second to be the Council of the French Union, elected by local organisations in France and the territories overseas and to include representatives of all forms of local interests. This Council must have wide powers both of remission and initiation in matters affecting the Union such as foreign affairs, defence and trade. He was unequivocal in describing the functions of the President. He must not be dependent upon the Assembly; he should be elected by a wider "college" which would include the Assembly but qualify him to be President of the French Union as well as of France. He must be above party, able to choose his ministers as he pleased, to dissolve parliament, to act as arbitrator amid party conflict, to give continuity to government and, if the nation were in peril, to be the "guarantor of national independence and the treaties concluded by France."[2]

It was a magnificent speech but it misfired. However unpopular the political parties might be, their leaders were just beginning to enjoy the power which seemed miraculously to have been restored to them. Yet here was de Gaulle making a bid for wider authority than had ever been accorded the head of a democratic state in Europe except in war. The French President, he was suggesting, should govern whether the majority in the Assembly agreed with him or not; parties should play a subsidiary role. At a time when demands for self-government were beginning to be heard throughout the overseas territories of France, de Gaulle proposed a loose form of federalism in which all real power would still remain with the mother country and indeed with the President himself. He would render his account to the nation and the Union only when his term of office expired.

The citizens of Bayeux applauded but the politicians remained unmoved. Blum declared bluntly that the elected Assembly must have the first and last word on the new Constitution. The Popular Republicans, to whom the speech was directed, were non-committal. The Communists were so alarmed by de Gaulle's thesis that they became more amenable to the draft under discussion. Only the parties of the Right, insignificant in the Assembly, showed approval. Within six weeks the Constitutional Commission had adopted a draft which ignored every major suggestion de Gaulle had made. The changes from the proposals which the country had rejected were insignificant. The new parliament was to be bicameral, but although the second chamber was to include representatives from overseas territories, it was to exercise no power over the government. The President was to be elected by the two chambers but apart from appointing the Prime Minister had few prerogatives. The Prime Minister had to be approved by the Assembly, which could be dissolved only if two ministerial crises occurred in two consecutive years. In the first year it could not be dissolved at all. The provisions for the French Union were less liberal than before. French sovereignty was to be maintained throughout and the doctrine of assimilation assured by the presence of overseas representatives in the impotent second chamber. No statute for the French Union was included in the draft and the nature of local assemblies was not defined.

Before the text of the new Constitution was debated in the Assembly de Gaulle returned to the charge. On August 27 he issued a statement to the press criticising the proposals in detail. He found them inadequate in every respect. The proposals for the French Union were vague and neither assured France her "pre-eminent responsibility" nor the overseas territories the development suitable to them. He remarked that, as far as France was concerned, the text did not contain either the words "government" or "executive power." The provision by which members of the government were "personally responsible" to the Assembly for their individual acts as ministers struck at the whole concept of collective responsibility. Under the draft a minister could be impeached by a simple majority vote. The right of the Assembly to initiate expenditure undermined executive responsibility for the budget. Finally the impotence of the President, who could not even sign decrees without the counter-signature of a minister and who could not communicate with the people except through messages addressed to the Assembly, destroyed all hope of continuity in government in the all too likely event of a ministerial crisis.

De Gaulle's statement was to be read and re-read in years to come by Frenchmen who wished to understand the General's concept of government, but it had little influence on the Deputies to the new Constituent Assembly. The Popular Republicans won a few minor concessions to de Gaulle's point of view, but as a whole showed themselves good parliamentarians. The rift between them and de Gaulle widened.

On September 30, the Assembly approved the new Draft by a large majority and submitted it to a national Referendum to be held on October 13. De Gaulle made one final effort. At Épinal, in the Vosges, where he had accepted an invitation to preside over the liberation ceremonies, he asked the country to reject the Constitution outright. As in August he enumerated its weaknesses point by point, ending with an appeal to all those whose "hearts he had touched" to join him in the effort to give France institutions worthy of it. On October 13 the people of France accepted the Constitution by a majority of more than a million votes with one third of the electorate abstaining. "A third of the French people are resigned to it, a third have rejected it, a third have ignored it," was de Gaulle's dry comment.[3]

For the third time in his career de Gaulle faced not only defeat but eclipse. Once more he consulted his small circle of devoted adherents, called, scurrilously, the "Imperial Guard." The elections for the first Substantive Assembly under the new Constitution had been fixed for November 10 which left barely a month for campaigning after the Referendum. Yet since nearly two thirds of the electorate had voted either against the Constitution or abstained it was tempting to assume that a majority of the people shared his view. For the first time a political party had been formed carrying his name and pledged to fight for the principles enumerated in the Bayeux speech. *L'Union Gaulliste*, under René Capitant, had attracted a few prominent individuals from other parties: Radicals like Chaban-Delmas, Giacobbi, Léo Hamon and Alfred Coste-Floret from the Popular Republicans, Clostermann and Malbrant from the *Union démocratique et Socialiste de la Résistance*. The party was too new to mount a major campaign itself but could back selected candidates from other parties in each constituency and so try and build up a true Gaullist political movement. Should he throw his full weight behind it?

In the end de Gaulle decided he would not. He knew that he would receive the support of the Right-Wing parties, who regarded him as a bulwark against Communism, but this was not the backing he wanted. On the other hand it was becoming plain that the people were getting tired of the constitutional wrangle and simply wanted the question settled. By attempting to postpone the answer yet again he might lose the following he still had. Except for a brief statement to the press on November 1, in which he urged the electorate to choose candidates who were "resolute" in their desire to change the bad institutions which the country had just adopted, he said nothing and played no part in the election.

For better or, as de Gaulle was convinced, for worse, the Fourth Republic came into being on November 10. The *Union Gaulliste* received a derisory vote; de Gaulle's influence had been negligible. France had decided to rebuild itself without him.

In the Chanceries and press of the world de Gaulle was regarded as finished. Some commentators took the precaution of pointing out that, so long as he was alive, he remained an elemental force in reserve upon which the French could call in an emergency, but the tone of their remarks revealed that they did not feel this was likely to happen. In Paris the politicians at last breathed freely. The country had shown that it preferred them to the General. The Communists themselves, having failed to find a partner, lapsed into opposition. Visitors from Britain and America received a welcome which they had not experienced since before the war. British Members of Parliament in particular found themselves treated almost as colleagues, as if their French counter-parts wished to make up for the rigidity of the previous administration. Ministers spoke patronisingly of de Gaulle. He had served the country and they would always be grateful to him but he did not understand politics. They hoped that he would accept the verdict of the country with good grace.*

But of this de Gaulle was incapable. For five months he stayed at Colombey, going seldom to Paris and seeing only the chosen few. To them he complained unceasingly. What maddened him was to watch men like Maurice Schumann, who owed everything to him, claiming still to follow him but taking office in the régime he condemned. Even worse was the spectacle of all the pre-war politicians, Blum, Auriol, Herriot, Ramadier, enjoying the limelight and beginning once more

* The author, as a Member of the British Parliament, paid one official and several unofficial visits to France at this time.

the game of ministerial general post, while those who had fought in the Resistance like Chaban-Delmas and Soustelle were ignored. His vocabulary of vituperation expanded. Eunuchs, drug-addicts of politics, pitter-patterers, anaesthetists, puppets, gigolos, dwarfs, no pejorative synonym was too coarse to be hurled at the men who were building the Fourth Republic. Occasionally an orgy of invective would be followed by a period of calm in which he would make up his mind to stand aloof, wrapping himself in mystery, and wait for the day when France would have need of him. But these moods never lasted for long. The politician in de Gaulle was always uppermost and the nightmare of his retirement was that he might be forgotten, that if he retreated into isolation men would come to think of him as part of history instead of looking to him for action.

De Gaulle did not always talk. Morazé, one of the ablest of his political advisers, Soustelle, Pompidou and Debré could make him listen, but there was never conversation nor even argument. Having listened, de Gaulle would hold forth on the absurdity of negotiating with Ho Chi Minh; the absolute necessity of holding Indo-China; the danger of German rearmament; the menace of the "Separatists," as he called the French Communists; above all the threat of invasion by the Soviet Army which was now so close to the French frontier.

It was this fear which finally impelled de Gaulle back on to the stage. As the war-time allies quarrelled and four-power control of Germany broke down, he became convinced that war between Russia and the West was imminent. He feared that America would hesitate to make use of the atom bomb and saw France once more being overrun. Somehow the people must be roused to their danger. From November to March he made no public speeches. Then he took his decision. He would re-enter the arena, if possible as a new Messiah, if not as a political partisan.

De Gaulle announced his intention to his small but faithful circle at the beginning of March. At once secret emissaries were sent out from Paris to contact former Resistance leaders, and war-time members of the association "Friends of Free France." The response was encouraging. Many of those approached had been discarded by de Gaulle himself when, in the first days of liberation, he had broken the Resistance as a political movement; but resentment was now buried in a new hope that, through him, they might once more exert an influence or take part in a new adventure.

The opening of the campaign was carefully staged. As a former Chief of State de Gaulle still enjoyed many privileges. He was entitled to a Guard of Honour and police protection whenever he appeared in public; he moved, with outriders, in a motorcade; his speeches were broadcast by the government-controlled radio. On March 30, at Bruneval, below the cliffs where Allied troops first disembarked in the invasion of 1944, this pageantry was harnessed to a setting calculated to evoke all the memories of the war, the Free French and the Liberation. From a platform not only draped with the *Tricolore* but flanked by standards bearing the Cross of Lorraine, de Gaulle addressed an audience of old comrades drawn from the Resistance and Free French sympathisers from all over France. The theme of his speech was no longer an appeal but a challenge. "The day is coming," he said, "when the mass of the French people, rejecting the sterile game of the parties and reforming the distorted framework of the State within which the nation is now going astray, will rally around France itself."[4] At Strasbourg a week later he was more specific. Ironically, the occasion was a ceremony in remembrance of American soldiers who had died in Alsace. "It is time," he said, "the *Rassemblement du Peuple Français* (R.P.F.) was formed and organised so that, *within the law*, it could promote and carry to fruition, above differences of opinion, a great effort for common safety and the reform of the State."[5] The following week on April 14, the R.P.F. was officially founded as an organisation with the same objectives: "the union of the people, the effort or renovation, the reform of the State."[6]

The Party leaders at once jumped to the conclusion that the phrase "within the law" was only a pretence and that de Gaulle's new movement was really revolutionary. All the old charges of Buonapartism and Boulangism were hurled at him again. Those closest to de Gaulle, however, did not believe he had any such clear intention. He wanted simply to rally behind himself the immense support he felt he still had in the country and then decide what to do. Since war was so close the Constitutional question might solve itself in a national emergency.

De Gaulle was not alone in thinking that war was imminent. More than a year had passed since Churchill, at Fulton, Missouri, had warned the world of the "iron curtain" that was falling across Europe and of Russia's revolutionary designs within the countries beyond it. Since then the curtain had come down. In January, 1947, the tragedy of Poland reached its climax. In farcical elections in which some of the results were declared before the votes had been counted, a Communist-dominated government was installed by the Russians, and the Poles, like every other country in Eastern Europe, were cut off from the Western world.* The cause for which Britain had made war upon Hitler had been finally betrayed. In Persia the Russian attempt to erect

* The author attended these elections as a representative of the British Parliament.

a Communist satellite state in Azerbaijan, supported by Soviet troops, kept the allies on the brink of war for many months. In Indo-China, after nine months of negotiation between the French Government and Ho Chi Minh, all hope of agreement was shattered by massacres at Haiphong and Hanoi. In January the eight-year war broke out.

The retaliation of the Western powers to this hardening communist attitude followed swiftly. In March President Truman abandoned his predecessors' belief in collaboration with Stalin and pronounced the Truman doctrine of aid to those governments which resisted armed minorities within their borders and pressure from without. At the beginning of May, 1947, after seven weeks of discussion, the Moscow Conference on Germany ended in deadlock. On May 14 Churchill made his "Europe arise" speech at the Hague Convention, launching the idea of a united states of Western Europe and advocating the reintegration of Germany into the Western world. In June came General Marshall's speech at Harvard. Although Molotov came to Paris with a large delegation to discuss with Bevin and Bidault ways and means of taking advantage of Marshall's offer, he and his entire delegation left Paris on July 2. The Russians were willing to accept aid but refused to collaborate in positive measures of reconstruction. Thereafter the Marshall plan followed the lines of the Truman doctrine. Wherever men looked, the Western powers and the communists seemed to be heading for collision. When de Gaulle spoke of national safety he was not, as his critics maintained, exploiting the feelings of the masses in the interests of his own movement. He was expressing a belief which was widely shared.

The *Rassemblement*, then, was well named. It was not intended as a political party but as a muster of the people, a call to a new resistance; resistance to the régime of the parties and the calamitous Constitution; resistance to the French Communists who had chosen "separatism" rather than patriotism; resistance above all to the threat of Soviet attack. From the start it was an authoritarian movement. Power was concentrated in the central direction which the President chose and where his word was law. The Executive and Departmental Committees existed simply to carry out instructions. The *Compagnons*, as the members were called, were organised regionally but also in factories where they formed *Groupes d'Entreprise*. The whole was intended to be a disciplined, social and political force working for the unity of France. Once a year they were summoned to the "*Assises Nationales*," a national congress where the leader gave them his orders. For all de Gaulle's denials, it was an appeal to the Buonapartist tradition in France.

Nevertheless it was an appeal that Frenchmen were prepared to answer. Twenty-four hours after de Gaulle had announced the formation of the *Rassemblement*, seventeen thousand members had enrolled. Within a fortnight the number of applications had reached eight hundred thousand, of which a hundred thousand were in Paris alone. Headquarters were set up at 5 Rue de Solferino and branch offices opened in every important town. The recruits were a mixed bunch. Most of the officials were veterans of Free France or the Resistance, old comrades who had been by-passed in de Gaulle's reorganisation but who now felt even more disillusioned by the return to the pre-war régime. Their background gave the *Rassemblement* a para-military character reminiscent of the Fascist parties before the war. The rank and file came from every walk of life. Generals and high-ranking officers, writers, churchmen, civil servants enrolled alongside wealthy speculators and black marketeers who saw de Gaulle as the bastion against Communism. The wave of strikes which swept over France that summer drove thousands of small business men into de Gaulle's arms. The response seemed to bear out all his predictions.

De Gaulle threw himself whole-heartedly into the growing movement, touring the country and making speeches to vast audiences in settings which looked more and more like those of the Nazi rallies before the war. He did not care. So long as the check-shirted young men touring the cities and flanking the squares with their jeeps chanted *"de Gaulle au pouvoir"* and made the crowds chant with them, he was content. When the Russians withdrew from the Marshall Plan he sounded the alarm. At Rennes, on July 15, before an audience of 60,000 people, he not only turned on the French Communists, denouncing them as fifth columnists plotting to turn France into a satellite, but painted a lurid picture of the Soviet Armies poised to strike within three hundred miles of the French border—a distance covered in less than two days by cyclists of the *Tour de France*. His feud with the United States seemed buried. The hope of France lay in Marshall Aid and American military protection. The war in Indo-China and rising nationalism throughout the French Empire were laid at the door of the Communists and of the régime which was too weak to control them. Federation, the vision of a union of self-governing countries, was discarded. French sovereignty must be retained in Algeria indefinitely and elsewhere for as long as possible.

The political parties did not take this onslaught lying down. The day after the *Rassemblement* was launched Ramadier, the Prime Minister, visited de Gaulle at Colombey to tell him that in future he would not be accorded a Guard of Honour when he appeared at other than official functions and that his speeches would no longer be broadcast over the French radio. After the Rennes speech the Communists demanded Committees of Vigilance for the defence of the Republic. The Executive Committee of the Socialist Party denounced de Gaulle's appeal as being without a programme, an appeal to rally round one man. The Popular Republicans forbade its members to join the *Rassemblement*. Officially only Radicals and Moderates were free to enlist under de Gaulle's banner without forfeiting their Party membership. By the autumn the stage was set for a trial of strength between the *Rassemblement*, the Communists and the parliamentary parties of the centre. It was to take place in the municipal elections.

On August 20 de Gaulle announced that the R.P.F. would fight the elections in every municipality in France. Since voting was to take place on October 19 and 26 this left only two months for preparation, but he kept his word. Funds poured into the Party Headquarters and de Gaulle threw himself into the election with furious energy. He spoke in fifty towns and drew tremendous audiences. Posters carrying his portrait appeared all over the country. He harped on the danger of war, he attacked the Communists and praised the free enterprise of the Americans. His opponents denounced him as a demagogue, a warmonger and a political quack, offering quasi-metaphysical remedies to cure material ills. But, as the campaign went on, they sensed that he was winning and began to speculate on what form a Gaullist dictatorship would take. Would the Communist Party and trade unions be dissolved? Would strikes be prohibited? Would the press be censored? In the tenseness of the struggle, commentators seemed to lose sight of the fact that these were only municipal elections and, however overwhelming the victory, the Assembly and the Government would still be there.

The results were a triumph for de Gaulle. Nearly forty per cent of the votes cast had gone to the *Rassemblement* or to candidates of the moderate or right-wing parties who had fought under de Gaulle's banner. In the large towns the R.P.F. had almost swept the board. In Paris, helped out by a strike which paralysed all forms of public transport, the *Rassemblement* gained control with a large majority. Only the Communists held their own and retained nearly a third of the votes cast.

After the elections the Gaullists celebrated. Mayors belonging to the *Rassemblement* were installed in fifty-two out of ninety-two of the principal French towns and cities. In Paris de Gaulle's brother, Pierre, was elected President of the Council. Abroad de Gaulle's victory was hailed as a triumph for the West: in the words of the *Daily Mirror*, "the best piece of news since the end of the war"; according to the *New York Times*, "the victory of the Marshall Plan over the fifth column."[7] In the general exaltation de Gaulle was confident that: "as the *Rassemblement* had conquered the cities so it would conquer the whole country except for the Separatists and a certain number of misanthropes, melancholics and general staffs without any troops."[8]

But how could he use his success? There was only one way. He had to persuade the Assembly to dissolve itself. Some of his supporters urged him to reach agreement with the Socialist or Popular Republican leaders so as to secure the two thirds majority needed to call a new general election. But bargaining was not in de Gaulle's nature. Instead he threw out a challenge. In a statement issued on October 27 he declared, "An immense force has arisen, the rally of the French people, born only six months ago, whose organisation is only just beginning, and which won at the first encounter more votes than all the parties combined. French men and women have discovered the path of salvation . . .

"Those who at present hold public powers find themselves shorn of their legitimate basis—the nation's confidence. Their powers stem, in fact, from a combination established among the parties which, it is clear, represents only a feeble national minority. In this situation there is no duty or democratic solution other than to go to the country. The present National Assembly must be dissolved as soon as possible."

After saying that, before a general election took place, the electoral system must be changed and the British system of majority voting adopted, de Gaulle ended: "The rally of the French people will continue in its national task. Open to all who wish to serve the cause of France, it will spread and organise to ensure the nation's salvation against any eventuality."[9]

The statement was a boomerang. Instead of offering the moderate parties some means of aligning themselves with popular feeling by collaborating with the R.P.F., it branded them all as enemies. The implication in the last sentence of de Gaulle's speech was that, if the Assembly did not do what he wanted, the *Rassemblement* would mobilise opinion in some unspecified way to bring about its downfall. It was a thinly veiled threat of unconstitutional action.

The effect was instantaneous. Already on October 22, when the first electoral results were known, Ramadier had reorganised his Cabinet, dismissed men like André Philip, Tanguy-Prigent, who were associated with dirigisme, and Moutet, who had negotiated with Ho Chi Minh, and replaced them with "moderates" who were in fact conservatives. Now all the party leaders not directly associated with de Gaulle rallied to the Republic. That same evening the Communists issued a statement branding de Gaulle's message to Parliament as an "ultimatum." Next day in the Assembly Ramadier, Herriot and a procession of other speakers suddenly roused themselves in defence of the Assembly and the democratic institutions which gave it life. As Claude Bourdet, an old Resistance leader who had at first hoped that the R.P.F. would revive the idealism of Resistance days, wrote, "de Gaulle has shocked the rank and file of the people—all those to whom a bad Republic is preferable to [a] good tyranny." De Gaulle had become "enemy number one of the Republic he had helped to resurrect."[10]

The defenders of the Republic lost no time in taking advantage of the opportunities de Gaulle had offered them. A month after the elections Ramadier, unable to cope with the strikes which were still paralysing the country, resigned. The President, Vincent Auriol, first asked Blum to form a Cabinet and, when he failed to get the necessary majority, chose Robert Schuman. On November 22 Schuman was elected by every non-Communist vote. Whatever support de Gaulle once had in the Assembly had already vanished.

Schuman's adoption was the death knell of the *Rassemblement*. It was the beginning of eight years of conservative rule, during which France not only recovered economically but to a great extent reasserted her leadership in Western Europe. Schuman did not attack de Gaulle but simply stole his clothes. His programme was first and foremost anti-Communist. To maintain order he called up 80,000 Reservists and then passed a law to protect the right to work in such broad terms that it became practically impossible to strike legally. During the debate, in which the Communists called Schuman everything from "Boche" to "assassin," free fights broke on the floor of the Chamber and Herriot had to suspend the sitting. But Jules Moch, the Minister of the Interior, used his powers ruthlessly. Thousands of strikers were imprisoned and pitched battles took place with the police in many towns. In Marseilles, where the strikers were under open Communist leadership, the Law Courts were stormed. But the Government stood firm and the strikes were broken before Christmas. Meanwhile, like Churchill in Britain in 1951, Schuman made a bonfire of controls. Free enterprise was restored, rationing abolished; the black market began to disappear. With the banning of four Communist newspapers and the splitting of the trade union movement into the Communist C.G.D. and the new democratic *Force Ouvrière*, opposition became disorganised.

The composition of the Government itself was a blow to de Gaulle, for it included not only Popular Republicans and Socialists but several

Radicals and Independents, whose parties had supported him in the municipal elections. These men preferred office to opposition. In the country it was the same. Gradually the Conservatives and Liberal Socialists who had feared for their freedom, the bourgeoisie and peasants who had feared for their property, the wage earners who resented the Communist-inspired strikes, found in the Schuman government and those which succeeded it the security they had been looking for. The *Rassemblement* became unnecessary. Instead of appearing as a saviour de Gaulle began to seem like an agitator.

* * *

During the following year some of de Gaulle's speeches hinted at a *coup d'état* and perhaps some of his advisers urged it. André Malraux is credited with the remark that "de Gaulle marched at full speed to the Rubicon and then told us to get out our fishing rods." De Gaulle had rejected revolution when he controlled the army three years before; he was not likely to attempt it now. No doubt he toyed with the idea and used it as a threat, but whenever he considered the question seriously he always came to the same conclusion; he could see how to enter upon a dictatorship but he could not see how to come out. Yet if he would not form an alliance with any of the parties what was he to do? One after another his supporters in the Assembly tried to bring about an understanding between the *Rassemblement* and the moderate parties; but de Gaulle always refused.

Constitutionally de Gaulle's only other means of exercising pressure on the Assembly lay in the elections for the General Councils, due in October, 1948. They would choose the new Second Chamber, the Council of the Republic. Although the authors of the Constitution had deliberately curtailed the powers of the Council, it was just possible, if the *Rassemblement* gained an overall majority, that by constant obstruction it could bring government to a standstill and force an election. However, the party leaders awoke to the danger and the government first postponed the elections and then altered the electoral law. De Gaulle, on a tour of South East France, became menacing. "If anarchy should gain further ground," he said at Annecy on September 19, "if bankruptcy should overcome us as it threatens to do; and if servitude should continue to approach us from within and without—in short if we should move towards our final collapse—then, and I say this in full conscience before France, the same duty would arise as in 1940 and it would be necessary to safeguard the public welfare against such people."[11]

But the government was not intimidated. At Grenoble on September 18 there was a riot after de Gaulle's meeting. Communists tried to break through the cordon of police and Gaullist strong-arm squads, who were marshalling the crowd. In the fighting one communist was shot dead and fourteen other people seriously injured. Several jeeps used by the Gaullists were burned. An immediate inquiry was ordered and on September 21 Jules Moch, the Minister of the Interior and the man who in 1946 had told de Gaulle he had no right to abdicate from power, gave his report to the Assembly. He said that it had been found that all the Gaullists and police hurt in the affray were injured by stones or blows, whilst the Communist demonstrators were hurt by bullets, that none of the Communists searched was found to carry arms, and that the police had not used their arms either. The inescapable conclusion was, therefore, that the shots were fired by supporters of General de Gaulle.

Speaking of the General's bodyguard, Moch stated that this consisted of two kinds of formations: the *Service d'Ordre*, trained and commanded by Colonel Rémy (a well-known Resistance figure and head of General de Gaulle's secret service in France during the occupation), which numbered six thousand in Paris and ten thousand in the Provinces and were not armed, though having all the makings of a shadow army; and the "shock formations" which followed General de Gaulle on his tours, were composed of men of all sorts, a number of them coloured, and, though not armed by the movement, were almost all found to carry arms.[12] It was these men who had driven their jeeps into the crowd on several occasions during the demonstrations and who had been responsible for the shooting. After saying that such a "private and motorised police" was inadmissable in a democracy, Moch mentioned that he had sent over eight hundred police to Grenoble to keep order, that the cost to the State of security measures during the General's provincial tours since January 1 had exceeded ten million francs and that the army had provided General de Gaulle with a number of cars, lorries, motor cycles and loud-speaker equipment and the squad of gendarmes for his personal protection. All this, Moch declared, was allowed to General de Gaulle as liberator of France, but it was impossible now to ignore the fact that he was the head of a political party. Next day Ramadier announced that, although the State would continue to take measures to ensure General de Gaulle's safety, this special bodyguard would henceforth be withdrawn.

The dialogue continued. On October 10, a week before the local councils were due to elect the delegates, de Gaulle gave his first press conference for nearly a year. Asked whether he would feel impelled to "go beyond legality" to save France if the Communists were included in the Government, he replied that "discretion was necessary in discussing any such plans." He went on to say, however, that in his view the existing government had already passed the bounds of legality by refusing new elections when the municipal votes of the preceding year showed that it no longer represented political opinion in France. But when another questioner asked him what means he would use to gain power he again chose "democracy." "I maintain that the country must be consulted," he said. "As long as the democratic way is still open, the decision is up to the country. I am at her service."

But the country did not want him. In the primary elections the Gaullist poll dropped heavily. In the new Second Chamber the R.P.F. only won fifty-six out of 320 seats and, even with individual allies in other parties, were still in a minority. There was no hope whatever of forcing an election.

De Gaulle was now truly at the parting of the ways. He had failed to overthrow the Constitution by political pressure; a general election was three years away. Either he could retire and await the catastrophe he still prophesied, which would provide the occasion of his recall to power, or he must really enter the party game. Yet he did neither. Instead he chose the role of critic.

He turned his attention first to the conduct of French foreign policy. In the summer of 1948 the blockade of Berlin by the Russians, successfully countered by the allied air lift, had finally shattered four power occupation. The ending of the zones of occupation and the formation of what is now Western Germany had become imperative. The necessary measures had been agreed between the United States, Great Britain and France in London. In speech after speech de Gaulle not only deplored the London agreement but reverted to his idea of a Germany of states. He sounded more like an opponent of Bismarck than Stalin. And although Marshall Aid was bringing about the recovery of France and American nuclear power was the sole guarantee of Western Europe's independence, he once again adopted an anti-American tone, criticising the entry of American big-business into Europe and suggesting that the Pentagon was only interested in certain European outposts, Britain and perhaps the Iberian Peninsula, and would sacrifice the rest. France alone, he argued, must be the core of European defence and for that purpose a great and modern army must be created at whatever cost. Towards the growing idea of Western Europe he remained coldly indifferent.

De Gaulle reaped his reward. In the single year, 1949, membership of the *Rassemblement* declined from more than a million to three hundred and fifty thousand. The Conservatives, frightened by his anti-Americanism, dropped away in their tens of thousands. Rank and file Liberals and Socialists, who had defied their party leaders to support him, saw in his programme a check to recovery and a risk of annihilation. In their place former *cagoulards* and fascists began to infiltrate the *Rassemblement*, making it more militant than ever. In June, sixteen of its members, including two municipal councillors, were arrested on suspicion of preparing a *coup d'état*. The case was not proven and de Gaulle may have been ignorant of the plot, but it shocked the public. Throughout France municipalities began to shun de Gaulle's rallies and refuse the facilities of their town halls and market squares. Attendances sank so low that de Gaulle threatened to refuse to speak.

Incredibly de Gaulle had suddenly become a pathetic figure. He had been much more alone in 1940, but no one had thought of pitying him. Now, in 1950, he was shunned by many of his old admirers, deserted by those who had sought to use him, derided rather than feared by his opponents; the men who spoke most loudly in his favour were either adventurers or belonged to the anti-Republican right-wing splinter groups which he had always mistrusted and despised.

As the general election of 1951 drew near de Gaulle again embarked on a speaking campaign, this time no longer as a national hero but as the leader of one of the two extreme parties—for that is what the *Rassemblement* had become. A new electoral law, by which parties in alliance were able to amalgamate their votes, had been passed specifically to weaken him and the Communists—and for the most part Gaullists fought alone. Helped by the Korean war, which de Gaulle heralded as the beginning of the third Armageddon, the *Rassemblement* did better than was expected, and, polling four million votes, emerged as the largest single party in the Assembly with 118 of the 627 seats.

Yet the position was hopeless. The Government parties had a clear majority over Gaullists and Communists together, and any understanding between the two was out of the question. De Gaulle, as leader of the largest party, at once offered to form a government, but as in the same breath he announced that he would do so only in order to reform the Constitution and give France the strong state she needed, there was not the slightest prospect of any major group supporting him. After several weeks, during which three ministers failed to form a government and one refused to try, Pleven succeeded in gaining investiture. The Gaullists, once more condemned to opposition, proceeded to destroy themselves.

Already Gaullists had been expelled from the party for supporting an unofficial candidate and Rémy, the great resistance leader, had been forced to leave the Executive for advocating the rehabilitation of Marshal Pétain. Malraux and Soustelle quarrelled with de Gaulle over Church schools, and Catroux soon resigned over Colonial policy and de Gaulle's opposition to the Schuman Plan. The decisive split came in the spring of 1952. When Pinay sought investiture as Premier, de Gaulle ordered his followers to abstain, but twenty-seven Gaullists rebelled and Pinay was elected. Shortly afterwards, in a vote on a bill to regulate wages, a third of the Gaullists voted for it, a third against, and a third abstained. De Gaulle appealed for unity, invoking the names of Joffre, Clemenceau and Poincaré, but when he tried to re-impose discipline twenty-six of the rebels left the party. The R.P.F., which eight months before had been the largest party in the Assembly, was no more than a rump.

Yet de Gaulle still could not bring himself to admit defeat. Although he himself virtually retired from public life, he allowed the *Rassemblement* to disintegrate for another year. In the summer the split in the Assembly was repeated in the Paris *Commune* and the Gaullists lost their majority. In November he emerged from Colombey to attend the "*Assises Nationales*," the last great rally the *Rassemblement* was to hold, and delivered a scathing attack on French foreign policy and in particular the European Defence Community. "They are inviting France to work for the King of Prussia—openly this time—," he went on. "Best of all it is our diplomacy which pursues a policy of presents. It gives away everything, the Saar, the bases, everything. Our friends the Germans want sovereignty? Here it is. Our friends the Americans want to install themselves in North Africa? Agreed. You desire the Supreme Command in Europe? Excellent. And in the Mediterranean as well? Bravo!"[13] He struck a chord, but it did not evoke an electoral response.

In the spring of 1953 the municipal elections came round once more. The *Rassemblement* lost two thousand of their three thousand, three hundred and twenty-seven seats in the larger towns and a similar proportion in the smaller *communes* on the second ballot a week later. This was not defeat but annihilation. Three days after the final results had been announced de Gaulle issued a statement to the press dissolving the *Rassemblement* as a political party. "The efforts I have made since the war," he wrote, "seconded by resolute Frenchmen, to enable our country to find its unity at last and to put at its head a government which really would be a government, have so far been without results. I acknowledge this without equivocation." Having traced the causes of failure he stated bluntly that the *Rassemblement* must disassociate itself from "a régime which is sterile and which it cannot for the moment change." De Gaulle then formally released the R.P.F. deputies from their allegiance, telling them that in future they stood as candidates or acted as deputies only as individuals. He ended by saying that the *Rassemblement* would remain in being, not as a political movement, but against the day when "the influence of a restless dissatisfaction could lead the French people to unite and the régime to transform itself. We behold the bankruptcy of illusion," he ended. "It is for us to prepare the remedy."[14]

Brave words, in which de Gaulle himself did not believe. From that moment the *Rassemblement* died. It held no more "*Assises Nationales*," de Gaulle addressed no more meetings. Within little more than a year the official Gaullist group in Parliament had changed its name twice and the few who kept in contact with de Gaulle himself had left it. The rebels joined the Government. From the summer of 1953 onwards only the insertion of the word "Gaullist" in brackets after the initials S.R. (Social Republicans) or A.R.S. (*Action Républicaine et Sociale*) reminded Frenchmen that de Gaulle had ever entered the political lists.

*   *   *

De Gaulle stayed at Colombey and continued to write the memoirs he had begun the previous year. To his friends he admitted that his political life had come to an end. Regularly, every Wednesday, he came to Paris to stay at the Hotel Lapérouse, but although he still often spoke as if France was on the brink of a national disaster, he was now convinced that, even if it came, the parties would somehow combine to prevent him playing any part. Gradually he came to accept defeat and retirement. Very occasionally he would emerge from his retreat to deliver a speech on Europe or the French Union and to give an occasional press conference. When in August, 1954, the Assembly finally rejected the European Defence Community under which the armies of France would have been merged in a supra-national European force, his spirits lifted. "The nation has roused itself. This healthy reaction could soon bring others in its train," and he went on to express again his belief in the grandeur and future of France.[15] But it was not a future in which he any longer had a role.

De Gaulle read and re-read the great authors of the past and present, Chateaubriand, Bergson, Nietzsche, Péguy, Barrès, Malraux, Mauriac, Sartre. He also enjoyed the novels of Françoise Sagan. After finishing Hemingway's *The Old Man and the Sea* in a night he remarked that he felt like the old man himself and only hoped that he would reach harbour before the sharks had made a skeleton of him. He began to study gardening. Because he was told that it might benefit his eyes he gave up smoking, announcing the decision to his friends so that he could not go back on it without losing face. From the midsummer of 1955 de Gaulle remained silent. What he had feared in 1946 he now accepted with resignation. He receded into history. In the newspapers he was referred to with respect, his journeys and occasionally his visitors were recorded. But he was a figure of the past, the "liberator" of France about whom children were taught in school but whose face was familiar only through pictures and whose voice, once so well known, was unrecognised by the new generation. Even his visits to Paris became an embarrassment to his staff because they experienced increasing difficulty in finding people who wanted to see him. Olivier Guichard, his personal assistant, was frequently obliged to fall back on old war-time associates to fill the gaps in his day, or to call on his publisher to come and discuss some detailed points in the memoirs.

The memoirs were his solace. He intended them to be at once his monument and a contribution to French literature. He succeeded in making them both. He wrote in long-hand, slowly and with much correction. His daughter Élisabeth typed out the pages. Except that he employed René Thibault to assemble the documents which he published as companion volumes, he did his own research. Each volume and each chapter had a theme which generally could be expressed in one word; for example, the last volume, "Salvation," has seven chapters, the titles of which read Liberation, Status, Order, Victory, Discord, Disunion, Departure. His writing, like his speaking, was rhythmical and lucid, but he made no pretence at impartiality. When a parliamentary commission inquiring into French policy in the thirties asked for his views he declined to give them, saying that a man could not be judge and party in a case and he was plainly a party. He wrote his memoirs in the same spirit.

De Gaulle had a marvellous story to tell, the story of one of the greatest political adventures in this or any other age and he told it entirely from his own point of view. For example, although the circumstances of his departure from France were attested by General Spears, who made notes that very day in the aircraft, de Gaulle dismisses them with the words "there was nothing romantic or difficult about the departure."[16] He did not wish it to be thought that the British had arranged for him to leave France.

In his feud with Muselier he mentions none of the admiral's trenchant criticisms of the way he was running the Free French Movement and, in particular, the Intelligence Services. He omits the uncomfortable dialogue he had with Stalin in 1944 and glosses over the period when he contemplated breaking with the British and transferring his whole movement to Russian soil. He scarcely mentions that an American Division, operating in parallel with Leclerc's, took part in the liberation of Paris, nor does he mention his request to General Eisenhower for the loan of two American Divisions to strengthen his authority in the capital. Although they were fresh in his memory when he wrote, he dismisses the turbulent years of the *Rassemblement* in a single paragraph in which he does not even mention the movement by name.

But if one accepts the purpose of the memoirs, these omissions become unimportant. Like an advocate defending a case in which he feels the verdict has already gone against him, de Gaulle was saying what could be said not only in his own defence but in defence of his vision of France. Every phase of his relations with Churchill and Roosevelt is described so as to suggest that it was France they were humiliating when in fact they were infuriated by his own behaviour. He barely mentions the opposition to his attitude within his own National Committee of Liberation. It is because he instinctively identifies himself with France that he can often write of himself in the third person. The memoirs will live and through them posterity will see de Gaulle as he saw himself.

De Gaulle began to write seriously in 1952. By January, 1954, the first volume was finished and was offered by Pompidou, de Gaulle's faithful *Chef de Cabinet*, to the publishing house *La Librairie Plon*. A contract was quickly signed and de Gaulle, honouring a custom of northern France, gave a lunch to the heads of the publishing house and their wives. The first volume was published in October, 1954, the second in May, 1956, and the third in September, 1959. De Gaulle refused to allow the book to be serialised in newspapers remarking that "one could hardly imagine Saint Simon allowing detached pieces of his work to appear in Paris daily."[17] In France alone about one and a quarter million copies of the three volumes have been sold. Although de Gaulle made a considerable sum from the first two volumes he gave much of it to a charity for handicapped children which he had founded in memory of his daughter Anne. The proceeds of the third volume, which appeared when he was again President of France, were entirely divided between charities and the parish of Colombey-les-Deux-Églises.

As he wrote the closing pages at the beginning of 1958, however, such a twist of fortune still seemed utterly remote. A crisis in Algeria was approaching but de Gaulle no longer believed it would open up the road for his return. To those who still came to see him, Béthouart, his contemporary at St. Cyr, his old *Commissaires* of the days of the liberation, Mairey and Triboulet, he repeated his refrain; the system was entrenched, too flabby even for a crisis to arise. He could do nothing, would never come to power. Since he had presented the awards at St. Cyr a year before he had made no public utterance and he showed no inclination to break his silence. He lived at Colombey, visited by his children and grandchildren, taking long walks in the countryside—he made the odd calculation that he had walked round his little estate fifteen thousand times—meditating rather than reading, for his eyes were already giving him trouble and he was soon to undergo an operation for cataract, becoming almost a country squire. He continued his weekly visits to Paris but those who met him remarked that he now listened more than he talked. The bitterness that he had felt in 1952 had turned into a profound pessimism. He claimed that solitude had become his friend but no one really believed him. "Old man," he wrote in the closing lines of his memoirs, "exhausted by ordeal, detached from human deeds, feeling the approach of the eternal cold, but always watching in the shadows for the gleam of hope!"[18] It was a farewell to public life. The watch in the lengthening shadows stretched out before him.

CHAPTER XIX

ON THE BRINK

While de Gaulle was writing his memoirs, Western Europe was being born. The idea, centuries old, was reconceived as the "iron curtain" was finally drawn across the Continent. De Tocqueville's prophesy of the partition of the world into American and Russian blocks was being fulfilled. The descendants of the tribes which Charlemagne had briefly united turned towards the Atlantic.

They found an eager sponsor. By injecting aid, inducing co-operation and offering protection to the countries struggling to rehabilitate themselves, the Americans stood godfather to Western European unity. In the decade from 1948 to 1958, while de Gaulle was losing his battle for personal power, a whole new family of institutions came into being. The largest and for some time the most effective was the Organisation of European Economic Co-operation which embraced seventeen nations and was the chief instrument for the planned use of Marshall Aid. In the narrower field there burgeoned the Council of Europe, Western European Union, the European Payments Union, the European Defence Community, Euratom, Europhema (which began the co-ordination of transport), European organisations for postal services, nuclear research, agriculture, the Coal and Steel Authority with its attendant court and parliament. Finally, on New Year's Day, 1958, the Common Market came into being.

Not all the institutions survived. The European Defence Community, for example, having been proposed by France as a means of containing Western German rearmament within a European framework, was finally rejected by the French Assembly because Britain would not join and the French feared German domination of an international defence force. Some of the other institutions were merged in the general organisation of the Common Market agreed upon in the Treaty of Rome. But by the beginning of 1958 the idea of Western Europe had taken enduring shape. The Common Market was so sound and vital a core that neither internal dissension nor external pressure could shake it. Russian attempts to intimidate its members through the

Warsaw Pact merely consolidated its growth. British proposals to dilute it into a wider Free Trade Area were resisted. More prone to illusions of grandeur even than de Gaulle, British statesmen sacrificed the leadership of Europe for a nebulous Commonwealth, membership of which became increasingly a licence to blackmail rather than a bond of co-operation. The major Continental countries went ahead without her.

These achievements owed nothing to de Gaulle. Ever since 1940, his attitude towards Europe had vacillated between a Western bloc and a community stretching from the Atlantic to the Urals, according to whether he was courting or opposing the Soviet Union. But on one aspect he was adamant. Europe, if it were to exist as an entity at all, must be a Europe of nations; nationalism must not be submerged. A loose confederation, with few but simple institutions through which the heads of governments met and discussed common interests, occasionally consulting their peoples on the great issues by referendum, was his ideal. De Gaulle, therefore, opposed every phase of the development of an integrated Western European community. In his rare public appearances he concentrated upon "the half-baked idea" of a European Defence Community and was jubilant when it was defeated. Privately he opposed the Schuman Plan for the Coal and Steel Authority as well as the Common Market because both depended upon "supra-national" institutions and were to be administered by stateless civil servants. He reiterated his theme that France must have absolute control of her economy, foreign policy and defence. Had he been in power the Treaty of Rome would never have been signed.

France and the Western world, therefore, benefited from de Gaulle's political isolation during the 1950s. Although it would be an exaggeration to claim that France always took the lead, men like Schuman, Pleven, Bonnefous, Pflimlin, Monnet, and Pinay initiated some of the most important schemes which evolved into the Common Market and provided much of the dynamism. And France itself recovered in the process.

In the latter part of the decade, peasants, bourgeoisie, and businessmen began to thrive as never before. Monnet's plans for the modernisation of French industry were bearing fruit. The curse of the black market disappeared. Wages lagged but social benefits brought the general standard of living at least to the level enjoyed by neighbouring countries. In 1955, in preparation for the Common Market, France was able to remove restrictions from three-quarters of her imports and repay large sums to the Payments Union. The party system, which de Gaulle so despised, served France well in many ways and might have carried the Fourth Republic into the age of affluence. But this promising harvest was blighted by the French Empire.

For all the time that France was building Europe, France was also at war. From the beginning of 1947, Frenchmen had been fighting continuously, first in Indo-China and then from one end of French North Africa to the other. When the Geneva Agreement put an end to the war in Vietnam in 1955, successive French governments had spent more on the war in the Far East alone than they had received in aid from the United States and the cost of fighting in North Africa was steadily increasing. Instead of benefiting from a surplus which the indomitable capacity of the French people had earned, the country remained in debt. The initiatives so evident on the European continent were paralysed when faced with the problems of the overseas territories.

This paralysis was partly due to the measures de Gaulle himself had taken while in power. In his youth de Gaulle had been sceptical of the value of the French Empire. After 1940, however, his attitude changed. It was the adherence of the French West African territories and in particular of Governor Félix Eboué, which gave to the Free French movement the independent base upon which its ultimate success depended. De Gaulle was not only grateful but deeply impressed by the loyalty and courage of his colonial supporters. He had given expression to his feelings at the Conference of Colonial Governors and officials which he summoned to Brazzaville. "In French Africa," he said in his opening address, "as in all the other territories where men live under our flag, there will be no progress unless the inhabitants benefit materially and morally in the countries of their birth, unless they can raise themselves little by little to the level where they are capable of taking part in the management of their own affairs in their own homelands."[1]

This sounded like a radical departure from the traditional concept of integrating French overseas territories with Metropolitan France and an invitation to the African and other French subjects to begin an evolutionary progress towards self-government. But de Gaulle had not thought out the steps by which this progress could be made. He recognised that the fall of France, the Japanese conquest of the Far East, and the pervasiveness of American anti-colonial influence had stimulated nationalist movements throughout the old empires of the world and he knew that some expression must be given to them. At the same time, as leader of the Free French Movement, he had pledged himself to preserve French sovereignty wherever it existed. He was the more determined to do this because his direct contact with the

African peoples had convinced him that the masses were backward and primitive and incapable of governing themselves for many decades.

This ambivalence emerged in every step he took until he left office in 1946. The Brazzaville Conference was followed by the suppression of forced labour throughout French Africa, the authorisation of African trade unions and a new penal code; an announcement was also made that the Constituent Assembly which would decide upon the French Constitution after the war was over, should contain sixty-four Deputies from the Overseas Territories, half of whom should be elected by the indigenous peoples themselves. Local Representative Assemblies were to share responsibility for local government and the French Union, as the Empire was henceforth called, was to have its own parliament sitting in Versailles and a loose form of federal cabinet under the President of France. Nevertheless de Gaulle always resisted the idea of independence, even though he admitted it might become inevitable.

The results were predictable. Africans and Asians felt that they had been encouraged to set up the machinery of representation and naturally assumed that this would lead to self-government and, eventually, to independence; French administrators, on the other hand, gave priority to the maintenance of French sovereignty. Clashes occurred at once. In Algiers Ferhat Abbas issued a manifesto demanding a republic which was supported by an overwhelming majority of Moslems. De Gaulle countered with his Ordinance of March 8, 1944, creating two classes of Algerian voters. But the nationalists continued agitating until on May 8 a demonstration at Setif was bloodily suppressed by the French and thousands of Algerians were killed. This massacre was scarcely mentioned in the French press and the facts only came to light several years later; but before de Gaulle resigned in 1946, the seeds of the Algerian war had been sown. In Morocco the pattern of events was repeated but bloodshed was avoided by an agreement between the Sultan Ben Youssef and de Gaulle under which the former agreed to accept a protectorate until independence could be negotiated with a properly constituted French government.

However it was in Indo-China that the contradiction in de Gaulle's policy produced the most disastrous results. Until the last months of the war Admiral Decoux, on behalf of Vichy, had preserved the semblance of French sovereignty by allowing the territory to be incorporated in the Japanese defence system and to be used as a base for Japanese operations in South East Asia. But, as the war in Europe neared its end in the spring of 1945, the Japanese turned on the French, whom they now regarded as enemies, massacred, disarmed or drove them out of the country and installed Bao Dai as their puppet emperor. When the Japanese in their turn began to withdraw, the people of Vietnam, led by the Communists in the North and Nationalists in the South, rose against Bao Dai and forced him to abdicate. In Hanoi a Communist school master, Nguyen Ai Hoc, known from then on as Ho Chi Minh, took over the administration, proclaimed a republic and appointed a young revolutionary, Giap, whose wife and child had died in a French prison in 1943, as General of the Army of Liberation. In Saigon the Japanese handed over to more moderate nationalists. The Vietnamese, therefore, were not only in control of their own country before the allies entered it but were already divided among themselves. This division was accentuated when, under the terms of the Potsdam Agreement, the British "liberated" the South and the Chinese, then still ruled by Chiang Kai-shek, the North. The French in August, 1945, had no foothold at all.

Although Bao Dai and Ho Chi Minh had proclaimed their independence and demanded the end of French rule in any form, it never occurred to de Gaulle to take them seriously. He was determined that French troops should take part in the defeat of Japan and, when Truman welcomed French help, made it a condition that an Expeditionary Force be landed in Indo-China. In other words, he decided to reconquer the country. In March, 1945, he had made a proclamation saying that a federal government under a French Governor-General, should be established, and in the summer he ordered General Leclerc to occupy Southern Vietnam, and sent Admiral d'Argenlieu as High Commissioner with clear instructions to "liberate" the whole territory in due course. Leclerc had no difficulty in occupying Cochin-China, where the British quickly made way for him, but when d'Argenlieu arrived he found a bloody revolution in full swing in North and Central Vietnam, which Ho Chi Minh could only partially control. However, he managed to hold elections in January, 1946, and Ho Chi Minh was returned with an overwhelming majority. It was at this point that General de Gaulle resigned.

His legacy made war almost a certainty. Both Leclerc and Saintenay, one of de Gaulle's Commissioners in Hanoi, recognised that the majority of the people were behind Ho Chi Minh and were opposed to any attempt to reconquer the North by force. Ho Chi Minh himself was in a difficult position since neither Russia nor China had recognised his independence and he could not fight both the Chinese and the French at the same time. He, therefore, came to an agreement with Saintenay which allowed French troops back into Hanoi on the understanding that independence would be granted to the whole country. The French induced the Chinese to leave and Ho Chi Minh went to France to conclude a treaty of alliance. But he had reckoned without the French whom he left behind.

D'Argenlieu, who always maintained that he was faithfully interpreting de Gaulle's orders, quickly came under the influence of those who wished to restore French sovereignty at all costs. Encouraged by some pro-French Vietnamese, he proclaimed a separate and independent state of Cochin-China. This was in complete defiance of the agreement Saintenay had made with Ho Chi Minh and, unless the latter could persuade the French Government to countermand d'Argenlieu's proclamation, any hope of a treaty had disappeared. But Ho Chi Minh was unlucky. Not only was the political climate in France hardening against the Communists, but none of de Gaulle's successors was prepared to compromise the "prestige" which he had so miraculously restored to a vanquished country by lowering the French flag over any part of the empire. Even Thorez gave him no encouragement. Ho Chi Minh, therefore, returned to Hanoi without a treaty but with a promise of further talks in Paris in January, 1947.

By now, however, the situation was passing beyond his control. Giap's guerrillas controlled large parts of the country and were waging an open civil war. D'Argenlieu was in Paris. In his absence his supporters decided to teach the Vietnamese a lesson. Brushing aside the mediation of the French civilian authorities and the advice of the French General in Hanoi, the local French commanders at the port of Haiphong seized the occasion of a customs dispute to issue an ultimatum to the Vietnamese Army to evacuate the city. When the ultimatum expired the French troops attacked and the cruiser *Suffren* shelled the Vietnamese quarter, killing several thousand civilians. Ho Chi Minh appealed to Blum, the new French Premier, for a general settlement, but although Blum talked of granting independence, his method of opening negotiations was to send d'Argenlieu back to Hanoi. It was a fatal mistake. On the night of December 19, some of Giap's troops in Hanoi murdered forty Europeans and carried off another two hundred as hostages in reprisal for Haiphong. The war had begun.

This is not the place to go into the details. It was never popular in France and was given only half-hearted support by successive French governments which, while refusing to negotiate with Ho Chi Minh, refused also to send reinforcements. No conscript went to Indo-China. The battles were fought by a volunteer professional army consisting of the Foreign Legion, manned mainly by Germans, the paratroops

and Vietnamese officered by Frenchmen. The war was finally lost by
bad generalship. For if General Navarre had accepted de Lattre de
Tassigny's advice, withdrawn his troops into the Tonkin Delta, and
told his government flatly that if they would not send reinforcements
they must negotiate, a peace which would have left France a role to
play might well have been possible. But even after the Communists
had gained control of China in 1949 and given open support to the
Viet Minh, the French generals continued to treat Giap's troops as
mere guerrillas and to believe that, if they could lure them to a pitched
battle, they could annihilate them. Hence the "crowning idiocy" of
Dien Bien Phu, an isolated strong-point supplied only by air, which
was destroyed not only by guerrilla infantry but by artillery which the
French refused to believe could be manhandled through the jungle.

De Gaulle had always insisted that the French must stay in Indo-
China, otherwise it would be the end of the French Empire. In this at
least he was proved right. The French defeat in Indo-China was the
beginning of the end, not only of the French Union but of the Fourth
Republic. Throughout the French Overseas Territories the extreme
nationalists, who had hitherto been in a small minority, became convinced that the French would neither be supported by her Anglo-
Saxon allies in maintaining her sovereignty nor be able to sustain it
alone. Asians and Africans who had favoured association with France
became afraid that the French would be defeated in the end and leave
them at the mercy of their nationalist enemies. The ranks of the
nationalist movements began to swell. On the other hand, among
Frenchmen and particularly in the army, opinion hardened. Many
Socialists and Liberals who had been in favour of a loose federation of
self-governing French territories, had second thoughts. If the Anglo-
Saxons, who were still urging France to merge her armies in a European defence force, were not prepared to support French interests
overseas, then France must begin to look after herself. After Dien
Bien Phu there was never a chance that the European Defence Community would be ratified by the French Assembly. The French were
determined to keep control of their army and to use it as and where
they pleased.

The army itself had changed its character as the result of the Indo-
Chinese war. It had acquired what de Gaulle had pleaded for in the
nineteen-thirties, an élite, mobile, professional force as its spearhead,
consisting entirely of volunteers. This professional army had been
fighting almost without respite since the North African campaign in
1942, and fighting well. Whether at Bir Hakim, in Italy, the Ardennes
or the swamps of Indo-China, French soldiers had proved themselves

the equals in courage and endurance of any in the world. Yet since the war their devotion and sacrifice seemed always to have been rewarded by defeat. They had been evicted from Syria and the Lebanon and now were to leave Indo-China. Inevitably they felt let down by the politicians who, in Indo-China in particular, had asked them to do the impossible. Officers and men returned to France feeling bitterly hostile to the régime, burning to avenge defeat and prepared to play an independent political role. They might not be able to hold all the French Empire but at least they could preserve the land which Frenchmen had settled. The stage for the Algerian tragedy was being set.

The final disintegration of the French Union as bequeathed by de Gaulle to his successors, followed hard upon the heels of Dien Bien Phu. Laniel's government in Paris fell and Mendès-France, a consistent opponent of the Indo-Chinese war, was endorsed as Prime Minister by an overwhelming majority in the Assembly. He went to Geneva to make peace. The great powers, which had been convened at Eden's instigation to try and settle the problems of South East Asia, had been deadlocked since April; now, within two months, they had reached agreement. The Russians, who feared the Chinese Communists might spread the war to the whole of South East Asia, brought pressure to bear on Chou En Lai, the Communist Foreign Secretary. The British and Americans did their best for Mendès-France. Vietnam was partitioned like North Korea two years earlier. By 1956 elections had been held and Diem, the one Nationalist non-Communist leader who had not compromised himself by collaborating with the French, became Prime Minister of South Vietnam and carried his country into precarious independence. He, and the rulers of Laos and Cambodia, which had hitherto been states in association with the French Union, rejected the French connection altogether and turned for protection to the United States. To de Gaulle's lasting chagrin Indo-China passed out of the French orbit.

A chain reaction was at once set in motion throughout the French Union. In the former French Protectorates of Tunisia and Morocco, nationalist parties had set out to capture the local representative institutions and to use them to acquire independence. In both countries French settlers were able to dominate whomsoever the government in Paris sent out as Resident General and block the evolutionary movement for reform. De Gaulle's friend, Sultan Mohammed V of Morocco, nurtured the Istiqlal but also tried to restrain it in the hope of achieving the "Agreements of Co-operation" which de Gaulle had forecast in 1945. But the reforms were never granted and the situation became explosive.

In 1952 a strike in fast-expanding Casablanca, called because Ferhat Hashed, the Tunisian trade union leader, had been murdered in Tunis, was bloodily suppressed. Four or five Frenchmen and between four and five hundred Moroccans were killed. In 1953, when the Sultan refused to confirm decrees which would have given the French disproportionate representation in the institutions, he was deposed by an alliance of the French administration and the Berber Pasha of Marrakesh, El Glaoui, the next most powerful man in Morocco. A puppet Sultan was set up and the "co-sovereignty" of the French and Moroccans was established by decree. Sultan Mohammed was exiled to Madagascar and at once became a national hero. A wave of arrests silenced opposition but, after the defeat of the French in Indo-China, arson, sabotage and murder spread until, by 1955, a subterranean civil war was being waged. In June, 1955, Lemaigre-Dubrueil was murdered by the Red Hand, the French terrorist organisation, for being too liberal in the views he expressed in his newspaper *Maroc-Presse*. At last the French Government acted and Faure, the Socialist Prime Minister, sent out Gilbert Grandval, a great resistance leader who was later to become one of de Gaulle's ministers, to replace the Resident General with instructions to depose the puppet Sultan, establish a Regency Council and institute reforms. Grandval was bitterly opposed by the French settlers and the government in Paris hesitated to support him. On August 20, the anniversary of the Sultan's deposition, the Moroccans rose, massacred French citizens and were massacred in turn. Shortly afterwards the Berbers turned against the French and started an armed rising. Finally in October the eighty-seven-year-old El Glaoui demanded the return of the Sultan. When he arrived, hurriedly brought by the French from Madagascar, El Glaoui prostrated himself at Mohammed's feet and begged forgiveness. Within six months Morocco gained its independence and became not a member of the French Union but of the United Nations.

In Tunisia the pattern of revolt was similar but only a little less bloody. The Nationalist Party, the Neo-Destour led by Habib Bourguiba, demanded self-government in association with France, and in August, 1950, a half-French, half-Tunisian Government was formed. The *colons'* lobby in Paris, playing on the government's fears of a Communist take-over in North Africa, blocked all progress towards representative government. In 1952, Bourguiba and the other Neo-Destour leaders were arrested and exiled; Bourguiba on an island and the others in the desert. Riots broke out and were met with the usual reprisals. In December Ferhat Hashed was murdered by the Red Hand. For the next two years pro-French Tunisians, nick-named *"Beni-oui*

oui" by the Nationalists, co-operated in a repressive colonial government under de Hauteclocque, the Resident General. In the spring of 1954, Britain agreed to evacuate the Suez base and Egypt became the focal point of Arab nationalism. Then came Dien Bien Phu and the Geneva Agreement. Mendès-France realised at once that the French defeat, coming on top of the British evacuation, imperilled the whole French position in North Africa. In July, while he was being congratulated in Paris for ending the Indo-Chinese war, murder and counter-murder flared up in Tunisia. At the end of the month Mendès-France and his Gaullist minister for Morocco and Tunisia, Christian Fouchet, flew to Tunisia, taking Marshal Juin with them to calm the suspicions of the settlers. Mendès-France's object was to make an agreement which would preserve French sovereignty but allow internal self-government. He succeeded and four members of the Neo-Destour returned from exile and became ministers. But the dam of French sovereignty had been breached and although the Tunisians quarrelled violently among themselves, within less than two years they had obtained independence.

In black Africa, where there were no French *colons*, the road to independence was smoother and the French Union served as a vehicle rather than an obstruction. A revolt in Madagascar in 1947 was brutally suppressed; thereafter African leaders like Houphouet-Boigny of the Ivory Coast and Leopold Senghor of Senegal used the Council and Assembly of the Union in Paris as a base from which to strengthen representative institutions at home. Obsessed with Indo-China and North Africa, French politicians allowed more and more power to be decentralised. After the defeat in Indo-China the future lay with the African leaders themselves. The struggle was no longer against France but between Africans who wanted a close association with France and those who wanted a loose federation or no special association at all. In the final solution de Gaulle was once more to play a hand.

By the spring of 1956, therefore, the French Union, as conceived by de Gaulle, was rapidly dissolving. The Associated States were associated no longer; the black African colonies were evolving towards self-government. French sovereignty, the lynch pin of de Gaulle's plan, was being fully exercised only in those territories which were governed as part of France, the old Colonial West Indies, the Enclaves and Islands in the Indian Ocean, and in Algeria.

Whereas West Indians and Indians were reasonably content, Algerians were not. The French had ruled Algeria since 1830, far longer than any other African territory. Of nearly nine million inhabitants, more than a million were European and of these about half were

French. Many had been born there and some families had made Algeria their home for four generations. Quite apart from the influence of the rich *colons*, there were tens of thousands of artisans, railwaymen, civil servants, small shopkeepers and farmers who had relations up and down Metropolitan France and made the French people aware of Algeria in a way that had not been true of any other French overseas territory. There were also some hundreds of thousands of young Arabs from Algeria who had settled in France and brought Algerian problems to many French doorsteps. The countries were inter-locked, not always happily but, as it seemed to many, indissolubly.

Since the war there had been an economic boom in Algeria. Under the Monnet Plan immense sums had been invested in communications, schools, hospitals and agricultural development. With improved medical services the population increased rapidly. The mass of Arabs remained miserably poor, but the Europeans and particularly the large land-owners were immensely prosperous, and a growing class of Moslem entrepreneurs began to feel that their interests were bound up with those of France. In 1954, oil had been discovered in the Sahara and this confirmed a belief among men of all French political parties that Algeria was economically vital to France. Even French Communists were lukewarm towards Algerians who claimed independence, not wishing to support a policy which might undermine the growing prosperity of the French working-class.

Instead of paving the way for Algerian independence, therefore, the French withdrawal from Indo-China, Tunisia and Morocco simply stiffened French resistance. Algeria was different. It was a part of France and if France could not hold it then she was doomed to become a small European nation. Whatever they might say in opposition, Socialists and even reformers like Mendès-France, vied with Conservatives in support of "*Algérie Française*" once they came to power.

And behind the politicians was the army. For once the soldiers and politicians seemed to be at one. In Indo-China the professional army had not only learned to fight guerrillas but had been taught the arts of psychological warfare. They felt traitors to the loyal Vietnamese they had deserted and were determined not to be guilty a second time. To the soldiers Algeria was not only an opportunity to avenge Dien Bien Phu but the last chance to serve a steadily diminishing France. Even conscripts, who were sent to Algeria in 1956, became impregnated with the professional soldiers' point of view. From then on it was clear that, if the politicians wavered over Algeria, they would have to reckon with an army that might take the law into its own hands.

To begin with, the course of events in Algeria ran parallel to those in Tunisia and Morocco. Ferhat Abbas, the moderate national leader who had been educated in France and had married a French woman, tried to use representative institutions to establish an autonomous republic within the French Union. In the elections for the Consultative Assembly in France in 1946 he swept the board and led his eleven Deputies to the French Constituent Assembly. But under the Algerian Statute, which was passed in 1947, *colons* and conservatives had their revenge. Under a socialist Governor-General, Naegelan, the elections for the Algerian Assembly, local authorities and later for the French Parliament were so blatantly rigged that the Nationalists were totally excluded and men whom Soustelle was later to describe as "pseudo-elected members currently known by the name of 'pre-fabs' . . . most often illiterate and frequently dishonest," were installed in their place.[2] For five years Algeria simmered with unrest under this sham régime which shelved one liberal proposal for reform after another. By the time the war in Indo-China came to an end the moderate Moslems were discredited and discouraged, and the revolutionaries saw their chance. They struck on November 1, 1954, in the Aures district. Within six months of the Cease Fire in Indo-China the Algerian war had begun.

The crucial year was 1956. In January general elections were held in France and Guy Mollet, the Socialist leader, replaced Mendès-France as Prime Minister. Whereas Mendès had declared unequivocally that Algeria must be forever French and that the rising would be put down, Mollet came to power with more progressive ideas. He advocated free elections in Algeria and was prepared to negotiate a new constitution with whatever leaders the election threw up. To win Moslem goodwill he appointed de Gaulle's old supporter, General Catroux, as Minister for Algeria with a seat in his Cabinet. But when Mollet flew to Algiers he was greeted by riots staged by the *colons*. Mollet, who was dependent upon Conservative support for his parliamentary majority, gave way. Catroux resigned, to be succeeded by Robert Lacoste; Mollet's policy was abandoned; in April, Ferhat Abbas arrived in Cairo to join the F.L.N., saying that the methods he had defended during the last fifteen years, co-operation, discussion, persuasion, had proved ineffective.

No government of the Fourth Republic was ever again in full control either of the Algerian situation or of France. On his return to France Mollet decided to strengthen the army in Algeria and by May practically the whole of the French fighting strength of four hundred thousand men, half of whom were conscripts, were engaged with the

F.L.N. As the war spread the rulers of Tunisia and Morocco became increasingly alarmed for their newly won independence. F.L.N. troops were constantly retreating across their frontiers and using their territory as a base for operations, bringing upon the heads of the Sultan Mohammed and Bourguiba the wrath of France and the threat of reoccupation. On the other hand support for the F.L.N. was so widespread that compliance with French demands involved the risk of internal revolution. In October, 1956, the two rulers attempted to mediate and arranged a conference at Tunis between themselves and the F.L.N. leaders. But the French pilot of the aeroplane carrying Ben Bella and four of his colleagues disobeyed orders and landed at Algiers where his passengers were at once seized and imprisoned. The French Air Force had been guilty of mutiny, but no one was ever reprimanded and both Mollet and Lacoste approved the action they should have condemned.

From the end of 1956, there was never any real chance of a negotiated peace except upon F.L.N. terms. The French Government joined enthusiastically in the Suez operation in November in the hope of bringing down Nasser and depriving the F.L.N. of its source of supply; but when Massu's paratroops were halted within a few hours of Cairo this hope vanished and France was left without an ally in her Algerian policy. In France itself the war was becoming unpopular among the electorate. Terrorism had spread across the Mediterranean and murders occurred every day on French soil.

In France itself government was breaking down. Successive Prime Ministers were unable to depend upon their own Cabinet or civil servants. The Minister of Defence had connived at the arrest of Ben Bella and his colleagues, but was retained at his post. Six months later, when the government invited Ben Bella's lawyer to Paris for talks, the lawyer was arrested by the Minister of the Interior and the talks never took place. Normal democratic life was gradually being paralysed, meetings held to protest against the war and atrocities were broken up by thugs in the pay of the *Ultras* but, instead of the thugs being prosecuted, meetings were banned. Journalists and writers who exposed the tortures inflicted by French troops upon their captives in Algeria were arrested without trial or prosecuted, while the torturers often went unreprimanded. Newspapers were confiscated under emergency powers. Civil servants withheld papers from their Ministers and Ministers covered up the actions of their subordinates in their reports to Cabinet. The police were openly partisan and in Paris were soon to demonstrate against the Assembly and the Government whose orders they were supposed to obey. A Prime Minister who attempted to impose his will was faced either with the prospect of civil war or dismissal by the Assembly.

In May, 1957, Mollet's Government fell, pulled down by the Conservatives who had forced him to continue the war but refused him the taxes to pay for it. Bourgès-Maunoury, Mollet's Defence Minister, succeeded him and met a similar fate. He passed the *loi-cadre* which, by dividing Algeria into provinces, some dominated by Moslems and some by Europeans, opened the way for possible partition. But, since the law put Moslems on the same voting role as Europeans, so giving them effective power in the country as a whole, the *colons* rejected it. Bidault and the *colons'* lobby were once more able to bring the government down. On September 30, 1957, Bourgès-Maunoury resigned and for the next five weeks France was without a government. Anarchy was very near.

* * *

De Gaulle had made no public pronouncement on Algeria since the war began, but in private he had spoken volumes. His attitude was always ambivalent. He despised the Arabs, "these miserable people, these infants in breeches," as he had said to General Juin when reviewing Algerian troops towards the end of the war;[3] yet he wanted them to develop under the tutelage of France. In launching the French Union as Head of the Provisional Government he had never allowed the word "independence" to appear on any text. However, when Indo-China fell and the Algerian war began, he became pessimistic. "Algeria is lost. Algeria will be independent," he had said to Edmond Michelet in 1955.[4] To Maurice Clavel he said the same in the following year: "I tell you Algeria will be independent. It is in the nature of things."[5] When he met Prince Moulay Hassan, later to become King of Morocco, he said that, whether one wanted it or not, Algeria would become independent; the great question was, how? What he meant he later explained to a Gaullist Deputy, to whom he said that, if he had remained in power, he would have kept France's position, not indefinitely, but perhaps for fifteen years.

As always de Gaulle blamed the régime. The miserable, incorrigible régime was losing everything he had given or given back to it; Indo-China, the Saar, the Indian Enclaves, Tunisia, Morocco and now Algeria. It was not what he had wanted. To him the loss of each territory was like the amputation of a limb. Yet if he had been in power there would have been no need for surgery. Everything would have happened differently. In his own mind, therefore, there was nothing inconsistent in saying, on a visit to the Sahara, that France must keep it or she would no longer have any weight in the world; or in telling an old Gaullist, Léo Hamon, that the presence of the European community meant that Algeria must never go the way of Tunisia or Morocco. He was expressing what he felt was right, but possible only if he was in control.

Nevertheless, de Gaulle had said so much to so many that his own supporters did not really know where he stood. Soustelle, Debré, Pompidou and the rest of the faithful little group used to lunch regularly together through these years of the Algerian struggle either at the Hôtel de Lassy, the headquarters of the Speaker of the National Assembly, or at the house of Émilien Amaury, the proprietor of a chain of newspapers which supported de Gaulle. If anyone began a sentence with the words, "The General told me . . ." he was at once drowned in a chorus of protest, for all knew that he had told each of them something different. Soustelle and Debré, in particular, realised that de Gaulle did not go the whole way with them in wishing to keep Algeria an integral part of France, but, like the others, believed that salvation lay in bringing him back to power. They could try to persuade him to accept their point of view afterwards. Two things only were clear. De Gaulle would say nothing in public until he judged the moment ripe. Visitor after visitor to whom he had said that Algeria must be independent begged him to say so openly. He always refused. Nor would he be bound by what he had said privately. "Everything which I have not put in writing I deny," he said to Louis Jacquinot,[6] and in 1957 his staff issued a public warning that the only people who could be called to account for words attributed to de Gaulle in private conversation were those who published them. "When General de Gaulle thinks it useful to make known the opinion he holds he will, as everyone knows, do it himself and do it publicly. This applies particularly to Algiers."[7]

De Gaulle did, however, write to Soustelle. This was significant for, ever since Soustelle had accepted Auriol's invitation to form a government after Pinay's fall in 1952, there had been some tension between them. It had happened during one of those "*cascades*" of Ministers descending on the Elysée when a government fell, and as soon as Soustelle received the invitation he had gone to see de Gaulle. The General had told him that the parties would never allow him to succeed but had otherwise made no objection. However, when Soustelle began seriously to try to form a government, de Gaulle was beside himself with indignation. Who did Soustelle think he was? Was *he* going to join the circus? Was he going to speak on the objects of Gaullism?

Was he going to blabber in front of the microphone? With heavy sarcasm and equally heavy mimicry he turned to those around him, saying that they must wait for the Prime Minister; they could take no decisions without him; they must know the Prime Minister's programme. It would be interesting to know further what post the Prime Minister would offer General de Gaulle. Perhaps the Under Secretaryship of State for the Fine Arts or Physical Education? Soustelle abandoned his attempt, but the outburst of jealousy was not forgotten.

However, when Soustelle's book *Loved and Suffering Algeria* appeared in December, 1956, de Gaulle wrote to congratulate him; "I do not think that one can contradict seriously what you propose, nor doubt the good faith of your actions . . .

"The final result is another matter . . . A French success in North Africa and particularly in Algeria demands great political skill. Local action of vast scope to ensure a genuine association of the two principal elements; powerful and continuous action on opinion in France to rally it for the effort required. Determined action abroad going, of course, as far as sacrificing the Atlantic Treaty if the need arises."[8] The régime being incapable of such skill de Gaulle feared the opportunity would be lost.

Soustelle was not entirely satisfied. At the beginning of the year he resigned as Governor-General of Algeria and founded the "Union for the Safety and Resurrection of Algeria" whose aim was a country in which Algerians and Frenchmen lived in absolute equality. But although he would have preferred a government of public safety under himself or Bidault he knew that only de Gaulle stood any chance of rallying sufficient following and, as de Gaulle's grand strategy could comprehend his own, Soustelle based his future support upon the latter.

In that winter of 1958, France was in many ways like Russia at the beginning of the century. Men of every political complexion were convinced that the régime was doomed and were plotting revolution. Conservatives, Poujadists, leaders of Old Comrades Associations were in league with Generals like Cogny, who had defended Dien Bien Phu, or Chassin, who had already been involved in Algerian intrigues and wanted a government of public safety under Bidault or Soustelle. Marshal Juin and General Koenig were not unsympathetic to some form of military rule. "*Ultras*," as the extreme *colons* in Algeria were called, were contemplating partition in the formation of an autonomous white republic in the provinces of Oran and Algiers. None of these groups looked to de Gaulle; hence de Gaulle's pessimism.

However, behind the scenes de Gaulle's disciples were hard at work. Only a few were closely in touch with him and even those could not always be sure how far he approved their plans, for de Gaulle would not commit himself. But from the end of 1956 onwards, more and more individuals began to speak of him as the country's only hope. Gilbert Grandval who, as Resident General of Morocco, had warned the French Government of the effects of deposing the Sultan, had formed study-groups to determine what the effect of de Gaulle's return to power would be upon Algeria, Black Africa, the economy of France and the constitution. Writers like George Boris, who had joined de Gaulle in 1940, Roger Stephane, who had been one of the resistance leaders in Paris, Jean Marie Domenach, editor of the magazine *Esprit*, and the communist secretary of the C.G.T., Pierre Lebrun, all of whom passionately believed that Algeria must be granted independence, began to suggest that de Gaulle was the only man with sufficient stature to save the Republic from its own impotence. Their voices were joined by those of René Capitant, André Malraux and François Mauriac, who had supported Sartre and other writers in protesting against the tortures inflicted by the police and soldiers on their captives in Algiers.

But the core of the Gaullist movement was the rump of the R.P.F. in the Assembly, renamed the Social Republican Party and led by Debré, Soustelle and Chaban-Delmas. When de Gaulle had dissolved the *Rassemblement* he had severed his official connections with his party followers, but he still kept in close touch with several of them. He saw Chaban-Delmas frequently and knew all that went on in the many governments which Chaban-Delmas served. Through Debré and Soustelle, who kept up a running fight against the régime in the Senate and Chamber respectively, he was informed of the trends of opinion in the party. He knew, without formally endorsing, the steps they were taking to influence opinion in the country. Chaban-Delmas, as Minister of Defence, appointed Léon Delbecque, a reserve officer and former R.P.F. official, to his staff to organise Gaullist cells among the officers of the army through special courses on psychological warfare; Debré, through his party machine in the constituencies, rallied the most ardent of those who had once flocked to the *Rassemblement* and, if he did not instigate, certainly kept track of all the many plots that were being hatched. Towards the end of 1957, the same sort of "spontaneous" surge of opinion as had occurred ten years before began to show itself. Old resistance fighters, disgruntled bourgeois who had voted for Poujade, former Vichyites who had backed de Gaulle when he turned on the communists, adventurers who longed for action even if it meant civil war, began to meet and talk of de Gaulle as the country's saviour. They were not yet a movement but a breeze, which, fanned by Debré, was beginning to blow up storm clouds and create the sort of climate de Gaulle had always hoped for.

It was not surprising. At the end of 1957, the impotence of the French party system was again exposed to the whole world. For five weeks after Bourgès-Maunoury's resignation, during which the Algerian war threatened to spread to the whole of North Africa, France was without a government. One leader after another accepted President Coty's invitation to form a Cabinet, only to find he could not command a majority in the Assembly. When finally Félix Gaillard, a comparatively young man and a Radical, succeeded on November 5, the situation in North Africa had already gone beyond his control. The F.L.N. army had virtually occupied the Algerian-Tunisian frontier and for weeks had been raiding French outposts, killing and capturing French soldiers and then retreating into Tunisia. French local commanders retaliated and, according to Bourguiba, carried out at least fifty reprisal raids into Tunisian territory. Bourguiba, who was in the absurd position of being dependent upon France under treaty for the defence of his country while at the same time harbouring and helping the Algerian insurgents who were fighting the French, appealed for arms to defend himself against both the French and the F.L.N. When France refused to supply them he accepted them from Britain and America.

Then, after due warning, the French bombed the village of Sahkiet Sidi Youssef on February 8, 1958, killing sixty people including women and children. The raid coincided, or perhaps was provoked to coincide, with a visit of the International Red Cross in the area. Bourguiba at once appealed to the Security Council of the United Nations to stop French "aggression." The British and Americans offered to mediate and Gaillard accepted the services of a "good offices" team, which consisted of Harold Beeley, an English Arabist who was later to be Ambassador in Cairo, and Robert Murphy who returned to the scene of his controversial war-time mission. But when the French Prime Minister presented the terms of the proposed settlement to the Assembly he was accused of having allowed foreigners to interfere in French affairs and was defeated by the same combination which had brought down his predecessors. On April 15, Gaillard, in his turn, resigned. Once again, as had been the case for one day in four in the last eleven months of the Fourth Republic, France was without a government. De Gaulle now realised that his opportunity might be near.

CHAPTER XX

THE RESTORATION

René Coty, the President of France, was not by nature a man of action. He had inherited the famous business of scent manufacture and become the Deputy for the Upper Seine. At the beginning of 1954 he had been elected to his high office only on the thirteenth count and because the parties could not agree on any of his rivals. In the various crises over which he had since presided he had behaved correctly, but he lacked the personality and had nothing like the influence of his predecessor, Vincent Auriol. Now, during six tempestuous weeks, he was to play a decisive part in shaping the history of France.

As soon as Gaillard fell Coty began the usual round of ministerial conferences. He first turned to the "Four Musketeers" of *Algérie Française*, Soustelle, Bidault, Duchet and Morice, but it was soon clear that, although they and their following had brought down two governments, there was no parliamentary majority for a "Government of Public Safety" pledged to win the Algerian war. The President then turned to René Pleven, but the name of Pleven was connected with the surrender in Indo-China and many Deputies refused to serve. Then suddenly, while Pleven was talking, others began to act. First the army. On April 25, at Pleven's invitation, General Salan flew to Paris from Algiers for consultation; in fact he delivered an ultimatum. The only terms acceptable to the army, he told the Prime Minister Designate, were that the rebels should lay down their arms and, having surrendered, be granted a general amnesty. Pleven saw that his "Charter" had no chance of being accepted and gave up the struggle.

Next the Gaullists made their first move. After Gaillard's resignation Delbecque had formed a Committee of Vigilance in Algiers. The most important collaborators were Alain de Sérigny, who led the rich *colons*; a fascist movement with seventeen hundred members headed by Robert Martel; the Poujadists, led by Doctor Bernard Lefèbvre; the students' and schoolboys' unions led by Pierre Lagaillarde; and the Ex-servicemen's Associations under Alexandre Sanguinetti. The object of the committee was ostensibly to ensure that only a government pledged to *Algérie Française* was formed in Paris and, failing that, to declare Algeria independent. In reality Delbecque was hoping to manoeuvre the members of his committee to declare for de Gaulle. As a preliminary exercise he announced a great demonstration in the streets of Algiers for April 26. Although Lacoste, the Resident Minister, was sympathetic he banned it for fear of massacre and demanded Delbecque's recall; but the army commanders refused to enforce the ban. The march took place and Lacoste's fears proved unfounded. Delbecque felt that he had won the first round.

Delbecque now went to see de Gaulle. He asked him directly what he would do if an appeal were made to him from Algiers to take over the government. De Gaulle made the first of his many oracular pronouncements: "I would know," he said, "how to assume my responsibilities."[1] Uncertain but not discouraged, Delbecque then persuaded Lucien Neuwirth, Deputy for Algiers and friend of Soustelle, to follow up his visit. Neuwirth was received by de Gaulle on May 3 and to the same direct question received an even loftier reply: "I would give you an answer."[2]

Meanwhile in Paris an approach to de Gaulle was being made from a more surprising quarter. On May 5 President Coty secretly sent General Ganeval, his Military Secretary, to see Colonel Bonneval, de Gaulle's aide-de-camp, to ask what the General's conditions would be for taking office. De Gaulle demanded emergency powers for eighteen months and a reform of the Constitution. That same day the President said openly to a visitor that, if the parliamentary parties could not agree, it might be necessary for him to appeal to General de Gaulle. On May 8 Coty made a second approach. The General was more moderate, and agreed to submit his candidature to the Assembly but refused to appear before it in person. The Deputies must vote him their confidence in his absence. Surprisingly, Coty found this condition unacceptable and sent for the man who had supplanted Bidault as leader of the M.R.P., Pflimlin. Pflimlin was a Moderate and every soldier and settler in Algeria believed that he would abandon them. When the news was published that Pflimlin had succeeded in forming a Cabinet and would seek investiture on May 13, all the plotters went into action.

The army, led by General Salan, the Commander-in-Chief in Algeria, entered the field officially as an independent political force on May 10. A telegram signed by Generals Salan, Allard, Massu and Jouhaud and sent to General Ely, Chief of the General Staff, for transmission to the President of the Republic, stated that the army in Algeria would regard as an outrage the abandonment of loyal French and Moslem citizens and that it was impossible to forecast its "reaction of despair" if this happened. The generals asked Ely to call the President's attention to their "anguish, which only a government firmly committed to defend our flag in Algeria could assuage."[3]

As Coty well knew, this ultimatum was not an empty threat. A plan to seize power by force and install the government the soldiers desired had been carefully prepared. "Operation Resurrection," as it was code-named, was not simply a wild scheme to invade France with paratroops but a comprehensive military operation which involved most of the Metropolitan army and air force. The leader of the revolt was to be General Miguel of the South-Western Command whose headquarters were at Toulouse. Four of the nine Regional Commanders in France were openly involved and most of the others gave clandestine support, including General Beaufort, Ely's aide-de-camp, who was to lead the operation in Paris. The navy was expected to assume a role of benevolent neutrality.

The morning of May 13, the day when Pflimlin was to present his Cabinet to the Assembly, the first phase of Operation Resurrection was set in motion. General Petit of the Air Force sent his transport aircraft to Algiers to be ready to embark the parachutists under General Massu's command. His action was confirmed by the Commander-in-Chief of the Air Force.

The Committee of Vigilance had separate plans. Their object was to bring the people of Paris and Algiers into the streets and create such civil disobedience that Pflimlin's government, if it ever came to power, would be shown to be impotent. In Paris they prepared mass demonstrations, in Algiers they called a general strike for 1.0 p.m. on May 13. However, on May 11 two French soldiers were executed in Tunisia in retaliation for the death of a Tunisian; the committee at once added to their programme a short ceremony of remembrance at the War Memorial in the evening.

Delbecque's plan was that the Committee of Vigilance should meet after the ceremony and elect Soustelle, who had promised to be there, as its chairman. It would then wait to hear the result of the vote in the Assembly, which most people thought would go against Pflimlin, and issue a manifesto in favour of a government of Public Safety. He intended that the Committee should occupy the government buildings in Algiers the following morning and remain in occupation until such a government was installed in Paris.

But Delbecque's control over the Committee was minimal. Within a few days of its formation an inner group of seven had been formed who were not only opposed to Delbecque but to de Gaulle as well. Some of their names were soon to reverberate round the world:

Pierre Lagaillarde, Robert Martel, Dr. Lefèbvre, Joseph Ortiz. Without informing Delbecque they decided to launch the revolt and occupy the government buildings before the vote in the Assembly had been taken and immediately after the memorial service. They informed some of the army commanders of their plans.

Lastly there were the Communists. Torn between fear of the army and de Gaulle they were prepared to back Pflimlin and the Fourth Republic if it stood firm against the rebels. But their leaders had laid plans for a general strike and for massive demonstrations in Paris and in the industrial north. If the strike was successful they hoped to blackmail the Socialists into a popular front and form a government with emergency powers. If the army took over, the Communists, who had accumulated considerable stocks of arms, were prepared to launch an insurrection. France was on the verge of civil war.

De Gaulle was in a state of almost unbearable suspense. He not only knew that a revolt was to take place in Algiers but that it might spread to France. Through Chaban-Delmas and Ely he was aware of the role certain army commanders intended to play. But he could not be sure that the rebel generals would not prefer to collaborate with the *Ultras* than with him, nor whether a firm stand by the government might not yet hold Salan and the army to its allegiance and enable Pflimlin to quell any rising. If he showed sympathy with the plotters he would destroy his chance of being called upon to form a legal government; if he waited too long he risked seeing a government of Public Safety established by the army. Still sceptical but more convinced than ever that he alone could save the country, de Gaulle waited at Colombey.

*   *   *

May 13 began calmly in Algiers. The general strike was a complete success and by the early afternoon crowds of young men were strolling in the streets. They knew nothing of the conspirators' plans and, although a group sacked the American Cultural Centre, the majority were orderly. At five o'clock a loudspeaker van manned by members of the Committee of Vigilance began touring the city and whipping up feeling against Pflimlin. But when, just before six o'clock, the generals appeared for the memorial service the crowd fell silent. Five minutes later the generals departed and the crowd began to disperse.

But they had forgotten the teenagers. Having heard a rumour that the University students were going to attack the Government-General Building, the school children decided not to be outdone. While the memorial service was in progress, several hundred shoolboys, led by Roseau, the President of their Association, streamed up the wide steps leading to the forum, the wide open space in front of the Government Building. They were met at the top by the special riot police who used tear gas. Infuriated, the schoolboys began to attack the police in earnest. They were soon joined by the senior students who had been belatedly rallied by Lagaillarde, wearing the uniform of a paratroop lieutenant. The police charged and cleared the forum but were then, mysteriously, ordered to withdraw. As they did so the parachutists arrived, but instead of stopping the students, urged them on and lent them a truck to batter down the gates of the Government Building. From behind the gates the riot police again used tear gas and at one moment fired a few shots in the air; but urged on by Lagaillarde who had got into the building and was haranguing the crowds from a first-floor window, the students pressed home their attack and the police once more withdrew—this time for good. By seven o'clock the Government Building was in the students' hands. They sacked the offices and burned the library. Parachutists prevented them from getting at the security files some of which, however, conveniently disappeared. One student carried off the bust of Marianne, symbol of the Republic, at the sight of which an officer remarked: "No casualties fortunately, except the Republic and that's not serious."[4] Under Lagaillarde's leadership the students then set up a committee of Public Safety.

A student riot is not a revolution and had anyone in authority acted with determination order could still have been restored. Authority lay with Salan. But although officials telephoned his headquarters, which were connected with the Government Building by a secret tunnel, Salan did not appear. At seven-thirty Massu arrived and at first seemed determined to crush the students; but when, a quarter of an hour later, Salan finally showed himself and was howled down when he tried to address the crowd, Massu changed his mind. He agreed to Lagaillarde's request that he hide the Committee of Public Safety and read out the names of its members from the balcony. Four were Moslems, all were *Ultras*, none were for de Gaulle.

Delbecque had not only been taken by surprise but had been let down by Soustelle. For, in the belief that Pflimlin would be rejected, Soustelle had been persuaded by Chaban-Delmas, acting on de Gaulle's instructions, to stay in Paris. De Gaulle did not want a potential rival in Algiers. When Delbecque finally arrived at the Government Building, therefore, he was without a leader; the best he could do was to get himself elected Vice-President of the Committee of

Public Safety in Soustelle's name. Several other names were added, including that of Roseau, who at once cancelled the summer examinations for the school children.

The initiative now swung back to Paris. The Deputies heard both of the student revolt and Massu's action during the dinner hour, rallied to Pflimlin and invested him with power by a majority of one hundred and forty-five, the Communists abstaining. France now had a legal government. The Cabinet met that night, resolved to crush the revolt, declared a blockade of Algeria, closed the aerodrome and put a guard over Soustelle. A demonstration by some six thousand marchers, mostly ex-servicemen and leaders of extremist right-wing parties, clashed with the police in the Place de la Concorde but was dispersed. Fifty people, including six high-ranking army officers, among them General Challe of the air force, were arrested. However, this show of firmness in the capital was followed by a confession of impotence towards Algiers itself. Although Pflimlin deplored the "insurrectionary" attitude of certain Generals, the Cabinet unanimously decided to accept the word of Massu that he had only headed the rebellion in order to control it and confirmed Salan in the full exercise of civil and military power. President Coty backed up this action with a personal appeal to all ranks of the army to be loyal to the Republic.

In the early hours of May 14, therefore, responsibility was virtually passed back again to Algiers. Salan was in control, yet no one knew exactly where he stood. However, the Gaullists regained some initiative. Lucien Neuwirth had managed to get control of the radio and at one o'clock in the morning announced that the Committee of Public Safety had appealed to General de Gaulle to form a government "free from the régime of the parties" and capable of "maintaining Algeria as an integral part of France." This was the first mention of de Gaulle's name since the revolt started. It was followed a few hours later by an appeal from General Massu, again on behalf of the committee, that the General break his silence and form a government of Public Safety to save Algeria from surrender. Apparently Massu also sent de Gaulle a telegram, but it never arrived and although de Gaulle certainly knew of Neuwirth's appeal he refrained from answering it. Outwardly he behaved as if nothing unusual was happening. He paid his weekly visit to Paris but was careful whom he saw and spent most of his time with his publisher, Charles Orengo. Privately, however, he told his faithful aides, Guichard and Foccard, at all costs to find out what Delbecque was doing and what was the attitude of the generals in Algiers towards him. For de Gaulle realised that everything now depended upon the army and particularly upon Salan.

Salan was still an enigma. During the morning of May 14 he had several long telephone conversations with Pflimlin and, at eleven-thirty, issued a proclamation saying that he had "provisionally assumed civil and military powers" and calling upon the population to have confidence in the army. Still no one knew whether he was exercising those powers on behalf of the government in Paris, on his own account or in the name of the committee. Salan could not make up his mind. If he declared for Pflimlin he might face a mutiny in Algiers and find himself under arrest; if he declared for the Committee of Public Safety he ran the risk of Court-Martial should Pflimlin succeed in asserting his powers. But he was not known as the "Chinese General" for nothing and seems to have hoped to maintain a middle position, controlling the rebellion through the power vested in him by the Government, yet at the same time forcing the Government to change its policy or resign. Delbecque sent frantic messages to de Gaulle during the afternoon begging him to reply to the committee's appeal, but the General refused to move. The turning point came the following morning.

Pressed by Delbecque and the committee to back up their appeal to de Gaulle, Salan asked his principal military advisers, Admiral Auboyneau and Generals Allard, Jouhaud and Dulac for their opinions. Auboyneau had succeeded Muselier as Commander of the Free French Navy and was still an ardent Gaullist. The other three had served Pétain. With some reluctance they agreed that the best solution seemed to be an appeal to de Gaulle. Still Salan was unsure. He left them to address the crowd from the balcony of the Government Building, made an adroit speech which still did not disclose where he stood, and ended with the traditional farewell, "*Vive L'Algérie Française, Vive la France.*" As he stepped back, this time to ringing cheers, Delbecque at his elbow hissed, "*Vive de Gaulle.*" Salan, visibly undecided, paused and then stepped forward to the microphone again. "*Vive de Gaulle,*" he cried.

This was the signal for which de Gaulle had been waiting. It did not matter that Salan had uttered the words as an afterthought; when he returned to his headquarters he was bitterly upbraided by his wife and several colleagues and could give no satisfactory explanation. But Salan confirmed over the telephone to Paris that he had made the declaration and de Gaulle was determined not to let him go back on it. Since Salan held legitimate power in Algiers and had appealed to him, he would give a reply as he had promised. That afternoon de Gaulle issued a statement which he sent in advance to Pflimlin and published at 5.0 p.m., which ended with the words, "Once before, from the depths of the abyss, the country gave me its confidence to lead it back to salvation. To-day, with new trials crowding in upon it, it is right that it should know that I am ready to assume the power of the Republic."[5]

There was consternation in Paris. The Communist Party denounced de Gaulle for siding with the rebels in order to set up a military dictatorship. The socialists announced that the Republic was threatened and declared themselves ready to join Pflimlin's government. The trade unions set up special committees to defend liberty. The press, almost unanimously, noticed that de Gaulle had not denounced the rebels and assumed that from now on he would head the insurrection. The Government itself, typically, said nothing.

In Algiers, on the other hand, de Gaulle's statement produced almost hysterical rejoicing. The Committee of Public Safety replied at once to his statement expressing its "deep pleasure" and sent a telegram to President Coty demanding that he appoint "the Liberator of the Fatherland" the Head of a Government of Public Safety. Next day an extraordinary demonstration took place which has sometimes been called "The miracle of May 16." A crowd estimated at more than a hundred thousand, at least half of whom were Moslems, demonstrated in front of the Government Building in favour of de Gaulle. Soustelle's dream seemed to be coming true. And Soustelle himself had already escaped from Paris. The daughter of a friend who lived in the house where he was under guard smuggled him out by taking the cushions out of the back seat of her car and covering him with luggage. He crossed into Switzerland, chartered an aeroplane and reached Algiers next day. But he did not receive the welcome he anticipated.

The day before, Salan had issued an order to the army announcing once more that he had been charged by the French Government with exceptional civil and military powers, that he intended to discharge those instructions by maintaining order and ending, "I alone am informed of the exact situation and I alone am qualified to take the necessary decisions arising out of the duties entrusted to me."[6] It looked as if Salan was regretting his appeal to de Gaulle and was veering back towards a lone hand or even support for Pflimlin. The telephone conversations which Delbecque's supporters monitored between Salan and Paris confirmed these suspicions. Delbecque and Neuwirth demanded an interview with Salan that same evening. They arrived at his headquarters carrying arms and tried to convince him that he had gone too far to draw back. Salan still prevaricated and when he heard that Soustelle had arrived at the airport the following morning prevented him from coming into the city and went out to meet him. Soustelle, a former Governor-General, was so popular in Algiers that, once he showed his face in the city, he would be bound to assume leadership of the revolt. The two men had a flaming row during which each contemplated arresting the other (Delbecque had managed to send some tanks to the airport to support Soustelle) but finally reached a compromise. Salan agreed to telephone Pflimlin to see if he intended to resign, in which case Soustelle undertook to return to Switzerland. Salan telephoned, found Pflimlin adamant and arranged to meet Soustelle in the forum later that day in front of the crowd. The cheers which drowned their greetings, music to Soustelle, rang a knell in Salan's ears.

Nevertheless, Soustelle's escapade was no more than a diversion; the real drama was being played out in Paris. Having made his offer on May 15 de Gaulle remained at Colombey to watch its effects. After their initial outbursts the party leaders began to reflect. De Gaulle had not mentioned Algeria in his statement and his reference to the Republic suggested that he was prepared to act constitutionally. On May 16, while Algiers was celebrating, Guy Mollet, the Socialist leader and now Vice-President of the Council, spoke of the great esteem and admiration he had for the General and asked for further explanation. Would de Gaulle denounce the rebels? If asked to form a government would he observe the Constitutional procedure and submit himself to the Assembly for investiture? De Gaulle made no immediate reply but on May 18 announced that he would hold a press conference in the afternoon of the following day.

By delaying de Gaulle was taking considerable risks. The communists had already called for a general strike on May 19 which, if successful, might bring down the Government and induce a majority of the socialists to enter a Popular Front. De Gaulle also knew, through Delbecque, that four separate missions had left Algiers for France on May 17 to make final preparations for Operation Resurrection. This too was planned to take place on May 19 and might result in an authoritarian government under Bidault and Duchet from which de Gaulle would be excluded. On the other hand, if he satisfied Mollet and the moderates, he ran the risk of being rejected in the Assembly by a combination of the communists, left-wing socialists and the parties of the extreme Right, who were backing the insurrection, but whom he would have disowned. He would have lost his chance of returning to power constitutionally. Through Guichard and Foccard therefore, de Gaulle used every contact he had in the army and the Establishment to postpone the military operations. In particular Colonel Paillole, Giraud's Intelligence Chief in North Africa, who was at the centre of the plot, was persuaded by Poniatowski, a friend of Guichard's and Pflimlin's *Chef de Cabinet*, that de Gaulle would never accept power at the rebels' hands. As de Gaulle drove from Colombey to the Palais d'Orsay where twelve hundred correspondents had assembled under the strictest security, he still did not know whether he had succeeded.

As de Gaulle entered the great hall everyone fell silent. As he rose to speak he knew that his chance of returning to power with a free hand to do what he thought best for France, uncommitted either to the régime or the rebels, depended upon what he said. He began calmly and affably by reminding his audience that it was three years since he had "had the pleasure" of seeing them. He then traced the course of events in Algeria and asked, rhetorically, why he might be useful. His answer was that he had a certain moral capital, that everybody knew the régime could not solve the Algerian crisis and that he was "one man alone," not associated with any party. He had taken no political action for six years and made no speeches for three, in short he was a man "who belongs to nobody—and belongs to everybody." He repeated that, if the people wished it, he was ready to take the leadership of the French Republic.

De Gaulle then answered a series of questions without notes, questions which on this occasion he had no opportunity of arranging in advance. What exactly did he mean by "assuming the powers of the Republic"? He answered, "The powers of the Republic, when one assumes them, can only be those which the Republic itself has delegated. That is perfectly clear." Nothing that he added made his meaning any more plain. The next question was crucial. How did he judge the uprising in Algeria and the attitude of the army? "In Algeria," de Gaulle replied, "there is a population which for years has been in the midst of war, murders and violence. That population has seen that the present system established in Paris cannot solve its problems . . . How can you expect this population not to rise up at last? How could it not seek a recourse for its misfortunes elsewhere than in parliamentary procedure? This inevitably is what has happened.

"And then the Algerians cry *Vive de Gaulle*, as Frenchmen do instinctively when they are in the depths of anguish or on the heights of hope . . . Finally, they give the best proof that the French of Algiers do not at any price wish to break away from Metropolitan France. For one does not shout *Vive de Gaulle* if one is not on the side of the nation."

Asked for a reply to the question Guy Mollet had put to him in the Assembly, de Gaulle launched into a panegyric of the Socialist leader, describing among other things how Mollet had been at his side when he addressed the people of Arras from the Town Hall balcony during the liberation—an incident that was either a lapse of memory or an invention, for Mollet had not been there. But all he would answer was that exceptional powers would need exceptional procedures.

Asked if his press conference was not giving new courage to sedition-mongers, he asked in return why he should label as "sedition-mongers" men whom the régime had not denounced and to whom it had even granted full powers—an obvious reference to Salan and Massu. Pressed again about what he would do in Algeria he replied that it would be necessary "to hear the parties involved. What would a judge be who gave his judgment before the hearing?"

Then came the final question: "Some people fear that if you return to power you will attack public liberties." The reply: "Have I ever done so? On the contrary, I restored them when they had disappeared. Is it credible that I am going to begin a career as a dictator at the age of sixty-seven?" After adding a few sentences about the plight of France and its power of recovery, he ended: "If the task should fall on me to lead the State and nation out of the crisis I would approach it without presumptuousness for it would be hard and fearsome. I have said what I have to say. Now I shall return to my village and I shall remain there at the disposal of the country."

It had been a superb performance and convinced the audience, if nothing else, that de Gaulle in his retirement had gained rather than lost in political stature. He had sympathised with the Algerian "population" in their war and misery and in their revolt against the parliamentary régime; he was plainly including the Moslems among the "French of Algeria" who had cried *Vive de Gaulle* and proved that they did not want to break with France. He had praised the army for preventing disorder and said that he could "well understand" the action of the military command; he added, however, that the army must remain the instrument of the State. He had said that it would be absurd and lamentable to destroy the bonds between France and Algeria.

In short de Gaulle had given the impression, to those who wished to believe it, that he intended to keep Algeria French but only because that was what, by its recent demonstration, the population had shown that it wanted. He had hinted, to those who could take the hint, that the links between the two countries might not always remain the same, but had left himself free to decide what the ultimate links might be. This was de Gaulle's first and most important public utterance on the subject of Algeria—all subsequent speeches were amplifications of it—

and it allowed every Frenchman to read into it what pleased him. It is not surprising that soldiers like Massu and Petit should have been convinced that de Gaulle was saying "Yes" to their demands; on the other hand Soustelle remained sceptical and the press and extremist politicians condemned him as a compromiser.

The effect of the conference was almost exactly what de Gaulle had hoped. The general strike, called by the communists that very day, had been a failure everywhere except in the northern coal mines—largely because the workers respected de Gaulle and were waiting to hear what he would say. The army coup had been postponed for the same reason; moderates in the parties and throughout the French Establishment began to turn to him. Although the Government made no reply to his press conference, there was intense activity behind the scenes. Mollet, now anxious to see de Gaulle, was in constant touch with Guichard; Pflimlin urged Bidault to visit the General; an exhortation which Bidault declined. The ice was broken by Pinay. Having consulted Pflimlin he went to Colombey three days after the press conference and came back a convert with a message to the Prime Minister that de Gaulle would be glad to meet him. As a result of these talks de Gaulle put out further feelers. He invited Georges Boris, his collaborator in 1940, and convinced him, without committing himself to any solution, that by opposing him the Socialists were driving him into the arms of the rebels. De Gaulle approached General Lorillot to send a message to Salan asking for a report on recent events, and Lorillot complied. De Gaulle, therefore, had established links, if not with the Government, with those who served its chief Ministers.

Meanwhile in Algeria the Committee of Public Safety had extended its authority over the whole of the country including the Sahara. On May 23 a new and enlarged committee under the joint Presidency of Massu and Sid Cara, a Moslem who had been Minister of State in Gaillard's government, issued a declaration claiming that it had achieved in three days what no government had been capable of in three years, the complete union of ten million Frenchmen in Algeria. To this General Salan added his own "Statutory Declaration," affirming "the indestructible union of the army and the nation" and calling for a government under General de Gaulle to preserve the existing unity between the peoples of the French Republic and the French Union. Soustelle, who was acting as political adviser to the committee and to Salan, made a lightning tour of the country, speaking passionately and eloquently of the "humane revolution" which would not only sweep away the former hatreds but unite all Frenchmen under de Gaulle. Pflimlin realised that Salan had irrevocably committed himself and abandoned any idea of a further approach to the military in Algiers.

By the end of the week following his press conference, therefore, de Gaulle knew that he would be asked to assume power; he still did not know by whom. As each day passed it was more and more evident that the Government could not check the rebellion. Would the ministers yield before the army decided to drive them out? Would he be invited to form a government or would he be installed by a revolution? There can be no question which solution he preferred. He had rejected military dictatorship before, he hoped to avoid it now. On the other hand, if the army acted he was no longer in a position to refuse office at its hands. Through General Ely, de Gaulle learned that Lagaillarde had arrived in France on May 21 to complete arrangements for Operation Resurrection. In Algiers Massu did not deny that he was ready with his paratroops. But Salan was still hesitating to take the final step and, with Massu's help, Delbecque and Neuwirth were able to disrupt Lagaillarde's plan. On Saturday, May 23, they persuaded Salan to authorise the seizure of Corsica.

The action, which had been carefully planned, was a brilliant and bloodless success. Many Corsicans lived in Algeria and the Corsican population sympathised with the settlers. The garrison consisted mainly of paratroops to whom Massu was the legendary hero. Pascal Arighi, a resistance fighter who had become a Corsican Deputy, had been waiting in Algiers for a signal. At 5.0 p.m. on Sunday, May 25, Salan sent him to Corsica in a special aircraft to start the revolt. Within a few hours the paratroops and police, including one hundred and twenty riot police flown from Nice by the Government to prevent just such a rising, had been won over. A Committee of Public Safety under the Presidency of Henri Maillot, a relation of Madame de Gaulle, was immediately formed, and enthusiastic demonstrations in favour of General de Gaulle and General Massu were held in the main towns. In the evening Colonel Thomaso, the Commander of the Algerian Territorials and a friend of Delbecque, arrived to take over the Military Governorship of the island.

Corsica was a master stroke. It revealed finally and absolutely the impotence of the Government not only to all Frenchmen but to the world. The Cabinet met on May 25 and decided upon the immediate recapture of the island. Orders were given to the fleet. But the navy mutinied. The mutiny was denied and disguised, but at five thirty on Monday, May 26, Admiral Nomy saw both Pflimlin and President Coty and within half an hour the order to sail was cancelled. The Admiral's objections, which included false weather reports, had proved insuperable. The rest of the measures the Government proposed were equally ineffective. No "disciplinary" action against officers or officials in Corsica could be taken since there was no one to enforce them. A blockade was impossible because the Corsicans in Marseilles would not obey it and neither troops nor police were prepared to make them. The army's transport aircraft were in Algiers and, since the fleet would not sail, the army could not move. The Government was powerless. It had no alternative but to resign. Yet for another two days ministers clung to office.

In Cabinet on May 25, Guy Mollet, outraged by the Corsican affair, had spoken dramatically of moving the seat of government to "the red bastion" of the North, arming the miners and dying among them on the barricades. But the miners would not have marched and by the 26th, Mollet had changed his mind. On that day he wrote a six-page letter to de Gaulle, setting out his fears and laying down as a condition of his support that de Gaulle would denounce the rebellion. De Gaulle did not reply. That same day the independent group in the Assembly urged Pinay to suggest that de Gaulle call a conference of all the party leaders; then, at last, Pflimlin suggested a meeting.

But de Gaulle had already decided to act. He knew, as Pflimlin knew, that the army might move at any moment. If he was to retain any freedom of action he must persuade the Government to resign. He had already sent a message to the Prime Minister suggesting that they meet that night and adding that, if he refused, the fact would be published. De Gaulle also answered Mollet's letter, stressing the points on which they agreed, and expressing the hope that he would accompany Pflimlin. In the small hours of the morning, and in secrecy that was not broken for several days, de Gaulle met Pflimlin at the old Royal Palace of St. Cloud. Mollet's party had forbidden him to come. The two men talked for more than two hours, Pflimlin expressing the belief that he could persuade all the non-communist parties to make an appeal to de Gaulle if only the latter would disavow the rebels. De Gaulle refused. He explained to Pflimlin that to do so before he had become Prime Minister would be to destroy his position as an arbiter. He could only, he said, disavow once. They parted without agreeing, Pflimlin convinced that de Gaulle was not in league with the conspirators but knowing that, without the assurance he asked, he could not carry the Assembly; de Gaulle certain at last that both Pflimlin and Mollet now really wanted him to assume power.

De Gaulle reached Colombey at 5.0 a.m. but did not go to bed. Although he had persuaded Pflimlin not to issue a communiqué or reveal their meeting, he had decided already that the time had come to force Pflimlin's hand. He must issue a statement himself. The army might move at any moment. If he did not continue to take the initiative it might slip from his hands. At 11.0 a.m. he telephoned Guichard the text of a message which was issued at midday. "I began yesterday," it read, "the regular process necessary to establish a Republican Government capable of restoring the unity and independence of the country.

"I am convinced that the process will continue and that the nation will show by its calm and dignity that it hopes to see it end successfully.

"In these conditions any action endangering public order, from whatever side it originates, may have grave consequences. Even though I understand the circumstances I could not approve.

"I expect the land, sea and air forces in Algeria to maintain exemplary discipline under the orders of their commanders, General Salan, Admiral Auboyneau and General Jouhaud. To these leaders I express my confidence and my intention to make contact with them soon."[7]

As de Gaulle expected, this statement produced consternation in the Government and the Assembly. Pflimlin told the Deputies that he had seen de Gaulle but agreed to nothing; he was prepared to stay at his post. The Socialists by a hundred votes to three decided in a party meeting that under no circumstances would they "rally to the candidature of General de Gaulle" which, in the form presented, was "a challenge to Republican legality." The Independents, on the other hand, insisted that their four Ministers resign from the Government because Pflimlin had not accepted de Gaulle's terms. The debate in the Assembly was so violent that it had to be suspended twice. Communists and Socialists branded de Gaulle as a "dictator-usurper," and sneered at the Government for not standing firm. Mitterand, who was a candidate for leadership of a Popular Front, accused it of "shaking at the first puff of wind from Colombey-les-Deux-Églises." On the other hand the young Radical, M. Lecoeur, said that the whole of France wanted a change and if the Assembly, which was stagnant and rotting, continued with its "ridiculous" struggles he would leave it.[8]

The debate went on into the night until at six fifteen on the morning of Thursday, May 28, the Deputies passed by a large majority the Constitutional reforms they had been nominally discussing. The Cabinet was held immediately afterwards. Everything now depended upon Pflimlin. He was being pressed to stay not only by the Communists and Socialists but by the M.R.P. He had a majority in the Assembly. Yet Pflimlin had information which only a few of his colleagues shared. He had been told by Ely and Beaufort that Operation Resurrection was to have been launched that night. Moch, the Minister of the Interior, had heard the same thing through the American Consul in Algiers. He, above all, knew that if a coup was attempted it would succeed, for he could not even rely upon the police. Both men knew that, although the Gaullists had been able once more to postpone the operation, the delay would last only twenty-four hours. Operation Resurrection was now planned for May 29.

At last Pflimlin made up his mind. He told the Cabinet that he was resigning and would give as his reason the withdrawal of the four Independent Ministers. President Coty was informed at four in the morning, but insisted that Pflimlin stay at his post till a new government had been formed. Coty then sent for the Presidents of the two Assemblies, André Le Troquer and Gaston Monnerville, and asked them to see de Gaulle that evening. Coty also tried to persuade the former President, Vincent Auriol, to accompany them, but Auriol replied that he had written to de Gaulle some days previously and had not yet received a reply. In fact de Gaulle's letter was waiting for him at his home to which he had not returned. Early in the afternoon—it was still Thursday, May 28—Coty sent for the party leaders and told them that his choice lay between a Popular Front, which everybody knew would provoke the army to take control, or de Gaulle. He was going to do his utmost for de Gaulle.

Meanwhile de Gaulle was conducting a very different kind of interview. On the evening of May 27, while the Assembly was debating and in essence rejecting his offer to form a government, he had sent a message to Salan, officially transmitted by General Lorillot, asking the former to send a representative to see him. On May 28, de Gaulle received General Dulac, Salan's chief aide, and three other officers who had flown from Algiers. Although their mission was known and approved by the Government, which was confident that de Gaulle would try to restrain the rebels, precautions were taken to conceal their identities. As the two cars passed through the ring of journalists who were literally camping round de Gaulle's house at Colombey, each passenger buried his head in a newspaper. De Gaulle talked to Dulac alone. He was at his most affable and, to avoid interruptions, served drinks himself.

Accounts of the conversation differ. Soustelle, who saw Dulac immediately before and after his visit to Colombey, says that de Gaulle "gave the green light" to the insurrection. Dulac found de Gaulle depressed and convinced that the parties would somehow prevent him coming to power. "You must do what is necessary," he ended by saying. Merry and Serge Bromberger, who saw de Gaulle himself later on, say that de Gaulle urged upon Dulac the absolute necessity of restraining the army from taking any action until it was known whether he would be invited to form a government. Dulac assured de Gaulle that Salan intended to comply with his wishes, but warned him that, if there was prolonged delay or if the Committee of Public Safety came to the conclusion that de Gaulle was prepared to compromise with the régime and to disown the Algerian Movement, then Salan might not be able to control his officers and Operation Resurrection would take place.

But there is evidence, the source of which must remain anonymous, which suggests that other things may also have been discussed. Those commanding the paratroop units which were to land in France if the operation was launched had already received their detailed orders. One of these commanders was a man who had for some years been a member of de Gaulle's personal staff. His orders were precise. He was to be dropped with his troop at Colombey, where he was immediately to form a Guard of Honour, and to take de Gaulle to Paris. There was no question of these orders being a precautionary measure, nor was any provision made in them that, in case de Gaulle refused, he was to be put under house-arrest. It is inconceivable, therefore, that they should have been issued without de Gaulle's acquiescence.

The truth would seem to be that, although de Gaulle desired above all to be asked to form a government legally and although he had steadfastly refused to acknowledge the rebellion, far less put himself at the head of it, he was now prepared to accept power at the hands of the army if all else failed. If this does not exactly make him a party to the plot, which he succeeded in forestalling, it does help to explain the extreme bitterness which some of the plotters felt towards him when he began to pursue an Algerian policy contrary to their own.

The last act of the drama was now beginning. Towards midnight de Gaulle received a telephone call from the Elysée telling him that Le Troquer and Monnerville were on their way to St. Cloud to meet him. Once more he drove to St. Cloud, this time openly and with a full police escort. It was an unsatisfactory interview. Monnerville took little part in the conversation but Le Troquer, who had owed his election to the Presidency of the Assembly to communist votes, saw himself as the guardian of the Constitution and was as intransigent as de Gaulle. He insisted that de Gaulle denounce the rebellion and present himself in person to the Assembly, and he opposed de Gaulle's demands for emergency powers and a referendum on the new Constitution. The most he would concede was that the Assembly be put into recess for three months. After arguing heatedly for an hour, de Gaulle rose and said that, since that was how matters stood, he was returning to Colombey. He left the room, slamming the door, and went home to bed and to sleep.

Le Troquer and Monnerville went back to the Elysée where Le Troquer reported failure. Coty sent them away, saying he would take a decision later in the morning. It was now May 29.

In fact Coty had made up his mind. He knew that Operation Resurrection had only been postponed and that, in spite of de Gaulle's meeting with Dulac, it might take place that night. He rose at seven in the morning and in his own hand wrote out a message to the Assembly in which he warned the Deputies that France was on the verge of civil war. He stated that he had asked "the most illustrious of Frenchmen" to form a Government of National Safety and added that, if that proved impossible, he would have no alternative but to resign. In effect, he was giving the Assembly an ultimatum. Coty then announced to the press that his message would be read to the Assembly at 3.0 p.m. that afternoon and appealed for calm.

When Coty telephoned Colombey at 9.30 a.m. de Gaulle was still asleep. Coty envied him and told Colonel Bonneval to inform the General of the message he was sending to the Assembly. During the morning Le Troquer gave his Socialist colleagues an account of his interview with de Gaulle the night before. This, coupled with the rumours of Coty's message, hardened their opposition. At 3.0 p.m. Le Troquer mounted the Tribune to read the President's message to the Assembly. He was in an unenviable position. He disapproved of the message; on the other hand he knew that, if Coty resigned, under the Constitution he would himself become temporary President and would be expected to call for a Popular Front Government which would almost certainly provoke civil war. Le Troquer almost gabbled the message and when he had finished the Assembly broke into an uproar. The Communists shouted, "*Le fascisme ne passera pas*" and both sides broke into discordant versions of the "Marseillaise." The sitting was suspended.

The climax was now approaching. Throughout the afternoon General Miguel, Commander of Operation Resurrection, had been under severe pressure from the Toulouse Committee of Public Safety, and particularly from Moch's riot police, to ignore Salan and give the signal for the attack. In Paris every committee had assembled, several thousand civilian supporters had been mobilised, dissident paratroops, armed units and police were on the alert. General Chassin had been seen in the city, but Miguel held firm.

Then, as the Deputies streamed out of the Chamber, several things happened. At 5.0 p.m. the Socialist Minister of Information, Gazier, released the texts of the letters which had passed between Auriol and de Gaulle during the week. De Gaulle's reply showed him in such a different light from that which had been depicted by Le Troquer that the Executive Parliamentary Group of Socialist Deputies and Senators there and then reversed their previous decision and accepted the correspondence as a basis of negotiation. However, in the corridors of the Palais Bourbon something more sinister was happening. Lucien Neuwirth and Captain Lamauleatte, a spokesman for the *Ultras*, suddenly appeared, having left Algiers in disguise that morning. They told such Deputies as they met that the army would wait no longer and that, unless de Gaulle accepted power that night, force would be used. Lamauleatte carried a Black List of Deputies who would be shot and informed several that they were on it. However, de Gaulle was already on his way to the Elysée. He was greeted by a President almost speechless with pleasure and relief at the prospect of being supplanted in his office. De Gaulle left after an hour having accepted the task of forming a government on terms which were to be published a few hours later—exceptional powers for a limited period and a referendum to determine the new Constitution. He returned to Colombey.

When the news of de Gaulle's acceptance was announced pandemonium broke lose in Paris. Gaullists and Communists, plotters and police, clashed all over the city. Sometimes the police were on the plotters' side. But gradually all other noise was drowned by a vast eruption of motor cars, jamming the Champs-Élysées and spilling out into side streets and squares, their horns tapping out in extraordinary unison the beats of *"De Gaulle au pouvoir"* and *"Algérie Française."* In the early hours of Friday, May 30 Parisians went to bed believing that the crisis was over.

But there was still a final scene to be played. The Socialist hierarchy had agreed to "negotiate," but the Party in the Assembly had still to be won if de Gaulle was to secure investiture. On the morning of May 30 at Colombey he received three men, Vincent Auriol, ex-President and Socialist elder statesman, Guy Mollet and Maurice Deixonne, the last, one of his most stubborn opponents. With Auriol de Gaulle failed, for he wanted him as Vice-President of the Council and Auriol demurred. But de Gaulle defended himself with such passionate fervour against Auriol's imputations that he might use a referendum to free himself from parliamentary control that he made a deep impression. When Auriol again raised the question of denouncing the rebels de Gaulle asked, with unanswerable logic, why the Government had not done so. The rebels were still endowed with full civil and military powers. How could he do what the Government refused to do?

With Mollet and Deixonne he was more gentle and persuasive, setting out his plans for the French Union, which were more liberal than theirs, offering Mollet the Vice-Presidency of the Council which Auriol had just refused, agreeing to meet the Parliamentary leaders the following day and to present himself in person to the Assembly. He also assured Mollet that he would maintain the responsibility of Government to Parliament in his new Constitution. His previous obduracy paid off. He had been able to make concessions when they mattered. Mollet returned to Paris overjoyed, Deixonne overwhelmed. He had met, he said, a great and honest man.

But in Algeria and among the plotters the mood was different. The Committees of Public Safety had noticed that de Gaulle had never once used the phrase *"L'Algérie Française"* which had become the revolutionary symbol. His meeting with the Socialists alarmed them. They feared that he was being drawn into the web of the party régime and might become its prisoner. Extreme pressure was brought to bear on Salan in Algiers and on Miguel at Toulouse to launch Operation Resurrection that night, clear out the whole "stinking" régime and install de Gaulle in a manner that would make his acceptance of the revolution inevitable. It needed all the authority of Marshal Juin and General Ely to hold the Operation in check.

On Saturday, May 31, de Gaulle drove up from Colombey to his old haunt, the Hotel Lapérouse. To those whom he met in the morning he seemed in an ill humour, depressed by the opposition which still confronted him, particularly from men like Mendès-France. But in the afternoon, when he received all the party leaders except the Communists, he was relaxed and affable. He answered questions, assured the Deputies that he would not be influenced by the Committees of Public Safety in Algeria and undertook to include in his government members of all the parties in the room. A few, including Mitterand and Mendès-France, remained unconvinced; the great majority, including the indomitable Ramadier, were captivated. All returned immediately to meetings of their parties and carried them in support of de Gaulle. Only among the Socialists was the majority a narrow one.

De Gaulle gave a final unexpected twist to the great drama. On Sunday, June 1 he drove to the Palais Bourbon to make his speech of investiture in the Chamber which, twelve years before, he had sworn never again to enter. Le Troquer, congratulating himself that his intransigence had won this concession to parliamentary procedure and knowing that de Gaulle had recently recovered from an operation for cataract, suggested that the Premier Designate might prefer to speak from his seat where the light was less glaring than at the Tribune. But de Gaulle chose the Tribune and read his speech without difficulty. It was the shortest and perhaps the clearest that any premier had made since the war. It proposed immediate legislation to grant the exceptional powers and the referendum which were the conditions on which he had accepted office, confirmed the promises he had made to Mollet, announced that a new Constitution would be drafted and submitted to the people and then prorogued Parliament until the normal date fixed for the opening of the next session. When he had finished he left the Chamber to the applause of all but the Communists and a minority of Socialists. In the evening he was invested with power by three hundred and twenty-nine votes to two hundred and twenty-four.

The Deputies who dispersed that night did not expect to see de Gaulle again, for he had made it only too plain that he did not wish to listen to their debates. But next day, during the discussion on the exceptional powers, de Gaulle again took his seat and when he rose to intervene began by expressing "all the pleasure and the honour that I feel at finding myself among you this evening . . ."[9] Perhaps the sentiments were genuine. De Gaulle had confessed in his memoirs that, in spite of his contempt for party manoeuvres, the ardent and controversial life of an Assembly attracted him. After twelve years of frustration and despair and a fortnight of tension he may even have felt a glow of warmth and pride in taking his seat among men who had so recently reviled but now applauded him. Certainly the Deputies were transported, crowding round and wanting only to shake his hand. The following day, June 3, they passed his Bills and left for their constituencies; some anxious and thwarted, the majority feeling secure for the first time for many years. De Gaulle was once more governing France.

CHAPTER XXI

TRUTH OR TREASON

De Gaulle was now Prime Minister of that French Republic which he had denounced and reviled ever since it had been acclaimed by referendum in 1946. Before this anomaly could be removed, however, he had to draft a new constitution, submit it to the people, hold general elections and then receive the verdict of the Special College which would finally choose a successor to President Coty. All this would take many months. Meanwhile he and Madame de Gaulle moved into the Hôtel Matignon, the traditional home of French Prime Ministers. Since their stay was to be short—President Coty had already reserved rooms in the Hôtel Meurice so that the Palace of the Elysée could be got ready for them—they accepted it as it was and used it as little more than a *pied-à-terre*; for de Gaulle was to travel incessantly during the next few months and Madame de Gaulle preferred Colombey.

No one knew what was in de Gaulle's mind. In spite of the vote he had just received his position was far less secure than when he had ruled as the liberator of France. Then, within a few weeks of entering Paris, he had stifled the resistance—his only serious rivals in authority —captured the administrative machine and won the complete loyalty of the army. Now he could count for firm support only on a handful of his own followers. The Communists, whose leaders had joined his Government during the war, were against him. The Socialists were divided. Some of the members of the Centre Parties whom he most respected, like Mendès-France, Pineau, Mitterand, de Menthon, had opposed his investiture. Even those who had given him his majority had done so for such different reasons that he was bound soon to incur their enmity. Gaston Deferre, who was later to be a candidate for the Presidency against him, was convinced that de Gaulle meant to negotiate with the F.L.N.; Mollet that he would bring peace to Algiers through general integration; the Conservatives that he meant to keep Algeria for ever French. Ironically the army, whose mutiny had brought him to power, was suspicious of his intentions. Unless he committed himself irrevocably to "*Algérie Française*," he might soon find himself in exactly the same position as his predecessors, lacking the physical means of imposing any policy in Algeria at all.

Already de Gaulle was in trouble. The Government he had formed caused an outcry among the rebels. True to his word de Gaulle had included members of all parties except the Communists in his Cabinet of "National Unity." Along with men like Michelet, Sudreau, Malraux, and Debré, all of whom had fought in the resistance and joined de Gaulle during the war, appeared the names of Mollet, Pflimlin, Pinay, Buron, Berthouin, Lejeune, all men of the hated "system" which de Gaulle was expected to destroy. Soustelle had been left out and even towards the Communists de Gaulle was conciliatory, ceasing to call them "separatists" and regretting that he could not bring them into the fold. Alain de Sérigny, proprietor of *L'Echo d'Alger* and chief spokesman for the *colons*, at once cried out in "anger and disappointment." Massu, the day after the Cabinet was announced, told a *Daily Telegraph* correspondent that de Gaulle must decide in favour of integration. Delbecque flew to Paris to protest to de Gaulle and ask him to make the Committees of Public Safety the basis of civil administration not only in Algiers but in France as well. He claimed that three hundred and twenty such committees were already in being. But de Gaulle had anticipated him.

The morning of Delbecque's journey he had already summoned Generals Salan, Jouhaud and Dulac to Paris for consultations. Already he had abolished the press censorship and removed all restrictions upon communications with Algeria and Corsica. Now he told them that he himself would be entirely responsible for Algerian affairs and asked Salan to be his Delegate-General. He then discussed plans. Municipal elections all over Algeria were to be held within a month and he expected the army to see that they were fairly conducted. Various changes in command were agreed: Jouhaud became Operational Commander of all Land, Sea and Air Forces in Algeria; Massu, Prefect of Algiers. By the time the generals departed they clearly understood that it was the army that was to act as de Gaulle's agent and not the Committees of Public Safety. Delbecque and his friends had been ignored.

Two days later de Gaulle visited Algeria. This was the moment for which everyone was waiting. In Washington and London statesmen looked to him to end the war and allow France once more to play her part in the North Atlantic Treaty Organisation. In Cairo the Arabs waited anxiously to see whether he would side with the army and the *colons*. De Gaulle himself was sure of only one thing; he alone could find the solution. Over and over again since the Algerian war began he had used the phrase "if only I were in power . . ."; now was his opportunity. There is no doubt what he wanted. Though he believed independence must come eventually he still hoped it could be granted as a gift from France, strengthening rather than severing the ties between the two countries. In the month immediately before the May rising he had told visitors that he had the power to rejuvenate France and make the Algerians long to preserve the connection; the day that France had de Gaulle the F.L.N. would cease to exist. Soustelle was whispering that as soon as he declared himself unequivocally in favour of *"Algérie Française"* the Moslems would rally to him almost to a man. De Gaulle had reservations; his vision was not the same as Soustelle's, but he did believe that the Moslems trusted him and that he alone could win them over. Yet at the same time he had to reassure the army that he would not negotiate with the F.L.N. and that their sacrifices would not be in vain; and he must do this in spite of the fact that Lucien Neuwirth was already in touch with some of the F.L.N. leaders unofficially. Taking with him Soustelle as unofficial adviser, and two ministers belonging to the "system," Jacquinot and Lejeune, de Gaulle set out on what the Communists described as his "pilgrimage to the source of his power."

De Gaulle had a tumultuous reception. The streets were packed, mainly with Europeans but with a respectable sprinkling of Moslems all waving *Tricolore* flags. As he drove to the Summer Palace they yelled and shouted, *"Vive de Gaulle," "Algérie Française,"* and sometimes, to de Gaulle's extreme annoyance, *"Vive Soustelle."* It was a little like the liberation over again and, as at the liberation, de Gaulle began by emphasising the "legitimacy" of his rule. Instead of welcoming first the men of the rebellion he rather received all the traditional representatives of the civic power, the Mayor and Councillors, the Diplomatic Corps, the heads of the Church and the University. When Massu was finally able to present the members of the Committee of Public Safety and to repeat Delbecque's request that de Gaulle make them the backbone of his new revolution, he received a frigid reply. De Gaulle then announced that at seven o'clock in the evening he would address the people of Algiers himself from the balcony of the Government-General Building. A vast crowd, again mainly European, filled the forum some hours before and was harangued first by members of the Committee of Public Safety, who sang their hymn of hate against "the system" and, more moderately, by Salan and Soustelle, who repeated the theme of ten million people wanting to remain French. The cheers for Soustelle and *"Algérie Française"* were still echoing across the forum as de Gaulle mounted the stairs. Unknown to him the two ministers following in his wake were suddenly whisked into a room and locked in; no member of the "system" was to be allowed to appear at his side.

"I have understood you," began de Gaulle—and the entire crowd burst into cheers which lasted several minutes. He went on: "I know what happened here. I know what you wanted to do. The road you have thrown open in Algeria is the road of renewal and fraternity." He spoke of the renewal of the institutions of government and of the "magnificent spectacle" of the different communities joining hands. "From to-day," he said, "France considers that in the whole of Algeria there is only one category of inhabitants—only complete Frenchmen, having the same rights and duties." He praised the ardour, discipline, the "magnificent work of understanding and pacification" of the army and said he counted on it now and in the future. He promised that in three months all complete Frenchmen should vote on a basis of equality to decide their own destiny. "With these elected representatives," he added, "we shall decide about the rest." He even praised the courage of the F.L.N. and appealed to them to join in the vote. "I, de Gaulle, open to them the gates of reconciliation. Never have I felt more than I do tonight how beautiful, how great, how generous France is. *Vive la République. Vive la France.*"[1]

The speech was a masterly combination of rhetoric and ambiguity. Those listening to it could read into it what they desired—a pledge of integration on the one hand, a guarantee that the destiny of Algeria would only be decided after her own representatives had been elected, on the other. As he continued his rapid tour of the country, to Constantine, Bône, Oran and down the coast of Mostaganem, de Gaulle reiterated his theme and added to its ambiguity. At Oran he spoke sharply to a member of the local Committee of Public Safety who demanded an end to political parties and the substitution of the committees as the foundation of French political life. At Mostaganem, perhaps in compensation and certainly for the first and last time, he used the phrase "*Algérie Française.*"*

Again and again he stressed that it was the army which must control Algeria and guarantee that all its inhabitants could really *feel* French. Finally, before he returned to France, de Gaulle wrote a formal letter to General Salan appointing him Delegate-General and instructing him to re-establish "the workings of the regular authority." De Gaulle had intended to disband the Committees of Public Safety

---

* Later de Gaulle was to ask his colleagues whether he had ever actually used these words. On being assured that he had, he said he must have been carried away by the enthusiasm of the moment; the words were superficial.

J. R. Tournoux. *La Tragédie du Général*, pp.287-90.

altogether, but Salan dissuaded him. De Gaulle insisted, however, on their being used simply as vehicles for improving public relations and remaining strictly under Salan's control. On June 8 he was back in Paris.

De Gaulle could not yet tell whether his gamble had come off. He had staked his future on winning the allegiance of the army without committing himself to their policy. By putting Salan in complete charge of the administration in Algeria he had hoped to drive a wedge between the army commanders and the *Ultras*, Martel, Lagaillarde, Dr. Lèbfevre and Delbecque who controlled the Committees of Public Safety. The decision was practical as well as political for the war and the rebellion between them had virtually destroyed the civil administration and the *Sections Administratives Specialisées* of the army had for months been the only effective organisation. The soldiers were far more sympathetic to the Moslems than the civilian population. But would the army stand up to the *Ultras*?

First indications were not propitious. No sooner had de Gaulle left Algiers than the Committee of Public Safety for Algeria and the Sahara, on which fourteen senior officers still sat, passed an unanimous resolution asking that the municipal elections be postponed, and any administrative organs which emphasised the "individual status of Algeria" should be abolished, and, once more, that the political parties be dissolved. This resolution was accepted by Salan and forwarded to de Gaulle on June 10. De Gaulle replied tartly that he found the resolution "inopportune and irresponsible" and reproved Salan for having anything to do with it. He refrained, for the moment, however, from ordering all officers to resign from the committees. Meanwhile, in anticipation of the resolution which he knew was on its way, he announced the formation of a special Algerian Secretariat under René Brouillet, whose *Chef de Cabinet* was the equally liberal Bernard Tricot.

On June 13, de Gaulle gave his first press conference as Prime Minister. He said nothing new but pledged himself once more to bring peace to Algeria in a way that would "make her one with France for ever," and to "organise on a Federal basis" French relations with the associated peoples of Africa and Madagascar.

Five days later he gave a clear indication of the sort of federation he had in mind when he concluded an agreement with Bourguiba even more favourable to Tunisia than the proposals put forward by Beeley and Murphy which had brought Gaillard down a few months earlier. It provided for the immediate evacuation of all French troops, other than the garrison of Bizerta. However, it was still anyone's guess whether Algeria was meant to be an exception or to conform to the general federal pattern.

With Algiers simmering de Gaulle had little time for anything else. He helped launch Pinay's Loan which, like Pleven's in 1944, was designed to check inflation; he put Debré in charge of the committee which was to draft the new Constitution. In this he knew what he wanted and was determined to get it; so as to set a time limit he let it be known that the referendum to approve the Draft would be held on or about October 5. Then, at the beginning of July, he went back to Algiers, this time taking Mollet with him.

De Gaulle was by now aware that his first visit had not been an unqualified success, the *Ultras* were openly hostile and the army vacillating. The students who had cheered him in June were by now tearing down his poster portraits in the streets of Algiers. Nobody tried to stop them. Although a few extremist officers had been sent out of the city the only ones posted to France by Salan had been six generals who were reputed to have been lukewarm over the rebellion. This time de Gaulle set out deliberately to win over the army. Instead of visiting the big cities he went to garrison towns, especially those in the fighting areas. He mixed with junior officers, talked to the soldiers, praised the Foreign Legion, and made a fuss of the *paras*. He was informal, he listened. He already knew all about the "psychological" action undertaken by men like Colonels Goussault and Trinquier and he learned now about the army's network of spies and informers, the Black Lists drawn up, the training schools for village headsmen, the bribes and threats used to produce the demonstrations of "fraternisation." It was all supposed to have been copied from Mao Tse-tung's handbooks on guerrilla warfare which had been absorbed by French prisoners in Indo-China; much of it might equally have been copied from the British in Malaya. De Gaulle, however, drew his own conclusions both about the effectiveness of such methods among the Moslems and of their effect on the army. For the moment he said nothing. On the last day of his visit, when a delegation from the Committee of Public Safety of Algiers asked to see him, he refused; a similar request from the trade unions he referred to Mollet. De Gaulle then returned to France.

Back in Paris the courtship of the army continued. On July 7 de Gaulle appointed Soustelle to succeed Malraux as Minister of Information. Malraux, who had once had communist sympathies, terrified the soldiers with his vague and liberal phrases. At a press conference in June, Soustelle, on the other hand, had become less dogmatic about integration, saying that he was in favour of it only in so far as it was the opposite of "disintegration." He had supported de Gaulle's measures to curb the Committees of Public Safety. Since de Gaulle had been using Soustelle as an expert to brief his Cabinet colleagues on Algeria they had sensed and accepted this change of attitude.

De Gaulle then rounded off his military flirtation by announcing that a great parade would be held in the Champs-Élysées on Bastille Day, to which the Generals of May 13 would be invited. He heralded the event by a series of awards and promotions. Salan received the *Médaille Militaire*, one of the highest military honours, Dulac was appointed Salan's chief aide. Massu became a full General. Jouhaud and Challe were made Generals of the Air Force and Faure, who had been in disgrace since his "attempted coup" of 1956, was given an important Divisional Command at Tizzi-Ouzou, one of the active fronts against the F.L.N.

The parade looked like the celebration of the victory of the Algerian rebellion. Besides the rebel generals and the paratroops, several thousand Moslem soldiers took part in the march, Moslem dignitaries made speeches in favour of integration. The climax came when the forgotten President Coty drove down the Champs-Élysées with his Prime Minister by his side. But for de Gaulle this was the pay off. He was no appeaser and he had gone as far as he intended to go in winning to his side those whose "unconstitutional action" had forced Coty to summon him to power. The time had come to exact obedience.

*   *   *

De Gaulle now turned his attention to France. Hitherto his Government had been almost provisional. Now he had to give it a permanent framework, first by settling the form of the Constitution and then by holding the elections which would ultimately make him President. As his chief agents he used two men, Michel Debré, Keeper of the Seals and, therefore, chief draftsman, and Jacques Soustelle, Minister of Information, whose duty it was to sell the Constitution to the nation. Both were brilliant men whose sustained and contemptuous attacks had steadily undermined the authority of the Fourth Republic. Debré, an admirer of the British parliamentary system, genuinely desired to create a Republic in which a government could be strong while remaining democratic; Soustelle, caring less for the form, saw the Constitution as a means of building a multi-racial state and uniting fifty million Frenchmen.

De Gaulle had no such illusions. He had already laid down the essentials, the powers of the President, the separation of the Executive and the Legislative, the use of the referendum. He chaired the Ministerial Committee to which the many drafts were presented but was bored with the details; he appeared only once before the sub-committee which was preparing the drafts. When Debré boasted that no less than one hundred and twenty texts had been considered, de Gaulle threw up his arms in despair. "What cheek," was all he could say. When the final text was published on September 4 it contained few surprises. It was a Constitution not only for France but for the new "Community" which it was hoped the Overseas Territories would now enter.

The key was the Presidency. The President was to be the Head of both France and the Community. He would be elected by a Special College drawn not only from the Assemblies in Paris and Overseas but from Departmental and Municipal Councils as well. He would serve for seven years. The President would appoint his Ministers, none of whom must be Members of Parliament. He would preside over the Cabinet. He would appoint all civil and military officials and be Commander-in-Chief of the Armed Forces. Parliament would control the budget but, if it rejected it, the President could dissolve it or, under certain conditions, rule by Decree. In a national emergency he could suspend the Constitution altogether. Bills dealing with the "organisation of the Public Authorities" could, if thrown out by the Assembly, be submitted to a referendum. The Government was responsible to the Assembly only on a vote of censure which could be proposed once during a Session. If defeated the Government must resign; but it was still open to the President to appoint another rather than hold an election.

De Gaulle himself led the campaign. He opened it at a great rally in the Place de la République and spoke in four other cities, Lille, Bordeaux, Rennes and Strasbourg, and three times on radio and television. None of his speeches was long and most of what he said he had already said and written a hundred times before. "This Constitution," he declared in the Place de la République, "has been drawn up for the people we are and the world and century in which we live. It means effective direction; a national arbiter above political rights; a Government which will be capable of governing, a Parliament which represents the political will of the nation without exceeding its role . . .With all my heart and in the name of France, I call upon you to answer 'Yes' on September 28. If you do not do so we shall on that very same day revert to the mistakes that you know so well."[2] His vast audience listened attentively and applauded soberly.

Within a week the prophets were forecasting an affirmative vote of at least sixty-five per cent. But Soustelle was working to produce something better. On July 17, ten days after he became Minister of

Information, he announced that he was forming a new movement, the Union for the Renovation of France, to campaign in the Referendum and later in the election. This movement was soon to become the U.N.R., the second great Gaullist Party, far more powerful and successful than the first; for the moment, however, it acted as Soustelle's propaganda machine. As Minister of Information he wielded powers possessed by none of his counterparts in Western democracies. Radio and television have always been subject to government control in France and Soustelle took full advantage of it. He manned his Secretariat with good Gaullists like Neuwirth and Terrenoire, and carried out a thorough purge of the staff. When a group of Deputies protested, he replied blandly that he had to make sure that Communists were eliminated from sensitive posts at such a vital time. Opposition parties were allowed exactly five minutes each on the radio and television and the rest of the time was packed with Government propaganda. His powers went further. As Minister of Information he was able to "co-ordinate" the information supplied by government departments and feed the news reels which appeared in the cinemas; through the Mayors and Prefects throughout France he saw that not only Government posters but private posters of which the Government approved were widely displayed in every Commune. Through the *Centre de Diffusion Française*, roughly the equivalent of the British Council, he was also able to feed a mass of material to "fringe" radio stations like Luxembourg and to the foreign press. Money was no object since it came from the State and Soustelle spent milliards of francs.

De Gaulle received some unexpected help. The world did not stand still while France wrestled with her internal problems. On the day that de Gaulle held his great parade in Paris, King Feisal and Nuri Said were murdered in Baghdad and the Middle East was thrown into turmoil. President Chamoun of the Lebanon appealed for protection to the Unites States, Britain and France. De Gaulle sent the cruiser *Grasse* to Beirut but before it arrived Eisenhower had ordered United States troops to land and sent the ubiquitous Mr. Murphy on another peace mission. British troops, at the request of King Hussein, were sent to Jordan. In the ensuing settlement the French played little part. All this was grist to de Gaulle's electoral mill. He was able, with justification, to claim that, because of her internal weaknesses, France was ignored in parts of the world where she had traditional interests. He managed first to block the Anglo-Soviet proposals for a summit conference and then get Mr. Khrushchev's blessing for a private meeting of "the Big Four" which included France. He also arranged talks with the Italian

Prime Minister, Fanfani, and the German Chancellor, Adenauer. The meeting of de Gaulle and Adenauer on September 17 lit a candle of hope in every Frenchman's heart that at long last Franco-German enmity was to be buried. With miraculous timing Khrushchev cancelled the meeting to which he had agreed and made a slashing attack on de Gaulle, comparing him with Hindenburg and suggesting that French big business was using him to set up a fascist dictatorship.

An outbreak of terrorism instigated by the Algerians also played into the hands of de Gaulle. For months rival factions of Algerians had been murdering each other in France, but on August 24 a co-ordinated campaign against Frenchmen began. Four policemen were shot dead in Paris. Petrol dumps, post offices and power stations were bombed and set on fire from Normandy to Narbonne. An attempt to destroy the Eiffel Tower by placing a time-bomb under a ladies' lavatory seat on the top story was discovered. Thousands of Algerians living in France were rounded up but the attacks continued, culminating on September 15 in a point-blank attempt on the life of Soustelle himself.

With his face in sticking plaster he described what happened an hour later at a press conference. As he was getting out of his car to go into his office a man standing on the pavement opened fire with a tommy-gun. Soustelle saw him just in time and threw himself down in the gutter. The man missed and ran off. As Soustelle rose he saw another man a few yards farther away taking aim. He threw himself down and was again missed. The second man was caught. Soustelle stressed that his assailants belonged to a "fanatical minority" and should not be identified with all Moslems in France; but he turned the incident to the advantage of the "one man" who could bring peace to Algeria and save France from the Communists whom he claimed were behind the F.L.N. A new poster "F.L.N. and Communism = assassins" was distributed by his Ministry only to be capped by a sticker handed out by the Gaullist movement reading simply "Oui-Nyet."

Nevertheless, press, public and Government were all surprised by the results of the Referendum. In France, out of an eighty-five per cent poll, de Gaulle received eighty per cent of the votes. This was as "massive" a "Yes" as even de Gaulle could have hoped. In Algeria the vote was still more overwhelming. In a slightly lower poll, ninety-six per cent of the voters, who for the first time included Moslem women, had said "Yes." No one, however, imagined that this was a true reflection of Moslem feeling. De Gaulle had publicly appealed for an impartial vote and had not only sent a special civil commissioner to supervise the elections in Algeria but had published his instructions to Salan that no pressure was to be brought upon the electorate by the army. But the private instructions issued by his Ministry under his signature were very different. From Salan de Gaulle demanded two things, a massive Moslem vote to show that the people were being consulted, and a majority for the Constitution. Salan had carried out his orders.

In face of an F.L.N. threat to murder anyone who went to the polls, the army had afforded much more than protection. It ran the campaign, policed every town and village on polling day, drove voters to the poll in lorries, and through its psychological department, made it abundantly clear that not to vote would be an error. There was no vernacular press and no opposition on the radio except from Cairo and other neighbouring stations. To remove all doubts, the voting forms were of different colours; white for "Yes" and purple for "No." With soldiers outside every polling booth it needed not so much courage as foolhardiness in a Moslem to ask for a purple form. Out of nearly three and a half million voters only a hundred and nineteen thousand did. In the Overseas Territories—Algeria, of course, was a Department of France —the results were equally impressive with one exception: Guinea opted out of the Community altogether.

*   *   *

The referendum authorising a new constitution had been won; next must come a general election. As the Algerian war was uppermost in people's minds he decided that at last the time had come to show his hand. At Constantine, on October 4, he made a bid for Moslem allegiance which was nothing short of a New Deal for the whole of Algeria coupled with some strong hints that his mind was open as to its future political form. "The whole of Algeria must have its share of what modern civilisation can and must bring by way of human dignity and well being," he said. In the next five years at least one tenth of all those salaries were to be brought up to the level of those in France; half a million acres of new land were to be distributed to Moslem farmers; industry and housing were to be developed to the tune of four hundred thousand jobs; two thirds of all Algerian children would be sent to schools. Then he turned to politics: "As regards the political status of Algeria I consider it quite useless to commit myself to any particular words . . . In two months from now Algeria will elect its representatives in the same conditions as France. It is essential that at least two thirds of these should be Moslems. As for the future it is natural that Algeria should be built on the dual basis of its personality and its close solidarity with Metropolitan France." Finally he appealed once more to the F.L.N. "Why kill people when you must make them live? Why destroy when your duty is to build? Why this hatred instead of co-operation? Stop these absurd battles! The moment you stop them you will see hope blossoming all over the land of Algeria. The prisons will empty themselves; and there will be a great future for everybody, particularly yourselves," and he ended: "*Vive la République. Vive L'Algérie et La France.*"[3]

This was de Gaulle's vision, the culmination of years of thought, the final expression of his hopes. No doubt much of the programme was impractical. Where were the teachers to come from and who would meet the cost? But if he could convince the Moslems of his sincerity he might yet keep Algeria French in some more intimate sense than membership of the Community he had already offered to the other Overseas Territories. But to do this he had finally to disown the *Ultras*. He began at once.

The Constantine Committee of Public Safety was so angry that it asked Massu to allow an anti-de Gaulle demonstration there and then. Massu refused and, when the Committee tried to send a delegation of protest to de Gaulle, he declined to see them. Then on October 9 he wrote a peremptory letter to Salan telling him that in the coming elections in Algeria electoral lists representing all shades of opinion—"I repeat all shades of opinion"—should be able to compete on a basis of complete equality. This time his private instructions were consistent. "What we should aim at," he wrote, "is that a political Algerian élite should freely emerge from the election; it is only thus that the political vacuum can be filled which has opened the way for the leaders of the Algerian rebellion." Civil servants and army officers were forbidden to stand as candidates and all officers were ordered to resign at once from the Committees of Public Safety.[4]

The *Ultras* were thunderstruck, but when they tried to call a general strike they found even the Europeans against them. The army obeyed de Gaulle. Within a week Massu and all other officers had resigned from the committees. Then on October 23, de Gaulle gave a press conference in Paris at which he made the offer of a "peace of the brave" to the F.L.N. He suggested that any F.L.N. commander in the field who wanted a Cease Fire should "use the wise old custom of the white flag of parley," in which case he guaranteed they should be received and treated honourably; secondly if delegates wanted to discuss a Cease Fire at national level he guaranteed their safe conduct in and out of France. For two days, while de Gaulle waited for an answer, hopes of peace rose throughout the world.

Although the F.L.N. had scornfully rejected de Gaulle's earlier appeal to take part in the Referendum and had retaliated by forming a government-in-exile before the vote was taken, Ferhat Abbas had that same month publicly renewed his offer to meet French delegates and "put an end to the trial of strength which had been going on in Algeria for four years."[5] What the public did not know was that he had been in touch with de Gaulle through intermediaries for some time and had let it be known that he was prepared to come to Paris with Belkacem and Lamine Debaghine, his War and Foreign Ministers respectively, to deal with de Gaulle in person. When de Gaulle's offer was made public, however, it soon emerged that the F.L.N. was divided and the commanders in the field were obdurate. The extremists seized on the phrase "white flag" and, ignoring the rest of de Gaulle's speech, labelled it a demand for surrender. On October 25, in a communiqué given over Cairo radio, the government-in-exile rejected de Gaulle's offer. The refusal of the F.L.N. shattered de Gaulle's hopes. So long as they continued to fight he knew that he could not hope to win the Moslem population. His spirits sank and he began to talk of the pacification of Algeria as an operation *de longue haleine* which would only be concluded successfully by a new generation in a totally new spirit.[6]

Nevertheless the French people showed their overwhelming confidence in him. The General Election, held on November 23 and 30, returned the U.N.R., Soustelle's new Gaullist party, and the Conservatives with a massive majority. The Communists were reduced to ten seats, the Socialists to forty.

For a moment de Gaulle hesitated. With so many extremists in Parliament it might be wise to remain Prime Minister so as to control them more directly. In a mood of unusual humility he consulted Coty, who, although he would secretly have liked to see his seven years' term of office through to the end, strongly advised de Gaulle to take the Presidency. De Gaulle was easily convinced and on January 9, 1959 the two men, according to custom, drove in the same carriage to the Arc de Triomphe where Coty formally handed over his office. De Gaulle thanked him, saying that he was a great citizen who was surrendering his mandate with great dignity; but either because he forgot or was too preoccupied with the crowd, he omitted the courtesy of accompanying Coty to his carriage.

* * *

President at last, and on his own terms, de Gaulle prepared for the next round in the Algerian struggle. Slowly and painfully he was coming to the conclusion that independence was inevitable. He was well aware that he was approaching one of the most dangerous crises in his long life and began to lay the foundations for his clash with the army. He chose Debré for Prime Minister rather than Soustelle, judging that he could count more certainly on his loyalty. He then turned once more to Algiers. Since Salan had exceeded his instructions during the elections in Algeria he brought him home and made him Governor of Paris. He posted another general and several extremist colonels and, so as to keep Algerian affairs firmly in his own hands, abolished the office of Delegate-General and appointed a civil servant, M. Delouvrier, Resident Minister directly under himself. From now on de Gaulle kept a close watch on all offices in Algeria, changing them constantly so as to prevent their contamination by the *Ultras*. It was a policy that was only partially successful because, even at St. Cyr and the *École Supérieure de Guerre,* the doctrine that the army must concern itself with civilian morale, and therefore with politics, had become part of the curriculum. But the posting of a thousand officers in the next three years did make it more difficult for the extremists to organise a military coup.

De Gaulle balanced this severity by ordering General Challe, who became Commander-in-Chief when Salan left, to clean up the rebellion once and for all. Since the F.L.N. had refused to negotiate a Cease Fire, de Gaulle was determined to show them that they could not win and to bring them to their senses. In conjunction with Delouvrier, Challe embarked upon a policy of clearing Algeria of terrorists sector by sector. As the army moved in to a district its civil administration would uproot whole villages and resettle the inhabitants in special camps where they could be protected from the terrorists. Within three years more than a million people were moved in this way. But although large areas were freed from the F.L.N. the cleaning-up was never complete; the F.L.N. filtered back into their strongholds as soon as the army moved on. Delouvrier's transplantations reduced the number of mass arrests, but his strict instructions about police and military methods of interrogation were not always observed. One army camp still gave courses in torture and it was practised on both sides. In spite of the exercise of clemency by which several thousand prisoners were released on de Gaulle's assumption of the Presidency, thousands more were still being held on suspicion and without trial.

Nevertheless, the schism between de Gaulle and the army grew and spread to the Government itself. In his tours of the Provinces in France de Gaulle was continually stressing the inevitability of the Algerian deciding their own destiny. On the other hand, the Government under Debré was applauding the success of General Challe's military operations and Marshal Juin and the Generals of May 13 were speaking as if the rebellion were already over and integration a fact, which Algerians must accept.

In the Algerian municipal elections in March, 1959, the army again defied de Gaulle's instructions and no liberal Europeans or truly representative Moslems dared to stand as candidates. The *Ultras* in Algiers boycotted the anniversary of the revolution and were openly speaking of de Gaulle as a traitor. Cries of "de Gaulle to the gallows" and "*Vive Pétain*" were heard round the forum, during their demonstrations. De Gaulle countered in a press conference in which he again talked of the "Algerian personality" and, in an interview with Pierre Laffont, editor of *L'Echo d'Oran,* derided the political significance of the slogan "*Algérie Française*" with the equivocal observation that there was no point in using it since it was already fact. "Those who shout loudest for integration," he went on, "are those who were formerly against it. What they want is to be given *Algérie de Papa,* but *Algérie de Papa* is stone dead and if they do not understand they will die with it."[7]

De Gaulle was quietly preparing his next move. Up till now he had insisted that negotiations with the F.L.N. should only concern a Cease Fire; but he had already spoken of an "Algerian personality" and the time had come to define it. On August 26 he held a special Cabinet to discuss Algerian policy. This was unusual because, as Minister for Algeria, he normally confided in no one but simply issued instructions. Now he asked each minister in turn his opinion. As they stated them it was clear that they were divided. Debré and the majority were in favour of yet another Algerian Statute under which French sovereignty would be maintained, but with a proviso that some time in the future Algeria might choose her own destiny. Soustelle and Cornut-Gentille, the Minister for Overseas Territories, were unalterably opposed to any idea of an Algerian State at all. Malraux and one or two others wanted the right of Algerians to opt for independence to be announced right away. De Gaulle neither agreed nor disagreed but, at the end said, "Gentlemen, I thank you. In this sort of business one must either go forward or die. I propose to go forward, but that does not mean that one may not also die."[8]

His meaning was soon made clear. On September 16, in a broadcast, de Gaulle "in the name of France and of the Republic" offered Algeria the right of self-determination. They had three choices, secession, which meant independence; "francisation," or out and out identity with France under which Algerians and Europeans would enjoy absolute equality; and association, which was broadly the status enjoyed at the time by the majority of the other Overseas Territories. The offer was hedged with conditions and contained many obscurities. De Gaulle would not negotiate with the F.L.N. as the sole representatives of Algeria. On the other hand the F.L.N. could take part in the negotiations and the voting along with other Moslems. Peace must be established and life returned to normal before the offer could be made good. The rights of the European minority must be safeguarded and, if necessary, the Europeans must be regrouped into areas where they could assure those rights themselves. In other words, if the Algerians chose independence they might find themselves faced with the partition of their country. At all costs French exploitation of the oil in the Sahara was to be guaranteed. Finally the French people as a whole must endorse the Algerian choice by referendum.

De Gaulle also made his own preference clear. Some people, he said, believed that secession would bring independence. In his own view it would result in "appalling misery," chaos and eventually a bellicose Communist dictatorship. It would mean inevitably the end of all help from France. "Francisation" he described factually and without enthusiasm. The solution he favoured was plainly association so that the various communities living in Algeria could be given guarantees for their own way of life and a framework for co-operation.

For all its ambiguities the speech was a landmark. It was the first time that any French Government had admitted the possibility of Algerian independence. Although many of the conditions were offensive to the F.L.N., the goal it had been fighting for was within its grasp. A surge of hope that the war might end swept through France while Government and people once more waited for the F.L.N. reply.

It came in the form of a qualified refusal. On September 28 the F.L.N. leaders, after consultation with the Moroccan and Tunisian Heads of State, issued a statement which acknowledged that the right of the Algerian people freely to decide their destiny had at last been recognised by the Head of a French Government. But they went on to claim that it was the success of their own arms which had brought about this change of heart and declared themselves ready to negotiate only if all French Forces were withdrawn from Algeria. They also protested against the right of the French people to endorse the Algerian decision and against any idea of partition or surrender of Algerian rights to the Sahara oil. On the other hand—and this was a concession—they claimed the right to act as "trustees" for the Algerian people only until the latter had decided the future for themselves.

Further discussions took place and then on November 20, the
F.L.N. leaders gave their final reply. They would still not agree to a
Cease Fire until the necessary conditions for a free vote in Algeria had
been guaranteed. But they were prepared to talk and nominated as
plenipotentiaries the four leaders imprisoned on the Île d'Aix off the
French coast near Bordeaux, who had been kidnapped on the airfield
at Algiers two years before.

De Gaulle turned down their offer that same day. He considered the
appointment of the imprisoned leaders as an insult and remarked
acidly, "We have told those who are fighting what they should do if
they want peace as we do . . . I am, of course, speaking to those who
are fighting, not those who are *hors de combat*."[9] He gave instructions
that Challe's "pacification" should be intensified and also that General
Councils should be elected in all twelve Departments of Algeria so
that the process of preparing the country for self-government should
begin. If the F.L.N. refused to take part, self-determination should go
ahead without them.

But the door was not really shut. The offer of self-determination,
once made, could never be withdrawn. Integration was dead. And
although de Gaulle might pronounce himself disillusioned with F.L.N.
leadership, he had made a considerable leap forward. The National
Assembly endorsed his offer by an overwhelming majority. Every
political party in France, including the Communists and excepting
only the die-hard Integrationists, supported him. Only nine members
of the U.N.R. resigned, a minute proportion considering the conservative character of the movement. Most of the Moslem Deputies
were behind him.

*   *   *

In Algeria de Gaulle's offer caused a storm. On the last day of the
debate in the Assembly Lucien Neuwirth, a loyal U.N.R. Deputy in
spite of his previous support for integration, announced in a press
conference that "commandos and killers" had crossed the Pyrenees to
assassinate certain political leaders. Next day his point seemed proved
when François Mitterand's car was riddled with bullets in the streets
of Paris. Mitterand had noticed he was being followed and escaped by
stopping his car round a corner, jumping the fence into the Observ-
atory gardens and hiding in the bushes while the firing went on. In the
inquiry which followed some doubt was thrown on Mitterand's story.
It seemed possible that the shooting had been arranged between himself and a political colleague to discredit the "Activists." However,

many Deputies did receive threatening letters and there was certainly a plot to overthrow the Government and make Bidault Prime Minister. The police scotched it and Bidault was placed under "protective custody"; the protection did not last long for within a month Bidault was again in Algiers speaking on behalf of a new committee uniting the various European extremist organisations. In January 1960, *L'Aurore*, the official organ of the right-wing Conservatives, violently attacked de Gaulle, calling him a "monarchist" and a "Napoleon." Shortly afterwards Pinay, the Finance Minister and the one member of the Cabinet capable of standing up to de Gaulle, attempted to find out what the President's offer of self-determination really meant and was dismissed.

But as always it was opinion in the army which was critical. Immediately after de Gaulle had made his offer Challe asked for an interview to discuss the role the army was to play under self-determination. Challe was only partially satisfied and on January 14 de Gaulle announced a second conference to be held on January 22, to be attended by the ministers concerned with Algeria and Generals Challe, Zeller, Jouhaud, and Massu. Then came a bombshell. On January 18, an account appeared in the *Süd-Deutsche Zeitung* of an interview given by Massu to a German journalist, Herr Kempski, in which the General not only disassociated himself from de Gaulle's policy but implied that the army might once again take things into its own hands. Massu denied having made the remarks but, on the morning the conference was to take place, he was relieved of his post. When the meeting began in the afternoon it was dominated, not by de Gaulle, but by Massu's empty chair.

Again de Gaulle's future was at stake. He knew that the *Ultras* were trying to persuade the army to remove him by force and that everything depended upon the High Command. Challe made it plain that he had come to find out what de Gaulle really thought and to inform him of the army's "profound anxiety." De Gaulle prevaricated. He congratulated the generals on the progress of "pacification" and assured them that it would continue. He reminded them that the Government had refused to negotiate with the F.L.N. He stressed, which was not quite true, that he had hoped for the solution which would be most French and guaranteed that the army would still be in Algiers when the vote on self-determination was taken. This last comment would certainly have been interpreted by the F.L.N. as inconsistent with his pledge that the voting should be entirely free; but it was also a statement of fact. With Algeria as it was, no referendum at all would have been possible unless the army had been there to keep order. Backed up by Ely, the Chief of the General Staff, de Gaulle carried the day. Jouhaud said bluntly that he thought de Gaulle was wrong, but the generals returned to Algiers committed to carry out his orders.

They arrived just in time to have their loyalty put to the test. On the morning of Sunday, January 24, crowds of Europeans led by territorials in uniform, began to converge on the University Building near the forum in Algiers. Troops patrolling the streets let them pass. By mid-afternoon all the old leaders of the main rebellion two years before were haranguing the crowds to cries of "de Gaulle to the gallows" and "Massu, Massu." Barricades were erected and La-gaillarde and Ortiz each announced that they and their followers were going to stay where they were until the policy of September 16 had been reversed.

At around 6.0 p.m. a squadron of mobile gendarmes charged the crowd near the War Memorial with rifle butts. Shots rang out from Ortiz's section of the barricades. Fourteen gendarmes and six civilians fell dead and one hundred and twenty-three gendarmes and twenty civilians were wounded. The gendarmes withdrew, taking their dead and wounded with them. The second rebellion had started.

What would Challe do? To begin with the soldiers had fraternised with the territorials, talking and joking with them as they built the barricades. But by seven o'clock a cordon of troops had been thrown round the rebels, who numbered about two thousand armed men; shortly afterwards General Costes, in command of security in the city, announced a curfew. At 8.0 p.m. General Challe came on the air to denounce "the rioters" who had fired on the police and to tell the crowds that he had ordered troops from the interior of Algeria to move on the city. The army seemed to be holding firm.

Yet the insurgents still clung to the barricades. No attempt was made to dislodge them or to end the general strike which the insurgents had called. On January 25, de Gaulle sent Debré to Algiers to report, but the Prime Minister did not try to alter the army's passive role. Delouvrier at one moment seemed to be losing his nerve and spoke of "shaking hands" with the rebels when all was over. Challe told the army that if it joined the rebellion it would lose Algeria and probably France, but moved his headquarters out of the city. At the end of five days the issue still hung in the balance. Everything depended upon de Gaulle.

At first the President was stunned. He could not believe that the army would sustain an attitude of passive resistance. He motored at once from Colombey and had an appeal for loyalty broadcast in his name; then he held a Cabinet. It was an atmosphere you could "cut with a knife" wrote Soustelle later.[10] De Gaulle, his face as white as marble, would then and there have ordered the army to destroy the barricades even if it meant opening fire. One after another the ministers agreed and disagreed. Debré, who had once said he would write until the pen fell from his fingers, speak until he could no longer utter a word in defence of French Algeria, gave a factual account of what he had seen and left the discussion to others. Malraux, Buron, Sudreau, Michelet, were with de Gaulle; Cornut-Gentil and Soustelle against. Sarcastically Soustelle suggested that, since the atom bomb was ready to be tested, they should explode it among the barricades and settle the matter. Juin, when consulted, was contemptuous. De Gaulle could do what he liked with his Marshal's baton; if he gave the order to fire Juin would come out publicly against him. In the end de Gaulle postponed his order to open fire to see if the army could subdue the rebellion without bloodshed.

Before the rebellion had begun de Gaulle had announced his intention of broadcasting to the nation on January 29. He stuck to his plan and appeared before the cameras in uniform. He spoke of "the foul blow" which had been struck at France by the rebels and then turned to the people of Algeria. "Frenchmen of Algeria, how can you listen to the liars and conspirators who tell you that by giving Algerians a free choice France and de Gaulle want to abandon you, to withdraw from Algeria, and to surrender it to the rebellion? Is it abandoning you, is it wanting to lose Algeria, to send and maintain there an army of five hundred thousand men . . . to devote to it this very year a thousand million old francs for civil and military expenditure, to undertake vast development work, to extract oil and gas from the Sahara at great effort and great cost and to carry them to the sea? . . . Above all, can you not see that, in rising against the State and the nation, you are destroying yourselves, and at the same time running the risk of causing France to lose Algeria at the very moment when the decline of the rebellion is becoming clear? I beseech you to return to law and order."

It was an eloquent appeal, although neither de Gaulle not his listeners can really have been taken in by it. The vast majority of Moslems had shown no enthusiasm for the sort of co-operation he was preaching and most Europeans still wanted L'Algérie de Papa. But it served as an introduction for his appeal to the army. "I say to all our soldiers, your mission does not admit of any equivocation or interpretation . . . What would the French Army become but an anarchic and derisory collection of military fiefs if certain elements were to make their loyalty subject to conditions . . . no soldier, on pain of committing a grave offence, must at any time associate himself, even passively, with the rebellion."

Miraculously the appeal succeeded. Next day the generals in Algiers switched from passive containment to suppression of the rebellion. The general strike which Lagaillarde and Ortiz had organised was brought to a stop. The territorials were mobilised. The crowds were prevented from reaching the barricades. General Gambiez, whose loyalty had been half-hearted, was posted. On February 1, 1960, the rebels marched out from the barricades and surrendered.

De Gaulle had won his first trial of strength and opinion polls showed that in France he was at the peak of his popularity. The army had obeyed him not only in suppressing a revolt with which it sympathised but in furthering a policy which every soldier knew in his heart must lead to the independence of Algeria. The way seemed open for negotiations which could bring the war to an end. Yet for two more years, during which he courted not only further mutiny but assassination, de Gaulle hesitated to make the only sort of offer which the provisional government of the F.L.N. would accept. At first he acted firmly. In an extraordinary session of Parliament a bill was immediately passed giving him special powers for a period of one year. Once again he was virtually a dictator. The leaders of the rebellion, with the exception of Ortiz who disappeared, were promptly arrested. Soustelle and Cornut-Gentil were dropped from the Cabinet and Soustelle expelled from the U.N.R. Challe was promoted to a European Command and succeeded by Crepin, a war-time Gaullist with no connections in Algiers. The territorials and psychological units of the army were disbanded and all activist organisations suppressed. *L'Echo d'Alger* was banned and its proprietor, Alain de Sérigny, was imprisoned. The administration of Algeria was taken out of the hands of the army and entirely reformed.

Then suddenly, just as he seemed to have reached the crest of a new wave of authority, de Gaulle drew back. At the beginning of March he again flew to Algeria and again went on a *tournée des popotes*, visiting the army units, talking to the officers, ignoring the civilians. But instead of ramming home the lessons of the recent revolt he seemed to be giving way to just those views he had so recently denounced. He spoke of the necessity of winning a complete military victory unless the rebels laid down their arms. He talked of the war going on and on and urged the troops to go and seek out the rebels if they would not surrender. He stuck to his theme, that in the end the Algerians must decide their own destiny, but that now the end seemed postponed indefinitely. "You are not always destined to be the French Army in

Algeria," he told the soldiers, but his listeners certainly believed that they would remain so until the rebellion had been utterly crushed.[11]

In France the reports of his speeches caused dismay. Just when everybody had been led to believe that the war would end, here was de Gaulle talking of it continuing indefinitely. Prices were rising, the peasants were complaining loudly. Soon after his return in March a majority of the Deputies asked that a special session of Parliament be called under Article 29 of the Constitution. Without referring the matter to the Constitutional Council, de Gaulle refused. Guy Mollet, now in opposition, protested and later in the summer Vincent Auriol, President of the Constitutional Council, resigned because of the way it was being ignored. De Gaulle's popularity slumped.

For a brief moment substance seemed to be given to de Gaulle's hopes of a military victory when three rebel leaders in the field inquired what were the conditions for a Cease Fire; but although de Gaulle met them personally in France in great secrecy, one of them changed his mind on returning to Algeria and the other two were arrested by their own colleagues. Both were shortly afterwards killed. Encouraged by these signs of war-weariness de Gaulle, in June, reiterated his offer of self-determination and appealed to the F.L.N. leaders to come to Paris to meet him. This time Ferhat Abbas accepted and sent two emissaries to arrange for his own visit. Conversations took place at Melun, but, as soon as the Algerians realised that de Gaulle was still only proposing a Cease Fire and that there was no question of serious political negotiations, they broke off the talks.

De Gaulle was now getting the worst of every world. Once again he had enraged the Europeans in Algeria and their supporters in France led by Soustelle and Bidault. The army again began to doubt his intentions. Yet by sticking to his refusal to negotiate anything but a Cease Fire and insisting that the Sahara must be treated as a separate problem he was forfeiting all hope of ending the war. On average fifty French soldiers were being killed each week, Europeans and Moslems continued to be murdered, and in spite of Delouvrier's instructions, to be tortured. De Gaulle seemed to be incapable of making up his mind. His friends begged him to speak out, to tell the army and the country that the sooner independence came to Algeria the better it would be for France. He could not bring himself to do so. It was already clear that the commissions composed of Moslem Deputies and Councillors who were ostensibly preparing for Algerian self-government would command no allegiance among their countrymen unless they were joined by representatives of the F.L.N.; it was equally clear that in France his supporters, who were still in a majority, were getting impatient. Young conscripts began to refuse to bear arms in Algeria and, when they were prosecuted, won enormous sympathy. Students demonstrated in Paris in favour of negotiations and provoked counter-demonstrations. Juin and his retired colleagues protested against the "policy of surrender." Things seemed to be drifting towards another explosion.

Then, without any warning, de Gaulle suddenly changed his tune. He had recorded a broadcast to be delivered on November 4, the text of which had been seen by Debré and several other members of the Government. In great secrecy he then recorded a second version and had the tape sent by special aeroplane to Algiers. While the aircraft was in flight an official told Debré what had happened. The Prime Minister listened to the second version and protested violently; for de Gaulle, while excoriating the F.L.N. leaders, had spoken of their claims to represent "the Algerian republic which would one day exist."[12] It was tantamount to a promise of *de facto* recognition.

De Gaulle blandly told Debré that he had not meant to use the phrase but that, having done so, it was better that it should stand. Juin, the only living Marshal of France, issued a formal denunciation of the President through his staff. A wave of despair swept through Algiers. Jacomet, Secretary of the Governor-General, resigned and Delouvrier had difficulty in dissuading many of his colleagues from following suit. Salan, now living in Spain, urged the European community to rise in revolt.

De Gaulle prepared to meet a new crisis. First he relinquished his own post as Minister for Algeria and appointed Louis Joxe, who had won a reputation in France for the ruthless suppression of violence. He then announced that a referendum would be held on January 8 to approve his policy. As Delouvrier had so nearly lost his nerve the year before, de Gaulle could not risk leaving him to deal with the second revolt and replaced him by Jean Morin. Then he went himself, for the last time, to Algeria.

It was a strange visit. He was cheered, perhaps more enthusiastically than ever, but the cheers were from Moslems who for the first time took charge of the streets crying *"Vive de Gaulle"* and *"Vive L'Algérie algérienne."* The European quarters were either empty or peopled by sullen young men in black caps and shirts who confronted as enemies the special police and army units which had been sent from France to keep order. De Gaulle expressed nothing but pleasure that the Moslems at last felt free to show their true feelings and caused great offence by referring contemptuously to the European demonstrators as "braggarts." During his visits to the army he now said what he had been expected to say in the spring; that Algeria had become a nation and that "in a world which does not resemble the world at all which I knew when I was young" this nationhood was bound to find expression. He reminded the officers that "the army serves no clan, no faction, no interest. The army, quite simply serves France . . . The soul of France is with us and I repeat that the entire country has confidence in you, beginning, gentlemen, with myself."[13]

On January 8, 1961, the Referendum gave de Gaulle the answer he wanted. Although nearly a third of the electorate abstained, the majority in favour of auto-determination was overwhelming.

It was all the more incomprehensible, therefore, that when in the following month de Gaulle again got into touch with the F.L.N. and arranged for a conference to be held at Evian, he should still have taken his stand upon a Cease Fire and the separation of the Sahara from Algeria. The time had long since passed when either was acceptable as a basis for discussion. When Joxe spoke of including a rival but totally discredited nationalist organisation in the talks, the whole conference had to be postponed. De Gaulle might argue that he could not throw away such bargaining points in advance, but in his broadcast on April 11 he clearly warned the French people that, in his opinion, Algeria would vote for independence and that it might be necessary for all Frenchmen living there to return to France. What was he waiting for?

The *Ultras* no longer cared. They had no illusions about their chances of success. France they knew was against them. The generals and colonels, who were now listening to Salan, had no serious hopes of saving Algeria but were set only on revenge. If Algeria must go it should go in ruins. The F.L.N. should inherit misery. And since de Gaulle was the chief traitor, de Gaulle must die. The Algerian secret army, notorious as the O.A.S., had been born. Throughout France and Algeria organised terrorism spread, so that plastic bombs exploded almost every day. The Mayor of Evian, Camille Blanc, received letters threatening him with death unless he refused to make arrangements for a renewal of the conference. On March 31 he was killed by a bomb which blew up his house. To every act of French terrorism the F.L.N. replied. The civil war which de Gaulle had been elected to prevent was beginning.

Then, on the night of April 21, the mutiny which de Gaulle had feared for so long broke. A directorate of four retired generals, Salan, Challe, Jouhaud and Zeller, seized control in Algiers and declared a military government. They quickly gained control of the city and proclaimed a state of siege and the setting up of a military tribunal to try all those who had betrayed Algeria. The Minister for

Public Works, Buron, who was visiting the city, was arrested and sent into the Sahara. With the spread of the rebellion to Oran, Constantine and other Algerian cities on the following day it began to look as if de Gaulle had lost control not only of Algeria but of his army as well.

For a moment de Gaulle was shaken. He had expected a revolt, but not by the generals; that Challe, above all, should break his oath outraged him. Outwardly, however, he remained icily calm. Code messages from Algiers radio seemed to presage a descent by parachutists upon Paris. De Gaulle at once announced that such an attack would be resisted by every means and ordered soldiers and police to open fire. He assumed full emergency powers under Article 16 of the Constitution and ordained a complete blockade of Algiers. He declared that all the rebel officers would be court-martialled and appealed to the troops in Algeria to disobey their officers if they joined the rebellion.

Privately he was less confident. He knew that the only troops capable of resisting a landing were too far away to be of use, even if he could rely on their loyalty. He did not trust the police, even less civilian volunteers. If the paratroops landed he expected to be killed. On the Saturday morning, after Challe's first announcement, he gave a sealed envelope to one of his most faithful followers saying that it was his political testament, to be returned to him the following Wednesday, if, by then, the revolt had collapsed. Then, listening constantly to the radio, he waited.

Meanwhile, the Government had panicked. Debré, believing an airborne invasion was imminent, appealed to the citizens of France to defend the capital. Thousands of volunteers, many of them carrying tin helmets and odd bits of equipment which had been lying about in corners since the war, poured into the streets during the night and made for the Ministry of the Interior, where Frey told them to form themselves into units and prepare to receive arms. There were no arms and what such a rabble could have done in face of an airborne invasion of highly trained troops no one stopped to think. De Gaulle was scornful and asked Frey the reason for the grotesque tumult he saw beneath his windows. As Sunday wore on he became more confident. To Chaban-Delmas he confided that, if he had been in Challe's shoes, he would have already landed. When Monday came and still no invasion, he knew he had won. Challe, after all, was not a revolutionary, not a de Gaulle.

De Gaulle was right. On Tuesday, April 25, the revolt suddenly collapsed. As Challe had said over the radio, there had never been a plan to invade France, only to hold Algeria; yet without invasion he could not break the blockade. When the troops began to disobey their officers and some commanders resisted his orders, he saw that he could not hold the army without bloodshed. He gave himself up.

Yet even now de Gaulle seemed incapable of taking the last inevitable step. He was severe enough in dealing with the mutineers and rebels. All the leading officers of the rebellion were cashiered and put on trial. The army, police and even the judiciary in Algiers were thoroughly purged. Regiments were disbanded and European activist organisations and newspapers suppressed. But when negotiations were reopened with the F.L.N. at Evian in May, de Gaulle still insisted that the Sahara, the hinterland of Algeria and inseparable from it, must remain French. Inevitably the F.L.N. broke off negotiations and did the same again at Lugrin where they were resumed in July. It was not until September that de Gaulle gave way and not until October that he offered to renew the talks.

Meanwhile terrorism ran riot. By the end of the summer the F.L.N. were carrying out about forty acts of terrorism in Algeria every day and the O.A.S. retaliating with an equal number. Since the O.A.S. concentrated upon Government supporters, including soldiers and the police, the army had to fight a defensive war on two fronts. In France the F.L.N. attacked the police, many of whom were killed. When Algerians staged a mass demonstration in Paris in protest against police reprisals they, in their turn, were shot down and thousands were arrested. Algerians began to be forcibly repatriated in large numbers. On September 8, the special commando of the O.A.S. which had been formed to assassinate de Gaulle, made its first attack. A bomb exploded in front of his car as he was driving from Paris to Colombey. No one was injured and the General drove on.

But serious negotiations had started at last. They began in secret in Rome and Geneva in January, 1962, continued at Bousses, a winter sports resort, during February and finally returned to Evian in March. There, on March 18, Joxe and Belkacem signed an agreement covering a Cease Fire and the provisional arrangements for a transfer of power. On March 19, the French Cabinet endorsed the agreement and de Gaulle announced that yet another referendum would be held to confirm it. Christian Fouchet, one of de Gaulle's earliest supporters, was appointed the first High Commissioner to Algeria. General Fourquet, an airman, was made Commander-in-Chief to carry out the terms of the Treaty. On April 8 the French people endorsed the peace by an overwhelming majority, and in June the Algerians followed suit. On July 3, 1962, Algeria became an independent state after one hundred and thirty-two years of French rule.

So ended an eight-years' war in which some fifteen thousand Frenchmen and perhaps one hundred and fifty thousand Moslems lost their lives, forty-two thousand acts of terrorism were officially listed as having been committed and tens of thousands of people were injured. But peace did not yet come to Algiers. Generals Salan and Gardy, two of the leaders of the mutiny, were in hiding in the city and, as soon as the final negotiations with the F.L.N. began, Salan interrupted the normal broadcasts from Algiers with a secret transmitter calling upon Europeans to demonstrate against the "surrender." From then onwards O.A.S. murders and F.L.N. reprisals increased to unprecedented levels. Upon the day the Evian agreement was signed, General Salan again interrupted de Gaulle's broadcast with an appeal which completely drowned the President's voice. On behalf of the newly-formed "National Council of French Resistance in Algeria," he called on all French soldiers to desert the army and join the O.A.S. On March 25, General Jouhaud was caught. On April 20, a red-haired man with a moustache, living in a block of flats with his wife and daughter, who gave his name as Louis Carrière, was interrogated by the police. It turned out to be Salan, by nature blond and clean-shaven. But Gardy was still at large and terrorism continued.

The aims of the O.A.S. varied as circumstances changed. At first they hoped to provoke the Moslems into breaking the Cease Fire. They failed because the discipline imposed by the F.L.N. was too strong. Then the O.A.S. tried to prevent Europeans leaving Algeria. They failed again. Finally they sought revenge on individuals and on the country. During May and June, General Gardy announced a "scorched earth" policy which was designed to leave as much of Algiers and Oran in ruins as possible. Town halls, government and university buildings, hospitals, post offices, telephone exchanges, tax-offices and schools were systematically blown up. In the first five days of May one hundred and twenty-seven Moslems were murdered in Algiers alone. No power on earth could prevent reprisals and for the first time since the Cease Fire began, the F.L.N. retaliated by shooting down seventeen Europeans in the street. As O.A.S. killing went on several hundred Europeans were kidnapped, many never to be seen again. Although both Generals Salan and Jouhaud appealed from prison to their supporters to end the massacres General Gardy refused to comply. It was not until July that he fled the country.

But if the secret army had nothing more to hope for in Algeria, the hard core still had a "duty" to perform in France. Colonel Bastien Thiry, a brilliant young Air Ministry official who, under Colonel Argoud, headed one of the commandos which was dedicated to the assassination of de Gaulle, was a devout Catholic who, having consulted priests, persuaded himself that tyrannicide was justifiable under certain conditions. In his view the conditions were fulfilled by de Gaulle.

Bastien Thiry had already planned five attempts on de Gaulle's life. The first, the bomb explosion in front of the President's car, had failed only because the plastic element in a massive explosive mixture had failed to ignite. Two other attempts were foiled by changes in de Gaulle's movements and two were discovered in time by the police. Now he decided to make certain of his man.

In the evening of August 22, 1962, as the President and Madame de Gaulle were passing through the village of Le Petit Clamart on their way from Colombey to Villacoublay Airfield, a man standing on the pavement at a bus stop opened a newspaper wide and appeared to be reading it. It was Bastien Thiry. Four accomplices in a shooting-brake some way ahead opened fire. De Gaulle's son-in-law, Captain Alain de Boisseu, who was sitting by the chauffeur turned and yelled to de Gaulle and his wife to duck, which neither of them did. The chauffeur accelerated and, although two tyres had been burst by bullets, managed to hold the car on the road. A hundred yards farther on a second burst of fire came from a blue car parked in a side-street. Again de Gaulle's car was hit, one of the bullets passing within a few inches of his head. The chauffeur drove on and stopped after passing a cross roads where there was traffic. The police escort had neither opened fire nor been able to stop the conspirators from driving away. De Gaulle got out, surveyed the damage, and remarked that it had been "a near shave." When he realised that his assailants had got away he added that those who were trying to protect him were as incompetent as those who were trying to kill him. He then got back into his motor car with his wife and drove to the airfield.

The attempt failed because de Gaulle's car was travelling faster than had been anticipated; the shots from the shooting-brake missed altogether and men in a third car mistook Bastien Thiry's signal and never got their guns off at all. Nevertheless it was a miracle that de Gaulle survived.

The failure marked the end of the O.A.S. Bidault, pathetically prostituting a more glorious past, issued a statement on behalf of a newly constituted "National Council of Resistance" praising the conconspirators as "patriots" and declaring that the attempted assassination was "an act of resistance intended to liberate France from a perjured dictator." The O.A.S., he announced, had sworn that "de Gaulle must be shot like a mad dog." The statement, which was enclosed in an official envelope of the National Assembly and posted within the precincts of the Palais Bourbon, reached the President a few days later.[14]

But by then a gigantic police operation was already under way. The identity cards of more than a million people were checked and within a month nine of the conspirators, including Bastien Thiry, had been arrested. Meanwhile the special counter-espionage service, founded by Jacques Soustelle in the days of the Free French and now purged and headed by General Paul Jacquier, had determined to break the O.A.S. once and for all. For some months Jacquier had been recruiting special anti-O.A.S. units consisting largely of old Resistance fighters who, for high pay, were prepared to take abnormal risks. They were nick-named *les Barbouzes* (the Bearded Ones), in mockery of their love of cloak and dagger methods, but they had already proved ruthless enough to bear comparison with the Black and Tans of the Irish rebellion. They were now to earn their money.

In February, 1963, a further plot to shoot de Gaulle with a telescopic rifle as he crossed the courtyard of the Military Academy on his way to address the students was betrayed to the police. Frey, the Minister of the Interior, at once went to de Gaulle to ask him not to visit the Academy. De Gaulle with a smile replied that, as Frey was so well informed, no doubt he would be able to protect him. Frey pounced and the conspirators confessed. They also divulged that Colonel Argoud, the head of the assassination commando, was at that moment staying in Munich.

Frey at once demanded that Argoud be extradited, but the German Government refused. *Les Barbouzes* then went to work. One evening as Argoud crossed the foyer of his hotel on the way to the lift two men in Tyrolean hats and coats, the traditional dress of the Bavarian Criminal Investigation officer, barred his passage and, in perfect German, demanded his passport. Before he could answer they seized him, hustled him through the door and into a car manned by two more men similarly dressed. At this point Argoud seems to have realised that his captors were not Germans and began to resist. He was knocked out and finally driven across the French frontier in a military vehicle which was immune from search.

On Tuesday, February 25, a head of the C.I.D. in Paris, M. Bouvier, received a telephone call "from the O.A.S." informing him that Colonel Argoud, for whom he had long been searching, was waiting to be called for. "The package is well tied up," said the voice, "and is waiting almost on your doorstep." He was then told to look in a blue beach-wagon in a street behind Notre Dame. Bouvier thought it was a hoax but investigated and found Argoud bound, gagged and unconscious where the voice had said he would be.[15]

With the capture of Argoud the O.A.S. collapsed. Bidault, the nominal leader, remained in hiding abroad and some of the gunmen escaped and disappeared. Bastien Thiry was executed. Argoud took no part in his trial, refused either to stand up or answer questions and eventually resisted all attempts to drag him to Court. He was sentenced to life imprisonment. Within three years de Gaulle felt strong enough to grant an amnesty to all except one man. When Challe emerged from prison in January, 1967, only Salan remained. Juin, deprived of his Marshal's right to remain on the active list, was denied an official funeral within a month of Challe's release.

Gradually the ghost of *Algérie Française* was laid. Throughout the summer of 1962, while the final stages of Algerian independence were being achieved, the Algerian French were streaming back to France. They queued in their thousands at the harbours and airports, often fighting each other in their anxiety to get away. By the end of 1963 nearly four hundred thousand settlers had returned and only a few thousand remained in Algeria. One after another the links between the two countries were cut. In 1963 the property of absent Frenchmen was confiscated by the Algerian Government; in 1966 Algerian wine was excluded from the French vintage. As Ferhat Abbas was replaced by Ben Khedda, Ben Khedda by Ben Bella and Ben Bella by Boumédienne, Algeria drifted away from France and into the arms of those who believed that revolution is synonymous with progress. While chaos spread in Africa, in the Congo, in Nigeria, in Burundi and Zanzibar, Algeria like Ghana under Nkrumah, became a training ground for guerrilla fighters dedicated to the overthrow of governments which retained close ties with the West. The prophecies of both de Gaulle and Bidault were being fulfilled.

De Gaulle had survived a hideous experience, of which the attempts on his own life were perhaps the least harrowing part. During Challe's rebellion, while waiting for the paratroops to land, he announced that if he left the Elysée it would be feet first. A man who sees himself as a redeemer cannot afford to be afraid. Yet de Gaulle had suffered. When heart-broken supporters reproached him for abandoning Algeria he would reply: "Do you think I enjoy what I have to do?" The betrayal of faithful Moslems, thousands of whom he knew must die, the sacrifice of all that France had contributed, the tortured conscience of loyal officers, above all the final surrender to the F.L.N., were wounds the effects of which he could not entirely hide. He was capable of sustaining them because he believed, like Stalin whom he admired, that in the end it was only the State that mattered and that he was its incarnation. Some writers have called him "a sacred monster," yet de Gaulle was not insensitive; on the other hand his philosophy enabled him to do things of which most men would have been ashamed. Over Algeria he deliberately misled his Ministers and his generals. Men like Bidault came to regard him as no better than a common cheat. Yet Bidault was wrong. By liberating France from Algeria de Gaulle had truly served his country; no other Frenchman could have done the same.

13. De Gaulle greets General Giraud on arrival in Algiers, May 30 1943. (*See page* 202). *Below*: De Gaulle with General Massu

14. Mr. Harold Macmillan's visit to France in December 1962. From left to right: Madame de Gaulle, Lady Dorothy Macmillan, General de Gaulle,

KING AT LAST

"How can you govern a country which produces 246 different kinds of cheese?" De Gaulle's outburst is justly famous. He had no illusions about the French. They were capable of grandeur because, as he also remarked, every Frenchman at some time in his life saw himself playing the role of Joan of Arc. The people were also apt, perhaps more frequently, to lose their sense of nationhood and become obsessed with the petty things of life. The aphorisms on this theme attributed to him are legion. "It is good to guzzle, but it does not amount to a national ambition." "Every Frenchman desires to enjoy one or more privileges. It is his way of asserting his passion for equality."[1]

These contradictions in the French character were given free rein after the fall of the Second Empire, and produced a unique parliamentary system. The revolutionary tradition bred suspicion of the least sign of personal power; yet individuals were so jealous of their opinions that they found it impossible to combine except in small and constantly shifting groups. Hence the fitful and futile coalitions of the Third and Fourth Republics.

All his life de Gaulle had longed to rescue his people from this self-imposed frustration. Now he had his chance. He believed he could combine firm government with popular sovereignty. After he had been officially installed as President he began to give the new Constitution his personal stamp.

He made no bones about his intentions. France had already experienced his rule and everyone who had served in his Provisional Governments in Algeria and Paris knew what to expect. He and he alone made policy; his Ministers, including the Prime Minister, were there to explain this policy to the Assembly and pass measures which would implement it. Ministers, he said to an old colleague, were in a sense secretaries to the Chief-of-State, each responsible for carrying out his wishes in their own Departments.

Debré's government was an excellent example. Most of its members had held office before, but only eleven out of twenty-one were professional politicians and by the end of that first year only two of those eleven remained. The rest were civil servants and experts, not policy makers but executives whose future depended entirely upon the success with which they interpreted de Gaulle's wishes. Often those wishes were made known by some public pronouncement without even the Minister concerned being consulted. For example, de Gaulle's offer to the F.L.N. of a "peace of the brave"—a total reversal of his previous policy—was only communicated to the Cabinet a few hours before he broadcast it. The text of his letter to Macmillan and Eisenhower, demanding a fundamental change in the North Atlantic Treaty Organisation was never submitted to Ministers. The first that anybody knew of his invitation to Khrushchev to visit France was an announcement in the press. Although Pinay was with de Gaulle in Africa at the time, he learned only from the local papers that Guinea had been granted independence.

As 1959 wore on it became clear that although under the Constitution the Government was technically responsible to Parliament, it tended to ignore parliamentary opinion and to act as an agent for the President, presenting Bills which the Deputies were expected to rubber-stamp. Since the Deputies could overthrow the Government only on a motion of censure and the same group of Deputies could only introduce one such motion in a session, they seldom had any option. Far from being sympathetic, de Gaulle steadily strengthened his position. In a dispute over standing orders he refused, through Debré, to allow a vote to be taken on Private Members' resolutions and had his refusal confirmed by the Constitutional Council. Over the highly controversial Bill allowing grants to be made to Church schools, he rejected all but one of the amendments proposed by the Assembly's Cultural Commission and got the Bill through on an issue of confidence. Chaban-Delmas, the President of the Assembly, might speak of a "Presidential sector" and an "open sector" of government, but by 1960 many Deputies had come to the conclusion that the only thing "open" to them was to choose an issue once in a while on which they could try and bring down the Government.

De Gaulle was unruffled by the growing opposition among the old parliamentarians. What was happening was exactly what he had intended; his powers as President were being extended, those of Parliament curtailed. In January, 1960, he coolly accepted the resignation of Pinay, his Minister of Finance, and appointed Wilfred Baumgartner in his place. This was a milestone. Apart from Mendès-

France, Pinay was the most respected politician of the Fourth Republic and the only man in the Cabinet capable of standing up to de Gaulle. Pinay had opposed the President openly and consistently, not only upon financial questions but whenever de Gaulle's policies relating to defence or foreign affairs seemed to him to be prejudicing the economic condition of the country. He asserted in Cabinet the right of Ministers to speak on all subjects for which they were collectively responsible. He protested when the French Mediterranean Fleet was withdrawn from N.A.T.O., cross-examined de Gaulle on his pronouncements of auto-determination for Algeria, criticised the creation of an independent nuclear deterrent, opposed his measures of nationalisation and drew attention in Cabinet to the fact that Ministers frequently learned from newspapers of Government decisions which they were supposed to have approved.

De Gaulle would have liked to keep Pinay—on his own terms. Not only had he carried through a successful devaluation of the franc and set France on the road to economic recovery, but he had been the first parliamentarian to approach de Gaulle in the crisis of 1958. When de Gaulle reminded him of the fact, Pinay replied that he hoped that he would not live to regret his actions. When de Gaulle reproached him for expressing his disagreement so openly in Cabinet, Pinay made the obvious retort that it was the one place where he felt obliged to do so. This de Gaulle could not tolerate. De Gaulle offered Pinay the post of Minister without Portfolio, observing that he regarded him as a statesman rather than a politician; but Pinay refused. He resigned, saying, as oracularly as de Gaulle himself, that he was leaving politics altogether for the moment but would remain at the disposal of the country.

A colleague who stayed on in the Government remarked that, with Pinay gone, de Gaulle's Cabinet became not a shadow but a morgue, the difference being that in the Council of Ministers the dead spoke. Certainly de Gaulle became increasingly autocratic. After the revolt of the barricades he once more assumed exceptional powers under Article 16 of the Constitution and, with general approval, exercised them for nine months. As Mollet, the Socialist leader remarked, although eighty per cent of the population might be against de Gaulle on most things, eighty-five per cent were with him over Algeria. In March he openly flouted the Constitution. The hoary problem of farm prices was causing such unrest among the peasants that Deputies representing agricultural seats were lobbied into demanding an extraordinary session of Parliament. The demand received more signatures than the Constitution required, but de Gaulle refused to sign the necessary Decree on the grounds that there had been already two extra sessions that year and that, as the Deputies were unable to pass legislation augmenting the budget, such a session was futile. Socialists and radicals used up their precious vote of censure in vain.

De Gaulle's high-handedness did not stop there. Mali and Madagascar had demanded the right to complete independence and the other members of the Community had signified their intention of following suit. De Gaulle realised that, if France was to retain her influence in those former colonies, their wishes must be met quickly. As the procedure laid down was cumbersome and made no provision for "independent" countries to remain within the Community, he proposed, through Debré, simple amendments to Articles 85 and 86 of the Constitution which would allow for the new development by agreement between the States concerned. The Legalists and Fourth Republicans accused him of breaking his own Constitution and of further detracting from the role of Parliament; de Gaulle replied loftily that events were more important than constitutional texts, of which France had had no less than seventeen in one hundred and fifty years. He got his amendments carried in May by using the "block" vote provided for in the Constitution under which the Bill and all opposition amendments were taken together.

Gradually a guerrilla war developed between de Gaulle and the Assembly. Paul Henri Teitgen complained that the Cabinet was being short-circuited on all important matters by technical committees consisting of de Gaulle's nominees, and that de Gaulle was so centralising power in his own hands that no one could take his place. Even Chaban-Delmas, a loyal Gaullist, warned the Government against behaving like an autocrat who claims rights in order to abuse them.

De Gaulle not only ignored them both but undertook a reform which would strengthen his position still further. In April, 1961, at a press conference, he spoke of changing the method of election of the President from the College of Notables, which was laid down in the Constitution, to a plebiscite. Plots to assassinate him had been already uncovered and he suggested that unless his successor, who might be called upon suddenly to take office, had the support of the nation, he might lack the necessary authority. It was a shot across the bows of Parliament, but since the Algerian war was still in progress no party fired an answering salvo. In September the bomb explosion in front of his car at Pont-sur-Seine underscored his message; no one at that stage wished to take his place.

De Gaulle's real reason for desiring to change the constitution was less altruistic. He had accepted the principle that the Government must be responsible to Parliament because it was the only way in which he could win the allegiance of party leaders. While the Algerian war lasted they had all allowed him largely to evade that obligation. But with the end of the war in sight he realised that they would begin to assert their responsibility and make it impossible for him to govern as he wished. The parties, other than the Communists, were unanimous in opposing his attitude towards N.A.T.O., his insistence upon an independent nuclear deterrent, his refusal to promote a fully integrated European Community. Reports from the Prefects throughout the country suggested that, at the next Presidential election, Pinay of all people might be chosen in his stead. As de Gaulle himself remarked, he had not saved France for people like that.

*   *   *

De Gaulle's first opportunity to test the electorate came in the Referendum, held on April 8, 1962, by which the people of France ratified the Evian Agreements and gave independence to Algeria. The Referendum itself was unconstitutional because Algeria was a Department of France and could not be alienated legally; however, except for the *Ultras* and a few extreme Conservatives, no one opposed the Algerian settlement and de Gaulle saw in the Referendum a chance to prepare the French people for a new phase in the life of the Fifth Republic. The struggle which had dominated French life for eight long years, and which he had been called back to resolve, was over. He had triumphed, not over the Algerians, but over the French Army and those who had plotted to destroy the Republic. All sorts of new horizons might be opened and the Republic enter a new and glorious phase if the people would show by a massive vote they approved his policies and had confidence in him.

On March 26 he appealed in a broadcast for such a vote: "I can and must say this—the massive Yes vote that I am asking for will mean that the French people will support me as Chief-of-State . . . that in my hard task—of which the Algerian affair is only one part—I have their confidence to-day and to-morrow." On the day of the Referendum he gave a broader hint of what was in his mind. "We are going to consecrate the use of the Referendum as the clearest, most frank and most democratic practice possible. Provided for in the Constitution, the Referendum thus passes into our way of life, adding something essential to the legislative work of Parliament. Henceforth every citizen will be called upon . . . to undertake his responsibilities on every issue of vital importance to the country. There is no doubt that the character and working of the institutions of the Republic will be vitally affected by it . . ."

When the electorate gave him the answer he wanted, approving the granting of independence to Algeria by a majority of over ninety per cent, de Gaulle at once exploited it. Debré, his loyal Prime Minister who had suffered tortures and eaten volumes of his own words over Algeria, proposed an immediate general election. Having endured the strain of a hostile Assembly for so long, Debré saw in the good will shown in the Referendum an opportunity of gaining a Parliament with which, even if the Gaullists did not have an overall majority, it would be far easier for the Government to work. But with Algeria out of the way, de Gaulle was sure that the parties, in whatever strength they were returned after an election, would exercise their rights under the Constitution far more vigorously than before. He did not believe that the U.N.R. could gain a majority; he did not care whether Parliament was easy to work with or not. What he needed was time, first to let people forget about Algeria and then to focus attention on the future. Above all he wanted an occasion for a Referendum, the answer to which must be a vote of confidence in himself and nothing else. Only then could he hope that a general election might give him a clear majority.

De Gaulle acted brutally and swiftly. The day after Debré had made his proposals de Gaulle secretly dismissed him and equally secretly appointed Georges Pompidou in his place. It was a significant choice. Debré, who had a long and distinguished political career and whose government had lasted longer than any in republican history, gave way to a man who had never been a member of either House of Parliament, but who had been de Gaulle's political adviser during the life of the R.P.F. and, for the last seven years, managing director of the Rothschild Bank. When the change was announced at the end of the week, every parliamentarian at once recognised that, though Pompidou might bear the title of Prime Minister he, like Couve de Murville at the Foreign Office, would be little more than a disc recording his master's voice. De Gaulle was giving notice to France and to the world that in future, even more than in the past four years, he was going to exercise personal power.

He turned first upon Europe. In April de Gaulle, Adenauer and Fanfani had proposed to their partners in the Common Market the beginnings of political collaboration through regular meetings of the Heads of State. Belgium and Holland had refused, partly because they believed in political fusion rather than loose confederation and partly because they did not wish to make any political move until it was known whether Britain, which had applied to join the Common Market, would become a member. On May 15, at a press conference, de Gaulle denounced the idea of a "supra-national" Europe in favour of a Europe of the nations: "I do not believe that Europe can be a living reality without France and her Frenchmen, Germany and her Germans, Italy and her Italians." Dante, Goethe and Chateaubriand, he went on, pointedly omitting Shakespeare, belonged to Europe because they were an Italian, a German and a Frenchman. "They would not have served Europe much if they had been of no nationality and had thought and written in some form of Esperanto or Volapük." The five members of Pompidou's Cabinet belonging to the M.R.P., the party on which de Gaulle depended for his majority, at once resigned and were replaced by under-secretaries. The Government was more subservient and less responsible to Parliament than ever.

In July de Gaulle once more deliberately and openly flouted the Constitution. He had already broken one of its most vital principles—the independence of the judiciary—by setting up special courts under judges whom he selected to try political crimes against the State. Because of the terrorism which had plagued France during the Algerian war, neither the public nor the political parties had greatly objected. But in May his own special court failed him by refusing to condemn Salan to death, largely because of a widespread feeling that Salan, like the other generals, had been misled and betrayed by de Gaulle himself. De Gaulle was outraged. He dissolved the court and set up a new military tribunal consisting of six officers and six N.C.O.s to try crimes against the State over which he commanded General de Larminat to preside. De Larminat, a Free French hero and one of de Gaulle's oldest supporters, committed suicide rather than accept the office.

De Gaulle was approaching a crisis. He was in open warfare not only with the parties in Parliament but with every traditional republican who regarded a written Constitution as the only guarantee of individual liberty. The trials of the Generals became their forum. Men like Isorni, Pétain's former Counsel, and Tixier-Vignancour, the right-wing Deputy and advocate, who defended Salan and Challe, thundered against the infamy of de Gaulle's policies, the shame of his betrayals, the immorality of his breaches of the Constitution. Their words echoed throughout France. It was true that previous Republicans had used special tribunals for political crimes and in particular, under a law of 1881, to judge those who gave public offence to the Head of the State; but none had abused the independence of the judiciary as flagrantly as de Gaulle. Although the terrorism of the O.A.S. and the F.L.N. provided a reasonable and immediate excuse, his special courts bore an uncomfortable resemblance to the "People's" court of Nazi Germany and the infamous tribunals of the Vichy régime. To traditional Republicans it seemed that only the existence of Parliament stood between the French people and absolute dictatorship.

De Gaulle brushed aside such legal quibbles. Terrorism, he argued, demanded exceptional measures and he was exercising exceptional but statutory powers. He had twice refused to become a dictator and was not likely to make the mistake now. Power must derive from the people through universal suffrage and he intended to become wholly and directly dependent on that suffrage. What could be more democratic?

As de Gaulle's intention of altering the constitution became clear, the parties began to organise. Paul Reynaud, independent but still a powerful voice, Guy Mollet for the Socialists and Maurice Faure for the Radicals informed de Gaulle that they were unalterably opposed to any change in the methods of electing the President. They decided to make the credits for the nuclear plant at Pierrelatte, the basis of de Gaulle's nuclear *force de frappe,* the occasion for a motion of censure before the Assembly arose for the summer recess. De Gaulle survived by only forty votes. Had it not been for the O.A.S., which many Deputies considered an even greater threat to the Republic than de Gaulle, he would almost certainly have been defeated.

Then, ironically, O.A.S. assassins came to his rescue. The attempt on his life at Petit Clamart enabled him to present his case for a reform of the Constitution as a matter of urgency, since at any moment he might be taken from the scene. On September 12, the principles of de Gaulle's reform were published; they were considered by the Cabinet in a series of sessions beginning next day. In essence de Gaulle posed two questions to his colleagues. Could the Presidency, the keystone of the Fifth Republic, be exercised unless the President was elected by universal suffrage? Should the suffrage take the form of a Referendum? With the exception of Pierre Sudreau, Minister for Reconstruction, every member of the Cabinet obediently supported de Gaulle's views. It was not without legal force. Although the Constitution under Article 89 laid down that any revision must be the subject of a separate vote in each House before being submitted to a Referendum, Article 11 gave the President the power to submit to the people *any* Bill "dealing with the organisation of public authorities." In other words the Constitution was obscure and de Gaulle's interpretation was at least arguable.

Sudreau pleaded with him not to become a symbol of illegality but was coldly thanked. On September 19, the Cabinet approved de Gaulle's plans. Next day he broadcast to the nation. Taking his stand firmly on Article 11, he explained that, in 1958, he had not bothered much about the method of election of the President, because he had taken office in a crisis and with overwhelming support; now he had to look ahead and consider the position of his successor who might suddenly be called upon to take office. It was a plausible appeal, although no one close to de Gaulle or with an understanding of politics really believed that he was thinking of his successor.

During the recess, opposition built up. Sudreau resigned a few days after de Gaulle's broadcast and was replaced by Joxe who combined the declining Ministry for Algiers with that of Education. Then, one after another, the party conferences condemned de Gaulle's proposals as illegal. Their main argument, which Debré had affirmed when he was Prime Minister, was that as the method of revising the Constitution had been clearly laid down in Article 89, the powers granted to the President in Article 11 were obviously only intended to apply to other forms of legislation. Gaston Monnerville, President of the Senate and the man who would have to assume the Presidency if de Gaulle were to die or be assassinated, said at the Radical Party conference that de Gaulle was planning "a deliberate, calculated and outrageous attack on the Constitution in order to establish a system of personal power." But although there were many meetings between party leaders and a loose "*Cartel des Nons*" was formed, there was no unanimity on any alternative scheme. Socialists and some Radicals clung to the old idea of a sovereign Assembly. Others favoured a Presidential régime on the American model in which the powers of the President and Parliament would be separate and clearly defined. There was agreement on only one point; de Gaulle must be prevented from changing the Constitution in the way he proposed.

As the day for the opening of the new session approached the parties received impressive juridical support. On October 1, the Council of State, to which the Government was obliged to submit the proposals without being committed to accept its decision, pronounced, with only one dissentient, that they were unconstitutional. The Constitutional Council, on the other hand, of which de Gaulle's predecessors René Coty and Vincent Auriol were ex-officio members and which, under Article 61, could have declared the proposals *ultra vires*, said nothing, although Léon Noël, the President and a Gaullist of long standing, Coty and several others were known to have been critical. Auriol, who had refused to attend the Council because of the disrespect with which it had been treated, emerged from retirement to denounce the "violation" publicly.

Next day, when Parliament met, the Assembly received a formal message from de Gaulle recommending the Bill through which the people would once more use the Referendum, "that sovereign right" which he had restored to it in 1945, to elect their President. The debate was opened by Paul Reynaud, who was later to declare that he was more proud of his opposition to this measure than of any other action in his long political life. But although one speaker after another rose to praise and then denounce de Gaulle, there was an aridity in their arguments which communicated itself far beyond the confines of the Chamber. The opposition was defending a text; de Gaulle was proposing an innovation. The party leaders admitted the need for a change but could not agree what the change should be; de Gaulle, with utter consistency, was pursuing the goal he had outlined at Bayeux fourteen years before. When Pompidou, winding up the debate, spoke of the conflict as between "two epochs, that of the Fourth Republic and that of the Fifth," he was sounding a truer note than his opponents, even though the note was but an echo from the Elysée.[2] Nevertheless, for the first time in the life of the Fifth Republic the Government was defeated. On October 5, two hundred and eighty Deputies, thirty-five more than the required number, voted for the motion of censure. Next day Pompidou offered de Gaulle the resignation of himself and his Government.

De Gaulle had twice told the Assembly that, if his Bill was rejected, he himself would resign. He did nothing of the sort. Having invited the challenge of the old Republicans he met it dramatically by demonstrating the difference between his régime and theirs. Under previous Republics France would now have been without a government and the President have been conducting a fevered search for a leader who could command a majority; de Gaulle, without a majority continued to govern. He "noted" Pompidou's offer but requested him and his Cabinet to stay in office until November 27. Then, acting with propriety according to his own interpretation of the Constitution, he dissolved Parliament and decreed that a Referendum on his Bill should be held on October 28, to be followed three weeks later by a general election. While the world held its breath, not over France but over Cuba, de Gaulle entered upon the last round of his decisive fight with the French political parties.

De Gaulle's campaign was less flamboyant than that which he had conducted with the help of Soustelle four years earlier. The militants for *Algérie Française* who then spearheaded his attack were now muted, some in gaol and some in exile; the U.N.R. had become obedient and docile. Yet if there were fewer posters and great rallies de Gaulle left little to chance. The secret instructions which Pompidou sent to every Prefect stated explicitly that, although government servants were to adopt an attitude of neutrality in the general election for the Assembly, they were to exert themselves with the "utmost energy" to secure the vote for the President of the Republic in the Referendum. The Prime Minister even set out the "clear and simple arguments which they could use to rebut suggestions that the Referendum was undemocratic or contrary to the spirit of the Constitution."[3] All over France the influence of the Prefects and public servants generally was considerable.

De Gaulle's second weapon was the government-controlled radio and television service. Party leaders were allowed five minutes each. De Gaulle, on the other hand, spoke three times, twice before the Referendum and once after it, and at greater length; Pompidou and Christian Fouchet each spoke once. But the real power of television and radio was exercised through the news and discussions which accompanied the campaign. These programmes were so biased in favour of the Government that on October 17, technicians struck and refused to transmit. Thereafter reporting became a little more objective.

The opposition had massive resources. Except for the U.N.R., every political party from the Communists to Bidault's new National Resistance Movement which fathered the O.A.S., recommended their members to vote "No" in the Referendum. In addition eighty thousand Notables, the members of the *Conseils Généraux*, the Mayors and Deputy-Mayors of almost every town in France, who under the 1958 Constitution elected the President but now faced disenfranchisement, were hostile. The press overwhelmingly supported the political parties and the peripheral radio stations like Radio Luxembourg gave opposition speakers a generous share of their time. And yet there was no real change in the nature of the opposition.

The "*Cartel des Nons*" was never more than a façade. Socialists, some Independents and members of the M.R.P. had agreed on an alternative Constitution, but in every party except the Communists there were important dissident groups proposing different policies. Although there was an interval of three weeks between the Referendum and the general election the campaign was fought as a whole, and it was soon clear that there would be no effective alliance to defeat de Gaulle and the U.N.R. Giscard-d'Estaing and a group of Independents refused to accept their party instructions to vote "No"; the M.R.P. was too divided to make more than a weak recommendation; Mollet wanted to collaborate with the Communists where they were likely to win seats in the second ballot of the general election, other Socialists and Moderates refused to have anything to do with them. By the time de Gaulle made his second broadcast on October 26, every elector knew that if the country rejected de Gaulle—and that was what the Referendum was about—France would return to the régime of party coalitions and unstable governments from which he had rescued her.

The polls, if not the country, gave a decisive answer. Although nearly a quarter of the electorate abstained on October 28, sixty-two per cent of those who went to the polls voted for de Gaulle. Remembering that the Communists, who had supported him in the April Referendum over Algeria, were now against him, this was as good a result as he could expect. He had failed, for the first time since his return to power, to win an absolute majority of those on the electoral role; but he could reasonably regard abstention at such a moment as tacit acceptance of his rule. He did so at his first Cabinet, welcoming the result of the Referendum with enthusiasm and moving straight on to the second phase of the campaign.*

It began with a victory. Immediately after the Referendum, Gaston Monnerville, President of the Senate, exercised his right under the Constitution of inviting the Constitutional Council to declare illegal the Bill which had been the subject of the Referendum. But although only three members had been appointed by de Gaulle and both Auriol and Coty attended, the Council once more evaded the issue saying that, although it had power to pronounce against laws passed by Parliament, nothing in the Constitution gave it similar powers in regard to laws passed by Referendum. On November 7 de Gaulle promulgated the Bill as law. As Monnerville said, the Council had committed suicide by its cowardice.

That same day, ten days before the general election, de Gaulle made his final broadcast. He still had everything to lose or gain. It was of no use to him to have won the election for the Presidency by universal suffrage if that same suffrage then returned a Parliament which was opposed to him. The Constitution he was remodelling so drastically was not designed to create a Presidential system on the

---

* In the general election only those who won a clear majority over all opponents and a quarter of the votes on the electoral roll in the constituency were elected on the first ballot. In the second ballot, held a week later, the candidate with the highest number of votes won.

American model. There was no question of Parliament performing its functions separately or even in opposition to the President and the Government. Theoretically, if Parliament refused to pass the budget or threw out every Bill which the Government presented, de Gaulle could still govern by decree. He could refuse both to accept the Government's resignation or to dissolve Parliament; but such a course of action would really be assuming the dictatorial powers which he had always rejected and he had made it plain that he would resign rather than attempt it. What de Gaulle was demanding, therefore, was something which no French political leader had ever achieved under the Republic, a clear majority of his own supporters over all the other parties in the Assembly.

De Gaulle's speech was uncompromising. There was no question any longer of his being the national arbiter, or the source of national unity. He was back in the days of the R.P.F., a lone political leader taking on all the rest. He made no concessions to any other party which might have resulted in an alliance. If he was "above party" it was only in the sense that he derided all others than his own as "parties of the past" which had failed France in 1940 and 1958 and would fail it again if they won a majority. Certain individuals, he said, had abilities which could still be useful if they served the "national" rather than party interests, but he begged the country, which had already voted in the Referendum for national rejuvenation, not to throw away what it had just won.

The hope of the opposition, which had been badly shaken by the Referendum, lay in a tight alliance which would eliminate all but one anti-Gaullist candidate, if possible on the first ballot, certainly at the second. But only a handful of alliances were declared and although several hundred candidates dropped out before the second ballot, the impression of continued divisiveness had been given and was reflected in the opinion polls taken in the final week of the campaign.

De Gaulle triumphed. The U.N.R. just failed to win half the seats in the Assembly, but with the thirty-three "Independents" led by Giscard-d'Estaing who fought under U.N.R. endorsement, de Gaulle had a working majority. Nominally he was dependent upon Giscard-d'Estaing's support, but it was extremely unlikely that this little group would risk turning out the Government, for without Gaullist backing the Deputies would certainly lose their seats. Of the two hundred and eighty Deputies who had voted against Pompidou in October, only one hundred and thirteen were returned in November and among the losers was Paul Reynaud who had led the attack.

De Gaulle, therefore, could look forward to five years of power comparable in extent with that of a British Prime Minister who commands a secure majority in the House of Commons. In practice his power was even greater because his own authority stood so far above that of any of his supporters that a Cabinet crisis was unthinkable. Pompidou and the twenty-five members of the new Government were not only de Gaulle's nominees, they derived such authority as they had entirely from the fact that he chose them. If he dismissed any one of them he ran no risk of some powerful trade union or business lobby aligning itself against him; and since no Minister could remain a Member of Parliament, dismissal became easier still. As Paul Reynaud remarked in the Assembly, after the general election de Gaulle now combined the role of an English king and an English prime minister. He was no longer an "accidental monarch," but a twice-elected monocrat. His reign truly began.

*   *   *

Like an English Tudor King, de Gaulle believed in showing himself to his people by going on "progresses" through his realm. In the first decade of his reign he made no fewer than twenty-five such tours, some lasting only a few days, many from two to three weeks. Every Department in the country received him and experienced all the pomp and ritual which such a reception entails. Even in Paris, where he spent most of his time, he visited borough by borough, suburb by suburb.

Each visit was planned in advance down to the smallest detail. Everybody responsible for the organisation was issued with a booklet containing the time-table of events, and except when de Gaulle got lost in a crowd, the schedule was rigidly adhered to. If the Department was within reasonable distance of Paris de Gaulle travelled by car, at great speed with a large police escort of motor cycles, followed by a cavalcade, each vehicle keeping its numbered place in the queue. At the principal town of the Department he was met by the Regional Prefect, who at once presented the Mayor, who presented the Councillors. The judges and other dignitaries took their place according to protocol.

In the early days of his rule, when the crowds were large, de Gaulle would make a speech from a balcony in the main square; but as the people became less curious, officials chose some spot where a few thousand or even hundreds could be made to look a packed audience. The speeches varied in length according to the importance of the town and were full of local and historical allusions. In Languedoc he talked of wine-growing, in Lyons of textiles; on the coast he saluted a seaport which he was sure would continue to prosper. For each town he had a special epithet, beautiful, vigorous, historic, interesting. He complimented the Mayor and Councillors and told the crowd that with such leaders their prosperity was assured. Sometimes he lashed out at his opponents in his own brand of invective: "There are many people who piss vinegar, but I tell you that things are not going badly."[4] Occasionally he was facetious: "With all that you produce in the way of meat, corn, wine, shoes, clothing, cider-presses at Chalonnes sur Loire I begin to wonder how one could eat, drink, be shod, dress or press wine if there were no Chalonnes. Fortunately there is Chalonnes . . ."[5] In important cities the speeches contained references to national or world affairs which had previously been given to the press and even the local allusions were carefully vetted by the Presidential staff before they were finally issued for publication.

Lunch was invariably taken at the Sub-Prefecture and dinner at the Prefecture itself, the menus in both cases having been sent in advance from the Elysée. De Gaulle might spend the night in the Prefecture or in a hotel. Between meals and speeches he toured the villages. Flags and bunting, a few cheers and always the Mayor and Councillors greeted him. Like a Member of Parliament visiting his constituency, he was well briefed about local conditions. He asked about the water supply; if the village was not on the mains he asked about the quality of the wells. If there was no electricity he assured the Mayor that it would not be long in coming. If the roads were bad he might make a pun, remarking that from the splendid health of the children he could see that the village was well on its way. And always, where there was a crowd, he would at some point go down into it on his own, shaking hands endlessly, saying "Good day" to mothers, babies, the old, the workers. Sometimes the immersion would last half an hour while de Gaulle, the centre of a human whirlpool, crossed and recrossed a street, caught sight of some old woman standing in her doorway or of the *curé* on the steps of the church. The police, who occasionally arrested people carrying weapons and even hypodermic syringes ahead of him, were frantic, the officials terrified; de Gaulle was truly happy. He might emerge with buttons missing from his coat, his hands scratched, his *képi* askew, but he had been among his people, literally entrusting his life to them. Crowds, more than anything, were the intoxication which sustained his spirit.

For the Ministers, journalists and officials who accompanied de Gaulle, these journeys through France became as much an ordeal as an Elizabethan progress was for the Queen's courtiers. To relieve the tedium of the routine the journalists made collections of de Gaulle's sayings, counted the number of times he used the same phrase or epithet, or even played practical jokes, like telling a policeman standing out in front of the crowd that his "flys" were undone. The political correspondent of *Le Monde* amused himself by pushing himself to the front of the crowd and seeing how many times in a day de Gaulle would shake his hand—for de Gaulle was apt to pick on any face which seemed familiar. Yet the progresses served a purpose.

De Gaulle might not be loved, but in many parts of France he was venerated and almost worshipped. Opinion surveys had shown that much of his support in the referenda came from parts of France where there were the smallest number of television sets; it was the legend as much as the face or the voice which counted. Occasionally the sick had been brought into the street to touch him, as they had to touch previous monarchs. Nevertheless, de Gaulle had one great advantage over his predecessors—television. In *Le Fil de l'Épée* de Gaulle had written that a leader must always be conscious of the effect that he makes upon other people, take care over his appearance and the gestures he uses. When television arrived de Gaulle put his precept into practice. Unlike many politicians who assume that all that is necessary in order to make a good impression is to be yourself, he rehearsed for long hours in private. An actor from the *Comédie Française* coached him in elocution and in the gestures which are effective when seen on a small screen. He practised before a mirror. Since his memory was as good as ever he could do without notes and, even more important, avoid the endless "ers" and "ums," the irritating "ye knows" with which so many performers punctuate their sentences. As a result de Gaulle never wasted a word and became a master of intonation. When, during the revolt of the barricades in Algeria, he cried "*Français, Françaises, aidez moi!*" he evoked a response which was felt far beyond the frontiers of France; from the lips of a Coty or even Paul Reynaud, the appeal would have seemed merely pathetic.

De Gaulle learned to use television as his kingly predecessors used the "audience." Louis XIV rose and went to bed in public; the people to whom he spoke were noted and the words he let fall repeated far and wide. De Gaulle in his broadcasts and particularly in his press conferences, shared his thoughts not only with those present but with several million Frenchmen and sometimes, on Eurovision, with eighty million Europeans. The conferences were elaborately staged. The platform was set up on one side of the great Salon in the Elysée with seats for the Cabinet to the left and for Ministers to the right. In front, under magnificent chandeliers, there was room for nearly a thousand people, batteries of cameras were arranged so that both platform and audience could be seen. Then, when everyone was in their place, de Gaulle appeared.

In the early years of his reign de Gaulle would speak first and then answer questions; but occasionally things went wrong and a journalist who was not on the list would slip in a question unexpectedly. Later all questions were taken first and de Gaulle gave a packaged answer, grouping them under subjects and making sure that no topic which he wanted to cover had been omitted. It was a superb performance and over the years de Gaulle used the press conference both to startle the world with a declaration of policy and to enlist the sympathy of the French in his struggle with the forces of evil, whether they were the Russians, the Americans, the British or the "degenerate" political parties of France. He was conscious of his own virtuosity and often remarked that, just as he fought the war with the radio, so he beat the politicians with television. But his boast was only partly true. In 1958 not more than a few hundred thousand homes in France had television sets. Ten years later a peak audience might be between ten and twelve million, of whom perhaps half were adults. That is still only a quarter of the electorate. The magic that surrounded his name had other ingredients.

*   *   *

In so far as the de Gaulles had a private life it was simple. When de Gaulle was not working he liked to watch television, play cards, or go for walks. Madame de Gaulle liked to go for drives and do her own shopping. When Lady Dorothy Macmillan stayed with them she found that the subject in which Yvonne de Gaulle was most interested was the price of the things she had to buy, particularly the General's favourite cheeses, Mi-Mollete and Brébis de Pyrénées. As the wife of the President, Madame de Gaulle bought her clothes from a famous couturier, but they were always simple and the General always approved them before they were actually purchased. Some visitors felt that in his home de Gaulle was a tyrant and that his wife had a most difficult life. If so it only increased her devotion. She was austere and a shrewd enough judge of character to make every member of de Gaulle's entourage stand in awe of her. According to a friend who passed many long hours with her, she spends most of her time knitting

—an accomplishment which drove André Malraux almost out of his mind—reading the paper and waiting for the General.

In public the de Gaulles were truly regal. When M. Viansson-Ponté, political editor of *Le Monde* throughout the first decade of de Gaulle's reign, entitled his delightful book *The King and his Court*, he was not being wholly satirical. De Gaulle set a tone to the official life of his capital as distinct as that of Queen Victoria. The ritual was elaborate and subtle. To begin with, those who had been through the divorce courts had, wherever possible, been removed from the government and Presidential staff. This rule was made on the insistence of Madame de Gaulle. If it was necessary to receive divorcées at a diplomatic function, the welcome was formal and distant. Even for the largest receptions, to which a thousand or more people were invited, the guest-list was carefully scrutinised and no one who was politically out of favour with the General (which was not the same as simply being a member of the opposition) was included. One concession to republicanism was made. The President and Madame de Gaulle did not wait until their guests were assembled before making their appearance. They received them standing, with guests of honour at their side. There was the usual crush on the stairs, the usual queue, the stentorian announcement and mispronouncement of names, followed by hand-kissing. The President kissed the hand of the ladies, the ring of a Cardinal or Bishop; Madame de Gaulle's hand was kissed by the men. During the reception the President moved slowly among the throng; Madame sat while ladies were brought into her circle.

There were degrees of magnificence and intimacy. The de Gaulles never staged anything quite so grand as the reception given by President Coty to Queen Elizabeth of England in 1957, when the Little Theatre of Versailles was especially restored and Paris illuminated with the most brilliant fireworks its citizens had ever seen; but they entertained many monarchs, each with some special mark of respect. For uncrowned Heads of State, whether they were the Russians or the rulers of small African republics which were once French colonies, Paris was decorated and de Gaulle always received them and talked with them alone. Although the house in which Lenin had lived while in Paris was "rediscovered" and renovated especially for Khrushchev's benefit, his visit was not a success. The closest he and de Gaulle came to each other was probably during those moments in a rowing boat on the lake at Rambouillet when, conversation being difficult without an interpreter, de Gaulle joined his guest in singing "The Volga Boatmen" Dr. Adenauer, on the other hand, was captivated by de Gaulle's charm and even found Colombey congenial. When, after signing the

Franco-German Treaty of friendship, de Gaulle suddenly stepped forward and kissed the German Chancellor on both cheeks, tears came into the old man's eyes. It was a statesmanlike gesture, watched by millions on Eurovision.

Of course, there were purely French occasions, dinners to Ministers and their wives, lunches for those who were to receive decorations to which the recipient's whole family were invited, cocktail parties for the military or for the hierarchy of the U.N.R., later called the Democratic Union for the Fifth Republic. The most important was the dinner given on June 18 each year to mark the anniversary of de Gaulle's first broadcast from London in 1940. It followed the ceremony at Mont Valérian where de Gaulle, leaving the parade, descended alone into the tomb where lay the ashes of fifteen Free French soldiers killed in action against the Germans. In the evening only the Old Comrades were invited, dinner was informal and was a real reunion. Yet sometimes the General must have felt a qualm, for it was not only death that was thinning the ranks of the faithful. Bidault and Soustelle were in exile and Rémy, the greatest Resistance leader of them all, who pleaded for Pétain's rehabilitation, was no longer invited.

De Gaulle's style—and he was a stylist in all things except perhaps in satisfying his voracious appetite—changed the life of Paris. Even by 1958 the hang-over from the occupation had not been fully cured. The black market had disappeared and the efficacy and integrity of the Civil Service throughout France had been so restored that a British Ambassador, Sir Gladwyn Jebb, considered it the best administered country in the world. But there were still many scars. Prostitutes had returned to the streets in force, homosexuals solicited unashamedly in public and drunkenness had increased alarmingly. In 1956 more than twenty thousand people died from alcoholism and nearly as many were admitted into hospital. Since the law allowed drink to be sold to children at the age of twelve, there were special homes for alcoholic children. At the root of the trouble lay the two and a half million *bouilleurs de cru*, owners of fruit trees and vineyards who, for one hundred and fifty years, had enjoyed the right of distilling pure alcohol for their own consumption or for sale, free of duty. Yet so strong was their parliamentary lobby that neither Mendès-France nor any other politician of the Third or Fourth Republics had been able to abolish their privilege.

De Gaulle dealt with the problem by Decree in 1960. The age at which alcoholic drinks could be sold to children was raised from twelve to fourteen; the right to distil in private was abolished in principle and was to be allowed to die out with its present owners;

subsidies were given to those who cut down cider-apple trees; a limit
was placed on the number of bars serving a given population and the
cost of licences drastically increased; employers were forbidden to
pay their workmen benefits in kind, which in heavy industries had
sometimes meant as much as ten pints of wine per man per day.
Prostitution and pimping was dealt with by a tightening of the law, a
heavy increase in fines and a welfare and maternity service to help those
who wanted help. No doubt it continued, but the streets of Paris were
free from soliciting for the first time in living memory and the risk of
running a *maison des dames* was so great that most went out of business.
And what de Gaulle did for life in the streets, Malraux extended to
their façade. As a result the character of the city in which de Gaulle
grew up, the city with which Stefan Zweig fell in love before the First
World War and Hemingway after it, no longer existed. There were
more students than ever, due to the educational reforms which de
Gaulle stimulated, but they were overwhelmingly French. Foreigners
were no longer popular, N.A.T.O. was expelled, tourists passed
quickly, driven on by the high prices, Americans were scorned. An
intense nationalism, inspired by de Gaulle, infused the younger
generation and made them arrogant and intolerant. It was possible for
a French child in the middle nineteen-sixties to be taught history without being aware of the existence of the Duke of Marlborough or of the
part that the British—let alone the Americans—played in the First
World War. The collapse of France in the face of Hitler was laid at the
door of the Allies who refused to support French policies in the
thirties.

And although the young polytechnicians would have indignantly
denied it, Paris was no longer the cultural centre of the world. Modern
painters found London, New York, Chicago or West Berlin more
stimulating; musicians looked to Moscow, New York, Warsaw or
Rome. There were brilliant French scientists, but the scope for their
talents in France was limited. The French theatre was ossified, television constricted by government control. Writers abounded and the
literature they produced was still infinitely various and often exciting,
but it was not, as young Frenchmen were apt to claim, the only literature in the world. The truth was that, under de Gaulle, France became a technocracy and Paris the centre not of the artist but of the
meritocrat. The eccentric gave way to the conformist. Examinations
dominated the life of students who knew that if they could win a
place at one of the *Grandes Écoles* their future was assured but that, if
they failed the *Bachot*, they would have to struggle. To enter journalism
or even to be a secretary the young needed a special diploma; it was

almost impossible for French men and women below the age of twenty-five to set up in business on their own, to try their wings in film-making or on television. Even pop was mainly foreign. Of course, there were exceptions. The young Europeans, the poets who gathered at the *Club des Poètes* to read their compositions to whoever was there, refused to conform. But they were conscious of being peculiar and many of them went abroad as soon as they left the University.

De Gaulle's enemies claimed that the decline of creative effort in France was due to government censorship and suppression; but this was only marginally true. Undoubtedly the greatest infringement of individual liberty came through his interference with the Courts of Law, the creation of special tribunals, the political appointment of judges. These measures stemmed from terrorism and their use declined with its decline. Nevertheless, de Gaulle used the courts to stifle criticism to an unprecedented extent. The law of 1881 made it an offence, punishable by fine or imprisonment, to insult the Head of State. At the time this was understandable, partly because of the extent of monarchical feeling and the contempt in which the Republic was held, particularly in the Army and the Church, but also because the President was above party and exercised only limited power. De Gaulle was in no such position. Yet whereas in the sixty-nine years of the Third Republic there were only six convictions under the Act and in the fourteen years of the Fourth Republic only three, under de Gaulle there had been three hundred and fifty convictions by 1968 and several more prosecutions were pending. The Act spread its net wide. Most of those prosecuted were writers, cartoonists and publishers; but a cinema-goer who blew a raspberry at a news film of de Gaulle was fined £13, a bystander who shouted "down with de Gaulle" as the President's motorcade drove down the Champs-Élysées was arrested, thrown into gaol and fined £25; a manufacturer of ash trays, which carried an unflattering cartoon, had his stock confiscated and was fined £425 into the bargain.

But although de Gaulle was sometimes unforgiving he was not vindictive. All but one of those who plotted against him in the O.A.S. had been released by 1968. Soustelle, living in Switzerland, published a book in Paris in that year. Michael Foot, the British Member of Parliament who was expelled from France after calling President Coty a traitor for demanding de Gaulle's return in 1958, was allowed by de Gaulle to return. Alfred Fabre-Luce, a strong supporter of Pétain whose satire *Le Couronnement du Prince* was banned in France, has written other books almost as scathing and still lives comfortably in Paris. *Le Canard Enchaîné* continued to lampoon de Gaulle who was one of its regular readers. Outspoken critics like Raymond Aron hold important Chairs in the University; outright opponents whose qualifications warranted it served on official committees or acted as technical advisers to the Government. De Gaulle would not forgive Pétain, but tens of thousands who venerated and served the Marshal also served his government.

Although some Frenchmen had less freedom under the Fifth Republic than under the Fourth, suppression moved in well-defined channels. The political parties, including the Communists, functioned much as before; it was their own failure to combine which cost them successive general elections. Members of Parliament had less freedom to harass and fewer opportunities to bring down governments; but their freedom of speech was untrammelled and the electorate showed that it preferred a greater degree of stability than the régime of the parties had ever been able to provide. Trade unions, never strong in France, were no weaker than before.

On the other hand, de Gaulle undoubtedly exercised pressure in the field of mass communications. Since the State controlled seventy per cent of French industry, a threat to withdraw government advertising curbed the exuberance of even the most hostile newspaper proprietors. Some newspapers were temporarily suspended. Editors were known to change the assignments of reporters who were too outspoken. But the sober criticism of *Le Monde* continued and every newspaper was free to publish signed articles by commentators and politicians who were opposed to the régime.

Radio and television were a different story. In the summer of 1964 an Act was passed which changed the status of O.R.T.F., (The Organisation of French Radio and Television), from that of a government department to a public corporation. However, as an opposition Deputy remarked, only the label was changed, not the bottle.[6] The Director-General still held office at the government's discretion and the majority of those appointed to the central and regional boards were strong government supporters. The government retained the right to make such pronouncements as it thought necessary and neither the opposition nor private citizens had any right of reply. During elections opposition leaders gradually won a fairer share of time but, year in year out, the bias of reporting and discussion remained heavily slanted in favour of the Government. For all this de Gaulle was directly responsible. He took a personal interest in "my television." On a free evening he would watch most of the programmes and, if they displeased him, he would summon the Minister of Information next morning and berate him. "My" television became "the" television or, in extreme cases and menacingly, "your" television. The strictures were at once passed on.

The outside world got a sudden glimpse of the way de Gaulle's censorship worked when, in December 1967, eighty-year-old Lady Asquith was invited to appear on a programme with four historians and a former French Ambassador in London, to discuss events at the turn of the century. Inevitably the question of the *Entente Cordiale* came up. Since de Gaulle had just reiterated his refusal to allow Britain to join the Common Market on the grounds that her economy was unsound and that she was not truly European, Lady Asquith let herself go.[7] She said that she felt "a lively nostalgic emotion" in discussing something which had been a fact for as long as she could remember but no longer existed. At once she noticed the red light go on in front of the compère who was sitting beside her and he picked up the studio telephone.

Smiling and guessing what was happening, Lady Asquith went on: "and if I have not arrived here this evening dressed in mourning, if I have not arrived here naked even—for this is the condition in which I understand General de Gaulle prefers to see Englishmen, and I presume that goes for English women too . . . it is because I think this discussion might give rise to the hope that, although the *Entente Cordiale* is now dead, it might one day be resuscitated."

The red light kept flashing, the compère gesticulating; in the gallery upstairs an English reporter heard the producer say over the telephone, "But no, my friend, how can I stop an old woman?" The programme went on. Lady Asquith recalled Churchill's offer of union between France and Britain in 1940 and de Gaulle's enthusiastic reception of it. Then, leaning forward and looking straight into the camera, she commented that Churchill had not asked after the health of the franc, nor said that it would take the French several years to get used to the British way of life. Lady Asquith ended by saying that the era of nationalism was dying but that de Gaulle, by his example, had revived it and made it respectable in Germany and, by contrast, had made Communism popular in France.

It was good, strong stuff, a little surprising perhaps from a woman and a foreigner, but child's play compared with the satire broadcast by the B.B.C. or printed in *Le Canard Enchaîné*. Yet, instead of maintaining a dignified silence, a Gaullist reporter not only attacked Lady Asquith in the party magazine *La Nation*, but did so inaccurately and maliciously. After making the elementary mistake of describing her as the daughter of Sir Edward Grey, Maurice Ferre alleged that she had insisted on a fee of £300 as well as her expenses, "an absolute lie" according to Lady Asquith. Although it was not contradicted by the producer, who knew the truth, the sequel was significant. Lady Asquith received a host of letters, all favourable and one thanking her for letting in some fresh air, light and truth into the programme. She was at once commissioned to write an article for *Paris Match* and to do a further broadcast for Radio Luxembourg.

De Gaulle was not to blame for all the gaffes of his supporters, but there was no question that he regarded radio and television as his special preserve, a weapon of State and the personal tool of the monocrat. Under his rule it was unthinkable that a Frenchman could emulate the Director-General of the B.B.C. and refuse to allow a Prime Minister to broadcast. No man capable of such action would have been appointed to the office. And for many years the people were satisfied. French women, in particular, liked to feel that the greatest Frenchman of their century was talking to them by their firesides. It was how he looked that mattered, not so much what he said. For days after a press conference, in any bar in France, you could hear people discussing the General's health, whether he seemed cross and if so with whom. Through television *Le Grand Charles* had become not only king but head of the family. It seemed that no monarch could ask for more.

ALONE UPON A PEAK

"All my life," de Gaulle wrote in his memoirs, "I have thought of France in a certain way . . . like the princess in the fairy story or the Madonna in the frescoes, as dedicated to an exalted and exceptional destiny . . . the positive side of my mind also assures me that France is not really herself unless she is in the front rank . . . France cannot be France without greatness."[1]

Like the late President Kennedy, de Gaulle always had his Grand Design for the organisation of the world. He sketched it to Winston Churchill in 1944, when, incredibly, he offered him the leadership of France in the reconstruction of Europe instead of that of the United States. He stated it in his memoirs. He returned to it in speech after speech. Very simply it was the idea of the "Third Force," to make Europe, as he put it himself: "one of the three powers of this planet and, if one day it becomes necessary, the arbiter between the Anglo-Saxon and Soviet camps."[2] The special twist he gave to this idea was, of course, that it should be under French leadership. He suggested to Churchill, and even to his enemy Roosevelt, that France should have a post-war army of fifty-five divisions; since then he has given France an independent nuclear striking force. The object was the same in both cases, to enable France to dominate Europe, to free Europe from American "hegemony," to allow it, under France, to expand in the only direction it can expand, which is eastwards.

De Gaulle began by freeing France from the obligations which had been laid upon her by the Fourth Republic. Since 1949, France had been a member of N.A.T.O. whose avowed aim was the merging of national armies into a European defence force under American command. In January 1958, the year that de Gaulle took office, the French government had signed the Treaties of Rome which launched the Common Market. That Treaty also stipulated that economic fusion was only a first step towards a wider political community in which the nations of Europe would merge their national sovereignty. To de

Gaulle the underlying implications of both Treaties were anathema. He decided to change or break them.

His first target was N.A.T.O. In September, 1958, he wrote an identical letter to President Eisenhower and the British Prime Minister, Harold Macmillan, proposing important changes in the organisation. The letter was never published but a West German newspaper, *Der Mittag*, got wind of it and a spokesman for the Federal Government, von Eckhardt, confirmed its existence. What de Gaulle suggested was an Anglo-French-American directorate for N.A.T.O. which would decide the political and military strategy of the whole free world, including the use of nuclear weapons. Atomic secrets and technical resources must be shared, and France must have an equal say with America and Britain in the structure of command. He ended by stating that unless his demands were met France would withdraw from the Organisation.

Of course there was a case for the reform of N.A.T.O. The world had changed greatly since 1949. Russia as well as America possessed thermo-nuclear weapons. The division of Germany was an established fact. China was emerging as a revolutionary force outside her own borders. Empires were vanishing, new and impatient countries taking their place. Closer consultation between America and Western European countries might have benefited them all. However, de Gaulle's proposition was preposterous. France had no nuclear weapons and, because of the Algerian war, had failed to honour many of her commitments under the North Atlantic Treaty. Yet de Gaulle proposed to raise France to a position above Germany or any other continental ally and to oblige Britain and America to seek her agreement for the whole range of their foreign policies.

As soon as the existence of the letter was known almost every member of the Organisation protested. Countries like Canada and Italy had no objection to American leadership, which was natural in view of its overwhelming preponderance of power, but they had no intention of being relegated to a status below that of France. After an interval of some weeks Eisenhower wrote a personal and courteous reply, agreeing that change was necessary although not in the form de Gaulle suggested; Macmillan had a careful study of the letter made, but sent no formal answer.

De Gaulle was not at all surprised. The mere fact that he had delivered an ultimatum showed that he had never expected his demands would be met. But he was not bluffing and immediately embarked upon the first stage of his grand design. It was a delicate operation. He had to disentangle France from her alliances without losing the protection of the American nuclear umbrella and to assert French sovereignty without strangling the new-born Common Market. Above all he had to gain time to equip France with a system of defence credible enough to be a deterrent on its own and to form the basis of a "European" Europe which could establish its independence of the two giant nuclear powers.

His first steps were comparatively easy. Since his allies in N.A.T.O. refused to support France's attempt to maintain sovereignty in Algeria, he felt justified in withdrawing the forces he needed from N.A.T.O. Command. After all, both Britain and America kept the bulk of their forces under their own control; he proposed to do the same. Nine tenths of the army was already in North Africa and he now resumed control over the French Mediterranean Fleet and several Fighter Squadrons. There were protests but, as he was doing little more than regularise an existing situation, no outcry. In June, 1959, he went further and refused to allow the Americans to stock-pile nuclear weapons on French soil, claiming that any such weapons launched from France must be under French control. The Americans immediately removed their Tactical Air Force to Britain.

For the next two years de Gaulle moved more cautiously. The Russians were pressing for the recognition of Eastern Germany and threatening to hand over to Ulbricht the control of East Berlin; Khrushchev was calling for a Summit Conference to endorse his proposals in a formal peace treaty. France, which was just carrying out the first of its atomic tests in the Sahara, was utterly dependent upon the presence of American forces in Europe. De Gaulle temporised. He allowed Couve de Murville to make a speech in the spring of 1960 stressing the "elemental necessity" of the Atlantic Alliance and of the presence of American troops; he confirmed that the French Fighter Squadrons on the Franco-German border formed part of the N.A.T.O. Command and pledged his full support for an integrated radar-warning system. Khrushchev visited Paris at de Gaulle's invitation, but their talks produced nothing more than an agreement for scientific and cultural collaboration and a certain disillusionment in de Gaulle who compared his guest unfavourably with Stalin. He at once balanced this exchange by himself visiting London and Washington where he spoke in glowing historical terms.

At home de Gaulle was more frank. In November, 1959, he had addressed the Centre for Advanced Military Studies in Paris in terms which left no doubt whatever of his ultimate intentions: "The defence of France must be French . . . if a country like France has to make war it must be her war . . . France must be able to defend herself in her own way . . ." and he went on to say that the system known as integration was already dead.[3] This was plain enough, even if the warning lay in the future. The following year, in France and even in Washington, he returned to his theme of a Europe from the Atlantic to the Urals and enlarged upon his hopes of a change in the nature of Communism, which would enable France to break down the barriers which divided Europe in two.

Speeches, however, were not enough. If de Gaulle was ever really to be able to dispense with the Atlantic Alliance he had to give France a system of national defence. Again the initial stages were not difficult. It was Guy Mollet, after the Suez débâcle, who had launched the programme for the separation of the isotope; Bourgès-Maunoury and Félix Gaillard had sustained it. All de Gaulle had to do was to confirm the time-table for the atomic tests in the Sahara, the first of which took place in February, 1960.

But neither Mollet nor his successors had envisaged a nuclear force separated from N.A.T.O. When, in December, de Gaulle made Debré, his Prime Minister, introduce a Bill to establish an independent nuclear striking force, he ran into opposition not merely in the Assembly and from his allies in N.A.T.O. but from most of the uncommitted world which was frightened at the spread of nuclear weapons, and from every political organisation in France except his own.

The arguments against him seemed overwhelming. To begin with, as the Americans pointed out, the North Atlantic Treaty provided for a general review of its clauses at the end of every ten years; if de Gaulle had asked for such a review in 1960 he must have been granted it and he could have laid his plans formally and constitutionally before his allies. De Gaulle did not dare take the risk. For by establishing a purely French nuclear force he was destroying the very essence of the Treaty whose object was to co-ordinate Western European defence and give it the strength and cohesion it had so plainly lacked when faced with successive German onslaughts. As Adenauer told the French Press Association in Bonn, the Atlantic Alliance could not be allowed to dissolve into a coalition of national armies; integration was its point and its strength and United States leadership natural. It was pointed out that the French action would encourage other nations like China or India, and perhaps Israel and Egypt, to develop nuclear weapons of their own; the British deterrent was no analogy since it was committed to N.A.T.O. and one of the two keys to its warheads was in American hands. If France had its own nuclear force Germany would in time follow suit and so perhaps provoke the very conflict the North Atlantic Treaty existed to prevent.

Frenchmen added their own reasons for opposing the Bill. The force was too expensive. The eight hundred and fifty million pounds, to be spread over five years, was only a beginning. France would be unable to fulfil her Treaty obligations (as it was she was only contributing two of the fourteen Divisions she had promised) and her standard of living would suffer. Only the Communists would gain. Finally, the force would be ineffective. Félix Gaillard described it as "a challenge to our friends without being a threat to our enemies."[4] The Mirage IV aircraft, which was to carry the atomic bombs, was so slow that it would never get through and, in any case, had not the range to return. Even if refuelling aircraft were bought from the United States, the operation would have to be carried out at low altitude over enemy territory. The number of thermo-nuclear weapons, if they were ever produced, would be so pitifully inadequate that they could not be a deterrent but might invite a pre-emptive strike to eliminate their nuisance value.

De Gaulle was quite unmoved. In spite of the fact that General Norstad, the N.A.T.O. Commander-in-Chief, was struggling to make his organisation the fourth nuclear power and was already planning a force of medium-range ballistic missiles under its command, de Gaulle continued to assert that integration was dead. He scoffed at the idea that Germans would ever want nuclear weapons which would be bound to invite immediate Russian attack. He cited the British deterrent as a precedent and consequently ignored the fundamental difference in what he was proposing for France. However all this was an exercise in dialectics. His decision was an act of faith. The nation alone counted in the world and even to reach the second rank, France must be responsible for her own defence. This meant a modern force in every sense of the word. De Gaulle was haunted by the thirties when the French High Command had refused to learn its lesson; he was determined not to fall into the same error. Of course he would have allies—so long as he needed them—but France would be a better not a worse ally for being strong.

But although these were the main arguments de Gaulle used at the time, his logic carried him further. If France were to be independent she must also be in a position to be neutral. For the moment he needed the Atlantic Alliance, but as he constantly emphasised, the Communist system might evolve, America's commitment to Europe weaken. Who could be certain that the United States would always come to Europe's defence? Might not America and Russia make a deal that imposed demilitarisation on the countries which lay between them? With its world interests, particularly in the Far East, America might drag Europe into a nuclear war in which she had no real interest.

Where so much was uncertain de Gaulle advanced the theory of marginalism. It was absurd, he argued, to make comparisons between French nuclear power and American or Russian. What mattered was not parity, but the possession of a force which, at a given moment, might tilt the balance between the two nuclear giants. French bombs might be few but they would still kill millions of people; if they were used they would probably provoke a nuclear war. Therefore a threat to use them would be as effective as if the force were a hundred times greater. Finally, and this was at the apex of his thought, if France alone had an independent nuclear force, then France alone would be in a position to lead Europe when the stalemate between Russia and the United States dissolved. Indeed it might even be possible to persuade his European neighbours to trust France rather than America long before that moment arrived because of the unanswerable logic of his case and the need for Europe to be, itself, free from the domination of America.

De Gaulle's Bill was thrown out by the Senate and met with such opposition in the Assembly that he was forced to make it an issue of confidence. But as the Algerian crisis was at its height there were just enough Deputies who feared to lose him, however much they disagreed with his military ideas, for him to win the vote. Once the programme had been launched he rightly judged there would be no turning back. By the beginning of 1961 de Gaulle had set France on a course which, in less than a decade, would take her out of the North Atlantic Treaty Organisation and virtually out of the Alliance as well.

*   *   *

Leaving N.A.T.O. was only a first step in the Grand Design. If France was to avoid isolation and to achieve her exalted destiny, Western Europe had to be weaned from American tutelage not only militarily, but economically and politically. A "European" Europe, "that exists by itself and for itself,"[5] had to be built. De Gaulle fixed his attention upon the Common Market.

Before he returned to power de Gaulle had promised Debré that he would tear up the Treaties of Rome. However, in 1958, he quickly realised that the Common Market might be just the instrument he needed if he could adapt it to his own ends. He therefore scrupulously carried out its economic provisions, greatly to France's benefit. What he opposed, and had always opposed in every discussion upon European union from 1943 onwards, was any idea of "supra-nationality." Yet this was the very essence of the Treaties of Rome. Under their provisions the Council of Ministers, the Executive of the Community, was to take decisions by majority vote after January 1, 1966. The Commission which administered the Community was able to make recommendations independently of the Member Governments. The High Authority for Coal and Steel had powers—which it has not used—to impose its decisions on Member States. Finally the Treaty provided for the ultimate election of a European Parliament by universal suffrage.

De Gaulle felt that in such a "hotch-potch" France would lose its identity. The States were "the only entities which have the right to order and the authority to act."[6] Therefore the union of Europe must be a confederation of states and any institution which could infringe national sovereignty must be suppressed or reformed. Above all, as he had said so often, France must be the "centre and keystone," the physical and moral leader of the confederation.[7]

At the same time, therefore, as he was preparing to torpedo N.A.T.O., de Gaulle set to work to reorientate the development of Western Europe. He began with Adenauer. One of the first questions de Gaulle had asked Couve de Murville when he appointed him Foreign Secretary was how much was left of his original policy of dismembering Germany. De Murville had replied "nothing." Starting anew, de Gaulle concluded that a "European" Europe could only be constructed on a close Franco-German understanding. Even while he had been advocating the dismemberment of Germany, de Gaulle had dreamed of the day when the Rhine would be a "street rather than a ditch" across which French and Germans must always fight each other; he now set out to bring about the transformation in the belief that what Germany and France decided upon, other Western European nations would be bound to follow.[8] His target was the grizzled old German Chancellor.

Adenauer had not only been warned against de Gaulle by the German Foreign Office but himself largely shared the views of those who believed in an "integrated" Europe. Acutely conscious of the "devil" that lurked beneath the surface of his own people, he believed that German nationalism could be exorcised only within a wider community. He was also convinced that the safety of both Western Germany and the democratic ideal depended on the presence of

American troops in Europe and upon the strengthening of N.A.T.O. Undaunted, de Gaulle began his courtship. Within a few months of assuming office he invited Adenauer to Rambouillet and treated him as his friend. He flattered him, talked with him alone, throwing in the occasional German phrase, reviewed the history of their two countries with all the mastery of which he was capable. The Chancellor was coy, but not unimpressed. The joint communiqué issued after the meeting spoke not only of "the end of the former hostility between France and Germany" but of the conviction that "a close co-operation between the German Federal Republic and the Republic of France is the foundation of all constructive effort in Europe."[9] A few weeks later de Gaulle paid the Chancellor a return visit at Bad Kreuznach on the Rhine. The ice was broken, the dialogue continued. The two statesmen met twice in 1959 and three times in each of the next two years; always de Gaulle played upon the theme of burying the hatchet and founding a new era on Franco-German friendship.

As Adenauer began to melt, de Gaulle felt that the time had come to bring his plan out into the open. The Common Market was succeeding beyond all expectations. The reduction of tariffs between the Six was several years ahead of schedule, trade was expanding fast, foreign and particularly American capital was pouring in to boost production. The Six were not only full of optimism but anxious to extend co-operation into the political field. De Gaulle, therefore, worked out a plan for the political organisation of Western Europe and submitted it first to Adenauer and then to the leaders of the other four Common Market countries. It was a straightforward blue-print for a confederation; regular meetings between the heads of government, the Ministers of Education, Defence and Economic Affairs; permanent commissions of civil servants to prepare these meetings; reform of the Treaties of Rome to unify the three autonomous communities (Euratom, The Coal and Steel Authority and The European Economic Community) and subordinate them to the new confederal "Cabinet"; a referendum throughout the Six to approve the new system.

At Rambouillet at the end of July, 1960, Adenauer seemed tempted but his own ministers warned him that de Gaulle's plan in reality meant the supercession of N.A.T.O. and the end of the supra-national character of the European organisations which were proving such a success. When the other leaders received the draft they expressed similar views. Nevertheless, de Gaulle prevailed upon them all to hold a preliminary meeting of the heads of government in Paris in February, 1961, and a second in Bonn in the summer. As a result, a committee of experts was appointed, under the chairmanship of Christian Fouchet,

15. De Gaulle with Dr. Adenauer at the Elysée, January 1963. (*See page* 422). *Below*: De Gaulle with Mr. Kosygin in the Kremlin, June 1966. (*See page* 426)

16. De Gaulle televised at a Press Conference early in 1964

then French Ambassador to Denmark, to put de Gaulle's proposals into the form of a draft treaty.

In October Fouchet reported. He had made considerable changes. The confederal Cabinet would have power to discuss and, if possible, decide upon a joint foreign and defence policy and to deal with cultural matters. Regular meetings of heads of state, of Prime Ministers and of the Ministers for Foreign Affairs and Education would take place; but instead of being subordinated to Ministers, as de Gaulle wanted, all the institutions in the Common Market would become responsible to a common parliament and the supra-national character of its civil servants would be retained.

The Federalists among the Six disliked the Fouchet plan, but they would probably have accepted it if it had satisfied de Gaulle. All were anxious to make a start towards a European political organisation. But de Gaulle had suddenly hardened. During the summer Khrushchev had withdrawn his ultimatum over Berlin and allowed the construction of the Berlin Wall. De Gaulle was now certain that the Russians would not risk a nuclear confrontation and that the threat to Western Europe had decreased. He therefore reverted to his wider vision of a Europe from the Atlantic to the Urals and proposed not only the subjugation of the autonomous institutions of the Common Market to the Council of Ministers but a reaffirmation of the rule that the admission of new members—Great Britain had already applied to join—could only be decided by unanimous vote. In other words he refused every concession to his partners. This killed his project. Although he visited Adenauer and Fanfani and won some support from both, neither Spaak nor Luns, the Belgian and Dutch Foreign Ministers, would consider a scheme which reversed all that in their opinion offered hope for Western Europe and threatened the Atlantic Alliance as well. To their refusal they added a rider that they did not wish to consider further any political organisation for Europe which did not include Britain. On April 17, 1962, at a full conference of the Six, de Gaulle's first attempt to create his version of Western Europe died.

Quite unabashed, de Gaulle changed his tactics. If he could not persuade his partners to accept French rather than American leadership, he would try bullying and dividing them. He began by trying to divide. In his long dialogue with Adenauer de Gaulle had already established a certain ascendancy. Although the German Chancellor set great store by the American alliance, he was genuinely moved by the prospect of ending a century of enmity with France. He admired de Gaulle, disliked the English, and was less wedded to supra-nationality than some of his followers. De Gaulle now turned the full force of his personality upon him. His object was simple. If he could form with Germany alone the sort of close understanding that had just been rejected by the five, if he and Adenauer and their respective Ministers could have regular meetings and co-ordinate their foreign and economic policies, then Germany and France would dominate the Common Market together and the other countries be bound to accept their pattern of development. In time he hoped Adenauer might come to see the American alliance through different eyes.

In July Adenauer was received in France with great ceremony. De Gaulle spoke of him as "a great German, a great European and a great man who is the friend of France" and went on to describe his visit as a "moment of truth" for the two countries. "The unity of Europe is a fundamental objective for both France and Germany. The great wonder of the age is that our two countries, having renounced their domination of the other, have discovered their common duty and recognised the senselessness of their old struggles."[10] Adenauer responded in the same vein, praised the French contribution to civilisation, reminded his audience that the Gothic style of architecture had originated on the Île-de-France, and thanked Frenchmen for the "rescuing hand" they had held out to Germany after the débâcle of 1945. It was all very emotional but not yet conclusive because, in the communiqué issued after the meeting, Adenauer insisted on expressing the hope that the negotiations with Britain would quickly succeed. But de Gaulle had made progress.

Then in September de Gaulle paid a visit to Germany. It was a euphoric occasion. The crowds were larger and more enthusiastic than they had been recently in France and in city after city de Gaulle's car was mobbed. He got out, threw security to the winds and dived into the crowds as if he were in France, shaking hands and greeting the people in German. In his speeches he harped upon the Franco-German theme. Europe needed a "massive centre," a "bulwark of power and prosperity similar to that of the United States in the new world"; this could only come on the basis of the solidarity of France and Germany.[11] In Hamburg he praised German military tradition and, forgetting his scholarship, said that neither country had ever achieved anything great without the help of the military. He addressed the German Staff College and spoke of a "joint and united defence." He was cheered by steel workers in the Ruhr. He left the country with cries of *Es lebe Frankreich* and *Vive de Gaulle* ringing in his ears. In October, at Adenauer's request, negotiations began for a formal Franco-German treaty. It looked as though de Gaulle had found a way of short-circuiting the resistance of his other Common Market partners.

Almost incidentally, de Gaulle's success in Germany killed the negotiations which Britain had been conducting for more than a year. When Macmillan made his formal application to join the Common Market in August, 1961, de Gaulle had given it a cautious welcome. "We know very well how complex the problem is," he said in a speech in September, "but it appears that everything now points to the wisdom of tackling it and, as far as I am concerned, I can only express my gratification not only from my own country's point of view but also from the point of view of Europe and consequently of the world."[12] It was a tactical move because an outright refusal would have seemed churlish at the very moment when he was launching his plan for a confederation of states which so exactly suited Macmillan's own conception of political association. In any case there seemed no harm, at that stage, in seeing how far Britain was prepared to go in modifying her relationship with the United States and the Commonwealth and adapting her economy, and particularly her agriculture, to suit the conditions of the Treaties of Rome. But, after his plan for political union failed, de Gaulle's attitude hardened.

The slow progress of the British negotiations had been due quite as much to British reservations towards the whole European idea as to any French intransigence. Britain's refusal to take part in any of the steps which had led to the Treaties of Rome, her efforts deliberately to prevent the formation of the Common Market by proposing a wider Free Trade Area and her subsequent but futile attempt to counterbalance it with a peripheral E.F.T.A., had aroused the antagonism of "Europeans" in all the Six countries. Before the negotiations began Professor Hallstein, the Chairman of the European Commission, told the European Parliamentary Assembly that unless Britain would accept the main provisions of the Treaties of Rome she would have to be content with association rather than full membership. Even such ardent well-wishers as Spaak were determined that Britain's entry should not weaken the fundamentals of the Common Market.

At first the British negotiators had laid down so many conditions to protect the Commonwealth and British economic freedom that resistance was almost unanimous. However, as the summer wore on they became more amenable and prospects seemed to improve. De Gaulle told Macmillan that he did not believe the British Prime Minister would ever be able to carry with him the Commonwealth or the Conservative Party. When they met at the Château de Champs in June, 1962, Macmillan was able to reply that he was doing both. The opponents of the Common Market within the Conservative Party had dwindled to a small group; Australia had reluctantly but definitely accepted that entry was in Britain's interests; New Zealand remained a special but manageable problem. Heath, the chief British negotiator, claimed that in his efforts to safeguard the position of former British Colonies he was asking no more than had been granted to France herself and, in the House of Commons, spoke more and more of "transitional arrangements" which he felt were reasonable and attainable. It seemed that the obstacles were gradually being overcome.

In reality one obstacle had already become insuperable. De Gaulle did not want Britain in. The longer the British negotiations dragged on, the stronger became de Gaulle's elemental fear that England would prove a Trojan horse within the European Community and end by strengthening rather than weakening American "hegemony." The British nuclear deterrent was dependent upon the United States and the British, like the Dutch, were constantly stressing the American theme that the Common Market should be "outward looking," with low external tariffs which would encourage world and particularly American trade. De Gaulle had always mistrusted American support for Britain's entry and his worst suspicions were confirmed when, in July 1962, President Kennedy launched his own grand design of a vast Atlantic zone of free trade.

De Gaulle's answer was his courtship of Adenauer. Although it was many months before the British negotiators in Brussels became aware of it, de Gaulle was turning his back on Britain by seeking a special understanding with Germany. As always, de Gaulle kept his own counsel, but from September onwards there was a marked difference between the political climate in Paris and that of Brussels where the negotiations were taking place. By October the staff of the British Embassy in Paris was convinced that the negotiations would fail, whereas in Brussels all was still optimism. Agriculture had been the last stumbling block, but when Heath and his colleagues accepted in principle both the financial pool into which levies on imports would be paid and the Continental system of guaranteed prices rather than the British system of subsidies, they felt that they were nearing the end of the road. In fact de Gaulle was simply biding his time.

Macmillan's visit to Rambouillet in December, therefore, was neither the cause nor the occasion of the rupture. Macmillan went because he believed that negotiations were reaching the final stage and he wanted to make sure there was no last-minute misunderstanding. Contrary to what has been said, on this occasion he never saw de Gaulle alone; full notes were kept of all their conversations. No doubt the French and British versions differ, but not in any vital respect. De Gaulle knew beforehand that the British nuclear programme was in difficulties and that Macmillan was to meet President Kennedy in Nassau later that month. Macmillan told him quite frankly that if the Americans could not deliver Skybolt, an air-to-ground guided missile capable of carrying nuclear warheads which would greatly extend the effectiveness of the British Strategic Air Force, he would ask for Polaris. De Gaulle expressed no particular concern. They parted friends and Macmillan had no reason to suppose that his coming talks with President Kennedy would have any particular bearing on the Brussels' negotiations.

Later, when Harold Wilson, then Prime Minister, accused Macmillan of having concealed from de Gaulle his intention of finding an American substitute for Skybolt, de Gaulle wrote to Macmillan to confirm that this had not been the case. There was no misunderstanding at Rambouillet, at least as far as the British nuclear proposals were concerned. Nor is it true that de Gaulle was not informed of what went on after Macmillan had left France. From Nassau, Macmillan dictated a special telegram every night and sent it to the British Embassy in Paris for transmission to the French President. De Gaulle knew at every stage what was being proposed in the Bahamas Agreement. He did not approve of the proposal for a multilateral nuclear force under the command of N.A.T.O., but he was certainly not surprised by it.

The sequence of events speaks for itself. The negotiations for the Franco-German treaty, which had been begun in the autumn, were completed by the end of 1962. The treaty was due to be signed on January 22, 1963. De Gaulle, believing that he had now found the true axis around which to build his "European" Europe, felt that the time had come to declare his hand. He therefore gave his famous press conference of January 14.

One thing was clear. De Gaulle's rejection of the British application was no sudden decision. In his press conference he was simply repeating what he had always thought and explaining why, although he had not opposed the negotiations taking place, he had never expected them to succeed. As he remarked a few days later when asked to comment on the chorus of criticism which his speech had provoked, perhaps one day Britain might evolve to a point where it would be possible for her to be truly European, but by then he himself would be dead. No doubt Macmillan's acceptance of Kennedy's plan made Britain a less desirable European partner than ever in de Gaulle's eyes, but this was incidental. De Gaulle's rejection was final and absolute and its timing was explained towards the end of the conference when he began to answer questions. Adenauer was expected in Paris the following week and de

Gaulle was asked how he visualised the evolution of Franco-German co-operation. "I believe," he replied, "that among the new elements that are shaping the world at present there is none more vital and fruit-ful than the Franco-German achievement," and he went on to stress that this friendship constituted "the condition and very foundation of the building of Europe." What de Gaulle was really bidding for on January 14, 1963, was a German guarantee of French leadership; Britain inevitably was brushed aside.

On January 22, de Gaulle seemed to have triumphed. The Franco-German treaty of friendship, embodying just those forms of political and military collaboration which had been rejected by the Common Market countries the year before, was signed in Paris. The Heads of State, the Ministers for Foreign Affairs, Defence, Education, their high officials, were all to meet regularly several times a year to co-ordinate their policies. Their declared aim should be to take a common stand on all problems affecting N.A.T.O., the Common Market and relations with the Communist and under-developed world. French was to be taught in German schools and vice versa, and students were to be exchanged. As long as de Gaulle was alive he seemed assured of a partnership which France would dominate and which, in turn, would decide the pattern of evolution of Western Europe. No wonder, that after the ceremony, he embraced the wizened old German Chancellor.

Yet, once again, de Gaulle had miscalculated. Adenauer proved a broken reed. For all his high standing among the German people, he could not persuade the Federal Parliament to become the tool of de Gaulle's ambition. Neither Chamber rejected the treaty outright but the upper Chamber, representing the States of Western Germany, qualified its ratification with a resolution inviting the Government to carry it out in a way that would further the aims of the Federal Republic and her Allies, mentioning in particular close partnership with the United States, re-unification of Germany, the integration of Allied Forces within N.A.T.O., the inclusion of Britain in the Common Market and the strengthening of its institutions. In July the lower Chamber went even further and, without consulting France, converted the resolution of the upper House to a preamble to the Treaty. The representatives of the German people had served notice on de Gaulle that, although they welcomed the end of Franco-German enmity, they were not ready to place their future in his hands. When de Gaulle visited Bonn that summer for the first of the regular policy meetings between Heads of State, the Treaty was already a dead letter. Only the exchange of students survived to remind people of what de Gaulle himself once compared to a love affair.

De Gaulle's failure was complete. For the second time in two years his partners in the Common Market had spurned his leadership and rejected the whole concept of his grand design. They were still bent on building Europe, but not in his image. Like him they saw the Common Market as a nucleus of a larger community, but they did not wish this community either to exclude Britain or to become a balancing "third force" which, in their opinion, would increase rather than reduce the risk of annihilation. On the contrary the signatories of the Treaties of Rome, including Frenchmen like Schuman and Monnet, who had been its first architects, still envisaged the European Economic Community as the core of a political system in which the narrow nationalisms which had torn Europe asunder for so long would gradually be fused into a single state. However long it took—and Schuman in particular recognised that the process could not be hurried—they were unwilling to see their brain child, which had made such a promising beginning, emasculated by a man who preached exactly the philosophy they were trying to overcome.

It was not only the Western Europeans who were indignant at de Gaulle's attempt to dominate Europe. After the signing of the Franco-German Treaty official notes of protest were presented in Paris by the Soviet, Polish and Czechoslovakian Governments. The Russians complained bitterly that de Gaulle was making a mockery of the Allies' solemn undertaking to destroy German militarism and scoffed at the idea that the French Army, standing "shoulder to shoulder with the Bundeswehr," could check the German instinct for revenge.[13] De Gaulle's rejection of Britain, made without consulting his partners, drew unofficial but almost unanimous protest from the Western hemisphere. In newspapers from New York to Rome he was hailed as a Buonapartist, the man who, for personal pride, was undermining the security of the Free World. The idea of de Gaulle as the world's "arbiter" was held up to ridicule.

But de Gaulle's conceit was impregnable. He recognised that his actions had postponed indefinitely any hope of political union in Europe and, through Pompidou, admitted as much in the Assembly; but he was incapable of realising the extent of his failure. He still believed that France alone was capable of leading Europe and that, if he continued to establish and assert her independence in every aspect of life, others would be bound to recognise the truth in time. The "genius of the land" must triumph in the end.

De Gaulle met his rebuff, as he had always done, by attacking those who opposed him. Jilted by Germany he turned on the Germans and made overtures to the Russians. Threatened by Kennedy's multi-

lateral nuclear force, he stepped up his own deterrent and opted out of
N.A.T.O. Isolated in the Western world he sought new friends among
the under-developed countries. Nearer home he rounded on his partners in the Common Market and by bullying and threatening them
tried to extract the maximum advantage for France while keeping up
a running fight against every development which might impinge upon
French sovereignty. He dealt with the Germans first.

While Adenauer remained Chancellor de Gaulle held his hand. The
old man had also been shocked by his failure to carry the German
Parliament. He lingered on in Office through the summer of 1963,
then in the autumn resigned. Like Gladstone, he meant to be the mani-
pulator of power in the wings, but Adenauer's failure had destroyed his
influence. When Erhard succeeded him the climate changed abruptly.
The new Chancellor at once reaffirmed his Parliament's view that
Europe must be democratic and integrated; Franco-German friendship could not be an end in itself. Although Erhard visited Paris early
in 1964 he had a cold reception.

Then de Gaulle struck. The essence of the Franco-German Treaty
was joint discussion of every major issue, particularly in foreign policy.
In the New Year, without consulting anyone, de Gaulle suddenly
recognised China. He followed it by equally provocative gestures,
sending a parliamentary delegation to East Germany and receiving
Nicholas Podgorny, one of the most prominent Russian leaders, in
Paris. The implications were clear. When Erhard attended the scheduled meetings of the Franco-German Cabinets that summer, he told de
Gaulle that the West Germans feared that France might be on the point
of recognising Eastern Germany. De Gaulle prevaricated. Returning to
Germany, Erhard protested publicly that Germany could not be relegated to a political no-man's-land or to the inferior rank of a country
without a history. De Gaulle retaliated in speeches that summer and
autumn in which he not only arraigned the whole range of German
foreign policy, from support of the Americans in Vietnam to support
for N.A.T.O., but openly threatened that unless they toed the line
France might change her direction. In fact she had already done so.

The Soviet Union caught France on the rebound. Bitterly disappointed at his failure to harness the Federal Republic to his Western
European chariot, de Gaulle had revived his youthful vision of an
understanding with Russia. As a historian he had always looked nos-
talgically towards the third great Continental land power of Europe and
in his military lectures in the 1930s, had regretted that the military
clauses of the Franco-Russian alliances before the First and Second World

Wars had never been implemented. The Bolshevik revolution had alarmed him, not because of the totalitarian régime it produced, but because it preached internationalism. Outside Russia Communists were "anti-patriots" or, as he called them in France, "separatists." But when Stalin emerged as a national hero in his struggle against Hitler, de Gaulle warmed to him and in 1944, just before his return to France, was still speaking of a permanent alliance with "our dear and powerful Russia."[14]

The Cold War and de Gaulle's own experience of Communism in France changed his attitude, but he never abandoned his dream of welding all Europe into one great confederacy and, although he never explained how Russia could cut itself off at the Urals, he constantly returned to this theme even when the Soviet Government was at its most aggressive. In Washington and London in 1960, in Paris in 1961, when Khrushchev was threatening to end four-power control of Berlin and de Gaulle was stiffening the attitude of the Anglo-Saxons he still lamented Russian methods and looked forward to the day when the Soviet Government would cease using threats and so transform itself that a dialogue would become possible. Then, like a flash of lightning, came the Cuban crisis.

De Gaulle supported Kennedy—unwillingly, if his secret service agent in America, de Vosjoli, is to be believed—but when Khrushchev climbed down and removed his rockets from the Caribbean, he drew his own conclusions. He was finally convinced not only that the Russians would never risk a nuclear war over Europe, but that this factor had altered fundamentally the scope and purpose of the North Atlantic Treaty. Since the American Strategic Air Force and Intercontinental Ballistic Missiles could both reach Russia directly from the United States, there was neither the same need as before for the preservation of American troops in Europe nor the same guarantee that the United States would risk a nuclear war in Europe's defence. De Gaulle went further. Kennedy had threatened Khrushchev with nuclear attack over Cuba without consulting his allies. Not all of them had even been informed. De Gaulle foresaw the possibility of America's N.A.T.O. partners being dragged into a nuclear war at America's heels over an issue in some far corner of the world in which their interests were only remotely involved.

De Gaulle was not alone in his thinking. Duncan Sandys, then British Minister of Defence, had cast doubts upon American willingness to risk a nuclear war in defence of Europe when defending Britain's own nuclear deterrent. Several of de Gaulle's opponents on the Continent shared his feelings. But whereas most people saw in the danger a reason for strengthening N.A.T.O. and giving America's partners a greater say, de Gaulle saw only a new opportunity for achieving his grand design and asserting French independence.

So long as any prospect remained of the Franco-German Treaty forming the basis of Western Europe, de Gaulle was content to be abused by the Kremlin as an accomplice of German militarism. As late as October, 1963, Couve de Murville was putting the blame for the Cold War squarely on Russian shoulders. But after Adenauer's resignation de Gaulle carried out his threat and changed direction. His recognition of China pleased the Russians because it embarrassed the Americans, who were deeply involved in Vietnam. Then in the next few months de Gaulle concluded an agreement with the Soviet Government for the combined exploitation of outer space under which French satellites would be launched by Soviet rockets, and a general agreement which greatly increased trade between the two countries. China bought French wheat in the summer of 1964 and the following year, when de Gaulle was boycotting the Common Market, both Russia and China took quantities which helped reduce the French surpluses. In February, 1965, de Gaulle pronounced that the reunification of Germany could only be attained in a Europe stretching from the Atlantic to the Urals, which was another way of saying not in the foreseeable future, and *Pravda* replied by praising his "realism." The next month the two countries agreed on the joint exploitation of the French colour television system with the help of a Soviet satellite. Gromyko, the Soviet Foreign Minister, visited Paris and in the following summer de Gaulle paid an eleven day visit to the Soviet Union. This was one more of those exercises in glamour during which, whenever possible, de Gaulle played his usual role of plunging into the Russian crowds, shaking hands and using the few Russian words he knew. He appeared on television, quoted Pushkin (in Russian) in his speeches, and was the only European statesman to have been allowed to visit the Soviet rocket base at Backomar in Kazahkstan. He crossed the Urals to visit Novosibirsk, apparently without noticing that he was no longer in Europe.

*　　*　　*

De Gaulle's eastern approaches were matched by brinkmanship in the rest of the world. Although he must rely on the American nuclear umbrella to protect him from some unexpected Communist eruption until the early 1970s, by which time he hoped the French deterrent would provide the marginal threat which was all he believed necessary, he set out deliberately to weaken American influence wherever he could. His tour of the ten South American Republics in 1964, during which he harped on the common Latinity of France and the countries he was visiting and openly attacked "hegemonies" of every kind, was blatant provocation. "We cannot accept," he said, "that some states should establish a power of political or economic direction outside their own borders—all and every hegemony must be banned from our world,"[15] and he repeated his theme over and over again. De Gaulle could supply nothing to take the place of American aid or investment in South America, yet even on the American continent he resented the presence of the United States. His Canadian visit served the same purpose, with the added spice that it embarrassed London as well as Ottawa and Washington. When de Gaulle turned on Israel, sent Mirage IVs to Iraq, made loans to Nasser and withdrew from Mers-el-Kebir ahead of schedule, he was playing the same game. If France was to achieve her "exalted and exceptional destiny" she must be seen to be free of all ties and alliances in every sphere, able to defy the most powerful of all states, capable of acting as a broker, if not yet as the arbiter, between the two worlds which were waging the Cold War and so retarding the progress of civilisation which France above all was destined to lead.

To sustain this defiance de Gaulle needed a modern and credible defence force; for no one would listen for long to a country that was militarily impotent. While he was courting Russia and flouting America, therefore, de Gaulle was pushing through the complete reform of the French fighting services which had been foreshadowed by the Act instituting the independent nuclear deterrents. It was uphill work. His plan had two elements; a *force de frappe*, a nuclear version of the armoured divisions he had begged for from 1935 to 1940, and a territorial army designed not to hold another Maginot Line, but to deal with fifth columnists and enemy parachutists, or hold sections of France specially suited for defence, like the Massif Central or Britanny, if the country were eventually overrun. Even in the 1950s co-operation within N.A.T.O. never played more than a minor role in his thinking. The *force de frappe* and the territorial army were to be wholly French.

The reorganisation got under way in 1960, when a five-year defence budget, itself an important innovation, was presented to the Assembly and several Ordinances were promulgated under the emergency powers granted to de Gaulle the year before. The immediate change was the centralisation of defence policy in a Committee, which gradually became known as the Defence Council, under de Gaulle's own chairmanship. This meant that the administration and supply of all three Services would be done centrally and that

Service Ministers were down-graded to little more than executive officers.

The creation of the *force de frappe* was more difficult. It was to consist of two branches, a nuclear striking force which could deliver first atomic and later thermo-nuclear bombs by land, sea and air, and a *force de manoeuvre* composed of six mixed armoured and infantry divisions, eventually to be equipped with tactical atomic weapons. From the start de Gaulle's plan ran into difficulties of every kind. The Algerians objected to nuclear tests being carried out in the Sahara and when, a few years later, de Gaulle transferred the tests to the Pacific, almost every country in the Far East protested. The United States tried to prevent Canada from supplying France with uranium. Because the French were starting from scratch and had no access to American, British or Russian secrets, delays dogged every stage of nuclear development. In Parliament the credits for the factory for the separation of radio-active isotopes, at Pierrelatte, were attacked at every stage, frequently defeated in the Senate and passed in the Assembly only because the Government made it a question of confidence in de Gaulle. Politicians criticised the basic conception of a national defence force divorced from N.A.T.O., soldiers deplored the reduction of conventional forces and questioned the efficacy of a nuclear arm whose development must fall further and further behind those of the existing nuclear powers. Where Britain had already found the effort too expensive it seemed mad to enter a race in which a single American laboratory would spend more on missile research than the French could afford in the course of their whole programme.

De Gaulle persevered. In speech after speech he frankly admitted that the purpose of the *force de frappe* was political. A national policy needed a national army, he told two thousand officers at Strasbourg in November, 1961; appalling though nuclear weapons were, "a great state that does not possess them does not control its own destiny."[16] Unless France became a nuclear power it would no longer be a sovereign nation but become an integrated American satellite; with the bomb, he argued, it would inevitably become the leader of Europe.

De Gaulle's Ministers and chosen Generals took up his theme. General Ailleret, who fathered the bomb from the beginning and became the first Chief of Staff of the Combined Forces, maintained that only by possessing nuclear weapons could France avoid building a second Maginot Line. General Gallois, fervent protagonist of the *force de frappe*, argued that, because no country would risk nuclear war in defence of an ally, all alliances were dead and France must look after itself and its neighbours. Defence Minister Guillaumat was upholding

the same theme when he told the Senate in 1959 that nuclear intervention should be powerful enough to permit the nation to act "outside all organisations."[17] Couve de Murville spoke of France becoming an equal partner of the United States within the Atlantic Alliance,
"a stable element of equilibrium" which foreshadowed peaceful
arrangements from the Atlantic to the Urals.

As the war in Algeria came to an end and the troops came home,
de Gaulle initiated a campaign of indoctrination to fit the new defence
plan. It was a difficult period. An army of more than a million men,
many of whom had suffered major defeats in two Colonial wars within
ten years, faced a reduction to less than half its size and adaptation to a
new and, in the opinion of many of its officers, dubious role. Somehow de Gaulle had to assuage wounded pride and enthuse men used to
fighting with the theory of a technical deterrent.

He revolutionised army education. Although National Service was
retained as "an enrichment"[18] for young men, its period was shortened
to fifteen effective months and not everyone called up was required to
fulfil his full term. A new form of Defence Service was instituted
which allowed conscripts not required in the army to serve their time
in civil life or to volunteer for service overseas. Several thousands
have done their National Service as teachers, doctors or technicians in
former French colonies. Exemption, particularly for those who had
lost a member of their family in the "country's service" was made
easier; conscientious objection was legally recognised in France for
the first time. De Gaulle's policy was to make the army a part of
national life rather than a life of its own. Military thought, he said,
was a branch of political thought, the child of general thought. Instead
of courses in psychological warfare, officers studied economics and
the political and social sciences. Promotion went more and more to
those who showed technical ability until General Valluy, a colleague of
General Challe, complained that the Army was becoming a career for
polytechnicians.

De Gaulle also make a tremendous effort to persuade the country
that military expenditure in the new form would benefit French
industries and stimulate scientific research. In the decade from 1960 to
1970 France will have spent more than ten billion pounds on defence,
about forty per cent of which will have been on the nuclear arm; and
although de Gaulle could claim that this was less in proportion to the
national budget than when he took office, there was no getting away
from the fact that, as the years went by, France lagged behind her
partners in the Common Market in her rate of expansion, and that
many people blamed de Gaulle's grandiose military ideas. Besides the

traditional arguments that the money might have been spent on housing, hospitals, schools and university buildings, scientists alleged that
sixty per cent of those engaged in atomic research were wasting their
time. De Gaulle's ministers denied it, and pointed to Franco-German
co-operation in building a fast nuclear reactor at Grenoble and an air
bus, co-operation with Russia in space and in the development of
colour television, co-operation with Britain in building the *Concorde*,
as direct or indirect results of the military effort and comforted the
entrepreneur with the information that, of the money spent on
Pierrelatte, ninety per cent went into private hands. It was an argument they thought they had won when, in 1967, the Assembly passed
the annual Defence Credits for the first time without opposition. As de
Gaulle predicted, the representatives of the people seemed to have
accepted his policies.

In spite of all the difficulties, by 1968 the new French defence force
was in being. The first Mirage IV strategic bomber went into service
in 1964 and in 1968 the full complement of sixty-two was operational.
The first nuclear-powered submarine, the *Redoutable*, was launched in
1967 and was expected to be operational by 1970. A rocket test-range
had been built on the coast near Bordeaux and sites for Intercontinental
Ballistic Missiles were already located in the Alps. Short and medium
range atomic rockets were under construction. Research was continuing on vertical take-off aircraft, hovercraft and the military uses of
space.

Meanwhile, the amorphous Colonial Army had been reduced to
less than half a million highly trained men and formed into a *force de
manoeuvre* of six divisions of three brigades each. Their equipment was
old, but thirty-ton tanks and helicopters were due by 1970 and tactical
atomic weapons soon afterwards. The Cinderella of the programme
was the territorial defence force, composed mainly of reservists with
antiquated small-arms, whose role has never been clearly defined.
Nevertheless, in de Gaulle's eyes, France in 1968 was an independent
military power. He behaved accordingly.

De Gaulle had hoped that the geographical position of France,
providing as it did the main room for manoeuvre and for the infra-
structure of the N.A.T.O. forces, would compel his allies to give in to
his demands. When it did not, when he saw that his letter to Eisenhower and Macmillan was being ignored, he decided then and there to
leave the Organisation. The divorce proceedings were protracted, not
because he had second thoughts but because he wished for time to
prepare his own defences. The stages were carefully timed. After
the initial broadside in 1959, banning American bomber stations and

withdrawing the Mediterranean Fleet, he did nothing until the Algerian war was over. Then, when the Allies were confidently expecting a strengthening of their Organisation, he announced that the divisions which had returned from Algeria would remain under French command. He would provide N.A.T.O. with only two of his quota of fourteen divisions. In 1964, when the first Mirage IV atom-bomber became operational, he declared himself the sole commander of all French nuclear forces. Whether N.A.T.O. founded a multilateral nuclear force or not, de Gaulle's finger alone would be on the French trigger. In 1965 he began shaping the *force de frappe* and withdrew the French Atlantic Fleet. In 1966 he gave notice of his withdrawal from the Organisation and in 1967 expelled it from French soil. Thereafter France shared only in the Early-Warning radar system; even the two French divisions in Germany were not under N.A.T.O. command. In December 1967, the Ministerial meeting of the N.A.T.O. Council was held for the first time in Brussels rather than in Paris, ironically and for the last time under the chairmanship of Couve de Murville.

By then de Gaulle had already thrown off the mask. All the time that he had been leaving the North Atlantic Treaty Organisation he had proclaimed that he was remaining a member of the alliance. But in his speeches he had also stressed that France would only belong so long as it was necessary, and his supporters, Gallois and Guillaumat, had said that in a nuclear age all alliances were dead and that the French defence force must operate free of any "association" whatever. With N.A.T.O. safely ensconced in Brussels de Gaulle came out in his true colours. Casually, in a speech in November, 1967, he mentioned that in future French defence would be directed "to all points of the azimuth."[19] In other words, although technically he still belonged to the Atlantic Alliance, he warned each of its members that he regarded them as potential enemies. In case his meaning had not been understood, he re-emphasised it a few weeks later in a speech to the *Centre des Hautes Études Militaires* where he told his Senior Officers that they must not only understand his new policy but "see it and acclimatise themselves to it in their thinking and in their studies."[20]

The die was cast. By the beginning of 1968, France was free not only of all political and military entanglements but had proclaimed her neutrality in the great ideological struggle which still split the nuclear world. This was independence indeed. And de Gaulle could claim some increase in French prestige and influence throughout the world.

By opposing the Americans in Vietnam, where the French had failed and where he was convinced no one else could succeed, he was speaking for a large minority—perhaps for a majority—in the Western world. In appearing to break down the barriers between Eastern and Western Europe he was answering the dreams of everyone who had seen with dismay the fruits of five years of war dissipated in failure to make peace. In championing under-developed countries he was appealing to men's charitable instincts. By rationalising his actions in speeches and press conferences he was able to pose as the one disinterested statesman, free from ideologies, seeking only the peace and well-being of mankind.

And yet the pose did not really carry conviction. For it was plain to anyone who paused to think that de Gaulle was the least disinterested of all the great leaders of this century. In foreign affairs he was actuated by only two motives, the grandeur of France and a pathological hatred of the United States; and in his mind the two were often inextricably interwoven. He had no sympathy with well- meaning idealists who sought to outlaw war or to create a world government which would prevent it. He scoffed at disarmament conferences and strenuously opposed any interference by that "ridiculous" organisation, the United Nations, in the "internal" affairs of other countries such as the Congo, Rhodesia, the Dominican Republic, and, of course, Algeria. Except for the peace-keeping force in the Gaza Strip, for which France voted, he refused to subscribe to the peace-keeping operations sponsored by the General Assembly. Of all men he understood that force ruled the world and that only a constant balancing of power could prevent the final holocaust. Yet he was less concerned with preserving this balance than in seeing that it was France that tipped the scales. When Russia and America invited him to sign the Treaty banning further nuclear tests, he refused, saying that so long as any power had nuclear weapons he was determined that France should continue to develop her own. Although he opposed the Communists in France he did not hesitate to encourage revolution in South America; for in many states that could be the only effect of his anti-American speeches. No doubt it was also jealousy of the United States which made him turn so suddenly on Israel and espouse the cause of the Arabs. According to de Vosjoli he even went so far as to pass information obtained from American Intelligence to the Russians. He was opposed to self-determination for the Saar and would have regarded with horror any suggestion of self-government for Alsace; yet he wantonly encouraged separatism in Canada and, in the opinion of the Flemish, was doing the same in Belgium. For years he had warned the world against the spread of Russian influence in the Mediterranean, but when Algeria became independent he expressed indifference to the Russian acquisition of naval bases on the North African coast.

This flamboyance, these hysterical changes of front, belied the statesmanlike appearances and ponderous speeches which de Gaulle so regularly made. His foreign policy was a failure. Instead of being a world leader, by the mid-sixties he had become the rogue elephant of diplomacy, feared for the wanton damage he could do but without any serious following outside his own country. At the end of a decade he was further away from the leadership of a "third force" than he had been when he took office. The Franco-German Treaty was in ruins. He had antagonised Britain without winning the support of a single Western European nation. He had deeply offended the United States without winning the trust of Russia or China. The countries of Eastern Europe were flattered by his attentions but uninterested in him as an ally. Among under-developed countries he had raised expectations he could not fulfil and encouraged revolt where he had been expected to give aid.

Frenchmen might applaud as each friendly nation was insulted in turn and foreigners, who preferred to be led rather than bear the burden of democratic decision-making, envy his freedom of action, but there was an unreality about the position in which he had placed France which caused apprehension. Certainly he had asserted political and military independence, but the result was isolation. France was neither courted nor followed. She was endured. No country had taken the threat of the azimuth policy seriously although defence ministers realised that, as de Gaulle's second generation of nuclear weapons came along, it might arise. Yet it seemed ludicrous to study the consequences of a French nuclear attack on London or Bonn. It was as if some large political bubble was floating above the international scene which everybody longed to prick but refrained for fear of causing embarrassment. There were few who would have prophesied at the beginning of 1968 that the deed would be done by the French themselves.

CHAPTER XXIV

PILLAR OF GOLD

De Gaulle's pretensions to influence in the world rested on his personal authority in France, and this in turn depended upon a general consensus among the people. No one knew this better than he. He was always conscious both of the source of his power and the precariousness of his position, and attached far more importance to French social and economic life than has generally been acknowledged.

In his youth the demographic problem haunted him. As he travelled France, preparing his studies on defence, the emptiness of the countryside, so vulnerable to a mobile attacking force, became an obsession. In his lectures, and later in his memoirs, he constantly referred to the losses in man-power that France had suffered and failed to make good. "At the beginning of the last century," he wrote, "our country was the most populous in Europe, the strongest and richest in the world; and her influence was unequalled."[1] He went on to note that whereas, since then, population had doubled in Britain, tripled in Germany and Italy, quadrupled in Russia and increased tenfold in the United States, in France it had remained stationary. This weakness, he believed, was one of the causes of the French disaster in 1940.

The failure of French industry to meet the demands of rearmament in the 1930s also appalled him. In spite of all the money that had been voted, delivery of almost every weapon had been behind schedule in 1939 and, in August, due partly to strikes, the production of aircraft practically ceased. When, during the war, he discovered that some French newspaper proprietors had accepted bribes from the Germans in the 1930s and saw how avidly other industrialists collaborated with the enemy, his dismay turned to disgust. He saw the *patronat* as men who preferred money to honour; the unions he despised. Inevitably industrial reorganisation formed part of the Gaullist revolution of 1944-45.

De Gaulle was not a socialist and his nationalisation programme owed little to Karl Marx. It was the corollary of his determination to restore the power and authority of the state. Public ownership of the mines, all forms of power, the banks and insurance meant that the comparatively small private sector would not only be largely dependent upon government orders but would have to conform to government policy. But de Gaulle's early influence on French economic life went much further. He began with reform of the Civil Service, he infused a new spirit into education and he encouraged French parents to have more children.

The reform of the Civil Service was forced upon him by the need to supplant Vichy officials; but it did not stop with the Gaullist takeover. De Gaulle believed in strengthening the central administration and increasing the power and authority of the Prefects. The process has gone on ever since. By founding the School of National Administration he not only provided the Civil Service with its own institute of administrative technology, but set the tone for the future development of education as a whole. De Gaulle believed in an élite. It had always formed part of his philosophy of leadership and was to be the core of his plans to rejuvenate France. During the war the *Grandes Écoles*, founded by Napoleon I, had languished; by adding to their number and encouraging the interchange of students, he improved standards and gave birth to the modern French meritocracy.

De Gaulle's attitude to the French working man has been alternately contemptuous and paternal. When the workers oppose him he dismisses them as "*la canaille*" or "cattle"; when he needs their votes they become the only true source of sovereignty. In 1944 he wished them to work and above all "to revive the French birth-rate, once so high it had nourished the spirit of enterprise and the greatness of our nation."[2] He, therefore, introduced a social security system greatly extending the family allowances which had been introduced by Pétain and including generous transitional payment for those declared redundant, unemployment and sickness benefits, appeals against dismissal, compulsory work councils. The Fourth Republic implemented and improved his plan, but it was de Gaulle who laid the foundations. Finally he instituted *Le Plan*. It was his means of integrating the public and private sectors of industry, of involving the Civil Service in economic planning, of ensuring that the country's resources were used to fulfil the military and civil targets of his grand design. The *Commissariat du Plan* no longer functions quite as he intended, but in the early years of France's recovery and in those preceding the formation of the Common Market it acted as an invaluable guide and stimulant to the whole French industrial effort. Whatever his critics say, even by 1946 de Gaulle had not been a negligible influence in the economic life of France.

In exile de Gaulle's economic thinking crystallised. He opposed the Common Market and it was fortunate for France that he was not in power in the early fifties. What impressed him, as he watched from Colombey, was the "servitude" which inflation and the balance of payments deficit imposed on each successive French administration. A country in debt or dependent upon foreign aid, whose currency was at the mercy of foreign speculators, was in a degrading position. Budgets had to be framed to repay debts or please foreign bankers. Social services had to be cut and wages held down to prevent a run on the franc. It did not matter to de Gaulle that in the course of this degradation France had staged a remarkable recovery, nor would it ever have occurred to him that what he considered servitude might be a form of salutary discipline. He was irritated by dependence of any kind.

Almost the only thing that pleased him during his years in the wilderness was the increase in the French population. It began to show itself in the 1950s when the primary school children increased by more than a third and those in higher education doubled their number. De Gaulle's vision expanded. If only, he would say to his visitors, France had a population of one hundred and eighty millions! In his mind's eye the empty spaces filled, factories burgeoned, French industry equalled the American, French forces dominated the Continent. In spite of a lack of mineral sources why should not France become a bigger and better Japan? Demography was against him. According to French statisticians the population of France by the year A.D. 2000 would be only sixty-five millions. Even so it was a beginning; France, he remarked, would soon have more people than Britain.

By the time de Gaulle returned to power in 1958, national economic strength had become the third pillar of his grand design. Without it, as had been shown at Suez, military and political independence were meaningless. He was determined that France should be freed from debt and placed in a commanding financial position. In spite of his preoccupation with Algeria the need to restore "financial order" was a main plank of his early speeches. In the forefront of his mind were the Common Market, which he had promised to abolish, inflation and the balance of payments. Lurking in the background was a smouldering resentment that the dollar and the pound were international currencies, whereas the franc was not, and a growing fear of the spread of dollar "hegemony" through American investment in French industry.

He tackled the immediate problems at once. Over the Common Market he turned a somersault. His advisers, Pinay, Pompidou and Rueff, persuaded him that, far from compromising French independence, the economic growth that the Market offered would greatly increase it. De Gaulle became the High Priest of the purely economic aspects of the Treaties of Rome. On the same advice he dealt with inflation and the balance of payments by the more mundane method of devaluation and restraint of demand.

To begin with de Gaulle was lucky. Gaillard's devaluation of 1957 had been far more successful than was realised. The reason why exports had increased so little was that it coincided with the recession in world trade. De Gaulle's second dose, making a devaluation of thirty per cent in all, caught world trade on the rebound. Although his measures of restraint on prices and wages were less successful than Gaillard's, production soared and exports increased by thirty per cent in a year, more than enough to cover the cost of imports. For the next five years, aided by the Common Market, France forged ahead with a steady increase in her gross national product, an average improvement of four per cent per man in productivity, and a healthy volume of investment. French post-war indebtedness was reduced by nearly half and French reserves in gold and currency climbed to 4.4 thousand million francs.

De Gaulle was delighted. Financial independence seemed easier to attain than he had expected. In speech after speech he boasted of the "brilliant results" of his policies. France had "espoused her epoch," was "accomplishing a vast renovation," "the transformation of man's lot in every sphere of activity."[3] He gave special credit to *Le Plan* which, he said, by co-ordinating science and economic planning, labour and technology, was steering France to prosperity and becoming a model for the world.[4] He was at least partly justified. His own ardour had fired the imagination of a disheartened and war-weary people and, although he may have exaggerated the role of the *Commissariat du Plan*, the targets it had set and the guidance it gave had helped French industry adapt itself to the Common Market. The combination of indicative planning, control over investment in the huge public sector and incentives in the private sector, seemed to have got the best of both the socialist and capitalist worlds. But clouds were on the horizon.

In the years 1962 and 1963, three-quarters of a million French Algerians were repatriated to France. This caused unemployment and heavy government expenditure. De Gaulle's quarrel with his Common Market partners reduced agricultural exports. Prices and unemployment rose; the dangers of inflation and of an external deficit loomed once more. In spite of his huge reserves de Gaulle decided on austerity. He remembered with regret rejecting the advice of Mendès-France in 1945 and determined not to make the same mistake again. Reserves, after all, were the hall-mark of independence to be preserved at all cost. In 1964 a "stabilisation plan," designed to keep a detailed control of prices and wages, was introduced. It worked only partially, perhaps because it was laxly—or intelligently—administered, but to de Gaulle's satisfaction gold and foreign currency continued to flow into France. On the other hand production stagnated. France was losing ground in the race with the other industrial countries. Economic independence seemed a little farther away.

Then another threat developed. In January, 1963, the Chrysler Corporation announced that it had bought a controlling interest in the Simca firm of motor manufacturers. A British journalist has described how, for the first six months after the take-over, American executives moved quietly about the factory watching, taking notes, but saying very little. Then one day one of them moved into the Managing Director's office, summoned the senior staff one by one, sacked some of them on the spot, promoted others. The results have shown that it was an injection of management technique which the company needed. But for de Gaulle the spectre of American economic domination suddenly became a reality. He was aware of the advantages which American investment brought to France, but, with many other Europeans, he feared foreign control over vital sections of French industry and the possibility of French factories being closed down in favour of those in Italy or Germany. He therefore set up a commission to study the effects and extent of American investment and himself turned his attention to a larger consideration—the supremacy of the dollar in the world.

Here de Gaulle was in his element. Patriotism and justice combined to uphold a contention which, by a happy coincidence, embarrassed both the Americans and the British. Quite simply, he felt that it was unfair, now that the Common Market countries had as much gold as the United States, that America and Britain should finance their deficit with paper money. This gave them an advantage over other states and particularly over France whose gold reserves were greater per head even than those in the United States. It was a dangerous over-simplification, but it appealed to others besides Frenchmen and de Gaulle felt that he was leading the fight for the economically underprivileged.

In 1963 and 1964, Giscard-d'Estaing, de Gaulle's Minister of Finance, took up the theme at meetings of the International Monetary Fund. He met with little response. Then de Gaulle entered the field himself. On February 4, 1965, during a press conference, he gave the world his analysis of the situation. Having traced the origins of the reserve currency system back to the Genoa Conference of 1922, and reviewed the way in which it had worked since, he came to his point. Inflation in America, he claimed, was being exported through dollar loans to other countries and by American investment in private industry abroad. This had conferred benefits, but contained the threat of expropriation of vital national assets. He continued: "We consider it necessary that international exchanges should rest, as was the case before the world's great misfortunes, on an indisputable monetary basis bearing the mark of no particular country.

"What basis? Truthfully in this respect no other criterion or standard than gold can be seen. Gold, which does not change its nature, which can be shaped equally into bars, ingots or coins, which has no nationality, which is eternally and universally accepted as the unalterable fiduciary value par excellence . . ." At the end of his speech he suggested that the International Monetary Fund should consider the question at a special meeting and make proposals for "the vast reform which is now necessary in the interests of the whole world."

It was a fascinating exposition, not because it recommended a return to the discarded gold-standard, but because it revealed de Gaulle's own alchemical view of gold. For him Keynes had not lived nor did the psychological factors which govern the exchanges have any meaning. But the statement was of great importance. For de Gaulle was doing in the financial world what he had already done militarily and politically, declaring French independence of all associations and alliances and challenging the existing system. He followed up his defiance by action. A week later a spokesman for the French Foreign Ministry in Paris announced that France had definitely abandoned the Gold Exchange Standard and would in future be converting all new foreign currency earnings into gold.

Once again de Gaulle was taking a great risk. Whatever the merits of the gold controversy, de Gaulle was pitting France against the four most powerful industrial countries and making open financial warfare on the United States. And he continued to do it even though the original cause of his onslaught proved unfounded. For when the commission he appointed reported later that year it found that American investment in Europe only amounted to two and a half billion dollars, whereas French investment abroad was as high as eight billion dollars. The commission did not consider American investments excessive and discouraged any curtailment. De Gaulle accepted the findings and dropped that particular part of his campaign; but he continued to attack the dollar and indirectly the pound. In June he informed the Central Banks privately that France was leaving the Gold Pool which financed the gold-exchange system at the pegged price of $35 an ounce. He kept quiet about it until the autumn. Then, when sterling was weakening under the impact of Mr. Wilson's government, he suddenly publicised the action he had taken in June. It was decisive. The next day the pound was devalued and the dollar came under heavy pressure.

However, once again de Gaulle had over-played his hand. Devaluation helped Britain, partly at the expense of France; and, although de Gaulle did his utmost to prevent it, the Central Banks of Belgium, Britain, Western Germany, Italy, the Netherlands and Switzerland combined with Washington to obviate a return to the gold standard. First they refused to sell forward gold, then they agreed to a double gold standard under which Central Banks continued to settle their deficits in gold or in dollars at $35 an ounce while the price of gold on the bullion market was set free. This did not help France and was not what de Gaulle wanted.

In March the bankers went further. Ignoring de Gaulle's continuing call for a world financial conference, the group of ten principal banking countries, including Western Germany, Holland, Belgium, Italy and Japan, agreed to meet in Stockholm in April to inaugurate a scheme of Special Drawing Rights within the International Monetary Fund which was intended to become the basis of a new international paper currency. Debré, de Gaulle's Finance Minister, dined with his Common Market partners beforehand in an attempt to dissuade them from attending the Stockholm Conference. He failed. He attacked them again in Stockholm itself. Debré won some concessions and France was able to opt out of the scheme when she pleased; but the scheme went through and instead of returning to gold de Gaulle found himself faced with a new reserve currency in the form of S.D.R., the preservation of the dollar and the pound in their old role, and a new supranational authority in the form of the Directorate of the International Monetary Fund. Undaunted, he turned his attention back to the Common Market.

* * *

De Gaulle had become an extremely rough partner. Since the Five would not accept his political plan he was determined not only to sabotage theirs, but to extract the maximum economic advantage for France from the Market itself. That meant establishing a common agricultural policy. France not only provided the Community with nearly half its arable land but had some ten million acres of virgin soil, a fifth of which could be productive if irrigated and farmed on a large scale: French farms were larger and more efficient than any within the Community except the Dutch. Unless the Common Market was going to provide an outlet for French surpluses at prices which enabled the farmers to share in the growing prosperity, de Gaulle might have to leave it whether he wanted to or not. For French farmers were in a militant mood and had already staged several strikes during which they blocked the main roads with their tractors.

In 1963, therefore, de Gaulle delivered an ultimatum. Unless farm policy was settled that year he would cease to co-operate with the Community. The threat was effective and in agreements signed in December, 1963, and December, 1964, agricultural policy was agreed. The price of wheat was fixed above that reigning in France but below the price in Germany; unified prices for all other products were to be agreed by July 1, 1967, by which time farm produce would circulate free throughout the Market. Even more important, French surpluses were guaranteed by her partners. In spite of increasing sales with the Market, three-quarters of French surpluses—which were likely to increase as agriculture became modernised—had still to be sold at a loss on the world market. France's partners agreed to make good these losses through levies on food from foreign countries and by straight budgetary subvention. In return they were to have free access to the French market for industrial goods by July, 1967, instead of 1970. De Gaulle had seemingly triumphed and the completion of the free market been advanced three years.

But the agreements had still to be put into practice and some of de Gaulle's partners, smarting under the treatment they had received, prepared a counter-attack. Led by the West Germans, who were suspicious of de Gaulle's overtures to the Russians and resented in particular French wheat surpluses, which they were financing, being sold to the East Germans, they concocted a secret plan with Professor Hallstein's Commission. Hallstein had supported de Gaulle in forcing through a common agricultural policy because he believed that it was the condition of all further progress, but he had bitterly resented de Gaulle's plans to curtail the Commission's powers. Now he planned his revenge.

At the beginning of 1965, all was optimism in Brussels. The most difficult hurdle had been jumped and trade and production were moving ahead fast. It seemed as if the hopes of the "Europeans" were being joyfully fulfilled. Admittedly a battle loomed ahead, for from July, 1966, decisions in the Council of Ministers were to be taken by a majority vote and all knew that de Gaulle would do his utmost to postpone the date. But since France had gained so much from the agricultural agreement it seemed possible that he might be prepared to give the system a trial. Then suddenly "a thunderbolt" came down from the sky. Professor Hallstein and the Commission challenged de Gaulle on the very issue on which he was most sensitive and which he thought had just been settled.

On March 21, 1965, the Commission proposed, without having consulted the Six governments, that it and not the Council of Ministers should take charge of the agricultural budget and that it should be responsible not to the Council of Ministers but to the European parliament. This meant an enormous increase in the powers of both the Commission, which would prepare the budget, and the parliament which would control it. It was part of Hallstein's plan that the Council of Ministers could modify the Commission's proposals only by a majority of five. No one was in any doubt who the sixth might be. The Commission added a rider. Sales of agricultural surpluses would only be financed if the exporting state accepted and strictly observed an agreed commercial policy towards a third state. France would be able to sell her wheat to the Communist world only by common consent.

De Gaulle accepted the challenge immediately. He saw it as an opportunity to demand a revision of the Treaty of Rome well in advance of the date when decisions in the Council of Ministers were due to be taken by majority vote. By chance it was Couve de Murville's turn to take the chair when the Council next met in June and, acting on instructions, he rejected the Commission's proposals at once. However three of the four Foreign Ministers supported them and urged their immediate adoption. Spaak suggested a compromise. But although Hallstein, on behalf of the Commission, offered to reconsider his paper, Couve de Murville suspended the sitting without a full discussion, saying that agreement was impossible. The meeting broke up in angry recriminations, the final agricultural agreements and the merger of the executives of the three European Communities, which had also been on the agenda, being left in abeyance. De Gaulle at once retaliated, withdrawing all his representatives from Brussels and boycotting the Common Market completely. Europe had come to a full stop.

De Gaulle was taking another great gamble. France had benefited enormously from the Treaties of Rome. Although her industrial production had risen less than that of her partners—thirty-eight per cent since 1958 against Germany's fifty-two per cent and Italy's seventy-two per cent—her exports within the Community had more than trebled. French manufacturers had reorganised to meet the challenge

and French farmers, slow to modernise, were pinning their hopes on
the agreements which had been negotiated. The French Territories
Overseas, by whose good opinion de Gaulle set so much store, had
received ninety per cent of the Community's foreign aid. Although
surveys showed that public opinion was behind de Gaulle in his stand
against the Commission, it was by no means certain that it would
support him if he carried out his threat of leaving the Community. The
Five, after all, had an alternative. They could join Britain and the Free
Trade Association, create a wider Customs Union which would include
North America, and face France with such competition that her industries and agriculture would be crippled if not ruined. The Presidential election was due in December and de Gaulle's boycott was
bound to be an issue. Yet de Gaulle held his ground. His political
instincts told him that the true "Europeans" would accept almost
any solution rather than drive France out of the fold, and his
advisers pointed out that increased American and British competition
would create almost as great difficulties for the Five as it would for
France.

On September 9, in a press conference, de Gaulle restated his case.
After tracing the histories of the Treaties of Rome he turned on the
Commission: "The Three Treaties each set up a semblance of an executive in the form of a Commission independent of the member states,
even though its members were appointed and paid by them . . . The
embryonic technocracy, for the most part foreign, was certain to en-
croach upon French democracy in dealing with problems which
determined the very existence of our country." He insisted that agricultural products should come into the Common Market at the same
time as industrial products and that "nothing of any importance
either in the initial planning or the later operation of the Common
Market" should be decided except by the national governments of the
Six. Otherwise the member-countries would lose their national identities, and "be ruled by some sort of technocratic body of elders, stateless and responsible to no one."

De Gaulle ended on a threatening note: "There is no doubt that it
is conceivable and desirable that the great undertaking which the
Community represents should one day be got under way again. But
that can take place, probably, only after a period of time the length of
which no one can foresee. Who knows, in fact, if, when and how the
policies of each one of our partners . . . will finally come round to facing the facts which have just been demonstrated once more?"

De Gaulle's speech was followed up by Couve de Murville, who,
on October 20, demanded an overall revision of the conditions under

which the Six operated. The Five were shaken. The following week
their Foreign Ministers passed a resolution reaffirming their principles
but suggesting a special meeting with the French in Brussels. By then,
however, de Gaulle was busy preparing for the Presidential elections
and was in no hurry to reply. Conversations dragged on.

The election was the turning point. For the first time de Gaulle
received less than half of the electorate's vote and only just over half of
the votes cast. Mitterand, his opponent in the second ballot, had come
within striking distance. The unknown Lecanuet, who made the
Common Market a special issue and said that if returned he would
make the relaunching of Europe within the spirit and the letter of the
Treaties of Rome a top priority, got over fifteen per cent of the votes.
For a few hours de Gaulle debated with himself whether to accept
office on such a narrow majority, but decided not only to do so but to
end the deadlock. The General Election was due the following year
and if, in the meanwhile, the Common Market had ceased to exist he
realised that he might lose his majority in the Assembly and be unable
to govern. He allowed his Ministers to accept the invitation of the Five
to a special meeting of the Council to be held in Luxembourg in January.

Nevertheless, out of near defeat de Gaulle plucked a victory. When
the Council met, de Gaulle no longer demanded formal revision of the
Treaties of Rome but suggested that the Commission should consult
the Six governments before making any proposals, should have Ambassadors it was sending abroad approved by those governments, and
should conduct all its business confidentially and in consultation with
the Council of Ministers which would also control its budget. The Five
not only agreed to this drastic curtailment of the Commission's powers
but, to de Gaulle's delight, were soon to accept Hallstein's resignation.
The most dangerous advocate of supra-nationality had been eliminated.
De Gaulle also persuaded the Five to proceed with the merger of the
three Common Market institutions, to sign the final agricultural
agreement and, although the Five refused to finance sales of French
surpluses to Eastern Germany, to allow France to export to other
Communist countries, which amounted to the same thing. Only on the
question of majority voting in the Council of Ministers did de Gaulle
receive a check. The Five refused to abandon their right to take decisions by majority vote if all attempts at unanimity failed. This right,
however, is one that has never been used.

De Gaulle had had at least a partial revenge. He was no nearer
winning acceptance for his grand design, but he had proved that his
partners set such store by the Common Market that they were pre-

pared to postpone indefinitely the creation of a truly federal system, and he had gained enormous economic advantages.

At the same time he had taken on a considerable challenge. For in return for common agricultural prices he had agreed that the entire market should be completed by July 1, 1968. This meant not only that goods of all kinds would circulate in absolutely free competition within the Six, but that all would accept a common external tariff which, on many products, would be much lower than the tariffs previously imposed by France. As further general tariff reductions, negotiated in G.A.T.T. under the Kennedy Round, would fall due at the same time, French industry in 1968 would face the stiffest competition it had ever known. Three years was not long in which to prepare.

Nevertheless, de Gaulle had reason for optimism. France had enormous advantages over her neighbours, for some of which he could claim credit. To begin with, thanks to de Gaulle, she had just won a guaranteed gilt-edged export market for her main industry. This was a marvellous foundation on which to build. Then, partly due to de Gaulle's encouragement in 1945, France had the youngest and fastest growing population in Europe. The realisation of this only hit the country in 1967, when it was discovered that the electorate, which had been the oldest on record for the Presidential elections of 1965, was the youngest on record two years later. Statistical projections showed that, as a result, the French labour force would increase by thirteen and a half per cent between 1965 and 1980, whereas that of Britain and Germany would remain static.

The French labour force was becoming more mobile and more productive than its rivals. Although in 1965 about ten times as many French men and women were engaged in agriculture as in Britain, the number was falling at a tremendous rate. Tens of thousands were quitting the countryside for the towns every year and in many Departments whole villages stood empty, leaving the land to large-scale mechanical farming. And, as the sons and daughters of peasants and small shopkeepers were becoming school teachers and their sons and daughters might well become polytechnicians, this trend was bound to accelerate. The new technocrats would not return to the land or to the small communes where they were born; they became available for new industries.

French workers were less inhibited by restrictive practices than their rivals in Britain or even in Germany. De Gaulle's grand "alliance" or "association" between capital and labour had never materialised, but his paternalistic interest in the French worker, whose unions have always been numerically and financially poor, had meant constant pressure on the employer to share profits and provide better security and conditions. Although profit sharing never got very far, fringe benefits were lavish in France. In return French employers were marvellously free in the way they could handle their labour. They could introduce new machinery and transfer men to different skills almost as they pleased. So long as earnings increased union leaders approved. Even when they didn't they were not always able to protest effectively, for over France as a whole only one worker in five belonged to any union at all.

Management could also call on a growing pool of skilled labour. Instead of a rigid system of apprenticeship, the young unacademic Frenchman was able to acquire skills, which would qualify him immediately for a job, by passing examinations in part-time courses or full-time technical schools. The *Formation Professionelle des Adultes*, founded to retrain prisoners of war, had continued as a state scheme to retrain workers from dying industries. With its help even the one-man or family businesses—an anachronism that will happily take a long time to die—were often able to make up in ingenuity and energy what they lacked in resources.

On top of all this, French management seemed superior to any other in Western Europe. In spite of the size and structure of French industry, too small as a whole and organised in too many small units, French income per head was already almost the equivalent of British and German. This too was in part due to de Gaulle, for the élite, which he had aimed to create in 1945, was coming into its own. By 1965, the French Universities were already hugely overcrowded, their students groaning under the rigidity of the curriculum; but above and outside the flow of graduates was the select little band who, having passed hideously difficult examinations, were taking the *"route Napoléon"* through the *Grandes Écoles*—the *Polytechnique*, the Institute of Political Science, the School for Engineers, the *École Supérieure Normale* (which trains dons), the National School of Administration which de Gaulle himself founded—and emerging as the ready-made leaders of France. Whether they went into the civil service as Inspectors of Finance, or industry as executives—and they frequently interchanged between them—these superbly self-confident young men introduced a new professionalism into all forms of management.

With Debré as his Finance Minister, de Gaulle did his best to seize these opportunities. Three years of austerity had built his reserves to the enormous total of five and a half billion dollars, of which five billion dollars were in gold. Comforted by this buttress to independence, de Gaulle began to relax controls and bring confidence back to industry. In 1966 production began to move and by 1967 was back to its growth rate of the "miracle" years, of four per cent per annum. Productivity per man kept pace so that by the beginning of 1968, the standard of life in France was probably rather higher than in Britain. Of course tastes differed. The French spent more on food and drink and less on plumbing; they owned fewer television sets and used fewer washing machines and household gadgets; but more French than British families ran a car and an astonishing number of middle-class families already had a cottage in the country. The whole Mediterranean coast, from Menton to Perpignan, was being transformed by gigantic development schemes into a vast holiday camp to which tourists were welcome if they could afford it, but which was mainly for the French themselves. Some civil servants, factory workers and workers in nationalised industries were underpaid by comparison with the general level and made regular protests through one-day strikes and demonstrations, but for the great majority of the people France seemed a better place than most in which to be alive. And when, in January, Debré felt able to reduce taxation and give a boost to demand and special incentives to investment, the country seemed poised for a leap forward which would leave her competitors standing and bring her quickly to the front rank of industrial powers. De Gaulle's dream of financial independence seemed about to be realised. And then, out of a blue May sky, came the student riots and the general strike.

CHAPTER XXV

THE BUBBLE BURSTS

No one has yet pin-pointed the origin of the student unrest which swept the world in the second half of the 1960s. It is tempting to attribute it to Mao Tse-tung and the Red Guards in China, and yet student riots on a massive scale had already occurred in Japan and, on a smaller scale, in England and America. No doubt, however, the spectacle of the leader of the world's most populous country throwing all he had so painfully built up to the whirlwind of armed school children in order that "the revolution" might be kept alive, had its effect. The Chinese "cultural revolution" was so crude that adults banded spontaneously together to resist it. In the civil war that still flickers intermittently throughout China thousands of lives have been lost, the economy has been ruined and power has been left in the hands of the army or, more accurately, of individual provincial commanders as in the 1930s. But a lust for destruction, unleashed in China, fanned out in a shock-wave across the planet. If that was "revolution," everyone of any age could play at it. So, while the Chinese were trying to get the Red Guards back to school, student violence spread from California through New York to London, Madrid, Berlin and—in different and more dangerous circumstances—even to Warsaw, Prague, Bucharest and Moscow.

It was not all spontaneous. In Western Europe it was clearly established that a group of trained international agitators, of whom Rudi Dutschke, Tariq Ali and Cohn-Bendit were examples, had travelled from country to country stirring up discontent and encouraging violence. Sixty were identified in London at the time of the Grosvenor Square riot in March, 1968 and, although some came from East Germany, there were more Trotskyites, Maoists and just plain anarchists than ordinary members of the Communist Party. Of course Communist Front organisations like the World Peace Movement or the World Federation of Trade Unions exploited the general unrest to whip up feeling about the Vietnam war, and there was evidence that the British Communist Party had planned a "winter of disruption" for

British industry. But although both these latter movements were reasonably successful, the only unusual thing about their strikes and marches was their violent undertone. France, however, had been immune from such disturbances and Frenchmen were understandably smug, some of them claiming that de Gaulle had implanted a new sense of order among his formerly turbulent people. Then, on May 3, the students of Nanterre came to Paris. Insurrection had begun.

The students had genuine grievances. The population explosion which de Gaulle had touched off after the war had hit the universities during the 1960s; but the universities were not equipped to cope with it. Successive French Ministers of Education had boasted of the splendid democratic tradition which gave every boy and girl who passed the *Bachot* the right to attend university, yet the facts were that, of more than six hundred thousand undergraduates in France, half fell away in the first year and between a quarter and a third of the rest never took their final examinations. In Britain, where there were only half as many students, a larger number actually took degrees. The French students, backed by many Professors and Assistant Professors, had been protesting about the wastage and overcrowding for years. They wanted more lecture rooms, more halls of residence, more contact with their professors and, above all, a less formal and rigid curriculum. A generation, so many of whom had travelled abroad visiting other universities or doing Voluntary Service Overseas, was not prepared to learn endless lectures by heart and reproduce unquestioningly the opinions of men and women only a few years older than themselves.

In 1966, Christian Fouchet, then Minister of Education, had drawn up a plan which had gone some way to meet these demands; but as it also made entry into the university more selective, Pompidou had never dared implement it. Then Peyrefitte, Fouchet's successor, suddenly introduced selectivity without, at the same time, granting reform. He announced at the end of 1967 that a mere pass in the *Bachot* would no longer qualify students to enter the university. Whether the students agreed with him or not they were indignant at his high-handedness and demanded a greater say in the government of the university themselves.

Nanterre, housing a part of the Faculty of Letters in the western suburbs of Paris, had better buildings and halls of residence than most other sections of the university. Yet, perhaps because various branches of sociology were taught there, it had always housed small groups of extreme militants. For a year these groups had been quarrelling with the authorities, particularly with their Dean, Pierre Grappin, a former resistance leader who had escaped from a Nazi concentration camp.

When some of the male students raided the girls' dormitories in the previous April and camped in the entrance hall, Grappin had taken the unprecedented step of calling in the police to evict them. Later students noticed strangers strolling about the campus, silently watching and reading notice boards. They were identified as police spies. However, nothing more happened for nearly a year. Then on March 19, 1968, during a Vietnam demonstration, a Nanterre student was arrested. Although the university was in recess a mass meeting was at once held in the Students' Hall and a group of left-wing activists, led by a red-haired, freckled refugee called Cohn-Bendit, hitherto comparatively unknown, invaded the administrative block, took the lift to the top floor and occupied the Council Chamber. No damage was done but during the occupation an alliance between all the left-wing activist and anarchist groups was formed under Cohn-Bendit's leadership. They became known as the Movement of March 22, the day on which the alliance was sealed.

Even so the unrest might have been contained if the authorities had acted with consistency. But Grappin, advised by Peyrefitte, blew hot and cold, exasperated the moderates and inflamed the extremists. Twice in March and April he closed Nanterre only to reopen it within a few days, each time making fresh concessions to the students. Violence was seen to pay—as Cohn-Bendit and his group were quick to point out. Then at the beginning of May Cohn-Bendit was summoned before the disciplinary committee of the Sorbonne, possibly to be expelled. His case was to be heard on May 3. On May 2, Grappin closed Nanterre once more. The students, led by Cohn-Bendit, marched on Paris.

If it had been left to the University authorities to handle their own affairs, it is just possible that order could still have been restored. The students would have struck, marched, perhaps rioted; but provided the University Council had coupled genuine reform with firmness, disciplining or even expelling those who had been the ring-leaders but giving the same concessions to the Sorbonne as Grappin had already granted at Nanterre, probably the students would have returned at the end of a week prepared to sit for their examinations. But Peyrefitte, on direct instructions from de Gaulle, had decided to teach the students a lesson. When they occupied the Sorbonne as they had occupied Nanterre, he told Jean Roche, the Rector, not only to summon the police but the *Compagnies Républicaines de Sécurité* (riot police). It was a fatal mistake. The riot police drove out the agitators but beat up as well harmless students who were leaving the Library and inquisitive bystanders. The news spread like wildfire.

Next day Roche became the first Frenchman for seven hundred years to close the Sorbonne. He had been preceded only by the Nazis. The professors' and students' unions jointly called a strike in protest and the students, barred from the Sorbonne, took to the streets. By Monday, May 6, what had begun as the agitation of a minority in one faculty had become a mass student movement. Over ten thousand young men and women roamed the Left Bank that night, building barricades and fighting the police who used tear gas for the first time. Three hundred and sixty students and passers-by and about fifty police were injured. It reminded the correspondent of *The Times* of the accounts he had read of the Paris Commune in 1871: "The lines of helmeted black uniformed police praetorians, charging slowly; the shouting, waving, singing student insurgents; the strains of the 'Marseillaise' and the 'Internationale' breaking now and then through the din; the first-aid teams rushing to the rescue with stretchers—it had all the markings of a terrifyingly realistic historical reconstruction . . ."[1] Then a strange thing happened. The population of Paris, which had hitherto held aloof, began to join the insurrection.

On the Tuesday a far larger crowd, most of whom had left their student days well behind them, gathered in the streets of Paris. From that moment the insurrection gradually slipped from the students' hands. During the rest of the week students continued to parade, supported by an increasing number of outsiders. On the evening of Friday, May 10, with the help of local residents, they occupied the whole of the hill round the Sorbonne (but not the University buildings) and erected barricades. Pompidou was away on a State visit to Iran and de Gaulle himself gave the order that the Sorbonne area was to be cleared. Since Grimaud, the Head of the Paris Police, had already told Fouchet, the Minister of the Interior, that his men were becoming increasingly unhappy at being used against students, this meant calling in the riot police again.

But de Gaulle had forgotten the radio. The official French radio and television service was still obedient, ignoring the riots altogether the first week and thereafter playing them down until the technicians themselves joined the insurrection; but although the French Government own a large share of Radio Luxembourg and a controlling one in Radio Europe I, both these stations had always retained editorial independence. Their reporters were in Paris. On that Friday night, as riot-police chased students in and out of houses round the Sorbonne, radio reporters went with them. French listeners were regaled with accounts of students left bleeding in the gutter, innocent householders beaten up and dragged away to Black Marias, smoke bombs being hurled into cafés and tear-gas into sitting-rooms full of women and children. A shudder went through the population.

Meanwhile, unknown to listeners, two critical meetings were taking place in the Sorbonne itself. For the first time in the history of the University the hundred and eighteen titular Professors held an emergency Senate to consider the demands which not only the students but the Assistant Professors and Lecturers were making. At the same time, eight hundred of the latter were debating in a hall next door. Faced with the prospect of a complete breakdown in university life, the Professors gave way. Overnight the Sorbonne was democratised. A new Senate was to be elected, to be composed half of junior staff and students and half of professors. Together they were to thrash out new rules and a new curriculum. When Pompidou returned from Iran that night, he realised at once that the students had won and, after visiting de Gaulle, called off the police and approved the new arrangement. As far as the students were concerned the insurrection could have ended then and there. The Government and the University Senate had capitulated.

But by then it was too late. Shocked by the behaviour of the riot police, thousands of French men and women spontaneously joined the students. By the middle of the week their demonstration had grown into a national protest. The trade unions became involved. The trade union leaders, and particularly Georges Seguy, the Communist General Secretary of the twelve hundred thousand strong C.G.T., had watched the student riots with increasing dismay. Although some of the rank and file, a few of whom had children at the University, had sympathised, union officials despised the student "*groupuscules*" and felt that they should be kept in their place. But as the week wore on they became alarmed. Although only one in five French workers belonged to a union at all, union leaders exercised an influence far wider than their membership and they saw it being suddenly eroded. The Friday of the barricades on the hill round the Sorbonne was decisive. Next morning Seguy and Eugène Descamps, General Secretary of the Catholic C.F.D.T.,* met the Lecturers and Student Unions, and after discussion decided to back them officially. They called a twenty-four hour general strike for Monday, May 13. The entire country was now involved.

Nevertheless the union leaders intended the insurrection to end the moment the strike was over. They had not wanted the strike, they did not believe in a revolution. Since the last elections the Communists in

* *Confédération Française démocratique du Travail*, with about four hundred and fifty thousand members.

particular had been looking forward to the moment when de Gaulle would resign or fall and they would become the dominant partners in a popular front government. They wished to appear both responsible and respectable. But, once again, something entirely unexpected happened. The general strike took place and was completely successful. Next day, with the exception of the Sud Aviation factory at Nantes which was dominated by Trotskyites, France returned to work. So as to keep control and steer whatever unrest remained into orthodox channels, the union leaders began formulating the demands which they would put to Government. And then, suddenly, the example of the Sud Aviation workers began to spread. Factory after factory closed down or was occupied spontaneously by its employees. There was little violence, proprietors and executives were politely expelled or kept out. Demands were vague, but in general seemed less concerned with wages and conditions than with loose phrases about "workers' control," which for the moment meant simply stopping all production. For the first time de Gaulle's name was being generally mentioned.

Desperately the union leaders tried to regain control. Seeing that they could not halt the movement Seguy, Descamps and even André Bergeron, General Secretary of the anti-Communist *Force Ouvrière*, joined forces at the end of the week and on Friday, May 17, called out the miners, railwaymen and engineers in an official strike. By the week-end organised life in France was grinding to a halt. The students, largely forgotten, watched bewildered as their protest developed into a tidal wave of civil disobedience. Airports were closed, airlines grounded. Petrol was unobtainable except at an exorbitant black-market price. There was no public transport and food was rapidly disappearing from the shops. Refuse and the remains of barricades blocked the streets of Paris, to be burned by rioters in the evening. Newspapers disappeared. Most significantly, from the Government's point of view, radio and television operators struck and refused to broadcast anything but a skeleton news service of their own editing. De Gaulle's own weapon was turning against him.

The creeping paralysis of public life shocked a few citizens into a sense of responsibility. On Monday, May 20, the union leaders managed to persuade the gas and electricity workers to stay on their jobs and so, at least, keep some essential services going. On Wednesday these same leaders published their demands, a forty-five per cent increase in wages and a forty, instead of a forty-eight hour week. Although to grant even half as much would make France uncompetitive and perhaps force her to leave the Common Market, Pompidou agreed to meet them and hinted at a general settlement. That same evening the

Government won a vote of confidence in the Assembly by twelve votes; it commanded little confidence outside.

The strikes and student rioting continued. With the closure of the Simca factories at Poissy and La Rochelle, and the Citroën works at Rennes, the entire automobile industry came to a standstill, bringing the numbers who had ceased work to something over eight million. The main ports closed down. Postal services were largely suspended and in Paris the last form of transport disappeared when the taxi-drivers took their vehicles off the street. Thousands of students marched on the Assembly to protest against Cohn-Bendit's expulsion from France.

For the first time politicians began to call for the Government's resignation. Waldeck Rochet, the Communist leader, demanded a popular front and declared that the Communist Party was "ready to assume all its responsibilities." René Capitant, the left-wing Gaullist, resigned from his party so as to avoid voting against it on the motion of censure. Mendès-France blamed the Government for the growing anarchy and said it was due to its "contemptuous monopoly" of all decisions during its ten years of power. There was near panic on the *Bourse* and only the closure of the Banks prevented a catastrophic run on the franc. Not only France, but the whole world was waiting for de Gaulle.

From the beginning de Gaulle had remained outwardly calm. He fulfilled his engagements and, having said that public order must be maintained, ostensibly left the details to his ministers. But everyone knew that he was directing his ministers behind the scenes. However it suddenly seemed that he had lost his touch. It was he who sanctioned the entry of the police into the Sorbonne; he was personally responsible for the employment of the riot squads. Yet when Pompidou returned from Iran and confronted him with the new situation in the University, he caved in so quickly that it looked as if he had panicked. Pompidou and not de Gaulle seemed to be in charge of the situation. To save face de Gaulle deliberately stuck to his State visit to Rumania and left Paris on May 14, the day after the one-day general strike. But when the strikes broke out again he cut short his stay and returned on Sunday, May 19. While still in Bucharest he had made his first public pronouncement: "Reform, yes, but shit in the bed, no."* It was oracular but unhelpful, the only immediate reply coming from the

* There are many refined translations of the phrase *"chi-en-lit."* Cassell's Dictionary gives "merry-andrew, masker, guy." But de Gaulle was undoubtedly using it in his barrack-room style, like *"pisse vinaigre."* Pompidou confirmed to the press that de Gaulle had used this phrase after the Cabinet Meeting on May 19.

Renault factory at Billancourt where workers in passive occupation of the buildings erected a banner inscribed "*Le chi-en-lit, c'est lui.*" Back in Paris, de Gaulle announced that he would speak to the nation on radio and television in the evening of Friday, May 24.

It was the ideal setting. Twice before in his life he had been called upon to save his country from disaster and twice he had succeeded. But neither previous crisis had arisen so unexpectedly nor seemed to depend so entirely upon him for its resolution. At least a hundred million Europeans were glued to their television sets to see or hear his speech. In Britain the ordinary programmes were interrupted with excerpts as he made it. It was a terrible flop. The gestures, the voice, the mobile eyebrows and the expressive mouth were all there as usual; but the message and even the authority were missing. It had been expected that he would sack some ministers, announce specific reforms, take charge of the situation by explaining to the people the consequences of their actions and urge them to return to work. He did none of these things. Instead he spoke in the vaguest generalities about the changes necessary and asked the people to show once more that they trusted *him*—in a referendum to be held in June.

Somehow it was all totally irrelevant. Things had gone far beyond a personal appeal. If de Gaulle had had some solution to offer or had even conveyed the impression that he was still in charge and would spell out his proposals day by day, the people would have rallied to him. But it was no longer a question of him or chaos. Chaos was already reigning and he had to convince the people that he knew how to replace it. As Robert Cottave, one of the leaders of the *Force Ouvrière*, said on British television immediately afterwards, "a referendum is a personal matter between the President and each individual; it has nothing to do with what is happening in France to-day." The proof of Cottave's dictum followed swiftly.

Within two days Pompidou had granted the unions a thirty-five per cent increase in the minimum basic wage and a shorter working week for the whole country, a surrender which could only result in inflation, loss of exports, a steep rise in the cost of living and perhaps devaluation. Yet when the union leaders presented their victory to the men occupying the factories, they would not accept it. "Take it back," they cried, "we want more." A few added "we want power," without knowing what it meant or how to get it. The strike went on. France was drifting into anarchy. De Gaulle's authority seemed to have evaporated completely.

That was also how it looked to the world. During the weekend following his broadcast de Gaulle was written off. In press and parliaments it was taken for granted that the referendum, through which he had hoped to confirm his authority, would not be held and that he would retire as soon as he could decently hand over to a successor. In France, as if to emphasise the futility of his intervention, violence reached a new peak within half an hour of his going off the air. In the Place de la Bastille thousands of students and young workers fought pitched battles with the riot police. They cut down trees, tore up pavements, overturned buses and cars to make barricades and answered tear gas with axe-handles and iron bars. Several hundred students stormed the *Bourse*, chanting "Temple of gold, temple of gold," smashed its windows, tore down the boards which displayed prices, and started a fire. Similar riots occurred in other cities. In Lyons a policeman was killed.

The Government began to give way. Pompidou met the trade union leaders and mortgaged the prosperity he had built up by conceding an all-round wage increase of rather more than ten per cent, a reduction in working hours and workers' contributions to social services, increased family allowances and pensions. He also announced that he had accepted the resignation of Peyrefitte, the Minister of Education.

Meanwhile the vultures crowded round the Gaullist bier. Mitterand, who had already said he was prepared to form a government, now announced that he was ready to offer himself as a candidate for the Presidency and proposed a provisional government of ten members. Mendès-France offered to lead this government so as to create "a new, more just, more socialist régime." Waldeck Rochet observed that no government of the Left could be formed without the participation of the Communist Party. De Gaulle himself remained supine, saying nothing and apparently bowing to the storm.

As he was later to admit, after the failure of his broadcast de Gaulle suffered one of his rare fits of despair. In his life he had contemplated total "withdrawal from history" after Dakar, during the Allied landings in North Africa, after his retirement in 1946 and after the failure of the *Rassemblement*. Now again, he was ready to resign. But he could not decide whether to try and secure the succession of Pompidou or hold an immediate general election and let him take his chance. Until he made up his mind there was no prospect of any leader coming forward who might combine the Centre and the Right and oppose the triumvirate who were so loudly staking their claim.

And then, as he was hesitating and not for the first or last time during those extraordinary weeks, the mood of the country began to change. As paralysis spread the people became afraid. There was rather less violence. The huge Communist demonstrations in Paris during the week-end in which the marchers chanted "*Adieu de Gaulle*," "*Pompidou à la Seine*," were perfectly orderly; although Cohn-Bendit had returned to France in disguise he seemed to have shot his bolt. But the collapse of de Gaulle's authority had produced a sense of shock which grew with uncertainty as to what might succeed him. Shopkeepers began to talk of revolution, to say that "they" wanted to kill everyone who owned property. In Switzerland it became impossible to find a room in a hotel because so many thousands of French people had gone there to exchange their money or buy gold. A few of the rich made preparations to send their children out of France. In many towns and in the universities die-hard Gaullists were reviving their commandos of *Rassemblement* days and laying in stocks of arms. There were rumours of intervention by the army and, for the first time since 1961, of the danger of civil war.

The whiff of change acted like oxygen on de Gaulle. On Wednesday, May 29 at 10.00 a.m. he left the Élysée with his wife and staff, ostensibly for Colombey. Travelling by helicopter it should have taken him less than two hours. He did not arrive until six in the evening. Although no one was to know it for certain for forty-eight hours, he had in fact visited the Commanders of the French Army in Germany, including his old friend and enemy General Massu, to find out whether he would have their support in restoring order. He got it on condition that he released the last of the O.A.S. prisoners, including General Salan. Sure of himself once more, de Gaulle acted. He ordered the release of Salan and eleven others including the notorious Colonel Argoud and announced that he would broadcast to the people that evening. In the afternoon, while he informed his Cabinet of what he was going to say, one of the largest counter-demonstrations ever seen in Paris was staged by his supporters. The French middle classes were bestirring themselves.

No one who heard de Gaulle that afternoon was ever likely to forget it. From the first few sentences in which he explained that, with things as they were, he was not going to resign, he was his old self. As he spat out the words "*Je ne me retirerai pas*," he electrified France and the listening world. Before he had finished he was in command of the situation. The referendum he brushed aside, saying that the situation prevented it being held. He refused to change his Prime Minister "whose worth, solidity and ability deserved the homage of all." He announced that he was dissolving the Assembly and that elections would be held "within the period laid down by the Constitution, unless an attempt is made to gag the entire French people, preventing them from expressing themselves at the same moment when they are prevented from living, by the same methods which are used to prevent the students from studying, the teachers from teaching, the workers from working."

As listeners sat up in their chairs he went on: "These methods are intimidation, deception, and tyranny exercised by groups long organised for the purpose by a party which is a totalitarian enterprise.

"If, therefore, this threatening situation continues, I shall be obliged, in order to maintain the Republic and in conformity with the Constitution, to adopt other methods than an immediate vote by the country."

Each listener knew that this reference to Article 16 of the Constitution, which gave him power to rule by decree in a case of national emergency, could not have been made unless de Gaulle was sure of the army. It meant that he was prepared once more to take emergency powers. After saying that he was conferring on the Prefects the status of his *Commissaires de la République* of Liberation days, de Gaulle ended: "France, in fact, is threatened by dictatorship. An attempt is being made to persuade her to resign herself to a power which would impose itself in the midst of national despair. That power would, of course, be essentially that of a conqueror—that is the power of totalitarian Communism. Naturally, to begin with they would colour it with deceptive appearances, using the ambition and hatred of discarded politicians. Afterwards, these persons would weigh no more than their own weight, which would not be heavy.

"No, the Republic will not abdicate. The people will recover their balance. Progress, independence and peace will triumph, together with liberty. '*Vive la République! Vive la France!*' "

The relief was almost tangible. After a month of growing anarchy, the voice of authority had sounded at last. Millions who would have been quite glad to see de Gaulle go a fortnight earlier and who had actually expected him to go at the beginning of the week, were now thankful that he was still there. It seemed that he and he alone could restore order. Next day, the beginning of Whitsun week-end, tanker lorries were again on the roads and stations distributing petrol. Chaban-Delmas dissolved Parliament in less than a minute and Pompidou announced his new government, shuffling Couve de Murville and Debré between the Foreign Office and Ministry of Finance. By Saturday the traffic along the Côte d'Azur resembled the height of the tourist season, with the difference that it was almost entirely French. Mitterand might comment that de Gaulle's broadcast was the "voice of dictatorship" and the Communists that it was "a real declaration of war," but nothing could dampen the spirits of the motorists who believed that the crisis had passed. By Monday men and women in their thousands began to return to work and by the end of the week only isolated factories remained occupied by strikers.

De Gaulle had pledged himself to restore order and hold a general election. He fulfilled both pledges simultaneously. He had outlined the basis of his campaign in his broadcast of May 30; now in a radio and television interview with Michel Droit on June 7 he amplified it. Although the Communist Party, as everyone knew, had been against the strikes and had done its utmost to act as "the fire-brigade" of the régime, de Gaulle used it as his bogy. The "totalitarian Communist enterprise" had exploited student unrest to try and paralyse the country and get rid of the President of the Republic. "One wondered, at one moment, whether our country was not going to slide into the void without reacting."[2] Of course he was right. As *The Times* was later to remark, the Communists had been doing their utmost to persuade the voters that they were not really a revolutionary party, but nice Left-wingers inspired as much by Pope John as Karl Marx. Yet no one doubted that they would have quickly discarded what de Gaulle called "walk-on characters" like Mendès-France and Mitterand and established their own system. Now their bluff was being called. The issue was simply "freedom or force." "The majority of the leaders of the revolt relish the idea of forcing the régime out of power . . . What is at stake is the freedom of the French people to choose their own government." Because it was basically the Communists that threatened that freedom, de Gaulle, and even more his campaign organiser Pompidou, hammered them until they earned the *Union Démocratique de la Cinquième Rèpublique* (U.D.V.), as de Gaulle's party was now called, the label of "the party of fear."

While the electorate was making up its mind to exercise its freedom, the Government restored order. The mass of workers returned peaceably to their jobs. Only at the Renault factory at Flins, where a student was drowned, and the Peugeot factory at Sochaux in Eastern France, where a young worker was shot dead, was there any serious fighting with the police. The hard core of students in Paris, on the other hand, having seen their revolt taken out of their hands, seemed determined to make a last stand. During the nights of June 10 and 11 thousands of them staged a pitched battle in the Latin quarter, erecting barricades once more, burning cars and buses, hurling paving-stones and home-made fire bombs at the police. The flames, the signal flares, the occasional loud explosion reminded onlookers of the uprising against the Germans in 1944. Seventy-two policemen and one hundred and ninety-four demonstrators were injured, hundreds of students were arrested, of whom thirty foreigners were deported next day.

By now the Government and public had had enough. The new Minister of the Interior, Raymond Marcellin, ordered the police to clear the Sorbonne and the Odéon Theatre which had been occupied by students for more than a month. Both were filthy and becoming a danger to health. On June 13 the police occupied the Odéon without serious trouble. Three days later the last students left the Sorbonne, which the Minister of Education announced would shortly be re-opened for educational purposes but "not as a hotel, a hostel or a hospital."[3] By July 1 peace had returned to the universities throughout France. Seven revolutionary students' organisations were banned. The people could go peacefully to the polls.

The results of the elections were staggering. In the first ballot, on June 23, the Gaullists won forty-six per cent of the votes cast and established a huge lead. Commentators pointed out that this could quickly be eroded if, as had happened before, de Gaulle's supporters failed to turn out for the second ballot when, in most constituencies, only one opposition candidate would stand. Both de Gaulle and Pompidou made impassioned appeals, begging the electorate to confirm its verdict by an overwhelming second vote. On June 30, it did. The U.D.V. won two hundred and ninety-nine out of four hundred and eighty-seven seats, giving them an overall majority of more than a hundred—a figure never remotely approached in the history of the Republic. The Communists were reduced to a mere thirty-four seats, the Federation of the Left to sixty. Giscard-d'Estaing's party, still an ally of de Gaulle's, rose from forty-two to fifty-eight seats. It was one of the most crushing victories ever attained in any democracy since the advent of adult suffrage. France had turned its back on anarchy and again rejected Communism. De Gaulle was more firmly in the saddle than ever.

What then had really happened during those turbulent weeks? Was the great uprising, which everyone recognised as a unique political event, simply a quirk of history? Had ten million French men and women been indulging in a bit of petulance, and were they now prepared to go back to normal, behave as if nothing had happened? Or was some deep current of unrest at work which would come to the surface again unless it were assuaged? During his days of uncertainty, de Gaulle had reflected deeply on these questions. As an avid reader of the press he was well aware that the Government had made mistakes. Overcrowding at schools and universities had become chronic, yet no Minister of Education had dared reduce the number of students or been able to accelerate the building programme. Slum clearance and hospital building were equally far behind schedule. Basic wages in industry had lagged behind prices and the gap between the wages of factory workers and the income of the lower executives or self-employed was widening. The unskilled had to work long hours to make ends meet. To add to the burden the Government had recently cut the share of medical expenses paid by the State and arbitrarily removed trade unionists from the Board of Management of the Social Security Fund.

De Gaulle's reform of the Civil Service had resulted in over-centralisation. Previously local government had been the life-blood of the French State. Mayors and "notables," members of the General Council and Municipalities ranked equally with the Prefects and carried a large part of the burden of administration. As members of the Electoral College which chose the President, they enjoyed consider-able local prestige. De Gaulle had not only destroyed the College and substituted a referendum but, by strengthening the office of Prefect, allowed Paris constantly to override local wishes. Gaston Deferre, Mayor of Marseilles, complained that he was unable to make the lowliest appointment or spend the smallest sum of money without consent from Paris.

But all these grievances were the normal stuff of politics, account-ing no doubt for the narrow majority by which de Gaulle's party had won the last general election and the speed with which it lost it in by-elections. They were neither acute nor wide-spread enough to produce a revolutionary situation. That was the strange thing. Apart from a few students and agitators, the French were not in a revolu-tionary mood. Neither the Communist Party nor any other recognised political organisation believed that a revolution had the slightest hope of success. France was prosperous. The day the riots started the London *Economist* remarked wistfully that, in spite of coming legislation to sanction the general rule of four weeks' holiday with pay, French workers were "still more concerned with the right to work than the right to laze."[4] Three weeks later the same journal was lamenting "the lunacy of virtually a whole people going on strike against itself with the thesis that it ought to pay itself more money for less work."[5]

But was it lunacy? Or was it exactly the opposite—a nation-wide release of pent up frustration held for the most part within civilised bounds? Except between students and the riot police, there was an absence of hate in this mammoth demonstration which was remarkable. Although a majority of those on strike belonged to the Socialist or Communist Parties, their attitude showed little of the traditional bitterness of the class war. Only two serious clashes between workers and police occurred, both in the motor car industry. Factory owners and managers talked freely to the men occupying their premises, professors argued patiently with students camping in the university buildings. Foreigners travelling through the country were often shown extraordinary consideration, Frenchmen going out of their way to find petrol and even lending them money. There was no hard and fast division between demonstrators and public. Property-owners, shop-keepers and civil servants marched with the rest, moved by an exaspera-tion which they found difficulty in expressing in a more precise way.

It seemed, therefore, that there was some deep-seated *malaise*, some stirring of the spirit which demanded more than mere adminis-trative reform. Although the young anarchists preached violence, beneath their preaching lay some genuine desire for new values. It was easy to laugh at their confused rhetoric when, in June, they were in-vited to appear on the B.B.C., but the question why these students, living in affluence, could find no satisfaction, still needed answering. If they sought only notoriety, what of the many thousands who inarticulately followed them?

De Gaulle was in no doubt about the answer. When, in his first broadcast, he had spoken of "the great mutation of society to which we must adapt ourselves," he had evoked no response because he was so plainly out of tune with what was happening in the streets of Paris. But it was neither cynicism nor electioneering which made him return to the subject in his interview with Michel Droit on June 7. In reply to Droit's question he admitted that our "machine civilisation" was bringing prosperity and new prospects, but he went on: "The trouble is that it is mechanical, which means that it catches man up, whoever he is and whatever he does, in a cog-and-wheel system so that the worker, for example, has no control over his own destiny, any more than ants in an ant-heap or termites in a termitary. Naturally, it is above all the Communist régimes that come to such a pass and that drive everything and everybody into dismal totalitarianism. But, in a differ-ent way and in different forms, capitalism also seizes and enslaves people."

De Gaulle's solution was "participation." "When people join together for a common economic task, for instance to operate an industry, by contributing either the necessary capital, or the directing, management or technical capacities, or the labour, the idea must be that they all form a firm together, a firm where they all have an interest, a direct interest in the output and efficient running. This requires that each of them be allocated by law a share of what the firm earns and of what it invests within itself thanks to its earnings. It also requires that they all be adequately informed of the way in which the firm is run and, through representatives, freely appointed by them all, are enabled to participate in the firm in its directing and its directing boards and thus to promote their interest, view-points and proposals. This is the course I have always thought was the right one. It is the course along which I have already taken a few steps, for instance in 1945, when, with my Government, I instituted joint production committees, and in 1959 and 1967, when I opened up the way to profit-sharing by ordinance. This is the course we must pursue."

Economists might sneer at the naïvety of de Gaulle's conception, but in every Western European democracy men had been searching for a formula to resolve the contradictions of capital and labour in a free but ancient society and as yet no one had evolved anything more specific. In Britain successive "declarations of intent" by governments, industrialists and trade unionists had produced more meagre results the more often they were repeated. De Gaulle, who had the power, might evoke the change of attitude which was needed. It was soon clear that he was going to try.

For a week after the elections the world waited to see what he would do with his renewed power. Then rumour began to spread in Paris. Once more de Gaulle was being dramatic and springing a surprise. Pompidou, the man who in the early days of the students' revolt had saved the Government, whose stature had so grown that even de Gaulle had felt constrained to praise him, of whom it was still being said that he was as indispensable to de Gaulle as de Gaulle was to him, was apparently to go and Couve de Murville to take his place. By June 9 rumour had become a certainty. Under the Constitution Pompidou would offer the President the resignation of his government the day the new Assembly met, Thursday, July 11. It would be accepted. Couve de Murville would take his place behind de Gaulle on the reviewing stand at the ceremonies of July 14, commemorating events which had so nearly been repeated.

Speculation ran riot. At first every political correspondent in Europe seemed determined that Pompidou was not being disgraced or discarded, but that he was being given a rest and remained the most likely successor to de Gaulle. The fact was that he was being relegated to the back-benches. Whether he ever re-emerged to accomplish another "mission entrusted to him by the nation," as de Gaulle suggested in his fulsome letter of dismissal, depended on his own inclinations, Couve de Murville's success or the direction that policy would now take under de Gaulle's fresh impulse. Soon it was being recalled that Pompidou had stood up to de Gaulle, first over Jouhaud's death sentence, recently over policy towards the students, and that de Gaulle could never work with people who opposed him. It was suggested that Pompidou, the grandson of a peasant, unknown until he became de Gaulle's political secretary, had begun to have ambitions of his own, to see himself as the heir-apparent; and that de Gaulle could never bear a rival, far less a Dauphin. All this was true and Pompidou's dismissal, like Debré's in 1962, was undoubtedly a sign that after the upheaval de Gaulle was again going to take things firmly into his own hands. However, there was another and more important reason for the change. Pompidou did not believe in "participation."

In addressing the newly elected Gaullist Deputies before the Assembly met, he had paid lip-service to the idea. "Whatever the resistance that might be conjured up, the interests one might wish to protect, it is necessary that these reforms be carried out. It is necessary to act, with prudence indeed, and with wisdom. But if we do not do it the country will turn away from us." He went on to eulogise de Gaulle: "It is no use, it is even criminal, to think of separating the government of General de Gaulle from the person of General de Gaulle . . . unity must come about in the name of General de Gaulle and the policy he conducts."[6] But loyal though he was, Pompidou's reservations were too obvious and too strong. As a banker he was never likely to accept the inefficiencies which must result from associating workers with management, particularly when the country had so much leeway to make up. Yet "participation" was de Gaulle's considered answer to the aspirations of the young and the frustrations of the workers. If it was to succeed it needed an executor who could obliterate his reservations in selfless dedication.

Whether Couve de Murville himself believed in the idea was doubtful, but also unimportant. As soon as his promotion was rumoured, journalists combed France for de Murville relations who could throw some light on the new Prime Minister's character. Surprisingly he was depicted as warm-hearted, generous, independent. Yet this calm, aloof member of an old French Protestant family had never given proof of independence in his long public life. Trained as an economist, he began his career as an *inspecteur de finance* and served successively the Third Republic, Pétain, Giraud, de Gaulle, the Fourth Republic and then de Gaulle again. He was the executor *par excellence,* and if any man could give "participation" practical application, it would be he.

Couve had already shown his hand. Two hours before de Gaulle nominated him Prime Minister, he had announced to the Assembly the measures he proposed as Finance Minister to meet the bill for the uprising. It had cost even more than had been anticipated—a vast increase in government expenditure due to the concessions Pompidou had made, and a run down of the reserves to defend the franc of between one and two billion dollars. Couve de Murville hoped to recoup at least part of this money by increasing the income tax paid by six hundred and fifty thousand of the richest people in France, by taxing companies, distilled spirits, and all but the smallest motor cars— a liberal-socialist approach plainly intended to earn the co-operation of workers in the innovations that were to come.

But "participation" lay in the future. Had de Gaulle other fresh impulses to offer? The answer came swiftly. Within a month of the elections he had shown himself in every other respect as overbearing and intolerant as ever. Although the completion of the Common Market within the Six on July 1 was the price he had agreed to pay for a common agricultural policy, he now did not hesitate to default. Without consulting his partners, he announced import quotas and export subsidies to protect French trade, breaking his engagements and postponing the completion of the market indefinitely. His partners, as always, meekly accepted his *diktat* and a few weeks later went further and withdrew their objections to applications for associate membership from Turkey and some African countries. Previously they had refused to discuss them before the British application for full membership had been properly dealt with. A tottering throne had not weakened de Gaulle's position within the Community.

He then turned on enemies nearer home. The strikers to hold out longest had been the radio and television journalists who were demanding assurances of greater objectivity in the presentation of programmes, particularly news. When, on July 12, they finally returned to work they issued a statement saying that, although they had received "no guarantee either of the impartiality of news or of television programmes," they were suspending their strike "as a gesture of appeasement." Like many gestures, it had the opposite effect. At the end of July the Government suddenly announced that, in the interest of efficiency, it was reducing the staff of the O.R.T.F. by forty per cent. Out of more than a hundred redundancies, sixty of those who had taken a leading part in advocating reform were dismissed or demoted. There was talk of suing the Government and of organising further strikes, but in the face of the electoral results it was soon clear that nothing would come of either move.

De Gaulle did not rest there. Police spies in jeans were again identified on the Left Bank as students returned for their examinations and it was reported that informers had supplied the police with a list of unofficial strike leaders in the factories. In the beginning of September, Jean-Louis Barrault, creator and director of the State Theatre at the Odéon, whom de Gaulle had specially elected for the post in 1959, was dismissed. Barrault had begun by protesting against the student occupation of the Odéon but in the end was won over by them and declared from the stage "Barrault, director of the Odéon Theatre, is dead." It was the humiliating function of his old friend, André Malraux, Minister of Culture, to tell him that his demise was official.

Having avenged himself upon those who had most obviously spurned him, de Gaulle turned to the world. It seemed that nothing had altered. He was as wayward and unpredictable as ever, interested only in proclaiming that internal unrest had in no way diminished the independence of France. The horrible Nigerian civil war was entering its final phase, with Federal troops poised to take the last few towns in Biafra and many thousands dying of starvation in the wake of both armies. The misery and slaughter had been seen on television and had shocked the world. Yet within the United Nations, the Organisation for African Unity and the British Commonwealth, governments had been unusually hesitant to take sides. The Ibos had first threatened the Federation by murdering the Northern and Western Federal Ministers two years previously, and however harsh the retaliation, every country which had recently gained its independence in Africa recognised that approval of the rebellion would only encourage similar movements among other tribes and might lead to more widespread rebellion and infinitely greater loss of life. In July the untiring efforts of Haile Selassie, the Emperor of Ethiopia, finally brought the two sides together in Addis Ababa for peace talks. No one was very sanguine about the outcome, but it seemed the last chance of ending the war by negotiation rather than by conquest. It was at this moment, on the very day that the delegates were assembling, that de Gaulle recognised Biafra.

It was a cynical gesture. If de Gaulle had thrown his weight behind Haile Selassie, if he had joined those who were protesting against the action of the British Government in honouring its treaty obligations and continuing to supply arms to the Federal forces, he could have claimed humanitarian motives. Although the British Government had good reasons for its decision, it was possible to differ honourably. But to recognise Biafra, without being able to do anything decisive to help it, could only stiffen the attitude of the Federal Government and make certain that the war would be ended by conquest rather than negotiation. De Gaulle did not care. His real reason for recognition was more squalid. French oil companies had been trying for months to wrest from Colonel Ojukwu oil concessions which belonged to Anglo-American firms. Recognition was the ultimate bribe with which de Gaulle hoped to sustain Ojukwu's resistance. With a shrug of distaste the governments of almost every country took note of the latest example of Gaullist independence.

But the horrors of Biafra were soon overshadowed by a greater tragedy. Since the beginning of the year, a drama more thrilling than fiction had been unfolding in Czechoslovakia. Provoked by the reintroduction of Stalinist methods in the previous year, Alexander Dubcek and a group of intellectuals in the praesidium managed in January to overthrow Novotny, the Stalinist General Secretary of the Czechoslovakian Communist Party. They then proceeded to humanise communism, revising the statutes of the Party, abolishing censorship of all means of communication, opening their frontiers and discussing with Western countries the possibility of economic and cultural cooperation. It was a metamorphosis planned to the last detail and carried through with a restraint which seemed at first to obviate interference. Czechoslovakia did not leave the Warsaw Pact as Hungary had done in 1956, nor denounce communism. Dubcek and his President, Svoboda, proclaimed their friendship with Russia, forbade organised opposition and acted only through the Czech Communist Party. But they had underestimated the catalytic effect of their actions.

For the past three years not only the Soviet Government but Gomulka in Poland, Kadar in Hungary and above all Ulbricht in East Germany had all been resisting liberal movements among the students and intellectuals of their own countries. Repression had once again approached Stalinist standards. Liberalisation to the extent proposed by Dubcek represented a threat to this conservative reaction which its leaders felt unable to contain. In July, the powers of the Warsaw Pact, minus Czechoslovakia and Rumania whose Prime Minister M. Ceausescu had supported Dubcek, met and issued the Warsaw Letter denouncing the Czech reforms as counter-revolutionary action instigated by Western imperialists. The Czechs stood their ground, proclaimed their loyalty both to the Warsaw Pact and to Communism and offered to meet their critics and explain. The Russians demanded a meeting outside Czechoslovakia. The Czechs refused but consented to military manoeuvres taking place on their territory. Russian, East German and Polish armour entered Czechoslovakia.

Reform and protest continued. When the manoeuvres were over the Russians refused to withdraw their troops, the Czechs refused to parley until they did. Eventually, on July 29, a meeting between the

Czechs, the Russians, Poles, East Germans, Hungarians and Bulgarians, took place at Cierna on the Czech-Ukrainian border. Unbelievably it seemed that the Czechs had won and Russian troops began to withdraw. But relief did not last long. Within a week the tone of the Russian press hardened and the Czechs were once more being accused of betraying Socialism and surrendering to counter-revolution. In spite, or perhaps because of a visit to Prague, Ulbricht became hysterical. Troop concentrations were reported on the Russian frontier and on August 21, Russian, East German and Polish units invaded Czechoslovakia. The occupation had begun.

Dubcek, the General Secretary of the Communist Party, Cernik, the Prime Minister, Smrkovsky, the President of the Assembly, were arrested at machine-gun point, manacled, abducted and thrown into Russian jails where they were treated little better than animals. But not even the three former colleagues of Novotny, who were believed to have invited the Russians to enter their country, could form a Quisling government, and Svoboda made it plain that he would not accept one if they did. For a week the world sat mesmerised while the television screen showed Czechs of every age shouting defiance at Russian soldiers, sitting down in front of their armour, setting fire to petrol tanks with burning paper, festooning guns with signs and slogans, telling the Russians to go home. "Workers unite or we will shoot you," read one of the bitterest cartoons, and at least eighty people died while the Russians kept up the pretence of "rescuing" the Czechs from counter-revolution. On August 23, Svoboda, with three ministers and three party members, two of whom were Novotny men, went to Moscow. As Svoboda refused to talk unless his other colleagues were present, Dubcek, Cernik and Smrkovsky were released from jail. For four days the Czechs resisted the Russian ultimatum. On August 30, they returned to Prague.

The price they had paid was the liberty they had tried so valiantly to give their country. The terms of the published "agreement" stipulated that censorship of the press should be reimposed and Russian troops be posted along the West German-Czech border; all other Russian troops would gradually withdraw. In return Dubcek's reforms were to be allowed to continue within the framework of socialism. But within hours it became clear that the Russians had no intention of honouring their side of the bargain. Tanks "withdrew" from some of the main squares and side streets, but no farther. Hundreds of Russian N.K.V.D. men landed at Prague airport and took over the administration. Cernik told pressmen that, in Moscow, Brezhnev had said he was prepared to wipe out three million Czechs to enforce obedience.

Pravda bore him out by speaking of a list of at least forty thousand people who were to be deported, no doubt for liquidation. Cernik advised "all the best brains" to leave the country, saying that, as he was not safe from arrest himself, he could not guarantee the safety of anyone else. An exodus began. The free radio-stations which had electrified listeners all over the world with the vividness of their reporting, went off the air. One announcer stopped in the middle of a sentence saying, "The Russians have arrived." With astounding rapidity darkness at noon descended once more upon Bohemia.

De Gaulle was apparently unmoved by this epic struggle. Czechoslovakia was not one of the countries he had visited in Eastern Europe and neither he nor France could claim even reflected credit for the courageous example the Czech people were setting. Usually so quick to comment upon other people's misfortunes or to take a side, he had no word of encouragement for the Czechs nor of approval or disapproval of his recent friends, the Russian leaders. While the French Communist Party roundly denounced the Russian action, de Gaulle's only recorded comment, during the first critical weeks of the Czech agony, was that it all stemmed from Yalta. The implication was that if France had not been excluded from that conference things might have been different, and that the agony of the Czechs was the fault not so much of the Russians as the Anglo-Saxons. De Gaulle's representatives supported the abortive resolution in the Security Council condemning the Russian action, but a demonstration in support of the Czechs was banned in Paris and only short excerpts of the thrilling scenes which appeared on British television were seen by French viewers.

De Gaulle's frustration was understandable. Dubcek's attempt to inject humanism into the communist world had not only stolen the political limelight, it had stripped the lasts shreds of credibility from de Gaulle's foreign policy. The *détente* with the Soviet Union for which he had sacrificed N.A.T.O., the vision of a Europe from the Atlantic to the Urals which he had dangled before a public baffled by his antipathy to the British, were finally exposed as chimeras. Domination remained the Kremlin's goal and de Gaulle's recent gestures of friendship could only be interpreted as serious errors of judgment. Once more France was in eclipse, yet de Gaulle had nowhere else to turn.

The explosion of the first French hydrogen bomb in the Pacific Ocean, which the world watched on television in between the processions of Russian tanks down the streets of Prague, no doubt gave some Frenchmen a comfortable feeling of security. What the Russians had done to Czechoslovakia they could not do to France with the same impunity. But the feeling was largely an illusion. It would be many years before France would become a credible thermo-nuclear power, if indeed she ever could. Meanwhile she was entirely dependent for her safety on the very forces with which she had refused to co-operate, the American, British, Dutch, Belgian and above all German troops under an integrated N.A.T.O. command.

Some Americans underlined the irony of de Gaulle's position. In the weeks before the Presidential elections, liberal delegates and candidates to the Party conventions dismissed the strangulation of Czech reform as just another quarrel among Communists. An article by Macnamara, until recently Secretary of State for Defence, stated that even if the United States did drop hydrogen bombs it could never avoid devastating retaliation, and this revived fears, which de Gaulle had often expressed, that the United States was interested only in its own freedom and would never risk nuclear war to defend Europe. Yet de Gaulle was not able to give Europe a lead. As the Russians began to threaten Rumania and Yugoslavia and the world to wonder whether the men in the Kremlin were afflicted with the same madness that drove Hitler into war, it was the German Chancellor, Dr. Kiesinger, who called for the rejuvenation of N.A.T.O. and President Johnson who warned the Russians against further aggression. De Gaulle, isolated, had nothing to say.

*   *   *

As parliaments and peoples returned from their summer holidays the whole great French exercise in civil disobedience began to recede into history. Compared with the Czech tragedy it soon looked no more than a frivolous escapade. In France life returned to normal. Everyone recognised that there would be difficulties but twice in de Gaulle's lifetime the French had lifted themselves out of greater catastrophes and it seemed possible they would do so again. Yet, as de Gaulle himself remarked, a nation cannot take three months' holiday and escape the consequences. By November the bills were being presented. The franc weakened. Those engaged in international business began to insure against loss by transferring cash into other currencies. To prevent a collapse the bankers met at Basle and offered France enough credit for a mild devaluation. The plan was put to de Gaulle.

But de Gaulle could not face the humiliation. Devaluation did not fit his vision of France. While negotiations had been going on he had said it was absurd; now he appeared on television to tell the country that it must make the sacrifices necessary to preserve the value of the franc. Demonstrations were banned, taxes increased and exchange rigidly controlled. Residents of France wishing to go abroad could only take two hundred francs with them and those who had more were liable to have their cars and jewels impounded at the frontier. De Gaulle, in 1968, was asking the French people to accept the austerity he had feared to impose on them at the behest of Mendès-France more than twenty years earlier.

It was a magnificent gesture, but how much sense did it make? What was needed was a revision of the international monetary system and this de Gaulle refused to contemplate except on his own terms. Yet he was not in a position to dictate. The Germans had stood up to him and refused to devalue the mark. Most mortifying of all, he had had to accept loans from the Anglo-Saxons. Even so, France was faced with a long and bitter struggle for recovery. Within a few days of de Gaulle's broadcast railwaymen and factory workers were complaining that the increases they had won in the summer had already been wiped out. The Unions were threatening to strike, the students grumbling that the promised reforms had not materialised. De Gaulle might hold down the lid of the cauldron through the winter, but there were few who believed that he could prevent it eventually from boiling over.

The truth was that the upheavals of 1968 had exposed the fantasies of Gaullism even to de Gaulle's followers. Until the summer de Gaulle had been able to persuade a majority of his countrymen that there was substance in his vision of a France independent of all foreign organisations, the arbiter of the civilised and patron of the under-developed world. Now most Frenchmen realised that they were as dependent upon the political and economic forces of the world as the rest of Western Europe. De Gaulle's own position had changed. Electorally his power was unassailable, yet he had won his victory in June not as the natural saviour but as the only leader capable of withstanding Communism. Had there been a viable alternative candidate in May, he would have been accepted with open arms.

*   *   *

But if the legend was wearing thin, de Gaulle was still a towering figure. It was more than forty years since he had first challenged fashionable thought in his lectures to the École Supérieure, and he had remained in the front line of protagonists ever since. Each decade had seen him in a different role. In the nineteen thirties he had been the military expert, lobbying politicians to accept his views. In the nineteen-forties he had become a rebel, first against the armistice and later against the resurrection of the régime of the parties and a sovereign Assembly. He had resigned rather than accept the role they allotted him. In the nineteen-fifties he had championed narrow nationalism and denounced the European Defence Community; in the nineteen-sixties he had crushed it by surrendering Algeria. Then, when the tide of unrest which was sweeping the world struck France at the end of the decade, he checked it almost alone and gave France—and civilisation— a breathing space.

Not all de Gaulle's policies have turned out well for France, but in every cause for which he has fought he has been true to his own vision. No breath of scandal, no hint of private interest has ever touched his name. Some men hate him for what he has done, more for the way he has done it. He has dissimulated, tricked and discarded those who served him. Sometimes he has been vindictive, often ruthless. He is capable of gratitude—to his comrades of Free France and to Lady Churchill to whom he has written regularly in his own hand since Sir Winston's death—but he does not easily forgive those who have turned against him. He does not seek to be loved, yet he is not a monster. No man has pursued his goal more relentlessly, yet de Gaulle has rejected dictatorship when it was within his grasp and both militarily and politically has sought to save lives rather than squander them. No statesman has been less careful of his own safety. By any standards de Gaulle has greatness.

Yet history may judge him more harshly than his contemporaries. If it emerges that in restoring self-confidence to the French people he has prevented the union of Western Europe, if his jealousy of the Anglo-Saxons leads to an expansion of Communism, then succeeding generations may revile rather than revere his name. A part of greatness is bestowed by events. As with other giants of the twentieth century, de Gaulle's stature must stand the test of time.

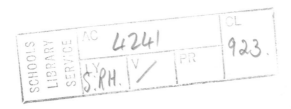

NOTES AND REFERENCES

CHAPTER I DESTINED FOR A SOLDIER

1. *War Memoirs of General de Gaulle. Volume I. The Call to Honour.* Translated by Jonathan Griffin. Collins. London. 1955. p.9.
2. *Letters of the Empress Frederick.*
   Macmillan. London. 1928. pp.76-7.
3. *France from Behind the Veil.*
   Count Paul Vassili. Cassell. London. 1914. p.35.
4. Op. Cit. *The Call to Honour.* Charles de Gaulle. p.10.
5. *Charles de Gaulle.*
   Philippe Barrés. Paris. 1941. p.22.
6. Op. Cit. *France from Behind the Veil.* Vassili. p.96.
7. *World of Yesterday.*
   Stefan Zweig. Cassell. London. 1943. p.114.
8. *La France et Son Armée.*
   Charles de Gaulle. Hutchinson. London. 1948. pp.135-6.
9. *Basic Vérités.*
   Charles Péguy. Translated by Ann & Julien Green. Random Books. New York. 1943. p.155.
10. Ditto. p.235.
11. Ditto. p.275.
12. Op. Cit. *The Call to Honour.* Charles de Gaulle. p.10.
13. *Charles de Gaulle. Général de France.*
    Lucien Nachin. Berger-Levrault. Éditions Colbert. Paris. 1944. p.22.
14. *Pétain et de Gaulle.*
    J. R. Tournoux. Plon. Paris. 1964. p.51.
15. *General Hering's Archives.* Op. Cit. *Pétain et de Gaulle.* J. R. Tournoux. p.381.
16. Op. Cit. *The Call to Honour.* Charles de Gaulle. p.10.
17. Op. Cit. *Pétain et de Gaulle.* J. R. Tournoux. p.51.
18. *Trente Ans avec Pétain.*
    General Sérigny. Plon. Paris. 1959. p.142.
19. *General Hering's Archives.* Op. Cit. *Pétain et de Gaulle.* J. R. Tournoux. p.383.
20. Op. Cit. *The Call to Honour.* Charles de Gaulle. p.10.

21. Op. Cit. *La France et Son Armée*. Charles de Gaulle. p.150.
22. Op. Cit. *Charles de Gaulle*. Lucien Nachin. p.28.
23. Op. Cit. *Pétain et de Gaulle*. J. R. Tournoux. p.55.
See also *Charles de Gaulle*. Lucien Nachin. pp.31-2.

CHAPTER II CLIMBING THE LADDER

1. Op. Cit. *La France et Son Armée*. Charles de Gaulle. p.98.
2. Op. Cit. *Pétain et de Gaulle*. J. R. Tournoux. p. 91.
3. Ditto. p. 387.
4. Ditto. pp. 88 and 389.
5. Ditto. p. 88.
6. Ditto. p. 96.
7. *Fantassin de Gascoigne*. André Laffargue. Flammarion. Paris. 1962. pp. 124–5.
8. Op. Cit. *Pétain et de Gaulle*. J. R. Tournoux. p. 98.
9. Ditto. p. 90.
10. Ditto. p. 101.
11. Op. Cit. *Charles de Gaulle*. Lucien Nachin. p. 48.
12. Ditto. p. 45.
13. *Bulletin de l'Association des Amis de l'École Supérieure de Guerre*. Signed J. H. July 1963. Also J. R. Tournoux. op. cit. *Pétain et de Gaulle*. pp. 124–5.
14. Op. Cit. *Pétain et de Gaulle*. J. R. Tournoux. p.104.
15. Ditto. p.104.
16. The text of the lectures was published in the *Revue Militaire Française* (March, 1928, June, 1930 and June, 1931). The lectures were also published by Berger-Levrault as brochures entitled *L'Action de Guerre et le Chef* (1928), *Du Caractère* (1930), *Du Prestige* (1931). Later de Gaulle expanded them into a book, *Le Fil de l'Épée* (Paris 1932) adding two chapters, one entitled *De la Doctrine*, which he had originally written for the *Revue Militaire Française* in 1925, and another *La Politique et le Soldat*.
17. *Le Flambeau. Revue Militaire d'Information*. Charles de Gaulle. Berger-Levrault Éditeurs. April, 1927.
18. Op. Cit. *Charles de Gaulle*. Lucien Nachin. p.54.
19. Ditto. p.56.
20. Op. Cit. *Pétain et de Gaulle*. J. R. Tournoux. p.129.
1. Op. Cit. *Charles de Gaulle*. Lucien Nachin. p.57.
2. Op. Cit. *Pétain et de Gaulle*. J. R. Tournoux. p.135.
3. Ditto. p.131.
4. Op. Cit. *Charles de Gaulle*. Lucien Nachin. p.56.
5. There is a photograph of the original letter in *Pétain et de Gaulle*. J. R. Tournoux. p.506.

CHAPTER III AGAINST THE GRAIN

1. Op. Cit. *Charles de Gaulle*. Lucien Nachin. p.58.
2. Ditto. p.59.
3. *Le Fil de l'Épée*.
   Charles de Gaulle. Berger-Levrault. Paris. 1944.
   Avant-propos p.VIII.
4. Ditto. p.154.
5. Ditto. *Avant-Propos* p.XII.
6. *Journal des Anciens Enfants de Troupe*.
   November, 1932. Quoted by Nachin in *Charles de Gaulle*. p.65.
7. *Memoirs. Volume I*.
   Basil Liddell Hart. Cassell. London. 1965. pp.103-4.
8. *Private Papers*.
   Basil Liddell Hart. A more moderate comment is given in his *Memoirs*.
   Volume I. p.274.
9. *Venu de ma Montagne*.
   Paul Reynaud. Flammarion. Paris. 1960. p.421.
10. Ditto. p.429.
11. Ditto. p.434.
12. Ditto. Annexe V. p.506.
13. *Nine Troubled Years*.
   Viscount Templewood (The Rt. Hon. Sir Samuel Hoare). Collins.
   London. 1964. p.160.
14. Op. Cit. *Pétain et de Gaulle*. J. R. Tournoux. p.159.
15. *Hitler: A Study in Tyranny*.
   Alan Bullock. Odhams. London. 1952. p.135.
16. Op. Cit. *Venu de ma Montagne*. Paul Reynaud. p.476.
17. Op. Cit. *Pétain et de Gaulle*. J. R. Tournoux. p.159.
18. *Mémoires: "Fragments."*
   Léon Blum. Albin Michel. Paris. 1944. p.114.
19. Op. Cit. *The Call to Honour*. Charles de Gaulle. p.31.
20. *Une Invasion est-elle encore Possible?* General Chauvineau. Berger-Levrault.
   Paris. 1939.
21. *De Gaulle Entre Deux Mondes*. P.-M. de la Gorce. Fayard. Paris. 1964.
22. Op. Cit. *The Call to Honour*. Charles de Gaulle. p.33.
23. See photostat of title page in *Pétain et de Gaulle*. J. R. Tournoux. p.511.

CHAPTER IV ONSLAUGHT

1. Op. Cit. *Charles de Gaulle*. Lucien Nachin. p.88.
2. Op. Cit. *Pétain et de Gaulle*. J. R. Tournoux. p.185.

3. *Au Coeur de la Mêlée.*
   Paul Reynaud. Flammarion. Paris. 1951. p.287.
4. Op. Cit. *Charles de Gaulle.* Lucien Nachin. p.90.
5. Op. Cit. *Pétain et de Gaulle.* J. R. Tournoux. p.185.
6. Op. Cit. *The Call to Honour.* Charles de Gaulle. p.33.
7. Op. Cit. *De Gaulle Entre Deux Mondes.* P.-M. de la Gorce. p.126.
8. Op. Cit. *The Call to Honour.* Charles de Gaulle. p.35.
9. Op. Cit. *Mémoires: "Fragments."* Léon Blum. p.116.
10. Op. Cit. *The Call to Honour.* Charles de Gaulle. p.34.
11. Ditto. p.37.
12. Ditto. p.40.
13. Ditto. p.40.
14. Ditto. p.41.
15. Ditto. p.43.
16. Ditto. p.43-4.
17. Op. Cit. *Pétain et de Gaulle.* J. R. Tournoux. p.195.
    Also *Documents.* p.412.
18. *Abbeville.*
    Major Gehring. Quoted by de Gaulle in *Call to Honour.* pp.52-3.
19. Op. Cit. *The Call to Honour.* Charles de Gaulle. p.46.

CHAPTER V THE BOTTOM OF THE PIT

1. Op. Cit. *The Call to Honour.* Charles de Gaulle. p.61.
2. Ditto. p.63.
3. *The Second World War. Vol. II. Their Finest Hour.*
   Winston S. Churchill. Cassell. London. 1949. p.138.
4. Op. Cit. *The Call to Honour.* Charles de Gaulle. p.70.
5. Op. Cit. *Their Finest Hour.* Winston S. Churchill. p.142.
6. Op. Cit. *The Call to Honour.* Charles de Gaulle. p.76.
7. Op. Cit. *Their Finest Hour.* Winston S. Churchill. p.181.
8. Ditto. p.187.
9. Op. Cit. *Au Coeur de la Mêlée.* Paul Reynaud confirms the danger of
   arrest. p.504.
10. Op. Cit. *The Call to Honour.* Charles de Gaulle. p.86.

SPECIAL NOTE

General Spears, in *Assignment to Catastrophe* has written a first-hand account of his departure from Bordeaux with de Gaulle and de Courcel which both the latter have contradicted. The contradiction will plague historians for years to come. I have accepted General Spears's version because it was too detailed and unusual a story for any man in those circumstances to invent, and he made his notes in the aeroplane at the time; and also because de Gaulle had every reason for concealing the fact that he was beholden to the British and had escaped with Spears's help. This does not mean that either de Gaulle or de Courcel were deliberately lying. On the contrary, I have found too many instances of people's memories (including my own) being coloured by what they have wished to think, to doubt their good faith. It was of immense importance to de Gaulle's purpose in 1940 that he could claim to be a Minister of the last independent French Government and therefore the heir to legitimate power; in support of this claim he naturally asserted that he left France of his own free will. Hence his insistence on the "fact" that Churchill had put the aeroplane at *his* disposal whereas the truth was that, by June 17, the movements of all British aircraft in and out of France were under British control—in this case that of the Ambassador.

CHAPTER VI THE LONE REBEL

1. Op. Cit. *Their Finest Hour*. Winston S. Churchill. pp.193-4.
2. Op. Cit. *The Call to Honour*. Charles de Gaulle. p.89.
3. *War Memoirs of General de Gaulle. Volume I. The Call to Honour. Documents.* Translated by Jonathan Griffin. Collins. London. 1955. pp.12-13.
4. Op. Cit. *The Call to Honour*. Charles de Gaulle. p.103.
5. Ditto. p.99.
6. Op. Cit. *The Call to Honour. Documents.* pp.26-7.
7. *The Eden Memoirs. The Reckoning.* The Earl of Avon. Cassell. London. 1965. p.127.
8. *De Gaulle contre le Gaullisme.* Admiral Muselier. Éditions du Chêne. Paris. 1946. p.13.
9. Op. Cit. *The Call to Honour. Documents.* p.20.

CHAPTER VII A LUCKY THROW

1. Op. Cit. *The Call to Honour*. Charles de Gaulle. p.121.
2. Ditto. p.133.
3. Ditto. p.133.
4. *"Into Battle."* Speeches by The Right Hon. Winston S. Churchill, P.C., M.P. Compiled by Randolph S. Churchill. Cassell. London. 1941. October 8, 1940. p.287.
5. Op. Cit. *The Call to Honour. Documents.* p.46.
6. Ditto. p.47.
7. Ditto. p.57.
8. Op. Cit. *The Call to Honour*. Charles de Gaulle. p.139.

CHAPTER VIII FROM GAMBLER TO PROPHET

1. Op. Cit. *The Call to Honour*. Charles de Gaulle. p.153.
2. Told to the author by Lady Churchill.

CHAPTER IX AT WAR WITH WHOM?

1. Op. Cit. *The Call to Honour*. Charles de Gaulle. p.192.
2. Ditto. p.195.
3. *The Memoirs of Lord Chandos*. Bodley Head. London. 1960. pp.247-52.

CHAPTER X FLIRTING WITH THE BEAR

1. *Le Journal Officiel (France Combattante)* is in the British Museum.
2. Op. Cit. *The Call to Honour*. Charles de Gaulle. p.216.
3. Op. Cit. *The Call to Honour. Documents.* p.251.
4. Op. Cit. *The Call to Honour*. Charles de Gaulle. p.246.

CHAPTER XI OUT IN THE COLD

1. *The Second World War. Volume III. The Grand Alliance.*
   Winston S. Churchill. Cassell. London. 1950. p.578.
2. *I Was There.*
   Admiral Leahy. London. Gollancz. 1960. p.74.
3. *Charles de Gaulle. The Crucial Years. 1943-1944.*
   A. L. Funk. University of Oklahoma. 1959. p.32.
4. *Diplomat Among Warriors.*
   Robert Murphy. Collins. London. 1964. p.151.

CHAPTER XII A WAITING GAME

1. Op. Cit. *Pétain et de Gaulle.* J. R. Tournoux. p.297.
2. Ditto. p.297.
3. *War Memoirs of General de Gaulle. Volume II. Unity. 1942-1944.*
   Translated by Richard Howard. Weidenfeld and Nicolson. London.
   1960. p.48.

See also *Appels et Discours du Général de Gaulle.*
1940-1944. Published in Paris during German Occupation. 1944. p.88.
4. Op. Cit. *Pétain et de Gaulle.* J. R. Tournoux. p.298.
5. Op. Cit. *Unity.* General de Gaulle. p.58.
6. *The Second World War. Volume IV. The Hinge of Fate.*
Winston S. Churchill. Cassell. London. 1951. p.569.
7. Op. Cit. *The Reckoning.* Earl of Avon. p.354.
8. Op. Cit. *Unity.* General de Gaulle. p.79.
9. *Roosevelt and Hopkins.*
Robert E. Sherwood. Harper. New York. 1948. p.340.
See also Op. Cit. *Diplomat Among Warriors.* Robert Murphy. pp.215-16.
10. Op. Cit. *Unity.* General de Gaulle. p.81.
11. Ditto. p.85.
12. Op. Cit. *Roosevelt and Hopkins.* Robert E. Sherwood. p.956.
De Gaulle originally said this to Admiral Stark who urged him to repeat
it to Roosevelt.
See also *Hostile Allies.*
Milton Viorst. Macmillan. London. 1965. p.144.
13. Op. Cit. *Hostile Allies.* Milton Viorst. p.144.
See also *The Blast of War.*
Harold Macmillan. Macmillan. London. 1967. p.257.
14. Op. Cit. *Unity.* General de Gaulle. p.105.
15. Ditto. p.107.

CHAPTER XIII THE DUEL

1. Op. Cit. *Charles de Gaulle. The Crucial Years.* A. L. Funk. p.131.
2. Op. Cit. *The Hinge of Fate.* Winston S. Churchill. p.729.
3. Op. Cit. *Unity.* General de Gaulle. p.114.
4. Ditto. p.119.
5. Ditto. p.120.
6. *Un Seul But, La Victoire.*
Henri Giraud. René Julliard. Paris. 1949. p.134.

CHAPTER XIV PLANNING A TAKE-OVER

1. Op. Cit. *Unity.* General de Gaulle. p.141.
2. Op. Cit. *Charles de Gaulle. The Crucial Years.* A. L. Funk. p.158.
3. Ditto. p.174.
4. Op. Cit. *Unity.* General de Gaulle. p.137.
5. Op. Cit. *Diplomat Among Warriors.* Robert Murphy. p.228.

6. Op. Cit. *Hostile Allies*. Milton Viorst. p.189.
7. *Three Years with Eisenhower*.
   Captain H. C. Butcher. Heinemann. London. 1946. p.404.
8. *Old Men Forget*.
   Duff Cooper. Rupert Hart-Davis. London. 1953.
9. *La IV République et sa Politique Extérieure*.
   Alfred Grosser. Armand Colin. Paris. 1961. p.18.

CHAPTER XV THE RETURN TO FRANCE

1. *The Second World War. Volume V. Closing the Ring*.
   Winston S. Churchill. Cassell. London. 1952. p.536.
2. *Histoire de La Libération*.
   Robert Aron. Fayard. Paris. 1959. p.79.
3. Ditto. p.81.
4. Ditto. p.84.
5. Op. Cit. *Charles de Gaulle. The Crucial Years*. A. L. Funk. p.280.
   See also Op. Cit. *I was There*. Admiral Leahy. pp.244 and 273-4.
6. Op. Cit. *Unity*. General de Gaulle. p.243.
7. Ditto. p.246.
8. *S.O.E. in France*.
   M. R. D. Foot. H.M. Stationery Office. 1966. Chapter XIV and Appendix 6.
9. *Is Paris Burning?*
   Larry Collins and Dominique Lapierre. Gollancz. London. 1965. p.145.
10. Ditto. p.216.
    See also Op. Cit. *Unity*. General de Gaulle. p.303.
11. Op. Cit. *Unity*. General de Gaulle. p.305.
12. Ditto. p.307.
13. Op. Cit. *Is Paris Burning?* Collins and Lapierre. p.318.
14. Op. Cit. *Unity*. General de Gaulle. p.308.
15. Ditto. p.309.
16. Op. Cit. *Is Paris Burning?* Collins and Lapierre. p.320.
17. Ditto. pp.332-3.
18. *De Gaulle Triumphant*.
    Robert Aron. Translated by Humphrey Hare. Putnam. London. 1964. p.94.
19. Op. Cit. *Is Paris Burning?* Collins and Lapierre. p.336.

CHAPTER XVI POWER AND GLORY

1. *Crusade in Europe.*
   Dwight D. Eisenhower. Heinemann. London. 1948. p.326.
2. *France 1940-1955.*
   Alexander Werth. Robert Hale. London. 1956. p.244.
3. Op. Cit. *De Gaulle Entre Deux Mondes.* P.-M. de la Gorce. p.340.
4. Op. Cit. *Histoire de la Libération.* Robert Aron. p.640.
5. *Le Procès du Maréchal Pétain. Compte Rendu Sténographique.* Albin Michel.
   Paris. Volume I. p.31.
6. Ditto. Volume II. p.891.
7. *War Memoirs of General de Gaulle. Volume III. Salvation.* 1944-1946.
   Translated by Richard Howard. Weidenfeld and Nicolson. London.
   1961. p.33.
8. Ditto. p.151.
9. Ditto. p.155.

CHAPTER XVII THE DIZZY HEIGHTS

1. *The Second World War. Volume VI. Triumph and Tragedy.*
   Winston S. Churchill. Cassell. London. 1954. p.217.
2. Op. Cit. *Pétain et de Gaulle.* J. R. Tournoux. p.329.
3. The minutes of the three Stalin-de Gaulle meetings were published by
   the Soviet Foreign Ministry in Moscow in 1959, *Soviatska-Frantsuzskie
   Otnosheniya.* 1941-1945.
   See *Russia at War,* 1941-1945. Alexander Werth. Pan Books. London.
   1965. pp.825 onwards.
   Also *De Gaulle.* Alexander Werth. Penguin. London. 1965. pp.183-4.
4. Op. Cit. *Salvation.* General de Gaulle. pp.8-9.
5. *Politics in Post-War France.*
   Philip Williams. Longmans, Green. London. 1954. p.13.
6. The three issues of *Les Vivants* are available in the Bibliothèque
   Nationale.
   See also Op. Cit. *France 1940-1955.* Alexander Werth. pp.250-251.
7. Op. Cit. *France 1940-1955.* Alexander Werth. p.228.
8. Op. Cit. *De Gaulle Entre Deux Mondes.* P.-M. de la Gorce. p.361.
9. Op. Cit. *Salvation.* General de Gaulle. p.130.
10. Ditto. p.294.
11. Ditto. p.278.
12. Op. Cit. *Pétain et de Gaulle.* J. R. Tournoux. p.361.
13. Op. Cit. *Salvation.* General de Gaulle. p.279.
14. Ditto. p.279.

CHAPTER XVIII DISILLUSION AND DEFIANCE

1. Op. Cit. *Salvation*. General de Gaulle. p.281.
2. *Le Monde*. June 17, 1946.
3. Op. Cit. *De Gaulle Entre Deux Mondes*. P.-M. de la Gorce. p.467.
4. Ditto. p.478.
5. *Keesing's Contemporary Archives*. Col. 8527 B.
6. *Major Addresses*. French Embassy.
7. Op. Cit. *France 1940–1955*. Alexander Werth. p. 375.
8. *Keesing's Contemporary Archives*. Col. 8948.
9. *Ibid*. Col. 8893.
10. *Combat*. October 29, 1947.
11. *Le Monde*. September 20, 1948.
12. *Journal Officiel de la République Française*. September 21, 1948.
13. *Le Monde*. November 11, 1952.
14. Ditto. May 21, 1953.
15. Speech. August 24, 1954. Quoted by P.-M. de la Gorce. Op. Cit. *De Gaulle Entre Deux Mondes*. p. 511.
16. Op. Cit. *Call to Honour*. Charles de Gaulle. p. 86.
17. *La Tragédie du Général*.
    J. R. Tournoux. Paris. 1967. p.234.
18. Op. Cit. *Salvation*. General de Gaulle. p.284.

CHAPTER XIX ON THE BRINK

1. *Journal Officiel de la République Française (Alger)*. January 30, 1944.
   See also *Keesing's Contemporary Archives*. Col. 6291.
2. *De Gaulle's Republic*.
   Philip Williams and Martin Harrison. Longmans. London. 1960. p.33.
3. Op. Cit. *Pétain et de Gaulle*. J. R. Tournoux. p.310.
4. Op. Cit. *La Tragédie du Général*. J. R. Tournoux. p.188.
5. Ditto. p.221.
6. Ditto. p.241.
7. Ditto. p.241.
8. *L'Espérance Trahie*.
   Jacques Soustelle. Éditions de L'Alma. Paris. 1962. pp.31-2.

CHAPTER XX THE RESTORATION

1. Op. Cit. *De Gaulle Entre Deux Mondes.* P.-M. de la Gorce. p.535.
2. Ditto. p.536.
3. *Les 13 Complots Du 13 Mai.*
   Merry and Serge Bromberger. Fayard. Paris. 1959. pp.137-8.
4. Op. Cit. *De Gaulle's Republic.* Williams and Harrison. p.55.
5. *Keesing's Contemporary Archives.* Col. 16258.
6. *Le Figaro.* May 17, 1958.
7. *Le Monde.* May 28, 1953.
8. *Journal Officiel.* May 27, 1953.
9. Ditto. June 2, 1958.

CHAPTER XXI TRUTH OR TREASON

1. *The de Gaulle Revolution.*
   Alexander Werth. Robert Hale. London. 1960. p.186.
2. *Le Monde.* June 5, 1958.
3. *Le Monde.* October 5, 1958.
4. Op. Cit. *The de Gaulle Revolution.* Alexander Werth. p.349.
5. Ditto. p.350.
6. *Press Conference.* March 25, 1959.
7. *L'Echo d'Oran.* April 30, 1959.
8. Op. Cit. *L'Espérance Trahie.* Jacques Soustelle. p.114.
9. Op. Cit. *De Gaulle's Republic.* Williams and Harrison. p.226.
10. Op. Cit. *L'Espérance Trahie.* Jacques Soustelle. p.141.
11. Op. Cit. *De Gaulle Entre Deux Mondes.* P.-M. de la Gorce. p.646.
12. Broadcast. November 4, 1960. French Embassy.
13. Op. Cit. *De Gaulle Entre Deux Mondes.* P.-M. de la Gorce. p.656.
14. *Keesing's Contemporary Archives.* Col. 19022.
15. *De Gaulle and His Murderers.*
    Joachim Joesten. Douglas, Isle of Man. 1964. p.107.

CHAPTER XXII KING AT LAST

1. *Les Mots du Général.* Ernest Mignon. Fayard. Paris. 1962. There are
   many versions of de Gaulle's aphorisms. M. Mignon has collected some
   of the best.
2. *Journal Officiel.* October 5, 1962.
3. Op. Cit. *La Tragédie du Général. Documents.* J. R. Tournoux. pp. 650–1.

4. Ditto. p.419.
5. *Paris-Presse*. May 22, 1965.
6. *Journal Officiel*. May 26, 1964.
Speech by Maurice Faure.
7. The programme was widely reported and excerpts were shown on British Television; but see, in particular, Linda Blandford's article in *The Sunday Times*. December 17, 1967.

CHAPTER XXIII ALONE UPON A PEAK

1. Op. Cit. *The Call to Honour*. Charles de Gaulle. p.9.
2. *De Gaulle and the World*.
W. W. Kulski. Syracuse University Press. New York. 1966. p.192.
3. *Bulletin d'Information du Ministère des Armées*.
4. *Annual Register*. 1960. p.256.
5. *Press Conference*. July 23, 1964.
6. *Broadcast*. September 5, 1960.
7. Speech at *Assises Nationales du R.P.F.* Marseilles. April 17, 1948.
8. Speech. March 16, 1950. Quoted by Roger Massip.
De Gaulle et l'Europe. Flammarion. Paris. 1963. p.54.
9. *Le Monde*. September 15, 1958.
10. *Keesing's Contemporary Archives*. Col. 18963.
11. *L'Année Politique*. 1962. p.672.
12. *Press Conference*. September 5, 1961.
13. *Keesing's Contemporary Archives*. Col. 19509.
14. *Discours et Messages*.
Berger-Levrault. Paris. 1946. p.440.
15. *Le Monde*. July 14, 1964.
16. *Le Monde*. November 24, 1961.
17. *Journal Officiel de la République Française*. June 14, 1962.
18. Speech of M. Herzog, High Commissioner for Sport. *Le Figaro*. June 11, 1962.
19. *Press Conference*. November 27, 1967. French Embassy, London.
20. *Le Monde*. January 30, 1968.

CHAPTER XXIV PILLAR OF GOLD

1. Op. Cit. *Salvation*. General de Gaulle. p.231.
2. Ditto. p.99.
3. Broadcasts. July 12, September 5, 1961. French Embassy.
4. Press Conference. October 26, 1966. *Le Monde*.

CHAPTER XXV THE BUBBLE BURSTS

1. *The Times*. May 7, 1968.
2. Text from the French Embassy.
3. *Le Monde*. June 17, 1968.
4. *The Economist*. May 3, 1968.
5. *The Economist*. May 24, 1968.
6. Quoted by Charles Hargrove. *The Times*. July 5, 1968.

BIBLIOGRAPHICAL NOTES

Most of the characters who have held the world's stage since 1870, when this story really begins, have left memoirs or written first-hand accounts of some particular event. Since a list of all the books consulted or read would be unnecessarily long I give here those I have found most helpful or stimulating at each phase of de Gaulle's long life. I have named separately books about de Gaulle which seem to me important and have listed at the end his own published works. In "Notes and References" I have given particulars of all books from which quotations are taken. I have included some other books but, except in cases where I have not easily found the book in library catalogues, here given only the author and title.

Of the standard histories I have relied upon the last two volumes of the New Cambridge Modern History, *Material Progress and World-Wide Problems* 1870-98 edited by F. H. Hinsley, and *The Era of Violence* 1870-1945, edited by D. Thomson; A. J. P. Taylor's *The Struggle for Mastery in Europe* 1848-1918, *English History* 1914-18, *The Course of German History*; *The Survey of International Affairs* issued by the Royal Institute of International Affairs. My one-time tutor C. R. M. F. Cruttwell's *History of the Great War* (Clarendon Press 1934) is still an excellent short outline. The many volumes of the Official History of the Second World War and the three volumes of *The Royal Air Force* 1939-1945 are a necessary corrective to the host of war memoirs.

FAMILY BACKGROUND AND CHILDHOOD

F. H. Simpson's two volumes on *Louis Napoleon* (de Gaulle's predecessor as a political adventurer) and A. J. P. Taylor's *Bismarck* set the scene for the catastrophe of 1870. Count Paul Vassili's *France behind the Veil* and Stefan Zweig's *World of Yesterday* bring the French collapse and aftermath to life. The best condensed account of the Dreyfus case I came across was in Barbara Tuckman's *The Proud Tower*. The temptation to delve was irresistible and I spent too long reading the articles and speeches of Zola, Clemenceau, Jaurés and Comte Albert de Mun. My justification was the effect of Dreyfus's conviction on the French army and therefore on the beginning of de Gaulle's career.

THE FIRST WORLD WAR

Sydney Fay's *Origins of the World War*, Harold Nicolson's *Lord Carnock*, Winston Churchill's *The World Crisis*, Virginia Cowles's *The Kaiser* between them offer a valid explanation of the unnecessary war. A taste of the war itself comes from *The War Memoirs of David Lloyd George*, *Lord Riddell's Diaries*, Duff Cooper's defence of *Haig* and (for pleasure), Siegfried Sassoon's *The Memoirs of an Infantry Officer*. Since Sir Edward Spears played such an important part in de Gaulle's later life it is instructive to remind oneself of the role he played in the First World War through his book, *Liaison, 1914*.

In 1925, Marshal Pétain wrote a report on the 1917 mutiny of the French army which has recently been published under the title *Une Crise Morale de la Nation Française en Guerre* (Paris: Nouvelles Éditions Latines 1966); a more vivid account is given by John Williams in *Mutiny 1917*. General Sérigny's *Trente Ans avec Pétain* throws fascinating side-lights on Pétain as a commander and man.

THE NINETEEN-TWENTIES

Marshal Pilsudski's reply in *L'Année 1920* (Paris: La Renaissance du Livre 1929) to Marshal Toukatchevsky's account of *The War Beyond the Vistula* gives one a glimpse of the beginning of modern Poland's tragedy in which de Gaulle played a minor but distinguished part. Harold Nicolson's *Peacemaking 1919*, Lloyd George's and Raymond Poincaré's memoirs, Chastenet's *Life of Poincaré*, J. M. Keynes's essay, *The Economic Consequences of the Peace* lead up to the French occupation of the Ruhr and the garrisoning of the Rhineland, in both of which de Gaulle took part. G. E. R. Gedye's *The Revolver Republic* is a first-hand account of the French attempt to set up a puppet government in the Ruhr; Eric Eyck's *History of the Weimar Republic* and Arthur Rosenberg's *History of the German Republic* tell the story from the German point of view.

THE NEAR EAST

Against his will, de Gaulle was deeply involved in the Near East. Of an enormous literature, George Antonius's *The Arab Awakening* still gives the most lucid account of the origins of the Anglo/French, Arab/Jewish conflict. *The Memoirs of Lord Chandos* and General Georges Catroux's *Dans La Bataille de la Méditerranée* are an antidote to de Gaulle's own account of the Free French role in Syria.

THE THIRTIES

Comparatively few people read Hitler's *Mein Kampf* when it was published, yet it is still vital to an understanding of this disastrous decade. I also reread Wheeler Bennett's great book *The Nemesis of Power* and Alan Bullock's

Hitler; A Study in Tyranny, and Denis Brogan's *Development of Modern France*. It was the period when de Gaulle was producing most of his own written work and challenging the military thinking of the High Command. Liddell Hart's brilliant studies of mechanised warfare originally published in *The Re-making of Modern Armies* (John Murray 1927) and now summarised in the two volumes of his *Memoires* were the basis of much of de Gaulle's thinking. General Chauvineau's *Une Invasion est-elle encore Possible?* (Paris: Berger-Levrault 1939), to which Pétain wrote a glowing foreword, expresses some of the defensive views which de Gaulle attacked. Paul Reynaud's *Venu de ma Montagne, Envers et Contre Tous* and *Au Coeur de la Mêlée*, Léon Blum's *Mémoires "Fragments,"* and above all the transcripts from the Riom Trials and the trials of Fétain and Laval, give the background.

Among English memoirs Antony Eden's *Facing the Dictators*, Duff Cooper's *Old Men Forget*, Vansittart's *The Mist Procession* and Harold Nicolson's first volume of *Diaries and Letters* (1930-39), present the counterpart of de Gaulle's struggle in France; they are balanced by Lord Birkenhead's perceptive life of *Lord Halifax*, Lord Templewood's *Nine Troubled Years* and Sir Neville Henderson's *Failure of a Mission*. Some of the threads are pulled together in James Joll's *The Decline of the Third Republic* (St. Antony's Papers. No. 5).

THE SECOND WORLD WAR
The three volumes of de Gaulle's own memoirs, *Call to Honour, Unity, Salvation*, need constant balancing by the relevant parts of Churchill's massive *The Second World War*. Arthur Bryant's *The Alanbrooke Diaries* (2 volumes) and Eisenhower's *Crusade in Europe* give more detached versions of some of the incidents. Chester Wilmot's *The Struggle for Europe* is an essential addition to the official histories. The other first-hand accounts fall within particular phases.

THE FREE FRENCH MOVEMENT
Sir Edward Spears's account of the departure from Bordeaux has been contradicted by both de Gaulle and Geoffroy de Courcel. For reasons given in a note on the chapter, I have accepted Spears's version in *Assignment to Catastrophe Vol. II. The Fall of France*. The most important book on the early months in 1940-41 is Admiral Muselier's *De Gaulle Contre Le Gaullisme*. The other reminiscences, Passy's (Colonel A. Dewavrin) three volumes of *Souvenirs*, Soustelle's two volumes, *Envers et Contre Tout*, generally corroborate the story de Gaulle tells himself. Henri de Kerillis's *I Accuse de Gaulle*, Admiral Decoux's *À la Barre de l'Indochine* 1940-45, and Robert Mengin's *No Laurels for De Gaulle* show how it was possible for honourable Frenchmen living abroad to reject de Gaulle's call.

VICHY AND PÉTAINISM

Paul Baudouin in his *Private Diaries*, Maxime Weygand in *Recalled to Service* and in *The Role of General Weygand: Conversations with his son* (Weygand, J.), Camille Chantemps in *Cahiers Secrets de l'Armistice*, Benoist-Mechin in *Soixante Jours Qui Ébranlèrent l'Occident* explained why a majority of Frenchmen refused to accept the policy de Gaulle pressed and Reynaud failed to execute in 1940. Professor Rougier's *Mission Secrète à Londres* establishes Churchill's unofficial understanding with Vichy. The cult of Pétainism is best understood by reading accounts and transcripts of the many trials in France from 1940-47, some of which have been collected in separate volumes and published by Albin Michel and Nouvelles Éditions Latines and all of which were fully reported in the Press; also through Fabre-Luce's books, listed among those dealing with de Gaulle. Robert Aron's *Histoire de Vichy* is an objective account of the régime. The Marquis d'Argenson's *Pétain et Pétainisme* makes a penetrating analysis of the attitudes which led to Pétainism. Admiral Leahy's *I was There* explains Roosevelt's policy.

NORTH AFRICA

Besides Leahy's memoirs, Robert Murphy's *Diplomat Among Warriors*, Harold Macmillan's *The Blast of War*, Henri Giraud's *Un Seul But, Le Victoire*, Kenneth Pendar's *Adventure in Diplomacy*, Soustelle's second volume of reminiscences, *D'Algers à Paris*, Captain Harry Butcher's *My Three Years with Eisenhower*, all give first-hand accounts of the North African epic. The American Government's reasons for supporting Vichy, Darlan and Giraud emerge from Cordell Hull's *Memoirs*, and Robert Sherwood's *Roosevelt and Hopkins*. Roosevelt's best advocate is William Langer in *Our Vichy Gamble*. Roosevelt's policy is ably criticised in Milton Viorst's *Hostile Allies*, Arthur Layton Funk's *Charles de Gaulle, The Crucial Years*, 1943-44 and Dorothy Shipley-White's *Seeds of Discord*. Renée Pierre-Gosset gives a glimpse of war-time life in *Algiers, 1941-43*.

THE RESISTANCE AND LIBERATION

I have only brushed the surface of the literature of the Resistance. Henri Michel's *Histoire de la Résistance* (Presse Universitaire de France 1950) and even more important *Les Courants de Pensées Dans La Résistance* (Presse Universitaire de France 1960), Michael Foot's *S.O.E.* and Robert Aron's *Histoire de la Libération de la France* are the standard works and tell an enthralling story. Rémy's (Gilbert Renault-Roulier) eight volumes of reminiscences and Emanuel d'Astier de la Vigerie's many short books are first-hand accounts by two of the great underground leaders. I would choose Rémy's *Comment Meurt un Réseau* and *Une Affaire de Trahison*, and d'Astier's *Sept Fois Sept Jours, Les Dieux et Les Hommes, De La Chute à la Libération de Paris*, which has excellent photographs and some interesting documents. Bruce

Marshall's account of Yeo Thomas's experiences in *The White Rabbit* is still horrifying.

Larry Collins and Dominique Lapierre give a vivid account of the Paris uprising in *Is Paris Burning?* Paul Serant gives a comparative analysis of retribution in different European countries after liberation in *Les Vaincus de La Libération* (Robert Laffont, Paris, 1964).

THE FOURTH REPUBLIC

Dorothy Pickles's *French Politics*, J. Fauvet's *Les Forces Politiques en France* (*Le Monde* 1951), Philip Williams's *Politics in Post-War France* are all objective studies of the political scene during the first five of de Gaulle's years in the wilderness; Alexander Werth's *France 1940-55* is a running commentary by an exceptionally well-informed left-wing journalist. For the later years Mendès-France's *La Politique et la Vérité: Juin 1955-Sept. 1958* (Paris: René Julliard 1958) contains reflections on the events leading to de Gaulle's return by the man who might have prevented it had he been able to resolve the contradictions of the French party system. It can be balanced by Raymond Aron's *Immuable et Changeante: de la IVe a la Ve République* (Paris: Calmann-Levy 1959). Alfred Grosser's *La IVe République et sa Politique Extérieure* answers many of de Gaulle's criticisms of the régime of the parties. Edmond Jouve, in his monumental *Le Général de Gaulle et la Reconstruction de l'Europe*, presents everything that has been said by de Gaulle about Europe and most of what has been said in opposition. It is an anthology rather than a book.

ALGERIA

The liberal side of the argument was given in *La Tragédie Algérienne* and *L'Algérie et la République* (Paris: Plon. 1957-58) by Raymond Aron and answered by Jacques Soustelle in *Le Drame Algérien et la Décadence Française: Réponse à Raymond Aron.* (Paris: Plon. 1957). Soustelle carries on his side of the story in *L'Espérance Trahie*, a telling indictment of de Gaulle's methods. Alexander Werth's *De Gaulle's Revolution* and Williams and Harrison's *De Gaulle's Republic* are objective political assessments. The Bromberger brothers' account *Les 13 Complots Du 13 Mai* is challenged by Georges Bidault in *D'Une Résistance à l'Autre* (Les Presses du Siècle 1965). Some of the polemical literature is listed under books dealing with de Gaulle, but the best source for the later stages of the Algerian drama are the accounts of the trials of Salan, Jouhaud and Challe. The attempts on de Gaulle's life are described by Joachim Joesten in *De Gaulle and His Murderers*. The confession and medical examinations of Colonel Bastien-Thiry are among the documents in J. R. Tournoux's *La Tragédie du Général*.

POST ALGERIA. 1963-68

Apart from interviews, in this latest period I have had to rely mainly on the daily press, reviews and magazines, parliamentary debates and records of broadcasts and television programmes. However, Professor W. W. Kulski's *De Gaulle and the World* is a remarkable study of the General's foreign policy. This policy is vigorously criticised by Paul Reynaud in *La Politique Étrangère du Gaullisme*. Edgar S. Furniss, Jr., in *De Gaulle and the French Army* gives a useful account of recent military reforms. For the chapter on the French economy in the last decade I was particularly indebted to a study by Norman Macrae which appeared in *The Economist* of May 18, 1968.

In the light of the student explosion of May, 1968, Michel Debré's *Jeunesse, Quelle France Te Faut-il?* (Paris: Plon. 1965) is revealing, as is Merry Bromberger's *Le Destin Secret de Georges Pompidou*.

BOOKS ABOUT DE GAULLE

The fullest biography of de Gaulle is Paul-Marie de la Gorce's *De Gaulle Entre Deux Mondes* written with the co-operation of de Gaulle himself. As a result the author has had access to people who would otherwise have hesitated to see him. Although de la Gorce generally takes de Gaulle's side, the wide scope of the book enables him to keep his subject in perspective. Other biographies by Frenchmen, including François Mauriac's *De Gaulle* (Grasset. Paris. 1964), tend to be sycophantic. Georges Cattaui's *Charles de Gaulle: L'Homme et Son Destin* remains the best authority for de Gaulle's childhood and family background.

De Gaulle's own memoirs, written in three volumes each with an accompanying volume of documents, are a brilliant justification of the part he played from 1940 to 1946. Of equal importance, and covering a far wider span, are his lectures, military essays and speeches. (A list of his published works is given at the end of this note.) There are many collections of his speeches from 1940-1945 and his major broadcasts and speeches from June 1958 onwards are available through the courtesy of the French Embassy. The intervening years are covered by collections like André Passeron's *De Gaulle Parle* or the R.P.F.'s *La France Sera La France*, of which Pompidou was one of the editors, and the press. Even during de Gaulle's years in the wilderness there was rarely an occasion when his speeches were not reported in *Le Monde* or *Figaro*.

That part of the argument over the need for an armoured striking force in the 1930s and a *force de frappe* in the 1960s which was waged in the Assembly and Senate is available in the *Journal Officiel*. Experts, including de Gaulle, wrote in the *Revue Militaire d'Information* in the 1930s, later in the *Revue de Défense Nationale*, and *Revue Politique et Parlementaire*, which are available in the Bibliothèque de Documentation Internationale Contemporaine, Paris. Of the many newspapers—de Quilici's Gaullist weekly, *La Marseillaise*, the independent daily, *France*, edited by Comert, Combault and

Levy, *Pour la Victoire*, which later became *France-Amérique*, edited by Geneviève Taboius and Henri de Kerillis, published in New York, are in the British Museum—the host of roneoed sheets and miniature pamphlets published by various resistance groups, in the Bibliothèque Nationale.

Another primary source is Lucien Nachin's little book *Charles de Gaulle, Général de France*. Nachin not only served with de Gaulle before and during the First World War, but was his constant correspondent up to 1940. Paul Reynaud also had a collection of 75 of de Gaulle's letters, some of which are quoted in his memoirs.

Two indispensable books which contain documents not previously published are J. R. Tournoux's *Pétain et de Gaulle* and *La Tragédie du Général*. Tournoux does not give references for all the conversations he quotes, but this is not surprising since both supporters and critics of de Gaulle are understandably chary of being quoted. Tournoux has probably interviewed more people connected with de Gaulle's life than any other Frenchman and those with whom I have discussed his work, whether members of the government or opposition, regard it as remarkably accurate.

In spite of repeated prosecutions, de Gaulle's opponents maintain a barrage of criticism which in volume will soon rival the literature in defence of Dreyfus. The most acid are Alfred Fabre-Luce, an ardent supporter of Marshal Pétain, Jacques Isorni, junior counsel for the defence at Pétain's trial, and Jacques Laurant, antagonist of Mauriac. Fabre-Luce's allegory, *Le Couronnement du Prince*, banned in France, is perhaps the most telling of all the general indictments. Georges Bidault's consuming hatred for de Gaulle comes out in *D'Une Résistance à L'Autre* and Paul Reynaud's indignation at de Gaulle's breaches of the constitution and policy of grandeur in *Et Après* and *La Politique Étrangère du Gaullisme*. Emanuel d'Astier de la Vigerie, who has completed the Gaullist cycle of admiration, opposition, dislike and back to grudging admiration, gives illuminating sketches and anecdotes in all his delightfully written books. Viansson Ponté's *The Court of the King* is a brilliant satire on the style of the Gaullist régime. Of the more detached critical essays I benefited from David Thomson's *Two Frenchmen* (London: The Crescent Press 1951), Sir Edward Spears's *Two men who served France* (London: Eyre & Spottiswoode 1966) and Robert Aron's *Explanation of de Gaulle* (Harper & Row, New York 1966).

WORKS OF GENERAL DE GAULLE

The more important writings of General de Gaulle are listed below, with the dates of their original publication.

La Discorde Chez L'Ennemi. (Paris: Berger-Levrault 1924).

Orientation De Nos Doctrines De Guerre. Extracts from The Revue Militaire March 1, 1925. (Paris: Berger-Levrault).

Rôle Historique Des Places Fortes Françaises. Extracts from the Revue Militaire December 1, 1925. (Paris: Berger-Levrault).

L'Action de Guerre et Le Chef. Lecture given at l'École Superieure de Guerre, April 7, 1927. (Paris: Berger-Levrault 1928).

Philosophie Du Recrutement. Extract from the Revue Militaire d'Infanterie, 1st term 1929. (Paris: Berger-Levrault).

Du Caractère. Extract from the Revue Militaire, June 1, 1930. (Paris: Berger-Levrault 1930).

Du Prestige. Extracts from the Revue Militaire, June 1, 1931. (Paris: Berger-Levrault 1931).

Le Fil De L'Épée. (Paris: Berger-Levrault).

Vers L'Armée De Métier. Extracts from the Revue Politique et Parlementaire, May 10, 1933. (Paris: Berger-Levrault 1933).

Métier Militaire. Extracts from Des Études. (Imprimerie J. Dumoulin. Paris: December 5, 1933).

Vers L'Armée de Métier. (Paris: Berger-Levrault 1934).

Comment Faire Une Armée de Métier. Extracts from the Revue Hebdomadaire, January 12, 1935. (Paris: Librairie Plon).

Les Origines de L'Armée Française. Extract from the Revue d'Infanterie No. 520, January, 1936. (Chales-Lavauzelle 1936).

La France et Son Armée. (Paris: Plon. Collection "Présences" 1938).

L'Avènement de la Force Mécanique. (Typescript circulated privately, January, 1940).

Mémoires de Guerre. (Paris: Plon. Vol. I *L'Appel,* 1954, Vol. II *Unité,* 1956, Vol. III *Le Salut,* 1959. (English translations published by Collins Vol. I, and Weidenfeld and Nicolson Vols. II and III).

OFFICIAL SOURCES

Journal Officiel de la République Française
    Lois et Décrets
    Débats de l'Assemblée Nationale
    Débats du Sénat

INDEX

Abadie, Doctor Jules, 201, 205, 210, 215

Abbas, Ferhat, 318, 326, 366, 375, 383

Abbeville, de Gaulle's tank action at (1940), 99-100

Abdullah, Emir of Transjordan, 65, 152

Abyssinia, Italian conquest of, 76, 77, 92; French part in reconquest of, 147-8

Action Française, L', 56

Adenauer, Konrad, his meetings with de Gaulle, 363, 402-3, 415-18, 421; signs Franco-German Treaty, 422. Mentioned: 390, 412, 420, 424, 426

Africa, *see* Equatorial Africa, North Africa

Agadir Incident (1911), 29

Ailleret, General Pierre Marie Jean, 428

Alexander, A. V., 167

Alexander of Tunis, General (later Field-Marshal), 232, 262

Algeria (Algiers), de Gaulle's early attitude towards, 40; proposals (1940) to move French Government to, 108, 113-14; Free French activities in, 179 *et seq.*; Darlan in control of, 181 *et seq.*, 188 *et seq.*; de Gaulle's first visit to, 201-2, 233 *et seq.*, 237; post-war situation in, 252-3; mounting crisis there, 313, 318; outbreak of civil war, 324-32; resulting in de Gaulle's return to power, 333-53; de Gaulle's further visit to and proposals for pacification, 354-8, 363 *et seq.*; his last visit, 376; suppression of generals' revolt there and final grant of independence, 377-84, 389

Ali, Tariq, 448

Allard, General, 334, 339

Allehaut, Colonel, 71

Allenby, Field-Marshal, 65

Amaury, Émilien, 329

Anderson, General Sir Kenneth A. N., 211

Anfa (Casablanca), meeting between de Gaulle and Giraud at (1943), 195-6, 200, 207, 222, 232

Antoine, *see* Fontaine, Major

Antoing, de Gaulle at College of, 18

Anvil (code name for invasion of South of France), 231-2, 234

Arcis-sur-Aube, de Gaulle's meeting with Huntziger at (1940), 106

Ardennes, de Gaulle's connexion with, 39; Pétain's view that Germans would not attack through, 81; German attack through (1940), 98; German offensive in (1944), 259, 270

Argenlieu, Captain (later Admiral) Georges Thierry d', joins Free French, 123, 126; takes part in Dakar expedition, 131, and capture of Libreville, 134; joins Empire Defence Committee, 136, 156, and National Committee, 161; accompanies de Gaulle to France (1944), 229; becomes High Commissioner in Indo-China, 295, 319, 320

Argoud, Colonel, 381, 382-3, 457

Arighi, Pascal, 345

Aron, Raymond, 406

Aron, Robert, 253

Arras, de Gaulle stationed at (1909-10, 1912-14), 23, 24-9; present at liberation of, 343

Asquith of Yarnbury, Baroness, 407-8

Astier de la Vigerie, Emmanuel d', 171, 178, 187, 192, 235, 278

Astier de la Vigerie, General François d', 192

Astier de la Vigerie, Henri d', 178, 191, 192, 200

Astier de Villatte, Major, 148

Attlee, Clement, 206, 282, 292

Auboyneau, Captain (later Admiral) Philippe, replaces Muselier, 167, 339, 347